COMPARATIVE LAW IN A CHANGING WORLD

Cavendish
Publishing
Limited

London • Sydney

COMPARATIVE LAW IN A CHANGING WORLD

Second edition

Peter de Cruz, LLB, LLM, PhD
Professor of Law
Staffordshire University

Cavendish
Publishing
Limited

London • Sydney

First published in Great Britain 1995 by Cavendish Publishing
Limited, The Glass House, Wharton Street, London, WC1X 9PX.
Telephone: +44 (0) 20 7278 8000   Facsimile: +44 (0) 20 7278 8080
E-mail: info@cavendishpublishing.com
Visit our Home Page on http://www.cavendishpublishing.com

Cruz, Peter de
Comparative law in a changing world
1 Comparative law
I Title
340.2

ISBN 1 85941 432 X

Printed and bound in Great Britain

PREFACE

When I began to write about comparative law in the early 1990s, the subject was considered to be 'in need of an audience' (Markesinis) and was certainly associated only with a highly theoretical and obscure enterprise which was the preserve of a few (mostly continental) lawyers and Leeds and Oxford stood out as two of the eclectic universities which actually had a course with that title. By being highly selective, my earlier work, *A Modern Approach to Comparative Law*, was confined to 343 pages of text. By 1995, there was a far greater interest in the subject and at least several more British universities now ran courses on comparative law which prompted the next edition of the book, which was expanded to 491 pages. Reflecting on comparative law at the end of the 1990s, looking to the millennium, I find that the basic premise upon which this book was first conceived, still remains. It still seeks to provide an overview of the comparative study of law and legal systems, primarily for undergraduate study, but also aims to serve as a resource for further study by postgraduates or practitioners who may wish to have some notion of the concept and techniques of comparative law. It still focuses on France and Germany as the main civil law jurisdictions and English law as the main common law example. These jurisdictions are both very different in their historical development, juristic style, ideologies and legal traditions, yet serve as typical paradigms of the civil law parent legal family because of their common characteristics, despite their many differences. This book continues to provide comparative illustrations of selected substantive areas of law within common law and civil law systems, using the three abovenamed jurisdictions as archetypal systems. Despite some criticisms of some of its content and/or approach I have, at least, for this edition, retained my basic approach to comparative law study. The definitive, all embracing, multicultural politically correct, up to the minute, totally comprehensive (covering the jurisdictions covered here and more) and seminal book has, as far as I am aware, certainly not yet appeared, certainly not from any of this book's reviewers. The impetus for this book grew from a series of lectures which I gave on the Keele University undergraduate comparative law course in the early to mid-1990s. Accordingly, the reader may find that I was highly selective in the coverage of topics and jurisdictions. I also developed a number of ideas which may be pursued in greater depth by researchers at postgraduate level.

The expression 'comparative law' was apparently first used in the 19th century and, although it is predominantly a method of study, it has also acquired a sufficient number of methodological principles which suggest that it is becoming a branch of social science in its own right. But, comparative law does not have a substantive core content as, for example, contract law or criminal law does in English law. Therefore, once key concepts, such as the sources of law and parent legal families, have been understood, there are several topics which equally merit comparative analysis.

As is often recounted, Aristotle collected something in the order of 150 city State constitutions in the 4th century BC in the course of devising a model constitution. Similar comparative enterprises have taken place throughout the centuries in most of what is now known as the civilised Western world. The process of codification also has a distinguished pedigree and a distinctive modern meaning in the context of the 19th century French and German Codes. The method of comparative law is, therefore, not a modern enterprise.

However, several things justify a fresh appraisal of comparative law as a methodological and socio-legal construct as we approach the new millennium. First, all other comparative law books used to assume that there are three main parent legal families – civil law, common law and socialist legal systems. This is no longer the case as a result of the disintegration of the former Soviet Union, the prototype of socialist systems and the rejection and demise of communism throughout Eastern Europe and in other parts of the world. We have therefore appeared to have returned to the pre-1917 position of having only two truly major legal families or parent systems. Socialist systems continue to exist, but are either returning to their civil law roots or undergoing a severe catharsis in ethnic conflict or are developing as part of a hybrid system of law. I have attempted to clarify the notion of parent legal families, legal systems and legal traditions in Chapter 1 and developed these points in Chapter 2. Chapter 6 provides an overview of the new Russian Federation Constitution reforms and an assessment of recent legal developments. This now assumes greater importance and poignancy in the light of dramatic and constantly changing developments in the 'new' Russia. Secondly, the impact of European Community law is gradually growing apace and must be taken into account as a unique supra-national legal order. This book addresses its continuing impact and the influence of European legal traditions on Community law as it is being developed by the European Court of Justice. Thirdly, none of the existing books or commentators on comparative law address adequately the techniques of comparison and no book offers a blueprint which is accessible, comprehensible, precise and practical. I have attempted to develop my original blueprint for comparison in Chapter 7. Fourthly, it has become increasingly clear that the common law distinction between contract and tort is only barely justifiable as being rooted in the difference between imposed and assumed duties and in their rules on remedies. I have attempted to provide some ideas for the future analysis of tort and contract as part of one law of obligations and this finds resonances in European civil law. Fifthly, despite a commentator's recent remark to the effect that comparative legal studies were not necessarily for everyone, implying that they were, arguably, too difficult and, if demystified, would be lacking in intellectual credulity, it is hoped that this textbook does provide an accessible historical and conceptual introduction to the development of civil and common law for undergraduates and postgraduate researchers and a concise, selective comparative overview of key topics, such as contract, tort, sale of goods and company law. Sixthly, developments in certain areas have also been considered – for example, the rise of the administrative tribunal in England and the blurring of the division between public and private law in English law, despite *O'Reilly v Mackman* [1983] 1 AC 147; the future of Hong Kong since it reverted to China in 1997; and the implications of German reunification are also considered, all of which have inevitably overtaken other existing texts. Finally, there is an overview of the current geopolitical map of the world as it has evolved in the 1990s and the last chapter provides a brief survey of the phenomenon of convergence of systems, as well as an evaluation of the possible reasons for any new world order that might be emerging.

I wish to thank John Morrow of University of Newcastle upon Tyne library for his continuing generosity in allowing me access to sources and materials unobtainable anywhere else. Without their help, even the earlier version of this book could not have been started. As always, all errors and inaccuracies remain the writer's sole responsibility. This book is dedicated to my wife, Lois, for her love, support and boundless patience and to my mother and late father, both of whom first sparked my enthusiasm in exploring a multiplicity of cultures in their legal and socio-legal context.

Peter de Cruz
Staffordshire University
July 1999

CONTENTS

Contents

Contents

Contents

Contents

LIST OF ABBREVIATIONS

ABGB ....Allgemeines Burgerliches Gesetzbuch fur
Österreich (Austrian General Civil Code)
AC ....Appeal Cases (English Law Reports)
AG ....Aktiengesellschaft (company)
AGBG ....Law on General Conditions of Business (German)
AJIL ....American Journal of International Law
Am J Comp L ....American Journal of Comparative Law
All ER...All England Reports
Asia Business L Rev..Asia Business Law Review
BGB...Burgerliches Gesetzbuch (German Civil Code)
BGH ....Bundesgerichtshof (Supreme Court, Ordinary Jurisdiction)
BGHZ...........Reports of civil cases of the German Federal Supreme Court
Canadian Bar Rev ....Canadian Bar Review
Chicago UL Rev ....Chicago University Law Review
Civ ....Cour de cassation, Chambre civile
CLJ...Cambridge Law Journal
CLR...Commonwealth Law Reports
CMLR ....Common Market Law Reports
Comparative Labour LJ...........................Comparative Labour Law Journal
Denning LJ...Denning Law Journal
DM...Deutsche Mark
ECR...European Court Reports
EEIG...European Economic Industry Grouping
EJIL..European Journal of International Law
EL Rev ....European Law Review
European Competition L Rev ....European Competition Law Review
FMSLR...Federated Malay States Law Reports
GEIE ....Groupement Européen d'Intérête économique
GG..Grundgesetz of 23 May 1949
GIE..Groupement d'Intérête économique
(Basic Law: West German Constitution)
GVG ....Constitution of Courts Act 1975 (Germany)
Harvard L Rev ....Harvard Law Review
Hastings LJ ....Hastings Law Journal
HGB...German Commercial Code
HKLJ...Hong Kong Law Journal
ICLQ....................................International and Comparative Law Quarterly
Industrial LJ..Industrial Law Journal
JBL ....Journal of Business Law
J Pub Law...Journal of Public Law
JSPTL...........................Journal of the Society of the Public Teachers of Law
KB ....King's Bench Law Reports
LQR...Law Quarterly Review
LS ....Legal Studies

Mich L Rev ....Michigan Law Review
MLJ ....Malayan Law Journal
MLR ....Modern Law Review
New Left Rev ....New Left Review
NJW ....Neue Juristische Wochenschrift: German Periodical
OJLS ....Oxford Journal of Legal Studies
Pennsylvania UL Rev ....Pennsylvania University Law Review
Req...Cour de Cassation, Chambre de requetes
RGZ....................Decisions in Civil matters of the German Imperial Court
SA ....Société Anonyme
SARL...Société a responsabilité limitée
Texas L Rev..Texas Law Review
Times Euoropean L Rev..................................Times European Law Review
Torts LJ ....Torts Law Journal
Tulane L Rev ....Tulane Law Review
ZPO....................German Code of Civil Procedure (Zivilprozessordnung)

CHAPTER 1

INTRODUCING COMPARATIVE LAW

INTRODUCTION

In order to appraise the development and use of comparative law in the modern world, it is necessary to examine the nature, scope and origin of the term itself. As a term of art, 'comparative law' must rank as one of the most unique within the scenario of legal research and study. If interpreted as a body of law, it is both potentially all-encompassing in its scope, in the sense of embracing all laws of all legal systems, as well as descriptive of a method of study and research (see Gutteridge (1949) p 1). In their work, *Major Legal Systems in the World Today*, David and Brierley proceed on the premise that there is little purpose in pursuing the traditional preliminary questions of defining the purpose of comparative law and emphasising the value of comparative law studies. Accordingly, they merely give a condensed account of these conventional concerns, and stress the more contemporary challenges, namely, to emphasise the general utility of comparative law, and convince any remaining sceptics thereof; and to provide means of assisting those who wish to use comparative law for their own purposes (see David and Brierley (1985) pp 3–4). Nevertheless, they also concede that it is 'only natural' that the traditional questions surrounding comparative law should be asked by those first confronted with the phenomenon called 'comparative law' (David and Brierley (1985) p 4).

This book assumes that its readers may not necessarily be experienced researchers or seasoned comparatists, but may quite possibly be 'first time' comparatists. It therefore discusses some fundamental questions, and also devotes some attention to reviewing the salient features of the literature dealing with definitional, terminological, methodological and historical questions. One reason for this initially traditional approach is that the events of the last 20 years and the last five years, in particular, in Western and Eastern Europe, and the former Soviet Union, have cast considerable uncertainty on the continued viability of the 'socialist tradition' and 'socialist legal system'. But, it would be impossible to appraise the current state of the civil law or the future of socialist systems in Europe, unless the ground rules for comparison were spelt out very carefully and unless the reader is given a sense of history.

What are the components of comparative law? How did comparative law develop? What are its functions or purposes? How may it be distinguished from the mere study of the law of a foreign jurisdiction? How may be it be distinguished from other legal disciplines? How has it been utilised in practical terms and in scholarly research?

Having examined these questions, we shall then undertake a brief survey of the scope of the notions of the 'common law' and 'civil law' families of legal systems, with reference to typical examples, and will return to this concept of 'parent' legal families in Chapter 2. The socialist system, long ranked alongside the common law and civil law as one of the three major legal systems in the world, is now in such decline that it no longer merits being analysed in juxtaposition with the other two systems. In the late 1990s, communist China is still very much a superpower and continues to cast its shadow over Hong Kong, particularly after 1997, being still wedded to the Leninist/Marxist ideology, although it claims to practise a new, 'open' form of communism which has seen fit to welcome the West in many more arenas than under previous regimes. The different versions of modern Chinese law are discussed in Chapter 6, which also discusses the basic concepts of the socialist system. It is submitted that, in the light of the continuing decline of forms of socialism, the socialist legal system, while deserving discussion, no longer warrants equal coverage as a major legal system in the late 1990s.

Instead, it will be considered predominantly in the context of its contemporary development and in relation to the general decline of socialism in Eastern Europe. A fresh appraisal of the study of parent or major legal families is necessitated by certain trends of convergence between civil law and common law, and by the collapse of communist regimes across Eastern Europe, including the disintegration and demise of the former Soviet Union and its subsequent fragmentation, 'republicanisation' and 'federalism'. A tentative assessment of the current Soviet legal situation, which has seen a number of changes in the last few months, will, therefore, be discussed in Chapter 6, as part of a discussion of unique legal systems, such as Japan.

There is some justification for considering the role of comparison in international law, for it is possible to consider international law as a separate legal system in itself. However, although there is a brief consideration of the international judge's judicial function and the value of the comparative method in providing him with the content of some of the principles he formulates at the international level, it has been decided, at least for the present inquiry, not to pursue this matter in any great depth. There is, of course, the ubiquitous difficulty of the comparability of rules which would have to be constantly overcome. Any domestic rule would have to fit in with the different conditions of the international community.

DEFINITIONS AND DERIVATIONS

Terminology: subject or method?

The first question that arises is: what is the nature of comparative law? Is it a branch of law, like family law or property law? Further, since law is sometimes defined as a 'body of rules', is there any identifiable body of rules known as 'comparative law'? The answer to both these questions is in the negative.

As an academic pursuit, it does not have a core content of subject areas and does not denote a distinct branch of substantive law. On the contrary, as Zweigert and Kotz put it, it describes 'an intellectual activity with law as its object and comparison as its process' (see Zweigert and Kotz (1977) p 2).

There are no less than 42 legal systems in the world, and comparison has traditionally focused on three major legal families in the world, namely the civil law system, common law system and socialist system. So, 'comparative law' can be said to describe the *systematic study of particular legal traditions and legal rules on a comparative basis*. To qualify as a true comparative law enterprise, it also requires the comparison of two or more legal systems, or two or more legal traditions, or of selected aspects, institutions or branches of two or more legal systems. The question of what constitutes a legal system and/or legal tradition is taken up in Chapter 2.

Legal systems, parent legal families and legal traditions

A *legal system* may be defined as the legal rules and institutions of a country (as in 'the French legal system') in the narrow sense or, as Winterton (1975) puts it, in the broad sense as the 'juristic philosophy and techniques shared by a number of nations with broadly similar legal systems' (such as the English common law system) (Winterton (1975) pp 69–70). This broad sense is really describing a *parent legal family*, such as the common law or civil law legal family. Perhaps somewhat confusingly, David and Brierley refer to these parent legal families as major legal systems, which is potentially ambiguous until it is appreciated that the so called major legal systems may also be called the parent legal families, since *either term* refers to either the common law, civil law, or socialist legal group because *the 'major' legal systems are the parent legal families*. In other words, to more readily identify and compare the various legal systems in the world, *a group of jurisdictions may be classified under a generic heading by virtue of having similar characteristics*. There is still a certain amount of academic disagreement over what these characteristics should be, but the key distinguishing features (according to Zweigert and Kotz (1998) pp 68–73) include: (a) the system's historical background and development;

(b) its predominant and characteristic mode of thought; (c) its particularly distinctive institutions; (d) its sources of law and the way it handles these; and (e) its ideology (however one might define this term). These matters are discussed in detail in Chapter 2. The theory of legal families is, therefore, in the nature of a taxonomic device, namely to group various jurisdictions with similar characteristics under certain generic headings – common law, civil law, socialist law – so as to make comparison more feasible and comprehensible. Hence, if one or two legal systems prove to be representative of two different legal families, the comparatist may then concentrate on these two systems as examples of the major parent legal families, such as the civil law and common law. It needs to be noted that there are, and have always been, many differences between the legal systems, such as France and Germany, but their history, predominant mode of legal thought, attitudes to law and the role of law, sources of law and characteristic legal institutions, nevertheless, justify placing them both clearly within the so called civil law parent legal family, rather than classifying them as common law jurisdictions.

A *legal tradition*, on the other hand, is not a set of rules about marriage, contracts, corporations and crime, but:

> ... deeply rooted, historically conditioned attitudes about the nature of law ... the role of law in ... society and the polity, the proper organisation and operation of a legal system, and about the way law is, or should be made, applied, studied, perfected, and taught. The legal tradition relates the legal system to the culture of which it is a partial expression. It puts the legal system into cultural perspective. [Merryman (1985) p 2.]

Thus, we have the common law, civil and socialist legal traditions, each with their characteristic attitudes to law, which enable comparatists to classify them accordingly, albeit from more general rather than highly specific detailed criteria. Any legal system, therefore, will have a number of legal traditions and sub-traditions (see Merryman (1985) p 6 *et seq*), historically conditioned, which, collectively, represent the heritage of that particular jurisdiction and, in themselves, provide an insight into the evolution of a given legal system.

Razi argues that a legal system in the wide sense 'is not made of rules alone but is also characterised by its institutions, practices, standards of research and even the mental habits of lawyers, judges, legislators and administrators' (Razi (1959) 5 Howard LJ 11). This, again, is much more akin to a legal *tradition* than to a system as such, although it really depends on the context of usage. If one is referring to the 'common law system' or 'civil law system', one is really using it in the wider or broader sense of a *parent legal family*. Reference to 'Country X' as a civil law system causes no confusion as such, and is *prima facie* the use of the narrow meaning (see Chapter 2, and Merryman (1977)), but it may be clearer to refer to it as a civil law jurisdiction (such as France) which, for the comparatist, means that the country/territory has a legal system which would fall within the civil law legal parent family, and possesses features which would be most closely associated with the civil law type of legal family.

Legal culture has been defined by Lawrence Friedman as 'ideas, values, expectations and attitudes towards law and legal institutions which some public or some part of the public holds' (Friedman (1997)). This is by no means a universally accepted definition, but it is nonetheless a useful way of describing measurable phenomena. It should be noted that some writers use the word 'legal culture' when they are referring to legal systems in general (for example, Ehrmann (1976)). The word 'culture' is, therefore, sometimes used synonymously with tradition (for example, 'This practice is part of the Asian culture', meaning their heritage). It is as well to be aware of these different usages of these terms to refer to similar phenomena. But, the whole enterprise of comparative law is to engage with these terminological variations, and to compare the various systems/traditions/cultures as part of the comparative law methodology.

Comparative law is, therefore, primarily a method of study rather than a legal body of rules. Accordingly, Edwin Patterson prefers to describe it by its French equivalent – *droit compare*. Other commentators have also labelled it comparative jurisprudence or comparative history of law or descriptive comparative law or comparative legislation. Nevertheless, the method theory has been advocated by such eminent commentators as Pollock, Gutteridge and David.

However, this has not been the view of a number of other eminent comparatists, such as Saleilles, Rabel, Rheinstein and Hall who have argued that comparative law should be seen as a social science, so that the data obtained should be seen not just as part of its method, but as forming part of a separate body of knowledge. It would appear that this social science theory has lost ground in more recent times. Yet, another view has been to accept both interpretations so that it may be seen both as a science in its own right, and as a method (see, for example, Winterton (1975) p 71).

There is no generally accepted framework for comparison, although most writers appear to assume that the comparative methods which should be employed are obvious. The basic concept, its aims, and its *raison d'être*, as well its methodology, have attracted somewhat disparaging critical comment (we take up the question of comparative techniques in Chapter 7). For present purposes, it should be noted that the subject's intellectual viability has undoubtedly benefited from the ringing endorsements of Professors Ernst Rabel and Otto Kahn-Freund, both of whom have, over many years, not merely defended, but championed its intrinsic worth as an academic and intellectual discipline. Rabel, for instance, declared: 'Comparative law can free the kernel of legal phenomena from the husk of their formulae and superstructures and maintain the coherence of a common legal structure ...' (cited in Coing, 'Das deutsche schuldrecht und die rechtvergleichung' (1956) NJW 569, p 670; translation by Grossfeld (1990)).

5

Modern comparative law draws from a range of disciplines, but is eclectic in its selection. It recognises the important relationship between law, history and culture, and operates on the basis that every legal system is a special mixture of the spirit of its people, and is the product of several intertwining and interacting historical events, which have produced a distinctive national character and ambience. Alan Watson, for instance, defines comparative law as:

> ... the study of the relationship between legal systems or between rules of more than one system ... in the context of a historical relationship ... [a study of] the nature of law and the nature of legal development. [Watson (1974) pp 6–7.]

Watson, therefore, places primary importance on comparative law as the study of the historical relationship that exists between legal systems, or between rules of more than one system. Legal history and the 'step beyond into jurisprudence' are what Watson regards as the essential ingredients of comparative law as an academic discipline in its own right. Of course, the significance of the legal history behind rules has been acknowledged by a long line of luminaries, including Dawson, Lawson, Merryman, Rene David and Kahn-Freund. Fritz Pringsheim (1961) even went so far as to say that 'comparative law without the history of law is an impossible task'.

Hence, mere comparison of rules *per se* does not constitute comparative law, so, if one accepts Watson's thesis, the comparison would have to be a study of the relationship between the rules of legal systems. What sort of relationships would these have to be? Watson himself suggests there may be three kinds of possible approaches: (a) the historical relationship; (b) the 'inner relationship'; and (c) the same pattern of development theory.

The historical relationship

In this category, it is perhaps most important to note that the private law of societies has nearly always been taken from others, thus tracing the historical background to a given system or rule usually brings insights into the present status of the rule.

The 'inner relationship' (Pringsheim)

This category, which is so described by Pringsheim (1933), appears to be based on an undeniable similarity between peoples or their development, and does not really depend on any actual historical contact, but on a spiritual and psychical relationship between the two different types of peoples, although various forms of 'influence' may well have been experienced by them in the course of historical experience. Watson points to the problems in applying this theory, such as its vagueness, which will make it difficult to define the relationship, and the fact that it will not exist in all areas or at all periods of development. He does, however, see its great value 'in the light which it can shed on major legal matters'. He cites the presence or absence of the trust as a good focus for the analysis of reasons why it has or has not developed in English and Roman law, respectively.

The 'same pattern of development' theory

This relationship has been suggested by commentators who believe that all legal systems in their early development underwent the same or similar stages of development.

While remaining flexible and open minded about the possible outcome of a comparative investigation, the comparatist seeks out those key, distinguishing features of a given society which have a common denominator and mirror image in other societies in the world. These features are then organised so as to form a backdrop to the 'black letter' law of the particular jurisdiction, so as to place it within its historical, social, economic and cultural context.

The elements of 'comparative law'

Despite the somewhat misleading nature of the term 'comparative law', and the suggestion of alternatives, such as 'the comparative study of laws' or 'comparison of laws', the appellation is now reasonably well established. Gutteridge, writing his first edition in 1946, felt that 'comparative law' as a term, although misleading, had become firmly established. It is with some satisfaction that we can confirm this even in the mid-1990s.

Types of comparative studies

What sort of comparative studies would rank as comparative law? Such studies may fall into several categories and Hug (1922) suggests five possible groups of studies: (a) comparison of foreign systems with the domestic system in order to ascertain similarities and differences; (b) studies which analyse objectively and systematically solutions which various systems offer for a given legal problem; (c) studies which investigate the causal relationship between different systems of law; (d) studies which compare the several stages of various legal systems; and (e) studies which attempt to discover or examine legal evolution generally according to periods and systems.

COMPARATIVE LAW DISTINGUISHED FROM OTHER DISCIPLINES

Commentators have sometimes attempted to clarify what comparative law is by saying what it does not include. For example, Watson (1974) states:

(a) Comparative law is not the study of one foreign legal system or part of one legal system, even though there are occasional or even frequent glances at one's own system. A study of one branch of foreign law remains a course on a foreign law, and not comparative law. Zweigett and Kotz (1977) agree with this view.

(b) It is not an elementary account of various legal systems or various legal families of law. Watson argues that there should be 'the necessary intellectual content'.

(c) Comparative law cannot properly be referring to an enterprise which is primarily a matter of drawing comparisons. Watson regards this as the most contentious of his three propositions, and concedes that, for example, those who disagree with this may argue that they may start from an individual legal problem which they regard as the same in more than one jurisdiction, and examine the legal response to it. Watson dissents on the basis that, if the starting point is the problem, the danger is that the main focus of the investigation will be on the comparability of the problem, rather than on the comparability of the law, so that it becomes merely a sociological rather than a legal inquiry.

While propositions (a) and (c) are reasonably well proved by Watson, proposition (b) is not so easily acceptable. What is meant by an 'elementary account'? Is it merely an outline? Surely, a logical starting point of any course on comparative law would have to be an introduction to the world's major legal systems. The writer cannot really imagine that any teacher on comparative law in any institution, apart from perhaps one teaching it as part of a global study subject in school, would leave the matter to rest after the introduction to the legal systems had been completed. Hence, his proposition stands, but its practical applicability must remain fairly unlikely.

Zweigert and Kotz (1977) stress that, in order for an intellectual enterprise to be considered as a comparative law enterprise, there must be 'specific comparative reflections on the problem to which the work is devoted', and that this is best done by the comparatist, stating the essentials of the foreign law, country by country, as a basis for critical comparison, concluding the exercise with suggestions about the proper policy for the law to adopt, which may require him to reinterpret his own system (see Zweigert and Kotz (1977) p 5). They also distinguish comparative law from other areas of law, such as, private international law and public international law. At this juncture, we outline the broad differences between comparative law and these other areas of research and law.

Private international law and comparative law

Private international law is a discrete body of law which is also known as the conflict of laws, or the laws of conflicts, because it is a form of private law which deals with situations, involving private individuals, in which there is a possible conflict of applicable laws. The function of private international law is to provide a solution as to which of several possible legal systems should be applied to a given case which has a foreign element.

Although it therefore appears quite distinct from comparative law, the two in fact interlink, since they both deal with the analysis of the operation of specific rules in several legal systems. The difference is that private international law is much more selective than comparative law, to the extent that the 'choice of law rules' are very narrow. In practice, every legal system will decide a particular problem according to its own rules, and there is still a lack of international consensus on the question of which rules to apply across national frontiers.

Public international law and comparative law

Public international law (often, simply, 'international law') refers to the body of law that governs relationships between States and is, thus, primarily concerned with the rights and duties of States *inter se*. Comparative law is a method of analysing the problems and institutions originating from two or more national laws of legal systems, or of comparing entire legal systems in order to acquire a better understanding thereof, or provide information, and insight into, the operation of the system's institutions or the systems themselves.

International law is a distinct body of law, and one of its sources is listed in the Statute of the International Court of Justice as the 'general principles of law recognised by civilised nations' (Art 38(1)(c)). The interpretation of this principle can only be rooted in the comparative law method.

Legal history, legal ethnology and comparative law

It has long been recognised that law and history are inextricably linked. Carl Joachim Friedrich called law 'frozen history' and argued that the history of the Western world was inconceivable without law. He went on to say: 'From feudalism to capitalism, from Magna Carta to the constitutions of contemporary Europe, the historian encounters law at every turn as a decisive factor' (see Friedrich, *The Philosophy of Law in Historical Perspective* (1963) pp 233–34).

All legal history uses the comparative method, as Maitland (1911) observed: '... history involves comparison and the English lawyer who knew nothing and cared nothing for any system but his own hardly came in sight of legal history ...' and in a forceful endorsement of the comparative method: '... an isolated system cannot explain itself, still less explain its history' (Maitland, *Collected Papers* (1911) pp 488–89).

Legal history is a vital precondition to the critical evaluation of the law and an understanding of the operation of legal concepts, which is a primary aim of comparative law. As some jurists have put it, comparative legal history is 'vertical comparative law', and the comparison of modern systems is 'horizontal comparative law'.

Legal ethnology has historically concentrated on those so called primitive societies which are not yet equipped with the trappings of modern civilisation. Yet, it is more correctly regarded as a branch of ethnology and comparative law, and it seeks generally to discover 'the origins and early stages of law in relation to particular cultural phenomena' (Adam, 'Ethnologische rechtsforschung', in Adam and Trimborn, *Lehrbuch der Volkerkunde* (1958) p 192). As Zweigert and Kotz explain, the task of modern legal ethnology is 'to study the changes suffered by societies already observed in adjusting to the intrusion of a higher civilisation' (Zweigert and Kotz (1977) p 9). Hence, legal ethnology is another branch of comparative law which contributes to the task of comparison and analysis through its own unique discipline and techniques of observation.

Sociology of law and comparative law

There are clearly many points of similarity and overlap between the sociology of law and comparative law. In view of its general aims, comparative law needs legal sociology as much as legal history and legal ethnology. Both legal sociology and comparative law are engaged in charting the extent to which law influences and determines man's behaviour, and the role played by law in the social scheme of things. One fundamental difference between the two is that sociology covers a much wider field than comparative law, and, as Zweigert and Kotz explain, while sociology of law, through field studies and empirical observation, simply observes how the legal institutions operate, comparative law concerns itself with the question of 'how the law ought to be', by studying the rules and institutions of law in relation to each other (Zweigert and Kotz (1977) pp 9–10). Watson has also emphasised the autonomy of law, legal ideas and legal tradition which transcend purely sociological or socio-historical explanations (Watson (1974) p 183).

A RATIONALE FOR COMPARATIVE LAW

Why does one need to look at other societies or other legal cultures? Is it not sufficient to make a detailed and thorough study of one's own culture to gain insights into it? One set of reasons is admirably put by Ehrmann (1976):

... only the analysis of a variety of legal cultures will recognise what is accidental rather than necessary, what is permanent rather than changeable in legal norms and legal agencies, and what characterises the beliefs underlying both. The law of a single culture will take for granted the ethical theory on which it is grounded.

THE ORIGINS OF COMPARATIVE LAW

Early comparative law

Ehrmann's opinion is not a new point of view and can be traced back to the ancient Greeks and Romans. The process of comparative law is believed to have begun in the ancient world, when some of the Greek cities adopted the law of other States, either in whole or in parts. The rationale for this appears to be that the laws or legal institutions of the other State were perceived as superior, or more advanced or sophisticated, and should therefore be deliberately imitated or adopted. It would seem that this imitation was not seen as an adoption of foreign law, but as an adoption of a law that was better than one's own. This process was probably repeated in various other parts of the ancient world.

Sources, such as the famous Twelve Tables, the oldest source of Roman law that has been discovered, indicate that the influence of the Greeks on the Roman culture and civilisation is undeniable. Both the writings of Cicero and Gaius appear to suggest that they believed the apparent legend that a legislative committee had been sent to Athens in order to learn from Greek law and legal institutions when Roman laws were being drawn up.

However, it was only in the classical period of Roman law that the further development of the *jus gentium* came to be influenced by comparative inquiries, and were therefore denationalised, and turned into a form of 'global law'; this was accomplished by a 'combination of comparative jurisprudence and rational speculation' (see Mommsen, *Romisches Staatsrecht* (1887) p 606 and Muirhead, *Historical Introduction to the Private Law of Rome* (1916) p 216). There appears to have been only one comparative attempt to collect diverse laws together dating from the later imperial period of the Roman empire, which was the *Lex Dei*. This was something in the nature of a combination of Roman law and Mosaic principles (the laws of Moses), and is also known as the *Collatio legum Mosaicarum et Romanorum*, which seems to date from c 400 AD. This appears to be one of the earliest known works on comparative law (see Sherman, *Roman Law in the Modern Law* (1922) p 111).

In the Middle Ages, after the fall of the Western Roman Empire, the principle of 'the personality of law' was applied in Western Europe, which meant that each individual was subject to the law peculiar to his nation or tribe. Hence, Roman and Germanic laws were being applied within the same territory. This unique co-existence of different laws suggests that there was familiarity with both Germanic and Roman law, although this did not result in any 'common law' or systematic comparative studies being established. When learning revived in the 900s, the Lombard school was the first secular group to undertake scientific studies on a comparative basis. Feudal law, and canon law, which were already part of the common law of Western Europe, were studied, together with fragments of Roman law in the pre-Justinian version. These medieval scholars, therefore, extended their knowledge to all the major legal systems of their time and civilisation, but it was left to the Glossators and their successors to bring about the great renaissance of Roman law which spread from Bologna (see Chapter 3).

For present purposes, it should be noted that 'the law from Bologna', which was received in nearly all the European countries, and achieved well nigh universal validity as *ratio scripta*, and which was taught in all the university centres of the time, was not really 'Roman law' in its ancient, unadulterated form. It was a combination of ancient law and Roman, and mediaeval and Germanic elements drawn from the Lombardic law, and that of the Italian cities (see Gierke, *Deutsches Privatrecht* (German Private Law) (1895) p 14). More precisely, it was not the law as derived from the Justinian text, but the law as interpreted by various schools of jurists (that is, the Glossators, Commentators *et al*). This version of Roman law and canon law enjoyed an absolute, unquestioned authority which also accounts for the lack of any interest in comparative study at that time. (Chapter 4 deals with the corresponding development of English law at this time.)

In the 16th century, a few comparative studies were produced, but these only dealt with the laws which were co-existing in the same country. In France, customs were reduced to writing at the beginning of the 16th century, but comparative studies were not then undertaken. Roman and Germanic laws were compared in countries like Spain and, eventually, Germany.

In the 17th and 18th centuries, national laws began to burgeon, and jurists on the Continent concentrated on analysis and mastery of their own traditional material, rather than on comparative analyses. Nevertheless, although there was no systematic, objective practice of comparative law evident during the 17th century, various personages like Bacon emphasised the importance of the lawyer freeing himself from the *vincula* (chains) of his national system, in order to make a true assessment of its worth. Leibniz suggested a plan for a 'legal theatre' which could undertake a portrayal of all peoples, places and times on a comparative basis. Subsequent natural law exponents, such as the Dutchman Grotius (1583–1645) and the Frenchman Montesquieu (1689–1755), used the method of comparative law to place their teachings of natural law on an empirical footing. Indeed, Gutteridge regarded Montesquieu as having a claim to being the probable founder of comparative law, since it was he 'who first realised that a rule of law should not be treated as an abstraction, but must be regarded against a background of its history and the environment in which it is called upon to function' (Gutteridge (1949) p 12). Kahn-Freund also appears to take the same view on the status of Montesquieu as the pioneer of comparative law (Kahn-Freund (1974) p 6).

In the 19th century, the influence of 18th century rationalism which led logically to a codification of laws took hold, so that unification and simplification of laws were the watchwords of the time. Various national codes were drawn up, giving rise to the period also being called the era of the 'Great Codifications' and, inevitably, jurists turned their main attention on the interpretation and analysis of these codes. Despite all these codifications, interest in foreign and comparative law eventually began to grow in Germany, France, England and the United States.

The roots of comparative law

Although various factors cohered to produce the comparative line of study, two distinct roots of modern comparative law may be identified:

(a) legislative comparative law; and

(b) scholarly comparative law.

Legislative comparative law

This refers to the process whereby foreign laws are invoked in order to draft new national laws. This process was possibly resorted to even in ancient Rome, although this has never been definitively established. It apparently occurred in Germany in the middle of the 19th century and grew with the movement for codification and unification of Germany. One may therefore exclude older codes, such as the 1794 Prussian General Land Law, and the 1811 Austrian General Civil Code, which are predominantly based on natural law philosophies. In France, the most influential code has been its Civil Code of 1804 which, at least to a certain extent, was an amalgamation of the customary Roman laws of Northern France, and the predominantly Germanic law of Southern France (see Chapter 3).

Among the notable German law examples are the General German Negotiable Instruments Law of 1848, the General Commercial Code of 1861 (which even included studies of the French Commercial Code), the company law reforms of 1870 and 1884, the extended reform process of German criminal law, involving nearly all the well known teachers of criminal law, which produced 15 volumes of comparative material. Nearly 20 years elapsed before a draft criminal code was produced. The most outstanding example of legislative comparative law, is, of course, the German Civil Code (BGB) which unified the private law of Germany from 1 January 1900. The comparative materials which were consulted in order to produce this work of scholarship include the Gemeines Recht, Prussian law, the French Civil Code, Austrian and Swiss law. Ironically, the completion and promulgation of this work gave it an almost encyclopedic and authoritative aura which meant that no recourse to the empirical and functional methods of comparative law resulted in the interpretation of this code, and it is usually only in the preparation of legislative material that comparative methods of study are utilised in Germany (see Chapter 3 on the BGB).

Scholarly comparative law

As an academic discipline, comparative law appears to have taken a long time to achieve recognition. The impetus for the modern methods of comparative law came around the middle of the 19th century, when the intellectual movement we now associate with evolution and Darwinism caught the imagination of intellectuals and scientists across Europe. In the same manner as comparative anatomy, comparative philology and comparative religion, comparative law was swept along in this welter of comparative disciplines engendered by the 'comparative method', hailed by the Victorian author Freeman as 'the greatest intellectual achievement of our time' which signified a stage in the progress of the human mind 'as great and memorable as the revival of Greek and Latin learning' (Freeman, *Comparative Politics* (1873) pp 1, 302).

It was, however, only in the second half of the 19th century that comparative law appears to have gained definite recognition as a branch of legal study, or at least as an approved method for the study of different legal systems. In England, in the 19th century, Sir Henry Maine, another contender for the distinction of being the founder of comparative law, published *Ancient Law* (1861) which had applied to the study of the origins of law, the process of comparison which Charles Darwin had employed in his *Origin of the Species* (1859). Writing in 1871, Maine declared: 'The chief function of comparative jurisprudence is to facilitate legislation and the practical improvement of the law' (Maine, *Village Communities* (1871) p 4). It was this view that was to have an important influence on the expositions of most of the legal comparatists who succeeded him (see p 16, below, for development of comparative law in England).

Various parallel events began to take place in Europe and England. In 1829, in Germany, the German jurists Mittermaier and Zachariae founded a journal for the study of comparative law in collaboration with other foreign jurists. In 1832, a Chair of Comparative Law was founded at the College of France, followed in 1846 by the establishment of a Chair of Comparative Criminal Law in the University of Paris. Other similar professorships were established. In 1869, the Corpus Chair of Historical and Comparative Jurisprudence was founded at Oxford, whose first occupant was Maine himself. In the same year, the French Society of Comparative Legislation was formed in Paris, followed in 1873 by the founding of the Institute of International Law which employed the comparative method in the investigation of the problems of private international law. Germany appeared to be content to devote itself primarily to comparative legal history, and had to wait until 1894 before founding a society similar to the French Society of Comparative Legislation, but full recognition of comparative law as a scholarly discipline was not achieved until after the First World War.

In 1894, the Quain Professorship of Comparative Law was established at University College, London and, in 1895, the English Society of Comparative Legislation was founded, which meant that there were now similar societies on both sides of the Channel.

By the end of the 19th century, France, Germany and even the United States had experienced a revival of interest in comparative law, with similar professorships being established in Columbia and Chicago, and a growing variety of graduate courses in comparative law.

The birth of modern comparative law

'Modern' comparative law is usually recognised as having begun in 1900 at the International Congress of Comparative Law held in Paris, where the first serious and organised attempts were made to formulate the functions and aims of comparative law. Although billed as an international conference, only one Englishman, Sir Frederick Pollock, took part as the representative of the English legal tradition. All other participants were from continental Europe. The conference *zeitgeist* was an optimistic faith in progress, and a strong desire for mastery of one's fate, and the forging of a common destiny. The Congress' two founders, Lambert and Saleilles, talked of a common law of mankind, a world law created by comparative law. Lambert expressed his vision thus:

> ... comparative law must resolve the accidental and divisive differences in the laws of peoples at similar stages of cultural and economic development, and reduce the number of divergencies in law, attributable not to the political, moral or social qualities of the different nations but to historical accident or to temporary or contingent circumstances. [Lambert (1905) Procès-verbaux des seances et documents; Congrès international de droit compare: cited in Zweigert and Kotz (1977) p 2.]

A great deal has changed since that time, not least in the cynicism that has replaced the idealistic, optimistic belief in progress, but also in the fact that comparatists are more knowledgeable and refined in their methods, and now realise that a comparison need not only be carried out between 'peoples at similar stages of cultural and economic development', since it really depends on the aims of the particular comparative investigation (see Chapter 2).

Another date which is also put forward as the birth of comparative law as an academic discipline is 1869, for reasons that we shall now examine.

COMPARATIVE LAW IN ENGLAND

In England, as in Europe, the first half of the 19th century did not see any significant growth in comparative studies, but Burge's *Commentaries on Colonial and Foreign Laws*, written for the practising lawyer, published in 1838, and Leone Levi's book comparing the mercantile laws of Britain with Roman law and the codes, *Commercial Law of the World*, published in 1852, were early attempts to apply the comparative method to practical aspects of law. Burge's work was later praised by Hug (in the United States), and Rabel who declared that the range and quality of the book's treatment made it useful as a substitute for a primer on comparative private law. Levi later proposed the formulation of an international unified code of commercial law and he is, thus, regarded as the first person to suggest the international unification of an entire area of law through the method of comparative law.

At that time, the Judicial Committee of the Privy Council, sitting in London, was also the highest court of appeal for all countries within the British Empire except Britain. This court had to apply the law to several different foreign systems and, apart from hearing appeals from common law jurisdictions, had to hear appeals from jurisdictions, applying Hindu and Islamic laws (India), Singhalese and Tamil laws (Ceylon), Chinese law (Hong Kong, the Malay States, Straits Settlements, Sarawak and Borneo), Roman-Dutch law (Ceylon, South Africa and Rhodesia), aspects of the French Civil Code contained in the Canadian Civil Code of 1866 (Quebec), Norman customs (The Channel Islands) and African and Asian customary laws. As Burge rightly pointed out, there was a need for 'more ready access to the sources from whence an acquaintance might be derived from those systems of foreign jurisprudence' (Burge, *Commentaries on Colonial and Foreign Laws* (1838) p v). The House of Commons' Select Committee recommended in 1848 that the universities establish Chairs in international, comparative, administrative and english law, but it was some years before this was implemented.

A seminal publication of the time was Maine's *Ancient Law*, published in 1861, but it is also possible to date the birth of modern comparative law as a separate academic discipline from the year 1869, when the French founded the Society for Comparative Legislation, and Maine took up his Chair of Historical and Comparative Jurisprudence. Sir Frederick Pollock followed in Maine's tradition who, in his pioneering work on English contract law, made it clear that he was simply translating Savigny's work on ancient Rome in his section on 'Intent to create legal relations'. Maitland also showed great interest in continental legislation, and Gutteridge himself became the doyen of comparatists of the time. Other great comparatists include Sir Otto Kahn-Freund and FH Lawson.

Apart from the establishment of journals, research institutes and a national committee on comparative law, a positive parliamentary step to encourage comparison of laws also occurred. In 1965, parliamentary recognition of the value of comparative law was given, with the enactment of the Law Commissions Act, which created two reform commissions, an English and Scottish Law Commission, whose function, *inter alia*, is to obtain information from other legal systems of other countries, as appears likely to facilitate their function of systematically developing and reforming the law of their country (s 3(1)(f) of the Law Commissions Act 1965). The Law Commission inquires into the function of the legal principle, the framework within which it operates, and, by consultation with foreign and local experts, ascertains whether or not the rule has been successful in achieving what it has set out to do.

There have been other instances of English law borrowing from foreign jurisdictions such as the Scots, for example, pleas of diminished responsibility in the criminal trial, the doctrine of the putative marriage and the procedure for the attachment of earnings. The English Ombudsman idea comes from Scandinavia and, in 1966, the House of Lords issued a statement through its Lord Chancellor which, although prompted by Lord Denning's tendency in certain prominent cases not to follow the House of Lords' rulings when he felt it would produce an unjust result, arguably had similarities with the age old continental practice of reserving the right not to follow any of its past judgments 'where it appeared right to do so' (see [1966] 3 All ER 77), which essentially indicated that they were prepared to correct any mistakes which had occurred. Although this power has been used sparingly, it represents an important judicial attitude which strengthens the law making function of the highest appeal court in the United Kingdom, and has given it a greater measure of flexibility. Continental courts have long regarded such a right to be part of their judicial duty.

An important stimulus for more comparative studies to take place occurred with Britain's entry into the European Community (EC) on 1 January 1973, which meant that the United Kingdom became a member of three European Communities to which all 12 members belong. Subsequently, the EC heads of government then committed themselves to establishing progressively a single market over a period expiring on 31 December 1992. This pledge has been included in a collection of treaty reforms known as the Single European Act 1986, which came into operation on 1 July 1987.

The key to effective comparative analysis is to collect sufficient materials and information which will enable the comparatist to place the particular legal rule or institution or branch of law in context. Norms and patterns of behaviour which one society may deem natural and legal may be categorised as reprehensible and unacceptable in another. In modern times, many of the more important advances have already resulted from 'cross-fertilisation' not just in law, but in science, literature and religion. Comparison enables a strong measure of objective neutrality and critical self-assessment to be applied.

THE CONTEMPORARY SIGNIFICANCE OF COMPARATIVE LAW

Functions and purposes of comparative law

Since its recognition as an academic discipline in its own right in the early 20th century and, indeed, since the 1920s, various comparatists have offered several suggestions on the actual and potential uses of comparative law, in the purely intellectual sense, in social science terms, in the domestic law arena and in the context of international law. We have noted Maine's belief in the legislative function of comparative law, and we have also seen how the 'scholarly' purposes of comparative law developed in Europe. A fair amount of academic ink has flowed under the bridge and crossed the academic Rubicon since then. Accordingly, let us examine the various functions and purposes of comparative law under the following headings:

(a) comparative law as an academic discipline;

(b) comparative law as an aid to legislation and law reform;

(c) comparative law as a tool of construction;

(d) comparative law as a means of understanding legal rules;

(e) comparative law as a contribution to the systematic unification and harmonisation of law.

Comparative law as an academic discipline

Teaching, studying and researching law

In the era of a crowded and ever expanding university law curriculum in which many 'black letter' and 'contextual' optional courses vie for student popularity due to practical value (for example, a company law course, which is seen as impressive to employers), rather than academic value, comparative law has had somewhat mixed fortunes. In 1936, Professor RW Lee, in a Presidential address to the Society for Public Teachers of Law, deplored the paucity of attention given to comparative law, saying 'what we are doing ... for comparative studies in this country [in contrast with] foreign countries is positively shocking' (Lee [1936] JSPTL 3). Since then, a few more universities have launched courses on the comparative method, although it remains confined to a handful of universities even in the 1990s. While many examiners and tutors consider that a PhD thesis should certainly contain some comparative studies covering foreign jurisdictional equivalents, the academic or educational advantages of comparative law has not attracted large numbers of undergraduates.

Comparative law as an academic tradition

Yet, as our historical surveys have shown, the comparative method is an essential part of any initial legal education and it has a more recent tradition going back to 1869 in England, when Maine took up his Chair of Historical and Comparative Jurisprudence, and an ancient tradition going back to the Romans and Greeks. Hence, in some form or other, it has formed part of the legal tradition in both the common law and civil law.

Are there any other justifications to include it in present day undergraduate and postgraduate courses? There are many educational reasons for doing so. First, the comparative method encourages the student to be more critical about the functions and purposes of the rules he or she is studying and to learn not to accept their validity purely because they belong to his or her own system of law. In other words, a wider knowledge of the possible range of solutions to legal problems, gleaned from other jurisdictions is, thereby, made available. Secondly, it will assist in sharpening analytical skills and methodological techniques. Thirdly, it will help to broaden the student's perception of the operation of a legal rule by seeing how it originated and currently operates within different systems, in either similar or different socio-cultural contexts. Fourthly, it gives the student an opportunity to study the interaction of different disciplines and to relate these to the formation and operation of legal rules, for example, when the student sees the interface between law and history. Fifthly, it provides a forum for the cross-fertilisation of experience, ideas, cultures and experience.

Using comparative law in research

The other important value of the comparative method lies in what Yntema called 'the constant refinement and extension of our knowledge of law' (Yntema, 'Comparative legal research: some remarks on "looking out of the cave"' (1956) 54 Mich L Rev 899, p 901), which forms an essential component of legal education.

Paton argues that it is impossible to conceive of the existence of jurisprudence without comparative law (Paton, *A Textbook of Jurisprudence* (1972) p 41), since all schools of jurisprudence, whether historical, philosophical, sociological or analytical, rely on the comparative research methodology. Yntema equated legal research with comparative law, saying the latter was just another name for legal science.

Comparative law as an aid to legislation and law reform

Perhaps the earliest example of the use of the comparative method for legislative purposes is when Greeks and Romans visited cities which they felt could provide them with models of laws that were worth enacting in their own country. More modern commentators have even regarded the aiding of the legislator as the prime function of comparative law. Maine's statement to that effect has been oft quoted, and examples of such borrowings can be found in Germany, England, Italy and Greece. Criminal law and bankruptcy law reforms in Germany have been based on extensive and comprehensive comparative research. Other examples of private law and commercial law areas include illegitimacy, divorce, personality, privacy, and vicarious liability. Italy and Greece have also enacted codes in various areas, based on the results of their comparative studies.

As we have already noted, statute law requires the English Law Commission to procure information from other legal systems, whenever this is seen as facilitating the performance of their function of systematically developing and reforming the law.

Grossfeld (1990) lists many examples of legislators borrowing foreign ideas. For example, the earliest legislation on companies was the French Commercial Code of 1807 which enacted the charter system, and formed the basis of the Prussian company law of 1843. The notion of income tax, which originated in England, was imitated by German legislators. The doctrine of proper allowances for dealings between connected enterprises, which has also been adopted in Germany, derives from the Internal Revenue Code of the United States (s 482). A number of ideas in the German Civil Code are derived from the Swiss Law of Obligations of 1881, and German civil procedure drew heavily from Austrian law. The anti-trust laws of Austria have also inspired German cartel law (see Grossfeld (1990) Chapter 3).

In addition, many so called Third World countries have adopted and adapted Western or socialist laws. One obvious reason has been colonialism and various wars which resulted in hybrid systems co-existing with native customary law. Another has been the ties that have resulted from Western influence which have led to expatriate Western academics setting up institutions of learning, or helping in the drafting of new laws more suited to the changing social and economic conditions of the particular society.

The American Law Institute was established in 1932 as a national institution which undertakes a wide range of comparative legal studies and research aimed at law reform and general restatement of laws. As set out in its constitution, the Institute's purpose is:

> ... to promote the clarification and simplification of the law and its better adaptation to social needs, to secure the better administration of justice, and to encourage and carry on scholarly and scientific legal work.

The leading State agencies, which have used extensive comparative legal techniques for legislation and law reform, are the Louisiana Law Institute and the New York Revision Commission.

A tool of construction

The comparative method has frequently been of practical significance to courts and the judicial process, in filling gaps in legislation or in case law, in providing the background and origin to legal rules and concepts which have been inherited or transplanted from other jurisdictions, in matters which are not covered by a code provision or statute or case law authority. In this way, a variety of solutions to the problem at hand will present themselves. A current, and important example of this, is in the practice of the European Court of Justice of the European Communities (the ECJ). By virtue of their legal background and origins, judges of the ECJ are bound to draw upon their own experience as lawyers within the Member States. The court seeks to evaluate and possibly utilise solutions provided by the legal systems from which the judges are drawn. For example, cases indicate that the French administrative law doctrine of *acte clair* might be followed in order to determine when it is 'necessary' for municipal court to make a 'reference' to the ECJ under Art 177 of the Treaty of Rome.

In *CILFIT Srl v Ministry of Health* [1982] ECR 3415, the European Court of Justice considered the application of Art 177 which requires, *inter alia* that, where a question is raised before a national court of a Member State, that court 'may' request the Court of Justice to give a ruling, 'if it considers that a decision on the question is necessary to enable it to give judgment'. The ECJ stated that 'the correct application of Community law may be so obvious as to leave no scope for any reasonable doubt as to the manner in which the question raised is to be resolved' (see [1982] ECR 3430). This follows the French doctrine of *acte clair*, under which, the theory is that, the obligation to refer does not apply, if the highest court concerned is of the opinion that there can be no reasonable doubt about the answers to the questions raised – there is no need to interpret a provision, if the meaning is clear.

Steiner (1990) suggests that what is clear to one person, may not be clear to another (see Steiner, *EEC Law* (1990) p 268). But, the ECJ has been very careful to point out that various points should be borne in mind in assessing whether the effect of a provision is clear and obvious: the various linguistic versions of the provision should be compared; comparability of legal concepts must be examined; every Community law provision must be placed in its context and interpreted in the light of the provisions of Community law as a whole, in the light of the objectives of Community law and its state of evolution at the date on which the provision involved is to be applied.

The few cases on this area have indicated that the spirit of co-operation and collaboration has generally prevailed among the Member States and the fears of the ECJ being powerless in requiring a national court to make a 'reference' have so far proved groundless. In other areas as well, the court often bases its opinions on comparative law. In Chapter 5, we examine how other municipal legal traditions and doctrines have been adapted and adopted by the ECJ in interpreting Community law – a practical and contemporary example of the use of the comparative method in the international and European sphere.

Aid to understanding legal rules

The comparative law method will increasingly be useful in a practical way for the modern and up to date practitioner. Recourse to comparative law has been at the heart of private international law (or conflict of laws) and, when you consider that so many systems have transplanted and borrowed so many concepts from the major legal systems and adapted them, it is becoming increasingly necessary to be *au fait* with a range of traditions and doctrines, not just because of closer interregional co-operation and trade, but also because of the setting up of transnational law firms, transnational litigation, the ever growing influence of American corporations in foreign countries, drafting of transnational contracts, and international credit arrangements.

International company law is another area where comparative law can make an extremely useful contribution to information, knowledge and understanding. The usual 'groundwork' needed before setting up an international company will usually involve acquiring a good understanding of the legal requirements with which the company will have to comply, and the legal framework within which the company will have to transact its business.

Further, in the ascertainment and application of foreign law in national courts, the comparative method is not just a requirement, but a necessity in order to resolve anything from domestic disputes across boundaries between American States and Mexico (see *State v Valmont Plantations* (1961) 346 SW2d 853), to the law that governs a drilling accident which occurred on a flagless drilling platform, fixed to the continental shelf, off the coast of Scotland. Even if one is inclined to set up a foreign tax haven, one needs to have some knowledge of foreign tax law, and who better to turn to than the lawyer who is highly conversant with tax havens around the world?

The time is coming when not just the European law specialist practitioner, but the comparative law specialist practitioner will be sought after, who will, with very few exceptions, be able to tell his clients dealing in foreign business which legal system they are going to deal with and, more importantly, what that means in terms of the legal requirements of that system.

Contributing to the unification and harmonisation of law

Early history

The idea of unification of laws is one that goes back to ancient history. However, the first movement for unification has been traced by Professor Gutteridge to King James I, who contemplated the unification of the laws of England and Scotland, but did not take it any further as a result of Bacon's discouragement. Unification on a worldwide scale was first proposed by Professor Leon Levi, to the Prince Consort, in connection with the Exhibition of 1851. The first organised measures taken towards unification occurred simultaneously with the revival of interest in comparative law studies, but were, at first, limited to the field of maritime and commercial law. All this was greatly assisted by the great expansion of international trade in the 19th century, which produced various unificatory international conventions dealing with private law, commercial law, trade and labour law, copyright and industrial property law, the law of transport by rail, sea and air, parts of procedural law, particularly in relation to the recognition of foreign judgments and awards. It is also worth noting the work of the Hague Conference in private international law, and the Rome Institute for the Unification of Law which has worked on the law of sale of goods, which has helped to produce the Hague Conventions on the Uniform Laws on International Sales of Goods (see Chapter 12), and the ongoing work of UNCITRAL which shows the continuing interest in some measure of unification in this century.

The Paris Congress

In 1900, the Paris International Congress of Comparative Law was held, and Lambert stressed the practical function of comparative law as being to provide material for the unification of those national systems of law which have attained the same degree of development or civilisation. The aim would then be to replace those national systems with an international common law.

Of course, the world has changed considerably since great jurists like Roscoe Pound and Hessel Yntema envisaged a world of common institutions, concepts and beliefs shared by all 'civilised' nations. The emergence of Africa, Asia, Russia and Latin America made this ideal a 'pious hope' by their sheer diversity of traditions and ideologies, and, even with the tremendous fillip for European economic union provided by the Treaties of Rome establishing the European Communities, the current schisms within Europe over the Maastricht Treaty illustrate the inherent difficulties surrounding European unification, let alone worldwide unification. Uniting the common and civil laws are also in doubt as a result of the current ructions in the European Community, although the creation of the European Community *per se* gives some glimmer of hope to the optimistic unificationist.

Unlike unification which contemplates the substitution of two or more legal systems with one single system, harmonisation of law arises exclusively in comparative law literature, and especially in conjunction with interjurisdictional, private transactions. Harmonisation seeks to 'effect an approximation or co-ordination of different legal provisions or systems by eliminating major differences and creating minimum requirements or standards' (Kamba (1974) 23 ICLQ 485, p 501).

The African situation

In the States of sub-Sahara Africa, there is legal pluralism, and two or three types of law or legal traditions all operate simultaneously in the same country. But, another tradition in West African and East African countries is that of Islamic law. The governments in these countries are, therefore, grappling with the problems of adapting indigenous customary law to the newly industrialised States, and evolving a single system from the different legal traditions. Comparative legal studies would be extremely useful in the process of unifying, or at least harmonising, the laws of these countries. It is in this context that it is perfectly feasible to look to the experience of countries at a different stage of legal, political, social and economic evolution. If the experience of the West is examined, it will be possible not just to modernise and modify the laws, but also to evaluate it and be highly eclectic in selecting which laws might be adopted and adapted to particular local needs and conditions. In this way, the comparative law method will assist in informing any efforts aimed at improving the laws in these countries so that their people may be the ultimate beneficiaries.

The international law dimension

A closely related field of comparative legal research is in the sphere of international law – the law which governs relationships between States. Utilisation of the comparative law method assists in the discovery, elucidation, and application of the 'general principles of law' which international and, occasionally, national courts are directed to apply. Article 38(1)(c) of the Statute of the International Court of Justice (ICJ) directs the International Court to apply, *inter alia*, 'the general principles of law recognised by civilised nations' and Art 215 of the Treaty of Rome 1958, establishing the EEC, provides that the non-contractual liability of the Community is to be governed by 'the general principles common to the laws of the Member States'.

With regard to Art 38(1)(c), Professor Schlesinger has said:

The phrase 'general principles of law recognised by civilised nations' refers to principles which find expression in the municipal laws of various nations.

These principles, therefore, can be ascertained only by the comparative method. [Schlesinger (1988) p 36].

There are, of course, difficulties which confront the international judge in using the comparative law method in the international sphere. Bothe and Ress identify some these problems (see Bothe and Ress (1980) p 61). First, there is the problem of deciding which legal orders should be compared. If he or she selected his principles from only a few legal orders and not others, this would undermine the confidence in the international judicial process of settlement of disputes. Recourse to principles of regional application are on a surer footing and, as we shall see, the recent decisions of the European Court of Justice of the European Communities show that English, French and German concepts are already making their presence felt (see Chapter 5). Secondly, there is the question of comparability or transferability of concepts and principles. It is certainly doubtful whether domestic law concepts can be transposed simply into the bases of international law decisions. It will also be misleading to assume that the guarantee of a certain human right in many State constitutions will automatically mean that States are, therefore, bound to observe that particular right. Nevertheless, there is certainly sufficient material in the internal law of the members of the international community for the international judge to perform a law creating and law making function. It should always be remembered that the comparative method is not intended to replace the judicial function, only to facilitate, clarify and inform it.

The only reliable method of ascertaining principles of law which can authentically be termed 'general' is through 'common core research'. This refers to that area of legal research which endeavours to find the 'common core', or highest common factor, of an area of substantive law (Schlesinger, *Formation of Contracts: A Study of the Common Core of Legal Systems* (1968)), or a legal institution in a number of countries, or of laws and institutions of a number of countries within the same legal system. Common core research will assist jurists and others seeking the international or regional unification of law to initially ascertain the extent of similarity and divergence among the legal systems to be unified, and to be in a better position to assess these features. Under Art 38 of the Statute of the ICJ, the comparative law method assists the International Court in applying international conventions and treaties, and to create new rules or abolish or modify old principles.

The comparative method also assists the international lawyer who requires information on the domestic law of a number of countries. Situations requiring this information might be when regional varieties of international law are sought to be compared (see Green, 'Comparative law as a source of international law' (1967) 42 Tulane L Rev 52, p 55), or when the law of a number of countries have to be studied in the course of preparing a draft treaty, and when international lawyers are required to advise on whether a country has complied with its international obligations (Hazard, 'Comparative law in legal education' (1951) 18 Chicago UL Rev 264).

Examples may be cited from international trade law, where the preparation of international conventions has necessitated reference to the laws of many countries, namely, the law of international sale of goods (see Chapter 12), shipping and transport and international bills of exchange.

The European Court of Justice of the European Communities has been utilising the comparative law method, in interpreting Community law and seeking to reach decisions by evaluating solutions provided by various legal systems, for example, in *Da Costa en Schaake NV* [1963] ECR 31; *French Republic v Deroche, Cornet et Soc Promatex-France* [1967] CMLR 351 (see Chapter 5). Hence, comparative law is a necessary but neglected element in interpreting the law of international organisations. In addition, national courts are increasingly being required to interpret and apply international law. The comparative legal method enables this to be done in a systematic, organised and comprehensive manner.

KEY CONCEPTS IN THE COMPARATIVE LAW METHOD

The parent legal family and legal traditions

Certain key concepts in the comparative law method may be highlighted. For purposes of comparison, we shall assume that we are using the 'parent legal family' or major legal family as our basic model for comparison. The notion of legal family has served as the organisational linchpin for the analysis of legal systems of the world. This concept did not originate with Professor Rene David, although his masterly exposition of the world's major legal systems in *Les Grands Systemes de Droit Contemporains*, 1950 (see, now, David and Brierley (1985)) has been regarded as a seminal work. The concept of legal families was certainly outlined by Montesquieu, so it is at least as old as the 18th century. It is discussed further in Chapter 2. Hence, when we refer to 'civil law countries', we are referring primarily to countries which have inherited the Romano-Germanic traditions (which are part of the civil law tradition) which have a distinctive juristic style. As we have seen, a legal tradition is not a set of rules within a particular jurisdiction, but a set of historically conditioned attitudes to the role of law in a particular society, its characteristic mode of legal thought and its legal sources and basic ideology. Within the civil law tradition, however, we have the French legal tradition *and* the German legal tradition. Both of these come within the civil law tradition because their legal system originates from Roman law and was based on compilations of the Emperor Justinian, as it was interpreted and disseminated by scholars from Bologna in the 12th century. They also share a tradition of devising systematic, authoritative and comprehensive codifications as their law making style, working from general concepts and providing solutions to problems. However, apart from differences in the structure of their codes, they are themselves distinguishable in their separate legal traditions.

The French legal tradition is based on a rigid separation between private and criminal law on the one hand, and 'public' or administrative law on the other; these form in reality two discrete systems of law, each with their own courts, their own unique legal concepts and their own commentators and learned authors. It also adopts a deductive method of reasoning, inferring its rules from broad maxims, and deriving solutions from those rules, through a sequence of logically correct deductions. This method is applied to (a) private and criminal law on the basis of the codes which resulted from the Napoleonic codification; and (b) to administrative law, elaborated and developed by the administrative courts, particularly the Conseil d'État, on the basis of the principles of legality.

The German legal tradition was greatly influenced by the 19th century Pandectist Movement, which was produced from the German Historical School of Law, whose only aim was the dogmatic and systematic study of Roman material. The eventual result was a conceptual, systematic law produced to a high level of abstraction in the German Codes, really very different from the French Codes in their tone, mode of expression and extraordinary precision.

But, these two traditions may legitimately be classed together since, for example, they both adopt codifications as their preferred style and both work from the general to the particular in their method of legal reasoning. Similarly, the primacy of legislation is therefore common to both systems, with codes and enacted law being primary sources of law.

The French and German legal systems have influenced a large number of countries where their codes and codificatory style have served as models of law making and legal philosophy. The civil law tradition, of course, is itself made up of several subtraditions: Roman civil law, canon law, commercial law, the French revolution and legal science (see Merryman (1985) p 6 *et seq*).

In contrast, the basic approach of the English common law tradition is case based law, founded on judicial decisions and the doctrine of judicial precedent (*stare decisis*). In more recent times, especially during the Conservative party's period of government in Britain, between 1979–95, cases have been heavily supplemented by legislation, which has taken over as the primary method of law making. Indeed, in a reversal of the earlier phases of common law history, judges have frequently been reminded by other more senior or traditional judges that their role is only one of interpretation, not law making, when it comes to the interpretation of statutes. Within this particular area, the common law frequently resembles the civil law in giving precedence (at least in strict theory, and sometimes in practice) to the 'intention of the legislature' and the 'intention of Parliament'. However, important decisions from the

House of Lords, sitting as a judicial body and the highest appellate court within Britain, have continued to shape and influence the law.

Accordingly, we shall compare the basic approaches, methodology, and ideology of civil law systems with the common law system as it functions and operates in present times as the mother system or parent legal family of the 'common law'.

Sources of law

Another important concept in comparative law is the term 'sources of law'. This can mean different things in different countries and, even in the same country, can mean different things according to different writers. As Professor David points out, however, all the divergent interpretations stem from one single fact: a lack of agreement on the meaning of 'law' (see David, 'Sources of law', in *International Encyclopedia of Comparative Law* (1981) Chapter 3, p 3). This, like sources of law, is partly attributable to the ambiguity of language and the difficulties in obtaining an authentic translation.

Generally speaking, the legislatures of the countries of the world have failed to address this question, presumably to reserve the right to decide what sources of law they will refer to, or change or abolish, according to the needs of the moment. Pragmatically, of course, the legislatures of various countries have simply had other more urgent matters to attend to, and usually concern themselves with regulation of a specific practical problem.

Even when statutes set out a hierarchy of sources, it is still necessary to refer to academic works, because the sources often include custom and tradition, which themselves are often undefined and variable.

In reality, 'the subject of sources of law may be governed by different principles, depending on the branch of law' (David (1981) p 11). Ideally, one would need to examine politics, sociology, psychology and many other areas to seek a definitive answer to the problem of defining a 'source of law'. In purely legal terms, we need only examine the historical background to a particular jurisdiction to see the factual and formal sources and deduce from those sources the current legal position. Hence, nearly every analysis of a legal systems or concept is preceded by a brief historical examination thereof.

The formal sources of law are legislation, codes, judicial decisions, custom, doctrinal or scholarly writing and equity. Each legal system has its sources which have a particular hierarchical structure. Thus, the main sources of law in civil law countries are the codes, enacted law, doctrinal writing, custom and decided cases. It should be noted that the role of cases as a source of law is officially a secondary one of supplementing enacted law or doctrinal sources. There is no legal doctrine of *stare decisis* in the civil law tradition, so that in theory, a case may simply be ignored and need not be followed by a subsequent court. The basic premise is that the legislator, not the judge, creates or makes law. In practice, of course, cases have played a pivotal role in developing the law in civil law countries, especially where the codes or statutes have not provided for novel or difficult situations.

Comparative law method

We shall discuss the different techniques that may be utilised in the process of comparison in Chapter 2. Initially, this will be based on the guidelines of Zweigert and Kotz (1977), but not entirely. Despite a number of features which distinguish one legal system from another, perhaps the litmus test of what is the heart and soul of a system, and its quintessential character, is not merely its language or terminology, its organisation, institutions or structure. As GW Bartholomew, when speaking about the common law, puts it:

> ... it is in fact no one single thing. It is neither a matter of substantive rules nor a matter of [procedures] in the administration of justice. It resides, it is submitted, in the mental attitudes and habits of legal thought that historically evolved ... and which are still used and followed by lawyers and judges.

By examining a system's history, mode of thought in legal matters, sources of law and legal ideology (collectively called the 'style' of a legal system by Zweigert and Kotz (1977) p 62) we may be better able to understand, appreciate and evaluate our own systems in a systematic and productive way. If used successfully, that understanding, appreciation and evaluation must be the greatest rewards that one may derive from comparative law.

As we approach the new millennium, perhaps more than in nearly any other period in world history, we need to appraise afresh the new world order. The Western and Eastern blocs of the world have now entered into various political, economic and cultural co-operative ventures which have presaged the gradual, but decisive, disintegration of the communist bloc that has swept across Eastern Europe, fragmenting and replacing the old Soviet Union with new independent republics and one rather tenuous 'Commonwealth', which is really more like a Federation of States, and which now wishes to be known as the Russian Federation. This has left only communist China reasonably intact as the last communist superpower still advocating the 'old' socialism. The catchphrase of the 1980s and early 1990s in the international context has been the 'global village' in which we now live, hence, it is surely counter-productive for lawyers, as much as for anyone else, to continue to exist in 'splendid isolation'. As McDougal appropriately expressed it as long ago as 1952:

> In a world shrinking at an ever accelerating rate because of a relentlessly expanding, uniformity imposing technology, both opportunity and need for the comparative study of law are unprecedented.

These words remain true even as we approach the year 2000.

SELECTIVE BIBLIOGRAPHY

Bothe and Ress, 'The comparative method and international law', in Butler (ed), *International Law in Comparative Perspective* (1980)

Butler, *International Law in Comparative Perspective* (1980)

Cotterrell, 'The concept of legal culture', in Nelken (ed), *Comparing Legal Cultures* (1997)

Dainow 'The civil law and the common law: some points of comparison' (1966–67) 15 Am J Comp L 419

David and Brierley, *Major Legal Systems in the World Today* (1985)

de Vries and Schneider, *Civil Law and the Anglo-American Lawyer* (1976)

Derrett, *An Introduction to Legal Systems* (1968)

Dutoit, 'Comparative law and public international law', in Butler (ed), *International Law In Comparative Perspective* (1980)

Ehrmann, *Comparative Legal Cultures* (1976)

Friedman, 'The concept of legal culture: a reply', in Nelken (ed), *Comparing Legal Cultures* (1997)

Glendon, Gordon and Osakwe, *Comparative Legal Traditions: Text, Materials and Cases on the Civil and Common Law Traditions, with Special Reference to French, German, English and European Law*, 2nd edn (1994)

Grossfeld, *The Strength and Weakness of Comparative Law* (1990)

Gutteridge, *Comparative Law* (1946); (1949); (1971) (reprint)

Kahn-Freund, 'Comparative law as an academic subject' (1966) 82 LQR 40

Kamba, 'Comparative law: a theoretical framework' (1974) 23 ICLQ 485

Markesinis, 'Comparative law – a subject in search of an audience' (1990) 53 MLR 1

McDougal, 'The comparative study of law for policy purposes: value clarification as an instrument of democratic world order' (1952) 1 Am J Comp L 24

Merryman, *The Civil Law Tradition* (1985)

Pringsheim, 'The inner relationship between English and Roman law' [1933] 5 CLJ 347

Sacco, 'Legal formants: a dynamic approach to comparative law' (1991) 39 Am J Comp L 1, p 343

Schlesinger *et al*, *Comparative Law: Cases, Text, Materials* (1988)

Schlesinger, 'The past and future of comparative law' (1995) 43 Am J Comp L 477

Von Mehren and Gordley, *The Civil Law System* (1977)

Vranken, *Fundamentals of European Civil Law* (1997)

Watson, *Legal Transplants* (1974)

Winterton, 'Comparative law teaching' (1975) 23 Am J Comp L 69

Zweigert and Kotz, *An Introduction to Comparative Law* (1977) Vols I and II, (1987)

Zweigert and Kotz, *An Introduction to Comparative Law,* 2nd edn (1992); 3rd edn (1998)

CHAPTER 2

THE CLASSIFICATION OF LEGAL SYSTEMS INTO LEGAL FAMILIES

TERMINOLOGY

Legal traditions and legal families

It has become established practice to classify the legal systems of the world into three main types of legal families or legal traditions: civil law, common law and socialist law. A legal tradition has been defined as a set of 'deeply rooted historically conditioned attitudes about the nature of law, the role of law in the society and the political ideology, the organisation and operation of a legal system' (see Merryman (1985)). Merryman goes on to suggest that whereas 'a legal system is an operating set of legal institutions, procedures and rules ... a legal tradition puts the legal system into cultural perspective'. Hence, he makes a clear distinction between a legal system and a legal tradition. On the other hand, David and Brierley prefer to talk of the three main legal families (that is, civil law, common law and socialist law) described as eponymous models, 'certain laws which can be considered typical and representative of a family which groups a number of laws' (see David and Brierley (1985)). In the same vein, Zweigert and Kotz (1977) also adopt the language of legal families, but emphasise, at great length, the pitfalls and problems that may be encountered in arriving at some sort of consensus among the comparatists, as to the set of criteria that should be employed, in order to classify the various legal systems into legal families, or according to their particular legal tradition. Efforts to achieve consensus on criteria have so far been largely unsuccessful. Consequently, in their third edition of 1998, while acknowledging that 'one's division of the world into legal families and the inclusion of systems in a particular family is vulnerable to alteration by historical development and change', and depends on 'the period of time of which one is speaking', and that objections to the method of classification must be taken seriously, Zweigert and Kotz could still confidently assert that, so far, no better (or 'worthwhile') method of classification has appeared (see Zweigert and Kotz (1998) p 67). However, it is submitted that there is, at root, far more concordance between the ostensibly divergent views because, in a sense, the matter turns on terminology and interpretation, and the different approaches are largely consistent with each other. Hence, to say that jurisdiction A belongs to the civil law tradition (which includes all the facets mentioned by Merryman) because it conforms to a certain set of civil law criteria is not inconsistent with saying that jurisdiction A should be classified within the civil law parent legal family because it conforms to similar criteria. The point is that jurisdiction A, or indeed legal system A (if that term is preferred), will, under either approach, be classified as a civil law jurisdiction or system. To a certain extent, therefore, some of the academic dialectic represents a distinction without a difference. Real problems and practical difficulties only arise if there is a disagreement over the classificatory criteria, which would assist in determining which law to apply to a given situation, and it is not possible to decide whether jurisdiction A (assuming it is an obscure country) belongs to a civil law system or tradition, or to any other major legal family. It might, for instance, be a 'hybrid' or mixed legal system, and knowledge of the laws of that legal system might be required, if the conflict of laws rule of a domestic forum points to the internal law of a foreign country as the law that governs the particular case. At this point, as a broad generalisation, it may be said that most legal systems in the world today possess characteristics which are predominantly identified with one or more of the three major legal traditions or parent families, that is, civil law, common law and (at least until recently) socialist law. This does not, of course, mean that this trichotomy encompasses every possible legal system existing in the modern world. In places like Asia and Africa and the Islamic countries, powerful elements of customary law (of non-European origin) still remain and are in evidence in varying degrees.

Classification of legal systems

At the beginning of the 20th century, a groundswell of opinion arose favouring widespread comparative studies and, in 1900, the concept of 'families of law' was introduced to comparative law. One of the ultimate aims of the comparative studies was to secure total or at least substantial unification of all civilised legal systems. As mentioned in Chapter 1, 1900 was the year of the First International Congress of Comparative Law which was held in Paris. In 1905, Esmein suggested a classification of legal systems into five families of law: Romanistic, Germanic, Anglo-Saxon, Slavic and Islamic. In 1977, Zweigert and Kotz divided legal families into eight groups: Romanistic, Germanic, Nordic, Common Law Family, Socialist, Far Eastern Systems, Islamic Systems and Hindu Law. Their criterion – juristic style – is discussed in detail below. In 1978, David and Brierley adopted a classificatory system based on ideology and legal technique, so that law families could be classified into Romano-Germanic, Common Law, Socialistic, Islamic, Hindu and Jewish, Far East and Black African.

Examples of each type of legal family

Countries that are usually classified as common law jurisdictions are England and Wales, Australia, Nigeria, Kenya, Zambia, the United States of America,

New Zealand, Canada, and various parts of the Far East, such as Singapore, Malaysia and Hong Kong. Civil law countries include France, Germany, Italy, Switzerland, Austria, Latin American countries, Turkey, various Arab States, North Africa and Madagascar. Socialist systems of law included Bulgaria, Yugoslavia and Cuba and, until recently, the former USSR, which has since disintegrated and is now comprised of 11 independent States who agreed to form the world's second commonwealth (initially known as the Commonwealth of Independent States (CIS)) and now wish to be called the Russian Federation, and four of the former soviet republics, who have declared their independence and remain outside the CIS. Examples of hybrid or mixed jurisdictions are The Seychelles, South Africa, Louisiana, the Philippines, Greece, Quebec in Canada and Puerto Rico. For these jurisdictions, there is some difficulty in classifying the legal family to which they belong, and even looking to the system to which they most are predominantly similar, will only be helpful up to a point.

The notion of legal families is not free from criticism and has been variously interpreted. Indeed, there is no consensus among commentators as to whether it is purely heuristic (David), basic and scientific (Knapp), or theoretically and descriptively useless (Friedmann). Even where the concept has been used, there has not been any consensus as to the criteria for classification, for example, Zweigert and Kotz prefer 'juristic style', while Glasson and Sarfatti focus on a system's historical origins as a distinguishing or identifying feature. There is equally no agreement on the groupings of the various legal systems. Undoubtedly, a range of alternative classifications will always be possible, depending on the data available and the particular interpretation of that data. It is certainly arguable that each classification will have some merit and, in factual terms, there are observable characteristics of each system which place it predominantly within one legal family or another (that is, the 'predominance principle'). The factual basis or antecedents of Canadian, American and Australian law are demonstrably English law. Similarly, the French influence on its eastern neighbours only becomes disputable when one has to decide the boundaries of this influence. Again, the widespread influence of Islam and the Koran is objectively observable in a number of countries. It is only when a comparatist seeks to classify various distinguishing features into groups of systems, and attempts to demarcate the parameters of those groups, that disagreement inevitably arises. Nevertheless, the question that should be answered with regard to classification is: What is the purpose of the classification? This takes us back to issues raised in the Chapter 1 and, essentially, it has been seen that factual, ideological, and historical characteristics may all be synthesised so as to enable a valid blueprint for comparison. By utilising the 'predominance principle', we move closer to a clearer classification of the various systems. It needs to be remembered, of course, that political, economic, social and moral factors all exert considerable influence on the profile of a legal system, and the fact that history is written by victors suggests that the political fortunes of a country will inevitably be reflected in its post-war or post-crisis legal, economic and social framework.

Criteria used to classify legal systems

Various criteria have been suggested as a means of determining the classification of a particular system, ranging from race and language (Sauser-Hall), culture (Schnitzer), 'substance' (substantive content of laws) (Arminjon, Nolde and Wolff), ideology, philosophy, conceptions of justice and legal technique (David), historical origins (Glasson and Sarfatti) and juristic style (Zweigert and Kotz). One should remember that the particular stage of development of a given legal system which is selected for comparison, will also play a significant part in the process of classification. It is proposed to examine the Zweigert and Kotz approach, with the proviso that the predominance principle should be applied. These two writers suggest that juristic style should be the crucial test which determines the classification of a legal system, which they suggest may be ascertained from:

(a) the historical background and development of the system;

(b) its characteristic (typical) mode of thought;

(c) its distinctive institutions;

(d) the types of legal sources it acknowledges and its treatment of these;

(e) its ideology.

EXAMINATION AND APPLICATION OF THE CRITERIA

Historical development

As far as historical development is concerned, it is widely accepted that the English common law development was fairly clear cut, wherein a large body of rules founded on unwritten customary law evolved and developed throughout the centuries with pragmatism, strong monarchs, an unwritten constitution and centralised courts being its typical features (see Chapter 4). This distinctive development justifies its separate classification. On the other hand, as we have already noted, non-common law systems have had a more chequered history and this has caused writers to label civil law systems 'Romano-Germanic' (David and Brierley). This reflects both the Roman law origins, strong influence of the French Civil Code and the subsequent influence of the German Civil Code. However, more significant has been the influence and reception of Roman law within a particular system. It was

Roman law, with its notions of codification, systematisation of concepts into categories, principles and divisions of law, which has left its lasting imprint on the French and German Codes. This was in stark contrast to common law adoption of substantive law principles which developed in an *ad hoc* fashion, in response to the need to resolve disputes, whose development was largely dependent on disputants bringing their case to the courts. As we shall see (see Chapter 11), there was no common law legislative tradition which sought to reform or redress the law by means of the legislature, unlike the civil law. The significant historical fact, therefore, is that common law was developed in and by the courts, giving judge made law considerable 'weight', whereas civil law was formulated, compiled and refined in the universities, later codified and then given statutory force by the legislature. This also explains some of the differences in approach and content. Eastern Europe and the former Soviet Union, of course, have traditionally been labelled 'socialist' legal systems, reflecting their Marxist-Leninist origins and ideology. It should be reiterated at this point that, in the light of the unification of East and West Germany in 1990, the continuing decline of Communist regimes in eastern regimes and the disintegration of the former Soviet Union in 1991, partly replaced by the new Russian Commonwealth of Independent States (comprising 11 of the former Soviet republics), the whole notion of 'socialist law' is now called into question. Even on the predominance principle, it has yet to be settled what type of legal system the new Russian Federation will eventually adopt (Chapter 5 discusses current Russian developments). Upon reflection, this identifying characteristic is reasonably helpful with the proviso that the non-occurrence of a particular type of historical evolution or historical experience in a given system does not, of course, mean that the particular system is not predominantly a common law, socialist or civil law system. We must therefore consider another significant, more wide ranging historical phenomenon: colonialism, of one form or another. For instance, outside Europe, the fact that a given jurisdiction was not dominated by a particular code, or not evolved through centralised courts, has, in many cases, nothing to do with its legal history and legal evolution. The historical explanation for Far Eastern, Antipodean and American jurisdictions is found in British, French and Dutch colonialism. In the first instance, British, French and Dutch control of places like Malaysia and India, Africa and Indonesia meant that predominantly common law or civil law was 'received' in these areas. However, in view of the diversity and uncertainty of local customary laws, codifications of laws were introduced into places like India and, to a lesser extent, in the Far East, so as to clarify, unify, modernise and adapt the foreign law to local conditions. Hence, the really significant historical development was the occurrence of colonialism which, ultimately, produced a plurality of laws. So, the first criterion is acceptable with the foregoing caveat: look to the history but consider other criteria as well.

Mode of legal thinking

As a generalisation, civil law, or Germanic and Romanistic legal families, tend to think in abstract, conceptual and symmetrical terms. Civil law, derived from universities and Roman law, is rule based and constantly seeks solutions to a problem before the court. It also thinks in terms of institutions, whereas the English common law is typical for its concrete, court based approach, seeking pragmatic answers to issues before the court. Where civil law proceeds from general principle to general principle, common law proceeds from case to case. Where cases have formed the primary source of the common law, statutes and codified law have been the civil law counterparts. While common lawyers think in terms of the parties and their particular legal relationship, civil lawyers think in terms of the existing enacted rules, codified or statutory, which may be applied to a given situation. Another consequence of the historical development which is reflected in the mode of legal thinking is the civil law penchant for planning, systematising and regulating everyday matters as comprehensively as possible. In contrast, the classic common law characteristic is to improvise, examining cases for possible precedents, which may or may not be 'binding' on the court currently hearing a case, and only deciding to legislate in any sort of organised and comprehensive fashion if the particular area of law happens to be confused, obscure or reveals a 'gap' in the law. Even when ostensibly comprehensive statutes are passed, the preceding case law is often relevant as a guide to interpretation since the enactment of the statute, is, generally, seen as a consolidation (and possibly clarification) of existing law. The common law statute, therefore, seeks generally to build or improve on existing case law, whereas the civil law equivalent has traditionally sought to enunciate universally applicable principles, clearly set out for either the citizen (as in the French Code), or the specialist (as in the German Code). It frequently sets out to establish new laws, and to do so explicitly. Of course, recent trends have indicated that the common law and civil law systems have been coming closer together in their use of cases and statutes. The United Kingdom Children Act 1989, which came into force in October 1991, while incidentally consolidating and integrating certain existing case derived rules and statutes, was enacted predominantly to effect 'the most comprehensive and far reaching reform of English child care law ever introduced' into the United Kingdom in the 20th century (Sir Geoffrey Howe: House of Commons Debates; 26 October 1989, vol 158, col 1071). On the other hand, civil law systems, particularly France and Germany, have begun to rely more and more on cases where, for example, the enacted or codified law has been found deficient in any way. Socialist law, as developed and based on Marxist-Leninist ideas, has also relied on codification (see explanations of the term, below) from early times, and on statutory rules to the exclusion of case law and with no doctrine of precedent as such. It had its roots in ancient Roman law and, thus, uses civil law legal terminology and civil law classifications and conceptualisations (see Chapter 6). However, its unique feature was that it simply viewed law as an instrument of State Policy, and merely as a vehicle for carrying out Marxist/Leninist ideals. Law was to be used for the purpose of implementing the State Plan in accordance with Marxist philosophy. In contrast to civil law and common law, it has traditionally seen law as created by the State and subordinate to the State. Clearly, therefore, so called socialist countries have, in many respects, been easily discernible and readily classifiable since, in the former Soviet Union, for example, the supremacy of the State machinery (the Russian Communist Party and the politburo) over any other organisation was manifest. The second criterion is therefore readily applicable at least in the first instance.

Distinctive legal institutions

In common law jurisdictions, the typical legal institutions are the trust, agency, tort principles, consideration and estoppel. In the Romanistic family, however, there is a strong tendency towards formalism and 'rules protecting the moral and economic integrity of the legitimate family against outsiders' (Zweigert and Kotz). There is also the direct action, oblique action, and abuse of right, to name but a few unique legal institutions. The Germanic family has institutions such as the abstract real contract, *clausulae generales*, the concept of the legal act, the notion of unjust enrichment, the doctrine of the collapse of the foundations of a transaction and liability based on *culpa in contrahendo*. Typical institutions in socialist legal systems included different types of ownership, unique notions of the role and status of contract in a planned economy, and the 'duty to rescue'. As parts of the former Soviet Union, which, since 1992, wishes generally to be called the Russian Federation, but which formerly called itself the Commonwealth of Independent States (CIS), lurches towards some form of capitalist economy and attempts to introduce social democracy, recent edicts passed suggest that there will be radical changes in ownership and the notion of contract and property for private persons and new entities created in the nature of Western style private companies. It is quite conceivable that Western commercial and legal notions will co-exist with more antiquated traditions rooted in civil law, but supported by a quasi-military government operating as a 'benevolent dictatorship' on the lines of certain Latin American countries. On the other hand, a predominantly social democracy, utilising civil law codifications, might yet emerge with the threat of military force being used simply to preserve order, peace and security. Changes paving the way for an independent judiciary have already been implemented (see Chapter 6), so that legal conceptions dealing with commercial and private enterprise will also change. On balance, therefore, the second criterion appears to be defensible and a positive aid to classification.

Choice of sources of law

The next identificatory feature suggested by Zweigert and Kotz is the much discussed topic of sources of law. Basically, the debate has centred on whether cases or statutes are the predominant source of law in any given legal system. Zweigert and Kotz argue that, although differences exist with regard to methods of interpretation, court structures and procedures, this topic is really of minor significance in the context of legal families and comparative law as a whole. They would attach far greater significance to the legal institutions of a legal system. It is not entirely clear why Zweigert and Kotz express this view. One obvious reason may be that all systems now use both cases and statutes (and/or codes) as sources, so that mere usage of one or the other is, *ipso facto*, inconclusive and, therefore, irrelevant to their classification. Nevertheless, applying the present writer's 'predominance principle', it is still true to say that, at the present time, the primary source of law in civil law countries, such as France and Germany, is still predominantly codified or enacted law, whereas, in common law countries, it is still predominantly case law. Exceptions to this general proposition clearly exist but, in this case, the exceptions certainly prove the rule. Moreover, it is also true to say that while common law and civil law courts use both cases and statutes as sources of law, their approaches to these sources, methods and techniques of abstraction diverge sufficiently to warrant differentiation. In short, common law and civil law jurisdictions both handle cases and statutes, but they do so in different ways (see Chapters 8 and 9). Civil law countries, like France and Germany, also have written constitutions, unlike the United Kingdom. However, the English common law based United States adopted a written constitution, which has played a fundamental part in the development of citizen's rights and responsibilities, in a similar manner to France and Germany. Thus, mere similarity of sources of law, at least in the context of written or unwritten constitutions, is of limited importance in ascertaining the true 'juristic style' of a legal system. Clearly, other criteria must also be taken into account.

Ideology of a legal system

This is interpreted by Zweigert and Kotz as meaning 'political or economic doctrines or religious belief'. This appears to be the least contentious of all the criteria, since it is widely recognised that the legal ideologies of Anglo-Saxon, Germanic, Romanistic and Nordic families are similar in all important respects. Equally, countries like China, Mongolia, North Vietnam, North Korea, and, until recently, Russia and many countries in Eastern Europe, have adopted a communist theory of law based on Marxist/Leninist philosophy, which warrants placing them in a separate category or legal family. Religious legal systems, such as Hindu and Muslim systems, also justify separate categorisation in view of their uniqueness. However, it is not so easy to classify the legal families of the West since their ideologies are so similar. They may be more readily classifiable according to their history, mode of legal thinking, and distinctive institutions. Sources of law are a distinguishing feature of Hindu and Islamic law and also help to separate the European continental from the Anglo-Saxon type of legal family. However, again as a consequence of recent momentous events in Eastern European and Russian jurisdictions, it has become extremely difficult to say what the eventual ideologies of these countries seeking independence will be. The better view would appear to be that some form of social democracy will emerge, although this will arguably be of a species still steeped in civil law legal approaches, and heavily dependent on State policy and enacted law. Hence, enacted law will continue to enjoy primacy, and only economic growth, followed by political maturity and experience, will lead to the emergence of a greater reliance on cases. In the case of 'mixed jurisdictions' or 'hybrid' systems of law, where civil law and common law co-exist, with or without local customary law, it will be even harder to apply the above named criteria (see Chapter 7).

CONVERGENCE THEORY AND LEGAL UNITY

As legal systems continue to resemble each other in their use of sources of law, there may well evolve a situation where both statutes and cases are being used in equal measure and even regarded as authoritative as each other. There is a discernible tendency to place more reliance on opinions of legal or doctrinal writers in common law jurisdictions, albeit for areas of law that are relatively undeveloped, such as medical law, and possibly a considerable reduction in the weight attributed to local custom in the 'modernisation' of systems of law. Would this mean that a convergence of systems had occurred, or would eventually occur? The debates over the Maastricht Treaty with regard to European co-operation, ongoing civil wars in parts of Eastern Europe, and the uncertainty over the future of the new Russian Federation and its uneasy relationship with the West over a range of critical issues, suggests that even European unity (between East and West, or among Western European countries) at the practical level is, at present, little more than an ideal. The 'euro' as a common currency was launched in early 1999, although, even in 2001, it will only be used by certain European countries. If closer European economic co-operation is eventually achieved, this will be but one small step towards some form of unity. As far as legal families are concerned, therefore, it is still relevant, useful and accurate to examine common law and civil law systems according to the criteria we have been discussing, and to reflect on the identifying characteristics of the few remaining countries which are still avowedly socialist legal systems. The convergence theories will be discussed in detail in the final chapter of this book, but suffice to say for the moment that, although convergence in certain respects is possible, deep seated differences in ideology, political attitudes, social and economic policies, not to mention fundamental moral values and philosophies, attitudes to law, and judicial, executive and administrative structures, would first have to be reconciled with each other. Wholesale integration is certainly not a likely prospect in the foreseeable future, but a preliminary attempt at harmonisation of elements of different systems has already begun in the context of the European Union.

SELECTIVE BIBLIOGRAPHY

Butler and Kudriavtsev (eds), *Comparative Law and Legal System* (1985)

Chloros, 'Common law, civil law and socialist law: three leading systems of the world, three kinds of legal thought' (1978) Cambrian L Rev 11

Dainow, 'The civil law and the common law: some points of comparison' (1966–7) 15 Am J Comp L 419

David and Brierley, *Major Legal Systems In The World Today* (1985), Pts 1–3

Eorsi, *Comparative Civil (Private) Law* (1979)

Friedman, 'Some thoughts on comparative legal culture', in Clark (ed), *Comparative and Private International Law: Essays in Honor of John Henry Merryman* (1990) p 49

Ioffe and Maggs, *Soviet Law in Theory and Practice* (1983)

Lawson, 'Comparative judicial style' (1977) 25 Am J Comp L 364

Lawson, 'Many laws', in *European Studies in Law* (1977) Vol I

Lawson, 'The comparison' in *European Studies in Law* (1977) Vol II

Markesinis, *The Gradual Convergence* (1994) Chaps 1 and 5

Merryman, *The Civil Law Tradition* (1985)

Pringsheim, 'The inner relationship between English and Roman law' [1933] 5 CLJ 347

Smith, 'The unique nature of the concepts of Western law' (1968) 46 Canadian Bar Rev 191

Sypnowich, *The Concept of Socialist Law* (1990)

Varga, *Comparative Legal Cultures* (1992)

Vranken, *Fundamentals of European Civil Law* (1997)

Zweigert and Kotz, *An Introduction to Comparative Law* (1977); (1998)

CHAPTER 3

THE CIVIL LAW SYSTEM

TERMINOLOGY

Different meanings of 'civil law'

It is important to clarify the terminology that is used to describe civil law systems and the civil law tradition, because the term 'civil law' is susceptible to several different meanings. Civil law, in one sense, refers to the entire system of law that currently applies to most Western European countries, Latin America, countries of the Near East, large parts of Africa, Indonesia and Japan. It is derived from ancient Roman law, and originated in Europe on the basis of the Roman *jus civile* – the private law which was applicable to the citizen, and between citizens, within the boundaries of a State in a domestic context. It was also called the *jus quiritum*, as opposed to the *jus gentium* – the law applied internationally, that is, between States.

In due course, this law was compiled and then 'codified' (see below) and many commentators often refer to civil law as primarily codified law. Some writers also prefer to label civil law jurisdictions as belonging to the Romano-Germanic family (see David and Brierley (1985) p 22), since this would include both the Roman heritage, and the contribution of German legal science in the development of its juristic style. However, although this alternative appellation is perfectly acceptable, and will indeed be utilised occasionally in this book, the present writer prefers the terms 'civil law system' or 'civil law tradition' because they are well established in content, and generally typify a distinctive juristic style which is widely recognised and accepted. Of course, 'civil law' has many other meanings in other contexts.

Civil law countries and common law countries

We speak of civil law countries (in the Roman law sense we have just described) as distinct from common law countries. Civil law countries are generally those countries which, according to the criteria we examined in the previous chapter, may be classified as such because of their sources of law (predominantly codes, statutes, and legislation), their characteristic mode of thought in legal matters, their distinctive legal institutions (and judicial, executive and legislative structures) and their fundamental legal ideology. All these elements determine their unique 'juristic style' (see Chapter 2). Common law countries are broadly those whose juristic style is based on the English common law model, predominantly founded on a system of case law or judicial precedent, and for whom legislation has not been traditionally regarded as a primary source of law, but usually regarded as mere consolidations or clarifications of legal rules and principles which are essentially derived from case law and judge made law.

Civil law and criminal law

Another usage of the term 'civil law' is in connection with the designation of the type of proceedings that might be instituted in a court of law, related to the distinct bodies of rules in common law countries which comprise civil law, which provides rules and remedies to regulate disputes between private individuals and criminal law, which provides rules, penalties and sanctions for those acts and omissions of individuals, which are seen as offences against the State, public order and society. In the context of comparative law, this is clearly not the sense in which 'civil law' is being used.

Civil law (private law) v public law

In civil law systems, there is a fundamental distinction drawn between private law and public law which is much more firmly rooted, and more sharply drawn, than in common law systems. In conceptual terms, both common law and civil law systems recognise that private law governs relations between private citizens and corporations, and public law concerns a dispute in which the State is a party. However, the distinction in civil law systems has far greater practical implications since, flowing from it, there are two different hierarchies of courts dealing with each of these types of law. The distinction between private and public law in English law has been largely effected for the purposes of academic analysis. The chief consequence of the distinction in English common law is the type of remedies that are available to the private individual in a case involving 'public law'. Apart from the specialised orders that are available (certiorari, mandamus and prohibition), the 1980s has heralded the rise of the public law remedy of judicial review of administrative action in England. No separate courts deal with public law disputes in common law jurisdictions which apply the same common law principles; the courts are used for other private law disputes to public law cases as well.

In civil law systems, the substantive body of private law consists, principally, of civil law (or *droit civil* in French law) which is further subdivided into various divisions of law, such as, the law of persons, family law, matrimonial property regimes, contractual regimes, property law and the law of obligations . It should be noted that commercial law is not included in this list, since it is not considered part of the private civil law in Romano-Germanic legal families.

Civil law and commercial law

The term 'civil law' is also used to describe the substantive body of private law which is based on the French Civil Code of 1804 (as amended), in contradistinction to the body of law known as 'commercial law' which is not regulated by the Civil Code. In common law systems, there is no distinction drawn between civil law and commercial law for the simple reason that, in common law systems, commercial law is part of their civil (as opposed to criminal) law. Moreover, as a term of art, commercial law is of fairly recent vintage in common law academic thought, although its content is traceable to ancient mercantile law (*lex mercatoria*), which was developed by international fairs and mercantile practice. In English law, commercial law has been defined as 'that branch of law which is concerned with rights and duties arising from the supply of goods and services in the way of trade' (Goode, *Commercial Law* (1995) p 35).

However, the content of the law is largely based on aspects of the law of contract and property which are relevant to business and commercial practice, and there is no jurisprudential, judicial or statutory recognition of a separate branch of commercial law, since the law is the same whether between professional traders or between friends.

It therefore contains elements of agency, commercial credit and export sales, but also deals with consumer credit and exemption clauses in contracts, the law of which applies equally to all legal persons. The only sense in which commercial law is treated differently in English law is in a separate procedural context where, for instance, it refers to commercial litigation, and cases involving areas of law mentioned above are usually entered on the 'commercial list' which is allocated to one of the judges of the Queen's Bench Division of the High Court. This judge will sit in, what has become known (since 1970) as, the Commercial Court where simplified rules of procedure apply. Nevertheless, the substantive rules applied in this court would be identical to the rules that would be applied outside this court.

In civil law systems, there are very important reasons for distinguishing between civil and commercial law. Commercial law in the civil law system is a distinct body of law which is usually contained in a separate code, such as the French Code de Commerce (Commercial Code) of 1807, which is administered by separate commercial courts at first instance. It governs, *inter alia*, companies, partnerships, negotiable instruments, trademarks, patents and bankruptcy (see, further, Chapter 11). Hence, in France, for example, this branch of law is not covered by the French Civil Code and lies outside the body of private law known as civil law, but is, nevertheless, part of French private law. Thus, yet another meaning of civil law within the Romano-Germanic legal family is the body of law applicable to ordinary citizens in relations with each other, and not the system of law which is generally contrasted with the common law system. Except where otherwise stated, we shall use the term as referring to the system of law modelled on the European Continental system, rather than to any other usage.

Meaning of codification in the civil law context

The meaning of the word 'code' will vary according to whether it is being used by lawyers trained in the English common law tradition, or lawyers brought up in the civil law tradition. In the civil law system, a code is an authoritative, comprehensive and systematic collection of general clauses and legal principles, divided into Books or Parts dealing in a logical fashion with the law relating thereto. Civil law codes are therefore regarded as the primary source of law, to which all other sources are subordinate, and often the only source of law on a particular matter.

Confusingly, codes have also been compiled in common law jurisdictions, particularly for procedure and, in terms of sheer volume, the United States have more 'codified' laws than any other country. However, the cardinal feature in a common law code is that it is based on pre-existing law (usually a combination of cases and statutes) and is neither designed, nor intended to be a formulation of all inclusive rules.

In other words, common law codes are generally enacted to consolidate the law on a particular area, or to clarify an area of law which has become unsettled, obscure or confused. It is exceedingly rare for a common law code to attempt to enact new rules or new concepts, although a salutary exception in 1991 was the United Kingdom Children Act 1989 which, although affirming many of the legal principles already established in the area, also created new concepts.

Despite the enactment or compilation of various codes in common law jurisdictions, cases (or judicial decisions) generally retain their clarificatory significance and will continue to be referred to as sources of law if there is any ambiguity in the statute, or if there is a perceived 'gap' in the legislation which could then be filled by an existing judicial decision. In terms of style and organisation, the format and structure of a typical common law statute is quite different from that of a civil law statute or code.

HISTORICAL DEVELOPMENT OF THE CIVIL LAW TRADITION

Roman law and western civilisation

Introduction

Civil law as an autonomous system of law originated and evolved in continental Europe and the influence of colonisation, legal science movements, and various key codifications, particularly those of the 19th century, have played a part in the formation of this type of law. In addition, this system evolved over more than a thousand years, inevitably undergoing significant changes in substantive content and procedure, and, in its early phase of development, being dominated for five centuries by the writings of jurists of the classical period. This type of scholarly pre-eminence was reprised in the 11th and 12th centuries in the universities when the study of Roman law was revived, and again in the 17th and 18th centuries when the natural law school exerted its philosophical influence. It is therefore no accident that doctrinal writing plays such a significant part, even today, in countries like France and Germany, since classical jurists actually created the structure within which the practice of law was created and developed.

The challenge of Roman law study

Roman law remains a challenge to modern scholarship and modern day historians, not least because weaving a tapestry from fragments of evidence and inconclusive evidence has proved an exceedingly speculative enterprise. Buckland pinpoints the problems one encounters when trying to discover what happened in the history of Roman law, when he declares that:

> Most ancient monuments and records ... perished when Rome was burnt by the Gauls, c 390 BC and what passes for the history of this time is largely a fabrication of later ages, or at best a vague tradition adorned with stories of gods and heroes ... [so] we cannot have any exact knowledge of the course of events.

It is also well established that there is little direct evidence for Roman law before the time of Cicero. Nevertheless, historians seem to agree that early classical Roman law was customary law rather than enacted law, which was probably derived from Romulus or one of the early kings. There also appears to have been a noticeable absence of professional judges during this period.

The two phases of Roman law in world history

In world history, Roman law appears to have undergone two distinct periods of development, the first period dating from the period of the Roman Empire and ending with the compilation by the Emperor Justinian (527–565 AD) of, *inter alia*, the Code and *Digest*, one bearing the imperialist heritage, the other the fruits of the juristic writing of Rome as it existed in the pre-Justinian era. The second period (sometimes referred to as the revival or Renaissance of Roman law, or the Second Life of Roman law (Nicholas)) began with the scholarly study of Justinian's works in the Italian universities in the late 11th century AD. The popularity of this intellectual pursuit spread to the rest of Europe and, to a certain extent, even to medieval England, leaving a lasting impression on juristic terminology and legal thought, as well as on the structure of European legal systems, which continued until the period of the 'great codifications' in the 19th century. Before we examine the impact of the great *Corpus Juris Civilis* of Justinian (see, further, *Justinian and the Corpus Juris*, p 53), let us consider some key features of early Roman law.

Public law and private law in early Roman law

The republican constitution protected the common citizen against abuse of power by magistrates who were from the aristocratic upper class of society. But there were no substantive rights given to the citizen which he could assert against the aristocratic classes or the State. A clear distinction was always drawn between public law which regulated the structures and powers of the State (public authorities) in relation to the individual citizen, and private law which governed the relations between citizens.

The praetor *and* iudex *in Roman private law*

In private law disputes, a State official usually officiated or arranged for a trial to be held after a preliminary hearing. In the conventional civil action, court proceedings commenced with a hearing before a *praetor*, a functionary who was one of a group of magistrates who were elected annually. This hearing identified the issues in dispute. The next stage consisted of a separate hearing in the manner of a trial before a *iudex*, an ad hoc judge, a private citizen, who was selected by consent of the parties and given authority by the *praetor* to try the dispute and to render a binding judgment; no appeal was available. In the majority of cases, neither *praetor* nor *iudex* had undergone any sort of legal training.

Laymen were also assigned the role of judges in the context of other tribunals and criminal proceedings where assemblies of laymen (sometimes numbering as many as 40) would sit in judgment. These men found on the facts, and also heard and rendered judgment on the whole case, after having heard various alternative arguments on the issues. This form of hearing resembled a form of arbitration before lay judges.

Case law and precedent in classical Roman law

A system of case law and precedent developed in ancient Rome under the *praetor-iudex* system. Although *praetors* had complete freedom to decide each case on an individual basis and could simply disregard previous rulings on similar cases, a practice of continuity began to develop so that new terms which were coined by the urban *praetor* were soon copied for future reference and used in subsequent cases. Clerks attached to the *praetor's* office kept records of the formulas used and these became available to the public.

From about the middle of the 2nd century BC, the litigant began to ask the *praetor* for a written summary of the claim, as well as any available defence, addressed to the judge, containing instructions on how to proceed with the case and to dispose of the issue accordingly. The plaintiff would then attempt to persuade the *praetor* to grant him a 'formula'. The *praetor* began to give advice to litigants on the conditions under which he would grant the action or allow the defence, and the judge would then resolve the case on the basis of this formula.

A consistent usage of certain terms and synopses eventually converted them into established formulas (the formulary system) and they assumed an air of certainty and predictability which began to serve as guidelines to litigants and legal advisers for future cases. As Allen puts it, 'there could be no more instructive example than this of a whole body of law built up by judicial practice' (Allen, *Law in the Making* (1968)). Remarkably, this system evolved without the publication of judicial opinions, or statement of reasons, or citation of cases, and without a theory of precedent.

The praetorian system appears to have evolved through the consistent use of well tested formulas and pragmatic patterns of action which determined the success or failure of an action, and whether a particular remedy or relief would be granted. The crucial form of development of the law appeared to be through remedies very much resembling the development of the early common law in England, where the system of writs was the early basis of legal rights and remedies. In other words, Roman law developed through procedure so that the Roman judge would issue an *actio utilis*, in the same way that a common law judge would later issue a writ. Furthermore, the two stage process and constant mix of officialdom and lay opinion meant that Roman law could respond to the changing needs of a developing society. But, it was not the *praetors* or *iudices* who became the custodians of the Roman law tradition, since their work was both ad hoc and temporal. That distinction went to the jurists.

Jurists, urban praetors *and sources of law*

In the absence of legal advisers, the *iudex* eventually turned to a select group of aristocrats, secular jurists who came to specialise in giving advice on legal matters. They were, in fact, self-appointed by their interest in the study and interpretation of the law and, in discussing legal problems, both actual and hypothetical, and writing about them, they established an enduring tradition which, through their writings, was then passed from generation to generation. These jurists advised a number of different persons, ranging from parties to litigation, and lay judges to the urban *praetor*, who was the most senior magistrate whose primary responsibility was litigation in the city of Rome. He was, therefore, chief administrative officer of the judicial system that regulated litigation between Roman citizens and, in the course of his duties, began to formulate the legal 'issues' (or matters to be decided/resolved) which were then presented to the trial judges.

During this period, the source of private law was very seldom to be found in legislation, although the Roman assemblies could usually 'amend' private law if they wished to do so. However, the cardinal source of law proved to be the formal edicts issued by the urban *praetor*, which also listed the legal remedies available, which accorded with the legal opinions of the jurists. The remarkable fact appears to be the manner in which, for many years, these jurists simply assumed the authority to interpret the law without any official authorisation. Throughout the republic, it was the aristocratic upper class of society which controlled and ran the city. In this world of social privilege and personal influence, 'the principal characteristic of Roman legal development was authority: the system was based not on principle as such but on the authority of those who expounded the law' (Smith (1968)). The jurists would therefore have had wealth, prestige and power to boost their standing in the community. We can only assume that the general public, who received this advice from the jurists, were satisfied with the quality of the legal advice tendered.

During the course of the first phase of the classical Roman Empire (the Principate), the authority of the jurists was further strengthened. The first emperor, Augustus, decided to invoke an obscure law and institute a system ('patenting') which authorised a select group of jurists to give their opinions, under his seal, so they could 'speak with the leader's authority or imprimatur' (*ex auctoritate principis*). This merely validated a system of Roman private law which had already taken root, and the jurists simply continued to give advice as they had done in the past, modifying their advice occasionally to take account of social or economic changes.

From the latter part of the 1st century, jurists were regularly appointed to be part of the emperor's council (cabinet), and often held top ranking imperial positions. This became established as a tradition and a thread of continuity began to be woven. The interpreters of the law were always members of the ruling class, whose position encouraged them to ignore public law and to develop private law. This explains in part why public law was not developed or seen to be developing for a considerable period.

Juristic writings included general commentaries, analyses of specific topics, elementary treatises, collections of opinions, or problems, in which the jurist submitted arguments which eventually led to his particular solution. Their work ranged from the drafting of wills and contracts, advising litigants on forms of action and possible defences, to revising praetorian formulas. As Dawson (1968) puts it: 'They were problem solvers, working within [the] system and not called upon to solve the ultimate problems of mankind's needs and destiny.' The similarities with English common law techniques of argument based on law and fact may be detected, particularly, in the typical style of these jurists of working on a case to case basis. This meant that apart from quoting each other, which they did frequently, they were usually only concerned with finding the solution to an individual case, not to formulate a principle for all time and for all societies.

The Twelve Tables: first landmark in Roman legal history

The jurists did not create their rules purely from customary law. They had access to one of the earliest known codes of laws, the Twelve Tables (c 450 BC), the first unequivocal landmark in the history of Roman law. These tables, which were drawn up by specially appointed commissioners, consisted mainly of Latin custom with certain borrowings from Greek law, which formed the basis of the law. This was a collection of basic rules, rather than a comprehensive or definitive piece of legislation, yet it came to be regarded by Romans of later ages as the starting point or fountainhead of their legal history. Livy called it 'the fountain of all public and private law'. Nevertheless, even after the Twelve Tables, a great deal of the law remained unwritten, and it continued to be interpreted by the pontiffs, until the jurists began to interpret the law.

The influence of Greece

It is widely believed that another reason for the brilliance of Roman law was the fact that, at an important point in its history, during the time of their territorial expansion in the 2nd century BC, it was enhanced by Greek ideas and philosophy which the Romans absorbed and modified, to bring to near perfection a system that was already adaptable, enduring and pragmatic. From 146 BC, after the Romans had conquered Greece, Greek culture was assimilated into the Roman Empire and, despite being the captive nation, Greek arts, literature and philosophy began to infiltrate into Roman society and, indeed, wield a dominant influence over it. This was hardly surprising since the Roman intelligentsia had been brought up on Greek philosophy, logic, rhetoric and scientific methods so that the next step was the utilisation of Greek philosophical approaches, to bring logic and order to the many collections of Roman court rulings which had accumulated. A considerable fillip to Roman jurists, to interpret, clarify and synthesise fully the corpus of the law, was given by the Emperor Hadrian (118–138 AD) when he commissioned the jurist Julian to consolidate the edict in such a way that, once it was published, it could no longer be altered. This, in effect, turned the edict into a permanent statute which could then be generally available and susceptible to varying interpretations.

The first systematic collection: the Institutes

Our knowledge of Roman law before the time of Cicero would be so much poorer if it were not for a remarkable book which was presumably written purely as an elementary introduction to law – the *Institutes* by 'Gaius'. This was the first trace of a systematic compilation of Roman law, a palimpsest of which was discovered in 1819, written by someone who adopted the name of Gaius, a jurist who lived in the 3rd century BC, and whose *Institutes* appeared around the 2nd century BC. Roman writers adopted *noms de plume* just as the English writer who called himself 'Glanvill' did, in medieval England. Gaius' book sets out Roman law in rudimentary terms, but in an extremely well organised and accessible manner. As one writer puts it, the *Institutes* offer 'priceless direct testimony to the state of classical law' (Smith (1968)). For example, it tells us that the content and concern of the law is threefold: it deals with persons, or things or actions. It then explains the scope of each of these headings, and further subdivisions or subclassifications are then given. It would have been extremely difficult to have understood Justinian's later codifications if not for the discovery of this book.

In the 3rd century AD, Rome experienced severe economic crisis, political instability and disruption. There were something like 25 emperors in the first 262 years of the Roman Empire and a further 21 emperors in the next 50 years. These factors, as well as the fact that great writers, like Ulpian and Paul, had explored Roman law so comprehensively so as to leave very little left for future jurists to analyse, led to the sudden decline of jurisprudence, from the 3rd century AD. In the later years of the second century, the Republican structure began to disintegrate, with the growing gulf between the wealthy landed class and the proletariat, dwindling numbers of citizens to fill the army, and, arguably, by the absorption of Greek morals which were more liberal than those of the Romans of the time, and which eventually led to Rome's moral degeneration.

Collapse of the Western Roman Empire

Once the Roman Empire in the West had collapsed and fragmented, this signalled the end, for some considerable time, of the only political and cultural power capable of maintaining political and legal unity. The Barbarian Invasion in the 5th century maintained the Mediterranean as the Roman world's chief artery of commerce, but the rise of Islam in the 7th century led to Western Europe regressing into a purely agricultural state, becoming a rural civilisation from the 8th century, when land became the sole source of subsistence, and social existence was founded on property or on the possession of land. This resulted from the closing of the Mediterranean to Western Europe. Law and the political order were, therefore, fragmented, although the Church preserved a great deal of Roman culture and civilisation in its laws.

In the Eastern Roman Empire, the demise of the Western Empire made Emperor Justinian determined not just to recapture it, but to restore Rome to its former glory in the legal context so that the genius of Roman law and its authors could be a lasting monument to Roman achievement.

Justinian and the Corpus Juris

In the 6th century, when the Western Empire collapsed, perhaps the most significant single event that took place in the East, where the Roman Empire continued, was the decision taken by the Emperor Justinian (527–565) to enact or re-enact a comprehensive compilation, systematisation and consolidation of all the existing law, from every source. The intention was to codify the law based on a selection of the decisions and enactments of the emperors, and from all juristic writings, with all the necessary modifications necessitated by the passage of time and the change in social and economic conditions. This great enterprise produced four compilations which became collectively known as the *Corpus Juris Civilis* or the *Corpus Juris*, for short. Various committees of lawyers were appointed, all from the East and probably all Greek speakers. The contents of the *Corpus Juris* are:

(a) The Institutions (or *Institutes*) – a systematic treatise, issued as an elementary textbook for first year law students, based on Gaius' earlier *Institutes*.

(b) The *Digest* or *Pandects* – a compilation of edited fragments from Roman juristic writings, arranged according to titles or headings derived from the classical period, but including material from the very late Republic to the middle of the 3rd century. This is the most important part of the *Corpus Juris*, and the classical period writings are still regarded as the most illuminating.

(c) The *Codex* – a collection of imperial enactments including edicts and judicial decisions, dating from the time of Hadrian, arranged chronologically within each title, so that it is possible to trace the legal evolution of a concept, as the facts in a case were distinguished from apparently similar facts in earlier cases.

(d) The *Novels* – a collection of imperial legislation enacted by Justinian himself, based on private collections, issued subsequent to the publication of the other three parts which were promulgated between 533 and 544 AD. No official edition of the novels was ever issued.

Since Justinian ordered the compilers to edit the juristic writings and the enactments, the law as presented in the collection is not really representative of either classical Roman law (the Principate) or of the law as it existed in Justinian's era. It is a greatly modified pastiche of legal rules and opinions. However, with the fall of the rest of the Roman Empire, the *Corpus Juris* fell into desuetude, and 'vulgarised', crude versions of Roman civil law were applied by the conquerors to the inhabitants of the Italian peninsula. This consisted, in part, of a fusion of Germanic customs and Roman law. Indeed, the German conquerors did not seek to destroy everything Roman in the style of Gaul. Hence, a number of Germanic Codes emerged, written in Latin, designed for Romans and Germans, drawn from various Roman imperial enactments (for example, *Codex Gregorianus* and the Theodosian Code), but the wording tended to be paraphrases or reconstructions of the original – thus, 'vulgarised'.

The revival of Roman law studies in the middle ages

Over the 11th and 12th centuries, in keeping with the Renaissance in philosophy, canon law and theology, Roman law studies also experienced a rebirth and revival, or a 'Second Life' (Nicholas). It is difficult to assign a single reason for this event, but some writers place central importance on the lectures given by Irnerius (c 1055–1130), in the late 11th century, who gave the first university lectures on the *Digest* at Bologna, the first modern European university where law was a major subject. The crucial point is that it was Justinian's *Corpus Juris* that was being studied, not the vulgarised Germanic versions, nor customary law derived from the law of the fairs (*lex mercatoria*), nor laws devised by local townships or minor rulers. Various reasons can be found for the success and popularity of Roman law at that time:

(a) The political and economic conditions of the time were conducive to the study and acceptance of works like the *Digest*. In political terms, there was a great need for a legal system that could unify and organise the social conditions of that era. Governmental power required centralisation so as to prevent its fragmentation. Economically, a society that saw the emergence of centres of commerce, trade and industry needed a law that could cope with the rapidly changing commercial trade, revival of maritime commerce and the decline of feudalism. Roman law could provide the legal techniques that could promote and strengthen commercial life.

(b) The *Digest* possessed a sense of authority because it was in book form, written in Latin and a relic of the old *imperium romanum*, Rome in its heyday, all conquering, glorious and supreme and a symbol of unity, offering a hope for a unified law. These images of Rome had never quite left people's minds. A book was a rare entity in the Middle Ages, so that almost any book had an aura of authority, particularly to the average citizen. Latin remained the *lingua franca* in the civilised world and had become the language of communication for the Western Church, intelligible to the clergy as well as the language of educated and cultured people.

(c) The *Corpus Juris* was also the product of Justinian who was regarded by many as a Holy Roman Emperor and, therefore, his work carried the authority of the Pope and the Emperor, and was really a form of imperial legislation. Italian lawyers therefore almost had a special duty to study the *Digest*.

(d) The *Digest* was an intellectually challenging compilation to the lawyers of the Middle Ages, difficult to follow in its language and the order in which it treated various topics, as well as in its unfamiliarity of legal treatment, being based on an ancient system of remedies, yet often merely listing decided cases with no guiding concepts. Its study attracted men of high intellectual ability who later became specialists in its study and acquired a professional skill in its interpretation. This ensured that they guarded their knowledge jealously and trained others only in a professional capacity, but also created a tradition of scholarship.

(e) Roman law as contained in the *Corpus Juris* also provided detailed solutions and approaches to practical problems. It also possessed a conceptually powerful structure, with clear distinctions which could be adapted to almost any situation or problem with simplicity and clarity. Property and obligation were distinguished, the former being indefeasible against the world, the latter merely a bond between two persons, whose legal effects varied according to whether the parties wished to create rights against one another, or on a reciprocal basis.

(f) Finally, it has been said that it was the 'rational character of Roman law and its freedom from relativity to any particular time or place' (Lawson (1977)) that also accounts for the huge success of Roman law.

Growth of Roman law: 12th to 19th centuries

Irnerius' lectures at Bologna heralded the study of the *Corpus Juris* in Western Europe as a coherent, systematic, body of law. By the middle of the 12th century, there were about 10,000 students in Bologna. The Italian universities became the centre of learning for scholars all over Europe, from whence it spread. There later ensued a succession of schools of thought (most prominently, the groups of scholars known as the Glossators and the Commentators) about the correct way to study and interpret the *Corpus Juris*. Scholars of Roman law acquired such tremendous prestige that university doctors of law were appointed to the royal councils and were made judges in many local courts. Those who had studied in Bologna returned to their homelands where they promoted the study of the *Corpus Juris* according to the interpretations and approaches of the Glossators and, subsequently, the Commentators. This really laid the foundations for a common law of Europe.

The Glossators were a group of scholars, who were apparently founded by Irnerius, who initiated the systematic study of Roman law by analysing the individual texts of the *Corpus Juris* and attempting to reconcile them in a logical manner with other texts. The development of the law, from the 12th century onwards, was determined by the manner in which the Glossators used the Justinian texts, not Roman law as Justinian might have intended, or as it might have existed in classical Rome. Their style is, therefore, characterised by the short notes or glosses which they appended to particular passages, for purposes of comparison with each other, in order to pose a question or suggest a solution. As time passed, the work of the later Glossators developed from gloss to commentary.

The Glossators were succeeded in the 13th century by scholars known as the Commentators (or post-Glossators). Although it is not always easy to distinguish where the late Glossators ended and the early Commentators began, it is generally correct to say that the Commentators could be identified by their systematic commentaries on, and synthesis of, the law.

This different approach was required because:

(a) the *Corpus Juris* was no longer the only set of texts on which the academic study of law was based. Canon law gained ascendancy and became a university subject in its own right. This was followed by theologians and philosophers turning to systematic analyses of the writings of Aristotle. The study of his *Ethics* and *Politics* eventually produced a systematic philosophy of natural law and what later became known as the Natural Law Movement (see below); and

(b) by 1200, Roman law had actually been 'received' into Italy as binding law, applicable in the absence of any local custom or contrary statute. It was therefore necessary to bring it up to date and to adapt it to local conditions and practical matters, and to reconcile it with the medieval legal tapestry. Several 'receptions' of Roman law took place which resulted in its authoritative acceptance in court practice in most of Western Europe.

A third group of writers, the Humanists, emerged during the 16th and 17th centuries, based in the French University of Bourges. They were opposed to both the Glossators and Commentators' approaches to the study of Roman law, and advocated the return to the original Roman texts and sources. They believed that the only authentic method of studying Roman law was to scrutinise the classical Roman texts unadulterated by commentary or gloss. Their approach did not, however, convince the practising lawyers who needed a living law which was practice orientated, and this particular philosophy never gained any widespread popularity or acceptance.

Eventually, through the Bologna lectures and the dissemination of Roman law through its scholars filtering through to the courts and legal practice, Roman civil law, as interpreted by the Glossators and Commentators, became the basis of a common body of law and legal commentaries, a common legal language and a common approach to teaching and scholarship. This is often called the common law of Europe, or the *jus commune*. Hence, from the 12th to about the 16th century, the *Corpus Juris* became the basis for legal science throughout Europe. Judges could apply Roman law and not local laws or customs to cases that came before them because of the existence of a 'pluralism of legal sources' (Coing (1973)), which meant that courts were free to apply the law from a number of possible sources and, thus, from any book of authority, not being confined to local customs if they were found lacking. Roman law was later accepted in the Italian courts as part of the custom of the courts.

As far as other 'Receptions' of Roman law were concerned, large scale instruction in Roman law in France only took place in the 13th century (see, further, 'History of French law', p 59, below). Of course, in Italy, Spain and southern France, Roman law had never completely disappeared. In northern Europe, only customary law remained, which varied from place to place. In northern France, the Reception began much earlier than in Germany, but was less widespread and happened somewhat gradually. The German courts did not receive Roman law until the end of the Middle Ages, around 1495 (see, further, 'History of German law', p 79, below). By all accounts, the Reception was completed in the course of the 16th century.

The common law of Europe that eventually emerged towards the end of the Middle Ages was, therefore, a mixture of local statutes and customs, a form of Roman law as interpreted by the various schools of thought and canon law. The unity achieved by the reception of Roman law into the civil law was further reinforced by canon law, which had become the universal law of the Western Church and which remained in use even in the darkest days of Roman law. English courts, on the other hand, never received Roman law at all, despite the fact that it was early known and taught, due to centralisation of courts at an early stage, powerful monarchs and the pragmatic character of early English law.

During the 16th, 17th and 18th centuries, despite the intervening revival of classical learning led by the School of Humanists, the influence of the Natural Law Movement gained ascendancy and played a significant part in the development of the civil law by:

(a) posing a challenge to the authority of the *Corpus Juris* as the only authoritative Statement of definitive legal rules. It did so on the basis of rationality and reason, which it claimed had to be satisfied, and, although frequently following the Roman solution, argued that there was no obligation to do so. The members of this School were highly conversant with Roman law and preferred to rely on the original wording of the unannotated Roman text to solve a particular problem. They clearly overlapped with the Humanist thinkers, though not in all matters; and

(b) transforming the methods of systematisation of the civil law. By utilising a deductive method, they started with a small number of very general concepts, which were then deductively developed in successive ranges of fewer and fewer general abstractions, categories and principles, until the lowest level of abstraction was reached, whereupon specific rules were enunciated which were applied to actual factual situations.

The Natural Law Movement represented an upsurge of rationalism and the belief that 'the law for any society could by the use of reason be derived from principles inherent in the nature of man and society' (Nicholas (1962)). The Dutchman Grotius (1583–1645) was the first great natural law exponent, and he applied it to the formation of a body of international law. However, his treatise on the jurisprudence of Holland considerably influenced the course of Roman-Dutch law. But it was in the international law field that the School of Natural Law was most influential, although it led to the elimination of the more irrational or 'authentically Roman' features of the law which were replaced by liberal doses of 'logic' in the law.

The Natural Law Movement gave rise to a renewed interest in codification, which appeared to be the best way of preserving a logically consistent set of principles and rules. In retrospect:

(a) it was responsible for the revival of public law, the division of law that regulated the relations between government and citizen but which, in practical terms, had remained relatively dormant in Roman law for many centuries;

(b) it led to codification, bringing to fruition and consolidation many centuries of learning in Roman law, which was then actually transformed from the theoretical taught law of the universities into the living law of the land. This was thus a watershed in civil law history;

(c) through the phenomenon of codification, a fusion of practical and theoretical law was created as well as a unified set of laws, from a sometimes confusing diversity of customs and practices;

(d) through codification, a set of systematic expositions of the law was formulated to suit the conditions of 18th century society;

(e) the Natural Law Movement also reaffirmed the power of the sovereign to play a major part in defining and reforming law. Hence, a form of legislative Positivism was also revived by the natural law ideas.

Some early codes were compiled in 1756 and 1794 but the most important codificatory event was the enactment of the French Napoleonic Civil Code in

1804. This proved to be a momentous event, not just because it meant France had a single system of law, but because many countries adopted, adapted or copied the Code throughout the world. Although its adoption was partly the result of Napoleon's victories, its enduring attraction survived long after his final defeat. This was partly because of the clarity and cohesion of the Code and partly because of France's status and prestige in the 19th century. Jurisdictions such as Belgium, Italy, Spain, Holland, Louisiana, Quebec, Egypt and parts of South America adopted the Code in one form or another.

In Germany, the French Code was not adopted primarily because of the jurist Savigny (1779–1861), but also because conditions were then not quite right for the Code's acceptance (see, further, 'History of German law', p 79, below).

History of French law

Pre-revolutionary French law

Multiplicity of customs

For several centuries, France consisted of a multiplicity of customs, existing in over 60 separate geographical areas, each with its own rules. When Gaul was part of the Roman empire, Roman law prevailed in it, but it appears likely that, in accordance with the practice of the time, certain local customs were allowed to subsist. There was certainly no common law in France in its early Roman period, either dealing comprehensively with private law matters, or administered with the imprimatur of a sovereign. In the 4th century AD, the sources of French law were the Codes of Gregorius and Hermogenius, the *Institutes* of Gaius and Paul's Sentences. By the 5th century, the Code of Theodosius had been compiled, but by this time, part of Gaul had already been occupied.

Despite the collapse of the Western Roman Empire in 476 AD, Roman law survived (as the law for peoples of non-Germanic origin) in the Germanic States which succeeded it and continued to do so in the course of the 5th century, particularly in the kingdoms of the Visigoths, Burgandians and Franks. A key factor that contributed to the continued existence of Roman law was the enactment of a statute – *Lex Romana Visigothorum* – passed by the Visigoth King, Alaric II, which contained a summary both of the *Leges* and of the *Jus* and, *inter alia*, a summary and commentary of the Code of Theodosius.

The *Lex* consisted of the various documents called constitutiones – which were opinions, enactments and decisions which had been handed down directly from the various emperors. The *Jus* consisted of the writings of the jurists – their interpretation and development of the older legal sources, extending back to the middle of the 3rd century AD. The terminology (*lex* and *jus*) appears to have originated in the 5th century, and the terms corresponded to the English distinction between statute and common law (see Amos and Walton (1967) p 26).

System of personal laws

During the 6th century, the Franks secured control and dominion over the whole country but, instead of removing Roman law from the newly acquired Roman subjects, adopted a system of personal laws. The Franks, Visigoths and Burgandians lived each according to his own law and permitted the Roman Provincials to live by theirs. For some 500 years in this Frankish period, the main source of law for the conquered Gauls was the *Lex Romana Visigothorum*. In the south of France, therefore, Roman law continued to survive, unlike the case in northern France, where the Franks chose to apply their own customary laws of Germanic origin, which were later consolidated into statutes.

Feudal system

In the course of the 9th century, this personal system of laws began to disintegrate, giving way to a feudal system which then engaged in a struggle with local, seigneural judges and the emerging royal, central power. While the great lay and ecclesiastic lords enjoyed widespread privileges, their 'inferiors' suffered ever diminishing loss of powers and privileges. A form of 'territoriality of law' (Amos and Walton (1967)) started to develop, with different laws in different localities, the population divided into different classes of people (nobles, middle class, serfs) with correspondingly different legal status.

A further jurisdictional conflict also developed between the power of the Church and that of the developing State, as to which Von Mehren and Gordley commented:

> Jurisdictions overlapped. The administration of justice was notoriously slow, complicated and expensive. No institution existed with a sufficiently general and exclusive jurisdiction to permit the development of a body of common law. [Von Mehern and Gordley (1977) p 14.]

Two geographical zones

It was during the course of the 13th century that the law of France became the law of two geographical zones:

(a) the area of *droit écrit* (written law) in the South; or *pays de droit écrit*; and

(b) the area of *droit coutumier* (law of customs) in the North; or *pays de coutumes*.

In the Southern Provinces (the Midi), the Land of Written Law, Roman civilisation and Roman law were paramount. Roman law was the common law of the country so that, when the Renaissance or the Second Life of Roman Law took hold, and the *Corpus Juris* came to be studied, there was a relatively easy reception of that law which came to be accepted as the practical, living law of the land.

In the Northern Provinces, local customs based on Germanic customs were in force. This was a larger area than the Southern Provinces, covering three-fifths of the country. The customs were varied, some applying to a whole province or large territory (*coutume generale*) numbering about 60 or so; others were in force only in a city or village (*coutumes locales*) numbering about 300.

There was, however, no complete division since the *pays de droit écrit* had, at least in the earlier periods, written customs influenced by Roman law, but containing Germanic elements. Eventually, all other local customs died out and Roman law was the only governing law. Similarly, in the North, although the *coutumes* were the common law, the law of contracts and obligations used Roman law as a supplementary law since the *coutumes* were silent on these matters. Similarly, Roman law was invoked if the *coutumes* were ambiguous or had nothing to say on other areas of law. In both zones, any matters which fell under the jurisdiction of the Church, such as marriage, were governed by canon law.

The monarchical period

Four main events took place in the period 1500–1789, during which, even by the end of the 15th century, royal power had been consolidated and became more dominant:

(a) the compilation of customs;

(b) the passing of royal ordinances and the grand ordinances;

(c) the Custom of Paris; and

(d) the emergence of a common law.

In view of the multiplicity of customs, Charles VII ordered the official compilation of all customs in his Ordinance, Montils-les-Tours of 1453. Hence, by the end of the 16th century, most of French customary law which was officially recognised had been reduced to written law. But, uniformity had by no means been achieved.

During the course of the 14th to the 17th centuries, many royal ordinances were passed, mostly dealing with administration or with civil or criminal procedure, but these must be distinguished from a series of grand ordinances, such as the Code of Commerce and Code of Civil Procedure, which were codifications of a branch of law. However, these royal ordinances eventually regulated substantive private law as well.

Two major legal figures in the era of Louis XIV (1643–1715) were Jean Baptiste Colbert (1619–83) his chief minister, and Guillame de Lamoignon (1617–77) who was the first president of the Parlement de Paris, the judicial branch of the king's court. In 1665, on Colbert's advice, Louis set up a special commission, the Conseil de Justice which consisted of eminent jurists and members of the King's Council, requesting memoranda from the provincial Parlements, and various legal experts, suggesting areas of law that required reforming and possible remedies. The jurists on the Commission were aware that Lamoignon had already produced an outline for a code. The Ordinance of 1667 on Civil Procedure, produced as a result of the Commission's work, intended to provide a complete and detailed systematic codification of civil procedure, but supplementary edicts were later found to be necessary. In 1670, another Ordinance on Criminal Law and Procedure was produced with the co-operation of the Parlement throughout the preparatory sessions, which owed much of the drafting to Lamoignon. His book, outlining a scheme for a single code based on customary law, was extremely influential, being used by jurists of the 18th century and relied upon by Louis XV's chancellor, Daguesseau (1668–1751) in the compilation and issue of various royal ordinances which were really mini codes on donations, wills and entails. These ordinances were later incorporated into the Civil Code.

The Custom of Paris was a collection of laws laid down by the judges of the various courts of justice, emanating from the Parlement de Paris which had become independent towards the end of the 13th century. Various provincial courts (parlements), were established between 1443 and 1775 which covered a wide area; the influence of the capital city, their intrinsic merits and the eminence of their commentators combined to give these laws a pre-eminent position. They were regarded by many as the common law of France since judges were applying a broad range of customs and tended to develop unitary rules.

The publication of the various customs made them more accessible and led to a more detailed study of them. General principles were discerned which were seen to be readily applicable to the whole of France. But, it was really the work of great jurists such as Dumoulin, Coquille, Loysel and Pothier (1699–1772) who provided the draftsmen of the Code with both material and a format. Pothier's elegant and lucid style was so impressive that some parts of the Code are really mere summaries of his statements.

Hence, despite the multiplicity of customs, the royal ordinances exercised a certain unifying force and they were generally in force throughout the kingdom. As in early English law, canon law also played its part in providing a common source of law and, indeed, influenced certain branches of French law, such as family law. It was a combination of all these factors that led to the emergence of a common French law, but it is equally important to realise that the 'tradition of local independence' retained its force in the provinces (see Von Mehren and Gordley (1977) p 48). Each particular province appeared to regard its particular law as a heritage guaranteed by the pact that had incorporated it into France (Von Mehren and Gordley (1977)).

The revolutionary period

The Revolution of 1789 ended the *ancien régime* or period of ancient law, and also marked the beginning of the transitional period usually called the period of 'intermediary law'. Reform was directed at the fields of public law and the law of political institutions. The old institutional structures were destroyed and political power and the machinery of government were now centralised as never before in France. Feudal laws were abolished, as were ancient privileges, Frenchmen were declared to have equal rights under the law, 21 was made the age of majority, marriage was secularised, divorce introduced, individual liberty was guaranteed and the protection of private property was reinforced.

Codification attempts began with the vote by the Constituent Assembly on 5 July 1790 'that the civil laws be reviewed and reformed by the legislators and that there would be made a general code of laws simple, clear and appropriate to the constitution'. The First Title of the Constitution of 1791, therefore, concluded with the promise that 'a Code of civil laws common to the whole kingdom will be enacted'. Nevertheless, actual work on codification only began under the Convention (1792–95). Various drafts were formulated until Napoleon appointed a commission of four to prepare yet another. By 'consolidation, moderation and compromise', Napoleon, working with a small team of lawyers, 'transformed the laws of the Revolution into a workable system of codes' (Schlesinger *et al* (1988) p 267, fn (c)) and, after several political wrangles with the various organs of the legislative body, the Civil Code was eventually enacted in 1804.

The task of the Code was 'to fix, in broad perspective, the general maxims of the law; to lay down principles rich in consequences and not to descend into the details of questions which may arise on each topic' (see Portalis, *Discours Preliminaire*, cited in Rudden (1974) p 1011).

The Civil Code presented the law in clear, concise and readily understandable language, addressed to the average citizen of France. It is a novel piece of substantive law which fused the *droit écrit* and the *coutumes*, and created a unified law for the whole country. Its drafters declared that the Code is a collection of rules of civil law in that it derives from Roman law as it was practised in France – a *ius commune* – a modernised form of Roman law. However, it did not simply reproduce Roman law and there were obvious differences between the Code's approach to certain legal concepts, and that of previous interpretations of Roman law.

In his *Discours Preliminaire*, Portalis explains the thoughts of the drafters of the Code:

(a) a code ought to be complete in its field;

(b) it ought to be drafted in relatively general principles rather than in detailed rules; and

(c) it ought at the same time to fit together logically as a coherent whole and to be based on experience (cited in Tunc, 'Methodology of the civil law in France' (1976) Tulane L Rev 459, pp 459–60).

In practice, however, it has not been possible to adhere absolutely to these aims and objectives.

By 1811, four additional codes had come into force: the Code of Civil Procedure, the Code of Commerce, the Code of Criminal Procedure and the Penal Code. These Codes were all subsequently amended or replaced with more modern provisions and, today, only the Civil Code remains in much the same state it was in when first enacted.

The Civil Code has, however, been amended in relation to status, family law, matrimonial property and security interests. Several attempts have been made to produce a more fundamental revision of it, but a comprehensive revision has never materialised. It has dominated the Prussian Rhine provinces for 100 years, been imitated by the codes of Belgium and Luxembourg, greatly influenced the codes of Italy, Spain, Portugal and the Netherlands, as well as Egypt, South America and Louisiana.

Structure and overview of the French Civil Code

The Civil Code is composed of three 'Books' or Divisions, following Gaius' *Institutes*, and commences with a Preliminary Title, which really seems to introduce the purpose of the Code, namely to implement the 'publication, effects and the application of the laws in general'. Book One is headed 'Of Persons', Book Two 'Of Property and Different Kinds of Ownership' and Book Three 'Of the Different Ways of Acquiring Property'. Each Book is divided into Titles, such as Enjoyment and Loss of Civil Rights, Marriage, Divorce, Domicile, and Adoption. These are again divided into Chapters and, in several instances, these Chapters are divided into Sections. The ultimate units are the Articles and there were originally 2,281 of these. These are typically short, not exceeding more than eight or 10 words.

Book One deals with matters such as marriage, divorce, the status of minors, guardianship and domicile. Book Two deals with property, usufruct and servitudes. Book Three consists of 20 Titles and deals with a rather odd assortment of topics: gifts, wills and intestate succession, but also obligations in general, including contract, quasi-contract and tort. In addition, it covers marriage settlements, sale, lease, partnership and other special contracts, as well as mortgages, liens and pledges and prescription.

Book One has been heavily revised, from about 1965. Title I of Book One used to contain particular rules as to the acquisition and loss of French nationality, but these rules were subsequently extracted and placed in a special, frequently amended statute called the Code of French Nationality. Civil law countries tend to treat citizenship as a public law subject which should not, therefore, be covered in a civil code. In France, the question of nationality assumes a considerable significance because it has an impact on the jurisdiction of courts and, to a certain extent, on choice of law. French and European commercial publishers, therefore, tend to include excerpts from the Nationality Code, in the light of its special significance in French law.

One in three of the Articles in the Civil Code has been repealed, amended or enlarged. More than half the Articles in the Code deal with the organisation of the family, and over half the Articles have been considered by the legislators at some stage. The strong preoccupation with the family is particularly noticeable. The reforms that have been made have dealt with removal of restrictions upon the capacity of married women, modernisation of the matrimonial regimes, facilitation of marriage and augmentation of the rights of illegitimate children. The continuing influence of religion and its tension with more secular philosophies is evident in the somewhat chequered history of French divorce law, and is reflected in Code amendments relating to the family.

The Code proceeded on the basis that judicial decisions shall have no authority beyond the cases in which they are rendered, and that there shall be no authoritative interpretation by anyone except the legislature itself. If the Codes did not cover a particular matter, a judge was directed where to turn in order to decide the case.

The following Code provisions emphasise the obligation of the judge in a French Court to resolve a dispute that comes before the court. Article 4 of the Civil Code states that:

> If he refuses to adjudicate a case for the alleged reason that there are no provisions in the law applying to this case or that the provisions to be found in the law are obscure or insufficient, a judge may be prosecuted as guilty of the criminal offence of refusal to administer justice.

But, in Art 5, it states: 'Judges are forbidden, when giving judgment in the cases brought before them, to lay down general rules of conduct amounting to a regulation.' This prohibition stemmed from the separation of powers doctrine, and the underlying purpose seemed to be the limitation of the power of the judiciary associated with the power of the Parlements.

After a century of experience, French jurists conceded that it has not been possible to keep to the letter of Art 5, and that judges are in fact making law, even though this may never be expressly acknowledged as a matter of strict theory.

A strong moral and ethical core of values runs through the Code, as illustrated by Arts 6 and 1134. Article 6 states: 'No derogation is allowed, by way of private conventions, from statutes which affect public order or good morals.' Article 1134 states:

> Agreements legally entered into have the force of laws for the parties thereto. They may be revoked by the mutual consent of such parties only, or for the causes allowed by the law. They shall be performed according to good faith.

After nearly 190 years of the French Civil Code, the words of Portalis, when he was writing about the role of courts in a codified system of law, bear reiterating. He singled out three main tasks of the judges in those circumstances:

(a) to clarify the meaning of the rules in the various circumstances which are submitted to the judge;

(b) to clarify what is obscure in the law and to fill in its gaps;

(c) to adjust law to the evolution of the society and, to the extent possible based on the existing texts, to provide against the inadequacy of the law in the face of contemporary problems (see Tunc (1976) pp 463–64).

In a more recent appraisal of civil law codes published in 1987, which includes a reference to the 'tort provisions' of the French Civil Code, Professor Hein Kotz illustrates the many similarities that actually exist between civil codes and English law and stresses that 'the legislative style adopted in each country is the result of the particular political, historical and social circumstances existing where and when the codes were drafted'. He continues, in relation to the French Civil Code, that 'a code can hardly be more inventive and sophisticated than the collected legal experience existing at the time it is drafted' (Kotz (1987) 50 MLR 7). He emphasises that a Code is a child of its time, and must be judged in its true historical context. Although the Civil Code has undergone several revisions and amendments, and it has been overtaken in many areas by supplementary legislation, it has certainly stood the test of time as a model codification as a result of the clarity of its concepts, and the accessibility of its language to the ordinary citizen, and the fact that it was, in Portalis' words, 'grounded in experience'. It remains the prototype of civil codes in civil law jurisdictions throughout the world.

Sources of law

The sources of French law are:

(a) Primary Sources of Law: enacted law statutes, constitutional law (which is at the very top of the hierarchy of sources), Regulations (*règlements* and *arrêtés*), the five Napoleonic Codes, General Principles of Law and Custom; and

(b) Secondary Sources of Law: the judge, court decisions (jurisprudence), learned annotations of academic writers (doctrine), textbooks, commentaries, monographs by experts and writers of repute and decisions of foreign courts applying a similar legal system.

Doctrine

Doctrine, a term in use in French law since the 19th century, signifies:

> ... the body of opinions on legal matters expressed in books and articles ... [and] is also used to characterise collectively the persons engaged in this analysis, synthesis and evaluation of legal source material, members of the legal professions who devote substantial attention to scholarly work and acquire reputations as authorities. [David and de Vries (1958) p 122.]

The word is thus a *faux ami*, as is jurisprudence and is, therefore, best translated as legal writers/scholars' opinions or the writing of legal scholars.

In modern times, as a result of the impersonal and terse style of French judgments, which are generally devoid of any argumentative threads, the function of explaining and developing the law through argument and counter-argument is performed in France by legal scholars and those who are responsible for drawing up reasoned proposals for a decision in any given case. These scholars include not just professional lawyers, but also the members of State Counsel's Office in their submissions to the courts.

It would appear that it is these submissions of State Counsel that most closely resemble English style judgments because of their 'personal, argumentative, discursive style' (Weston (1991) p 116), and it is only because of the learned annotations by some distinguished legal scholar that it is at all clear whether a given decision 'affirms, modifies or departs from case law' (Weston (1991)).

Thus, as in Italy and Germany, it is the leading law professors and lecturers who are accorded a much more prestigious position in the legal profession than either their counterparts in England, or judges in France. Admittedly, legal textbooks are being cited more in the England of the late 1980s and early 1990s, but the prestige of doctrinal writers in France is greater and of much older vintage.

Modern doctrine places court decisions in their proper perspective and indicates the policies underlying legislation. However, it is not a binding authority on the courts, nor a binding guide to decision. It merely has persuasive authority much in the style of early English common law which accorded a certain status to old and established treatises, but did not regard them as sources of law *strictu sensu* (see Chapter 4). In a system that is rooted in codes and codification, doctrine can only assist in the interpretation and guidance of legal development within the established legal framework.

Status of judicial decisions (jurisprudence) in French law

What is the current position of case law in modern French law? Judicial decisions are not *per se* binding. However, as Blanc-Jouvan and Boulouis express it: 'Without having binding authority *de jure*, they at least have *de facto* authority. This authority varies according to circumstances' (Blanc-Jouvan and Boulouis, in *International Encyclopedia of Comparative Law* (1972) p F-61). They give further useful pointers of the factors which are especially relevant:

(a) the number of similar decisions which can be invoked;

(b) the importance of the court which rendered the decision; and

(c) the way in which the judge has expressed himself.

It would appear that when a harmonious line of cases has accumulated, in which a single authoritative principle consistently emerges, this phenomenon is characterised in French law as *la jurisprudence constante*. If such a consistent line of case law has built up, French courts will tend to follow them, albeit as illustrations of a general principle. The single decision of a first instance court is given less weight than that of the Court of Cassation (particularly if this is given by the Plenary Assembly). A decision which expressly confines itself to the facts of the particular case will be less authoritative than a decision firmly based on principle.

There has never been a prohibition against reference to judicial precedent during the course of litigation. Thus, despite the absence of any formal doctrine of *stare decisis*, there is a strong tendency on the part of French judges to follow precedents, particularly those of the higher courts. The reasons for this have been conveniently summarised by David and de Vries (1958):

(a) the maintenance of professional dignity;

(b) the sharing of responsibility for decisions within the judiciary as a whole;

(c) the saving of time and research for attention to other matters where no precedent exists;

(d) the fulfilment of the expectations of parties who have relied upon previous decisions of the courts; and

(e) the avoidance of excessive or prolonged litigation where a uniform line of decisions clarifies doubtful issues (see David and de Vries (1958) p 117).

In other words, the reasons for the common law practice have resulted in a similar pattern of predictable judicial behaviour in France.

Ever since the famous speech by Ballot-Beaupre (1836–1917), delivered in 1904, in his capacity as president of the French Supreme Court (Cour de Cassation), there has been a 'no less than spectacular development' (David and Brierley (1985) p 120) since 1900 in the law of liability for civil wrongs which corresponds to the sentiments expressed therein, by giving new interpretations to the provision dealing with civil responsibility or delictual liability of persons, namely, the words of Art 1384 of the French Civil Code – that a person is responsible not only for the damage caused by his own actions and for those caused by the actions of persons for whom he must answer, but also for damage caused by 'things under his care' to develop a new law on delictual liability. This is an area where judicial decisions have filled a gap in the legislation to adapt to the changing conditions of French society, but it has to be viewed as exceptional in the context of areas of law governed by Code or legislative provisions, since it must be noted that the Code provisions remain central to the judicial process and, albeit expanded, provide the legal authority *strictu sensu* for the law regulating this area.

Key features of the French legal system

The basic notion of law under the French legal system is different from that which is typical of common law countries. As David puts it:

> The law is not a restricted domain. It is not the business of judges and practitioners alone, because the law is not limited to litigation. The law is seen as a method of social organisation, always changing, and is thus of primary interest to statesmen and in fact to all citizens. [David, *French Law: Its Structure, Sources and Methodology* (1972) trans M Kindred, p viii.]

Hence, a Frenchman and French lawyers have a much broader view of the meaning of the word 'law' than the typical English or common law lawyer, who sees it as mainly linked to the possibility of a court action. The French conception of law comprises:

> ... all the rules devised to establish the structures of society and to regulate people's conduct, and these include many which cannot give rise to an action in the courts but are none the less basic to the organisation of the State. [Weston, *An English Reader's Guide to the French Legal System* (1991) p 46.]

There are also different words that are used for different senses of 'law': 'a law' (or statute) is *une loi*; 'the law' is *la loi* or *'la justice'* as 'to fall foul of the law'; but the law as an academic discipline is *le droit* as it is for legal systems of different countries (*le droit anglais*) and for different branches of the law (*le droit penal*, etc) (see Weston (1991)).

French law, being derived from the Romans, is based on Roman law as interpreted by the Glossators and post-Glossators, and as practised in France. It is not, therefore, based on ancient Roman law. Its primary legal methodology is codification and its primary source of law is, therefore, legislation. Another point we need to bear in mind, as ever, is that the French approach to law is different from that of the common law tradition in its legal categories or classifications of areas of law, in its form and approach to legislation and case law and in its heavy reliance on doctrinal material as a source of law. It is also based on a rigid separation between (a) private law and criminal law; and (b) 'public' or administrative law. There has never been a distinction between law and equity in the sense of the common law distinction, and the concept of the 'trust' does not exist in French law.

There are distinctive legal institutions in France, such as special administrative courts and special doctrines, such as the abuse of rights, direct action and oblique action. There is also an important distinction between the ordinary courts and the administrative courts.

The court system

There are two words available in English meaning 'court', namely a general term 'court' and a narrower term 'tribunal' which refers to panels and bodies which exercise administrative or (more usually) judicial functions, but with limited or special jurisdiction. In France, it is as well to remember that French judges are not supposed to perform a law making function as a result of the doctrine of the separation of powers between the legislature, executive and judiciary. French courts are organised on the basis of general and limited jurisdiction. Weston makes several linguistic points on the comparative problems regarding an understanding of 'courts' in French law and English law (see Weston (1991) Chapter 6), the more significant of which we summarise here.

The higher courts are mostly called *cours*, and all deliver *arrêts*, while the lower ones are mostly called *tribunaux* and all deliver *jugements*. There is a third term in French law, *juridiction*, which appears to be superordinate to the other two. Any *cour* or *tribunal* (or an individual judge) may be described as a *juridiction*, whereas some *juridictions* are *cours* and others *tribunaux*.

Juridiction must be translated as court though, in the plural, as in *les juridictions françaises*, it would refer to 'courts and tribunals'. If, however, the special division of the Criminal Court of Appeal (the *chambre d'accusation*) and the investigating judge of the Criminal Division of the *Tribunal de Grande Instance*, the *juge d'instruction*, are referred to together as *juridictions d'instruction*, the term will then be best translated as 'judicial authority'. Hence, as Weston points out:

> The three French terms are in practice generally to be translated by a single English word because the distinctions between *cour, tribunal* and *juridiction*, in so far as they correspond to distinctions in the English language at all, are not reflected in the English language system. [Weston (1991) p 67.]

The French court system has a dual system of courts, ordinary courts (the *ordre judiciaire*) and administrative courts (*ordre administratif*). The ordinary courts, which are divided into civil and criminal jurisdiction, have jurisdiction unless a case involves the State or a State employee or corporation as a party, in which case the administrative courts will have exclusive jurisdiction. All English courts have jurisdiction to decide cases in administrative matters and to exercise control over administrative bodies and tribunals.

Another conceptual point to note is that the administrative courts really belong to the executive arm of the State and are seen as part of the administrative machinery. Hence, to the French legal mind, only the ordinary courts strictly belong to the judiciary (or in the French, *appellation-autorité judiciaire* – 'judicial power'). It is only these courts that a French lawyer thinks about when discussing the 'judicial' system. The distinction between ordinary and administrative courts is, therefore, far more significant in French law than the one they also have between civil and criminal courts.

The court system has three tiers, but there are only a few similarities with the English legal framework. In the lower tier, there are 485 *tribunaux d'instance*, which is roughly equivalent to the English magistrates' courts and county courts, that is, limited primary jurisdiction. This is the only court in France presided over by a single judge, and all other courts have a bench of judges. There are also a number of ordinary courts of first instance, which are specialised or special courts, only the first of which is a 'court' rather than a tribunal.

They are:

(a) the *tribunaux de commerce*, of which there are nearly 230, consisting of three lay commercial judges with a minimum of five years' experience, elected by their peers in the form of an electoral college comprised of traders' delegates. The English Commercial Court set up within the Queen's Bench Division of the High Court in 1970 has a similar jurisdiction;

(b) social security tribunals, with lay assessors, of which there are 110;

(c) employment tribunals: there is at least one in each department and numbering over 280, which are further subdivided into five divisions, corresponding to different sectors of employment;

(d) landlord and tenant tribunals, numbering around 400.

At the next level, in the second tier, so to speak, though not in an appellate sense, are the *tribunaux de grande instance*. These deal with civil actions involving sums higher than 30,000 francs, or with more serious criminal offences. There are 181 of these, exercising an unlimited jurisdiction, 175 of which are in metropolitan France. This regional court has several chambers or divisions and is often likened to the High Court of Justice in England but there are several differences:

(a) it is the normal court of first instance in civil matters (apart from the small claims dealt with by the *tribunaux d'instance*); they are therefore closer to the English county court but they have a criminal jurisdiction;

(b) the English High Court jurisdiction is primarily civil and it has appellate jurisdiction in both civil and criminal cases. The *tribunaux de grande instance* do not have any appellate jurisdiction;

(c) the English High Court is represented in large provincial cities by a district registrar, has the right to statutorily sit anywhere in England and Wales, although based in London. The *tribunaux de grande instance* is really a regional court.

In the second tier, there are 33 courts of appeal (*cours d'appel*), which are again decentralised and regional courts. They can hear appeals from each of the tribunaux of one or more départements. Each court of appeal has several divisions. Within its civil divisions, it hears appeals from the civil division of the *tribunaux de grande instance*, from the agricultural land tribunals, and the industrial conciliation tribunals.

A Social Division hears appeals from the social security appeal tribunals and a Commercial Division hears appeals from the commercial courts. Within its criminal jurisdiction, appeals are usually heard by a Criminal Division, except for those involving a minor, which will be heard by the Juvenile Division.

There is a crucial difference between the English Court of Appeal and the French version. The French cour d'appel conducts a re-examination and rehearing of the whole case and can, therefore, substitute its own view of the facts or the law for that of the original court that heard the case. The English Appeal Court has the power to do this, but very rarely disagrees with the trial judge's view of the primary facts, since he had the opportunity to see and hear the witnesses, and evaluate the evidence first hand. The normal practice has been for the appeal court to overturn the original court's view only if new or fresh evidence comes to light (as in the spate of recent English criminal cases involving alleged terrorist activities), or forensic evidence proves that the original verdict was not 'safe' and could no longer be upheld. In addition, the English Appeal Court will overrule a lower court decision if it is proved that the original court acted in such a way that no reasonable judge would have acted, either excluding evidence that should have been included, or misinterpreting the evidence which he did take into account.

Another notable difference between the French and English appellate courts is that, in England, there is predominant reliance on oral evidence gleaned from the adversarial process in one continuous hearing. The facts in a French case are obtained through a rigorous investigation of the court itself, the results of which are then complied in a written dossier. It is obviously easier to review this dossier at the appellate stage.

The Supreme Court, with jurisdiction over the whole of France, is the Cour de Cassation. This consists of five civil chambers and one criminal chamber. The first three are called the First, Second and Third Civil Divisions, the remaining two the Commercial and Financial Divisions and the other the Social Division.

A minimum of three (and usually five) judges hear a case from a single division and there are more than 100 judges in all. The first three divisions or chambers deal with litigation arising out of general private law; the Commercial and Financial Divisions deal with trade and economic law cases and the Social Division deals with litigation arising out of labour and social security matters. There is no civil jury, but there is one for criminal cases.

The Cour de Cassation is known as a court of error, which means that it only deals with cases that appeal on a point of law, such an appeal being known as a *pourvoi en cassation* (or sometimes known as a *recours en cassation*), which is an appeal on points of law – a form of application to have a judgment set aside purely on legal grounds. It does not appear to have any direct equivalent in English law, although the nearest would seem to be the English application for judicial review, which asks the court to review not the merits of the case, but the legality of an administrative decision.

However, this court does not fulfil the same function as the House of Lords. If it finds the *pourvoi* justified, it has no power to substitute its own decision, but merely to quash it. The case will then be remitted for further consideration to another court of equal jurisdiction to the first court that heard the case. If this lower court takes the same view as that of the original court, the matter will be referred to the Assemblée Plénière (Plenary Assembly) of the Cour de Cassation on which all five divisions are represented, with 25 judges presiding. If the Assemblée Plénière again quashes the lower court's decision on the same grounds as before, the Assemblée Plénière will then remit the matter to a third court, which is then obliged to follow the view taken by the Assemblée. Recent time saving reforms have made it possible for either the division which has dealt with the first *pourvoi*, or the Assemblée Plénière to enter a final judgment if its decision on the particular point of law in question leaves nothing further for the court below to consider.

Cases may be referred direct to the full court by a joint bench or even by an ordinary bench. If this is done and the lower court's decision is quashed, the Assemblée's decision will be binding on the court to which the case has been remitted.

The primary function of the Cour de Cassation is to secure uniformity of interpretation, a task which, in England, is carried out by the Court of Appeal. The whole ethos of the Cour de Cassation is different from the House of Lords, which, as stated by the former Lord Chancellor, is not a court you should usually appeal to unless the case is one which is not covered by the law. The Cour de Cassation's philosophy is that there should be unrestricted access to the courts for every litigant who wishes to argue a particular issue in law. In pursuance of this, there is no filter division such as the Appeals Committee of the House of Lords, and there are 127 judges in the Cour de Cassation.

The House of Lords only hears something like 70 cases a year as opposed to the 15,000 that the Cour de cassation's five civil chambers hear per year. The number of cases that go to the Cour de cassation have tripled in the last 10 years and it is currently facing a severe overloading problem with an increasing backlog. The Procureur Général and the Premier President of the

Court have drawn attention to this crisis last year and the latter suggested having a filter to vet cases that were appealing to the Cour de Cassation.

Finally, all courts, except for the *tribunaux d'instance*, are collegial in that they act as a bench of at least three judges, or at least seven in the Cour de Cassation, but that they are seen to act as one body. At the end of a case, they issue one judgment; there are no published reports of dissenting judgments. Moreover, the actual judgment tends to be exceedingly terse and laconic by English law standards, as little as one sentence if thought appropriate. Thus, reliance has to be placed on the opinions of doctrinal or academic writers whose written opinions are termed doctrine . While the English judge is often a public figure, whose views and even physical features may be relayed and displayed on a television screen or 'tabloid' newspaper in an important case, the typical French judge remains anonymous.

Public and private law

Introduction

English law has devoted relatively little attention to the problem of classification in the law, primarily because of the late development of legal science in England. However, the distinction between public law and private law:

> ... seems to many Continental European lawyers to be fundamental, necessary and, on the whole, evident. Institutional works, student manuals and treatises contain discussions of the dichotomy, often in confidently dogmatic terms that put to rest incipient doubts. [Merryman, 'The public law-private law distinction in European and American law' (1968) 17 J Pub Law 3.]

The distinction itself is traceable to the Roman jurist, Ulpian, who drew the distinction (usually placed at around 200 AD). His statement appears near the beginning of the *Digest* and is repeated on the first page of Justinian's *Institutes*: 'There are two aspects of this subject: public and private law. Public law deals with the State ... private law with the well being of individuals' (quoted in Kahn-Freund, Levy and Rudden (1991) p 10).

As we have seen, there is one Supreme Court (Cour de Cassation) which deals with private law matters and another (the Conseil d'Etat) for public law matters. There is also the Conseil constitutionnel, created by the 1958 Constitution, and the closest equivalent to a constitutional court that France possesses, although its powers are much more restricted than those of the United States Supreme Court. It has a dual function: adjudicative and advisory. It vets all election cases, parliamentary standing orders, and parliamentary legislation. This has become more closely approximated to a constitutional court, since its decisions are binding on the Cour de Cassation, the Conseil d'Etat, the legislator and government, and it has a very strong influence on other judicial authorities.

However, it cannot declare an Act of Parliament unconstitutional once it has been promulgated, nor can it review the constitutionality of regulations, and it is not a supreme appellate court, such as the US Supreme Court. The question will remain as to whether it can properly be called a court.

Content of public and private law

Public law (*droit public*) governs relations to which the State (or a subdivision of it such as a département, or a State owned enterprise or a public authority) is a party (this means relations between public bodies *inter se* and between public bodies and private persons), while private law (*droit privé*) governs the rights and duties of private persons and corporations. Public law administers State run bodies that provide public services, schools, hospitals and municipalities, as well as regulates the legal position of persons who serve the State (such as civil servants or soldiers).

It is important to note that the divisions of the law are firmly fixed in the minds of civil lawyers, but the divisions themselves are by no means immutable as a result of at least two factors. First, the existence in many countries (including France) of a special hierarchy of courts dealing with administrative matters and, secondly, the involvement of the State in certain cases where the central parties are private persons.

On the first point, it would be incorrect to assume that the scope of the administrative courts' jurisdiction is the scope of public law. Many disputes to which the State is a party, and which would belong to the province of public law, are within the domain of the ordinary courts of law.

On the second point, in many cases, although the parties to a given relationship are private citizens (or companies), the State is not indifferent to this relationship. Rules are accordingly provided to regulate such relationships, to which the parties are obliged to submit. A typical example is the area of marriage and divorce. Parties are bound to abide by most rules formulated dealing with the marriage ceremony, or of its effects, or its dissolution. The point is that the essential feature of marriage is that it is a private relationship between persons, but it is one in which the State (or society) has particular interests, such as the protection and security of the vulnerable party (generally, the wife) and children of the relationship. Accordingly, these rules are imposed as a result of what English law would call 'public policy'. It may, of course, be provided that private law rules shall apply to a given relation, although the State is a party to such a relationship.

The separate hierarchy of administrative courts

As a result of the separation of powers, the French executive is not subject to the jurisdiction of the ordinary courts but it is subject to the control of the central organ of the executive, the Conseil d'Etat, created in 1799 by Napoleon, which, in this capacity, performs a function very much like a court. Thus, the executive can only be 'kept in check', so to speak, by a court that is part of the executive system itself. The Conseil d'État (literally: 'Council of State') has been supplemented by a number of other lower level administrative courts, and together with these courts, forms a self-contained hierarchy of courts with three tiers as well. The Conseil d'État is the supreme administrative court at the top of this hierarchy.

The lowest tier of the administrative court structure consists of the *tribunaux administratifs* (administrative courts), which are regional courts, numbering 26 in metropolitan France, and, since 1989, by virtue of an Act of 31 December 1987, there is now an intermediate tier of appellate administrative court: the *cour administrative d'appel* (Administrative Court of Appeal). This system is a regional set up, with five courts having been established at Paris, Bordeaux, Lyon, Nantes and Nancy. From these courts, appeal lies to the Conseil d'État in the form of a *recours en cassation* ('appeal on points of law'). It is worth noting that the law that is applied by these administrative courts is almost entirely case law and is found in the decisions of the Conseil d'État, and there is now a voluminous literature which informs this area of law.

These administrative courts have a dual jurisdiction:

(a) they exercise a review jurisdiction, called the 'annulment jurisdiction' from which even statutes are not necessarily immune, ever since a 1975 decision of the Cour de Cassation which held that a treaty took precedence over a later Act of Parliament; and

(b) they exercise a *pleine* jurisdiction (full jurisdiction) which allows them to award damages to those who have suffered injury or damage as a result of a wrongful act on the part of a public servant acting in the course of his duties. This entitles the court to substitute the administrative decision which is being challenged.

Two categories of executive or administrative acts which are not subject to review by the administrative courts are:

(a) those 'connected directly with, or forming part of, the legislative process and parliamentary proceedings'; and

(b) 'those concerning the government's relations with foreign countries or with international organisations' (see Weston (1991) p 87).

Current status of the distinction

The whole question of the dichotomy has been under scrutiny and undergone criticism over the last 10–15 years, but it has remained, at least in its basic structure. The problem is that there are occasions when a civil or criminal court will have to apply administrative law, for example, when a person charged with an offence created by an administrative regulation wishes to challenge the legality of the regulation. Or, an administrative court has had to take cognisance of private law on several occasions. It is also a moot point as to whether criminal law should be classified as public or private law. In the context of crime prevention, it seems to fall within public law, but criminal cases are brought before the private law courts. The fundamental distinction really seems to be between administrative law and private law, since public law encompasses constitutional law, which lies outside the jurisdiction of the administrative courts. As a preliminary proposition, it appears that the distinction between public and private, in the strict, conventional sense, is breaking down as the frontiers of State intervention begin to encroach into private law matters.

Conflict of jurisdiction

There is also the Tribunal des Conflits, a sort of Jurisdiction Disputes Court, dealing with matters such as whether a case should be heard in the ordinary courts or in the administrative courts. The main area of conflict has been the case where a private citizen sues a public servant in the ordinary courts and the administrative courts wish to argue that the matter belongs properly to the realm of public law. If the local prefect enters a plea of no jurisdiction, arguing that the ordinary court in question has no jurisdiction to hear the case and the court rejects this plea, the prefect may apply to the Jurisdiction Disputes Court for a final ruling. This ruling must be given within three months. If the original court accepts the plea, the plaintiff must either sue in the administrative courts, or else appeal to a higher ordinary court. Conflicts of jurisdiction between the civil and criminal ordinary courts are decided by the Cour de Cassation.

Distinctive French legal doctrines and concepts

Abuse of rights

Among the distinctive doctrines of French law is the notion of the abuse of rights. This is a kind of fault based action which consists in the abusive (that is, wrongful) exercise of a right motivated by the desire to cause harm. The reported cases dealing with this type of situation suggest that they occur most often in the context of the law of property. The basis of the action appears to be quasi-delictual rather than delictual. The closest English law analogy is the English tort of nuisance. If a person's land is adversely affected by smells, vapours, smoke or any 'dangerous thing' for an appreciable period of time, the person causing such effects will generally be strictly liable, under English law, regardless of fault in the tort of nuisance to the occupier of that land (see, for example, *Stone v Bolton* [1950] 1 KB 201; *Rylands v Fletcher* (1868) LR 3 HL 330).

Direct action (action directe)

In French law and, indeed, in the Romanistic legal family, the *action directe* (direct action) makes it possible for a person who is only indirectly represented to intervene in a contract concluded on his behalf by a middleman. Thus, in a few specified instances, the French Civil Code gives a person an independent right of suit, if that person has a special interest in a contract concluded between two other parties (see Arts 1759, 1798 and 1994).

English law only allows such actions as an exception to its general rule of privity of contract – that only parties to the original contract may sue – unless one of the many exceptions may be successfully invoked (such as trusts, agency or assignment).

Examples of this action in French law are:

(a) where a landlord can proceed against a subtenant, if the tenant is in arrears with the rent; or

(b) where a principal may claim directly against a third party to whom his agent has delegated the performance of the authorised task; and

(c) in the realm of the law of insurance.

If a tortfeasor is covered in respect of an accident by a policy of insurance, the victim can sue the insurer direct. In the case of the *action directe*, it is the legislator who decides, on the basis of an abstract balancing of the interests involved, that the third party should have a right to intervene, regardless of whether this accords with the intention of the parties or not.

Oblique action

This is an action whereby a suing creditor is empowered to exercise, in the insolvent debtor's name, all the latter's rights and actions, except those which are purely personal. This is what is stated by Art 1166 of the Civil Code. Thus, the creditor is allowed to stand in the place of the debtor, but can only exercise the right belonging to the debtor by bringing an action. The personal rights and actions may be either: (a) ones which are not primarily of a pecuniary nature; or (b) ones which the debtor may decline to exercise for conscientious or other personal reasons (Amos and Walton (1967) p 241).

In order to bring the action, the creditor(s) must have a 'personal interest' in bringing the action (see Civ 11.7.1951, p 586). The debt has to be certain, due and liquidated (see Req 25.3.1924, DH 1924.282, S 1924.1.67) and there will be no such 'personal interest' if the debtor is solvent, or if he is already prosecuting the claim in question himself (see Amos and Walton (1967) p 242). The main purpose of the oblique action is to prevent the debtor from negligently allowing his rights to be lost.

A practice that has developed outside the Code is that the creditor bringing the oblique action usually joins the debtor as a party to the action.

Any defence which would be good against the debtor is good against the creditors because the action belongs to the debtor, but is simply brought by the creditors in his name. This will apply to defences which have become available after the bringing of the action.

The creditors instituting the oblique action do not obtain any priority or charge with regard to what is recovered. If the action is successful, the property recovered will simply be included in the general estate of the debtor. Indeed, if the other creditors wish to do so, they can prevent the creditor, who filed the action, from applying the proceeds to his own claim (Amos and Walton (1967) p 243).

Thus, there is little incentive for a creditor to institute the oblique action and its use is relatively rare, because there is the more effective remedy of attachment (saisie-arret) under the Civil Procedure Code (see Art 557 et seq).

History of German law

Early German law

In the Middle Ages, the law of Germany consisted mainly of customs and traditions, as did medieval law generally. The private law of the German territories before 1400 thus took the form of local custom. Although originating in common Germanic ideas, they were locally developed in each part of the territories of Central Europe which were part of the 'Holy Roman Empire of the Germanic Nation'. Some of these customs were applied in a single city, some over large stretches of territory, yet others were confined to a single village or manor or to a special group of persons. The revival of the title of Roman emperor and its assumption by German kings did not result in the rules of the *Corpus Juris* being applied, either as legislation, or to fill in gaps where local custom was silent.

Roman law was taught in cathedral and convent schools, but some Germans travelled to Bologna, while others began to attend Italian and French law schools. These private law rules were highly localised, 'orally transmitted and immensely diversified' (Dawson (1968) p 153).

However, many of these customary rules were privately collected and expanded in law books, some of which eventually attained high status as works of authority, rather like the early books of English law by Bracton and Glanvill, such as the *Mirror of Saxon Law* by Eike von Repgow (*Sachsenspiegel*), produced around 1225, which predates Bracton. The central power in the Empire did not, however, attempt to implement Roman law to all German territories as a form of common law to supplant local customs.

Nevertheless, in the 1450s till nearly the end of the 15th century, a great deal of factional strife, frequent anarchy and the lack of a strong central authority were factors which convinced all reformers that there should be an end to private warfare. Emperor Maximillan (1493–1519) sought to restore the power of the monarchy and to secure lasting peace and unity.

In 1495, for reasons which remain mysterious, and which have never obtained consensus from various historians, Roman law was adopted by the newly established imperial court, the Reichskammergericht, the operative ordinance stating that judges were ordered to decide cases coming before them 'according to the common law of the Empire', which meant, according to Roman law. The ordinance of 1495 placed 'statutes' and 'customs' on an equal footing.

Reasons for reception of Roman law

Many reasons have been adduced for the 'reception' of Roman law, bearing in mind that there was no complete displacement of German law by Roman law. Von Mehren and Gordley (1977), in reliance on various researchers' findings, suggest six reasons:

(a) lack of legal unity within Germany;

(b) lack of written law often made it difficult to ascertain the rules;

(c) lack of written law was seen as a major cause for the unsystematic nature and lack of rational structure of the Germanic law;

(d) as a result of the highly fragmented nature of the legal order, neither a strong legal profession nor one with extensive knowledge of Germanic laws had been produced. In England, for instance, the legal profession fought to prevent any takeover by Roman law;

(e) legally skilled administrative personnel were increasingly needed to replace the 'unlearned, noble administrator' and the only source of such personnel was students trained in Roman law at the Italian and other universities;

(f) the whole body of Roman law was given the status of statutory law in Germany through the 1495 regulation which reduced greatly the practical significance of German law.

The Roman law that was received was not the 'unadulterated' sixth century *Corpus Juris*, but the version that had been modified by the Glossators and Commentators. Some parts were actually ignored and Germanic Commercial Law, for example, remained intact. The degree of reception was also far from uniform with the more northerly regions retaining their Germanic law and, when some cities reformed their legal systems in the 14th and 15th centuries, they again retained many of the original Germanic elements.

Hence, instead of having a sophisticated university derived Roman law and Canon law which co-existed with local customary law, by the middle of the 16th century, there was a reasonably homogeneous common law based on post-classical Roman law principles, adapted and 'harmonised' to suit daily life, but which co-existed with a mixture of Germanic principles (see Forrester, Goren and Ilgen, *The German Civil Code* (1975) p xxiii). This brand of 'common law', or Usus Modernus Pandectarum, continued to exist in certain parts of Germany, subject to many local variations, until 1900. A great disadvantage with these laws was their sheer bulk, so that even commentaries on them could not ensure legal uniformity or legal certainty.

The Pandectists

During the 16th, 17th and 18th centuries, Roman lawyers in Germany and elsewhere were producing syntheses of modern Roman law in the name of the law of nature and the law of reason. The whole style and characteristic philosophy of these movements was to present this adapted Roman law in a logical and orderly progression of concepts. It was out of this natural law and law of reason that the German branch of the movement, so to speak, emerged – the Pandectists. They sought to promote the dogmatic and systematic study of Roman law. Their plan was to study all historical sources which had shaped German legal history, and they viewed law as a closed system of ideas, principles and institutions derived from Roman law. Their methodology was a scientific, logical approach to the solution of legal problems. Law was therefore approached outside any ethical, moral or religious considerations, and, at least for the resolution of problems, was a mathematical process determined by a 'conceptual calculus'. The German Civil Code (BGB) is a product of the Pandectist School, in its abstraction, precision and logical symmetry. Ethical and moral considerations were not, by any means, irrelevant, but law's basic methodology did not, *prima facie*, utilise such concepts.

Diversity of political entities

The situation was not helped by there not really being a united political entity which could be called Germany, but rather hundreds of independent political entities varying enormously in size and influence, each with its own judges and courts and all steadfastly clinging to their own customs as far as they could. This was despite the fact that there was an Emperor, and the German territory was meant to be part of the Empire. Natural law philosophy, and the merging of various smaller States into larger political units and the rise of an absolute monarchy led to territorial codifications, which partly preserved the pre-existing law as a residual source, which would be applied in the absence of statute. With the formal dissolution of the Empire in 1806, State legislation reigned supreme for some time.

Political unification: 1871

In the early 19th century, at the Congress of Vienna 1815, the German Confederation was established. This was a loose association of States which included Austria, Bavaria and Prussia. It lasted until 1866, when Prusso-Austrian rivalry led to a conflict which Prussia and her allies from the North German States won. After Austria's defeat, a new North German Confederation was set up, but there was no final coalition between the northern and southern States until nearly five years had passed. In 1870, a war broke out between France and an alliance of German States. The German alliance won, which saw the French army surrender at Sedan in September 1870, and Paris fall in early 1871. Bismarck, the Prussian Chancellor accordingly proclaimed the new German Empire, or Reich, at Versailles in 1871.

Legal codification

For most of the 19th century, after the establishment of the Congress of Vienna in 1815, various attempts were made to achieve codification. Several German States had already adopted national codes, such as Prussia (1794), and the French Code had been adopted by certain Rhineland States, during the Napoleonic wars. These wars strengthened the feeling for national unity, but one of the major obstacles to German codification was the celebrated dispute between two distinguished German scholars, Carl von Savigny (1779–1861), leader of the Historical School of Jurisprudence, and Professor Thibaut of Heidelberg, the leading spokesman for the natural law school of jurisprudence, who argued for codification. This powerful conflict of learned opinion set back the success of codification for several decades. Some have portrayed this opposition as a conflict between the Romanists (such as Savigny) and the Germanists (such as Thibaut).

Thibaut's views ultimately won the day and natural law elements have been integrated into the German Civil Code (BGB), but the sharp disagreement between two such prominent thinkers deprived the codification movement of considerable impetus for some time.

Nevertheless, several discussions did take place between members of the Confederation, to formulate uniform laws governing bills of exchange, and to work to produce a uniform commercial code. A number of States also proceeded to draft civil codes which all remained unadopted in 1871, except for Saxony, which produced a Code of Civil Law in 1863, which, in its Pandectist approach and structure, was a forerunner of the BGB.

In 1871, an extraordinary constitutional and legislative situation existed. As one set of commentators put it, 'There were more than 20 kingdoms, grand-duchies, duchies, free cities, principalities, and one imperial territory' (Forrester *et al* (1975) p xiii). As these writers go on to explain: '... each of these had their own hierarchies of courts and their own laws, or at least their own particular combination of ancient codifications, Rom-German law, modern codifications and local custom.' In fact, more than 10 codifications were in force, but the point was, they did not necessarily apply if they contradicted local custom. Even more confusingly, different texts applied in different areas within individual States.

Of course, a fairly uniform law merchant, or commercial law, did exist and it was mainly in the field of family law and succession that the greatest uncertainty existed, as a result of the diversity of laws.

Upon establishment of the German Empire in 1871, the new Constitution gave the federal government power in a variety of fields, including civil procedure, organisation of courts, criminal law and criminal procedure, and bankruptcy. The first law enacted by the new German Empire in 1871 was the Criminal Code, which was most easily achieved because the Northern German League had adopted a Criminal Code in 1870, which the Reich took over.

The system of courts

There are five different sets of courts in Germany, apart from the Federal Constitutional Court. There are courts of ordinary jurisdiction (civil/criminal law), labour courts, administrative courts, social insurance courts and tax courts. Each set of courts is generally three tiered; there are courts of first instance, courts of appeal and a federal supreme court. The first instance courts and the courts of appeal are courts of the several regions (*Länder*), so it is up to the individual region/district to staff, maintain and equip these courts, which will involve employing, paying, promoting and pensioning judges who sit in them. Only the courts of last resort are federal courts whose judges are federal judges.

The jurisdiction of these courts is determined by federal legislation. Although the basic law (Art 74, para 1) provides that the constitution of the courts and court procedure fall within the area of concurrent legislative competence, the federal Parliament has legislated so comprehensively in this area that it utterly dominates this area of law leaving little scope for the *Länder*.

It is the ordinary jurisdiction courts, with which the average citizen has most contact, which has more judges than any other jurisdiction and hears nearly all matters of civil and criminal law. At first instance, small claims are brought to the lowest civil court, the Amtsgericht, but claims exceeding DM6,000 must be brought in the regional court, the Landgericht, where each party has to be represented by a German lawyer who has *locus standi* at that court. The Amtsgericht is also the forum for the enforcement of judgments, and handles non-contentious business, such as the maintenance of the land register and the commercial register, the supervision of guardians, testamentary administrators and trustees in bankruptcy. Civil cases in the Amtsgericht are heard by a single judge, which is also the case for criminal cases, unless serious crimes are involved. In that sort of case, two lay judges sit on the bench with a professional judge. The Landgericht also sits as a trial court in cases unsuitable for the Amtsgericht, in which event, the case is heard by a special division of the Landgericht called the Schwurgericht.

This consists of three professional judges and two lay judges who have the same voting power as the presiding professional judges, and have the right to consider issues of fact and law in the case. Both the sentence, and the verdict, must be approved by a two-thirds majority of the judges.

Most of the work of the Court of Appeal consists of civil matters, since appeals from criminal convictions rendered by the Landgericht usually go direct to the federal court. The Appeal Court hears appeals from decisions of the Landgericht, sitting as a Court of First Instance, and from decisions of the Amtsgericht, sitting as a Family Court. The Appeal Court judges sit in divisions, called senates, which comprise three judges, each presided over by the one who has the highest rank or seniority.

Civil cases falling outside the jurisdiction of the Amtsgericht start in the Landgericht, or District Court. The Landgericht also hears appeals from first instance decisions of the Amtsgericht. But, if the Amtsgericht was sitting as a Family Court, the appeal goes directly to the Appeal Court (Oberlandesgericht). In principle, decisions of the Landgericht are made by a panel of three professional judges, but it is quite common for a single judge to be delegated to hear straightforward cases.

The Landgericht has a special chamber for commercial cases (as defined in Art 95 GVG) which is usually dealt with by a panel of three judges – two experienced commercial men, acting as honorary commercial judges and one presiding professional judge.

Appeals can be made against both the decisions of the Amtsgericht, and the Landgericht but, in civil matters, the amount has to be at least DM1,200 in order to obtain leave to appeal. A further appeal to the Federal Court on points of law is possible against the decisions of the Court of Appeal, in cases involving amounts greater than DM60,000, or in disputes involving matters of fundamental importance (see Bocker *et al*, *Germany: Practical Commercial Law* (1992) p 3).

In criminal cases, the Landgericht hears appeals from convictions from decisions handed down by the Amtsgericht.

The highest of the courts of ordinary jurisdiction is the Federal Supreme Court (Bundesgerichtshof), which sits in Karlsruhe and consists of 15 senates, 10 for civil matters and five for criminal matters. There are five federal judges in each senate, one of whom presides. Appeals from the decisions of the Appeal Court are heard by the criminal senates. As the matter stands, an appeal is available to the Federal Supreme Court only if the Appeal Court has given its permission, or, if the case is one which it believes concerns a matter of principle, or that its decision deviates from a decision of the Appeal Court (Art 546 of the ZPO (Code of Civil Procedure)).

Labour courts have jurisdiction over disputes concerning labour law, such as matters involving employment contracts, collective bargaining agreements and works agreements. The appeal system is three tiered with two regional courts in every German district and a Federal Court, which has jurisdiction over the whole country to determine appeals on points of law.

Administrative courts deal with disputes relating to the acts of public authorities. Cases start in the Administrative Court, then proceed up on appeal to the Administrative Appeal Court and, finally, to the Federal Administrative Court in Berlin, which must be on a point of law.

There is also a special branch of social courts, the Court on Social Matters, which deals with social insurance and allied matters, and which contains two lay judges at each of the three levels. There is, however, one professional judge in the Court of First Instance.

Disputes of revenue law are heard by a special set of tax courts, but there are only two levels of court in this context because complaints against decisions of the tax authorities first come before special committees.

In addition to these five systems, there is the Federal Constitutional Court, to which anyone can bring a formal case lodging a 'complaint', alleging an infringement of his constitutional rights through an act of public authorities. There is always the possibility of challenging a new law or a final judgment as unconstitutional if it is a case involving human rights. This court has built up a store of cases. The Constitutional Court may declare any law or judgment null and void.

Enactment of the BGB

After a long period of drafting, discussion and more redrafting, the final draft was submitted to the German legislature, in June 1896, for debate. No less than 125 speeches were made on the draft code, and over a third of these dealt with rights and liabilities related to game and domestic animals! This illustrates the predominant outlook of the legislators to the draft. Speakers also spoke on habitual drunkenness as a ground for placing a person under guardianship, divorce on the ground for insanity, civil marriage, parental consent to marriage, holograph wills and parental authority.

The Burgerliches Gesetzbuch (BGB) – Civil Code – was officially promulgated on 18 August 1896, and entered into effect on 1 January 1900, and effectively unified the private law in the German Empire. It regulates the relations between private persons who are regarded as equals, rather than as subordinate to the State as under public law.

Its main objectives were clarification and consistency in the law, and it represents a harmonisation of pre-existing law in the various parts of the Reich. The political values of 19th century liberalism appear to have set the agenda for the contents of the rules of the Code. Its key themes are the individual and his need for freedom. The BGB thus gives parties great freedom in contracting and in the realm of property, reflecting the view that equal freedom for all individuals would ensure the smooth functioning of social justice.

The BGB is not written for the layman, unlike the French Civil Code. It is addressed to the legal profession, giving precedence to precise solutions, and predictability of outcome. Its commentaries are, therefore, regularly updated, with detailed analyses of myriad situations and a range of available solutions. It often looks to the economy, not the law, to secure social justice. Some commentators, like Bochmer (1965), have therefore said that it reflects the end, rather than the beginning of an era, because its structures, the choice of approach, and the code's values all come from the 19th century. As Von Mehren and Gordley point out, although Romanist in inspiration, the influence of the Germanic tradition is seen in a number of its paragraphs, for example, dealing with: joint ownership (paras 705, 1416, 2032); the contract of inheritance (para 2281); the law applicable to executors of wills (para 2197); the concept of acquisition in good faith from unauthorised persons (para 932); the introduction of the land register (para 873); the concept of contracts for the benefit of a third party (para 328) and the assumption of debt (para 414) (Von Mehren and Gordley (1977) p 79).

The BGB has been used as a model for codes in many countries: the Japanese Civil Code (1898), the Swiss Civil Code (1907) and the Swiss Code of Obligations (1911), as well as the revisions for the Austrian Code in the 1910s, and, indirectly, the Turkish Code of Obligations (1926). In the light of strong legal ties between Italy and Germany, the drafters of the Italian Code have also been influenced by the BGB.

Structure of the BGB

The format adopted by Justinian's *Institutes* was to divide the codes into self-contained chapters, subdivided into sections which are called 'paragraphs' dealing with different topics such as persons, obligations, property and succession, though by no means in that order. The BGB does not actually follow this tradition and calls its Book One the 'General Part', followed by the words 'Book One', which is followed by 'Books' or chapters on obligations, property, family law and succession.

Thus, Book One (General Part) contains paras 1–240, Book Two (Law of Obligations) contains paras 241–853, Book Three (Law of Property) contains paras 854–1296, Book Four (Family Law) contains paras 1297–1921, and Book Five (Law of Succession) contains paras 1922–2385. The paragraphs are equivalent to an English statute's 'sections'.

This format is similar to the method adopted by Roman scholars, such as the judge and scholar, Professor Heise of Heidelberg, who adopted a similar style of analysis. He divided his teaching of Roman law into five sections, the first dealing with the basic principles of legal behaviour and the methods of creation of legal relationships (see Forrester, Goren and Ilgen (1975) p xiv).

Book One provides the definitions and legal vocabulary which govern the remaining four books. It commences by describing the types of persons (who may be physical or juristic) who can have rights and obligations. It also defines the different types of property, and outlines the principles underlying the creation and dissolution of legal obligations. Book Two starts off with 200 paragraphs containing general principles relevant to all obligations, and the next 400 deal with 30 specific types of obligations, which illustrate the approach of commencing with the general concepts, then moving to the specific examples but, in order to ascertain the scope of a particular obligation, you would have to refer to Book One, the first part of Book Two and the specific provisions pertaining thereto in Book Two.

Using the Code therefore requires a high degree of familiarity with its contents and its particular style, since it constantly requires cross-referencing from the specific Title to the relevant provisions of the General Part. Accordingly, in modern practice, there is now a 2,000 page book, printed on extra-thin paper, which is called a Short Commentary on the BGB (*Kommentar zum BGB* (1974)), edited by judges of the imperial and federal courts, which contains a collection of cases – judicial decisions on the various paragraphs – which no practising German lawyer is ever seen without when engaged in interpretation of the BGB. There is also a Commentary on the BGB, which is regularly updated, consisting of a seven volume collection analysing the BGB, but which also gives a great deal of coverage to the views of academic writers (see, for example, *Munchener Kommentar zum BGB* (1978), (1987), (1993)).

Amendments to the BGB

The BGB has undergone alterations and amendments in the course of its long history which spans nearly 100 years. Some of its sections were repealed during the Nazi era, and the practice developed of enacting special laws outside it. Accordingly, it is necessary from time to time to refer to legislation which supplements the BGB. New social legislation, either included within the Code's framework, or through supplementary legislation, has been the trend for several decades, and has accelerated apace in the 1980s and 1990s.

By the 1970s, there were nearly 60 statutory modifications of the Code, and more than 800 of its 2,385 paragraphs have been repealed, modified, renewed, undergone insertions, and even declared unconstitutional by the Federal Constitutional Court.

Some of the more important alterations to the Code have occurred in relation to family law, particularly in respect of matrimonial property (implementing a new marital property regime), celebration and dissolution of marriage, the status of illegitimate children and a number of provisions dealing with the welfare of children in need of protection by the Guardianship Court. Other changes have occurred in the field of property law, and employment law.

Style of the BGB

The legal language of the BGB is generally seen as being rather abstract and complex, but it is precise in what it says about the particular area of law. But the main difficulties lie in the need to be familiar with the various concepts, as interpreted by the courts and in practice, a knowledge of technical language and the need to cross-reference. For example, para 157 states: '... contracts shall be interpreted according to the requirements of good faith, giving consideration to common usage' and para 242 states: '... the debtor is bound to effect performance according to the requirements of good faith, giving consideration to common usage' (see translations in Forrester *et al* (1975) p xvi). It will be noticed that key phrases such as 'good faith' and 'common usage' are not defined, and you would therefore need to consult the case law on the subject. In fact, para 242 is the most utilised section in the whole BGB, having been used by the courts to create a whole corpus of law, to vary and supplement contracts, using 'implied' terms much in the same way as in English law, thereby creating flexibility within formalism.

Paragraph 242 has become a controlling statutory enactment of the general principle of 'good faith' which dominates the entire legal system (see Horn, Kotz and Leser (1982) pp 135–45; and Chapter 12 of this book, for a comparative study of good faith).

The significant point that this illustrates is that, despite the key civil law principle that gives supremacy to legislation (and, of course, has ultimate allegiance to the Constitution), no civil lawyer is able to answer or resolve questions and issues of law without some recourse to case law. Further, in accordance with the civil law ideology, the opinions and writings of doctrinal or academic writers have to be consulted, as in the French system, in order to obtain a considered view on a particular provision. General and abstract statements of principle clearly have to be elaborated upon in order to be applied to specific circumstances not covered by the Code. Paragraph 133 provides that, in construing legal texts, the underlying intention and not the literal meaning of the words should prevail. This is sometimes referred to as the teleological approach, or purposive method of interpretation.

Another point worth noting is that the BGB does not have any 'foreign' non-German terms in it, eschewing Latin for German translations. Terms, such as *bona fides*, or conduct *contra bonos mores*, have been translated as *treu und glauben* and legal transactions *gegen die guten sitten*, respectively. This was the result of its 19th century background in that the BGB is a national and strongly German code with a powerful strain of nationalism and patriotism running through it. Again, the case law is the only way in which it is possible to know what these particular terms will mean in a given context.

Bearing in mind the importance of cases to the Code's interpretation, what is the legal method employed to accommodate the legislative supremacy principle?

Interpretation of the BGB

The fundamental point to note about the judicial style in Germany is that the judge is not permitted to simply cite a case as an authoritative source of a legal principle. Some legislative provision or Code provision has to be cited, or some well established, general legal principle, for example, the notion of *culpa in contrahendo* (liability due to fault existed before contracting) which does not appear in the BGB, but which has been cited by the courts. Thus, the courts would have to say: 'According to § XYZ of the BGB (or, according to the general principle of ...) as interpreted by the BGH (the Supreme Court), we find that the legal position is ...' To emphasise the point, although an English court does the same in cases turning on the interpretation of a statute, usually citing the need to ascertain 'the intention of Parliament', this general approach in German law is applicable to all cases, not just those involving statutory interpretation.

Thus, the BGB is interpreted in the manner illustrated above, and, as has been stressed, by consulting the case law on a particular provision. Another important point to note is that, since there is no doctrine of precedent in German law, the cases on the provision need not necessarily be followed. However, cases of the Supreme Court tend to be followed, but will be departed from if seen as out of date or inappropriate to the particular case.

Application of the BGB

A sixth 'Book' or 'Chapter' was included in the 1895 Draft of the BGB which dealt with the relationship between imperial and State laws and other private international law problems. Although removed from the Code itself, it was enacted separately, after modifications, as the Introductory Law (*Einfuhrungsgesetz zum Burgerlichen Gesetzbuch*) (EGBGB) at the same time as the BGB and is still in force, but it is of far less utility today than it might have been in the early 20th century. The EGBGB has a long list of the fields in which the laws of the States may survive, and in which they lapse, but there are now far fewer civil law (private law) areas which are regulated by State legislation than there used to be. Some remaining areas are forestry, water rights and mining.

The EGBGB also contains rules which govern conflicts between the BGB and foreign law. They also cover situations where the BGB and the *lex locus delicti* (law of the place of commission of the act) differ in the extent of available remedies. These provisions of the EGBGB would need to be consulted in cases where a foreign element is involved.

Of course, the BGB does not, and cannot, govern all legal disputes or controversies, but is only meant to provide an authoritative guide to disputes of a civil (private law) nature between citizens. Its delict provisions, for example, have no penal significance. It has no application to questions of public law involving the federal government or the States. Commercial law is regulated by a separate Commercial Code (HGB), which deals with merchants and their commercial transactions. There are also Codes dealing with employment, tax, patents and copyright and other public law topics. There are also separate hierarchies of courts dealing with tax, social security and administrative law.

Local district courts (*Amtsgerichte*) are the greatest users of the BGB, and these are spread all over the country. Not all these courts perform full judicial functions, however, as they often deal with very small cases. Higher up the hierarchy, the Code is also referred to, but not with such frequency, particularly because of the increasing supplementary legislation that has been passed in the last two decades or so.

Other important legislation affecting the BGB

Finally, there is also a book containing a collection of laws known as the basic law, which was a form of constitution adopted in 1949, while Germany was still under military occupation, by the States now comprising the Federal Republic of Germany. This document was not the constitution of a unified Germany but only the expression of the will of a number of German States. Accordingly, it was called a basic law rather than a constitution. It lays down certain directly enforceable fundamental human rights and citizen's rights, which are recognised in all constitutional States in the West, and which are covered by the European Convention for the Protection of Human Rights. Thus, it contains, *inter alia*, the following principles: that everyone has a right to life, corporeal integrity and the unhampered development of his personality (Art 2); that everyone is equal before the law (Art 3); that freedom of belief, conscience, religion and ideology is inviolable (Art 4); and that everyone has the right to express himself freely in speech, writing or pictures (Art 5).

It is worth noting that Art 3 has already had a far reaching impact on the law relating to rights over marital property as laid down in Book Four of the BGB and this was confirmed by subsequent legislation.

Evaluation of the BGB in the modern world

The BGB has certainly proved its durability over a period spanning two world wars, political, economic and military upheavals and, in the last two years, the re-unification of East and West Germany. Although it is written in an abstract style and requires frequent cross-referencing, it has withstood amendments and alterations, and been supplemented by two Short Commentaries, case law and the basic law, not to mention the opinions of learned commentators. It remains an impressive testament to the Pandectist school of thought, but in the modern world, will provide a basic law of another sort, namely, one with basic concepts, principles and fundamental values, which will continue to require adaptation and modernisation in order to cope, not just with a new Germany, but with a new European order.

Key features of the German legal tradition

We have seen therefore that German law, as influenced by their particular legal heritage, has developed in a systematic, logical, abstract and conceptual manner. This is traceable to the Pandectists and their philosophy. German law thinks in terms of general principles, rather than in pragmatic terms, conceptualising problems, rather than working from case to case. The legal terminology and central method of law making – to codify laws in a comprehensive, authoritative and precise manner – distinguish it from the common law approach. Flowing from this, the primacy given to enacted law and specific statutory provision is, at once, typical of the Continental style of law. Further, although cases have grown in importance in interpreting the Codes and statutes, they are still primarily considered to be illustrations of general principles which are universally acknowledged, or illuminations of statutory provisions which embody such principles. However, there is no doubt that the last 20 years has seen a significant rise in recourse to case law in the interpretation of the BGB and, as these develop a consistent pattern, some notion of precedent might be followed in practice, though not in strict theory.

As the United States experience has shown, once case law reaches unwieldy proportions, it becomes necessary to systematise, abstract and collate them in an organised fashion. Hence, the American Restatements resemble the Continental Codes, at least in their structured and systematic approach to legal topics, wherein they commence with the general principle, and in their technique of providing illustrations to the general principles. The difference is that the American compilations are not statutes and are, at best, secondary sources of law (see, further, Chapter 4). In constitutional terms, Germany now accepts its Constitution as being at the apex of laws, having priority over all other law, and as it is written, German constitutional law has closer affinity in some senses to the United States than the United Kingdom which has no written constitution. Indeed, in the German Constitutional Court, if a Constitutional Court holds any law as being incompatible with the Constitution (that is, the basic law) that law will henceforth be applied no longer. Court decisions are, therefore, regarded as being authoritative pronouncements of the law, which is certainly an unusual feature in a civil law system. Of course, case law is also the main source of law in the special administrative courts in France (see above).

Political unification of Germany

The unification of the two German States, East and West Germany, which took effect on 3 October 1990, was the culmination of a process of change exemplified by the opening of the Berlin Wall on 10 November 1989. It occurred with a speed that surprised most commentators and citizens, both German and non-German. It is not intended here to discuss the many legal implications of this dramatic and undoubtedly historic event. This section is by way of a coda to our discussion on German law, and seeks to highlight the brief background to the division of Germany and to identify some of the more salient implications of German reunification.

The 1945 position

Following the defeat of Germany in 1945, the Four Powers (the United Kingdom, United States, Soviet Union and France) assumed authority over Germany, including the right to decide its status and frontiers. It was expressly emphasised by them that this was not an annexation. Hence, Germany retained her status as a State. The original intention was to prepare Germany for a peace settlement with its former adversaries but, unfortunately, co-operation broke down among the Western powers and the Soviet Union and, in 1949, two new States, the Federal Republic of Germany (FRG) and the German Democratic Republic (GDR), which would be effectively under the control and administration of the USSR. On 23 May 1949, the basic law (Federal Constitution) (see, also, above) came into force in the FRG, according to which the FRG is a democratic, social and federal State based on the rule of law. It is characterised by its separation of powers. The Constitution controls the exercise of all the State's powers.

However, the Four Powers, at every critical stage, maintained the existence of rights and responsibilities with regard to Germany as a whole. This continuous assertion of rights over Germany 'as a whole' has caused some writers to think that there was in fact a third German State in addition to East and West Germany, over which all the Four Powers retained certain rights and responsibilities (see, for example, Piotrowicz (1991) p 636).

The road to unification

By 1989, there were two German States which existed relatively independently, but not without several wrangles over the true status of each of these States in relation to each other. Nevertheless, West and East Germany entered into negotiations that their mutual relations had to be resolved and the Four Powers were also involved in seeking to establish the place of the single German State in Europe. Two major Treaties were concluded between the FRG and the GDR on the road to political unification. First, there was the Treaty of 18 May 1990, establishing a Monetary, Economic and Social Union. It, *inter alia*, recognised the introduction of the social market economy in the GDR as the basis for further economic and social development. In addition, the monetary, economic and social union was seen as 'an initial significant step ... towards national unity'.

The Preamble to the Treaty provides that the parties are moving towards national unity 'in accordance with Art 23 of the basic law' (Constitution) of the FRG. Article 23, thereof, provides that the basic law is to apply in all parts of Germany under West German control plus West Berlin. It then declares that 'In other parts of Germany, it shall be put into force on their accession'. Of course, this was drafted in 1949 and the feeling in the FRG seems to be that it was the 'real' Germany. By agreeing to this, the East Germans almost appeared to be saying that they agreed with this view. The GDR has, in fact, acceded to the West German Constitution and has become a part of the FRG. As one writer sees it: 'No new State has been created; one has ceased to exist, having been incorporated into the other, which has consequently expanded its territory' (Piotrowicz (1991) pp 639–40).

Secondly, the Treaty on the Establishment of the Unity of Germany was signed on 31 August 1990 and entered into force on 3 October 1990. This agreement actually established the unity of the two States and brought about the end of the GDR. It also mentions Art 23 of the basic law.

This Treaty deals, *inter alia*, with the coming into force of the basic law in the former GDR, the amendment of the basic law, the harmonisation of laws and the application of treaties of the two States. Piotrowicz and Hailbronner see the accession by the GDR to the FRG as an instance of State succession, or universal succession, since this is a case where one State, with its consent, is absorbed by another, 'thereby forfeiting its own separate legal identity' (Piotrowicz (1991) p 640) and where, 'with regard to the Federal Republic's treaties, only an enlargement of territory has taken place' (Hailbronner (1991) p 32).

The Moscow Treaty: Final Settlement

A third Treaty, the Final Settlement with Respect to Germany, also known as the Moscow Treaty, was concluded, after the six countries had met in Bonn, Paris and finally Moscow. These negotiations towards a final settlement were known as the Two-plus-Four Agreements – the two Germanies and the Four Powers. It signifies the final acceptance by Germany that it has an obligation to live within its borders. Article 1(1) states:

> The united Germany shall comprise the territory of the Federal Republic of Germany, the German Democratic Republic and the whole of Berlin. Its external borders shall be the borders of the Federal Republic of Germany and the German Democratic Republic and shall be definitive from the date on which the present treaty comes into force. The confirmation of the definitive nature of the borders of the united Germany is an essential element of the peaceful order in Europe.

This Treaty resolves the controversial question that surrounded the nature of Poland's tenure over the Oder-Neisse territories: they are conclusively Polish territories. Hence, no other State may have any claim to them. The most important point that this Treaty settles is that all the States which might possibly have had any claim to any rights in this matter have now accepted the border question as definitively resolved under the unification arrangements.

Article 7 of this Treaty also terminates the rights and responsibilities of the Four Powers over Berlin and Germany as a whole; this effectively dissolved all corresponding agreements, decisions, practices and institutions which the related Four Powers were involved in.

On 4 March 1991, with the deposit of the last ratification of the Treaty by the Soviet Union, Germany became a full sovereign State.

Unification – a late 1990s postscript

A postscript to unification would seem to indicate that the new, united Germany has experienced a great many problems in coping with the transformation of the former GDR territory of the FRG, from a State run economy, to that of a market economy. Three years after the 'unification' saw a total breakdown in the East German economy, which has also seen severe levels of rising unemployment, and the continuous flow of migration from East to West has not abated, all of which have given rise to even more problems ranging from racial tensions to neo-fascist demonstrations.

All these points are mentioned because one of the central themes of the comparative law methodology is that an understanding of the societal and ideological conditions of a particular jurisdiction is essential, if the legal landscape that one is attempting to put together is to be put into its true perspective. No comparatist should, therefore, be surprised if State intervention does increase, if only to restore higher levels of order, organisation, employment, and to secure economic progress for the whole of the re-unified Germany.

Application of EC law in the former GDR

As a result of the accession of the former GDR to the basic law of the FRG, the territory of the former GDR automatically became part of the EEC without any amendment of the Treaty of Rome. Indeed, the European Council has confirmed the legal integration of the GDR as an enlargement of the territory of an existing Member State and the integration became effective as soon as the unification had been legally established, subject to the necessary transitional arrangements (European Council Doc/90/1 of 28 April 1990). By virtue of Art 227 of the EEC Treaty, EEC law takes immediate effect in the new German *Länder*, since it provides that the EEC Treaty is applicable to the Member States in their respective territories, unless special provisions, like Art 227, para 2, apply. Hence, as Hailbronner points out, the principle of 'moving treaty frontiers' may be applied to supranational organisations like the European Community in the same way as it does to States (Hailbronner (1991) p 37).

OVERVIEW OF THE CIVIL LAW TRADITION

Although the oldest extant legal tradition in the Western world, the civil law tradition continues to go from strength to strength, while continuing to adapt to changed and changing social, economic and political situations. It has developed different subtraditions and, as a broad church, encompasses both the French and German legal traditions. It has exported its ideology and legal ideas throughout the world and spawned many imitators and acquired many admirers. It operates on the basis of principles and thinks in concepts and, in German law, in sophisticated abstractions. Yet, its case law has been invaluable when it has needed to adapt to different conditions and to develop progressive legal concepts. It has influenced the law of the European Community in structure, style of judgment and ethos, and we wait with interest to see how much it will influence the shaping of the new European law that appears to be at a crucial turning point and which, in the view of some, is on the brink of being subsumed under a 'European law' banner which will eventually destroy its inherent beauty and priceless heritage.

It is undoubtedly 'converging' with the common law, at least to the extent of its increasing reliance on case law, albeit still citing cases merely as illustrations of general principles, not as authoritative pronouncements of principle. Its volume of case law continues to grow in the field of administrative law. However, at its heart and in its ideology, it remains very much a unique tradition in its own right by virtue of its constitutional protection of the individual, vigorous moral and ethical principles, reliance on elaborations of statutory and codified precepts, separate and specialised courts, collegiate judiciary, attitudes towards access to justice and, particularly in the case of the French codes, the pre-eminence accorded to individual liberty and freedom of expression.

SELECTIVE BIBLIOGRAPHY

Buckland and McNair, *Roman Law and Common Law* (1952)

David, *English and French Law* (1980)

David and Brierley, *Major Legal Systems in the World Today* (1985)

David and de Vries, *The French Legal System* (1958)

Dawson, *The Oracles of the Law* (1968)

De Vries and Schneider, *Civil Law and the Anglo-American Lawyer* (1976)

Dickson, *Introduction to French Law* (1994)

Foster, *German Legal System and Laws* (1996)

Hailbronner, 'Legal aspects of the unification of the two German States' (1991) EJIL 18

International Encyclopedia of Comparative Law: Vols I and II

Lawson, 'The comparison', in *European Studies in Law* (1977) Vol II

Lawson, *A Common Lawyer Looks at the Civil Law* (1950)

Lawson, Anton and Brown (eds), *Amos and Walton's Introduction to French Law* (1967)

Mehren and Gordley, *The Civil Law System* (1977)

Merryman, *The Civil Law Tradition* (1985)

Piotrowicz, 'The arithmetic of German unification: one into three does go' (1991) 40 ICLQ 635

Pringsheim, 'The inner relationship between English and Roman law' [1933] 5 CLJ 347

Robinson, Fergus and Gordon, *An Introduction to European Legal History* (1987)

Rudden, 'Courts and Codes in England, France and Soviet Russia' (1974) 48 Tulane L Rev 1010

Smith, 'Roman Law', in Derrett (ed), *An Introduction to Legal Systems* (1968)

Varga, *Comparative Legal Cultures* (1992)

Vranken, *Fundamentals of European Civil Law* (1997)

Zweigert and Kotz, *An Introduction to Comparative Law* (1987) Vol I; 3rd edn, (1998)

CHAPTER 4

THE ENGLISH COMMON LAW SYSTEM

INTRODUCTION

The English common law system, which consists of several characteristic legal traditions, is rightly regarded as one of the two major legal systems in the world, as well as one of the two most influential. Although not the oldest legal system in existence, it is the oldest national law in existence common to a whole kingdom. It is also comparable to the oldest, the civil law system, in the extent of its spread throughout the world, and in its remarkable influence, having been adopted by a wide range of countries and cultures, even in their post-colonial era. As with the civil law system, the English legal system has been spawned from a particular sequence of historical events, a set of *distinctive legal sources, ideologies, doctrines, institutions, and a distinctive mode of legal thought* which, *collectively, constitute* the English *common legal tradition*. This legal tradition was successfully 'transplanted' from England to many countries throughout the world which are culturally, as well as geographically and linguistically, different from England and English culture. Those traditions, in places, such as Australia, South East Asia, India and Hong Kong, were then formalised and made part of the predominant legal system of that particular jurisdiction. Remarkably, this uniquely English set of sources, institutions and laws co-existed with the indigenous culture, religions and local customs of those places, and a dualist system often emerged. Indeed, despite respecting and preserving local culture, the administration of justice and government was soon transformed into an infrastructure which was readily identifiable as the English style of government and administration. This 'legal transplantation' (Watson) is a testimony to its genius and its adaptability, particularly where the 'reception' of English law was not legislatively imposed but voluntarily adopted.

Initially, reception of English law was the result of British colonisation, trade missions and the dominance of the British empire during vital periods in world history. However, several former colonies, well into their post-colonial era, and after their 'nationalist' stage of development, continue to use the common law approach and legal philosophy in their legal system.

Key events which shaped English legal history were the early centralisation of courts, mainly brought about by Henry II, wherein the royal courts (the common law courts) became the main source of the law common to the whole country, the writ system which ensured a particular style of development geared to existing writs, which were later supplemented by the creation of the Courts of Chancery, which developed a separate body of law (known as 'equity'), both of which gave rise to a remedy orientated, pragmatic approach which had no need for scholarly input or advice. Therefore, English law developed through judicial decisions (or 'case law') and equity could, up to the late 19th century, only be administered by the Courts of Chancery. Equity and the common law were eventually 'fused' by the Supreme Court of Judicature Acts of 1873–75 in their jurisdictional application, but continue to exist as separate bodies of law, which may now be utilised by one and the same court.

English law never 'received' Roman law in the way that it was received in civil law countries. The rigidity of the common law procedures, the need to conform to the framework that had been created, and the centralised courts, all helped to mould a diversity of local customs and primitive Anglo-Saxon practices into a law that was followed by the whole country, which thus became a common, unified law.

It has been said that the common law 'dates from time immemorial', but it really dates from about the middle to the late 12th century when a common law was identifiable and could be said to be in place. Furthermore, at the time of the 12th and 13th century, when there was a frisson of Roman law 'intellectualism' running through continental Europe, consisting of learned treatises on the *Corpus Juris*, Romano-Canonical treatises on procedure, customary law and royal legislation, all of which had undergone a massive absorption of Roman law, English law had already experienced its era of 'modernisation'. The English common law tradition and the common law courts were already established and were, by that time, impervious to any 'reception' of Roman law or, indeed, any foreign law.

English law also created prerogative writs (certiorari, mandamus and prohibition) which enabled administrative decisions of State organs and officials to be challenged, which, therefore, rendered unnecessary any separate administrative courts such as those that developed in civil law countries.

Examples of common law jurisdictions are Australia, the United States, Singapore, Malaysia, New Zealand, large parts of Africa, India, Pakistan, South East Asia and North America. Despite acquiring independence, several Commonwealth nations have maintained links with the United Kingdom and, although they have adopted written Constitutions, their judges have continued to interpret these in accordance with typical English legal methods, doctrines and legal conventions.

TERMINOLOGY

A legal tradition is not the same thing as a legal system, although the legal system inevitably forms part of the legal tradition and *vice versa*. The term 'legal system' may been used to refer to of an operational set of legal rules, procedures and institutions (Merryman (1977)). Such a system may be grouped within the category of a so called *parent* legal system or *major* legal system such as the *civil law* or *common law* systems. Systems possessing common characteristics associated with each of the main legal families may thus be *prima facie* classified as belonging to its corresponding legal family. A system that relies heavily on codes as definitive statements of the law with very little reliance on case law would, *prima facie*, qualify as a civil law type of system, because of the predominance and pre-eminence of the codes. On the other hand, you could have a common law system which uses comprehensive codes for one area of law, such as criminal law (as in India), but their predominant mode of interpretation and weight attached to case law, in applying these codes, will usually determine their eventual classification. As we have seen, writers, such as David and Brierley (1985), also refer to three main *legal families*, that is, the common law, civil law and socialist law generic groups. However, the term 'legal tradition' suggests certain forms of legal practice, or legal rules or norms, substantive or procedural, which have been established over a period of time and whose origins are not of recent vintage. It also suggests a well defined, consistent and reasonably well established, 'historically conditioned set of attitudes' (Merryman (1977)) about the relationship between legal rules, law and society. The term 'legal tradition' will be used particularly, but not exclusively, in referring to those legal systems which are not the parent legal system or family.

The term 'common law' may refer to:

(a) the English legal system developed in, applicable to and common to England (and Wales, but not Scotland);

(b) that part of English law which was created by the king's courts, or common law courts (and developed as case law) in England from about the 12th century, rather than 'statute law', or the law enacted by Parliament as opposed to the body of rules and principles of equity, as established by decisions of the courts of equity (or, as they were otherwise known, Courts of Chancery) which began to be developed from around the 14th century;

(c) the modern usage, which includes English cases and statutes, including principles developed and established by common law courts and the courts of equity; and

(d) that part of English law which has been 'received' by a given jurisdiction and which applies, therein, either through colonisation, or via unilateral and voluntary enactment by that jurisdiction.

The common law should also be distinguished from international law, which applies between States, and canon or ecclesiastical law, which derived from the church and was administered by the church courts. Although the common law is not derived from Roman law, it is, in many respects, closer to ancient Roman law, in some of its jurisprudential content and procedural practices, than the modern civil law systems.

If the law on a particular topic happens to be identical under English law and in American jurisdictions, it is frequently referred to as the Anglo-American legal position. Despite the radical 'Americanisation' of the law in the United States, English law continues to be a major source of law or, at least, still represents the primary source of law in relation to several major areas of law in the United States. It may be argued, with some justification, that, in many cases, it is no longer accurate to use the term 'Anglo-American' law in the way that has been done since the early 20th century because American law has now developed a character of its own and diverges from the English common law in so many different ways (see Atiyah and Summers, in *Form and Substance in Anglo-American Law* (1987), an Anglo-American academic enterprise).

THE ENGLISH COMMON LAW TRADITION

The key features of the common law tradition are:

(a) a case based system of law which functions through analogical reasoning;

(b) an hierarchical doctrine of precedent;

(c) sources of law which include statutes as well as cases;

(d) typical institutions like the trust, tort law, estoppel, and agency. Although some of these institutions appear in one form or another in other legal systems, the 'trust' concept is unique to the common law system. Civil law jurisdictions have utilised a general notion of unjustified enrichment (see Zweigert and Kotz (1977) Vol II, p 208 *et seq*) to cope with situations where English law has utilised a 'trust' concept;

(e) a distinctive improvisatory and pragmatic legal style;

(f) categories of law such as contract and tort as separate bodies of law as well as two main bodies of law: common law and equity, which may, nevertheless, be administered by the same court. Remarkably, in classical Roman law, there also existed two bodies of law that bore a remarkable resemblance to English common law and courts of equity, but the fact that modern civil law, as embodied in its codes, is a product of the last two centuries, and was able to combine precise general rules and equitable principles, rendered an 'equitable' jurisdiction unnecessary in civil law countries; and

(g) no substantive or structural public/private law distinction as that which exists in civil law systems.

The common law tradition is typically identified with a case based system but although cases play a dominant role, the primary sources of English law include not just case law, which is a body of principles derived from court decisions regulated by the doctrine of precedent (*stare decisis*), but also statutes, which is the law contained in legislative enactments. In more recent times in England, legislation has become not just an authoritative source of law, but sometimes the primary source of law where no cases are relevant to the issue at hand, or even where decided cases do exist. The law applicable may depend on the particular facts of the case and/or the interpretation of the 'intention of the legislature' in the statute concerned.

The doctrine of precedent governs this case law system. Thus, decisions of higher courts are generally binding on lower courts, a practice which probably originated around 1800 when law reports acquired a degree of reliability sufficient to sustain the consistent application of such a doctrine. That part of the case which is considered binding on a subsequent court is the *ratio decidendi* (the reason for the decision), which is broadly the principle established by the case. Any other comments of the judge are, *prima facie*, classified as *obiter dicta*, or comments uttered in passing which are not strictly binding on the court. However, depending on the particular area of law, the ultimate status of a judicial pronouncement may depend on what a subsequent higher court says about it.

The English Court of Appeal generally disposes of between 800–900 cases a year and the House of Lords hears between 50–70 appeals. This may be contrasted with the thousands of cases (25,000 cases in 1987) which the French Court of Cassation handles per year. However, the courts in France are regionalised, they have far more judges generally, particularly in the Cour de Cassation, and are more specialist. There is, it would seem, a very different attitude between civil and common law to the right of appeal.

The typical common law style may be called pragmatic and improvisatory, primarily geared to the adjudication and resolution of disputes. One reason for this is that English law is not codified, in the civil law sense of being contained in enacted collections of authoritative and *prima facie* exhaustive rules of law. Civil law, *ex facie*, is codified in the authoritative sense. Countries like France, Germany, Italy, Spain and Portugal all possess a collection of codes, including a Civil Code, a Commercial Code, a Code of Civil Procedure, a Penal Code and a Code of Criminal Procedure, but England has not, by tradition, enacted any code on the lines of the Continental codes, and the only area in which it has attempted to 'codify' the law is in commercial law, and, to a certain extent, company law. Unlike France and Germany, England has no written constitution or any comparable, comprehensive piece of constitutional legislation.

Although statutes are an authoritative and burgeoning source of law in English law, the typical English legal attitude towards statutes, with some rare exceptions, is that statutes are passed to consolidate or clarify existing law, and are intended to build on existing case law, which may legitimately be invoked to interpret any ambiguities or uncertain meanings in a statute. Hence, while civil law codes (and, therefore, judges) think in terms of solutions to problems, derived from systematic and authoritative expositions of the law and work towards solutions, from general clauses and principles, English law judges see their primary function as the arbiters of disputes and that their task is to resolve disputes. They therefore pay special attention to the particular facts of a case, examine the legal question to be decided (the 'issue') and make a ruling based on a careful study of whether that case 'fits' into any previously decided case whose facts happened to be similar. If they found that there was a similar case decided by a higher court (such as the Court of Appeal or the House of Lords), they would usually apply the *ratio* of that case to the present one.

If an English judge did not wish to follow a previous decision, he has the option of 'distinguishing' it (that is, decide it is not applicable) on the basis of its facts, or law, or both. If there is a statute that appears to govern the instant case which is in conflict with a judicial decision, the rule is that the statute would prevail.

Another source of law in Britain today is the law of the European Communities, which is supposed to take direct effect in the United Kingdom without the need for implementing legislation to be passed. This is the result of Britain's accession to the Treaties establishing the European Communities and the UK European Communities Act 1972.

Academic or scholarly writings are cited occasionally in English courts, but not usually in a favourable light. The notable exceptions are cases where the law is relatively uncharted as in medical ethics cases or child law cases dealing with novel issues of courts sanctioning, what it regards as, 'life saving' medical treatment despite an adult refusing consent to such treatment (caesarean section cases). Doctrinal writing in common law countries does not have the status of authoritative sources of law as in Continental countries, but the situation may well change, particularly in the newer areas of law.

The public law/private law distinction was recognised in England, at least, by the late 19th century. In civil law countries, it is crucial to the process of allocation of the court which has jurisdiction to hear the case, whereas English common law makes a distinction between the procedure to be used, depending on whether the purpose of the case is to enforce the public duties of a State agency or State body, or the private rights of a citizen. English academic writers have used the term 'public law' to cover both constitutional and administrative law. When English lawyers think of public law, it is thought of primarily in terms of the application for judicial review.

The practical importance of the distinction in English law is that, if a private citizen wishes to question the exercise of a public law function by an administrative body, the special procedure for doing so is known as an application for judicial review. This will not be heard by any special administrative court, since there is no separate administrative court system within the 'ordinary' civil courts' system. However, there are specialist administrative tribunals, but these are still subject to the normal review and appeal powers of the ordinary courts of judicature, and have never really caught the imagination of the general English public.

Judicial review is similar to the Court of Cassation's powers which merely pronounces on the legality of actions, and the court has no power to substitute the original decision with its own. There are no English public law rules separate from the general principles of common law. Contracts between private citizens and the State will be subject to the same principles as those which govern contracts between citizens. The English judiciary do not generally see a sharp and clear dividing line between public and private law. This was confirmed by two House of Lords' cases, *Davy v Spelthorne* [1983] 3 All ER 278 and *Roy v Kensington and Chelsea and Westminster Family Practitioner Committee* [1992] 1 All ER 705. The result of *Roy* has been to render meaningless the so called rule in *O'Reilly v Mackman* [1983] 1 AC 147, whereby procedural law had been separated from the substantive law. Lord Diplock has argued that public law cases must normally be pursued under the special procedure under Ord 53 of the Rules of the Supreme Court, whereas private law cases (even those involving substantive issues of judicial review) must be pursued in the ordinary courts.

The historical reasons for English law's traditional dislike of the public law/private law distinction have been well documented (see Samuel (1988); Beatson (1987); Harlow (1980); Weir, *International Encyclopedia of Comparative Law* (1971) Vol II). The disputes of the early 17th century culminating in the abolition, in 1641, of the prerogative courts were really concerned with the nature and scope of the 'absolute' prerogative of the English Crown. The relationship between the 'public' and 'private' capacities of the Crown remains a source of confusion and debate even today.

However, in most continental legal systems, apart from criminal matters, the jurisdiction of the ordinary courts is generally limited to disputes governed by private law. When the ordinary courts found it difficult to cope with the increasing volume of public law disputes, special administrative courts were set up in France, headed by its Conseil d'État and this was then imitated in other continental countries.

The existence of special prerogative orders (formerly prerogative writs), as well as tort actions against public officials who would be sued in their individual capacity, meant that there were legal devices available for dealing with alleged abuses of power by government agencies and officials. No immunity attaches to public officials simply because of their status. Certiorari prohibits a tribunal from exceeding its jurisdiction and mandamus compels a government official to carry out his duty. The writ of prohibition can prevent a tribunal from exceeding or abusing its jurisdiction.

Although the ordinary courts have jurisdiction over matters of public and private law alike, there are many hundreds of specialist administrative courts, called tribunals, of which there are 70 different types. The law established and developed by these administrative, industrial and domestic tribunals, often consisting of professional and lay assessors, which deal primarily with small cases, has been growing very rapidly and is notable for its sheer volume. These have been created to determine claims by citizens against public authorities or vice versa and deal solely with public law matters. They exercise administrative and/or judicial functions, but have limited or special jurisdiction and were created to provide a means of settling disputes efficiently and speedily, without the formalities of a court of law. Tribunals hear about six times the number of contested disputes heard by the High Court and county courts of law. Their proliferation has been a distinctive feature of the development of judicial administration in Britain, over recent decades, and the workload of these tribunals greatly exceeds that of the High Court and county courts (The Royal Commission on Legal Services, Cmnd 7648, 1979, London: HMSO, para 15.1, Tables 2.1 and 2.2). Their main defects are the lack or limitations of rights of appeal, the limited efficacy of claimants' remedies and preclusion of legal representation by certain administrative tribunals.

The French tribunal does not correspond to the English term 'tribunal', in its narrow sense, and none of the French terms (*cour*, *juridiction* and *tribunal*) are reflected in the English language. The French Conseil d'État and the hierarchy of administrative courts represent the deluxe model of administrative courts on the Continent, and have earned deserved admiration from most countries in continental Europe. The Councillors of State are legally trained and are competent to adjudicate on all conflicts in which public authorities are involved. These courts have built up an imposing body of case law, and have generally succeeded in protecting the citizens' civil rights and pecuniary interests against the errors of bureaucracy and officialdom. They have the right to annul administrative acts, decisions and regulations and have the right to award damages to those who have suffered injury or damage as a result of a wrongful act on the part of a public servant acting in the course of his duties.

In the United States, there is a multiplicity of administrative tribunals and regulatory agencies which deal with most areas of social and economic life. Access to these bodies is, as in Britain, easier and cheaper than to the ordinary courts. A major preoccupation of the United States Supreme Court has been the review of administrative actions. Around one-third of its full opinion cases generally deal with such issues, whereas only a quarter of the Supreme Court's cases have adjudicated on constitutional law issues proper.

The civil law and commercial law distinction, common in civil law systems, does not have a great deal of significance in English law. In English law, the subject may be fragmented into subjects such as agency, bailments, and sale of goods. Commercial law, having developed separately from common law, is now part of the English common law and 'consists in an extension of the general principles of contract law to special transactions of a mercantile character' (Gutteridge, 'Contract and commercial law' (1935) 51 LQR 91). For the most part, common lawyers do not draw a sharp distinction between civil law and commercial law and most textbooks indicate that such a distinction is either not perceived or, by not being mentioned, is actually obscured (see Weir, *International Encyclopedia of Comparative Law* (1971) Vol II, p 111 and books cited therein).

THE COMMON LAW IN THE UNITED STATES

Preliminary observations

When we look at how the English common law has fared in the United States, several points should be borne in mind. First, the law of the United States comprises Federal and State laws as well as constitutional law. It is therefore an example of English law being transplanted into a legal and constitutional set up which is radically different from the common law homeland. Secondly, both English law and the laws of the United States have now reached a stage in legal evolution when a long, hard look needs to be taken to decide if it is any longer legitimate to maintain this 'Anglo-American' unity of appellation. Thirdly, by virtue of the first point, given the complexity of the territory, its unique cocktail of foreign influences, systems within systems, as in Louisiana, and its immense size and pace of development, it is very rarely possible to state what the 'American law' is on a particular subject. Clearly, this often varies from State to State, but it might also depend on whether there is a possible conflict between State law, Federal law or constitutional law. Clearly, all these factors make meaningful comparisons difficult.

The United States has undergone profound changes not just in technology, economics and culture, but in its development of concepts and principles of law which have transformed its legal scenario, with themes like individual liberty, checks against abuse of power and the pre-eminence of the Constitution. Many articles and tomes have been written about these far reaching and significant developments. The following section merely presents an overview of a selection of areas for comparison.

Linguistic issues

The famous observation by the English playwright, George Bernard Shaw, that England and America were 'separated by a common language' rings true today even more than it did nearly 50 years ago. At the most basic level, there are problems of translation – not least because there is 'American English' and also 'American legal language' which is not always equivalent to English legal language. For example, in American usage, 'High Court' refers to the United States Supreme Court whereas, in England, it refers to the only court of first instance with unlimited jurisdiction. Another striking example is the term 'judicial review', which we have examined earlier with regard to English law where it refers to the power of the English High Court to scrutinise the legality (but not the merits) of a decision taken by an inferior court or a public body. In America, judicial review is 'the power of any court to hold unconstitutional and hence unenforceable any law, any official action based upon it and any illegal action by a public official that it deems to be in conflict with the 'United States Constitution' (Abraham (1952) p 251). On a broader comparative note, it is a power that ordinary courts possess in Australia, Brazil, Burma, Canada, India, Pakistan and Japan.

History of American law: some observations

Early legal development

The story of the development of American law in the 50 different States, has been told elsewhere and it is not my intention here to recount it in any sort of detail. However, certain historical events may be highlighted which may give some insights into the way it has developed since that first English settlement occurred, in 1607 at Jamestown, Virginia.

Legal development in the original 13 colonies occurred at different stages, since the colonies were established at different times, and each had its own separate charter, being separate units under the English Crown. As with other British charters of this nature, most of the colonies' charters provided for limited local autonomy. But, there was diversity as to the extent of Crown control, and the dates of settlement.

English settlers brought with them the law with which they were most familiar. Thus, if they came from provincial towns and villages, the law they were most conversant with was really that of local customs as they existed in their boroughs, manors and villages, not the 'common law' administered by the royal courts of Westminster. But, the English common law was increasingly utilised when society became more complex, which was inevitable when the population grew, and shipping, commerce and industry also developed. Appeals from the colonial courts were still directed to

London, but ecclesiastical courts were never established in the colonies. Significantly, the institution of trial by jury in both criminal and civil cases was adopted with great enthusiasm, and one of the key grievances of the colonists, in their struggle with England, was their resistance to any attempts by the British Government to shift political cases to vice admiralty courts where there were no juries.

The First Continental Congress

In 1774, the First Continental Congress was formed and met in Philadelphia and this comprised about 55 delegates from almost all the colonies. This was one of the first concrete signs of union among the colonies and of war against England. There was strong feeling among the colonists that the individual rights of the English and the Bill of Rights of 1689 should be followed and introduced into the American colonies.

Post-revolutionary status of English law

Once independence had been won in 1776, it was clear that the English common law had become the basis of the legal systems in each of the 13 colonies. By that time, English law had come to be highly regarded and, indeed, essential to the needs of increasing commercial enterprise and to support effectively grievances that were expressed to the Crown. Each colony had a Bar of trained, able and respected professionals, capable of working with a technical and refined system of rules. The colonial legal profession had also achieved considerable economic success and social standing. Of 56 signatories to the Declaration of Independence, 25 were lawyers (see Farnsworth (1987) p 8).

But, different 'cut off' dates (as to when English law would cease to apply) were statutorily enacted by different colonies. Indeed, after the Revolution, some colonies exhibited a reaction against the application of English law, and their legislatures prohibited the citation of English decisions which had been rendered after independence. The adoption of a written constitution was seen as a break with English tradition. Louisiana, when purchased from the French in 1803, and admitted to the Federation in 1812, continued to maintain the French law tradition, and, indeed, traces of its period of Spanish rule. Louisiana adopted several codifications based on the French model, including the French Civil Code.

Around this time, there was a period of uncertainty caused by anti-British sentiment and since there was no adequate body of American case law to replace the 'banned' English decisions, the American Bar lost a number of their most able lawyers and, despite the fact that law reports began to be published at the end of the 18th century, they were too few in number to be used effectively. French and Roman law were considered as possibilities to replace the gap left in the law, and European writers were cited as authorities, especially in the field of conflict of laws and commercial law. But, civil law failed to make its way into the United States, primarily because there were insufficient numbers of judges who were conversant with foreign languages, English reports and treatises were still available and the French Civil Code did not appear until the beginning of the 19th century.

In early American legal history, English common law principles were applicable only insofar as they did not contradict the constitutional, political, or geographic conditions of the new States (see Rheinstein, *International Encyclopedia of Comparative Law*, Vol I, p U-137). However, the law actually administered was apparently a 'simplified version of the law of England' (Rheinstein). The law that was being relied upon was gleaned from books such as Blackstone's *Commentaries of the Laws of England*, which first appeared in America, in 1803, and acquired a wide American readership. This ensured that legal language, legal methodology and basic concepts of private law in America were to remain firmly rooted in the English legal tradition.

But, there was no formal or organised system of legal education in mid-18th century America and it was not until the beginning of the 19th century that the American law school and scholarly writing tradition began, with the establishment in 1829 of the Harvard Law School by Justice Joseph Story who wrote a set of treatises on the main branches of the law. A steady flow and ever burgeoning number of textbooks, many written by professors of the increasing number of law schools, marked the co-operation that was to distinguish the special relationship between legal practice and scholarship, which has played a dominant part in shaping the development of the law in the United States.

The early part of the 19th century witnessed a revival of interest and a return to the English tradition with the publication of the works of James Kent and Joseph Story, which eventually replaced Blackstone. The growth of agriculture and trade began to dominate the economy as efforts were directed to shaping English law to fit the westward expansion that had gathered momentum. The foundations of contracts, torts, sale of goods, real property and conflict of laws were laid during this period, mainly by a reappraisal of pre-Revolutionary English law, but sometimes the law was derived simply from local customs and usages. This occurred in the case of farmers and gold miners and cattle raising, where English principles were adapted to suit the different conditions.

Codification was seen as an important issue in the 19th century and, while English common law was seen as unwieldy, the French Code was considered an impressive model. Codification first took root in Massachusetts, which was followed by New York. The famous Field Code of Civil Procedure drafted by David Dudley Field, a lawyer, was accepted by New York in 1848 and codification started to gain impetus. But, by 1865, Field's Civil Law Code was greeted less enthusiastically because the codification movement had begun to lose its popularity.

Diversity of American cultural influences

The diversity of religions, nationalities and economic groups gives some idea of the range of cultural, religious and linguistic influences America was enriched by. Although the English were in the majority, there were also Dutch, French, German, Irish, Scots and Swedish settlers. Of course, several States were under Spanish rule and so there is also a trace of this heritage in the law of marital property and the law relating to Spanish-Mexican land grants. But all the community property States (such as Louisiana, Texas, New Mexico, Arizona, California, Washington, Idaho and Nevada) have experienced modification and modernisation of the old laws. The Spanish tradition continues to play a dominant role in the Commonwealth of Puerto Rico which was acquired from Spain after the Spanish-American War, in 1898. Spanish remains the predominant language in Puerto Rico, but common law concepts govern most private law fields of endeavour, the law of procedure and a large area of public law matters.

Constitutional developments

There was no official reception of English statute law since 1776 and English common law developments after that date were not considered as having to form part of American law. In 1776, State constitutions began to be adopted, but not without considerable political debates and bitter inter-State hostilities. A movement away from the loose Confederation gathered momentum among the delegates at the Constitutional Convention, in 1787, who were seeking to preserve the union. A vitally important decision taken at the Convention was that there should be a central government with extended powers designed to have control over individuals, not States.

In September 1787, the Federal Constitution was signed and submitted to Congress. It become effective with a two-thirds majority of the States in July 1788, and the first president, George Washington, was inaugurated in April 1789. It contains the notions that the people are sovereign and that their government is based on a social contract. However, there was no guarantee of basic human rights. This was soon introduced under 10 amendments to the Constitution which were proposed by Congress in 1789, and ratified in 1791.

Separation of powers

Three Articles in the Constitution expressly delineate the three major governmental powers: legislative, judicial and executive which represented the concept of the doctrine of 'checks and balances', or separation of powers between these three limbs. Americans were undoubtedly familiar with the writings of Locke and Montesquieu and they had long experienced the practical operation of the doctrine in their own governments in the colonial period. Although the distribution of governmental powers was contained in the Constitution, it was only in 1803, with the landmark case of *Marbury v Madison* 5 US 1 Cranch 137 (1803), that the scope of judicial review of these powers was clarified. In 1789, Congress had passed the First Judiciary Act which appeared to contemplate Federal judicial review of State court decisions in certain cases. The Act implemented the judiciary Article of the Constitution, by creating lower Federal Courts and, by defining their jurisdiction together with that of the Supreme Court. The new Federal Courts began to declare State legislation as contrary to the Federal Constitution itself.

In the famous case of *Marbury v Madison* (see above), the Supreme Court refused to give effect to a section of a Federal statute, on the ground that Congress had exceeded the powers granted it by the Constitution when it enacted that statute. The court held that its review powers, under the First Judiciary Act 1789, were not limited to the review of State law for its constitutionality, but included examination and review of Federal legislation. Federal government had limitations on its powers, as defined under the Constitution, and thus, Federal legislation would be subject to judicial review in the Federal Courts. This decision was not based on any express provision in the Constitution, but was derived from the basic philosophical approach of the Americans, honed by colonial experience of the problems caused by excess of powers and from constitutional tradition. It gave effect to the principle of separation of powers. *Fletcher v Peck* 10 US 6 Cranch 87 (1810) was subsequently decided by the Supreme Court, in 1810, which confirmed the authority of the Federal Court under the Federal Constitution to review the constitutionality of State legislation. These decisions helped to unify the law in this area, making the principle of separation of powers an actionable claim for the observance of the 'rule of law' in the United States. Equally, a State court can also refuse to enforce a State or Federal statute on the grounds that it violates the Federal Constitution, but its interpretation is subject to review by the United States Supreme Court.

State law and the Federal Courts

Another important matter is the scope of powers of the Federal Courts. The essential is that Federal law is supreme only in limited areas. In either a State or Federal Court, an action based on a right derived from State law may be met by a defence based on Federal law. Alternatively, a case based on State law may be met by a defence based on Federal law. Hence, Federal Courts frequently apply State law, but the role of State law in the Federal Courts should be noted briefly.

The landmark case of *Swift v Tyson* 41 US 1 (16 Pet) (1842) saw the United States Supreme Court recognising the duty of the Federal Courts to give effect, on questions within the law making competence of the States, to State law that was 'local' in character, for example, State statutes and decisions which interpreted these. However, where the State law was regarded as part of the 'general law' or general provisions of the common law, the Federal Courts were under a duty to ascertain the relevant legal principles independently and to apply them irrespective of what the courts of the particular State would have done.

The Supreme Court therefore declared that the Federal Courts have developed a 'Federal common law' that was uniform throughout the United States, which finds its ultimate expression in United States Supreme Court decisions. This Federal common law was, therefore, binding on Federal Courts but not on State courts. The outcome of litigation might, therefore, depend upon which court, State or Federal, heard the case and many felt that this would cause uncertainty, injustice due to 'forum shopping', and the frustration of State policies.

Swift v Tyson was eventually overruled by the United States Supreme Court in *Erie Railroad Co v Tompkins* 304 US 64 (1938) which held that the Constitution of the United States did not empower the Federal Courts to create any common law of their own, that the common law was entirely State law and that, in areas reserved by the Constitution to the States, the Federal Courts were bound to apply State law, just as they were bound to apply the statute law of States. Subsequent cases have established that the exclusive State law character applied, not only to the substantive common law, but also to the branch of the common law known as the conflict of laws. A nationally uniform law of conflict of laws thus exists only in relation to those matters which belong to the sphere of Federal regulation, as indicated under the Constitution.

In cases involving choice of law, in order to determine what foreign law to apply, the Federal Court must, in cases where it is giving effect to State law, follow the choice of law principles of the State in which it sits. In cases involving a diversity of jurisdiction, therefore, a Federal Court adjudicating claims arising from State law must arrive at substantially the same outcome as would a court of the State in which it sits. The law in this area appears to be unnecessarily complex and could probably be resolved by legislation. It will not, however, be a simple matter to reconcile the difficult jurisdictional and constitutional issues which bedevil this area.

The demands of a rapidly increasing industrial society led to the need for a stable system of law which could cope with the developments in corporations, public service companies, railroads and insurance. During the final quarter of the 19th century, the judge's role changed from a law creator to a systematic applicator and interpreter of the law. It is therefore only in the 1800s that it is possible to speak of any sort of distinctive 'American law' existing as such.

By the end of the 19th century, the general consensus was that the system of judicial decision on a case by case basis had failed to match the speed of political, economic and social changes. Legislation began to come into its own as an instrument of change, consolidation and adaptation, and was used extensively to cope with the needs of a newly emergent society.

Reception of equity

The move to integrate law and equity began in 1848 with the adoption of the Field Code in New York. This provided for a single civil action and laid down that 'the distinction between actions at law and suits in equity, and the forms of all such actions and suits heretofore existing are abolished'. Fusion of the two systems was accomplished for the Federal Courts in 1838 and, in 1947, New Jersey reorganised its court system, and retained a Chancery Division. The only States which still administer law and equity separately are Alabama, Arkansas, Delaware, Mississippi and Tennessee.

Uniformity and diversity in American law

Continuing differences

There is no common Supreme Court of Law and Equity, since the Supreme Court has limited itself to matters of constitutional importance which involve the Constitution of the United States and to Federal legislation, including international treaties. For most States, the Supreme Courts' decisions are final. But, there is a considerable diversity among the various States in:

(a) their matrimonial property regimes, where the majority of States have separation of assets (as in English law) but eight States of the South and West (as well as Puerto Rico) have community property regimes;

(b) the law of real property;

(c) the laws of divorce.

However, State laws have all been built on the basis of the English common law, and the same conceptual and institutional frameworks are applied by the judiciary who follow the same basic approach and procedure.

A simplification of procedure has taken place so that there is far less formality in court proceedings, and a number of changes were made to abolish professional monopolies, and to make the criminal law more humane. Judges are publicly elected in the United States for set periods ranging from 10 to 20 years and have to justify their re-election. The judge has been characterised by Roscoe Pound as a 'social engineer' who can only perform his job effectively if he understands the full circumstances of each case, and the full consequences of his decision. Hence, a notable difference in American court judgments, apart from the single judge delivering the main judgment in appellate cases, is the court's approach to medical information, psychiatric information, economic considerations and criminological facts. English courts also refer to medical and psychiatric information, but the significant difference is that all the experts called in an American court are seen as participating in a joint exercise, to assist the court, to ascertain the 'best' decision to be made in any individual case. A somewhat wider range of experts may be called in than in a comparable English court.

Finally, legal education in the United States is often conducted not just by law teachers, but jointly with political scientists, sociologists and doctors, which indicates a far more multidisciplinary approach to law.

Unifying influences

Three influences have been identified as unifying factors which have served to preserve the fundamental unity of the laws of the United States. First, the National Conference of Commissioners on Uniform State Laws (NCCUSL); secondly, the American Law Institute; and, thirdly, the legal scholars or doctrinal writers.

The NCCUSL has specialist commissioners who prepare draft statutes which, when approved by the Conference, are then recommended for adoption by all States. These commissioners are appointed by the governors of all the States in pursuance of the original objective of the American Bar Association, to promote 'uniformity of legislation throughout the Union'. This organisation can only recommend adoption to national legislatures, which they may or may not adopt, with or without amendment. It has been most successful in the area of commercial law where, in conjunction with the American Law Institute, it produced a Uniform Commercial Code which was adopted in 1967 by all States, except Louisiana, which has only adopted parts thereof. Revision of the Code has also been effected. The Code has 400 sections, is divided into nine major substantive Articles which correspond to the 'Books' of the civil law, and these are divided into 'Parts' which correspond to 'Titles' in civil law codes, and these are further divided into 'Sections' which correspond to 'Articles'. It fills over 700 pages containing comments and took over a decade to prepare. It is perhaps the most modern collection of commercial law concepts currently available.

The second organisation which assists in unifying American law is the American Law Institute, which was organised in 1923 to overcome the uncertainty of American law, and consists of a group of about 1,800 lawyers, judges and law teachers. They have worked on a wide variety of projects, each under the supervision of a prominent scholar in the field, but their most outstanding achievement has been the Restatement of Law, which is an extensive collection of laws covering the following fields: agency, conflict of laws, contracts, foreign relations of the United States, judgments, property, restitution, security, torts and trusts. The Restatement also resembles civil law type codes. The common law rules are stated in a systematic and precise style. Each section is followed by explanatory comments and illustrations. The drafts of these laws were subjected to scrutiny by several bodies before being published under the name and auspices of the Institute.

The Restatement does not possess official authority and does not have the status of legislation. On questions on which there is no universally accepted legal principle or rule, the Restaters selected the one which they considered most accurate in reflecting the common law tradition and current policy. Nevertheless, it has been cited to many judges over many years who, in accepting the validity of many of its rules, have contributed to the unification of 'American principles'. It is regarded as representing the considered opinion of some of the leading American scholars and, although it is not followed as a code, it appears to enjoy a stronger 'weighting' than a doctrinal treatise. The American Codes now far outnumber the civil law codes. Nevertheless, it is still true to say that despite superficial similarity, the American Code cannot be equated with civil law codes and really represents a half way house between a full blown authoritative and binding source of law, and a mere source of reference. They are certainly closer to English style legislation in their intention to clarify and consolidate the law. The rate of citation of the Restatements to appellate courts – 4,000 times a year – suggests that they exercise an appreciable influence towards unification of the law.

These Restatements are guides to the law, particularly for foreign lawyers, but there is no guarantee that a stated legal principle is the current principle governing an area of law. The usual recourse to case law and statutes still needs to be made to ensure its accuracy.

The final unifying influence is that of legal scholars who have stamped their academic influence of the shape of American law in its formative years. It is well known that Professor Christopher Columbus Langdell (1826–96), a New York lawyer, introduced, through his casebooks, the case method of instruction into American Law Schools and it is clear that brilliant scholars, such as Corbin, Williston, Kent and Story, have played a major part in unifying the law and guiding the courts in its application. Unlike the English tradition, treatises and articles of the leading professors of law are often cited with approval in American appellate courts.

On a comparative note, we may reiterate the powerful influence of doctrinal writers in the civil law and their continued influence in the modern continental setting.

The American judge v the English judge

Atiyah and Summers (1991) (Chapter 12) have noted certain divergences and similarities between English judges and their American counterparts and this section is based on their main observations. First, apart from their different backgrounds and mode of training and selection, they note that the system of written briefs and more 'office' like procedures of American appellate courts, makes an American appellate judge more politically and socially orientated than his English colleague, which he needs to be able to perform satisfactorily within the American system. Secondly, as a result of different pay scales, English judges are invariably drawn from the leaders of the practising profession, whereas American judges are not, being far less well paid than their colleagues in private practice. Thirdly, English judges may be characterised by their formal, pragmatic and professional attitude to the resolution of disputes, born of many years' experience as a barrister in writing briefs which tend to identify the law and apply it to fact, expressed in neutral terms. American judgeships are far more politically based; they usually have to attract attention in some way, often have to align themselves with a political party and are not seen as lifelong jobs unless they become Federal judges, so that the 'American lawyer is sometimes less interested in impressing other judges or practising lawyers, and more interested in impressing scholars, law reviews and the academic community generally' (Atiyah and Summers (1991) p 351). Fourthly, the English judge is far more homogeneous than his American counterpart, with the vast majority coming from the same upper middle class background. All English professional full time judges come from the Bar, whereas there is a wide range of ethnic and educational backgrounds represented in the American judiciary. There is no such thing as a single legal culture in America. Accordingly, Atiyah and Summers also make the important point that, contrary to the opinion in certain quarters, the 'indeterminacy of rules' in the English legal system is far less pronounced than it is in the United States. There is, in fact, 'wider agreement about the criteria for determining the validity of rules'. English law is formulated in terms of formal rules which are usually applied strictly in accord with their terms, giving them a 'high mandatory formality'.

The 'background factor' appears to explain the greater willingness of the American judge, when compared to the English judge, to cite academic literature in his opinions and to pursue theoretical and intellectual issues.

Finally, the American judge appears to be dealing with a different set of sources, different types of legislation and cases. As Atiyah and Summers point out, among the many questions an American State Supreme Court judge may have to face is whether his or her court should follow a prior decision when most of the State Supreme Courts have pursued a different line. This is the sort of question which no English judge has to consider (see Atiyah and Summers (1991) p 358). Despite all these differences, the basic American judicial approach most closely resembles the English common law tradition than any other.

Comparative overview

Both England and America had similar sources of law in their formative phases of development and both use similar divisions of law and approaches to law, but, as Atiyah and Summers put it, 'these two legal systems embrace very different conceptions of law' (Atiyah and Summers (1991) p 417). This also applies to legislation, where it is not surprising that the American conceptions of legislation as a form of law are also different from the English conception.

Certain fundamental American approaches in terms of legal vocabulary, basic philosophy and principles and concepts, have generally not deviated greatly from their original English roots. Farnsworth isolates three main English law ideas which, he argues, still dominate American legal thought:

(a) the concept of supremacy of law, best illustrated by the notion that the State is subject to judicial review;

(b) the tradition of precedent; and

(c) the notion of a trial as an adversarial, contentious proceeding, in the American context, usually before the jury, 'in which the adversarial parties take the initiative and in which the role of the judge is that of umpire rather than that of inquisitor' (see Farnsworth (1987) pp 11–12). It should be noted that the American version of judicial precedent is very different from the English notion (see Farnsworth (1987) pp 45–52).

Differences between the American legal scenario and the English one may be explained by divergences in their historical experience, in their constitutional structure, the different political and social conditions, the diverse geographical and climatic conditions, in their remarkable technological advancement, and by the distinctive judicial and academic personnel, who have played a major role in shaping the destiny and substantive content of its current legal scenario. However, in Rheinstein's view:

> ... in spite of all its local variations and differences, the United States constitutes one single nation, economically, politically and socially. Everyone regards himself as an American first, an Illinoisian or New Yorker, Californian or Louisianan second.

It is, perhaps, this nationalist fervour that best unites the vast American continent.

THE COMMON LAW TRADITION IN SOUTH EAST ASIA

The countries covered by the term 'South East Asia' (SE Asia) include Burma, Thailand, Cambodia, Laos and Vietnam, the Philippines, Malaysia, Singapore and Indonesia. However, since our discussion is concerned only with the countries that may be classified as predominantly 'common law countries', we shall be here looking in detail only at the representative legal systems of Malaysia and Singapore, which are within the group of countries Professor Hooker has labelled as the 'English legal world'. A brief reference will, however, be made to India, which is part of the common law family but has several differentiating features.

Historical introduction to the English legal world in South East Asia

The colonial territories in which English law eventually became the general law of application were the Straits Settlements, the Federated and Unfederated Malay States, the British Borneo Territories and Burma. The Straits Settlements comprised Penang, Malacca and Singapore. The last of these has been an independent republic since 1965. Penang and Malacca were incorporated into the Federated and Unfederated Malay States and the Borneo Territories (British North Borneo and Sarawak) and became part of the State of Malaysia. Burma is now an independent republic. These countries all share a common reception (see, further, 'Reception of English law in Singapore and Malaysia', p 121, below) of English law in which all had the following features: English law was made the general applicable law and the English courts were courts of general jurisdiction. Hence, once reception of English law had taken place, even when native courts had been established, native law was applied, subject to English legal principles and to the overriding jurisdiction of the general courts. Reception of English law did not, however, take place at the same time, and general reception in Malaya only occurred in 1951–56.

As Hooker puts it:

... the history of the English legal world in South East Asia is a history of the accommodation between English principles and the indigenous laws, resulting in the latter being absorbed within the English legal system by way of both statute and case law. [Hooker (1978) p 123.]

The term 'indigenous' as applied in older works refers to native, religious, customary or tribal laws. Hooker continues: 'The legal history of the area is not so much a history of institutions as of the formation of special precedents giving effect to local laws' (Hooker (1978)). These special precedents, therefore, became part of the whole body of the English common law which was applicable in the territories concerned.

The prevalent and characteristic legal methodology in this English legal world in South East Asia, from about the 18th century, was a case law method, and the substantive law consisted of the English common law as it existed at the time (that is, English court decisions and statutes) and local customs were usually given effect, but not without inevitable uncertainty and confusion in all quarters.

In 1807, a Charter of Justice was granted by the Crown establishing a Court of Judicature in Penang, with the jurisdiction and powers of an English superior court, which had several justices and judges, and the powers of an ecclesiastical court, so far as the several religions, manners and customs of the inhabitants would admit. The law which the court was to apply was the law of England with the necessary modifications, that is, subject to local customs, religions and local legislation.

British colonisation of the Malay Peninsula began in 1786 when the English East India Company acquired the virtually uninhabited island of Penang from the Sultan of Kedah. The British had occupied Dutch Malacca since 1795, but returned it to the Dutch in 1818, under the Treaty of Vienna of 1814. Having lost Malacca, the British turned to Singapore, which was also virtually uninhabited except for 150 Malay fishermen and a few Chinese. Under a treaty of friendship and alliance, concluded with an official of the Malay Sultanate, the English East India Company obtained permission to establish a trading post on the island and, in 1819, the British Crown acquired full sovereignty over the island of Singapore. In 1824, Malacca was ceded to the British under the Anglo-Dutch Treaty of the same year.

The Dutch later formally transferred Malacca to the English East India Company in 1825, following the cession of Malacca. Subsequently, the courts were required to apply English law to all three Straits Settlements, with due regard for 'native customs, usages and law' under their Charters (the Charter of Justice 1826) which applied to Penang, Malacca and Singapore. It was generally accepted that the Charter of Justice of 1826 introduced English law into the Straits Settlements, but doubts existed over the definitive extent of the modifications necessary to take into account religion and local custom. In 1858, *R v Willans* (1858) 3 KY 16 defined a local custom within the meaning of the Charter as excluding a pre-existing European law. The rule was eventually settled that the Charter did not sanction local law, but merely admitted it as an exception (see, also, *In the Goods of Abdullah* (1835) 2 KY Ecc Rs 8 and *R v Willans* (1858)).

The subsequent history of English law in the Straits Settlements is predominantly a history of an accommodation of the law to local circumstances, given the variety of races (Malay, Chinese, Indian) and of religions (Islam, Hinduism and a potpourri of Chinese religious customs). A regime of 'personal laws' sprang up, rather in the way it did in the interregnum between the First and Second Life of Roman law. Laws were applied to persons of a named religion or race as part of the general common law of the territories. From 1942 to 1945, British Malaya was occupied by the Japanese in the course of the Second World War, but after the Japanese surrender, the British resumed control. By then, the spirit of nationalism had begun to grow and, indeed, after the war, the movement for independence started to grow in European colonies throughout the region.

In 1957, independence was proclaimed and what was then the Federation of Malaya became a sovereign State within the British Commonwealth. Singapore won internal self-government in 1959, and was briefly merged with Malaysia in 1963, but, in 1965, political differences between the two countries led to her secession and she remains an independent republic.

Reception of English law in Singapore and Malaysia

Meaning of 'reception' of law

The phenomenon of reception appears to be a universal one. It appears to have been used as a technical term in connection with the introduction of Roman law into Western Europe and also refers to the spread of law of the metropolitan countries into their colonies.

The common law interpretation of the term appears to date from the early 17th century (*Calvin's Case* (1608) 7 Co Rep 1a; 77 ER 377), acknowledged through the 18th century and reaffirmed in the classic case of *Campbell v Hall* (1774) 1 Cowp 204; 98 ER 1045.

A distinction was drawn between settled and ceded (or conquered) colonies. For settled colonies which were either uninhabited prior to the settlement, or only inhabited by a nomadic population without the arts of cultivation, the settlers carried with them, as their birthright, the law of England (see Bartholomew (1985) p 6). In the case of ceded (or conquered) colonies, the law existing prior to the conquest continued in force 'until the royal pleasure was known' (Bartholomew (1985)).

The effect of subsequent Letters Patent was to declare that, to a lesser or greater extent, English law should be applied. English law thereby spread throughout the territories of the British Empire, but was subject to a number of qualifications and restrictions. Blackstone, in writing of settled colonies, agreed that, in uninhabited territory which was discovered by English subjects, all the English laws, which are then in being, are immediately there in force but added:

> This must be understood with very many and very great restrictions. Such colonists carry with them only so much of the English law as is applicable to the condition of an infant colony ... The artificial requirements and distinctions incident to the property of a great and commercial people ... are neither necessary nor convenient for them, and therefore are not in force ... [See Blackstone, *Commentaries on the Laws of England* (1765–69) vi, p 107].

The accepted view is that the same restriction applies to ceded (or conquered) colonies in which English law applies by virtue of the royal will.

However, stating the rule did not settle the question of which laws were applicable to the various colonies, and to what extent.

Reception of English law in Singapore

The reception of English law in Singapore appears to have been settled in the following way. Despite the passing of a Third Charter of Justice in 1855, this was not regarded as effecting a re-introduction of English law as it stood at that date. Unlike the Second Charter of 1826, which created a new court for Singapore, the Third Charter had been passed to reorganise the structure of the existing court (see Sir Benson Maxwell CJ, in *R v Willans* (1858) 3 KY 16, p 37). Thus, through the Second Charter of Justice 1826, Singapore received:

(a) a court system based on the prevailing English structure; and

(b) as a result of judicial interpretation of the language of the Second Charter of Justice 1826, it received English law 'as it existed in England' on the date of the Charter, 27 November 1826.

So, any English statute passed after that date is not applicable in Singapore. Arguably, there was no 'cut off' point, but the matter has never been definitively resolved. This dual reception is known as the 'general reception of English law'. Hence, the foundations of the infant Singapore legal system were laid, which place it unequivocally within the English common law family or tradition.

Moreover, only English law of general policy and application was to be received (*Choa Choon Neo v Spottiswoode* (1869) 12 KY 216, p 221, *per* Sir Benson Maxwell CJ and *Yeap Cheah Neo v Ong Cheong Neo* (1875) LR 6 PC 381, p 384), and such English law was to be applied subject to local customs and religions and local legislation.

The Singapore Parliament has now enacted the Application of English Law Act 1993 (AELA) which 'seeks to remove the uncertainty as to the extent of the applicability of English law to Singapore, particularly in regard to statute law'. The AELA repeals s 5 of the Civil Law Act 1985, so as to abolish the continuing reception of English law under the section. However, the new statute declares (in lists contained in its annexed schedules) those English statutes which continue to be applicable in Singapore, and the English common law (including principles and rules of equity), which was in force before the commencement of the 1993 Act, continues to be in force and part of the law of Singapore. Hence, the AELA's prime contribution is to clarify the applicability of English statute law to Singapore. It is therefore now possible to make a compilation of all the English statutes which are made applicable via this Act. (For a full account of the 1993 Act, see Yeo (1994) 4 Asia Business

L Rev 69.) Singapore therefore continues to remove some of the trappings of its colonial past while retaining elements which it considers necessary to its future progress, prosperity and development.

Reception of English law in Malaysia

Malaysia was initially divided into the Federated and Unfederated Malay States. A feudal system existed in Malaysia and, in a purely formalistic sense, still does. Each of the States had a king (the Sultan) who was an independent monarch in his own right. When Malaya became a federation, all these sultans retained their sovereignty except to the extent that they would owe primary obedience to the Head of State, the Yang di-Pertuan Agong, the Chief Sultan, who by tradition resides in the capital, Kuala Lumpur.

Unlike the Straits Settlements, the Malay States were not colonies in the formal sense, but really protectorates whose rulers continued to exercise power in most formal matters of administration, but effective and ultimate power was exercised by the British Resident, a sort of governor, who was a representative of the British Government.

The position, established by a number of cases, is that the Sultan retains his independent sovereign status, despite the fact that they had bound themselves by treaty not to exercise some of the attributes of sovereignty (see *Mighell v Sultan of Johore* [1894] 1 QB 149; *Duff Development Company v Kelantan Government* [1924] AC 797 and *Pahang Consolidated Co Ltd v State of Pahang* [1933] MLJ 247).

Even after the residency system had taken effect, and up to the early 20th century, English law was not applicable *simpliciter* in these Malay States. As far as Malays were concerned, they were subject to Islamic law and Malay *adat*, a form of customary law. Islamic law was not a foreign law, but a local law of which the courts were obliged to take judicial notice (*Ramah v Laton* (1927) 6 FMSLR 128). Each of the Federal Malay States (FMS) had legislation regulating the administration of Islamic law.

There was also legislative recognition of Chinese family law, and Hindu law was considered on a par with Chinese law since the courts recognised Hindu law, and local variations thereof, on substantially the same grounds as Chinese law. Since the higher ranks of the judicial hierarchy were filled with English lawyers trained in English common law, some English rules were certainly starting to appear in the 19th century. Recourse to English law appeared to be necessary to fill lacunae that appeared since, in certain cases, it was not possible to ascertain what law, if any, applied.

In 1937, English law was legislatively introduced into the FMS by the Civil Law Enactment No 3 of 1937, and extended to the Unfederated Malay States by the Civil Law (Extension) Ordinance of 1951. This was later repealed in

1956 by the Civil Law Ordinance of the same year (s 3(1)) which repeats the provision, appearing in the earlier Acts, providing for the application of English law 'subject to such qualification as local circumstances render necessary'. This was, therefore, merely according legislative recognition to *de jure* judicial practice. Judicial precedent from each State jurisdiction may be freely cited in modern Malaysia and this can only be subject to later legislative amendment.

Malaya is now known as West Malaysia, and the law that applies to all its States is a mixture of English common law, English rules of equity, local legislation, imperial legislation and group personal (customary/religious) law (that is, the law that is applicable by virtue of membership of a defined racial, religious or ethnic group).

Unlike England, both Singapore and Malaysia have written constitutions but, in Singapore in particular, the Constitution does not dominate the availability of legal rights and remedies in the way that it does, to a great extent, in the United States, France and Germany. The Privy Council remains the highest Court of Appeal for Singapore, but not for Malaysia. This refers to the judicial committee of the English Privy Council, and the origin of this practice is traceable to the days when the English Sovereign ruled by, and with, the advice of the Privy Council. Appeals to the Privy Council from courts in Singapore were radically curtailed, in 1989, by the Internal Security (Amendment) Act 1989 and the Judicial Committee (Amendment) Act 1989. It is expected that, as a result, there will now be very few appeals to the Privy Council, although it remains nominally the highest appellate tribunal within Singapore. The eventual abolition of all appeals to the Privy Council for both criminal and civil cases is now on the cards.

By virtue of the Judicial Committee Act 1833 (as amended in 1844), a committee was set up within the Privy Council to hear appeals from overseas either under the Act or under the customary jurisdiction of the Privy Council. Until 1966, only single opinions were given, but dissenting opinions are now permissible.

In criminal cases, the jury system was abolished in Singapore by the Criminal Procedure Code (Amendment) Act 1969. This is certainly not in keeping with other major common law jurisdictions.

It can be seen, therefore, that where Portuguese and Dutch influence centred on Malacca for predominantly trade motives, English influence eventually extended over the whole peninsula and was to leave a permanent legacy to the political and legal institutions of the country. Of course, Indian culture and religion were transplanted through the Indian immigrants who settled in Malaya, bringing with them Hindu law and Hindu customs, as was the Islamic religion and the law of the Muslims. However, the *adat*, or native Malay customary law, prevailed and, indeed, has a direct link with the feudal set up. Thus, the influence of customary law was allowed to flourish despite the 'general applicability' of the English common law, but the ethos of English law, and its culture, traditions and philosophy, is still very much in evidence in Singapore and Malaysia.

THE COMMON LAW IN INDIA

The vast majority of people who are natives of the Indian sub-continent are Hindus, but this does not mean that Hindu law, which is a law based on a religion and particular way of life, governs India. It is worth bearing in mind that, although the Indians themselves were either Hindus or Muslims by religion, neither Hindu nor Muslim laws were the laws that governed the country from the 16th century onwards. On the contrary, India is traditionally classified as a common law jurisdiction. The history of the current Indo-British jurisprudence originates from the formation of the London East India Company in 1600, in the reign of Elizabeth I. The charters of Queen Elizabeth and James I granted to the company the power to make laws which were necessary, so long as these were not contrary to the laws, statutes and customs of England. The Dutch, Portuguese, French and English who came to India, however, were, as in the case of the Straits Settlements, primarily interested in establishing strong trade links with India rather than attempting to colonise it. Eventually, the British gained a legal, political and even cultural foothold in the country through the making of numerous treaties between Indian princes and the East India Company, and intermittent military ventures.

Vast territories were governed by the East India Company and the British Crown then created special royal courts, applying English law, which were later replaced by Supreme Courts staffed by English judges, which also applied English law except in inappropriate cases involving inheritance, marriage, caste and religious disputes. By the end of the 19th century, English common law became the law which applied to most of India. The judicial norm, in cases other than those mentioned above, was to determine them in accordance with 'justice, equity and good conscience'. Reception of English law (see, also, p 121, above), therefore, took place through the many laws drawn up by English jurists, such as Macaulay who was the originator of the Indian Criminal Code, and the codes that were formulated and applied. A veritable host of such codes were drawn up including a Code of Civil Procedure and Criminal Procedure. Other statutes which codified the common law of India included the Evidence Act 1872, Contract Act 1872, Transfer of Property Act 1882 (amended 1929) and Succession Act 1865. In fact, by 1861, the administration of justice in India was regularly carried out in the country by judges trained in the English common law. Codifications were, however, used to reform and clarify the law and not merely to consolidate existing laws. New rules were created and enacted without inhibition in the spirit of improving on the existing English common law, for example, in the law of contract and wills.

Nevertheless, the law of India, prior to independence in 1947, would certainly have conformed to the English common law prototype in its juristic style, ideology, sources of law, judicial and administrative hierarchy, and fundamental concepts. The doctrine of binding precedent was not merely recognised, but officially endorsed and promulgated. The judge is given a high profile, as in other common law jurisdictions, and dissenting opinions are part and parcel of this approach, as are publications of law reports, which were first published privately.

Procedure in legal issues, and the primacy of the rule of law are other distinctive common law features. Unlike England, however, no centralised system for the administration of justice has been set up and, apart from the Federal Supreme Court, there exist only State or territorial courts. The Federal Supreme Court itself is headed by a chief justice and 13 judges.

The gaining of independence, in 1947, did not radically alter the basic characteristics of Indian law, but there are some distinguishing features from common law. For example, Indian courts try to establish precedents which are tailored to the particular local facts of a case and might, therefore, deviate from a blanket acceptance of an English precedent, if appropriate. There is no distinction between common law and equity in India. The English legal terminology for the law of property is used purely in a technical sense, and applied to regulate a land tenure system that differs markedly from the English system. India has a written Constitution which created a union of States, another feature which distinguish it from the English position. This Constitution contains a list of basic rights rather like the Russian Federation Constitution (see, further, 'The new Russian Federation Constitution', p 195, below), the infringement of which may be held void by the High Court, which is the highest court of the Member States, or by the Federal Supreme Court of India, the highest tribunal in the country. The Supreme Court has the power to decide appeals against judgments of the High Court, in cases involving more than a designated monetary limit, and may also hear an appeal where permission has been given to do so by a High Court or by the Supreme Court itself. The Supreme Court seeks to ensure respect for the Constitution and it will hear cases where a breach of a 'fundamental right' has been alleged.

In view of the great diversity of Indian society, such as its 15 officially recognised languages, and the uneasy co-existence of Hindus and Muslims, which led to the creation of Pakistan in 1947, the English common law can be seen to have united the country in a way that appeared intrinsically impossible, even to the native population. However, as a former Attorney General of India put it: 'The massive structure of Indian law and jurisprudence resembles the height, the symmetry and the grandeur of the common and statute law of England.' This is because: 'The English brought into India not only the mass of legal rules strictly known as "the common law", but also their traditions, outlook and techniques in establishing, maintaining and developing the judicial system' (see Setalvad (1960)).

However, one needs only to read about Indian culture and literature to obtain a firm impression of the legacy of the English tradition in India extending far beyond the law and the administration of justice. It appears true, even today, that the legacy of the English in India can still be seen in their fundamental approach to many aspects of life but, predominantly, only among the more privileged and 'educated' classes. Its unique culture and customs have survived, but its legal and political ethos still bears strong imprints of the English common law traditions.

THE COMMON LAW IN THE FAR EAST: HONG KONG

In early times, the island of Hong Kong was apparently inhabited by some peasants and fishermen who lived there under Chinese rule and custom. The law to which they were subject at the time was that of the Qing dynasty, partly codified by the Qing Codes. The colony of Hong Kong was acquired by the British in three stages; in 1842, 1860 and 1898. Hong Kong was not, however, acquired for settlement or territorial expansion, but as a base in the Far East to advance the commercial, diplomatic and military interests of Great Britain (see Endacott, *A History of Hong Kong* (1973) p 38).

The legal system (such as it was) that existed in Hong Kong in the 1840s, was not suitable for these purposes. On 5 April 1843, Hong Kong received a local legislature and English law was to be received into the colony, but not in cases where it was considered not suitable for its inhabitants or to the circumstances of Hong Kong. Although there was no differentiation in the types of English law, there was, in practice, a distinction drawn between statutes and cases. The 'cut off date' for Acts was 5 April 1843: all Acts contained in the English statute book on that day, provided they were general and not purely local in character, and not unsuitable to the circumstances of Hong Kong or its inhabitants, were automatically applicable to Hong Kong. All English Acts passed after that date were not applicable to the colony unless they necessarily applied by their own terms, or were specifically imported by prerogative legislation or local ordinance. Common law, in the sense of case law, was considered unchanging and, therefore, remained applicable even after the cut off date, since these cases were seen as merely declaratory of the law that had always been applicable. This quaint concept has been discarded, but the continued reception of contemporaneous judicial decisions meant that there was possibility of Hong Kong being left with a set of ossified legal decisions.

However, it became increasingly problematic to ascertain which English Acts were in force in 1843 and to discover accurate texts. Hong Kong's own legislature, nevertheless, continued to produce statute law specifically adapted to the colony, so that a voluminous collection of English law was rendered nugatory.

New legislative formula

In 1966, a new legislative formula was introduced through the Application of English Law Ordinance 1966. It divided English law into two types: (a) enactments; and (b) common law and equity, dealt with each separately and abolished the cut off date.

Under s 3(1) thereof, English common law and the rules of equity shall be in force, so far as they are applicable to the circumstances of Hong Kong or its inhabitants, and subject to such modifications as such circumstances may require. Common law and equity may be amended by legislation, but their operation in the territory is only to be affected by statutes which themselves have effect in Hong Kong. Thus, Acts of Parliament apply if extended by their own terms, or by other legislation including the schedule of the Application of English Law Ordinance itself (s 4).

Various anomalies resulted from this Ordinance, since it applies some English Acts to Hong Kong (for example, the Justices of the Peace Act 1361 and the Distress of Rent Act 1689), but not others. Case law then established that the effect of the Ordinance would seem to be that, if a common law rule was affected by English legislation, it was the amended common law which applied, irrespective of whether the amending Act of Parliament took effect in Hong Kong or not. Hence, an Act passed in England, though without reference to conditions in Hong Kong, or the wishes of the Hong Kong Government, and not itself directly in force in Hong Kong, would, if it impinged upon the common law, indirectly affect the law that was applicable in the colony (see Wesley-Smith, *An Introduction to the Hong Kong Legal System* (1987) p 37).

The local legislature, therefore, amended the Ordinance, so that it was made clear that the common law and equity are to be applicable in the colony, notwithstanding amendment of them as part of the law of England made at any time by legislation not in force in Hong Kong. This did not resolve other potential anomalies, but the current position appears to be that 'the common law imported into Hong Kong can be affected by legislation made as part of the law of England which does not apply to Hong Kong, provided that such legislation was formerly in force under the old formula' (Wesley-Smith (1987) p 38). Ironically, therefore, the cut off date retains its significance because all statutes which were part of English law on 5 April 1843, and which abolished common law or equity, will still have that effect. Section 3 will only apply to

English legislation passed after 5 April 1843, or to earlier legislation which did not previously apply to the colony.

Hong Kong after 1997

In 1997, Hong Kong once again came within the sphere of China's control. In order to ensure that, by then, Hong Kong would possess a comprehensive body of law which owes its authority to the legislature of Hong Kong, it was necessary to replace British legislation by local legislation on the same topics. A legislative programme has been adopted to achieve this. The Hong Kong Act 1985 provides for the Hong Kong legislature in specified fields with Hong Kong ordinances, and the Hong Kong (Legislative Powers) Order 1986 specified the fields of civil aviation, merchant shipping and admiralty jurisdiction. A further order was made in 1989 which confers similar powers to enact legislation, to give effect to international agreements which are applicable to Hong Kong. At the basic level of compatibility of laws, Hong Kong's case law will have to be codified if there is to be any hope of the two systems being harmonised with each other.

At midnight on 30 June 1997, Hong Kong became a Special Administrative Region (SAR) under the direct authority of the Central People's Government (CPG) of the People's Republic of China (PRC) and, according to the promise of Deng Xiaoping in 1982, there was then 'one country, two systems'. The National People's Congress (NPC) of the PRC enacted a basic law for the Hong Kong SAR pursuant to Art 31 of the Constitution of the PRC. The Basic Law is a sort of mini-constitution for the future Hong Kong SAR, designed to provide a constitutional framework for the maintenance of Hong Kong's present legal and economic system post-1997.

Article 5 of the basic law draft states that:

The socialist system and policies shall not be practised in the Hong Kong Special Administrative Region and the previous capitalist system and way of life shall remain unchanged for 50 years.

Article 8 goes on to provide:

The laws previously in force in Hong Kong, that is, the common law, rules of equity, ordinances, subordinate legislation and customary law shall be maintained, except for those that are inconsistent with this law, or have been amended by the legislature of the Hong Kong Special Administrative Region.

Thus, problems of integration of policy, culture, ideology and politics apart, Hong Kong will continue to receive, for 50 years after 1997, the English common law. Hence, it will continue to apply the doctrine of precedent and appeals from its Court of Appeal will still lie to the Privy Council. Article 83 allows the courts to refer to precedents from other common law jurisdictions. Hong Kong's Court of Appeal held in 1973 that any relevant decision of the

Privy Council is binding on the Hong Kong courts. Hence, decisions of Chinese courts will have no impact on Hong Kong until 2047.

Judges are meant to be appointed from within Hong Kong, and Arts 81 and 91 of the draft basic law permit the appointment of judges from other common law jurisdictions to sit on the Court of Final Appeal and other courts respectively. A continuing problem has been the difficulty in procuring judges of sufficient calibre and experience to sit on the Bench.

It must be appreciated that the Hong Kong transition is unique because, under paras 1 and 2 of the *Joint Declaration (JD) of the United Kingdom of Great Britain and Northern Ireland and the Government of the People's Republic of China*, there is no transfer of sovereignty as such. The Government of the People's Republic of China declares that 'it has decided to resume the exercise of sovereignty over Hong Kong' with effect from 1 July 1997 (see *Joint Declaration of the Government of the UK of Great Britain and Northern Ireland and the Government of the People's Republic of China on the question of Hong Kong with Annexes*, Cmnd 9543, 1985, London: HMSO). Thus, that document, which the British Government described as the highest form of commitment between two sovereign States, merely prescribed the timing and modalities of the resumption of Chinese rule over Hong Kong, subject to certain transitional arrangements for the next 50 years. In a sense, therefore, China recognised the legitimacy of British administration which lasted for 12 years. As far as implementation of the JD is concerned, there is no dispute settlement provision and the UK would, therefore, not be able to respond militarily to any forcible occupation of Hong Kong by China. China does not recognise the compulsory jurisdiction of the International Court of Justice.

However, until 1 January 2000, a formal mechanism for bilateral consultation will exist in the 'Joint Liaison Group' (JLG) which was established under the Joint Declaration. This will be of some utility because Annex II of the JD makes it clear that the functions of the JG are limited to liaison, so it is not intended to operate as an organ of power, and plays no role in the administration of Hong Kong or the Hong Kong SAR. It also has no supervisory role over the administration of the former colony.

However, there are several factors which suggest that China will abide by the terms of the Joint Declaration, most of which could be said to be public policy grounds (see Slinn (1997)):

(a) The JD is a freely negotiated international agreement. There is, thus, an obligation to observe such an agreement in good faith, which is a fundamental principle of international law. China has a reasonably good record of observing such agreements.

(b) The 'object and purpose' of the JD is clearly stated in the preamble as 'the maintenance of the prosperity and stability' of Hong Kong, which China has identified as a vital Chinese interest to be satisfied by respect for the autonomy and for the 'capitalist lifestyle' of the Hong Kong SAR.

(c) Since the agreement came into force, the practice of the parties has been to accept the existence of a binding agreement.

(d) Serious breaches of the JD would endanger the already delicate relationship between China and Taiwan, and China's relations with third States and with international organisations. Efforts to end the separation between Taiwan and the mainland are still very much on China's agenda. Indeed, the 'one country, two systems' formula was seen as a slogan for unity between China and Taiwan. As far as relations with third States and international organisations are concerned, any breach of China's undertakings towards Hong Kong's status would affect adversely an extensive multilateral and bilateral network of treaties in areas such as extradition, investment protection and air services.

(e) The Chinese leader has underlined the importance China has placed on maintaining Hong Kong's stability and prosperity.

(f) Arrangements have also been made for the Hong Kong SAR to continue to participate in a wide range of international organisations, and these arrangements assume the SAR's autonomy.

The United States Hong Kong Policy Act 1992

In addition, the USA has enacted the United States Hong Kong Policy Act 1992 which gave legislative effect to US policy, which is predicated on Hong Kong remaining a fully autonomous territory from 1 July 1997, in respect of economic and trade matters. This agreement will mean that the US will continue to expand trade and economic relations, which will include entering into bilateral economic and air services agreements. They will also support Hong Kong's participation in multilateral agreements and organisations in which Hong Kong is eligible to participate. If the SAR does not retain sufficient autonomy to discharge its international obligations under the JD, Hong Kong will lose any benefits which are available under the Act. This Act apparently elicited protests from China which claimed that it was tantamount to interference with China's exercise of sovereignty in domestic affairs. The Act gives sanction to US support for compliance with the JD.

Can socialism and capitalism co-exist?

The study of Puerto Rico's legal history by JA Morales, which illustrated how American common law transformed the fragmented Puerto Rico's Spanish civil law tradition, has suggested that the domination of a law in a country which already had an indigenous law, or which has already been ruled by another law for many years, may be due to several factors: the choice of legal language; the content and style of legal education; and the type of legal personnel it produced (Morales, 'Puerto Rico: two roads to justice' (1981) 79

Revista de Derecho Puertorriqueno 293, cited by Epstein, in 'China and Hong Kong', in Wacks (ed), *The Future of the Law in Hong Kong,* pp 60–61). If common law and socialist law begin to co-exist after 2047, experience in other jurisdictions suggests that one of the systems will prevail. Given the obvious military might of China, that system might arguably be imposed from across the sea from the Mainland.

China falls into the category of a socialist legal system since it shares with the few remaining socialist countries common economic, ideological and political foundations. China has primarily looked to civil law codes and, indeed, codification as a preferred style of legalism, but socialist law was not created in a vacuum. It was in 1927, when the 'Chinese Soviets' were established in Jiangxi and Hunan, that Soviet law began to make a lasting impression on China and the Mainland Chinese leaders. The policy of the Chinese Communist Party (CCP) at the time clearly played no small part in China's eventual 'conversion'. True to Marxist/Leninist ideology, Chinese Marxist orthodoxy views all law as an extension of the economic system and the system of ownership which determines the mode of production. Law is an integral part of the political structure, but is also merely the instrument of the political will of the ruling class.

A new form of 'preliminary socialism' has entered into China's official ideology relatively recently and this argues that, because socialist China emerged from a semi-colonial, semi-feudal period, without passing through a stage of highly developed capitalism, its productive forces have lagged far behind those of developed capitalist countries. China would first have to undergo a long period of preliminary socialism, wherein the private economy will be allowed to co-exist with the socialist public economy and, by allowing mixed economic forms, the CCP has been given the latitude and discretion to reform China's economic and social systems without undermining their leadership or their socialist ideology. The capitalist productive forces of Hong Kong are seen as a means to an end of 'preliminary socialism'. The question that must lurk in the back of one's mind, therefore, is when will the period be seen to have served its purpose so that the socialist State can move on to the next stage of development? Can China's economic and ideological systems co-exist with Hong Kong's capitalist system?

The future of the common law in Hong Kong

As far as Hong Kong and China are concerned, there are fundamental ideological, institutional, philosophical and economic differences between them which need to be resolved before any sort of successful integration and co-existence will be possible. It should be remembered that the system proposed for the post-1997 Hong Kong is not a Federal system of power sharing, and that Hong Kong's law making competence will derive from the

NPC and, ultimately, from Art 31 of the Constitution. Hence, the basic law is not really a mini constitution in the way that one would expect. It will be an NPC law which can extend or restrict the application of the Chinese legal system to Hong Kong as the NPC thinks fit, subject to amendment or repeal like any other NPC legislation. However, as long as it remains in force, it will constitute a fetter, or check, on the application of Chinese law in Hong Kong.

In essence, China's legal system remains incompatible with that of Hong Kong. Mainland China's historical roots are overwhelmingly rooted in civil law and their predominant socialist law ideology means that they give very little recognition to private rights, since everything is generally geared to the State plan, and the best economic interests of the State. Mainland China retains a legislative jurisdiction in defence, foreign affairs and other matters outside the limits of Hong Kong's 'high degree of autonomy'. Other factors which will influence the shape of things to come will be the Mainland's control of legal language, personnel, and the weight and popular appeal accorded to public policy and morality, counterbalanced by Hong Kong's devotion not just to the money market and prosperity, but also to its own sense of justice, human rights and democracy. At present, most legal proceedings in Hong Kong are conducted in, and nearly all law is published in, English – a language which is not the mother tongue of 98% of the inhabitants. Its District and Supreme Courts, and Lands Tribunal function only in English. Interpreters are provided for non-English speakers. However, the government has committed large resources to translating the entire statute book into Chinese and to draft new ordinances and subsidiary legislation into both languages, with both languages to be equally authentic. Legal education, on the other hand, will continue to be in English only, but some secondary literature in Chinese is beginning to emerge. These elements may all be irrelevant if Mainland China were to exercise their military powers, or play their public order card, and simply take over the island and rule it as they deem fit. When Chris Patten took over as Governor of Hong Kong, there was something of a 'roller coaster' relationship between himself and Chinese representatives from Mainland China. In his capacity as representative of the British Government, Patten continued to insist that, even after the British handover in 1997, certain fundamental civil liberties would be constitutionally protected in the former colony. This met with a cool reception from the Chinese leaders, not as a matter of principle, but because of the implications of actually spelling out such laws. Negotiations continued for some time and it is believed that some sort of compromise was eventually achieved. Only time will tell whether the terms of such a compromise were effective in maintaining civil liberties in the Hong Kong of the 21st century.

The process of implementing the JD, over the period 1985–97, proved to be a highly rigorous exercise in scrutiny of an international treaty to 'exhaustive textual exegesis' (Slinn). It provides a memorable example of international legal co-operation, which was necessary to ensure the Hong Kong SAR's international status as an autonomous trading and economic entity.

The Hong Kong Bill of Rights Ordinance

The Hong Kong Bill of Rights Ordinance entered into force on 8 June 1991 (Cap 383, Laws of Hong Kong). Its purpose is to incorporate into the law of Hong Kong, the provisions of the International Covenant on Civil and Political Rights (ICCPR) as applied to Hong Kong (see Chan (1998)). The Bill consists of three parts: (a) Pt I provides for the commencement of the Ordinance, the principles of interpretation, the scope of application, permissible derogation in times of emergency, and remedies and jurisdiction of the courts; (b) Pt II contains the Hong Kong Bill of Rights, consisting of 23 Articles, which replicate the substantive rights provisions of the ICCPR; (c) Pt III sets out certain restrictions and limitations on the scope of the Bill, replicating the reservations entered by the United Kingdom when it ratified the ICCPR. It also contains s 14, which freezes the operation of the Bill in relation to six specified ordinances, for a period of one year. The Ordinance is not entrenched, but retains the status of an ordinary ordinance. Section 3 provides that all pre-existing legislation shall be construed in a manner consistent with the Bill of Rights and if it cannot be so construed, be repealed to the extent of the inconsistency. Section 4 provides that all subsequent legislation shall be construed consistently, not with the Bill of Rights, but with the ICCPR as applied to Hong Kong. If it cannot be so construed, the Bill of Rights Ordinance says nothing about its validity. However, the Letters Patent, which was the constitution of Hong Kong, shall be *ultra vires* the legislation and, hence, null and void.

So far, the Hong Kong courts have been quite prepared to look beyond the ICCPR to examine established law and practice, and seek to evaluate them against contemporary international human rights standards. It is envisaged that there will be a fresh jurisprudential approach (see the leading case of *R v Sin Yau Ming* [1992] HK CLR 127). However, the Privy Council (the highest Court of Appeal for Hong Kong) in *AG v Lee Kwong-Kut* (1993) 3 HKPLR 72 has not been enthusiastic about the Hong Kong Court of Appeal's approach. Although conceding that international and comparative jurisprudence may give valuable guidance to the interpretation of the Bill of Rights Ordinance, Lord Woolf also pointed out that these materials, such as Canadian cases, were limited when it came to interpretation of domestic legislation. The court believed that the common law was quite able to provide its own judicial guidelines for interpretation of legislation. In the light of this cool reception from the Privy Council, international and comparative jurisprudence has played only a minor part in the interpretation of the Hong Kong Bill of Rights. The Privy Council also cast doubt on the relevance of European jurisprudence, in *AG v Ming Pao Newspapers Ltd* (1996) 6 HKPLR 103. Lord Jauncey emphasised that the role of the European Court of Justice, in relation to the domestic legislation of contracting States, differed markedly from the role of the Hong Kong courts in legislation, which is claimed to contravene the entrenched provisions of the Bill. The Hong Kong courts are more supportive of reference to international and comparative jurisprudence as aids to legislative interpretation, if these sources reach a similar conclusion to the common law position. Up to mid-1997, the Hong Kong courts have delivered approximately 300 judgments on the Bill of Rights (see Chan (1998)) and, apart from the observations already made, the common law notion of 'Wednesbury unreasonableness' tends to creep in (see Associated Provincial Picture House Ltd v Wednesbury Corporation [1948] 1 KB 223). This is partly due to the uncertainty of wandering into unknown territory located within international law. The mood of the courts has been described as 'conservative, inward looking and parochial, showing excessive deference to executive policies and legislative sovereignty, and demonstrating only half hearted commitment to fundamental human rights' (Chan (1998) p 335) and, most worryingly, this writer argues that the general outlook of the Hong Kong courts is that 'Human rights are regarded as a necessary evil, which have to be kept in close control'.

In the first few judgments on the basic law, there is no suggestion that this approach will change, as far as the courts of the SAR are concerned. In HKSAR v David Ma [1997] 2 HKC 315, the Court of Appeal held that the Hong Kong courts had no jurisdiction to question whether a decision of the Standing Committee of the National People's Congress, setting up the provisional legislative council, was consistent with the Basic Law. Further, in Cheung Lai Wah v Director of Immigration [1997] HKLRD 1081, the Court of First Instance upheld an amendment to the Immigration Ordinance depriving retrospectively children, born in Mainland China to parents who are Hong Kong Permanent Residents, of their right of abode in Hong Kong saying that, although this right is conferred on them by the basic law, it is also justifiable under the basic law.

In a very practical sense, the survival of the common law and concomitant Western principles regarding human rights and civil liberties in Hong Kong, might also ensure the survival of a democratic society and greater freedom for the citizen of Hong Kong in the 21st century. Indeed, it is expected that Hong Kong will continue to function pretty much as before the handover in 1997, right up to 2047 – a free market will only really thrive in a free society. For the foreseeable future, China appears to wish to preserve the Hong Kong phenomenon.

COMPARATIVE OVERVIEW

As with the civil law system, the common law tradition has inevitably undergone notable changes over its nine centuries of existence. In its parent country, where legislation was once regarded as a necessary evil and occasional inconvenience, a remarkable proliferation of legislation has taken place, particularly, in the latter half of the 20th century. Its basic philosophy has remained the resolution of disputes, rather than the provider of, or vehicle for, universal truths and general solutions. However, it has both explicitly and implicitly been ready to posit principles, based on standards of morality, social policy and commercial probity. In this, it has many parallels with civil law systems.

Its basic legal technique remains firmly rooted in a process of abstraction, operating at different levels of generality, and reasoning by analogy and by precedent, in reliance on decisional law or judicial precedent, rather than primarily in applying and interpreting statutes. A crucial difference with the civil law approach is that, with some exceptions, in order to determine a point of law, instead of consulting a code or statute, the common lawyer and judge will consult cases and textbooks of cases before looking at statutes and, primarily, in order to resolve a dispute or an alleged breach of legally enforceable rights.

The vast proportion of cases in more recent times have been decided by the lower courts and specialist tribunals, the latter presided over by judges and arbitrators outside the ordinary courts' structure. But, the appeal courts and the House of Lords continue to exercise control and influence over the shape and progress of legal development. There is still very little evidence of English law being subsumed within, or markedly influenced by, European Community law, although the highest Court of Appeal for English domestic courts is now the European Court of Justice of the European Communities, and EC law is applicable to Britain under the European Communities Act 1972.

The doctrine of precedent, despite its flaws, potential rigidity and inability to play a pro-active role in law reform, has, at least in England, been assisted by the expedient of legislation, particularly in the area of company law, commercial law and family law. In countries to which the common law has spread, it has been adapted considerably, so as to acquire different characteristics and features; in countries like America, it has had to accommodate rapidly changing social, political and economic conditions. It has thrived in the former colonies of Britain, and has managed to co-exist quite successfully alongside indigenous customary law, primarily because of its potential for flexibility.

In England, there has been a remarkable increase in the number of cases of judicial review, especially over the last decade, and questions must be raised over the efficacy of the ancient prerogative writs to secure for the citizen, acceptable standards of justice and to provide sufficiently strong protection against governmental power and control. There appears to be a discernible trend, in common law jurisprudence, to broaden the juristic base for the articulation and enforceability of the rights of the individual, particularly against the State and State interests, and the potential removal of any remaining distinction between public and private law in England, except in a small proportion of cases.

Judges remain in the forefront of the common law legal tradition, both at home and abroad, and it is their role and function that is currently undergoing closer scrutiny than ever before.

Case law has also been steadily acquiring a higher profile in civil law countries, like France and Germany, whereas, in England, the so called law making function has been carried out in far greater measure in the last decade by the legislature than in the past. But, as far as convergence of legal systems is concerned, judgment has to be reserved. The preceding survey will have at least indicated that, although several similarities exist between common and civil law countries, several more ideological, jurisprudential, institutional and procedural dissimilarities will first have to be reconciled before any sort of true 'harmonisation of laws' can occur.

SELECTIVE BIBLIOGRAPHY

Alder, 'Hunting the chimera – the end of *O'Reilly v Mackman*?' (1993) 13 LS 183

Angus and Chan (eds), *Canada-Hong Kong Human Rights and Privacy Law Issues* (1994)

Bartholomew, in Harding (ed), *The Common Law in Singapore and Malaysia* (1985) Chap 1

Buckland and McNair, *Roman Law and Common Law* (1952)

Chan, *An Introduction to the Singapore Legal System* (1986)

Chan and Ghai (eds), *The Hong Kong Bill of Rights: A Comparative Approach* (1993)

Chan, 'The jurisdiction and legality of the provisional legislative council' (1997) 23 HKLJ 374

Chan, 'Hong Kong's Bill of Rights: its reception of and contribution to international and comparative jurisprudence' (1998) 47 ICLQ 306

David and Brierley, *Major Legal Systems in the World Today* (1985) Pt III

Farnsworth, *An Introduction to the Legal System of the United States* (1987)

Hall, *The Magic Mirror: Law in American History* (1989)

Harlow, 'Public and private law: definition without distinction' (1980) 43 MLR 241

Hay, *An Introduction to US Law* (1976)

Hohmann, 'The nature of the common law and the comparative study of legal reasoning' (1990) 38 Am J Comp L 143

Hooker, *A Concise Legal History of South East Asia* (1978)

Hooker, *Legal Pluralisms* (1975)

Horwitz, *The Transformation of American Law* (1977)

Hurst, *Law and the Conditions of Freedom in the 19th Century in the United States* (1975)

Ingman, *The English Legal Process* (1992)

Levy-Ulmann, *The English Legal Tradition* (1935)

Manchester, *Modern Legal History of England and Wales* (1980)

Matson, 'The common law abroad: English and indigenous laws in the British Commonwealth' (1993) 42 ICLQ 753

Pound, 'The development of American law and its deviation from English law' (1951) 67 LQR 49

Rheinstein, *International Encyclopedia of Comparative Law*, Vols I and II

Schlesinger *et al*, *Comparative Law: Cases, Text, Materials* (1988)

Setalvad, *The Common Law in India* (1960)

Slinn, 'The Hong Kong transition' (1997) 9 Wig & Gavel 35

Tunc, 'The not so common law of England and the United States, or precedent in England and the United States, a field study by an outsider' (1984) 47 MLR 150

Van Caenegem, *The Birth of the English Common Law* (1988)

Wacks (ed), *The Future of the Law In Hong Kong* (1989)

Yeo, 'Application of English Law Act 1993: a step in the weaning process' (1994) 4 Asia Business L Rev 69

Zweigert and Kotz, *An Introduction to Comparative Law* (1987) Vol I; 3rd edn (1998) Vol I

CHAPTER 5

EUROPEAN COMMUNITY LAW

INTRODUCTION

Having considered the two major families or systems of law known as the common law and civil law systems and their respective traditions and legacy, we now examine the law of a special, single, political entity, the 'European Community' or European Union, which has given rise to a unique legal system which is at once *sui generis*, separate from either civil or common law parent families, yet 'supranational', a regional system and a distinctive legal order in its own right. As 1993 and the planned implementation of the European Single Market came and went, it remains increasingly important to recognise the importance of the law of the European Community (EC) as a legal order, in the sense of 'an organised and structured system of legal rules, with its own sources and its own institutions and procedures for making, interpreting and enforcing those rules' (Isaac, *Droit Communautaire Général* (1983) p 111). In some respects, of course, it is a particular kind of 'hybrid' legal system, but the term 'hybrid' is not usually associated with this sort of legal system (see Chapter 6 for examples of 'conventional' hybrid systems). Even more importantly, it is now not possible, with the formation of the European (then Economic) Community, to contemplate studying civil law systems in Western Europe or, indeed, English law without also examining the impact of EC law on these systems:

> The European Community, founded on the Treaties of Paris and Rome, is governed by a quadripartite institutional system – novel in its conception, unique in its assignment of powers, different from all previous national and international systems, a Community system in letter and in spirit.

This is how the *European Documentation on the Court of Justice of the European Communities* describes the three European Communities generally referred to as, the 'European Community', or the 'EC' which usually refers to the Economic Community. Although it is, in law, three Communities (see below), there is only one set of institutions for all three. Thus, it has become generally acceptable to refer to the three Communities as the European Community.

It is widely recognised that the Treaty of Paris (1951) and Treaty of Rome (1957) have had an unprecedented effect and impact on the major European countries by virtue of their creation of the European Communities: the European Coal and Steel Community (ECSC), the European Economic Community (EEC) and the European Atomic Energy Community (Euratom).

Just as there developed a 'common law' in England, the Treaty of Rome appears to have laid the foundations for the evolution of a common European law, a new *ius commune* which is being implemented both by the institutions setting up the Treaty, and by law making and law enforcing agencies of the Member States. This law is also capable of being invoked by individuals of those Member States. It included the written law of the EC and certain 'general principles of law' which are unwritten, but now encompass the protection of human rights.

The impact of EC law has been seen in the use of continental approaches to statutory interpretation by English judges and in the many EC Directives that have become part of the established legal language, affecting areas such as company law, where harmonisation of national company laws has been embarked upon by the European Commission since 1968. Further implications and effects of EC law on English and continental law are discussed towards the end of this chapter.

SCOPE OF CHAPTER

There is now a vast and ever burgeoning body of literature on the European Community (EC) and its law and case law continues to grow, dealing with topics ranging from human rights to agricultural policy, but the purpose of this chapter is to place EC law in its contemporary and comparative legal context, outlining its key characteristics and comparing them with those of the legal systems which we have already analysed. We shall also examine the sources of EC law and its relationship to national laws, the influence of French, German and common law traditions on its structure and development, and speculate on its future directions, and potential role and development as a unique form of European law. This chapter is, therefore, highly selective and will examine community law primarily within a conceptual and comparative framework.

MONISM, DUALISM AND THE ACCESSION OF BRITAIN

An international treaty, such as the Treaty of Rome, will usually come into force when it has been signed and ratified by its signatories. However, since treaties are governed by international law, the implementation of the Treaty into the domestic laws of the Member State depends on whether that State has a monist or dualist form of constitution. Broadly speaking, a monist constitution accepts that international law obligations are of the same nature as, or are even superior to, national law obligations. According to this constitutional approach, a rule of customary international law, or a rule established by an international treaty to which that State is a party, is automatically part of that State's national law. Hence, once a State has concluded a treaty guaranteeing certain rights for its nationals, those rights are automatically protected by national law. For example, it may be said that both the French and Dutch constitutions are monist constitutions.

A dualist constitution, which is the category into which the British constitution broadly falls, is one under which only limited status is given to rules of international law until, or unless, they have been transformed (that is, implemented) into national law by some method of national enactment, for example, by an Act of Parliament.

However, it is inaccurate to categorise a State as being wholly monist or dualist, and it is more correct to say that, in the first instance, a State is governed by its monist or dualist tradition. This is because a State with a monist constitution may retain the power in its courts to decide which provisions of a treaty are binding (as under the Dutch regime), and a 'dualist State' may have a general judicial presumption that its Parliament does not intend to legislate contrary to international law and this will extend to obligations imposed by treaties, as well as by general principles of international law (as in the United Kingdom). As far as Britain was concerned, therefore, Community law was not automatically applicable when it ratified the EC Treaties.

Britain's attitude to membership of the Community has been characterised by some as antipathy and disdain, throughout the many years of the Community's genesis, but this attitude changed in the 1960s and, eventually, having signed the Treaty of Accession on 22 January 1972, on 1 January 1973, Britain joined the Community. English, Danish and Irish became official Community languages and the translations into these languages of the EEC and Euratom Treaties were declared to be authentic texts (see, further, below).

As a result of Britain's accession, the European Court of Justice (ECJ) ranks above the House of Lords as the ultimate court. However, this is only so in disputes involving Community law and Community generated law. Thus, the ECJ is, for the most part, a 'court of reference' rather than a Court of Appeal, which means that it deals primarily with questions relating to the interpretation and validity of Community law. It will, therefore, still be up to the national courts and tribunals to apply the interpretations handed down by the ECJ. The House of Lords remains the final Court of Appeal in Britain in internal, domestic cases.

By virtue of the United Kingdom European Communities Act 1972 (the Act), Britain has adopted the provisions of the Community Treaties, but has not adopted either a strict monist approach (leaving the courts and administration to work out the exact implications of the Treaties) or a highly specific dualist one (that is, by detailing precisely the changes that will take place in United Kingdom law under the Treaties). It has chosen a middle line and opted for flexibility rather than rigidity.

Generally, under s 2(1) of the Act, European Community law, whether arising from the Treaties or from Community Regulations, and whether such law has already been made or is to be made in the future, is to take direct effect in the United Kingdom without the need for the United Kingdom Parliament to pass a statute each time. Hence, it recognises the principle that the Treaties should determine the extent of these rights in the United Kingdom and permits the direct enforcement of these rights in the United Kingdom.

In addition, under s 2(4) of the Act, 'any enactment' (and this is wide enough to include a statutory instrument as well as a statute) passed, or to be passed, in the United Kingdom must be construed with directly applicable Community law in mind. Hence, there appears to be a presumption that United Kingdom statute law is to be read subject to European Community law. Thus, if there is a conflict between European Community law and domestic English law, Community law will override domestic law wherever the former is directly applicable. Recent cases appear to confirm the supremacy of Community law over domestic or municipal law (*Duke v GEC Reliance Ltd* [1988] 1 All ER 626; *Factortame Ltd v Secretary of State for Transport (No 1)* [1989] 2 All ER 692; *Factortame Ltd v Secretary for Transport (No 2)* [1991] 1 All ER 70; *Kirklees Borough Council v Wickes Building Supplies Ltd* [1991] 4 All ER 240).

It should be noted that all these above cited cases are House of Lords decisions, apart form the last which is a Court of Appeal decision. In *Duke v GEC Reliance Ltd* (see above), the House of Lords affirmed their previous position that they will not deliberately misconstrue the meaning of a United Kingdom statute in order to enforce against an individual a Community Directive which has no direct effect between individuals. Section 2(4), in the words of Lord Templeman (p 636), with whom the other Law Lords expressly agreed: 'Section 2(4) applies and only applies where Community provisions are directly applicable.'

The European Communities Act 1972 does not expressly forbid Parliament from amending or repealing that Act itself and, indeed, under the constitutional doctrine of constitutional supremacy, the 1972 Act could be repealed. Until that happens, the 1972 Act provides a legislative bridge which links Community law to English law, so that those provisions of Community law which it requires to become part of the national legal system automatically become part of the United Kingdom legal system, in accordance with the definition of its meaning and effect laid down by Community law.

Recently, the European Court gave an affirmative answer to the question which the House of Lords referred to it, which was:

Under Community law, must a national court ignore its own national law and provide interim relief for a person with directly enforceable Community law rights, who would otherwise suffer irreversible damage because of delay in having those rights determined?

In *Factortame Ltd v Secretary of State for Transport (No 2)* [1991] 1 All ER 70, the ECJ not only replied in the affirmative, but further stressed that, under Community law, a national law (whether legislative, judicial or administrative in character) must be set aside by a national court, if it prevents the application of Community law.

Since this decision, the late Lord Denning has criticised the impact of Community law upon English law, departing considerably from his famous 1974 *dictum* of the 'incoming tide' of Community law which could not be held back, by describing it as a 'tidal wave bringing down sea walls and flowing inland' over British fields and houses, 'to everyone's dismay' ((1990) *The Independent*, 16 July). He called for the amendment of the 1972 Act and suggested that European Court decisions and Community Directives should only be binding if they are approved by, respectively, the House of Lords and the relevant British Government minister.

However, in the *Factortame (No 2)* case (at pp 107–08) (above), Lord Bridge said that criticisms of the European Court were based on a 'misconception' and that:

... there was nothing novel in according supremacy to rules of Community law in those areas to which they apply, and to insist that, in the protection of rights under Community law, national courts must not be inhibited, by rules of national law, from granting interim relief in appropriate cases [which is what was done in the case itself because of the two year wait which had to be undergone, before an ECJ ruling could be procured] is no more than a logical recognition of that supremacy.

In April 1998, the English Court of Appeal held that breaches of EC law by the United Kingdom (under the Merchant Shipping Act 1988 (the 1988 Act)) were sufficiently serious to give rise to liability for damage caused (see *R v Secretary of State for Transport ex p Factortame Ltd and Others (No 5)* [1998] 3 CMLR 192). The applicants were Spanish trawler owners and managers and had succeeded in establishing, before the UK courts and the European Court of Justice, that the 1988 Act, which precluded those who did not meet its criteria from registering to fish, was illegal and that the UK had, therefore, breached EC law. The Court of Appeal held that the various provisions of the 1988 Act discriminated against citizens of other Member States of the European Community. There was a liability to pay damages, but not exemplary damages.

In the light of these recent developments, Community law, for the moment, retains its primacy over domestic legislation and only time will tell if it will be eventually truly integrated into English law.

THE SINGLE EUROPEAN ACT 1986

Various other treaties and amendments have been agreed upon and passed, but proposals to move towards this 'ever closer union' have had a stormy reception. The 1980s experienced further attempts to revive the sense of excitement and adventure which existed in the 1960s and, despite attempts to devise a thoroughgoing reform of the original Rome Treaty, in fact, the EC heads of government met in Luxembourg and agreed only to various amendments to the Rome Treaty, which constituted the Single European Act 1986. Under this Act, which came into force on 1 July 1987, its signatories pledge themselves to establishing progressively a single market (that is, a complete free internal market between Member States) over a period expiring on 31 December 1992. The Act defines a single market as 'an area without internal frontiers in which the free movement of goods, persons, services and capital is ensured in accordance with the provisions of this Treaty'.

The Act also seeks to assist the free movement of goods by, *inter alia*, breaking down technical barriers (for example, different national product standards), national restrictions and subsidy policies. It also aims to expedite EC decision making by extending majority voting to most major areas of the single market programme, which replaces the unanimous voting requirements which applied before the Act took effect. It therefore amends the EEC Treaty so as to provide a clear legal authority for Community programmes on economic and monetary policy, social policy, research and technical development, and the environment. It further states as an aim of the Treaty the achievement of a common foreign policy, and encompasses the political co-operation procedures within the scope of the Treaty, which is another innovation.

The Single European Act (SEA) represents an important commitment to the achievement of a single market, but it is clear that its future success is by no means assured. Apart from nationalistic antipathy, the drafters of the SEA did not appear to have given a great deal of thought to the implications of grafting amendments onto a dynamic and living legal system, which has already been shaped and formed by case law from the European Court of Justice. This, in itself, will conceivably pose not inconsiderable problems of interpretation for Member States and for European Community administrative and judicial bodies.

THE INSTITUTIONAL FRAMEWORK OF THE COMMUNITY

The legislative and judicial machinery of the EC consists of four main 'institutions' which are: the Council of Ministers, the Commission, the European Parliament (EP) and the European Court of Justice (ECJ). These have been set up under the following Treaties: ECSC (Art 7), EEC (Art 3), Euratom (Arts 1 and 9), the Merger Treaty and the Convention on Certain Institutions Common to the European Communities (Arts 1, 2(1), 3 and 4(1)). The first three are political institutions. These four institutions carry out political, legislative, executive and judicial functions of the Community and have jurisdiction over all the Member States. They are autonomous, and independent of Member States. So, are they really different from traditional international organisations?

EC institutions and traditional international organisations

At first glance, the EC institutions appear to be very similar to a traditional international organisation, such as the Organisation for Economic Co-operation and Development (OECD) or the North Atlantic Treaty Organisation (NATO). For example, those sorts of bodies have also been created by multilateral treaties, possess a distinct legal personality and act through the agency of institutions created and regulated in accordance with the terms of the parent treaty. However, several comparative comments may be made on the general nature of EC institutions. First, they do not correspond to the classic 'separation of powers' format, because, for instance, the EP (formerly 'the Assembly'), as it has been known since 1962, is primarily a consultative body and has no power to affect the content of legislation, but is merely to be consulted on proposed legislation in many, but not all, cases. The EP's powers of consultation were increased by the co-operation procedure introduced by the Single European Act (see below). In practice, the Council is the dominant force in the Community and the progress of the Community is usually determined by the speed at which the Member States, thereof, act to pursue or promote proposals or resolve difficulties.

Secondly, another unique feature of the institutions is that they are involved with, and often exert a considerable degree of regulatory control over, matters which have traditionally been within the exclusive jurisdiction of individual States. Their capacity to make rules which are directly and automatically binding, not just on the Member States, but also on individuals and corporate bodies within those States, make them *sui generis* and endowed with a supranational character since, in so doing, they are unlike any conventional institutional organisation.

Thirdly, the EC institutions were conceived of as a collaborative enterprise and must, therefore, be analysed in their 'team' context.

Finally, it should be noted that, unlike other international institutions, they were created with the primary goal of European political integration and, as such, the European Court of Justice even makes its decisions with the goal of European integration in mind.

The Council of Ministers

This is composed of Ministers from the Member States' governments (Art 2 of the Merger Treaty) and is a collegiate body of the Community which advises and supervises the Commission on many important areas of decision making under the ECSC Treaty. It has been described as the Community's 'decision making body' which takes the final decision on most EEC legislation, concludes agreements with foreign countries and, in conjunction with the Parliament, decides on the Community budget. However, the Council does not possess the requisite administrative machinery to put these decisions into practice. The actual implementation of decisions is, therefore, carried out by the Commission.

The Minister who usually represents a Member State is its Foreign Minister, but this may be varied and specialist Ministers frequently represent their countries, depending on the subject matter being discussed. The Council possesses legislative powers under the EEC and Euratom Treaties and has responsibility for the co-ordination of Member States' economic policies, but it basically agrees legislation based on the proposals put forward by the Commission.

The office of President of the Council is held on a strict rota basis and determined alphabetically, and it is only held for six months per presidency. This means that each State will hold the presidency at least once every six years.

The Treaty prescribes three methods of decision making:

(a) simple majority: Art 148 of the EEC Treaty states this as the norm; at least seven members must vote in favour;

(b) qualified majority: Art 148(2) sets out a system of weighted voting based on the population of Member States; the largest countries, United Kingdom, France, Germany and Italy have 10 votes each, Spain has eight and so on; and

(c) unanimity, which is prescribed by a large number of Articles, for example, in relation to admission of new members, and the provisions dealing with supplementary legislative powers. Despite this elaborate voting procedure, the vast majority of decisions are taken by consensus.

The Single European Act extended the applicability of the qualified majority voting procedure, especially with regard to matters dealing with the internal market, and this has expedited decision making.

The heads of government of the Member States have met regularly for a number of years as the 'European Council', but this body must not be confused with the Council of Ministers which we have just been discussing. This European Council had no formal recognition in the original Treaty, but has always had a wide agenda which did not confine itself to matters within the scope of the Treaty, but dealt with matters of general policy, and left its conclusions to be consolidated by the Commission and the Council of Ministers via the normal legislative process. It has evolved into 'the most politically authoritative institution' of the Community (Bulmer and Wessels, *The European Council* (1987) p 2). Article 2 of the Single European Act 1986 gave official recognition to the existence of the European Council, but did not make it an official institution as was envisaged by the draft of the EP. Article 2 also describes neither the functions nor the powers of the Council, and this perhaps emphasises the informal nature of the Council and its flexibility.

Each Council meeting deals with a particular area of policy and, since 1975, the Council has met, on average, three times a year, primarily to break deadlocks in negotiations which it has done several times. Article 2 of the Single European Act stipulates that the Council shall meet at least twice a year and, in the view of some commentators, this indicates the intention of the parties to return the responsibility for taking important decisions to the other major institutions. The deliberations of this Council are specifically excluded from the jurisdiction of the ECJ (Art 30) which means their decision will not be legally enforceable under Community law.

The European Commission

This is the body that proposes EC policy and legislation, and consists of 17 members. All must be nationals of a Member State, one at least from each State. It carries out decisions taken by the Council and supervises the day to day implementation of Community policies. It also negotiates agreements between the EC and non-EC countries. Of the 17, there are two each from France, Germany, Italy, Spain and the United Kingdom, one each from Belgium, Denmark, Greece, Ireland, Luxembourg, The Netherlands and Portugal. Commissioners are appointed unanimously by the Council for four year terms. Each Commissioner, upon appointment, renounces national allegiance and gives a solemn undertaking to be completely independent in the performance of duties and not to seek or take instructions from any government or any other body. As such, they are appointed to act not as national delegates, but in the interests of the Community as a whole. Each Commissioner is in charge of an area of Community policy and formulates proposals, within that area, aimed at implementing the Treaties.

The powers and functions of the Commission are set out in fairly broad terms in Art 155:

(a) The Commission shall ensure that the treaty provisions and the measures taken by the institutions pursuant, thereto, are applied.

This is the policing function of the Commission, which involves detecting breaches of Community law (Art 213 gives supervisory powers to collect necessary information and to carry out necessary checks). It also gives the

Commission primary responsibility for taking legal action against Member States in breach of the Treaty, the most common procedure being under Art 169. Under this provision, a Member State is given maximum opportunity to remedy an infringement before being taken to court by the Commission. The other key area where EC policy 'bites' is in the enforcement of its rules against individuals and corporations in competition policy, where violations of the Treaty's competition provisions, under Arts 85 and 86, may be punished by substantial fines. Article 86 deals with 'abuse of dominant position' (see below).

(b) The Commission shall formulate recommendations and deliver opinions on matters dealt with by the Treaty, if it expressly so provides or if the Commission considers it necessary.

Although recommendations and opinions have no binding force, this forms a major part of the Commission's work to sustain the spirit of integration and provide institutional relations.

(c) The Commission shall have its own power of decision and participate in the shaping of measures taken by the Council and the Assembly (now the EP) in the manner provided for by the Treaty.

It should be remembered that the main method of legislation is for the Council to act on a proposal of the Commission. However, the right of participation in the legislative process, and to be physically present at meetings of the EP, is possibly the most important feature of the Commission's role as promoter of integration. The Commission has the right to amend its proposals at any time before they are adopted by the Council. The Commission's view must also be sought formally by the Council before the latter may be allowed to act on the issue in question.

(d) The Commission shall exercise the powers conferred upon it by the Council for the implementation of the rules laid down by the Council.

As has been pointed out, although the Council is styled as the primary decision making body, it lacks the administrative machinery to transform decisions into practice. Hence, this particular function is the task of the Commission, which broadly carries out: (a) administrative tasks; and (b) legislative tasks.

Included under administrative functions will be the supervision of policies, the power to grant exemptions, investigate complaints and impose fines, a chief example of which is in the area of competition law. Within the second category of tasks is the detailed implementation of policy by secondary or subordinate legislation, particularly in relation to agriculture policy.

The European Parliament

This was originally called the Assembly, and is a directly elected body with 518 members, which exercises political control over the Community. There are 81 members from the United Kingdom. It possesses consultative and advisory functions. Its name was officially changed by Art 3(1) of the Single European Act. The Commission is accountable to the European Parliament (EP). As mentioned above, this Parliament does not have any legislative functions as such, but two relatively recent innovations have improved its position:

(a) A new conciliation procedure may now be initiated at the request of the EP in order to reach agreement between itself and the Council, if the Council intends to depart from the opinion of the EP.

(b) Articles 6 and 7 of the Single European Act, provide for a 'co-operation procedure' between Council and the EP in the passage of certain types of legislation, and requires the assent of Parliament, by an absolute majority of its members, to the admission of new Member States and to association agreements with non-member countries.

The co-operation procedure applies to legislation under 10 Articles including Art 7 (elimination of discrimination on grounds of nationality); Art 49 (free movement of workers); and Art 118a (protection of the working environment). When it applies, the legislative procedure will proceed in the usual way (and include the consultation of Parliament) until the stage when the Council would normally be ready to accept the act in question. At this point, instead of doing so, the Council will adopt, by qualified (that is, weighted) majority, a 'common position'. This common position will then be communicated to the EP together with a full statement of reasons which led the Council to adopt it, and a statement of the Commission's position. The EP will then have three months to decide how to act. It can approve or reject the common position, or propose amendments to it. If the EP approves the common position, or fails to make a decision, the Council will adopt the act in accordance with the common position. However, if the EP rejects the common position, the Council must be unanimous in order to pass the legislation at its second reading. The Council must act within three months or the proposal is deemed not to have been adopted.

If the EP proposes amendments, the Commission has one month within which to re-examine its proposal in the light of the proposed amendments. It has the option of adopting some or all of the amendments, but is not obliged to do so. The Commission then sends the proposal to the Council whether or not it has agreed to adopt the EP's amendments.

The Council may then either accept the proposal as amended by the Commission, for which a qualified majority will be sufficient, or it can amend it either by accepting amendments proposed by the Parliament, but rejected by the Commission, or by adopting amendments of its own. In the latter two cases, the Council must be unanimous if it wishes to pass the legislation.

Ultimately, the new procedure merely charges the Commission with a legal obligation to consider the EP's proposals and to give reasons if it rejects them. The centre of power and decision making has not really shifted.

The European Court of Justice

The Court of Justice of the European Communities, which is the full title of the European Court of Justice (ECJ), was set up by the ECSC Treaty to ensure that the law would be observed in the interpretation and application of the Treaties (Art 164 of the EEC Treaty). It is the fourth institution of the Community, and has a number of functions to fulfil. It is required to act as an international court (Art 170), an administrative court (Arts 173–76, 178, 184), a civil court (Art 215), an administrative tribunal (Art 179) and as a transnational constitutional court (Art 177).

Composition and organisation

There are 13 judges in the ECJ and six Advocates General who are appointed by 'common accord', which means they are unanimously elected by the governments of the Member States. That procedure strongly affirms the concept that the Court is one of the institutions of the Community. The judges hold office for a renewable term of six terms and three Advocates General are replaced or re-elected every three years. The independence of the judges is guaranteed by the Treaty and the rules of procedure contained in the Statute of the Court (which is a protocol to the original Treaties). It is based on three procedural principles:

(a) their deliberations are secret;

(b) judgments are reached by majority vote; and

(c) judgments are signed by all the judges who have taken part in the proceedings, although dissenting opinions are not published. This is certainly unlike most national courts (in the common law jurisdictions) and other international courts.

The President of the Court, who holds office for a three year renewable period, is appointed by the judges themselves by an absolute majority vote in a secret ballot.

According to Art 166 of the EEC Treaty, the function of the Advocates General is to act 'with complete impartiality and independence, to make, in open court, reasoned submissions on cases brought before the Court, in order to assist the Court in the performance of the tasks assigned to it'. These legal officers have no direct counterpart either in common or civil law, and their duties should not be equated with those of a public prosecutor or similar kind of functionary in a French court. The Government Commissioners (*Commissaires du Gouvernement*) of the French Conseil d'État is the closest civil law analogy, but they are not allowed to act independently and are specifically obliged to confer and deliberate with the conseillers (d'État) or senior ranking members of the Conseil d'État.

Several weeks after the lawyers have addressed the Court, there is a separate hearing in which the Advocate General will comment on the salient points of the case, weigh up the provisions of Community law, compare the case with previous ruling and propose a legal solution to the dispute. Thus, there is the influence of both civil and common law traditions (see, further, 'The influence of French law', 'The influence of German law' and 'The influence of common law tradition', pp 158, 160 and 161, below). The Court is not bound to follow the advice or opinion of the Advocate General and has been known to even reject them explicitly. In any event, the Advocate General does not participate in the deliberations of the Court and the opinions of the Advocates General have been an important source of the ECJ's jurisprudence.

The Court's powers

All the Treaties establishing the European Communities use the same formula to define the specific responsibilities of the ECJ, namely, to 'ensure that, in the interpretation and application of this Treaty, the law is observed'. Thus, the Court interprets and applies the whole body of Community law, from the basic Treaties, to the various implementing Regulations, Directives and Decisions issued by the Council and the Commission. However, the Court only has the power to interpret or rule on the validity of provisions of national law when an individual case arises concerning the failure of a Member State to fulfil an obligation. In this type of case, it will rule on the relationship of national law to Community law. On rare occasions, the Court may also be asked to apply and interpret national law in disputes involving contracts to which the Community is a party.

The ECJ is the Community's supreme judicial authority. Since the Treaties establishing the various Communities could not possibly cover every possible eventuality, the gaps that have appeared in the legal framework have been ably and aptly filled by the ECJ. However, it has also had a heavy workload, and so the Single European Act has made provision for the establishment of a Court of First Instance to be attached to the ECJ, which will have jurisdiction over a limited range of cases. A point that has been commented upon with regard to the ECJ is that there is no appeal from its judgments. Once the Court of First Instance is established, there will be a right of appeal on points of law to the European Court from the Court of First Instance.

The ECJ does not have any inherent jurisdiction, but only such jurisdiction as has been conferred on it by the Treaties. Case law has indicated that any attribution to the ECJ of jurisdiction outside the Treaties will fail. A case would need to be brought within one of the specified heads of jurisdiction before the Court could hear it. Recourse to the Court is relatively simple, but a fundamental distinction is drawn between (a) judgments; and (b) advisory opinions and rulings.

As far as judgments are concerned, there are two types of basic actions which may be initiated: (a) a direct action, which involves disputes between parties and which begins in the European Court; and (b) requests to the European Court for preliminary rulings, which are actions begun in a national court and which take the form of questions put to the ECJ by national judges.

If an action is begun in the European Court, it will end in the European Court, so that the Court's judgment will represent a final determination of the dispute between the parties, the Court will grant any appropriate remedies and the judgment (at least, until the First Instance Court is established) will not be subject to appeal. But, if a national court commences the action, it will, accordingly, end in a national court because the ruling of the ECJ will be transmitted to that court, which will then itself decide the case.

Direct actions may be divided into two main categories: (a) those in which there is an agreement between the parties, which gives the Court jurisdiction; and (b) those in which the Court has jurisdiction by operation of law. Applications in the first category are uncommon in practice and mainly concern actions arising out of a contract concluded by the Community, which contains a clause that gives the ECJ jurisdiction.

In the second category, actions may be further subdivided into cases in which: (a) the action is against the Community; or (b) the action is against a Member State.

Actions against the Community include: (a) proceedings for 'annulment' (judicial review); (b) plenary jurisdiction proceedings, which include:

(a) actions for damages for non-contractual liability (tort);

(b) appeals against penalties imposed on private individuals for violations of Community law; and

(c) actions brought by Community officials against the institution employing them.

The EEC Treaty adopts the philosophy that neither the legislature nor the executive are above the law of the Treaty, and has made the ECJ the supreme arbiter of the law. It has, therefore, introduced Arts 173 and 174, which are a form of judicial review. These Arts allow the ECJ, in specified circumstances, to review the legality of, and declare void, an act of the Council or Commission. As Brown and Jacobs (1983) have noted, the 'decisions of the

Court of Justice cannot be reversed by an act of the Council; on the contrary, any measure of the Council having legal effect can be annulled by the Court if contrary to the Treaties' (Brown and Jacobs, *The Court of Justice of the European Communities* (1983) pp 32–34). Of course, the Treaties also set out the limits of the powers of review of the ECJ.

The Treaty, therefore, talks in terms of 'review' and 'annulment' rather than 'judicial review' or declarations or injunctions. Actions may be brought for review of (a) Community acts; (b) failure to act or to fulfil obligations; and (c) actions may also be brought to dispute the legality of a Community Regulation.

Article 173(1) describes the four grounds on which an act (other than recommendations and opinions) may be annulled:

(a) lack of competence, which corresponds to the English legal concept of substantive *ultra vires*, alleging the Council or Commission have acted outside their authority;

(b) infringement of essential procedural requirements, which is similar to the English concept of procedural *ultra vires*, but the ECJ appear to take a much more active role than English courts in striking down decisions, for instance, on the ground of failure to give reasons for EC decisions;

(c) infringement of this Treaty or any rule of law relating to its application, which constitutes the most important ground, and somewhat overlaps with the previous two grounds. Its generality has made it the most used ground in annulment actions. Apart from procedural and substantive irregularity in procedure, the 'rule of law' limb of this ground has been used by the ECJ to develop a unique blend of European administrative law, on the basis that case law has established that there are certain 'general principles of law' which are widely recognised, and which underpin the Community legal order, and against which the legality of Community acts must be measured (see *Stauder v City of Ulm*, Case 29/69 [1969] ECR 419). This particular legal method is discussed further in our subsequent consideration of the Community legal order as a whole and its legal techniques (see, further, 'Community techniques of legal interpretation', p 169, below). A highly topical and important area of development has been in the field of human rights.

In *Stauder* itself (see above), it was clearly stated by the ECJ that, although the EEC Treaty made no specific mention of human rights, there were 'fundamental human rights enshrined in the general principles of Community law and protected by the Court'. This was echoed in *Internationale Handelsgesellschaft v Einfuhr und Vorratsstelle für Getriede und Futtermittel* [1970] ECR 1125, when the ECJ reiterated that there was a guarantee of human rights inherent in Community law, and that respect for human rights is 'an integral part of the general principles of law protected by the Court of Justice'. The principles which English law refers to as 'rules of natural justice', namely, the need for an absence of bias and *audi alterem partem* (hear the other side), have also been culled by the ECJ and used in other cases;

(d) misuse of powers: this ground derives from the French *detournement de pouvoir*, for which there is no precise analogy in English law, and involves the use of a legitimate power in an illegitimate manner or for an illegitimate purpose. It has now been overtaken by ground (c), above, in contrast to its early days when it used to be the sole ground for complaint in the ECSC Treaty.

Article 175 grants a remedy for a wrongful failure to act 'in infringement of [the] Treaty' on the part of the Council or the Commission, but there are at least two differences between this Article and Art 173, which it appears to resemble. First, proceedings cannot be brought under Art 175 unless a request for action has been sent by the complainant to the defendant. The defendant then has two months to comply and the action may then be brought within the following two months. Secondly, there is only one ground of complaint here whereas there are four under Art 173. However, although it seems clear that there must have been an infringement of a provision which imposed an obligation to act, it is not clear whether Art 175 can be extended to 'any rule of law relating to the application of the Treaty' which could apply to Community legislation or, indeed, whether it might further be extended to include infringement of a 'general principle of law'. These matters may well need to be resolved by the ECJ in the not too distant future.

Actions for damages may be brought by either a Member State or a private individual, and the applicant is required to prove that he has suffered loss as a result of Community action. In the case of contractual liability, where it is alleged that the Community is in breach of contractual obligations, the applicable law will be the law governing the contract, and the case may be heard by the national court or by the ECJ if the parties so decide.

In actions for non-contractual liability which have a five year time bar from the date the damage was suffered, the Community must 'make good any damage caused by its institutions or by its servants in the performance of their duties' in accordance with 'the general principles common to the laws of the Member States'. Case law in this area suggests that, before the Community will be liable for damages, there must be a sufficiently serious ('manifest and grave') violation of a superior rule of law intended for the protection of the individual (see *Zuckerfabrik Schoppenstedt v Council* [1971] ECR 175). There has been some controversy over the meaning of what is 'manifest and grave', but the current position appears to require that the complainant prove that both the extent of the loss and the degree of the Community's violation were manifest and grave, in other words, sufficiently serious to warrant compensation (see *Amylum v Council and Commission*, Cases 116 and 124/77 [1979] ECR 3497; and *Koninklijke Scholten-Honig v Council and Commission* [1979] ECR 3583).

With regard to actions against Member States, there are two methods whereby such actions may be taken against any Member State 'which fails to fulfil an obligation under [the] Treaty'. Article 169 of the EEC Treaty allows the Commission to initiate such an action, or a Member State may do so under Art 170 of the EEC Treaty. Thus, the Commission, as guardian of the Treaties and of the decisions taken by the institutions, may initiate proceedings for failure to fulfil an obligation. If it considers that a Member State, in some aspect of its administration, has not honoured a Community obligation, it will ask the Member State to make its comments on that view; after receiving that State's observations, or even if it has not received them, it will then issue a 'reasoned opinion', which will set out the reasons for the allegation and set a time limit, for the rectification of the situation, which is usually six months, but which may be shorter in more urgent cases. If the State does not act on the opinion within the stipulated time, the Commission may take the matter to the ECJ.

A Member State may also initiate this procedure after notifying the Commission and, again, the Commission will ask the Member State, against which the breach is alleged, to respond, after which it will issue its reasoned opinion. If the Commission does not produce the opinion within three months from the date of the request, the matter may be directly referred to the Court.

The ECJ may, if it agrees that the case is well founded, make a declaratory judgment stating that the obligation has not been fulfilled, which appears to be the only sanction, although Art 171 of the EEC Treaty states that the State is 'required to take the necessary measures to comply with the judgment'. There are no penalties available to enforce the ECJ ruling. In practice, it appears that Member States generally comply with the Commission opinions either before the proceedings are commenced, or during the course of proceedings, and the Commission tends to withdraw the case once the State has complied with the opinion. It would appear that the majority of Member States regard the declaratory judgment as a sufficient public and recorded blemish against them, and seek to avoid it. In the unusual event that a State refuses to comply, the Commission has the power to initiate a second action based on Art 171, and a declaration should be obtained stating that the first decision has not been complied with. Among the subjects of the actions, which have been taken against most of the Member States at some stage or other, have been customs duties and charges, and the ongoing Anglo-French saga involving fishery legislation.

The ECJ's role is somewhat limited in the context of the preliminary reference procedure since it merely seems to rule on an abstract point of law, leaving the national court to decide relevant issues of fact, and to apply the law – albeit as interpreted by the ECJ – to those facts.

Nevertheless, this particular procedure (provided by Art 177) maintains an extremely important link between Community and Member State because it affects the relationship between Community law and national law. By determining the scope of rights and obligations of private citizens in Member States, as laid down and interpreted under Community law, the ECJ is directly applying Community law within the Member States. Through this procedure, similar to the civil law practice of referring to the national constitutional court to ensure uniformity and conformity with the constitution, the Treaty seeks to ensure uniformity of application of Community law in all the national legal systems. Article 177 references were expressly stated to be heard by a full Court in plenary session, and not by a Chamber of the Court (Art 165(2)), but the sheer volume of applications invoking this procedure has forced the ECJ to abandon the initial requirement and hear such cases in Chambers.

Article 177 has, therefore, been called 'an instrument of transnational law' (Pescatore, 'Legal problems of an enlarged European Community', in Bathurst *et al* (eds) (1972)) and the ECJ has also been called a 'transnational constitutional court' drawing an analogy between the EEC Treaty and a written constitution (see Stein, 'Lawyers, judges and the making of a transnational constitution' (1981) 81 AJIL 1).

The role of the ECJ in this context is to provide an interpretation of the law, not apply it, since the latter function is the task of the national court, although Art 177 also permits the ECJ to rule on the validity of Community legislation. In certain cases, the ECJ has found it difficult not to transgress into the area of application of Community law. In such cases, the Court has managed to reformulate the question asked, so as to bring it within their jurisdictional competence. Hence, it is through this preliminary reference procedure that the ECJ has established the twin doctrines of direct effect and the supremacy of Community law over national law (see, further, 'Direct applicability and direct affect', and 'Supremacy of Community law', pp 165 and 168, below).

DIFFICULTIES IN COMPARISON

In the light of its complex institutional structure and its unique legal character, it is not easy to find a ready basis for comparison of the European Community with other political or legal entities. The Community contains features of other ordinary international organisations and, of course, the Treaty is an agreement governed by international law. However, the Community structure also contains features of federalism, which are most prominent with regard to the judicial and legal system, but rather weak in matters such as legislative and executive powers, taxation, defence and monetary issues. The reasons for this are rooted in history and the objective of creating a United States of Europe consisting of some form of European federation. Hence, the Community has hybrid features which must be kept in mind when examining its legal configuration. Its political organs, the Council, the Commission and the

Parliament, each contain international and 'federalist' features (see Hartley (1986)). A typical international organisation is a form of intergovernmental co-operation which operates on the basis of consent, so that no Member State may be bound without its consent.

Yet, Community law is said to be binding on the Member States, as well as on individuals, in many cases, and applicable by national or domestic courts. Further, Community decisions derive their force from the fact that they are taken by organs which have been given the power by the Community's constitution – the Treaties.

They do not, therefore, derive their power from the fact of consent by the Member States. This is why the Community legal order is sometimes described as supranational. However, case law from the European Court of Justice suggests that individual Member States are not necessarily bound by Community law, unless various implementation measures are enacted, and it will also depend on the nature of the legislation involved, and its date of implementation. In practical terms, the United Kingdom has generally proceeded to amend the legislation or law in question, so as to be in accord with the European Court's rulings, whenever national legislation has been called into question, on questions of discrimination at work or human rights issues involving access to children in care.

Community law has, of course, emanated from the civil law systems. As such, it has adopted some of the typically civil law judicial, administrative and legislative styles. It is on the basis of comparing the particular 'juristic style' of Community law with that of common law and civil law parent systems that the discussion now proceeds.

COMPARISON OF LEGAL STYLE OF COMMUNITY LAW WITH OTHER SYSTEMS

As we have seen in Chapter 2, the juristic style of a particular legal system (as suggested by writers like Zweigert and Kotz) may be determined by an examination of the following factors:

(a) its historical background and development;

(b) its characteristic mode of thought in legal matters;

(c) its distinctive institutions;

(d) the types of sources it acknowledges and its treatment of these;

(e) its ideology.

When we examine the historical antecedents of Community law, we see that its modern beginnings may be traced to the post-war sense of helplessness and fear of survival which was felt by European nations involved in the two global conflicts, coupled with the rise of power of America, on whom the West was growing increasingly dependent, and the rise of the Soviet Union and China as Communist superpowers. However, as we have seen, the common law of England was shaped by the powerful centralisation of courts and its visionary kings, judges and Statesmen; and the legal configuration of the modern civil law, although initially derived from Roman law and customary law in France and Germany, was determined by its rebirth in the Italian universities, the French Revolution and the German Pandectists.

Since civil law was the legacy of the European nations that first entered into the EEC Treaty of Rome, it is the European 'continental' legal style, specifically the French tradition, that the Community has adopted in its court structure and administration of justice, and, before the German and common law tradition made themselves felt, in the interpretation of codes, statutes and rules of procedure. In the 1980s, however, two further influences have started to make their way into Community law via the judgments of the European Court of Justice: the German legal approach and the English legal style (see below).

As has been stated time and again, history and law are generally inseparable and history clearly leaves its footprints in the shifting sands of legal opinions, legal literature and legal discourse.

Unlike common law jurisdictions, which have a case law orientated system, despite their increasing reliance on statutory law, many civil law countries, particularly France and Germany, approach legal problems in terms of general concepts and principles which are predominantly, but not exclusively, contained in its codes and statutes. European Community law has adopted and adapted a number of different legal styles, beginning with the French style then the German approach, in its earlier phase when there were only six in the Community; then, with the enlargement of the Community, it has slowly started to rely on previously decided case law in the style of the common law and has even begun to develop its own version of *stare decisis* (see Koopmans (1991)).

The influence of French law

In the modern period, a great deal of the continental and predominantly French legal ethos, ranging from sitting as a group or team of judges and delivering a collegial or collective judgment, to being permitted to consult travaux préparatoires and other extraneous aids to statutory or legislative interpretation, is evident in the judgments of the European Court of Justice (ECJ). However, one need not have looked far to see the initial influence of French administrative law, particularly in the period when there was only a Community of six.

For instance, take Art 173 of the EEC Treaty, dealing with provisions on actions for the annulment of Community decisions. This Article, *inter alia*, permits a natural or legal person to institute proceedings against a decision addressed to him. It confers jurisdiction on the Court to review the legality of acts of the Council and the Commission other than 'recommendations' or 'opinions', and Art 173(1) enables parties to attack a Community act on any one of four grounds: lack of competence; infringement of an essential procedural requirement; infringement of the Treaty or of any rule of law relating to its application; or misuse of powers.

These four terms are borrowed from French administrative law and the grounds of annulment are similar to those developed by the French Conseil d'État as forms of *'excès de pouvoir'*, which leads to annulment, in French administrative law. However, case law from the ECJ suggests that, despite their origin, and the fact that they are terms of art with definite meanings, they are now terms of Community law and must be taken in that context alone ([1957–58] ECR 133). Indeed, the ECJ has developed these terms far beyond the parameters of the French concepts.

Even more historically illuminating is the influence of the French administrative legal tradition generally on even the basic structure and legal philosophy of the Community institutions. For instance, among the draftsmen of the first Treaty of Paris was M Maurice Legrange ,who was one of the first Advocates General at the European Court. In a very real sense, one can see the link between the development of the French Conseil d'État and its pre-eminent position in France, and the creation of the ECJ. It was in Art 12 of the Law of August 1790 that it was stated that 'judicial functions are distinct and will always remain separate from administrative functions. Judges in the civil courts may not ... concern themselves in any manner whatsoever with the operation of the administration'. Read within the context of the history of the *ancien régime*, we then see a clear recognition of the necessity for a check on the unlimited power of the administrator. To this end, the Conseil d'État was set up in 1799 and, through a body of case law, has established rules by which the executive must regulate their affairs, so as to promote effective administration and protect the individual. If one bears in mind the fundamental division between public and private law in civil law countries and in the first six Community countries, one sees that the whole concept of judicial control over administration unites the laws of civil law countries within the Community since, 'from an ideological standpoint, all have been powerfully influenced by the French Revolution and Empire, and by the *liberalisme bourgeois* of the 19th century' (Auby and Fromont, *Les Recours contre les Actes Administratifs* (1971) p 449, cited and translated by Mackenzie-Stuart, in *The European Communities and the Rule of Law* (1977)).

Another sign of the French influence, apart from the concise single collective judgment, was the individual advisory opinion of the Advocate General which precedes the judgment, which finds its provenance in French law, in the Cour de Cassation, the Supreme Court in private law and criminal court. A similar function is performed in the Conseil d'État by the *Commissaire du Gouvernement* (Government Commissioner) although, unlike his counterpart with the same appellation in the other administrative courts, this official is not a member of the Conseil d'État at all, but is a senior civil servant who represents governments and is responsible for putting forward government views and projects. In France, at that level, he is a ministerial spokesman.

Of course, the fact that other members of the six included Belgium and Luxembourg, who have legal systems very similar to the French, and Italy, whose legal system is closer to the French style than any other, explains why the French influence was so dominant, and this was also noticeable in the style of legal reasoning, which was deductive and pitched at a high level of abstraction (Koopmans (1991)).

The influence of German law

However, the impact of the German legal tradition soon began to appear in the ECJ's case law. In accordance with the Court's attempts to identify general legal principles, one of the principles so earmarked was the principle of proportionality, derived from German administrative law, which is that administrative action should be proportionate to the ends that it seeks to achieve (Verhaltnismassigkeit). This had been fully developed in German law, but has now become an established part of Community law (see Art 30 of the EEC Treaty). The principle was illustrated in the famous German beer case (*Commission v FRG*, Case 178/84 [1987] ECR 1227), which dealt with 16th century German legislation on beer purity. This legislation required beer to be made from a limited number of natural ingredients, and had the incidental effect of preventing beers made in other Member States, which contained various additives or preservatives, from being sold in Germany. The basic issue was whether the German legislation could be regarded as fulfilling the mandatory requirements of protection of health or protection of consumers. On the first question, the Commission could show that all the preservatives or additives at issue were permitted under German law to be used in other foodstuffs. Thus, despite the German Government's arguments that beer was consumed on a large scale by German drinkers, the Court held that these preservatives and additives did not constitute a threat to health in beer. Another illustration is the Italian vinegar case (see *Commission v Italian Republic*, Case 193/80 [1981] ECR 3019). The principle from these cases is that, while national legislation may limit free movement of goods for reasons of public health, such restrictions can only be permitted so far as they were indispensable for ensuring public health.

Another concept borrowed from German law has been the concept of respect for legitimate expectations (Vertrauensschutz). Further evidence of the German influence can be seen in the way in which the ECJ's judgments have become 'less deductive and apodictic' (Koopmans (1991) p 502), and an examination of judgments in the 1960s and 1980s will reveal differences in the breadth of the Court's judgments and the tendency to be more discursive in its judicial style.

The influence of the common law tradition

With the accession of the United Kingdom, Ireland and Denmark, new traditions entered the Community. However, it was the common law that gradually wielded an influence on the character of Community law. This took some time but, during the 1980s, for example, a greater awareness of procedural problems developed in two ways:

(a) the Court showed a willingness to reopen a case for oral argument when it felt that it was possible to expedite a decision on the basis of arguments which had not yet been addressed by the parties (see *AM and S Europe*, Case 155/79 [1982] ECR 1575; *Lancome*, Case 99/79 [1980] ECR 2511, pp 2526–28; *Commission v UK* [1983] ECR 2265, pp 2268–70). The adversarial approach, derived from the common law, was clearly being encouraged where the Court felt it would expedite matters to do so;

(b) the Court began to recognise a company's right to a fair hearing in the decision making process before an administrative body or agency. This right was acknowledged even when the relevant Community provisions did not mention it (see *Transocean Marine Paint Association*, Case 17/74 [1974] ECR 1063). In this case, the English rule of *audi alterem partem* was utilised to strike down a Commission decision which had varied the legal position of the applicants, without giving them an opportunity to be heard, that is, to submit their views on the matter.

Commentators have also pointed out that the Court's judgments in anti-trust cases shifted from focusing on the effectiveness of competition rules and the scope of Community law, to the rights of companies accused of anti-competitive behaviour (see Korse, *EEC Anti-trust Procedure* (1988) Chapters 3–4; and Korah (1980) 33 Current Legal Problems 73).

It was during the 1980s that the Court began to rely on previously decided case law. But more significantly, it also began to develop the practice of declaring that it would follow a previous precedent because no new arguments had been advanced. It has repeatedly held that, in the system of preliminary rulings, national courts should never feel obliged to refer questions to the Court when a ruling on the matter has already been given. The Court has also emphasised that national courts are at liberty to submit new questions on the issue for the Court to consider, when they believe that these have not yet been determined by the Court (see *CILFIT v Ministero della Sanita*, Case 283/81 [1982] ECR 3415). Hence, the ECJ appears to be developing a form of *stare decisis* which is broadly in accordance with English common law tradition, but which is not exercised in exactly the same manner as in contemporary English common law. Previously decided cases are relied upon in later cases, but the scope of their applicability may be extended or restricted in accordance with the particular circumstances.

Another indication of the influence of the common law tradition is the fact that the Court's proceedings have now assumed a less formal atmosphere, in the context of the encouragement of some sort of dialogue between judges and lawyers. This is very much in the spirit of the English common law tradition. When it works, it appears to work very well indeed, but sometimes it is hampered or hindered by translation problems, for example, when the Court has to listen to oral interpreters who may not appreciate fully the vital nuance in the particular statement or give a literal, but not an accurate translation. This brings us to the tricky question of the 'language of Community law'.

The language of Community law

The difficulties of comparison of Community law with other legal systems are compounded when we look at the language of Community law. Indeed, a preliminary point to clarify is that what is referred to in this section is: the actual different languages used which require accurate translations to render them intelligible and meaningful to national systems and, if necessary, to the Courts, not the legal terminology *per se*. In the present context, therefore, it will be evident that there are several languages used to express Treaties and other enabling provisions.

Although the ECSC Treaty is in one authentic version in French, the other Treaties have been drawn up in a single document in several European languages, including German, French, Italian and Dutch, Danish, English, Irish and Norwegian, all said to be 'equally authentic'. Of course, this is an accepted form for a multilateral multi-lingual treaty. The 'equally authentic' formula ensures that all texts, having an equal status, can be cited as the authoritative statement of the law and no one text may, therefore, take precedence over another. The EC Commission has 1,000 staff who are employed in translating the mountain of documents – an enormous task necessitated by the nine official languages and the authenticity approach.

However, it is now becoming more widely recognised than ever before that translation of a legal text is much more than simply providing mere synonyms or literal equivalents for terms, and translators need to be very conversant not just with the operation of 'registers' (different levels, 'pitches' and contexts), legal registers and legal terms *per se*, but with the overall legal system into which the concepts fit. To use the title of an article on this matter, difficulties in giving accurate translations is a problem which no EC Directive can eliminate (see Reeves, '1992 Languages: the barrier no EC Directive can eliminate' (1989) Linguist 5).

An additional linguistic difficulty is that Community law has now developed several distinctive concepts whose meaning and application are far removed from their original or derivative meanings. Consequently, the Member State may well be unwittingly misled by the superficial similarity of terms. Finally, Community law must be interpreted in the light of its overall matrix, in the light of its objectives, its particular evolutionary stage and according to the contemporaneity of the issue. Thus, something decided in 1973 might not necessarily be interpreted or decided in the same way in 1992, if conditions have rendered the earlier decision obsolete or inappropriate.

As closer European integration approaches, it might well be essential for linguists, who are also trained lawyers, to work as interpreters and perhaps for many more 'exchange programmes' to be set up which could ensure a constant flow of cultural and legal ideas on both sides of the Channel and across Western (and, indeed, eventually Eastern) Europe.

The Community Regulations are drawn up in the nine official languages of the Community and published in the EC official gazette (Official Journal of the European Communities). As far as the ECJ is concerned, the official languages of the Court are: Danish, English, French, German, Italian and Dutch, but Irish (although not official) may be used. Generally, only one of the official languages may be used as the procedural language, but there is a certain amount of flexibility allowed to participants in the Court process. The applicant has a choice of language and, if the defendant is a Member State, or a person or corporation subject to a Member State, the procedural language will be the official language of that State. If so desired, the parties may jointly request the use of another official language as the procedural language, which the Court may allow and, in exceptional circumstances, the Court may authorise the total or partial use of another official procedural language if one of the parties so requests.

Legislation as language

At another level, the characteristic mode of thought in Community law is, in fact, derived from its secondary sources of law, which we discuss further, below. In other words, if one were to ask a European Community lawyer what his typical legal language is when he deals with Community law, his answer, at the basic level of generality, will be in terms of Regulations, Directives and Decisions. As we shall see in our discussion on Community law sources, each of these have a special, unique meaning and each of these, in the European context, are almost instantly associated with the legal language of the European Community. In the company law field, in particular, there has been a series of Directives emanating from the EC, some of which have already been implemented in national legal systems. Thus, the types of legislation that have been enacted within, and by, the Community have become part of the legal order and legal language of the Community and are now identifiable as such.

THE COMMUNITY'S LEGAL ORDER/REGIME

Nature of Community law

Community law has been described as a body of law that is 'at once hierarchical and autonomous' (Valee, 'Le droit des Communautes Européennes "que sais-je?"' (1983) No 2067, p 90). In considering what Community law represents, we might first say what it is not. It is not a super-State, nor a quasi-State nor a Federal State (Dagtoglou [1973] CLJ 259). The Treaty of Rome is not a federal constitution, although there may be some who would wish it were. However, Community law is a separate legal system, distinct from, though closely linked to, both international law and the legal systems of the Member States (*Van Gend en Loos* [1963] ECR 1). As the ECJ has put it, in creating the European Community, the Member States have 'limited their sovereign rights, albeit within limited fields, and have ... created a body of law which binds both their nationals and themselves' (*Costa v Ente Nazionale Per L'Energia Elettrica* (ENEL) [1964] ECR 585). The *Van Gend en Loos* case also emphasised that the Community treaties are more than mere international agreements. They also form the constitution of the Community (*Les Verts-Parti Ecologiste v European Parliament*, Case 294/83 [1987] 2 CMLR 343) and the rules of law derived from them constitute the internal law of the Community (*Federation Charbonniere de Belgique v High Authority*, Case 8/55 [1956] ECR 245, p 277).

In addition, it has been pointed out that, although it has been 'engendered by international law, it does not share all its characteristics, having more in common with branches of national law such as constitutional and administrative law' (Hartley (1988)). But national legislatures do not have the power to repeal or amend it and it will override any national law with which it comes into conflict. Its interpretation, in the final analysis, comes within the exclusive jurisdiction of the ECJ (*Van Gend en Loos* (above)).

Community law has, therefore, been conceived not simply as a supranational body of law, but was intended to be an integral part of the legal orders of the Member States and be enforced by the national courts as well as by the ECJ. As far as the United Kingdom was concerned, upon its accession to the Communities, the effect of the new legal order was clear. In the much quoted words of Lord Denning:

> ... when we come to matters with a European element, the Treaty is like an incoming tide. It flows into the estuaries and up the rivers. It cannot be held back. Parliament has decreed that the Treaty is, henceforward, part of our law. It is equal in force to any statute ... Any rights or obligations created by the Treaty are to be given legal effect in England without more ado. Any remedies or procedures provided by the Treaty are to be made available here without being open to question. In future, in transactions which cross the frontiers, we must no longer speak or think of English law as something on its own. We must speak and think of Community law, of Community rights and obligations and we must give effect to them.

Although this was uttered in the context of the United Kingdom, the impact of Community law on other European Member States is no less significant.

Direct applicability and direct effect

The first point to note about the so called principle of 'direct effect' is that it is nowhere explicitly mentioned in the Treaty. It is, therefore, a creation of the ECJ, which was first established in the case of *Van Gend en Loos* [1963] ECR 1, for a number of reasons which we shall explore presently. A more accurate term might, therefore, be 'direct applicability' which has been defined as denoting 'the ability of a provision of Community law to become part of the domestic legal system of a Member State without the need for formal enactment by national means' (Freestone and Davidson (1988) p 28). In other words, it is a concept that suggests that, in the appropriate case, Community law is directly applicable to national law and can, thereby, create rights in favour of individuals which national courts must protect.

The next point to note about this concept is that the concept of direct applicability is found in Art 189 (EEC Treaty) with regard to the effect of regulations. That Article declares that a regulation has general application and 'It shall be binding in its entirety and directly applicable in all Member States'.

The question of the direct applicability of Community rules first arose in the case of *Van Gend en Loos* (above). In September 1960, the plaintiff, Dutch haulage company Van Gend en Loos, imported an aqueous emulsion of ureaformaldehyde from Germany for use in the manufacture of glue. It received a claim from the Dutch customs authorities for duty at a rate higher than the rate current for the product, at the time when the Treaty of Rome entered into force. As a result of an agreement concluded between the Benelux countries, in July 1958, aqueous emulsions had been transferred from a category of products taxed at 3% to another category taxed at 8%. The glue manufacturer protested to the national authorities on the grounds that Art 12 of the Treaty prohibited the common market countries from increasing the customs duties that they applied as between themselves on 1 January 1958, when the Treaty entered into force.

In turn, the authorities concerned, the Dutch Revenue Appeals Tribunal (Tariefcommissie), using the procedure of Art 177 of the Treaty, put the following question to the ECJ:

> Whether Art 12 of the EEC Treaty has direct application [as argued by the plaintiffs in the action]; in other words, whether nationals of Member States can, on the basis of the Article in question, lay claims to individual rights which the courts must protect?

The German, Belgian and Dutch Governments submitted their observations to the Court. In their opinion, only Member States or the Commission could bring any alleged infringements of the Treaty before the Court. The Treaty, they submitted, conferred rights and imposed obligations only on the signatory States, and certainly not on private individuals who must remain subject to their national law. The Advocate General agreed, giving his reasons for his view.

However, the Court thought differently and, in another well known passage, said:

> The objective of the EEC Treaty, which is to establish a Common Market, the functioning of which is of direct concern to interested parties in the Community, implies that this Treaty is more than an agreement which merely creates mutual obligations between the contracting States. This view is confirmed by the Preamble to the Treaty which refers not only to governments, but to peoples. It is also confirmed more specifically by the establishment of institutions endowed with sovereign rights, the exercise of which affects Member States and also their citizens.

From these propositions, the Court could, therefore, declare that:

> The Community constitutes a new legal order of international law for the benefit of which the States have limited their sovereign rights, albeit within limited fields, and the subjects of which comprise not only Member States, but also their nationals. Independently of the legislation of Member States, Community law, therefore, not only imposes obligations on individuals, but is also intended to confer upon them rights which become part of their legal heritage. These rights arise not only where they are expressly granted by the Treaty, but also by reason of obligations which the Treaty imposes, in a clearly defined way, upon individuals as well as upon the Member States, and upon the institutions of the Community.

Hence, the Treaty has created in each of the Member States, whose constitutional law relating to the internal effect of international obligations differs widely, rules of substantive law which were enforceable by private individuals. In the instant case, the importer was, therefore, to be placed on the same footing as if there had been full observance of the Treaty.

It was perfectly possible for the Court to have reached its final conclusion by confining itself to a discussion of Art 12. However, it has been argued that it chose not to do so because:

(a) it wished to rebut the suggestions from the governments that direct effect was an exception;

(b) it felt that there was a need to defend the system created by the Treaties against the tendency to apply Community law purely in accordance with the subjective wishes of the parties rather than as a system that stood on its own and functioned independently of the parties' wishes;

(c) it seemed to wish to promote the individual as the beneficiary of Community law and, thereby, be an effective instrument for enforcing a Member State's obligations (see Louis (1990) p 109).

Since that famous case was decided, the ECJ has built up a large body of case law elaborating on the tests to be applied, but this is not the place to pursue the many ramifications which arise from the principle. Suffice to say that, to be directly applicable, a provision must itself be legally self-sufficient (Freestone and Davidson (1988) p 31) and, according to statements made in cases like *Reyners v Belgian State*, Case 2/74 [1974] ECR 631, the tests to apply, in deciding whether a provision meets this requirement are: (a) the obligation it establishes must be clear and precise; (b) the obligation must be unconditional; (c) the obligation must not be dependent upon further action by either the Community or national authorities.

Recent cases have sought to clarify the scope and operation of Directives which had a direct effect, that is, were directly enforceable. Basically, directly effective provisions of EC law, whether Treaty Articles or provisions of Council or Commission Regulations, Directives or Decisions create rights for individuals (including business entities). Such individuals may enforce these rights in a national court even though there were national provisions which denied such rights. This is the result of the principle of supremacy of EC Law (see, also 'Supremacy of Community law', p 168, below). However, such EC provisions must be unconditional, which means they must not be dependent on further action being taken at Community or national level and must be sufficiently precise.

Nevertheless, Member States neglected to transpose Directives into national law either correctly or within the prescribed time limits and, thus, denied individuals of their Community law rights and effective remedies in national courts. The European Court of Justice, therefore, allowed individuals to rely directly on the Directive, despite conflicting national provisions. Directives may, thus, create enforceable rights for individuals as plaintiffs or defendants, but only as against the State, which is not allowed to defend itself by pleading that their actions were lawful under national law. Directives, therefore, create rights for individuals (or business undertakings) in disputes between them and the State when the latter has failed to fulfil its Treaty obligations. A Directive can, therefore, not be relied upon by an individual against another individual (*Marshall v Southampton and SW Hampshire* AHA [1986] ECR 723, affirmed in *Paolo Faccini Dori v Recreb Srl* (1994) The Times European L Rev, 4 August). The *Faccini Dori* case (above) also made clear that the landmark *Francovich* case (*Francovich v Italy* (1991) ECR I-5357) now requires Member States to compensate any damage caused to individuals as a result of a failure to transpose a directive into national law.

Supremacy of Community law

Several months after the judgment in *Van Gend en Loos*, a Milan judge brought before the Court a request for interpretation of the Treaty in a case which required clarification of the situation, in the event of a conflict between Community law and national law. In the famous case of *Costa v Enel* [1964] ECR 585, Mr Costa, a shareholder in Edison Volta, argued that he had suffered injury through the nationalisation of the facilities for the production and distribution of electricity in the country. He refused to pay a bill for a few hundred lira presented by the new nationalised company ENEL. When summoned before a court in Milan, he submitted in his defence that the nationalisation law was contrary to the Treaty of Rome. The judge hearing the case, therefore, approached the ECJ. Meanwhile, the Italian constitutional court had intervened in connection with the law establishing ENEL. In its opinion, the situation was: since the Rome Treaty had been ratified by an ordinary law, the provisions of a later conflicting law would have to take precedence over those of the Treaty.

But, the ECJ disagreed and, in its judgment, pointed out that:

> By creating a Community of unlimited duration, having its own institutions, its own personality, its own legal capacity of representation on the international plane and, more particularly, real powers stemming from a limitation of sovereignty or a transfer of powers from the States to the Community, the Member States have limited their sovereign rights, albeit within limited fields, and have thus created a body of law which binds both their nationals and themselves.

> The integration into the laws of each Member State of provisions which derive from the Community and, more generally, the terms and the spirit of the Treaty, make it impossible for the States, as a corollary, to accord precedence to a unilateral and subsequent measure over a legal system accepted by them on a basis of reciprocity.

As if this were not forceful enough, they went on to add that:

> The executive force of Community law cannot vary from one State to another in deference to subsequent domestic laws, without jeopardising the attainment of the objectives of the Treaty ... The obligations undertaken under the Treaty establishing the Community would not be unconditional, but merely

contingent if they could be called in question by subsequent legislative acts of the signatories.

As in *Van Gend en Loos*, the Court then affirmed the precedence of Community law as laid down in Art 189, which, it added, is subject to no reservation and would be 'meaningless' if a State could unilaterally nullify its effects by means of a legislative measure which could prevail over Community law. Accordingly, the ECJ concluded that:

> ... the law, stemming from the Treaty, an independent source of law, could not, because of its special ... nature, be overridden by domestic legal provisions, however framed, without being deprived of its character as Community law, and without the legal basis of the Community itself being called into question.

This approach was confirmed in subsequent cases like *Minister of Finance v Simmenthal* [1978] ECR 629, where the ECJ confirmed that, in cases where national law and directly effective Community law came into conflict, national courts are under a duty to give effect to Community law, which would even override incompatible rules of national law which were passed subsequently. It stressed that Community law provisions are a direct source of rights and duties for all those affected thereby, whether Member States or individuals, and that national courts were under a duty to give full effect to Community law provisions.

Community techniques of legal interpretation

A reading of the case law decided by the ECJ reveals the particular legal approach or techniques of legal interpretation which it applies, when dealing with Community law. First of all, it considers the issue or dispute which has been brought to its attention in the light of any relevant Treaty provision, or piece of secondary legislation. If these are clear and unambiguous, it adopts the literal interpretation, very much as most legal systems do, whether common or civil law, unless there are good reasons for not doing so. Cases also indicate that the ECJ is conscious that the same standard of draftsmanship found in national legislation cannot be expected in treaties. The next interpretative principle is the logical interpretation of the text, wherein the Court will consider the provision within the context of the system. In considering previous judicial interpretations on a provision, the Court may also consider adopting the teleological interpretation which, although literal to a certain extent, focuses on the intention of the legislature in the light of the conditions prevailing at the time of the judgment.

Secondly, and not necessarily in the alternative, the Court has been known to adopt the following approach:

(a) It asks for comparative materials on the issue, based on legislation, academic opinion and case law of the Member States, on the existence and scope of the disputed rule or concept. It should be remembered that, in accordance with the continental courts' practice, and the close connection between continental judges to the academic world, the ECJ has found the contribution of learned writers' opinions extremely helpful to the clarification and development of the Court's jurisprudence. Nevertheless, the Court goes for quality rather than quantity, and is highly eclectic in its choice of doctrinal opinions, choosing only the most eminent of experts with established reputations in the field, and the actual number of judgments citing these writers' opinions are fairly few in number in relation to the abundance of writing on Community law.

(b) It invites the parties and the advocates or interveners to submit their views as to the existence and scope of the disputed principle.

(c) It reviews the case carefully, and then considers whether there are any 'general principles of law' which are sometimes, but not always, traceable to international law principles, municipal law concepts and institutions/doctrines or are simply not traceable to any recognisable source, for example, relating to equality and discrimination (see *Re Electric Refrigerators*, Case 13/63 [1963] CMLR 289, p 303) or on the status of international administrative tribunals (see *Bourgaux v ECSC Common Assembly*, Case 1/56 (1956) 2 Rec 451). As we have already indicated, the ECJ has also begun to adapt various concepts to suit the particular style of the Court and the needs of the parties. There is no doubt, however, that the Court makes extensive use of comparative material and is perfectly happy to utilise its own version of 'legal transplants' where it deems it appropriate, or necessary, to do so.

Distinctive legal institutions/doctrines

Under this criterion, the term 'institutions' refers to the characteristic legal concepts and doctrines of a legal system rather than the administrative, judicial or legislative organs of a particular entity. Hence, in the Romano-Germanic legal family, typical legal institutions include rules protecting the moral and economic integrity of a family against outsiders, the abuse of right, direct action, oblique action and their unique versions of the concept of good faith (see Chapter 9). In the Germanic legal family, there are concepts, such as that of the general clauses, the abstract real contract, the institution of unjustified enrichment and the doctrine based on collapse of the foundations of a transaction.

When we examine the European Community, we find that there is an inevitable mixture of concepts and civil law and common law influences, for reasons explained above, but also that many of these concepts have begun to be clothed with a distinctive EC flavour. As we have seen above, the doctrines or concepts that have become part of Community law are certain general principles of law, such as 'market freedoms', which are essential prerequisites of the integration of national economies: free movement of goods, free movement of workers, freedom to exercise professional activities and so on. Another set of principles concerns setting limits to the exercise of Community powers, and yet another set may broadly be called principles of legality developed in administrative law and practice in Member States, particularly, with regard to economic law and the protection of legitimate expectations. Prominent among these sorts of doctrines are:

(a) the principle of equality and non-discrimination;

(b) the principle of freedom;

(c) the principle of solidarity (against a Member refusing to fulfil its obligations);

(d) the principle of unity (that is, of the common market);

(e) the principle of proportionality;

(f) the rights of the defence, including the right to a hearing;

(g) confidentiality of correspondence between lawyer and client;

(h) prohibition of arbitrary acts;

(i) general principles of human rights;

(j) general commercial principles, such as good faith and fairness in dealing;

(k) abuse of dominant position (Art 86 of the EEC Treaty).

Choice of sources of law

The phrase 'sources of law' in the present context refers to the authority from which it is derived rather than the historical, social, political or economic reasons or causes of the law. Hence, the sources of Community law may be divided into primary and secondary sources of law. The primary sources of Community law are the founding Treaties (in particular, the EEC Treaty). As far as the Treaties are concerned, apart from the founding Treaties, other treaties, such as the Accession Treaties, the Merger Treaty of 1965, the 1970 Budgetary Treaty and the Single European Act 1986, would be included. Finally, any pre-existing Treaties such as GATT, treaties guaranteeing human rights (the UN Covenants and the ECHR) and treaties between the EEC and third States, would also qualify as primary sources.

The secondary sources of Community law are the law making acts of the Community organs which result in a body of law, namely, the administrative and judicial acts emanating from the respective organs:

(a) Administrative acts: Regulations, Directives and Decisions made by the Council or the Commission in order to carry out their task in accordance with the Treaty (Art 189 of the EEC Treaty). There is some confusion over the status of Recommendations and Opinions; the position appears to be that Opinions cannot be regarded as sources of Community law but Recommendations might be, although only under the ECSC Treaty.

(b) Judicial legislation: decisions of the ECJ.

As we have seen, cases are the predominant source of law in the common law tradition, although the modern trend is to have greater reliance on statutes wherever possible. Although codes and legislation are the main official sources of law in civil law countries, we have seen how they are sometimes merely a facade for the actual sources, which are court decisions.

Ideology of the system

The objectives of the European Community are probably the best guide to its underlying ideology in the sense of its motivating political and economic doctrines. It is in the Preamble to the EEC Treaty that we find a general and rhetorical statement of principles, commencing with the intention 'to lay the foundations of an ever closer union among the peoples of Europe', to which we have earlier alluded. But, the basic principles of the substantive law of the EEC are contained, firstly, in Art 2 of the EEC Treaty which sets out the objectives of the Treaty, and the means by which they are to be achieved. The objectives are:

> ... the harmonious development of economic activities throughout the Community, a continuous and balanced expansion, an increase in stability, an accelerated raising of the standard of living and closer relations between the States belonging to the Community.

From this Article, it appears that the goals of the Community are to be attained by the two mechanisms of a 'common market' and the 'progressive approximation of economic policies' of Member States. Article 3 then develops these means into 11 heads of activity, or statements of intent, such as:

> (a) the elimination, as between Member States, of customs duties, and of quantitative restrictions on the import and export of goods, and of all other measures having equivalent effect; (b) the establishment of a common customs tariff and of a common commercial policy towards third countries; (c) the abolition, as between Member States, of obstacles to freedom of movement for persons, services and capital.

Further categories then specify the adoption of a common policy on agriculture and transport and the application of procedures to co-ordinate the economic policies of Member States.

The wording of these heads suggests that they are, by no means, exclusive or limiting which is clear from Art 3 and Art 2. Each of these heads of activity is the subject of particular Articles of the Treaty containing specific provisions.

Some of these provisions constitute directly effective rights (and, in some cases, obligations) for nationals and enterprises of the Member States, directly effective obligations for the Member States and also obligations or powers to enable the Community institutions or the Member States to adopt implementing, or further regulatory measures.

A great deal has already been achieved to implement these objectives, such as a customs union and various measures intended to achieve the removal of restrictions on the 'four freedoms' – free movement of goods, persons, services and capital. The major step taken towards this goal was the Single European Act, a treaty agreed by the Member States in 1986, in force in the United Kingdom from 1 July 1987 (Cm 372/1988). This Act has set the further objective of the Community, of 'an area without internal frontiers in which the free movement of goods, persons, services, and capital is ensured' in accordance with the Treaty, to be achieved by 31 December 1992. There is now a common agricultural policy, and provision is made in the Treaty for the co-ordination of economic and monetary policies (see Arts 6, 102a–105). The Community has also been moving toward the goal of Economic and Monetary Union.

Among the stated objectives in Art 3 is the ninth head, which shows that the Community has also undertaken certain social objectives which are fully developed in Title III of the Treaty. They include equal pay without discrimination based on sex, improvements in the health and safety of workers, a common vocational training policy and the maintenance of a European Social Fund which provides assistance for such schemes as the retraining and resettlement of workers. The Single European Act deals expressly with the objectives of social and economic integration (including reduction of regional disparities), research and technological development, and protection of the environment. It also contains provisions which formalise political co-operation between the Member States in questions of foreign policy.

The objectives are supplemented, and intended to be promoted and realised, by certain fundamental principles in Arts 5, 6 and 7, which deal with the basic principles of Community loyalty and co-operation between Member States and institutions of the Community in the co-ordination of the economic policies of the Member States, as well as a general prohibition of discrimination on grounds of nationality. These encapsulate the principle of Community 'solidarity' which, under Art 5, imposes the obligation on Member States to take all appropriate measures to endure fulfilment of the obligations arising out of the Treaty. There is also an obligation on the national judge to ensure the legal protection which subjects derive from the direct effect of provisions of Community law. It should, perhaps, be noted that the general non-discrimination provision in Art 7 does not prohibit all discrimination, but only discrimination on the grounds of nationality.

The non-discrimination provisions only become specific when dealing with State commercial monopolies (Art 37 of the EEC Treaty), cartel agreements (Art 85 of the EEC Treaty), enterprises with a dominant economic position (Art 86 of the EEC Treaty) and dumping (Art 91 of the EEC Treaty).

It will be noticed, therefore, that apart from primarily economic objectives there are also social ones, and at root there is the historical motivating objective of a certain degree of European political unity or, at least, integration. Perhaps, at a rather prosaic level, as a generation of French political leaders has argued, uniting with one's neighbours could enable France and, ultimately, all European countries to play a much more dominant role in European economic and political affairs than they have done in modern times. It might also provide a safeguard against future domination by any major superpower in war or peace. The true objectives of the Community may well be characterised as being both regional and, ultimately, global.

The Maastricht Treaty, signed in December 1991, calls for European monetary union by 1999 and seeks to point the way to closer European co-operation in defence and foreign policy. In the light of the very narrow French referendum result ('le petit oui', as one French newspaper called it), on 20 September 1992, and the Danish rejection in its referendum, it remains to be seen if the objectives of this Treaty will indeed be a reality by the year 2000, given the current uncertainties and pan-European debates surrounding its implementation.

THE MAASTRICHT TREATY

On 11 December 1991, European Community leaders meeting in Maastricht agreed on the texts of a Treaty on European Union and Economic and Monetary Union and associated protocols. The texts are subject to ratification by all 12 national Parliaments of the Member States, a process which was expected to be completed by the end of 1992. The agreement extends Community action into areas not previously covered by the EC Treaties, especially Economic and Monetary Union and defence. The text states: 'This Treaty marks a new stage in the process of creating an ever closer Union among the peoples of Europe, where decisions are taken as closely as possible to (sic) the citizen.' Yet, as a British newspaper article put it: 'Never have so many argued over a Treaty that so few have read' ((1992) The Sunday Times, 11 October). The Treaty has certainly been the subject of a heated and frequently acrimonious debate. In 61,351 words, it expanded the scope of responsibilities in the European Community bringing new policy areas under the jurisdiction of its institutions. The Treaty has become a best seller in European countries, but remains unread by the bulk of the population in the United Kingdom.

The Treaty introduced the concept of Union citizenship and increased the decision making powers and right of enquiry of the European Parliament. A Social Chapter, agreed by 11 Member States, will not feature in the Treaty, but will be implemented via the EC institutions. It sets out a procedure for a single currency as part of an economic and monetary union, provides for a common foreign and security policy, and a common policy on judicial affairs and seeks to pave the way towards a common defence policy. The Treaty says that the Union should have a single institutional framework. It also introduces into EC law the concept of 'subsidiarity'. Here is a summary of certain key features of the Maastricht Treaty.

The general aims of the Treaty

The first section of the Treaty lists its general aims including the promotion of economic and social progress, abandonment of internal frontiers, establishment of a single currency and development of foreign policy and defence policy.

Steps to European Union

This consists of a number of amendments to the original Treaty of Rome of 1957. Articles 2, 3 and 3a set the objectives for European Union which include a commitment to non-inflationary economic growth, a high level of employment and social protection, and raising the standard of living and quality of life. There is also a timetable for the elimination of customs duties, a common transport policy and the modification of national laws to achieve effective functioning of the Common Market.

Subsidiarity

This controversial concept is covered in Art 3b. The principle of subsidiarity governs the limits of Community action with the Article stating that, for policy areas outside the Community's exclusive jurisdiction, the Community will act 'only if and insofar as the objectives of the proposed action cannot be sufficiently achieved by the Member States' and can better be achieved by the Community. Thus, 'Any action by the Community shall not go beyond what is necessary to achieve the objectives of the Treaty'. There is no clarification within the Treaty of whether subsidiarity is applicable to areas which do fall within the competence of the Community.

The legal significance of the concept of subsidiarity will doubtless evolve over the next few years.

European citizenship

The Treaty says that every person holding the nationality of a Member State shall become a citizen of the Union and will enjoy the rights conferred by the Treaty. These rights include the right to move and reside freely within the territory of the Member States, the right to vote and stand as a candidate in local elections for people living outside their own country and the right to vote and stand as a candidate for the European Parliament. A Union citizen in a non-EC country shall be entitled to diplomatic or consular protection by any Member State. There is also the right to petition the European Parliament or apply to an Ombudsman.

In 1999, the concept of a European citizenship is still circumscribed and the specific and limited rights, listed above, may well expand. The notion of European citizenship will, thus, probably evolve rather than be radically or rapidly changed.

A single economy

This is one of the key themes introduced by the Treaty, but Britain has secured an opt out clause which enables it not to participate in this aspect of the European Union at this stage.

Powers of the European Parliament

In certain fields, the European Parliament is to have new powers of joint decision making with the Council of Ministers, allowing it to reject a proposal by an overall majority of its members if agreement cannot be reached between the two institutions in a joint Conciliation Committee. The Commission and its President will be subject to parliamentary approval at the start of their mandate, which is to be five years from the beginning of 1995 coinciding with the parliamentary term. The European Parliament can request the Commission to submit any proposal where it decides, by overall majority vote, that new EC legislation is needed. This measure was apparently introduced to placate those who suggested that the EC did not possess sufficient democratic accountability.

Education

The Treaty exhorts the development of a European dimension in education. Community actions will include the development of the teaching and dissemination of the languages of the Member States, encouraging mobility of students and teachers and promoting co-operation between educational establishments.

Culture

The Community pledges, in Art 128, to 'contribute to the flowering of cultures of Member States, while respecting their national and regional diversity and, at the same time, bringing the common cultural heritage to the fore'. The cultural enterprise includes moves to improve knowledge of the culture and history of European peoples and conservation of cultural heritage of European significance.

Justice and Home Affairs

The Treaty identifies areas of common interest among the Member States, namely, asylum policy, crossing of the Community's external borders, immigration policy, combating drug addiction, combating fraud, judicial co-operation in civil and criminal matters, customs co-operation and police co-operation. In these matters, joint positions and joint action can be taken by the Council, which will have the right to decide that certain measures may be adopted by a qualified majority. Only Member States will have powers of initiative in criminal matters instead of the Commission, but the Commission will be fully associated with the work. The European Parliament will be informed and consulted and its views will be taken into consideration. There is particular reference to the European Convention on Human Rights and to the Convention of the Status of Refugees, regard being had to the protection given by Member States to persons persecuted on political grounds.

The Social Chapter and social policy

The stated objectives in the 1989 Social Chapter are to promote employment, improve living and working conditions, implement proper social protection and develop human resources with a view to lasting high employment. The social provisions include a minimum wage (which has proved very contentious for smaller businesses in the United Kingdom) and the principle of equal pay for male and female workers.

British opposition to the draft Treaty on social policy has resulted in no change to the social Articles in the Treaty of Rome, as modified by the Single European Act. The 12 Member States have agreed in a protocol that 11 Members States can borrow the Community institutions, with the Commission, Parliament and Court of Justice doing their normal jobs and the Council adopting measures by unanimity in some cases and qualified majority in others. This majority will consist of 44 votes out of 66 instead of 54 out of 76. But, with the advent of the Labour Party coming back into government in May 1997, the minimum wage has been implemented as the new Labour Government has been committed to its implementation.

The Council will usually try to achieve agreement on the basis of 12 Member States but, where the United Kingdom does not accept this, the British Government will not participate in the deliberations or decisions.

The 11 have agreed that the following matters can be decided by qualified majority vote: health and safety; working conditions; information and consultation of workers; equality at work between men and women; and integration of persons excluded from the labour market.

The following are issues requiring a unanimous vote: social security and social protection of workers; protection of workers made redundant; representation and collective defence of workers and employers; conditions of employment for third country nationals; and financial contributions for promoting jobs. Significantly, matters such as pay, the right of association, the right to strike or the right to impose lockouts, do not come within these provisions.

In Britain, towards the end of 1994, differences of opinion between those Conservative Members of Parliament in favour of European Union and those against it reached a crisis point, even within the last Conservative Government, when it came to voting on Europe and, although the Government just managed to hang on to its slim majority, the signs for the second half of the 1990s were that Maastricht would continue to be a serious bone of contention between the United Kingdom and the other EC countries as well as within the former Tory Government itself. The current Labour Government will doubtless have its opposing factions with differing views toward European integration within the Cabinet, and it is realistic to assume that true consensus will be a rare commodity in this area.

CONCLUSIONS

Even a brief examination of the salient features of the European Community reveals the wealth of legal traditions, legal institutions and doctrines that the Community embodies. Although a predominant legal tradition is the French legal tradition, both in Community institutional structure and methods of reasoning predominantly adopted by the European Court, there have also been concepts which, at least initially, derived from German law. Having been conceived, developed and promoted by Frenchmen, it is inevitable that French ideas and French legal philosophies also dominated the early legal and administrative development of the Community legal order. However, our brief survey also reveals that, like all great and enduring ideas, the Community legal order has now acquired a life of its own. Although rooted in French or German legal philosophies, it has started to adopt and adapt elements of the English common law tradition to the extent of developing its own unique system of precedent. Similarly, English judges have been using the teleological or purposive approach since the mid-1980s and have even been referring to it by this nomenclature. Hence, cross-fertilisation of concepts and principles between EC countries is well under way.

Its methods of legislative and statutory interpretation are a truly international combination of techniques and styles. Since the founding Treaties are really international agreements which are governed by international law, and the European Community is an international organisation, it is equally subject to the rules that govern international organisations. Yet, as a regional grouping, it has also created a unique relationship between the national law of Member States and Community law and even appears to traverse the interface between international law and domestic (national) law. For example, it echoes Art 38 of the Statute of the International Court of Justice, which refers to the general principles of law recognised by civilised nations, by also referring to general principles of law as well, and the ECJ's case law suggests that there is no limit to these principles and that they are traceable to, and reminiscent of, international law and national law concepts as contained in Treaties, codes and cases all over the civil and common law world.

Our comparative study shows that European Community law is unquestionably a unique form of European law, even at the most fundamental level, but has more practical and immediate significance than any other legal system by virtue of the twin pillars of its legal order. In other words, by virtue of its primacy over national law and the direct applicability of some of its provisions, it has already begun to direct the flow, if not actually turn the tide, of European law. Indeed, the ECJ has established the principle of liability of Member States towards their citizens for any breaches of Community law, first established in *Francovich v Italy* [1991] ECR I 5357: Cases 6 and 9/90. (See, also, *R v Secretary of State for Transport ex p Factortame ltd (No 5)*, above.)

As Van Gerven (1995) observes, the growing 'communitarisation' of national private law by EC law has the effect of diminishing the traditional gap between civil law and common law. The European Community is no longer the preserve of civil law countries and the hegemony of the European Court of Justice (ECJ) as the highest Court of Appeal for the EC countries serves to build up a Community tradition, case law and European integration. The EC harmonisation programme consists of Directives and Regulations, and national implementation of Regulations does not require parliamentary action. Areas such as inheritance law or family law are not easily 'harmonised' as are other areas, such as commercial law or labour law. However, the ECJ has developed general principles of law which, although based on national law, were in turn applied by courts in national legal systems. Wyatt and Dashwood (1993) have argued that certain fundamental rights have been declared by the ECJ to form an integral part of the general principles of law, although there is technically a difference between general principles *per se* and fundamental rights. The following have, therefore, been called general principles of law: the rule relating to proportionality; equality; legal certainty; and the protection of human rights (see Bronitt, Burns and Kinley (1995)).

As we approach the millennium, European lawyers are coming to grips with more and more Community law, and we continue to observe the frequently disorientating and fluctuating fortunes of Eastern Europe. The need to employ the comparative method, to be able to deal with different European systems of law, is becoming increasingly evident – to prepare for further developments and to understand the new legal order in an ever changing world, and to provide much needed assistance to ravaged Eastern European countries who will, one day, it is hoped, wish to return to some semblance of law, peace and order. The process of change, adaptation and transplantation has already begun, and integration and harmonisation will continue to pose challenges well into the next millennium.

SELECTIVE BIBLIOGRAPHY

Bronitt, Burns and Kinley, *Principles of European Community Law: Commentary and Materials* (1995)

Freestone and Davidson, *The Institutional Framework of the European Communities* (1990)

Furse, 'The role of EC law in UK, reform proposals' (1996) 17 European Competition L Rev 134

Green, Hartley and Usher, *The Legal Foundations of the Single European Market* (1991)

Hartley, 'Federalism, courts and legal systems: the emerging constitution of the European Community' (1986) 34 Am J Comp L 229

Hartley, *The Foundations of European Community Law* (1990)

Kapteyn and VerLoren van Themaat, *Introduction to the Law of the European Communities* (1990)

Keeton and Schwarzenberger, *English Law and the Common Market* (1963)

Koopmans, 'The birth of European law at the crossroads of legal traditions' (1991) 39 Am J Comp L 493

Lagenbucher, 'Argument by analogy in European law' (1998) 57 CLJ 481

Lasok and Bridge, *Law and Institutions of the European Communities* (1991)

Louis, *European Community Law* (1990)

Mackenzie-Stuart (Lord), *The European Communities and the Rule of Law* (1977)

Markesinis, 'Five days in the House of Lords: some comparative reflections on *White v Jones*' (1995) 3 Torts LJ 169

Mathijsen, *A Guide to European Union Law* (1995)

Shaw, *European Community Law* (1993)

Shaw and More (eds), *New Legal Dynamics of European Union* (1995)

Spencer, *1992 and All That: Civil Liberties in the Balance*

Turpin, *British Government and the Constitution* (1990) Chap 5

Van Gerven, 'Bridging the gap between community and national laws: toward a principle of homogeneity in the field of legal remedies?' (1995) 32 CMLR 679

Vranken, 'Statutory interpretation and judicial policy making: some comparative reflections' (1991) 12 Statute L Rev 31

Weatherill and Beaumont, *European Community Law* (1994)

Wyatt and Dashwood, *European Community Law* (1993)

CHAPTER 6

SOCIALIST LAW AND OTHER TYPES OF LEGAL SYSTEMS

SCOPE OF CHAPTER

In the early 1990s, the world saw the end of the old Soviet Empire and the dismantling, quite literally, of the Berlin Wall which had separated West from East Germany. It was thought by some at the time that this might well have signalled the end of communism as practised in countries like the old USSR and, in time, the People's Republic of China and Cuba would follow suit. However, the latter eventualities have not yet transpired so there is still some value in examining the socialist approach to law, not least, because the constitutional crisis in 1993 and events between 1998 and 1999 suggested that the new Russian Federation might even revert to its old form because of the highly volatile nature of its leader, President Yeltsin, and its many economic problems. This chapter, therefore, examines the socialist concept of law before discussing differences and similarities between civil law and socialist systems. It then conducts a brief inquest on the former Soviet Union which was the prototype of the socialist legal systems and ideology. It concludes that section with an appraisal of the current Russian reforms and hypothesises on the future development of the Russian Federation. We then examine the Chinese and Japanese concepts of law as examples of unique, *sui generis* systems of law.

THE SOCIALIST SYSTEM AND RUSSIA

The system of law that existed in the former Union of Soviet Socialist Republics (USSR) was the law that governed the world's second superpower and served as the communist system's prototype. In Europe today, the socialist legal system appears to have tailspun into terminal decline and is no longer the dominant and equal partner with civil law and common law parent legal families. Instead, it has been progressively relegated to the role of historical anachronism in most of Eastern Europe, becoming an example of just another legal system. Indeed, as a result of the events of the past five years in Eastern Europe and the former Soviet Union, it is arguable that many former socialist countries will return to their civil law roots, but if they retain some of their former ideology, or are 'converted' to capitalism and adopt Western style laws, they will certainly become 'hybrid systems' of law. If it is a combination of civil and quasi-military law, this will not conform to the classical notion of a hybrid system because, although the traditional conception of a hybrid legal system is one in which more than one legal system co-exists, this usually refers to a system where both common law and civil law types of law can be found, but which operate in different contexts and spheres.

The present section traces the typical features of the socialist legal system and the key characteristics that distinguished it from being regarded as a civil law system. This is followed by a very brief inquest on the former USSR before examining some of the decrees that have already emanated from the regime under President Yeltsin, and the reforms effected by the 1993 Constitution of the Russian Federation. At the end of that overview, we shall assess the possibilities of a successful transformation of this Federation into a viable form of civil society and social democracy.

The socialist concept of law

The word 'socialist', when used in connection with the law, means many different things to legal specialists. At its most basic, it signifies a philosophy and ideology which is based on what is commonly referred to as the 'Marxist-Leninist' school of thought. The socialist ideology is predicated on the principles, *inter alia*, that all law is an instrument of economic and social policy, and the common law and civil law traditions reflect a capitalist, bourgeois, imperialistic, exploitative society, economy and government. Marxist theory is founded on the doctrine of 'dialectical/historical materialism' which argues that a society goes through various stages or phases in the course of its evolution and development. It might begin with no legal system, then become a slave owning one, followed by a stage of medieval feudalism, before moving on to capitalism, then socialism, before law finally 'withers away' in a classless society with no necessity for any legal system, because all men will treat each other as equals.

Writers have long debated the 'true' meaning of terms like 'socialist' and 'socialism' and 'Marxism' and, even now, when communism appears to be in terminal decline in Eastern Europe, with a commensurate rise in social democracy, there is still debate on whether socialist law continues to wield a strong global influence, not least, because of the continued communist colours of the People's Republic of China.

Szabo believes that the socialist concept of law 'may be considered as part of a homogeneous scientific theory with a particular aim' (see Szabo, in *International Encyclopedia of Comparative Law*, p 49). That aim, of course, is the creation of a new legal system – socialist law. Quigley (1989) describes (rather than defines) socialist law as 'the law of countries whose governments officially view the country as being either socialist or moving from capitalism to socialism, and which hold a communistic society as an ultimate goal'.

In the preface to her book, *The Socialist Concept of Law* (1991), Christine Sypnowich defines 'socialism' as 'a society where private property in the form of capital has been eliminated and replaced by common ownership of the means of production thereby permitting a large measure of equality and fraternity in social relations'. She argues that it is incorrect to believe that an ideal socialist society would have no need of law. She concedes that left wing thought has long espoused the view that law will wither away under socialism, which was a view developed by Marx and Engels. It is also a view which has been supported by Western and Soviet thinkers in the Marxist tradition. But, she strongly disagrees with the conventional or common view taken on the nature of socialist legality. The classical doctrine of Marxism is that law and State are determined by, and subservient to, the economic structure of society and the political and economic aims of the State, as revealed in the State Plan. Marxist-Leninist theory extols the primacy of economic relations in society, which takes precedence over politics and law. On the domestic front, Stalinism could be described as one party rule comprising central planning and State ownership of the means of production. In international terms, it meant isolation from the West, occasionally leavened with selective interactions with foreign communist parties.

Law, when used by Soviet leaders, has therefore been a mere tool in the planning and organising of the economic and social structure of the country. It is simply part of the ideological superstructure which controls the material reality of the means of production; it is determined and defined in terms of its political function.

The groups of countries that have received socialist law may be divided into two main categories:

(a) the older socialist jurisdictions, such as Poland, Bulgaria, Hungary, Czechoslovakia, Romania, Albania, the People's Republic of China (see, especially, 'Different versions of communism in China', p 205 and 'Chinese law in the post-Mao era', p 206, below), the People's Republic of Vietnam, the People's Democratic Republic of Korea, Mongolia (the oldest national legal system in this group) and Cuba; and

(b) the newer or nascent socialist legal systems, such as the Democratic Republic of Kampuchea (Cambodia), Laos, Mozambique, Angola, Somalia, Libya, Ethiopia, Guinea and Guyana.

The Communist Party is the only real governing and planning body within the socialist legal system. Once it decides a particular policy, it communicates its plans to all its constituent organs and this policy will be carried out by its legislative, executive and judicial agencies.

Differences between civil law and socialist systems

The majority of Western scholars have argued that socialist law forms a family of law separate from the civil law family, and these include David, Hazard, Merryman, Ancel, Osakwe, Bogden and Constantinesco. However, Friedmann, Lawson, Losano and Ehrenzweig belonged to the school of thought that believed that socialist law is simply a member of the civil law group or subspecies of civil law. Many scholars identified the differentiating features of socialist law from civil law. As summarised by Quigley (1989), these were:

(a) socialist law is programmed to wither away with the disappearance of private property and social classes and the transition to a communistic social order;

(b) socialist countries are dominated by a single political party;

(c) in socialist systems, law is subordinated to creation of a new economic order, wherein private law is absorbed by public law;

(d) socialist law has a pseudo-religious character;

(e) socialist law is prerogative instead of normative.

Similarities between civil law and socialist systems

There are many similarities between the civil law and the socialist system. Quigley (1989) mentions the inquisitorial style of trial, codes and the passing of legislation/regulations as the basic style of law making, division of law into its civil (private) law categories and the method of investigation of crime (written documentation compiled by a law trained investigator). He also points out that socialist legal systems have utilised civil law institutions, methodology and organisation, (see Quigley (1989) pp 800, 803). Further, he refers to Hazard's observations that family law and the civil code provisions on interpersonal relations do not differ from those of other civil law countries (see Quigley (1989) p 803).

Indeed, Quigley argues that, despite significant differences between civil law and socialist law, 'when one looks at Soviet or socialist law from a global perspective, these differences do not erase the basic identity of socialist law as part of the civil law tradition' (Quigley (1989) p 804). He maintains that it is impossible to understand socialist law without viewing it within the tradition of which it is a part. He concludes that the points of difference between civil law and socialist law have not removed socialist law from the civil law tradition, and to think otherwise is to overlook the historical connection of socialist law to civil law and 'the continuing relevance in socialist law of civil law rules, methods, institutions and procedures' (Quigley (1989) p 808).

The Russian tradition of codification goes back many centuries. The *Pravda Russkaia* (Russian law), commonly thought to be oldest surviving compilation of Russian laws, was adopted in the 11th century. This was followed by many more in the 15th, 16th and 17th centuries. In 1830, Speranskii published a complete collection of the laws of the Russian Empire consisting of a 42 volume reproduction of more than 30,000 legislative edicts and enactments promulgated since 1649. In 1832, a 16 volume Code of Laws was published, which represented a systematic codification of the whole Russian law, dealing with it division by division. This contained 60,000 Articles covering all branches of law. In 1845, a new Criminal Code was enacted which preceded even more codes being promulgated, culminating in the last tsarist codes of 1903 and 1913.

After the Bolshevik Revolution in 1917, it was nearly five years before any codification took place and, although the new regime was overtly seeking to destroy all pre-Revolutionary law, during 1917 to 1920, a system of judge made law was utilised. It was only in 1922 that Soviet codification revived, wherein the existing codes were modified and promulgated afresh, the great legal philosopher Pashukanis being a dominant scholar of the era of codification.

The Soviet Civil Code was clearly influenced by the German Civil Code, the Swiss Civil Code and the Russian Draft Civil Code of 1913. The intention appeared to be to blend the best of German codification with the high aims of the French Code.

As with civil law systems, legal scholars constitute an extremely valuable intellectual source of law in all socialist countries. Since there are usually very few reported court decisions in most socialist countries, the legal expert or doctrinal writer actually writes legal opinions on judicial decisions giving not just the bare facts and ruling, but also the background and explanation of the consequences of a decision. For a case in point, one may cite the poignant 1971 case of Poltavskii, the stevedore, who saved a young child from certain death in a storm by flinging an electric cable that had entangled itself near the child away from the child's legs at the cost of his own life. This was not just reported by Stavisski, a doctrinal writer, but the aftermath of this case was then reported up to its remarkable conclusion: that the so called analogy of law could be used to award compensation to the stevedore's wife by virtue of the Electrical Company's lack of control over securing of electric cables; and that a legal precedent had, thereby, been created (see Hazard, Butler and Maggs (1977) p 466).

In other words, legal scholars play a major role in analysing, developing and disseminating legal doctrine. They also play a significant role in training all the members of the legal profession and are the most highly compensated of all lawyers. They are the most conversant with the law, of all the professionals, through their training and teaching of the law to future lawyers, and have wrought an invaluable influence on the law through their systematic commentaries, consultations of legislative drafting committees, and on consultative committees attached to the different Supreme Courts. Just as they have had a tremendous impact on the development of Soviet law in the early 20th century, perhaps the legal scholars of the 1990s will play a part in the radical restructuring (and Westernisation?) of the new Russian society.

Was the socialist system part of the civil law system?

The present writer respectfully disagrees with Quigley's overall conclusion that the socialist system was simply another extension of the civil law system. Even though he is perfectly correct to highlight the similarities between civil law and socialist law, as many other writers do, it is surely the powerful influence of the Marxist/Leninist ideology and its manifestations, that were once all pervading, all encompassing and totally dominant in societies like the former Soviet Union, that unquestionably distinguished it from civil law systems and any other legal system. The former Soviet Union punished any individual who made 'profits' derived from 'unearned income' which had been gained from private enterprise; it had no separation of powers; its agencies were not allowed to criticise Soviet laws; doctrinal writers could only criticise laws if they were obsolete laws and, even then, criticism had to be analytical rather than political and certainly not polemical. The courts simply carried out government policy or the Communist Party's policy. They developed the remarkable institution/office, known as the 'Procurator', which combined the roles of prosecutor, investigator, appellate agency, advocate and welfare officer.

Another important point of differentiation is that, whereas the French Code was seen as the epitome of French liberty and the Revolution, the Soviet Codes were regarded merely as a basis for the furtherance of political aims and objectives which would have to be modified, as socialist society changed, in accordance with the building of a truly communist society.

Yet another point of significance was in the socialist treatment of property. Under Soviet socialism, property was limited to two categories: socialist property and personal property. Personal property was that which individuals were permitted to own for their own consumption. Socialist property included property owned outright by the State, and property owned by 'public' organisations and collective farms. These nominally independent bodies functioned as if they were organs of the State. Four basic characteristics of the Stalinist-style economy are: 'collective ownership of the means of production; enterprise performance evaluated in terms of gross quantitative output targets; fixed prices bearing no relation to market forces; and a centralised hierarchical administrative apparatus' (see Stephan (1991) p 39).

Upon assuming power, President Gorbachev indicated his determination to face the problems of deteriorating standards of living and erosion of the nomenclature's position in society. Although initially imposing authoritarian measures to deal with these problems, the end of 1986 saw the leader altering his approach to address the increasing economic problems. In December 1986, the Law on Individual Labour Activity established a procedure whereby individuals could engage in small scale production of consumer goods, sell services such as repairs, and open family run hotels. By 1990, there was a distinct trend towards the full restoration and reinstatement of private property (see Stephan (1991) p 49).

In the field of foreign investment, access of Soviet firms to foreign markets was radically expanded, by 1988, together with the liberalisation of the rules governing joint ventures. In fact, the Law on Co-operatives of the USSR, which was enacted in the spring of 1988, legalised private economic activity. It permitted private firms, organised as co-operatives, to hire labour, sell shares and to 'engage in any kind of activity except those prohibited under legislation of the USSR and the Union Republics'. In October 1990, the Soviet legislature endorsed a plan for privatisation of the State economy. Since then, a number of State endorsed ventures have been initiated, although Russia continues to struggle against rampant inflation (around 2,000%, according to some estimates) and an ageing superstructure in need of radical refurbishment.

Inquest on the Russian Empire

The Empire in Russia really began in 1552, when Tsar Ivan IV ordained the building of the Cathedral of the Annunciation in Kazan to celebrate his victory over the Tartars. This was to mark the moment when Muscovy first conquered infidel territory and imposed its rule over non-Slav people. In the intervening years, the Russian Empire has been the largest in the history of the world and outstripped the British Empire in terms of sheer longevity. The Empire was unusual in that it made no clear distinction between metropolis and colonies. The colonised territories were not overseas, but all adjacent to or encircling the heartlands. Russians found it natural to resettle there as if they were simply moving into another region of their home territory.

Thus, until recently, Russians readily accepted the right of all citizens to move freely and live in different parts of the country. But, Russia continued to assert its control over the Eurasian expanses because of fear of subjection to some other power. The cost of defending and administering a huge and diverse territory has exacted its toll, and the price paid by the Russian people has been despotism, serfdom, heavy taxation and an oversized bureaucracy.

Alexander II (1855–81) attempted to create the institutions of civil society by abolishing serfdom and setting up elective government assemblies, the beginnings of land reform, reforms in local administration, a hierarchy of law courts and a citizen army based on adult male conscription. During his 'period of great reforms', judges were made independent of the administrative wing of the government for the first time.

Nicholas II then established an elected Parliament. But, the Russian people created institutions of their own, such as the soviets of workers', soldiers' and peasants' deputies, modelled on the village community. It was those soviets which, in 1917, seized power under the leadership of the Communist Party and then gave their name to the State which emerged from the ruins of imperial Russia.

Under the communists, the Empire acquired a fresh start and renewed vigour, but the new era was short lived. Although Lenin and Stalin managed to turn the Empire into the second mightiest State in the world, this had its price. While encouraging mass literacy in the numerous vernacular languages of the Soviet Union and creating virtually sovereign State structures for even small ethnic groups, all States were tightly controlled and severely restricted by the ethos of the planned economy and the centralised power, and the overweening influence of the one party rule of the Communist Party.

Thus, even small doses of *glasnost* (opening up Russian society) were enough to cause a stir and upset the odd balance of national fervour and repression of individual liberty that is typical of Russian society. Gorbachev's other innovation – *perestroika* – the restructuring of Soviet society, may have failed during his short presidential reign, but surely he has blazed a trail for others, the democratic and privatising aspects of which Yeltsin and his successors will surely endeavour to pursue.

The end of the USSR and the new Russian Federation

Marxist/Leninist ideology inspired the classical planned economy of the former USSR, and other socialist countries, which contrasted with the market economy of the West. The Soviet Union's form of communist rule began with the October Revolution of 1917 (or, strictly, 30 December 1922) and ended in December 1991. On 2 September 1991, President Gorbachev and 10 of the 15 republic leaders signed a declaration recommending that central government be suspended until a new constitution is signed. This declaration, presented at the opening session of the full Soviet Parliament, effectively declared the end of the USSR.

On 21 December 1991, 11 of the 12 remaining republics, who were willing to form a new confederation, met and signed a Treaty, establishing a new Commonwealth of Independent States, with Russia, under its President Boris Yeltsin, its acknowledged leader. This was pursuant to an earlier agreement signed between Russia, Belorussia and the Ukraine on 8 December 1991, which announced that the headquarters of the new Commonwealth would be not Moscow, but Minsk, the Belorussian capital.

The great ideological experiment, begun by Lenin's Bolshevik Revolution, lasted just over 74 years. The Soviet State, which had been constituted on 30 December 1922, ceased to exist a few days before its 70th year. In 1992, the former Russian Soviet Federative Socialist Republic (RSFSR) changed its name to the 'Russian Federation'.

The treaty creating the Commonwealth begins with a Preamble stating the objectives of building democratic, law governed States on the basis of mutual recognition and respect for sovereignty, and the 11 States then say:

> Co-operation between members of the Commonwealth will be carried out in accordance with the principle of equality through co-ordinating institutions, formed on a parity basis and operating in the way established by agreements between members of the Commonwealth, which is neither a State nor a super-State structure.

Crucially, it also states: 'With the formation of the Commonwealth of Independent States, the Union of the Soviet Socialist Republics ceases to exist.'

Republics which have not joined the Commonwealth are Estonia, Latvia, Lithuania and Georgia. Of course, the new Commonwealth is not a State; it has no central government or common citizenship. It has some attributes of both the British Commonwealth and the European Community, but is unlike either. It really resembles most closely a federation of States with each State retaining independence in many matters. However, like the former Soviet Union, it faces extremely serious economic problems and, once President Gorbachev resigned on 25 December 1991, the Russian President Yeltsin issued decrees which carried on the Gorbachev legacy of *glasnost* and *perestroika*, moving the new Commonwealth into an era of private enterprise, capitalism and some form of social democracy.

Russian law – return to civil law or hybrid system?

It should be noted that, during the era of the Soviet Union, the 1922 Civil Code of the Russian Socialist Federated Soviet Republic (RSFSR) was derived from the German Civil Code. Before the Revolution, Russia was, in fact, a civil law country. Accordingly, the style of law making in the USSR was through codes and legislation. In fact, a code or set of laws would often be enacted at Federal level and then expanded and adapted to form the version for the codes of the constituent republics. Hence, it is apparently President Yeltsin's intention, at the present time, to leave undisturbed any existing laws which do not conflict with civil liberties' reforms or economic and criminal law changes he is implementing (such as family law codes), or the reforms in private ownership which he has begun to introduce. Laws that were passed under the former Soviet regime were, therefore, all-union laws, being applicable to all republics, republic laws and local legislation.

The courts were used to promote and carry out State and government policy. All this was supposed to change under the new laws in the new Federation. If the old republic codes remain undisturbed for non-economic regulation, a hybrid system, which is similar to the African legal system, may eventually result. Certain socialist based procedures will remain, alongside new 'democratic' and capitalist laws, within a civil law legislative and judicial framework. We now examine a sample of some of the ongoing legal changes that are taking place in the Russian Federation in the late 1990s.

Russian Federation reforms

(a) Reform of the judiciary: The Russian Justice Minister announced, on 25 December 1991, that judicial reform had begun in Russia and that 'reliable guarantees – juridical and constitutional – have been created for the irreversibilty of this reform'. A 'very substantial' increase in the pay of judges and the removal of the budgetary system of judicial power in Russia is supposed to be introduced. Incentives have been promised to make it a competition to become a judge, so that 'from now onwards, jurists might consider it their greatest dream to become a judge as the peak of a juridical career'. Recruitment of people of the highest calibre will be sought.

(b) Institution of the jury: 'once again, the stage by stage introduction of this institution, whereby whether a person is guilty or not, will be decided by the public'; but 'only the issue of guilt or innocence, not the measure of punishment' will be their task.

(c) A new law on the pledging of security has been introduced.

(d) A new Criminal Code is being introduced. This had its first reading in the spring of 1992. For the first time, priority will be given for the protection of the individual's rights. The interests of owners will be recognised as paramount. Articles dealing with punishment for private enterprise 'crimes' have been annulled (repealed). There will no longer be any punishment of close relatives of a criminal for the failure to report the crime. The list of crimes punishable by death has been considerably decreased. The list of Articles under which capital punishment could be ordered has been reduced from 27 to three, and women and minors will not be included. The maximum period of imprisonment will probably remain at 15 years.

There are new Articles dealing with criminal responsibility, for example, for setting up fraudulent businesses.

On 29 January 1992, President Yeltsin approved a decree whose intention is to accelerate privatisation. This basically encourages applications of privatisation of State and municipal enterprises which may be submitted by work collectives of enterprises, their subdivisions, Russian and foreign legal persons and citizens on the basis of the RSFSR Law, On the Privatisation of State and Municipal Enterprises of the RSFSR.

Russian courts and Russian trials: the new Russia in action?

Several reforms have taken place with regard to Russian courts in the Russian Federation. For instance, there are the new style *arbitrazh* courts which are different from the previous *gosarbitrazh* courts. The *arbitrazh* courts are State sponsored tribunals which are responsible for resolving economic disputes. They remain institutionally distinct from courts of general jurisdiction and from the constitutional court. They are, of course, similar to institutions in France and Germany. However, the Russian innovations are: the lowering of fees for filing cases; parties must now bear the burden for assembling and presenting evidence; hearing cases by a single judge; requiring that judicial opinions include the rationale for the decision; enforcing decisions; and reforming appellate procedure. One of the most significant changes here is that petitioners now have the burden of proving their case to the court. The prior rules merely obliged petitioners to respond to requests by the judge for evidence, rather than for petitioners to demonstrate the liability of the defendant. Hence, for those courts which deal with economic disputes, the judge has to decide the case based on the evidence presented by the parties. These courts also have the right to decide in the petitioner's favour if the defendant fails to present evidence to support the claim.

Another innovation is that judicial opinions or written judgments must now comply with requirements in order to be valid: they must consist of introductory, descriptive, explanatory and determinative parts. Judges are, therefore, required to explain the basis for their decisions.

The major problem of implementation of judicial decisions has also been tackled. The burden of enforcing the judgment lies entirely on the petitioner and, if he wins, but the defendant does not have the money to pay the petitioner in the bank, the chances of recovery are very poor indeed. Assuming no appeal is made, the petitioner may obtain another court order to recover the judgment from the defendant's bank account but, if this cannot cover it, marketable assets may be seized by the judicial enforcer (equivalent to the British bailiff or US marshall) and these may be sold if buyers of those assets can be found. The whole process is fraught with difficulties and, although a whole new body of judicial enforcers (*sudebnyi ispolnitel*) has been created to assist with implementation, the current situation is still very much beset by the country's huge economic problems and is not proving very effective.

There is also a completely new Russian institution known as the Cassation Court, of which there are now 10, to which a litigant may appeal even after the case has been reviewed by the appellate court. Each court hears appeals from a specified geographical region, rather like the Federal Circuit Courts of the

United States. Some of its judges come from legal practice, others from academia. They are not, therefore, selected from the existing *arbitrazh* courts. The function of the Cassation Court is not to consider a case on its merits, but rather to review cases for legal errors. It is only concerned with mistakes, which might have been made in applying the substantive or procedural law, that might have caused an incorrect decision to have been made by the trial or appellate court. It has the power to uphold the appellate decision or reinstate the lower court decision. It may also overturn both decisions, remand the case for a new hearing or even make a new ruling. Any decision to change a previous ruling may be based on violations of substantive or procedural law.

In practice, the Cassation Courts have gone beyond merely substantive or procedural errors and considered other errors.

An unsuccessful litigant may also appeal to the Higher *Arbitrazh* Court. All existing remedies must be exhausted before the Higher *Arbitrazh* Court may be approached. The appeal is still called a 'protest', as in Soviet times, and the rules for such an appeal are unchanged – the litigant can only petition for a protest to be issued, and the only two sets of officials who have the right to issue protests are the chairman of the Higher *Arbitrazh* Court and his deputies, and the General Procurator and his deputies.

Observation of a Russian trial by the ICJ

The Justice Organisation reported, in its international section, on a visit to Moscow by its legal officer to participate in observation of a Russian trial. In October 1997, an International Commission of Jurists (ICJ) delegation went to Moscow to observe the trial of a female Nigerian student who had been detained for 21 months on drugs charges. The three person delegation included representatives from Sweden, Poland and the UK. The case illustrates the problems Russia faces as it seeks to comply with its Council of Europe obligations. Russia became a member, in February 1996, after it introduced domestic protection measures. These included the creation of a constitutional court and a Bill of Rights. The defendant was arrested on 16 January 1996, but was not brought before the court until 2 April 1996. Even more significantly, it was not until 9 October 1997, in the presence of the ICJ delegation, that the judge considered an application for her immediate release. This was refused and there was no appeal to a higher court.

The delay in the trial highlighted problems in the legal process: (i) There was no interpreter present at the defendant's arrest or when she was charged, despite the fact she spoke fluent English, but poor Russian. Repeated requests for a second English translation of the indictment (due to the incomprehensible first version of the indictment) were ignored. The defendant did not receive a copy of the indictment until September 1997, after a court hearing at which Amnesty International trial observers were present. Further adjournments were made as a result of the failure to find an English speaking interpreter for the trial. An interpreter was eventually appointed by the court in May 1997. (ii) The judge failed to use her power to compel attendance of witnesses, which included police witnesses, by way of summons; the trial kept being delayed on several occasions by non-appearance of these witnesses.

The trial was adjourned during the ICJ visit. The defendant was eventually tried and convicted in early November 1997. She was sentenced to eight years imprisonment. The prosecution called six witnesses, but only one attended the trial. An earlier defence application to call a witness on behalf of the defence was refused by the judge. The defendant is currently appealing.

Lack of accommodation was another problem: throughout her detention, the defendant shared a cell with 54 other inmates in a cell with 43 beds.

This is just a snapshot of one trial observed by an international organisation. It also involved drugs allegations, which remain a huge problem in Russia's volatile situation, and should not be taken as necessarily representative. But, it is certainly worth noting.

The new Russian Federation Constitution

The Russian Federation's Parliament debated its new draft constitution, which has undergone various amendments and, eventually, came into force on 12 December 1993, the day of the nationwide vote (referendum). Extracts from the latest December 1993 version are reproduced here. A number of salient points may be noted.

Its Preamble commences:

> We, the multi-ethnic people of the Russian Federation, unified by our common destiny on our land, seeking to advance human rights and freedoms and promote civil peace and accord, preserving a historically established State unity, guided by universally recognised principles of equality and self-determination of peoples, honouring the memory of our ancestors ... considering ourselves a part of the world community ...

Article 1 boldly declares: 'The Russian Federation ... shall be a democratic Federative law based State with a republican form of government':

(a) There is a clear statement in Art 2, Chapter 1, that 'Human beings and human rights and freedoms shall be of the highest value. Recognition of, respect for, and the protection of the human and civil rights and freedoms, shall be the duty of the State'.

(b) Article 3(1) declares that 'The multi-ethnic people of the Russian Federation shall be the bearer of its sovereignty and the sole source of authority in the Russian Federation', and Art 3(2) continues, 'The people shall exercise their power directly and also through bodies of State authority and also through bodies of local self-government'. It states, further, that 'Referendums and free elections shall be the highest expression of the people's authority'. It further declares that 'No one shall have the right to appropriate power in the Russian Federation. Seizure of power or appropriation of authority shall be prosecuted in accordance with Federal law'.

(c) The principle of 'government by the people' is stated in Art 4. This stresses, *inter alia*, that the elections of State authorities, specified by the constitution of the Russian Federation, are free and are conducted on the basis of universal, equal and direct suffrage by ballot. It also states that 'Citizens of the Russian Federation have the right to resist any attempt at the forcible elimination or revision of the current constitutional system'.

(d) Article 4(2) stipulates that 'The Constitution of the Russian Federation and Federal laws shall have priority throughout the territory of the Russian Federation'.

(e) Article 5 states that 'The Russian Federation shall be made up of republics, territories, regions, cities with Federal status, the autonomous region and autonomous areas, all of which are equal members of the Russian Federation'. Article 5(3) is particularly illuminating: 'The Federative make up of the Russian Federation shall be based upon its State integrity, a uniform system of State authority, the separation of jurisdiction and powers between the bodies of State authority of the Russian Federation, and the equality and self-determination of the peoples within the Russian Federation.'

(f) Article 5 also emphasises that 'Democracy in the Russian Federation is exercised on the basis of political and ideological diversity, a multiparty system and the participation of non-party persons'.

(g) Article 6 states that 'The system of State power in the Russian Federation is based on the principles of the separation of legislative, executive and judicial power, and also delineation of the terms of reference and authority between the Russian Federation and its constituent republics, *krays*, *oblasts*, autonomous *oblasts*, autonomous *okrugs* and local self-government'.

(h) Article 7(1) declares that 'The Russian Federation shall be a social State, whose policies shall aim at creating conditions ensuring adequate living standards and the free development of every individual'.

Article 7(2) goes on to say 'Citizens of the Russian Federation shall be guaranteed the protection of their work and health; a minimum wage; State support for the family, motherhood, fatherhood, childhood, invalids and aged people; the development of a system of social services; and the provision of State pensions, allowances and other social security guarantees'.

(i) Article 10 elaborates further 'State power in the Russian Federation shall be exercised on the basis of its separation into legislative, executive and judicial branches. The bodies of legislative, executive and judicial power shall be independent of each other'. In accordance with the reform of the judiciary, Art 120 declares that judges shall be independent and subject only to the constitution of the Russian Federation and Federal law. They are now irremovable, although their powers may be discontinued or suspended in accordance with the procedure and on the grounds established by Federal law.

(j) Article 11(1) declares that 'State power in the Russian Federation shall be exercised by the President of the Russian Federation, the Federal Assembly (Federal Council and State *Duma*), the government of the Russian Federation and the courts of law of the Russian Federation'.

Article 11(2) stipulates that 'State power in the members of the Russian Federation shall be exercised by the bodies of State authority established by them'.

Article 11(3) further states that 'the jurisdiction and powers between the bodies of State authority of the Russian Federation shall be delineated by this Constitution, the Federation Treaty and other treaties on the delineation of jurisdiction and powers'.

(k) Article 7 declares that the State and territorial arrangement of the Russian Federation is based on the principle of Federalism.

(l) Article 13 enshrines the principle that 'Ideological pluralism shall be recognised in the Russian Federation' that 'No ideology shall be established as a State or compulsory ideology'; and that 'political diversity and a multiparty system shall be recognised in the Russian Federation'. Indeed, it goes on to state that 'all public associations shall be equal before the law'. However, this Article concludes by declaring that 'The creation and activity of public associations whose purposes or actions are directed at forcibly changing the foundations of the constitutional system; disrupting the integrity of the Russian Federation; subverting the security of the State; creating armed units; or inciting social, racial, ethnic or religious strife, shall be prohibited'.

(m) Article 14 stipulates that 'the Russian Federation shall be a secular State. No religion shall be declared an official or compulsory religion'. Accordingly, 'all religious associations shall be separate from the State and shall be equal before the law'.

(n) Article 17 contains a ringing endorsement of Western style democratic principles. It declares that, 'In the Russian Federation, human and civil rights and freedoms shall be recognised and guaranteed under universally acknowledged principles and rules of international law and in accordance with the Constitution'.

(o) In the second chapter of the Constitution, headed 'Human and Civil Rights and Freedoms', there are enumerations of basic rights, liberties and obligations. Article 19 states, for example, that all are 'equal before the law and the court'. It also declares that 'The State shall guarantee equal human and civil rights and freedoms without regard to sex, race, nationality, language, origin, property or official status, place of residence, attitude to religion, persuasions, affiliation with social associations or other circumstances. Any form of restriction of civil rights on the basis of social, racial, national, language or religious affiliation shall be prohibited'. It continues: 'Men and women shall have equal rights and freedoms and equal opportunities to exercise them.'

(p) Chapter 2 also contains Articles which declare everyone's 'right to life', the right to freedom, and freedom of movement and choice of residence, and 'inviolability' of one's person and one's abode, the right to freedom of thought and speech, the unimpeded expression of one's opinions and beliefs and the right to renounce them. Article 22 stipulates that 'Arrest, taking into custody and holding in custody, shall only be authorised by a judicial decision. Without a judicial decision, no person may be subjected to detention for a period of more than 48 hours'. For lawyers and civil libertarians interested in the right to privacy, which does not have any statutory equivalent in England and Wales, Art 23(2) declares that 'Each person shall have the right to privacy of correspondence, telephone conversations, postal, telegraph and other messages. The restriction of this right shall only be allowed on the basis of a judicial decision'.

Article 24 then states that 'The gathering, storage, use and dissemination of information on the private life of an individual without the individual's consent shall not be allowed'. Further, 'The bodies of State authority ... local self-government and their officials shall be obliged to provide each person access to documents and materials that directly affect his rights and freedoms unless otherwise specified in the law'.

Article 26 guarantees freedom of worship – the right to freely confess any religion or not confess any religion, to choose, hold and disseminate religious, non-religious or other beliefs and to act in accordance with them, given compliance with the law.

(q) Article 29 deals with freedom of thought and speech and contains two illuminating sub-sections. Article 29(4) states, *inter alia,* that the list of data that constitute State secrets shall be fixed by Federal law, and Art 29(5) categorically states that 'Freedom of the mass media shall be guaranteed. Censorship shall be prohibited'.

(r) Under Art 36(1), 'Citizens and their associations shall be entitled to have land in private ownership'.

(s) Article 45 reiterates that 'The State protection of human and civil rights and freedoms in the Russian Federation shall be guaranteed'.

(t) Article 49 declares that each person accused of a crime has the right to have his case examined by a court of law. The presumption of innocence is also stated, thereunder, as well as the fact that a defendant is not required to prove his innocence. It also asserts that 'everyone has the right to a review of his case by a superior court' and 'the right to ask for a pardon or a lessening of a sentence'. Nobody may be sentenced for a second time for one and the same crime. The State shall also provide victims of crime or abuses of authority access to justice and compensation for damage.

(u) Under Art 123, proceedings in all courts shall be open. Hearings *in camera* shall only be allowed in cases provided for by Federal law. Judicial proceedings shall be conducted on the basis of adversary procedure and equality of the parties, and shall be conducted with the participation of a jury in cases provided for by Federal law.

(v) Compulsory labour is prohibited (Art 37).

(w) Article 34 declares that each person shall have the right to use freely his abilities and property for entrepreneurial or any other economic activities not prohibited by law.

(x) Chapter 7 deals with judicial power. Article 118 makes it clear that 'judicial power shall be administered by courts of law only. The judicial system shall be established by the Constitution of the Russian Federation and Federal Constitutional law. It is exercised by means of constitutional, civil, administrative and criminal judicial proceedings'. It goes on to say that 'the creation of emergency courts shall be prohibited'.

(y) Article 56 declares that individual restrictions on rights and freedoms, with an indication of the scope and time limits of their operation, may, in accordance with Federal law, be imposed in a period of a state of emergency to safeguard citizens' safety and uphold the constitutional system.

Belorussian reforms

On 23 April 1992, the Belorussian Parliament recognised the need to implement a legal reform as one of the conditions of building in the republic a rule of law State, and confirmed the basic provisions of the plan of the reform. The main purpose of the reform is the creation of a legal system capable of ensuring the functioning of a rule of law State, the assertion of an independent judiciary as the main guarantor of civic (citizens') rights and liberties, the implementation in the legislation of democratic principles of the organisation and activity of law enforcement bodies in accordance with generally recognised norms of international law. It was stressed that the 'judicial authorities' would be separated from the 'legislative and executive authorities' as well as from political parties and public associations.

Legal reform in Belorussia will be implemented in three stages:

(a) changes will be made to the existing legislation dealing with adoption of laws on the constitutional court, the public prosecutor's office, the bar, notary's service and national security service;

(b) organisational measures will be implemented to create basic elements for the new system of judiciary bodies, such as the jury, the investigating committee, and Courts of Appeal;

(c) the final aims of the legal reforms will be implemented, including the creation of the new system of judiciary bodies acting on the basis of the new legislation.

Towards a Russian social democratic State?

It would appear that the foundations have certainly been laid, in this most complex and contradictory of countries, for a social democracy to replace whatever form of socialism that existed. All the prerequisites of a democratic State seem to be there – civil liberties, separation of powers, independent judiciary, guaranteed freedoms, media freedom, the right to decide whether to join a trade union (Art 30 of the Russian Federation Constitution), even the switch to private ownership in the capitalist mode, intercountry economic ventures and a preponderance of leaders who, at least, say they wish to have a more democratic society.

But, new federations and newly declared independent States apart, the future of the new republics, or of the fringe republics, is far from assured. Old conflicts are unresolved, economic problems are ever escalating, scarcity of basic supplies is still prevalent, productivity remains low and new problems continue to emerge. The method of privatisation currently being favoured is a system of vouchers awarded to every Russian citizen in order to break up the old State companies into a number of democratically owned units. Yet, this system has never worked in capitalist countries, and the value of the vouchers is already falling as people try to exchange them for money.

President Yeltsin has also extended the special powers he was given by the Parliament last year, so that he has the right to 'hire and fire' ministers at will. He postponed the local elections, which were due by the end of 1992, and has an ambivalent attitude towards answering questions from MPs, but agrees to talk to the press 'as a favour' to the journalists. It is still unclear what the division of responsibility between Parliament and President is, but, rather than create a system of democratic institutions, Yeltsin prefers to rule by decree.

There is, therefore, no true accountability in the Russian Federation, such as an equivalent of the American system of regular presidential press conferences, and no equivalent of the Prime Minister's 'Question Time' in the British House of Commons.

In 1998, President Yeltsin dramatically dismissed his entire government twice in six months. It was only after the ousting of Sergei Kiriyenko, the new Prime Minister, in August 1998, that Yeltsin seemed to retreat into illness and make even fewer public appearances. His poor health is extremely well documented and there have been many calls for his resignation, which abated somewhat, in September 1998, when Yevgeni Primakov was appointed. Yeltsin's popularity rating in January 1999 was 1% of popular support.

The economic crisis in Russia ever deepens. Russia's government and private firms together owe US$194 billion of foreign debt to overseas governments and banks. The effect of Russia's parlous economic state is that it is now taking the world financial system ever closer to the edge, and the system is now so structured that the losses in one country are transmitted to another with the movements in financial prices greatly exaggerated by the speculative derivative markets. On the comparative front, the economic problems in South East Asia have not helped. Unemployment in Russia looks set to rise by at least half a million over the next two years and, perhaps, very much more.

In the light of its multifaceted problems, wholesale transformation of the Russian economic and political landscape is urgently required; a transformation which involves the hearts and minds of the people, with strong and positive leadership, so that the ingrained economic conventions of the people may be replaced by a spirit of enterprise. There is an urgent need for a body of commercial law to develop to elevate the concept of contract to a pivotal place in the market. Indeed, there is also a need to develop a system of tort law. Both these developments will lead to its citizens becoming more aware of their legal rights, and the need to defend such rights in court rather than depend on the State to do so.

But, political stability remains absolutely essential as a prerequisite.

Other recent developments

The brooding omnipresence and dissatisfaction of the reduced Russian armies maintains the dark cloud of a potential coup and an internal coup is never to be discounted. Even worse, the country retains a formidable arsenal which, even if not totally modern, could still wreak havoc. The battlegrounds in places, like Moldavia, Georgia and Chechenya, indicate that a lasting peace may not be possible without more bloodshed and suffering. Historians will doubtless continue to debate the question of whether the union could have been preserved and whether the old USSR was even truly 'socialist'. The recent war in the Balkans involving Serbia and Kosovo and the countries of the North Atlantic Treaty Organisation (NATO) (March 24–June 13 1999) demonstrated that Russia is still inclined to support its old allies, like the Serb leader President Milosevic, until international pressure is brought to bear on it. In this case, such pressure resulted in eventual co-operation with NATO after Milosevic eventually agreed to withdraw his troops from Kosovo, after 72 days of NATO bombing raids, to stop reported atrocities against thousands of ethnic Albanians who were driven from their home in the former Yugoslavia. Less than a month into the Balkans conflict of 1999, President Yeltsin had warned NATO that, unless NATO ceased their bombing raids, there could be Russian military action against them, sparking a European war or possibly even a world war. The uneasy relationship between Russia and the West is graphically demonstrated by this recent conflict, although Russia eventually co-operated with the West in presenting Milosevic with an international peace plan.

In terms of the development of legal systems, there were certainly clear efforts by Russian leaders, from the end of the 1980s through the 1990s, to achieve some form of social democracy, and this will probably develop within a civil law framework. But, the current signs of its wholesale, early implementation are not encouraging.

If the law of the new Russian Federation and non-member republics consists of a combination of civil law (based on Roman law or more recent continental versions) and a quasi-military government, in some ways resembling a South American junta or some form of benevolent dictatorship, or even a completely new version of social democracy, it will not really matter. What will matter is whether the Russian people will, ultimately, be allowed to live in a stable society which is able to provide the average family with minimum living standards, law and order, and the provision of their basic needs.

It remains to be seen whether this new Russian political and economic experiment will eventually succeed in transforming Russian society so that, in the words of the Russian Constitution, its people will be able 'to advance human rights and freedoms' and 'promote civil peace and harmony, preserve the historically evolved State unity ... ensuring Russia's well being and prosperity and preserve the immutability of its democratic foundations'.

HYBRID LEGAL SYSTEMS

Jurisdictions in which there is more than one system co-existing with one another are sometimes described as mixed jurisdictions or systems, or hybrid systems of law. Hooker (1975) uses the term 'legal pluralism' to describe the situation where two or more laws interact, often as the result of colonisation or annexation. The classic work on the operation of judicial decisions and doctrine was a collection of essays, published in 1974, edited by Joseph Dainow (see Dainow (ed), *The Role of Judicial Decisions and Doctrine in Civil Law and in Mixed Jurisdictions* (1974)). This book covers developments in Louisiana, South Africa, Scotland, Israel and Mexico.

Examples of jurisdictions where common law and civil law co-exist and interact include South Africa, Sri Lanka, Scotland, Louisiana, Quebec, the

Philippines, Japan, Mauritius, the Cameroons, St Lucia and the Seychelles Islands.

The Seychelles Islands, situated in the Indian Ocean, provide one example of this fusion of civil and common law. They have a civil law tradition dating back to 1756 when the original French settlers annexed it and promulgated the French Civil Code and Commercial Code in 1808 and 1809, respectively. However, they also have a common law tradition dating from 1814 when the islands were ceded to Britain. They became a Crown colony in 1903 and achieved independence in 1976. Hence, English common law was introduced by legislation passed after the British arrival, but, although these laws regulate daily administration, it is French substantive law and French codifications that continue to form the bedrock of Seychelles law. French case law is also relied upon, although there is no strict doctrine of precedent. Generally, judicial decisions in the Seychelles have high persuasive authority and will be followed unless there are good reasons for not doing so (Art 5 of the Seychelles Civil Code). English law applies to certain branches of its law such as maritime and shipping law, company law, banking, business and civil procedure. A new Civil Code was introduced in 1976 which, although printed in English, follows the structure and style of the original French Civil Code, but its content is a unique blend of English and French law updated to suit modern social and economic conditions.

OTHER TYPES OF LAW

The meaning of 'law' is a many sided question to which several eminent writers have responded with different conceptions and interpretations. There are, of course, other non-Western conceptions of 'law' such as the Muslim, Hindu, African, Chinese and Japanese conceptions of law. These are based on religious beliefs or customary law. It is not proposed to discuss these laws here, but salient points regarding Eastern laws, such as the Chinese and Japanese conceptions of law, will be highlighted.

Eastern legal conceptions

A number of general comments may be made on Eastern laws. First, these systems traditionally perceive law as playing a minor role in the sense that it is simply another vehicle for maintaining peace and social order. Secondly, law and the recourse to the courts is traditionally seen as a last resort, where all other methods of mediation, conciliation, persuasion and moderation have failed. Many Far Eastern countries adopted codes on Romano-Germanic lines, but a number of these then opted for the communist ideology. Countries like Indo-China, Japan, Malaysia and Burma also experienced major wars or uprisings or colonisation, in one form or another, which have left their imprint on the development and composition of their laws. Japan underwent codification using German and French legal models and then experienced a radical Americanisation of laws and culture in the aftermath of the Second World War which has, in no small measure, resulted in their spectacular economic development, to become, arguably, the leading industrial country in the world. These diverse influences have left Japan with a unique blend of Western and Eastern conceptions of law and legal tradition.

The Chinese conception of law

A predominant principle of the traditional Chinese conception of law has been the belief in a cosmic order of the universe, involving an interactive relationship between heaven, earth and men. The universe is seen as the basis of law. China's 3,000 year old history produced numerous philosophical ideas, with three main philosophical traditions influencing the development of the legal system in China: the Confucian, Legalist and the Buddhist. Chinese sources of law, thus, derive from these traditions.

While the Confucian believes in a natural harmony between man's ritual propriety and the natural principles of the universe, the Legalists' theory, which originated in the 3rd century BC, argued that there should be government by law (obeying legal prescriptions) rather than government by men. These theories proved too remote and alien to the Chinese of the time and, by 206 BC, Confucianism was re-established as the favoured philosophy and the ideology of the State by the Han dynasty.

Two levels of law operate within Buddhism or the Buddha-Dharma: (i) karma (action): the law of action and reaction; the most general of all laws, which includes good and evil, physical or psychic; (ii) the Buddhist law of causation: a belief that good and evil are a direct consequence of the actions of the mind. Buddhism draws much sharper distinctions between the intention to commit evil, or acts committed with intent, and actions committed without premeditation or forethought.

None of these traditions have been eradicated despite the outward conversion to communism in China.

Codification

Chinese Codes appeared at the time of the Han dynasty, but dealt only with administrative and criminal law matters. It continued to dominate all aspects of life for the next 2,000 years. In an attempt to unshackle themselves from Western ideas and Western domination, the Chinese adopted a series of Codes ironically based on Western prototypes. They passed a Civil Code in 1929–31 (dealing with private and commercial law), a Code of Civil Procedure in 1932 and a Land Code in 1930. Since Hong Kong was annexed by the British, these Codes were never in force there. Chinese law underwent a period of Europeanisation and, on one level, can be included within the Romano-Germanic legal family. But, if one lifted the veil of codification and legislation, one would find the old Chinese traditions and societal hierarchies, family and kinship networks still very much alive. In fact, despite the Codes and the apparent Westernisation of Chinese law, Chinese judges have been quite prepared to ignore the Codes and formalistic laws if they conflicted with more humane Chinese customs. Despite China embracing communism on 1 October 1949, the Buddhist ethics of motivation have continued to be followed up to today, although the government of the new People's Republic has officially adopted a Marxist-Leninist ideology.

Different versions of communism in China

Whenever a conflict between Maoism and older traditions has occurred, Chinese communists have been quick to follow the established tradition of advocating *li* (interpersonal law), rather than *fa* (new law based, *inter alia*, on punishment for compliance). Although avowedly Marxist-Leninist in ideology, the Chinese have been at pains to emphasise moral development and civic consciousness among its citizens, much more so than the former USSR. In the first few years of communism, law would be given primacy and urgent measures were taken to build a new society and new social order. All existing laws, decrees and courts had been abolished by the 'common programme' of 1949, so that speed was of the essence in rebuilding the social matrix. In fact, China adopted a Soviet model of Marxism until 1957, when relations between China and the former USSR began to deteriorate, and in 1960 China decided to pursue their own version of communism, emphasising a more individual based social transformation, in preference to economic growth, allowing greater participation by the managers and directors of enterprises, settlement of disputes rather than litigation, compromise by persuasion, repentance for misdemeanours and a return to ancient tradition. One noticeable consequence of these changes in philosophy, social relations and rejection of the 'principle of legality' has been the virtual disappearance of any transcendental philosophy linking man's behaviour with the cosmic order and nature.

The doctrines of Chairman Mao have replaced Soviet approaches to a Marxist run society. Some of Chairman Mao's most potent ideas became the subject of a 'Mao cult', motivated by the Socialist Education Movement, promoting the ideas that political leaders must share the concerns and lifestyle of the peasant or commoner, and that the masses are a progressive political force with revolutionary potential. There was a general wave of anti-elitism primarily among middle rank officials. Law was, once again, seen as the last resort and as a constant tension between right wing and left wing groups.

Almost no legislation was passed after 1949 right up to the death of Mao, in 1976. The traditional Chinese antagonism toward rigid forms of legislative prescription re-surfaced. Consequently, there is only a small body of judicial decisions, and a mere handful of reported Supreme Court decisions. No doctrine of judicial precedent is known. Neither have there been any substantial amounts of doctrinal writing.

Chinese law in the post-Mao era

In the aftermath of the arrest of the 'gang of four', China has developed two systems of justice: (i) 'popular' justice; and (ii) bureaucratic justice. The popular model is based on the radical ideals of continuing revolution and self-reliance, rejecting codification and opposing any sort of formalising legislation which would stultify current social structures, while social inequities still persist in China, which is still in a state of transition. The workers, farmers, women and neighbourhood residents play a large part in policing this sort of system. The bureaucratic model is based on the premise that law is necessary to consolidate past gains, to control and govern future changes, to maintain State control and ensure the continued progress and means of production. Police, courts and the Procurate (modelled on the Soviet quasi-military office) play an essential part in this sort of system. Co-operation and confrontation between the two models continued throughout the 1970s.

In 1978, a new constitution was enacted and legislation once again began to appear. Since 1979, laws have been passed on elections, court organisation, joint ventures, Chinese and foreign capital investment, marriage, local government and the environment, and there is now a Code of Criminal Procedure and a Criminal Code. With the passing of several more laws which, *ex facie*, appear to eradicate uncertainty and injustice, the new legal system has also sought to control dissent and centralise State power, as well as extend and unify Peking's modernisation programme. Maoist traditions have been breached by the favouring of expert management, rather than worker participation, and relying on material incentives, encouraging a more capitalist ideology, buttressed by making profitability a central goal, and borrowing from capitalist countries and encouraging foreign investment. There has been a growing emphasis on legalism, since law is seen more and more as a controlling mechanism, as well as an educative one.

The gulf between the elitist 'privileged' class of 'haves' and the 'have nots' has, unfortunately, been widened, so that any dissent or dissatisfaction has been dealt with severely. Although Chinese law has a positive input of revisionist and progressive laws, the shortage of lawyers, judges and courts, as well as the lack of legal education, and anti-legalist thought, all operate to repress rather than encourage the growth of jurisprudence or, more pragmatically, individual freedom of expression.

Current Chinese law is in a state of transition, and the events of Tiananmen square are only one manifestation of a country, rich with tradition and culture and caught between the need to modernise, under pressure from a body of youthful opinion wanting some form of democracy, coupled with the desire for China to take a more exalted place in the international community, and the perceived need to preserve its incomparable heritage with dignity. The success or failure of China, in coming to terms with this ongoing conflict, will determine the shape of its laws in the 21st century.

The Japanese conception of law

Background to Japanese law

It is well established that Chinese ideas exerted an extremely strong influence on Japanese culture and, ultimately, influenced the overall Japanese conception of law. The 5th century AD saw the infiltration of Chinese writing and, in the 6th century AD, the 'importation' of Buddhism. The major forces that have shaped Japanese conceptions of law are multifarious: historical, physical and cultural. Japan is an island nation which enjoyed relative isolation, which enabled it to achieve a national ethnic unity. This was maintained for thousands of years. It was also a rural agricultural nation, up until the last century, with settled populations in localised farming communities. Japan also possessed a stable hierarchical social structure, but this was disrupted by civil wars, which came to an end around the end of the 16th century with the ascendancy of the Tokugawa Shogunate. In the succeeding generations dominated by Tokugawa officials, Japan appeared to be permanently settled into a stable and regular routine of administering 'one big rice estate' (Henderson (1965)), where Shintoism, Buddhism and Confucianism continued to have an impact on Japanese traditional ideas.

It was Chinese Confucianism that had the single greatest impact on early Japanese thought and, in the way in which the Japanese have achieved acclaim with their globally renowned technological advancements and innovations in modern times, they earlier adapted Confucian ideas to the Japanese psyche and way of life. Nonetheless, there are several typically Japanese characteristics in their conception of law. First, there is the 'aversion to law', which refers to their general antipathy toward the law as the means of resolving disputes through the courts, resulting from their 'norm-conscious sense of values, combined with their emotional anarchism' (Noda (1971)), as well as their propensity towards intuition and emotion, and their belief that law is simply a corpus of legal rules without any connotations of legal or personal rights. It is only respected as a teacher of morals and an expedient for maintaining social order, and not a great deal beyond that. Other reasons for the Japanese aversion to litigation and preference for conciliation may be the fact that the earliest Japanese Codes were never seen by anyone other than the magistrates for whose use they were specifically designed. Further, the early Japanese Codes were descended from the Chinese Codes which were almost exclusively penal, so that law came to be associated with pain, punishment, constraint and the idea of prison which connotes severity.

Secondly, there is no room for Western ideas of logic in Japanese law, since logic is anathema to their subjectivity, emotion and honour. Life is seen as 'indeterminate, immensely varied and subtle' (Kawashima (1967)) and should, therefore, be accepted and lived as it is, not placed into neat segments by logic. This is partially explicable by their 'racial and cultural homogeneity of thought' (Noda (1976)) which has nurtured the environment of a common understanding and consensus about life experiences and life in general.

Thirdly, there is the belief that life should be governed by non-legal rules of conduct (*giri*) and the obligations incurred towards benefactors (*on*) such as parents, the Emperor, the nations and the law. The guiding principle is that it is one's duty to repay this lifelong debt which cannot, in fact, ever be fully repaid. These obligations must be fulfilled by a special friendliness towards the other party, so that the spirit in which a duty is performed should be one of affection and benevolence. The main duty is to avoid discord and achieve harmony.

European influences on Japanese law

In the 19th century, Western nations became extremely interested in trade with Japan which threatened the isolation sought by the Shoguns – the military overlords of the day. Initially, only the Dutch received special permission to enter specified harbours for the specific purpose of trading. However, with increasing interest from other Western countries, the so called 'unequal treaties' were entered into by the Shogun with the United States, which had sent a fleet of warships to cruise off the Japanese coast in 1853, and Japan eventually entered into treaties with England, Russia and The Netherlands. The essence of these treaties was to give foreigners the right to settle in specified cities, have the right to trade and have consular representation. These moves were met with considerable opposition from the people and were widely seen as a national humiliation, so that even the Emperor emerged from his semi-retirement, which had been forced upon him by the Shoguns, and led the opposition to these treaties. By 1867, the Shogun had no option but to withdraw and the Meiji Emperor was reinstated with full governmental powers. This heralded a remarkable Westernisation of Japanese legal thought and, in the next few decades, the army and administration were also modernised on European lines, Western technology was adopted and a new constitution was introduced in 1889. This followed a Prussian model which turned Japan into a constitutional monarchy, although the Emperor retained all powers of decision. Further Europeanising influences followed as a result of a number of factors:

(a) The Japanese were anxious to remove the discrimination of the unequal treaties which gave consular courts jurisdiction over Japanese courts in matters affecting foreign nationals. The French Professor Boissonade was, therefore, commissioned to draft a new Criminal Code and a Code of Criminal Procedure. This came into force in 1880 and was, inevitably, strongly reminiscent of French law. At the same time, the German Professor Roesler had also been asked to draft a Commercial Code, which he based on the French Civil Code, but left the family and succession law to be drafted by a Japanese committee. Both these drafts provoked criticism from the conservative and liberal wings of the Japanese Parliament when they were presented to them. As you might have expected, they were seen as too French and insufficiently Japanese, or that codification was inappropriate at that time.

(b) The preparation of the Japanese Civil Code was, therefore, handed to a commission of three Japanese professors who, ultimately, followed two drafts of the German BGB (Civil Code) in key points of structure and content, although there were French and English law traces as well. No one can be sure as to why the German model eventually won favour, but it is certainly possible that the BGB was rated as the most mature and sophisticated example of the continental art of legislation; that the French Code was already seen as having technical defects; that Japanese scholars found German conceptualism and systematic exposition attractive and in accord with their own systematic modes of theorising. It is also likely that, as the BGB was the product of the German Empire, this would have impressed the more conservative Japanese scholars. Perhaps the answer lies in a combination of these reasons.

The Japanese Civil Code and Commercial Code accordingly came into force in 1898 and 1899, respectively, both being based predominantly on the German equivalents. Indeed, the Japanese Code of Civil Procedure and their organisation of courts was also modelled on the German scheme. Inevitably, towards the end of the First World War, it was German legal philosophy that provided the main inspiration to Japanese private law scholarship

The influence of Anglo-American law

In 1945, after the Second World War, there is little doubt that Anglo-American law exerted a very strong influence on Japanese law. Whether it succeeded in transforming the essence of Japanese legal thinking or centuries of tradition remains a point of contention. In terms of actual changes to existing written laws, however, the following may be noted:

(a) The new Japanese Constitution has been based predominantly on American legal ideas, which included strengthening the position of judges, the status of public officials, reforming administrative organisation, and including a list of basic rights which the courts are required to enforce.

(b) Both the Codes of Criminal Procedure and Civil Procedure have been amended so as to curtail the judge's power to restrict the parties and their counsel in presenting evidence during the trial. The old Japanese family system has been abolished in favour of the principle of equality of husband and wife which is embodied in the Civil Code.

(c) Democratising laws were implemented, at the insistence of the American occupying force, in relation to company law, bringing in anti-monopoly laws, as well as more supervisory laws to regulate the stock market and share issue.

(d) Judicial review and conciliation are envisaged by law. A special pre-trial procedure (*wakai*) is available which usually suffices to settle the dispute but, if it fails to do so, the parties have the right to go to court.

Continuing influence of Japanese traditions

However, very much in line with indigenous Japanese philosophy, the Code of Civil Procedure requires the judge to attempt to bring the parties to reach a settlement; indeed, the judge plays the role of mediator as often as possible. In addition, there is a procedure that allows a panel of conciliators, composed of a judge and two conciliators, to adjudicate on a dispute (*chotei*) and the judge tries not to take an active part in the proceedings which must be seen to have been resolved without judicial intervention. There is an obligation in the case of family law or labour law for *chotei* to be referred to. As a result of a Supreme Court decision, it is now established that the *chotei* procedure is only possible if the suggested solution is voluntarily accepted by the parties. The procedure has been in decline since 1958, and the parties now tend to go before the court and request that it resolve the issue 'in strict law'.

Furthermore, in the case of Japanese contracts, should a dispute arise, there are clauses which require the parties to confer in good faith, or to settle the matter harmoniously by consultation. This is in sharp contrast to the typical Anglo-American contract which may refer the dispute to independent arbitration, but may also utilise a whole range of other legal devices to deal with the situation.

Finally, there is the principle of 'both parties are to blame' which Japanese law used to apply to disputes; in a quarrel, each party was seen as attacking the other so that there was no room for the concept of self-defence to be applied to acts committed in the course of a quarrel (see *Osada v Japan* (1932) Great Court of Judicature Judgment, 25 January). This case was subsequently overruled in 1957 and self-defence was accepted as a defence.

Future trends in Japanese law

At one level, Japanese thought and Japanese law continue to move inexorably towards the West. Newer types of legal actions are being brought to the courts fairly frequently and the Japanese popular press now devotes much more attention to law, litigation and international economic and political relations with the West. As we have seen, the post-war democratisation of government, Westernisation and modernisation of Japan has continued apace. This has occurred alongside dramatic reform of the traditional rural order through land reform, and demographic changes such as the movement towards, and concentration within, big cities, changing family values and relationships accompanying other changes in social conditions. But, despite their remarkable industrial and economic progress, Varley suggests that 'the Japanese remain strongly enthralled by their own unique heritage and uncertain ... of their moorings in the cultural gulf that still separates East and West in the modern world'.

On the other hand, Kawashima (1979) has maintained that, although Japanese legal thinking is predominantly influenced by German legal thought, this does not mean that the legal thinking of Japanese lawyers is completely Westernised. There are 'significant elements' which indicate non-Western ways of thinking. The reference to German thought has already been discussed and again, in many respects, Kawashima is correct. Nevertheless, it is probably true to say that Japan is in a state of flux and is a society in transition. In the mid-1990s, there appears to be a rise in the political and professional profile of women in Japanese society which has somewhat shattered the stereotypical 'geisha girl' mentality of many of the male population. If Japanese women do succeed in assuming a more egalitarian role in society, this will have a profound impact on Japanese political and social life as a whole and could also have far reaching legal and cultural repercussions.

However, despite undergoing radical legal transplants and massive injections of Western culture, the heart of the Japanese legal mind remains an Eastern one, operating on a different plane, in tune with different rules and still very much steeped in tradition and characteristically stern discipline. As with other Far Eastern legal conceptions, at many levels below the façade of written laws and codes, Japanese law remains, as Noda first expressed it, 'the law of the subtle mind' (see Noda (1971)) and an exotic example of a fusion of Western and Eastern legal traditions seeking to come to terms with the demands and pressures of modernity.

SELECTIVE BIBLIOGRAPHY

Butler, *Soviet Law* (1987)

Dainow (ed), *The Role of Judicial Decisions and Doctrine in Civil Law and in Mixed Jurisdictions* (1974)

Feldbrugge, *Russian Law: The End of the Soviet System and the Role of Law* (1993)

Hazard, Butler and Maggs, *The Soviet Legal System* (1977)

Hendley, 'Remaking an institution: the transition in Russia from State *arbitrazh* to *arbitrazh* courts' (1998) 46 Am J Comp L 93

Ioffe and Maggs, *Soviet Law in Theory and Practice* (1983)

Karim, 'Observing trials in Russia' [1998] Justice Bulletin 14

Kawashima, 'Japanese way of legal thinking' [1979] International Journal of Law Libraries 127

Kim and Lawson, 'The law of the subtle mind: the traditional Japanese conception of law' (1979) 28 ICLQ 491

Knapp (ed), *International Encyclopedia of Comparative Law*, Vol I, *National Reports*, Vol II, *Legal Systems of the World*

Lee and Lai, 'The Chinese conceptions of law: Confucian, legalist and Buddhist' (1978) 29 The Hastings LJ 1307

Quigley, 'Socialist law and the civil law tradition' (1989) 37 Am J Comp L 781

Rudden, 'Civil law, civil society and the Russian constitution' (1994) 110 LQR 56

Smith, *Reforming the Russian Legal System* (1996)

Stephan, 'Perestroika and property: the law of ownership in the post-socialist Soviet Union' (1991) 39 Am J Comp L 35

Sypnowich, *The Concept of Socialist Law* (1990)

Zweigert and Kotz, *An Introduction to Comparative Law* (1987) Vol I

CHAPTER 7

TECHNIQUES OF COMPARATIVE LAW

SCOPE OF CHAPTER

This chapter now moves to the heart of the comparative law enterprise by seeking to apply the various components of juristic style, which we have been examining in the various parent systems, to construct a comparative law methodology. It offers a theoretical and practical framework, containing a range of comparative techniques, within which a macro-comparison (comparison of two or more legal systems) and/or micro-comparison (study of a specific institution or problem which exists within legal systems, using comparative legal material) may be validly undertaken. Comparatists should be wary of the pitfalls and dangers of comparison, but this should not inhibit them from embarking on comparative analyses utilising the materials, tools and methods of comparison to the best possible advantage. Although comparative law as an academic and scholarly discipline has now existed for nearly 100 years, literature on its methodology or techniques has been somewhat scarce. This chapter seeks to examine the various approaches to effective comparison and provide a comprehensive guide to the process of comparison.

GENERAL CONSIDERATIONS

Initially, it is important to note some of the major pitfalls and perils that lie in wait for any comparative lawyer:

(a) linguistic and terminological problems;

(b) cultural differences between legal systems;

(c) the potentiality of arbitrariness in selection of objects of study;

(d) difficulties in achieving 'comparability' in comparison;

(e) the desire to see a common legal pattern in legal systems – the theory of a general pattern of development;

(f) the tendency to impose one's own (native) legal conceptions and expectations on the systems being compared;

(g) dangers of exclusion/ignorance of extra-legal rules.

Linguistic/terminological problems

In 1938, the late Professor Gutteridge wrote that 'differences in the language of the law constitute not the least of the barriers which separate the various legal systems of the world'. This is why he believed that 'the pitfalls of terminology are the greatest difficulty and danger which the student of comparative law encounters in his novitiate' (Gutteridge (1938)). This has been echoed by many comparatists over the last 50 years and, in more recent times, for example, by Winterton (1975) and Grossfeld (1990). Whereas physicians, chemists, economists, mathematicians and musicians have a common vocabulary, legal terminology is fraught with linguistic traps and potential minefields of misunderstanding which vary from country to country. Yet, language is the most important medium of communication for the lawyer, and legal concepts have precise linguistic configurations and parameters. All declarations in legal transactions are 'constitutive' in that they connote specific concepts which will give rise to specific consequences in precisely defined situations. Reciprocally, legal thinking is shaped by its technical terminology (see, for example, White, *The Legal Imagination* (1973)).

Any form of translation runs the risk of overlooking the conceptual differences between languages. Such conceptual differences must, first, be understood if the comparatist is to make sense of what he is comparing. The question arises as to the extent of the connection between linguistic structures and legal structures and to the consequences of translating a legal institution into a different language.

Some studies have been carried out which have investigated the post-colonial changes that have taken place in legal systems, such as Asia and Africa, when English gave way to native languages (see Marasinghe (1979) Lawasia 74). There have also been studies of law and language by Glanville Williams (see Williams (1945) 61 LQR 71) of the English legal system and in The Netherlands and Belgium, by Van den Bergh and Broekman (see Van den Bergh and Broekman, *Recht en Taal* (1979)). Unfortunately, none of these studies has had any illuminating effect on comparative law studies, although there is now a fairly extensive (and expanding) literature acknowledging the importance of language as a factor in comparative law (see, for example, Grossfeld (1990) especially Chapter 13).

One of the other ambiguities which should be noted is that, even in English speaking countries, homonyms may have different meanings. Hence, even if the basic legal concepts are similar, different terms may be utilised so as to create an impression of divergence, and this may even occur within the same legal family. Conversely, although the terms used may be identical, their substantive content or actual application, in practice, may be quite different.

A common law example: similar term; different in practice

An example of an identical term which is common to two jurisdictions within the same legal family is *stare decisis* ('let the decision stand'). Being common law jurisdictions, both the American and English legal systems have, *ex facie*, adopted the doctrine of *stare decisis*, but their actual operation within their individual jurisdictions are 'markedly different' (see Atiyah and Summers (1987)). The essential difference between American and English practice is that the lower courts in America are not bound to follow their own decisions, and the authority of a court's own prior decisions depends largely on the persuasiveness of the reasoning of the earlier courts. Indeed, unlike English courts which adopt a more formalistic approach, in America, subsequent judges at all levels have the power to disregard otherwise binding decisions (see Atiyah and Summers (1987) pp 113–34 for detailed discussion of differences between English and American practice). The result is that a 'binding' decision may not be absolutely binding because the court may believe that the previous ruling was clearly wrong when delivered, or inappropriate to different factual conditions or the composition of the court may have changed, so that the majority view has become the minority one.

Stare decisis is, in particular, likely not to be followed where a constitutional issue is involved, where the difficulty of legislative amendment cannot remedy a perceived defect in the law, or on a procedural question where retroactive overruling is not unusual (see, for example, *Burnet v Coronado Oil and Gas Co* 285 US 393 (1932) pp 406–08).

The doctrine of precedent in America has, therefore, never acquired the formalistic authority it is supposed to have in England for a number of reasons, such as the American judicial and political structure and hierarchy, the great volume of decisions, conflicting precedents in different jurisdictions and the remarkable speed of the changes which have taken place in social and economic conditions (see Farnsworth (1987) pp 44–52).

Similar terms in civil law and common law

There are, clearly, even more difficulties in translating alien legal concepts, since an authentic translation often demands more than mere linguistic accuracy. For a translation of a legal term to be meaningful, intimate knowledge is required both of the system being translated as well as that of the native system. Even if a term is translated faithfully and related to a comparable legal institution or structure, there is always the danger of being unaware of ambiguities of language which are found in every system of law. Hence, one has to guard against assuming that identical terms in two legal systems will correspond to the same juridical concepts in both these systems.

Equity

A term that is used both in civil law and common law which has different meanings is 'equity' (*Aequitas, equité, Billigkeit*). The continental Codes contain many references to it (see, for example, Arts 565 and 1135 of the French Civil Code, paras 315–19 of the German Civil Code (BGB) and Art 4 of the Swiss Civil Code). 'Equity' is not defined in any of the Codes, but it appears that European continental judges use the concept whenever they do not wish to adopt a formal or narrow interpretation of a legal principle, for example, because they wish to adapt such a principle to rapidly changing social conditions. In English law, the technical meaning of the term 'equity' refers to the body of law that developed separately from the body of law as laid down by the common law courts, from about the 15th century. The rules, maxims and practice of equity were shaped by the Courts of Chancery, presided over by the Chancellor of the Exchequer. These courts were later to be known as the 'courts of equity'.

Other common terms with different meanings

Other examples of identical terms which mean different things in different systems are the term 'possession', which has a different juridical meaning in French law to English law, the concept of good faith, which is used as a general clause of considerable significance in German commercial law, but is merely a synonym for honesty and fair dealing in English sale of goods law, although the term *bona fide* does have a special technical meaning in English property law.

As far as French law is concerned, there is now the excellent *English Reader's Guide to the French Legal System* (1991), by Martin Weston, which tackles the linguistic problems encountered in comparing the English and French legal systems. It is certainly true that the linguistic problem will continue to bedevil comparatists each time they indulge in comparative study.

Cultural differences between systems

Another factor to bear in mind is the question of cultural differences between systems. Anthropologists and sociologists have been prominent among those who have highlighted the many different meanings one can ascribe to the word 'culture', and many legal writers and historians have expounded on the uniqueness of legal systems and the link between law and culture. A commonly expressed view is that law, culture and society are inextricably linked, but this view has been challenged, for example, by Alan Watson, a leading Scottish comparatist and specialist in Roman and civil law. Watson

(1974) has argued that legal rules may not merely exist, but also happily endure, even in an environment that is far removed from its antecedents. Thus, he argues that 'legal rules are equally at home in many places' (Watson (1977) p 130) so that, irrespective of their provenance, private law can survive 'without any close connection to any particular people, particular period of time or any particular place' (Watson (1976) p 81).

In support of his thesis, he cites the way that Roman law survived, despite a radical change in circumstances, and that the civil law tradition subsists in countries as culturally and geographically diverse as Germany and Paraguay, and that German law was even received in Japan.

There is no doubt that the same legal ideas and institutions keep cropping up in many different and diverse jurisdictions but, as we have stated at the very outset of this book, every legal system is the product of its history and, very often, its political fortunes. It is therefore no surprise that the aftermath of Empire, colonialism and a peculiar mix of events, political, social, economic and cultural, has left vestiges of the past still very much in evidence in law, culture and society. Watson's view appears tenable insofar as it emphasises the enduring quality of law and its ability to be 'transplanted' (Watson) and to survive in many different cultures and environments. It further emphasises that a truly comprehensive method of comparing laws must include not just a sociological approach, but also an historical one.

On the other hand, it is surely necessary to acquaint ourselves with the particular cultural background we wish to study before we can really understand the foreign text, since the choice and meaning of the words in the text are determined by its cultural background (Fuller (1968) p 57). What sort of cultural elements should a comparatist look for in a legal system selected for comparison? Leon Friedman (1969) suggested that the cultural elements which the comparatist should seek to discover in a fully developed legal system are:

> ... the values and attitudes which bind the system together and which determine the place of the legal system in the culture of the society as a whole.

He therefore suggested that the following questions should be asked:

(a) What kind of training and habits do lawyers and judges have?

(b) What do people think of law?

(c) Do groups or individuals willingly go to court?

(d) For what purposes do people turn to lawyers?

(e) For what purpose do they make use of intermediaries?

(f) Is there respect for law, government and tradition?

(g) What is the relationship between class structure and the use or non-use of legal institutions?

(h) What informal social controls exist in addition to or in place of formal ones?

(i) Who prefers which kind of controls and why?

It is, of course, more difficult to become 'culturally acclimatised' to a legal system which does not accord with one's native system in terms of its juristic style or primary sources. However, the study of French law or German law is certainly not going to require as much cultural adjustment for a common lawyer residing in England, as for a common lawyer residing in a non-European country, or even in America. It is the study of Japanese law, Chinese law or legal systems based on religions which will require greater cultural attuning. Hindu and Islamic family laws are typical examples of laws based on cultural concepts unfamiliar to the Western lawyer. It is very often the social and cultural environment which informs the particular law and, if one is ignorant of 'local history', the true rationale of foreign laws will not be understood, so that some of these laws might appear 'backward' or eccentric. But, their very 'foreignness' should be a spur to the comparatist, not an obstacle.

Of course, Africans and Asians may also encounter the same cultural difficulties when studying Western law, but experience of Western colonialism and exposure to Western cultural concepts through television, overseas media services and student exchange programmes are helping to ensure that there is a greater awareness of, and exposure to, Western ideas and institutions. In today's world, the Internet provides a great deal of accessible information, and computer programs in schools, in many parts of the world, now provide enhanced visual education relating to societies around the world. A great deal of 'imported television' tends to be American in origin and, hence, this has also created its own cultural impact across the world, particularly in language and concepts. Satellite television is slowly transforming the cultural awareness of countries around the world.

It needs to be made clear at this point that the comparatist is not seeking to be judgmental about legal systems in the sense of whether he believes them to be 'better' or 'worse' than any other given system. What the comparatist is seeking to do is to evaluate the efficacy of a given solution or approach to a legal problem in terms of that particular jurisdiction's cultural, economic, political and legal background. To find that a system is different is almost the preliminary assumption. Of course, the comparatist should accept the differences as much as the similiarities. Given a set of priorities, the task is to assess the effectiveness of a solution in terms of achieving those aims and objectives. For example, if a legal system wishes to ensure equality of bargaining power between trading parties (which some might consider unachievable or too idealistic, anyway!), one method of doing so is to have a statute that prescribes minimum standards for fair trading, so that all parties are aware of all the facts regarding their product, the market conditions (usually relevant), current prices, protection from misrepresentations, fraud, freedom from duress or coercion, etc. If a given legal system does not have such a statutory provision, its courts, tribunals or some form of ombudsman would have to deal with disputes between contracting parties to provide a forum for a fair hearing and redress and compensation. But, these are measures which themselves assume a great deal. What if the system you are dealing with has no infrastructure to allow for any formal resolution of disputes? Suppose there is a local tribunal, but it only sits once every three months: is lodging a claim too time consuming and highly detrimental to normal business? The comparatist's task here would be to identify this situation, suggest means of dealing with it, explore the ways that contracting parties in that jurisdiction deal with it and comment on this, using the tools of the comparative trade, so to speak.

It has been asserted that it is impossible to perceive the significance of something which was written in a different period of history, and the example given is the difficulty of appreciating *The Merchant of Venice* because we could never understand the period related scene in which Shakespeare used the word 'Jew' (see White (1982) p 427). This is surely the height of cultural snobbery and the worst manifestation of cultural relativism. One wonders whether the writer of these remarks could have seen non-Europeans performing *The Merchant of Venice* with such authenticity that Royal Shakespeare Company experts were raving over their acting brilliance and their deep appreciation of the nuances of the play and, obviously, about the Jewish centrality of it. These comments about the difficulty of appreciation because of the sheer cultural and historical divide make several assumptions about the quality of scholars in the world today. They are the sorts of comments that are still made about 'foreigners' (that is, non-Europeans) never being able to fully appreciate or perform European (that is, mainly German) music because they do not have the cultural upbringing or background to do so. Many of the world's leading musical performers and interpreters of the 20th century (Zubin Mehta comes to mind) come from Asian backgrounds and it was the cultural exposure and their particular family background that enabled them to immerse themselves in Western music and to basically become world class performers of Western (and any other) music. The point that is being made is that the difficulties of getting 'under the skin' of a different culture should not deter a serious comparatist from embarking on the comparative enterprise.

Arbitrary selection of objects of study

This particular peril of comparison was highlighted by the late Professor Lawson who warned comparatists, in 1952, that he could not see how a comparison between two laws could be 'systematic'. Alan Watson ((1974) p 11) interprets 'unsystematic' as meaning that there is no single system and no set of criteria which would be useful for all purposes and acceptable to all scholars. However, he argues that there will have to be a considerable element of arbitrariness and subjectivity in the selection of legal systems, even if there is a clear relationship between them. He argues, however, that this is inevitable, in the very nature of things, since the choice of topic or institution for study can 'scarcely be made in full knowledge of all the relevant facts'. However, this will be reflected in any general conclusions, and 'no objective test will demonstrate that the aspects considered were the most appropriate and the only ones appropriate'. Comparatists may take heart, however, that, provided the comparison is carried out with circumspection and according to the criteria we shall outline later on in this chapter, patently unhelpful and inappropriate comparisons will be easily discoverable and may be discounted. Topics selected for comparison will, inevitably, depend on the primary purpose for which the comparatist is undertaking his research. As will be shown (see 'The quest for methodology', p 225, below), a combination of techniques may be utilised and adapted according to the nature of the materials being compared and the interim results obtained.

'Comparability' in comparison

General considerations

The comparability of legal systems depends on a number of factors, some constant, many transient. Grossfeld (1990) lists the following determinative factors: the cultural, political and economic components of a society, as well as the particular relationship that exists between the State and its citizens, its value system and its particular conception of the individual and the world in general. Other general factors include a society's 'cultural climate', a term used by Grossfeld which he describes as that 'resulting from the people's unconscious axioms, collective feelings and prevalent ideas of reality'. He also places importance on the 'homogeneity of the society' in question and 'whether it has a cultural consensus or not'. Other factors he mentions are geographical situation, language and religion and he stresses that, in order to ascertain the effect of legal solutions in different systems, a multidisciplinary approach is required.

Comparison of systems at similar stages of development

Comparatists have also warned against selecting for comparison systems which have no 'proper relationship', in the sense that they are not strictly properly 'comparable', because, for example, they are being examined at different stages of their legal evolution. No less a comparatist than Gutteridge seemed to think that, for instance, comparing the law of the ancient races of the East with modern European law would not be productive, and he quoted Pollock who thought such comparison might 'lead to ludicrous if not dangerous misunderstanding' (Gutteridge (1949) p 73). He also dismissed Montesquieu's 'occasional excursions into exotic research' and stressed that 'Like must be compared with like; the concepts, rules or institutions must relate to the same stage of legal, political and economic development', a view he further supported by referring to Buckland and McNair's comparative study of the principles of Roman and English law (*Roman Law and Common Law* (1936)), which he felt illustrated that 'institutions may be widely separated in time, but may be sufficiently similar to make comparison fruitful and valuable'.

Gutteridge's view was an affirmation of the view earlier expressed by Schmitthoff who had argued that, for the 'strict observance of comparability', the comparison 'must extend to the same evolutionary stage' of the different legal systems which are being compared (Schmitthoff (1939) p 96).

Despite this view, however, Gutteridge then goes on to say that it really depends on whether the subject matter lends itself to comparison and 'everything depends on the purpose which the investigator may have had in mind when applying the process of comparison'. With respect, this does appear to detract from the force of the whole thrust of his earlier comments, and commentators, such as Kamba, appear to think, and justifiably so, that this view of comparability is 'unnecessarily restrictive' (Kamba (1974) p 507). Lest we think that this was a view peculiar to the 1930s and 1940s, it should be noted that Alan Watson also wrote, in 1974, that one of the worst faults that may compound the inappropriate selection of systems is that the legal systems are examined at different points in their evolution. What then should we make of this apparent requirement of 'comparability'?

Main purpose of comparison: the ultimate test

Two responses may be made to this particular 'peril' or comparison. First, it is usually true that, in order to make meaningful comparisons, it is important to select systems which are at a similar stage in their legal (and often their political, economic and social) evolution, so that there is a baseline of similarity. For example, if one seeks to explain English commercial law relating to companies by referring to the law of a non-Western undeveloped society, which still utilises a barter system and where the notion of commercial law or companies in the Western sense is non-existent or relatively undeveloped, such a comparison will be of little *prima facie* value in comparing 'like with like'.

Secondly, as Gutteridge himself pointed out, this point of 'comparability' is not a serious problem if the purpose of the comparison is to illustrate the different influences that operate at different stages of legal, political and social evolution. Hence, it would be perfectly acceptable to examine the different approaches taken to cohabitation outside marriage in Western societies, and compare it to the non-Western countries where marriage is frequently regarded as the norm, in the sense of an officially sanctioned public contract, but where several consecutive polygamous marriages are permitted under religious or customary law. The same approach may be adopted (see Kamba (1974)) in explaining the African law of matrimonial property, for example, which is itself a fusion of Western and indigenous law, and a comparison of the Western approach to this topic in a society at a different stage of evolution would be extremely illuminating and useful. Hence, the choice of legal systems must, ultimately, depend on the main aims and objectives of the particular comparative investigation.

In practice, of course, comparatists will generally commence their research by comparing systems of law which are at similar stages of legal development, first, because of the accessibility of materials and, secondly, because for novitiates at least, there can be no better starting point than a study of the two major families of legal systems, civil law and common law, as a means of familiarising themselves with some of the greatest ideas that have ever graced legal history.

Viability of theory of a common legal pattern

To any researcher trained in a particular philosophy and legal system, there is always the temptation and desire to perceive a common legal pattern in all or many divergent systems. This may be called the 'theory of a general pattern of development'.

Sir Henry Maine, in his famous book *Ancient Law* (1861), took Roman law as his typical system of ancient law from which he drew a large number of analogies and, in *Village Communities* (1871), sought to ascertain the general process of legal evolution by comparing different legal systems and institutions. Subsequent research suggested that Maine was, in fact, incorrect in many of his assumptions about Roman law, so that his book is of little value in terms of accuracy of legal facts. Maine's theory of the similarity of legal development in all primitive systems has been echoed by Pringsheim in a well known article (see Pringsheim [1935] 5 CLJ 347). He argued that:

> A natural relationship exists at an early stage between all primitive legal systems; each system during its youth seems to pass through a similar process before the peculiarities of the nation are imposed upon its juridical order.

Alan Watson has strongly denounced this theory, declaring that 'the appearance of similar development is achieved only by the grossest misstatement of relevant legal facts. At times, it is as if a comparative anatomist were to say that lions and ants are similar and are at a comparable level of development, since both are warm blooded, have six legs and are always winged [sic]' (see Watson (1974)).

In essence, Watson warns against advocating a doctrine of assuming a general pattern of development because:

(a) although it is perfectly natural and conceivable that different peoples did, at various times, have the same basic responses to a situation, it is simply not possible to move from this commonplace observation to the formulation of a theory of general legal development applicable to all or many unrelated societies;

(b) legal historians, such as AS Diamond, have sought to enunciate historical hypotheses without reference to the best available evidence, relying on arguments drawn from the experience of other people who themselves had only second hand knowledge of the matters in question. Diamond's arguments for asserting that there is no reliable evidence for believing that the Twelve Tables were a legal code are, thus, flawed and can have no weight 'except to those who already believe in the pattern of development'. Further, Diamond does not even discuss the arguments which have persuaded other scholars to form the opposite opinion on the Twelve Tables.

Hence, a theory of a general pattern common to several societies may well obscure the discovery of the actual development of the legal system being studied.

Imposition of one's own legal conceptions

This point is linked to the earlier point on culture and law. Europeans and Americans must be constantly aware, when studying non-Western legal systems and cultures, that they must not approach or appraise these systems from their own Western viewpoints or judge them by European or American standards. For example, some Western lawyers concluded in the 1970s that China has no legal system because she has no attorneys in the American or European sense, no independent judiciary, no Codes and, since the Cultural Revolution, no system of legal education. Yet, this is surely to judge a non-Western system by Western standards, rather like the Western visitor who assumed that there was no 'proper' music played in China because he did not see any Western instruments in the Chinese concert hall he visited.

Surely, what is required is not to search for Western institutions or rules or concepts, but to look for the 'functional equivalents of legal terms and concepts' (Ehrmann (1975) p 11) in various cultures. In other words, he should ask: by which institutions and which methods are the four 'law jobs', identified by Hoebel, being performed? These four 'jobs' are:

(a) social control;

(b) conflict resolution;

(c) adaptation and social change; and

(d) norm enforcement (see Hoebel, *The Law of Primitive Man* (1954) p 10 *et seq*).

We can immediately see, from this sort of approach, that there is most certainly a Chinese legal system, but it is a unique system which does not necessarily 'fit' into Western conceptions of law or legal systems. As we have already seen in the previous chapter, in the case of indigenous Japanese law, logic in the Western sense has no place in Japanese thought.

Omission of extra-legal factors

A final error that the comparatist has to guard against is not to overlook 'extra-legal' factors, which may be informal customs and practices, which operate outside strict law, or various non-legal phenomena which ultimately influence the state of the law.

One of the benefits of the effective utilisation of the comparative law methodology is to deepen and widen one's knowledge of the social and economic *milieu* within which a legal system and legal rules operate. A systematic comparison, which is the essence of comparative law, seeks to explain the similarities and divergencies between the legal systems selected for comparison. The reasons for these differences and similarities are very often 'extra-legal' and cannot be causally linked to any legal rule or principle. Apart from obvious extra-legal factors, such as revolutions, coups d'états and wars, there are also peacetime events of momentous proportions, such as radical devaluations of currency, changes in government which prompt radical shifts in economic and legal policy, widespread unemployment, the introduction of wide ranging technological change, nationalistic fervour and the gaining of independence. As ever, the impact of historical events will play a part in legal development, whether in education, industry or commerce. In modern times, the signing of an international treaty may also result in the integration of laws which unite the particular system with several others, with inevitable effects on legislation, case law and even the everyday practice of law. Specific examples of extra-legal rules may be drawn from the law of contract, where informal rules are often observed by businessmen, for example, in Germany, which prevent offers from being binding (by insertion of terms like *'ohne Obligo'*) or from being legal offers at all; and, in England, where extra-legal devices curtail the capricious revocation of offers, although the law seems to allow revocation to take place without restrictions.

In property law, the appearance of insurance companies in America, which guarantee the insured against any loss that might be suffered against a third party's rights, has considerably shortened the long wait that has normally to be endured before 'searches' of deeds may be completed. This development has lowered the value of the particular piece of property. This is because any third party covenants imposing any liability on the buyer would be covered by the insurance company so there is no need to carry out inordinately extensive and expensive searches, the cost of which would have been added to the price of the property. The German land register tends to cut down the waiting time in much the same way.

THE QUEST FOR METHODOLOGY

Introduction

When the late Professor Gutteridge wrote his seminal book, *Comparative Law*, which was first published in 1946, he included a chapter, entitled 'The process of comparison', in which he expounded on the subject matter of comparison, the sources of foreign law and the materials for comparison. But he did not, except in the most indirect and incidental manner, actually outline the mechanics or techniques of comparison. Hence, as he made clear, he was merely going to discuss certain features of the process of comparison and characteristics of foreign law which had to be appreciated before the task of comparison could be undertaken. It was therefore left to other writers, utilising comparative methodology, to attempt to spell out the actual method of comparison. Most of these, with some notable exceptions, have tended to follow Gutteridge's example and have written (and argued) about the functions, objectives and subject matter of comparative law rather than proffered any precise plan of comparison. Of course, it is essential to agree on what the functions of comparative law are (see Chapter 1) and, more specifically, to decide on the purposes of the particular comparative investigation that one is planning to undertake, since this will determine the choice of legal systems or topics for comparison, as well as the method of comparison. We therefore begin with the question of functions, before formulating a blueprint of comparison.

Clarifying the general character of comparative law

Despite the establishment of comparative law as an academic discipline, confusion still exists on its functions and subject matter. For example, various commentators have disputed the theoretical question of whether comparative law is a method or a science in itself.

Those who have advocated the method theory include luminaries, such as Pollock, Gutteridge, Kahn-Freund and David who have regarded comparative law purely as a method of comparative study and research as applied to law. On the other hand, supporters of the social science theory include Saleilles, Levy-Ullman, Kohler, Arminjon, Nolde, Wolff, Rabel, Yntema, Rheinstein,

Hall and Brutau who regarded comparative law as a body of knowledge and, thus, a social science. As Professor Sussman put it:

> They tend to see this science as something which may well be arrived at largely through the application of the comparative method, but nevertheless as constituting a body of knowledge analogous to a science of language and linguistics growing to a substantial degree out of the comparative study of specific languages. [Sussman, 'Discussion: the nature and teaching of comparative law in the context of modern society (1970) Proceedings of Seventh International Symposium on Comparative Law 105, p 108.]

It is certainly the case that comparative law is a method of comparing legal systems, and that such comparison produces results on the legal systems being analysed. However, writers appear to be arguing over whether the data obtained should be regarded simply as part of the method, or whether they should be regarded as a separate body of knowledge.

Winterton (1975) avoided taking sides in the terminological debate by using the term 'comparative law' to include both the method and the data resulting from the application of it. The present writer would find no objection to this except to say that current thinking appears to have swung towards the direction of the 'method' theorists. More importantly, however, it is submitted that whichever school of thought one prefers does not affect the techniques or, indeed, subject matter of comparison which is the primary concern of comparatists wishing to translate theory into practice.

It is as well to remember that, as Gutteridge emphasised, comparative law serves a variety of purposes and it should not be confined to any narrow or exhaustive categories. We have already examined these functions in Chapter 1, but suffice to reiterate, in the present context, that there are several interrelated academic and practical aims of comparative law including the enhancement of academic study, aiding and informing the legislative process and law reform, elucidating the application of foreign law in the courts and contributing to the unification and harmonisation of laws.

The subject matter of the comparison

The subject matter of comparative law as a method has been defined as 'two or more legal systems; or parts, branches or aspects of two or more legal systems' (Kamba (1974) p 505). There has also been some discussion as to whether comparison of laws and legal institutions of different countries within the same legal family can be correctly called 'comparative law'. But, as Winterton (1975) points out, uncertainty has only been voiced in relation to comparisons within the common law systems. Few European comparatists would even begin to dispute the validity of comparison of German, French and Italian law as proper subjects of comparative law, although they all exist within the same legal family.

The source of the uncertainty of comparisons within the common law family might well stem from the fiction that the common law is a fixed and immutable body of law which has always existed and is substantively uniform throughout the so called 'common law world' (see the comments of J Windeyer, in *Skelton v Collins* (1966) 115 CLR 134, and Palmer (1965) 30 Law and Contemporary Problems 250, where he says: 'Canada has one common law, that of England'). As the present writer has sought to demonstrate (see Chapter 4), the law of the United States of America, often classified together with English law as 'Anglo-American' law, has very different characteristics from English law. This is by virtue of its constitutional law, but there are divergencies also in its judicial system, legislative norms, uniform laws and its other codifications. There are various other features, such as the content of a great deal of its legal language and socio-legal and instrumentalist approaches, which attest to the fact that the 'common law' in America is often applied differently from English law and has been modified so radically so as to constitute a law *sui generis,* whose resemblance to English law is often only in its basic terminology, but little else.

Macro-comparison and micro-comparison

It has now become reasonably well established to use the terms 'macro-comparison' and 'micro-comparison', which have been attributed to Rheinstein, to describe the two different species of comparative study that may be undertaken. Macro-comparison refers to the study of two or more entire legal systems; micro-comparison generally refers to the study of topics or aspects of two or more legal systems. It is noted that studies which have concentrated on a solitary foreign system of law have sometimes been called comparative law studies, possibly on the basis that there is an implicit comparison with one's own legal system. Such enterprises cannot be accurately described as comparative law which must involve, as its aim, the explicit and systematic study of at least two legal systems. Mere incidental reference to another legal system does not, thereby, qualify a study as 'comparative law'. As Le Paulle ((1922) p 853) put it:

> A legal system is a unity, the whole of which expresses itself in each part; the same blood runs in the whole organism ... An identical provision of the law of two countries may have wholly different moral backgrounds ... [or] brought about by ... wholly different forces and, hence, the similarity may be due to purest coincidence – no more significant than the double meaning of a pun.

In similar terms, Dean Pound stressed, in 1951, that a 'fruitful comparison' must involve more than comparison of legal precepts, but include comparison of systems of law as systems (see Pound (1951) 100 Pennsylvania UL Rev 1).

Suitability of topics for micro-comparison

We have already discussed the various issues that surround the choice of legal systems for macro-comparison (see above), that is, the question of which entire legal systems may usefully be compared. However, there is obviously a greater range of topics for micro-comparison and, again, the primary purpose or main aims and objectives of comparison will determine the selection of topics. Among the possible topics chosen may be:

(a) the institutions or concepts peculiar to the systems;

(b) the sources of law, judicial systems and judiciary, legal profession or even the structure of the legal system;

(c) the various branches of national or domestic law;

(d) the historical development of legal systems; and

(e) the ideological, socio-legal and economic bases of that system.

As with macro-comparison, the question of comparability or equivalence will inevitably arise but, again, the purpose of that particular comparison will be determinative. Is the comparative study designed to trace the development of a particular institution, in a comparable society, at a comparable stage of its legal and economic development? Or is the study aimed at illustrating the different varieties of responses to similar problems exhibited in societies which have a totally different perception of law, or 'rights', or have a different attitude to distributive justice or, indeed, a totally different conception of all three? If comparing non-Western institutions, it should be immediately realised that there is rarely any objectively ascertainable criterion of a 'better' or 'worse' institution except by Western standards of 'fairness' and 'reasonableness', which are frequently an example of imposition of one's own standards (see 'Imposition of one's own legal conceptions', p 223, above) to a foreign culture and society. Surely, the question here should be: how has that system's functional equivalent of this institution met the needs of that particular society in terms of social control, conflict resolution, adaptation to social change or norm enforcement? Personal preference will, of course, play a part in the selection of topics but, as always, the various requirements of systematic comparison must, by and large, be fulfilled. In addition, practical matters, such as the comparatist's own expertise or experience, availability of materials and the language factor will shape the final selection.

Comparative method: requirements

In the voluminous writing on comparative law, a recurrent criticism has been the 'general failure of legal scholarship to invent and employ a method adequate to the task of realistically describing and effectively appraising a flow of authoritative decisions through time, that is, for making fruitful decisions through time' (see McDougal (1952) p 28). One reason has been the semantic and theoretical debate over even the term 'comparative law' and, it must be said, a somewhat monolithic view of the process of comparison. Yet, it was as early as 1931 when Hug and Ireland articulated a somewhat idealistic view of 'the real purpose' of comparative law:

> To understand the history of the rule, to trace its principal sources, its developing vicissitudes and its final formation and acceptance, to appreciate its relation to other parts of the instant system and, most important of all, to learn its actual operation, to see what it does as distinct from what it says, by consultation of the commentators and, more importantly, by examination of the actual decisions of the courts to carry through this analysis for each of the great systems of law, classifying and discussing as many of the subdivisions as circumstances permit, to discover and set forth the similarities and differences of the existing solutions and then to make a summation of the whole resultant, with a view to an at least partial and temporarily valid prediction as to the tendency of current doctrine and lines of decision, more correctly constitutes the real purpose of comparative law.

We have already seen how the cultural, economic and legal context of a particular system (in the case of macro-comparison) or a particular branch of law or institution (in the case of micro-comparison) has to be taken into account in order to acquire a more complete picture of the system or topic being studied. Comparatists, dating from Gutteridge and up to Kahn-Freund, have stressed the importance of examining the socio-cultural context of the subject matter being investigated. It was more than 40 years ago when, in considering the proper materials to be examined in a comparative study, Ferdinand Stone wrote:

> We must study the history, the politics, the economics, the cultural background in literature and the arts, the religions, beliefs and practices, the philosophies, if we are to reach sound conclusions as to what is and what is not common. [Stone (1951) p 332.]

Taken to its logical conclusion, this suggests that the comparatist must be something of a polymath, highly learned in a variety of disciplines and extremely conversant with the socio-cultural backdrop to the subject matter of comparison. It must be remembered that, while it has always been extremely difficult to become a master of any single discipline, let alone two, it is even more difficult, not least in terms of the sheer volume of material, 40 years on from when Stone first expressed his opinion. In many respects, the purpose of comparative legal study is not, primarily, intended to be a means of becoming an expert, *ipso facto*, in legal systems, or in legal institutions or in any specific branches of law. Hence, for the purposes of a comparative study of legal phenomena or legal systems, a knowledge of the socio-cultural factors is necessary, but only to enhance the comparatist's overall perception of the subject matter under inquiry, not to be investigated in any great depth or detail for its own sake.

Furthermore, as Kamba points out, the extent of knowledge required of social context will also depend on whether the comparative study is a cross-cultural one or an intra-cultural one, and on the main aims and objectives of the comparison (see Kamba (1974)). In essence, a cross-cultural study is one in which there is a comparative study of two legal systems belonging to a Western and non-Western society. An intra-cultural comparison is one in which a comparative study is made involving two or more legal systems belonging to the same societal type, for example, Western society. Naturally, the fewer common denominators there are between the systems being compared, the greater the detailed background or socio-cultural knowledge that will be required. Of course, even when making comparisons of legal systems or institutions within the same socio-cultural grouping, for example, between two Asian countries, the comparatist must take nothing for granted, remain flexible and open to suggestions and be aware that a specific set of laws might have developed in a particular legal system as the result of a unique series of events, for example, wars and uprisings, Western colonialism or simply as a result of the monarchical regime that ruled the country for several years, which created a number of 'imperial laws' which co-existed alongside more liberal ones. In non-Western countries, in particular, the influence of customary law cannot be overestimated.

The test of functionality

Zweigert and Kotz (1977) emphasise that 'every investigation in comparative law begins with the posing of a question or the setting of a working hypothesis – in brief, an "idea"'. Their view appears to be that the usual reasons for embarking on such a study frequently stem from dissatisfaction with the solution in one's own system or purely from the intellectual pleasure of doing so.

Nevertheless, they believe that:

The basic methodological principle of all comparative law is that of *functionality*. From this basic principle stem all the other rules which determine the choice of laws to compare, the scope of the undertaking, the creation of a system of comparative law ... in law, the only things which are comparable are those which fulfil the same function [their emphasis].

They go on to suggest that the question to which any comparative study must be directed must be posed in purely functional terms. The questions that must be asked must, therefore, be: what function does the rule under scrutiny fulfil in its own society? Alternatively, which institution, legal or otherwise, fulfils the function under scrutiny in this particular society? This is certainly in line with points we have noted earlier, in the context of cultural equivalence, and the need to ascertain the functional equivalents of a familiar legal term, institution or principle.

Zweigert and Kotz also argue that:

> [Functionality] rests on what every comparatist learns ... that the legal system of every society faces essentially the same problems, and solves these problems by quite different means, though very often with similar results.

How far is this accurate? In an unpublished article ('Legal history and comparative law'), which I have had the opportunity of reading, Derek Roebuck agrees with the principle of functionality, but takes issue with the further observations of Zweigert and Kotz and argues that 'it can be shown that all societies do not have the same problems'. He gives several examples of how different societies have faced different problems:

(a) some societies make more of incest and adultery than others; they have more elaborate categories;

(b) other societies do not consider certain activities either morally or legally reprehensible, for example, marrying a second cousin, which others have made a capital crime;

(c) adoption laws vary from society to society; English law only provided for adoption in the 1920s, whereas far less sophisticated societies had adoption laws of great 'complexity and subtlety' in 'well defined and manifold categories' from a very early period in their history.

Several responses can be made. First and foremost, it must be realised that Zweigert and Kotz were clearly setting the scene for the detailed discussion to follow, wherein they certainly display their deep and detailed knowledge on a wide range of substantive topics. It cannot therefore be the case that they were unaware of the fact that different societies have historically approached and treated certain areas of human intercourse in different ways. However, secondly, while not disagreeing with the content of Roebuck's points, I would suggest that, at the general and basic level, Zweigert and Kotz are absolutely correct in their statements. It really depends on how you interpret what they are saying because:

(a) while different societies treat certain questions, like adultery and incest, differently, all societies face the need to resolve their particular domestic/local problems and, whether this is how to treat the requirements for a valid marriage, or adultery or incest, the basic problem is: how should the law deal with these situations? Should it require certain strict requirements? Should it criminalise certain behaviour? In other words, all societies, from Alaska to Australia, face the basic problem of how best to regulate their society and resolve conflict;

(b) hence, once a particular community has decided on its response to a given situation, it is at this point that we are sometimes merely examining the content of their laws rather than the reasons for it, or the functions it fulfils. Thus, different societies may have different specific problems, but their basic problems tend to be very similar to one another;

(c) on the second part of the quotation from Zweigert and Kotz, it is again true that societies frequently do solve their problems by quite different means (and here Roebuck's points are relevant as illustrations of the different ways of dealing with the situations). Some societies criminalise certain behaviour while others do not. Many other examples are actually given by Zweigert and Kotz themselves in their section on the method of comparative law (see Zweigert and Kotz (1977) Vol I, pp 29–30 and Vol II);

(d) on the final point, Zweigert and Kotz say that 'very often' (that is, not in every case, although more often than not) there are similar results, in other words, as in other systems. This must also be correct at least to the extent that, if agreements are breached, there are usually some forms of redress, criminal or otherwise. If there is a need for a child to be placed under the protection of an adoptive family because it has been orphaned or abandoned, all societies provide for some means of doing so. The point about English adoption, of course, is that, although there were no formal adoption laws which gave adequate protection to children until the 1920s, various informal adoption procedures did exist, as well as wardship procedures, whereby a family could be made to look after an abandoned child, and the criminal law was usually on hand to impose a criminal sanction where cruelty *per se* could be proven, though no child protection laws had yet been passed.

Thus, the final result, the protection of the child or some form of redress to the 'victim' or innocent party, is, at the basic level, the same in virtually every society.

The presumption of similarity of results

Zweigert and Kotz end their section by submitting that the many examples they have cited, drawn from different legal families, point to a *praesumptio similitudinis*, a presumption that the practical results are similar. They clearly believe this to be a valid presumption, since they argue that it helps the comparatist by telling him or her where to look in the law of a foreign system in order to discover similarities and, at the end of the study, also acts as a means of verifying the results. Indeed, they say (p 31):

> The comparatist can rest content if his researches through all the relevant material lead to the conclusion that the systems he has compared reach the same or similar results but, if he finds that there are great differences or ... diametrically opposite results, he should be put on notice and go back to check again whether the terms in which he posed his original question were indeed purely functional, and whether he has spread the net of his researches wide enough.

As far as what they call 'unpolitical' areas of private law are concerned, namely, business dealings, commercial and property transactions, there is certainly some justification in what they say. Indeed, in the law relating to married couples, Western laws on divorce have many similarities and achieve the same practical results, for example, in allocating responsibility for the children, awarding maintenance (or alimony, or financial support) for wives and apportioning property upon divorce between the spouses on an equitable basis.

But, it is too much of a generalisation to suggest that there should be a presumption that the practical results will invariably be the same in every, or even most, legal systems. To take one example, in the case of couples who cohabit outside marriage (cohabitants), in 1987, Sweden passed fairly radical legislation which practically accords statutory recognition (and, therefore, financial and other rights) not just to heterosexual cohabitants, but to homosexual ones as well. This has certainly not been followed in countries like England, America, Germany or France. More importantly, it is exceedingly unlikely it will be followed, at least in the foreseeable future, by non-Western countries. It must, surely, be more accurate to say that there is a general tendency for a similarity of practical results to be found in most jurisdictions for a number of legal institutions, but the comparatist should keep an open mind.

THE COMPARATIVE LAW METHOD

A three stage approach

Comparatists soon discover that none of the existing texts or casebooks on comparative law actually appears to provide a plan of comparison, outlining possible methods of comparison. The closest attempt by a recognised text at providing some guidance on method remains that of Zweigert and Kotz, which we have considered at length in the previous section. Of course, many comparatists have written copiously on what a proper comparative method should consist of, but, of the published literature, only Kamba has actually suggested some 'objective' practical comparative techniques, in the sense that they make no assumptions as to ideology, culture or political persuasion. Accordingly, we shall consider the efficacy of his approach.

Kamba (1974) suggests that there are three main stages involved in the process of comparison:

(a) the descriptive phase;

(b) the identification phase; and

(c) the explanatory phase.

The descriptive phase may take the form of a description of the norms, concepts and institutions of the systems concerned. On the other hand, it may consist in the examination of the socio-economic problems and the legal problems and the legal solutions provided by the systems in question. The identification phase deals with the identification of differences and similarities between the systems being compared. The explanatory phase is the stage in which an attempt will be made to account for the resemblances and dissimilarities between systems, concepts or institutions.

It is made plain by Kamba that these phases are not always distinctly separated from each other and may well be dealt with in a different order, but three further points are then made. First, all three phases must, at some point, be undertaken before the enterprise can be properly regarded as comparative law. Secondly, the ultimate test of evaluation of the techniques employed is: does the technique of comparison, employed adequately or effectively, fulfil the object or objects which the comparatist has decided on? For example, does it promote a better understanding of one's own law, assist in the formulation of reliable theories of law, promote law reform or unification? Can the results obtained be considered accurate? Thirdly, depending on the answers to these and similar questions, the proper execution of the three phases is greatly influenced by three further factors:

(a) the comparatist's jurisprudential outlook;

(b) the social context of the legal systems under comparison; and

(c) the legal context of the legal topics being compared in the case of micro-comparison.

The jurisprudential outlook, according to Kamba, refers to the comparatist's general attitude to law. In other words, if the comparatist favours a sociologically or historically orientated view of law, this will usually mean that a sociological or historical approach to comparative law will be adopted. A preference for textual material may also constitute another jurisprudential orientation. With respect, it must be said that this approach assumes that the comparatist is a fairly experienced researcher, with a certain amount of expertise in specialist legal research. The present writer's supervisory and teaching experience indicates that, even with postgraduates of high quality, their views on law and approaches thereto tend to be very much in the developing stage, and their experience of comparative research is usually minimal. Further guidance to the would be comparatist is, therefore, required (see 'A method of comparison: a blueprint', p 235).

The social context of comparative study has already been discussed but, as far as the legal context is concerned in micro-comparison, Kamba echoes the view of Schmitthoff who declared that 'the quality of a legal institution may differ according to the structure of the legal system of which it forms part' (see Schmitthoff (1939) pp 97–98). Hence, the topic being compared must be placed within the context of the entire legal system from which it is derived.

A method of comparison: a blueprint

Based on the preceding discussion, it is now possible to formulate the following approach or method of comparison:

STEP ONE: identify the problem and state it as precisely as possible. This follows Zweigert and Kotz's initial step.

Points to note here are: the framing of the particular issue is crucial; what is your timescale for completion? Is the topic extremely wide? Too narrow? Seek a second opinion, if possible; otherwise, commence initial research by reading some basic articles or textbooks which deal with the topic. On the other hand, remember that your title is provisional and merely a working title which can be modified, subsequently, in the light of your preliminary research.

STEP TWO: assuming that the 'home' jurisdiction is one of the jurisdictions being compared, identify the foreign jurisdiction, and, if possible, the parent legal family to which it belongs or may be identified with most closely, following the usual criteria: sources; mode of legal thought; ideology, etc. If it happens to be a hybrid system or a system predominantly based on a religious faith, this should be noted.

Analysis of socialist legal cultures

If the problem involves a socialist system of law, this may pose insuperable difficulties at the present time, particularly if it involves one of the countries currently engaged in civil war rather than civil law. As we have seen, the Russian system is in a state of flux and the world waits to see which type of legal system will eventually prevail, assuming the society, its government and its leadership remain stable or, eventually, achieve stability over a relatively long period. A comparative study of problems involving socialist countries or Eastern Europe might well involve different considerations. In an article published in 1996, it was argued that comparative studies tend to be 'reductionist' in nature, uncritical descriptions of law and merely confined to formal discourse written constitutions and to primary and secondary legislation (see Puchalska-Tych and Salter (1996) 16 LS 160). The clear response to this is that a comparatist has got to start somewhere and is not going to be able critically to evaluate a legal system or legal problem within it before first examining key texts, be they written constitutions, etc. We have also stressed, throughout this book, that the socio-legal, socio-political and socio-cultural background to a given jurisdiction are very important in order to gain an insight into the workings of that jurisdiction. The level of knowledge or information that one gains, or is able to access, will obviously vary depending on which jurisdiction is being examined and the aspects thereof which are being considered. The level of understanding that a comparatist may achieve is another thing altogether. This book can only provide the methods.

Puchalska-Tych and Salter (1996) also highlight the comparative errors most commonly committed in the analysis of socialist legal cultures:

(a) denial of the diversity of historical backgrounds of various socialist States (one has only to read David and Brierley (1985) to see an exception to this, which the writers do mention, and the list of articles cited in the last chapter of this book, for example, Osiatynski (1991), Agh (1991) and Elster (1991));

(b) denial of the socio-political and legal evolution of Eastern European societies (the articles cited under (a), above, do address this point);

(c) presentation of the socialist legal culture, as if frozen in time and space and as if the old totalitarian model still applied (Chapter 6, above, debunks this view);

(d) the one sided Western perspective: presenting the socialist situation and legal tradition as a deviation from the norm which is tacitly the 'Western model' of law and society.

They argue for a 'dialectical analysis', which requires 'cultural mediations' and contextualisation of phenomena, to analyse internal contradictions, phenomenological exposition and methodological reflexivity. In a nutshell, they wish all comparative study to be more than mere descriptions, but to recognise the living nature of the law, to be more orientated towards the point of view of the people being studied, and, citing Friedman (1990), that law should be studied as a culture not as a 'collection of doctrines, rules, terms and phrases'.

Clearly, we have been taking great pains to point out that there are many perspectives that should be adopted in comparative legal studies, and this book certainly does not advocate a preference for a so called 'Western' approach as being necessarily preferable to other systems.

Once identification of the system has been effected, move to Step Three.

STEP THREE: decide which primary sources of law are going to be needed or, even more importantly, which materials are available? Does your nearest library provide them? Will you need to examine a Civil Law Code? Is the solution contained in a statute, or would a statute provide merely the initial source of reference? Will a decided case provide the basis for the answer? If there is no obvious answer, move to Step Four.

STEP FOUR: gather and assemble the material relevant to the jurisdiction being examined. This should include primary and secondary sources of law. If you do not have particularly strong feelings on what the legal approach should be (that is, sociological or historical), it is suggested that you give equal weight to historical influence and socio-economic factors.

A useful checklist is:

(a) bibliographies culled from current law periodicals or texts;

(b) any available comparative encyclopedias;

(c) introductory works dealing with that particular system or with comparative law generally if the researcher is a 'first time comparatist';

(d) the Internet (if available);

(e) written constitutions, if relevant and available, of the jurisdictions being examined;

(f) law Codes (that is, the Civil Code, Codes of Civil Procedure and their equivalents);

(g) law reports;

(h) law and socio-legal journals;

(i) commentaries, textbooks and casebooks; and

(j) legal periodicals, wherein updated lists of available legal materials in particular areas of law occasionally appear. If there is difficulty in procuring any or all of these materials, the inter-library loan services are generally very helpful, failing which a visit to the Institute of Advanced Legal Studies in London is also recommended. Another valuable step may be to contact the embassy of the country in question, especially if it is particularly remote, in order to obtain up to date information. Many embassies are prepared to at least send some basic material or provide some helpful contacts for the researcher to deal with.

STEP FIVE: organise the material in accordance with headings reflecting the legal philosophy and ideology of the legal system being investigated. This may, initially, take the form of columns setting out the differences and similarities between the home jurisdiction's law alongside that of the system being compared. (This accords broadly with part of the descriptive phase in Kamba's analysis.) Of course, as with all research, the comparatist might well find that the initial hypothesis may begin to take on a life of its own, and there may be a need to modify and amend the basic formulation as the research takes shape.

A suggested working outline might include:

(a) the working title, subtitle and subtexts;

(b) the main sources of law of the systems under comparison – preferably with general bibliographies;

(c) the hierarchy of sources:

 – codes, statutes, enactments, edicts, custom, doctrinal writing; commentaries;

 – cases, statutes, other secondary legislation, textbooks, custom?;

 – encyclopedic works on targeted jurisdictions;

(d) background/socio-cultural material:

– treatises/periodical articles covering the jurisdiction and/or the topic being studied.

STEP SIX: tentatively map out the possible answers to the problem, comparing carefully the different approaches, bearing in mind possible cultural differences or socio-economic factors, where relevant, and exploring any other non-legal factors (such as local custom/local conventions/religious traditions) which may have influenced the current legal position in both jurisdictions. Throughout the inquiry, two questions should be posed constantly: how does the rule/institution really operate in practice? And, why? (That is, are the reasons historical, pragmatic, cultural or based on religious beliefs, economic practices or certain trade practices, etc?)

STEP SEVEN: Critically analyse the legal principles in terms of their intrinsic meaning rather than according to any Western or other standards. Check on the accuracy of the translations you might have had to scrutinise: have you considered the cultural rather than literal meaning of the term/phrase/concept? What purpose does the rule fulfil? What principle, if any, does it support or apply? What practical effects might it have on the parties involved?

STEP EIGHT: set out your conclusions within a comparative framework with caveats, if necessary, and with critical commentary, wherever relevant, and relate it to the original purpose of your enquiry. Indicate the relative importance that you gave to the nature of the systems being studied, their parent legal family, if any, or their hybrid nature, their historical or socio-cultural development and the possible repercussions of these developments on the legal development of the rule/solution/institution/branch of law, in relation to other legal systems. It will also be desirable to justify your preliminary conclusions with reasons, so that future researchers will be able to see the approach that you adopted, and why. An example of another outline might be:

(a) type of legal system: common law/civil law/socialist/hybrid/religious;

(b) branch of national law: commercial law/family law/property/corporate law, etc;

(c) issue: for example, 'to what extent does the rule relating to X operate within jurisdictions A and B?';

(d) aims and objectives of the study: short term/long term? Dissemination?;

(e) historical perspective: how has history (recent or ancient) shaped its present legal position?;

(f) primary sources: cases/written constitutions/Codes/treaty/ EC Directives/Regulations?;

(g) references: books, articles, monographs, unpublished theses sometimes available in library archives;

(e) method of analysis: empirical surveys, questionnaires, interviews, literature searches: library based?;

(f) law and language: linguistic considerations: any translations required; communicating with a scholar from the foreign jurisdiction to get first hand information about the operation of the rule in practice rather than merely from books?;

(g) background: socio-political, cultural and economic factors?;

(h) analysis: literature review of two jurisdictions;

(i) synthesis;

(j) case review and/or statutory interpretation: key cases and legislation?;

(k) critique: what does this mean for the future development of this area of law in the context of the legal development of this topic, in this particular jurisdiction?;

(l) conclusions: tying the threads of the argument together with the comparative perspective paramount.

This, then, is but one blueprint within which the comparative technique or methods may be applied. While taking account of the approaches of other comparatists, it also elaborates on the comparative method and integrates the latest position on the socialist countries. It also strives to integrate a socio-historical approach to law, but comparatists who have their own personal preferences may, of course, pursue them accordingly.

It needs to be emphasised that a blueprint is a plan of action – it is not meant to be exhaustive and its completion does not ensure or guarantee a deeper understanding of the areas being studied. It is also not meant to cover every possible approach to a particular comparative enterprise. It is, however, a beginning; no more and no less. Of course, every comparatist is unavoidably influenced by her background or training and experience. Similarly, linguistic differences can be a barrier because of the initial difficulties in understanding the cultural underpinning of the language, but a language can also build bridges between countries and comparatists. You need to know there is an iceberg beneath the surface before you can begin to examine the tip of it! This blueprint should give you some idea of the configurations to look for. The whole fascination of the enterprise must be the constant discovery and rejoicing in the differences (and similiarities) between systems and this spurs the quest for rationales and explanations. But, it is hoped that comparative exercise will broaden the mind and widen the researcher's horizons, so that she no longer pursues the study from a one dimensional perspective.

As with all comparative studies, each successful investigation marks the end of what should have been an illuminating inquiry, but it should also mark the beginning of a fresh outlook in studying the operation of different legal systems.

SELECTIVE BIBLIOGRAPHY

Atiyah and Summers, *Form and Substance in Anglo-American Law* (1987)

Collins, 'Methods and aims of comparative contract law' (1991) 11 OJLS 396

Farnsworth, *An Introduction to the Legal System of the United States* (1987)

Friedman, 'Legal culture and social development' (1969) 6 Law and Society Rev 19

Friedman, 'Some thoughts on comparative legal culture', in Clark (ed), *Comparative and Private International Law: Essays in Honour of John Henry Merryman* (1990)

Grossfeld, *The Strength and Weakness of Comparative Law* (1990) especially Chapters 1, 10, 11, 12, 13

Gutteridge, 'The comparative aspects of legal terminology' (1937–38) Tulane L Rev 401

Gutteridge, *Comparative Law* (1949) Chap VI

Kahn-Freund, Levy and Rudden, *A SourceBook on French Law* (1991)

Kamba, 'Comparative law: a theoretical framework' (1974) 23 ICLQ 485

Knapp, 'Comparison and the global problems of law' (1990) 59 Revista de la Universidad de Puerto Rico 749

Legrand, 'How to compare now' (1996) 16 LS 232

McDougal, 'The comparative study of law for policy purposes: value clarification as an instrument of democratic world order' (1952) 1 Am J Comp L 24

Nelken (ed), *Comparing Legal Cultures* (1997)

Puchalska-Tych and Salter, 'Comparing legal cultures of Eastern Europe: the need for a dialectical analysis' (1996) 16 LS 157

Rheinstein, 'Comparative law – its functions, methods and usages' (1968) 22 Arkansas L Rev and Bar Association Journal 415

Sacco, 'Legal formants: a dynamic approach to comparative law' (1991) 39 Am J Comp L 343

Schlesinger, *Comparative Law: Cases, Texts, Materials* (1988) pp 1–43, 868–98

Smith, *The Magic Mirror: Law in American History* (1989)

Stone, 'The end to be served by comparative law' (1951) 25 Tulane L Rev 325

Tumanov, 'On comparing various types of legal systems', in *Comparative Law and Legal System* (1985) p 69

Van Hoecke and Warrington, 'Legal cultures, legal paradigms and legal doctrine: towards a new model for comparative law' (1998) 47 ICLQ 495

Watson, *Society and Legal Change* (1977)

Watson 'Legal transplants and law reform' (1976) 92 LQR 79

Watson, *Legal Transplants* (1974)

Weston, *An English Reader's Guide to the French Legal System* (1991)

White, 'Law as language: reading law and reading literature' (1982) 60 Texas L Rev 415

Zweigert and Kotz, *An Introduction to Comparative Law* (1977) Vol I

CHAPTER 8

A COMPARATIVE STUDY OF JUDICIAL STYLES AND CASE LAW

THE MEANING OF 'CASE LAW'

It is important to distinguish two different usages of the term 'case law'. In the broad sense, this refers to a body of non-statutory rules as declared, or developed, by judicial decisions. This body of law is called 'jurisprudence' in French law.

In the narrow sense, case law refers to a method of using the rules, so produced, as a basis for deciding future cases. This, as mentioned earlier, is the method which is typical of the growth and evolution of the English common law tradition. The present chapter discusses the use of the term in the first, broad sense and then considers its recent application in the narrower sense.

CASE LAW AS A SOURCE OF LAW

A preliminary question is whether judicial decisions, or cases *per se*, actually constitute a source of law in the various legal systems. As we have seen, historically, cases have been the primary source of law in the English common law tradition, but have at best been regarded only as a secondary source of law in the civil law tradition.

The French Civil Code, in Art 5, expressly forbids judges to lay down general principles as a means of deciding cases (*par voie de disposition générale et règlementaire*), but Art 1 of the Swiss Civil Code, drawn up a century later, expressly directs the judge that, in the absence of statutory provisions or customary law, he should decide in accordance with rules which he would lay down, 'if he had himself to act as legislator', and that, in doing so, must be guided 'by approved legal doctrine and case law'. In French law, Art 4 of its Civil Code provides that a judge who refuses to render a judgment, on the basis that the law was silent on the matter, or obscure or inadequate, can be proceeded against personally for denial of justice. In other words, he has to render a decision.

We have also noted the movement towards convergence not just of sources in civil law and common law jurisdictions, but also of policies and theories, in the 1970s and 1980s, which has continued into the mid-1990s. Significantly, although legislation and Codes remain theoretically the official sources of law in civil law countries, theory and practice diverge to the extent that a study of the weight and authority given to cases in civil law countries has become an essential feature if we are to study the law as it functions in practice. This is particularly the case in French administrative law, wherein the Conseil d'État clearly exercises a law making role, and in German constitutional law. Both these areas of law have been, and continue to be, dominated by case law. Thus, there are at least two good reasons for a comparative study of case law. First, such a study reveals what the law really is in practice; and, secondly, cases highlight the contemporary problems that face a legal system at any given point in history.

KEY ISSUES

Although five styles of appellate judicial opinions have been identified, it is probably true to say that an examination of the form of judgments in European continental courts and Russian courts (as they existed pre-1990), at the time of writing, as contrasted with the form of English court judgments gives the student of comparative law a clear illustration of the differences between the three major legal traditions.

The following discussion focuses on three key issues:

(a) to what extent are cases in civil law or socialist countries treated as authoritative? Does a practice of *stare decisis* exist in European continental law or in the Russian legal system?;

(b) how far does the form or 'style' of European continental judgments and decided cases in Russian law differ from that of English common law?;

(c) what are the merits and demerits of *stare decisis*?

THE AUTHORITY OF CASE LAW IN NON-COMMON LAW JURISDICTIONS

The authority of case law in non-common law countries

Civil law countries

As we have seen, the Codes and legislation are given primacy, as formal sources of law, in civil law countries. Thus, if we consider the relationship between judicial decisions and statutory or enacted law, we find that the official attitude of civil law judges in the private law courts is an explicit adherence to statute or codified law. Any creative exercise by judges or judicial law making is, therefore, explained in the context of 'legislative interpretation'. The classic Romano-Germanic tradition, as mentioned earlier, is that the legal principle should be doctrinal or legislative in origin. In civil law countries, therefore, the fundamental principle is that the jurisdiction of the private law courts does not traditionally encompass the power to rely on a previous judicial decision as a basis for the judgment, since there is no theoretical equivalent of the *stare decisis* rule. This would mean that, in theory, the principles laid down by a court are, generally, always subject to rejection by another court. As we shall see, it is invariably 'the court' that arrives at decisions, and this collegial character of the judgment also encourages the notion of the judges as interpreters, not law makers. There is, moreover, no distinction between *ratio* and *dicta*, since judgments tend to be phrased in terms of general principles, or based on general clauses from which the eventual decision is reached. Civil law courts also treat many issues as factual which a common law court would regard as legal, that is, points to be decided by law. This further encourages the lower courts to have freedom from binding precedents *per se*.

An exception to this general rule is where there is a consistent line of precedents which have followed the same view on a particular question. In France, Mexico and the Spanish speaking world, the occurrence of such a harmonious line of decisions will have the practical effect of *stare decisis* or binding precedent.

In France, this phenomenon is called *la jurisprudence constante* and in Spain *doctrina legal*. As far as French law is concerned, Professor Tunc argued in 1955 that, as far as Court of Cassation judgments are concerned, a single precedent (that is, case) in point *pratiquement* establishes the law and that the *jurisprudence constante* theory is obsolete and erroneous. Nevertheless, in 1968, Professor Nicholas reaffirmed the continued existence of the *jurisprudence constante* approach, and it would now seem that the current position is that it co-exists with the 'single precedent' approach. Lambert and Wasserman have, thus, rightly declared that 'France has just as many leading cases as England'. The court's approach, thus, depends on the particular circumstances of the case before the court.

In countries governed by written constitutions and separate constitutional courts, such as Germany and Italy, there are also legislative provisions which allow for certain decisions to have binding force. Paragraph 31 of the Gesetz über das Bundesverfassungsgericht (law concerning the Federal Constitutional Court) deals with this situation in Germany. Similarly, Art 136 of the Italian Constitution provides that:

> When the court declares that a provision of law is unconstitutional, the provision shall cease to have effect from the day following the publication of the decision.

In practice, therefore, there are circumstances in which civil law judges have been known to follow a consistent judicial view which has been taken by a line of cases, particularly if the decisions have been laid down by superior courts.

Reasons for lower courts following superior courts' decisions

Subordinate courts have tended to follow superior courts' decisions but, although this practice has not been openly seen or acknowledged as a practice of precedent, it has, nevertheless, been carried out for the following reasons:

(a) Codes formulated in the 19th century could not possibly envisage developments in the 20th century. Hence, where there has been a gap in the law which is not covered by the Codes, or ancillary legislation, judges have had to consider whether to indulge in some sort of 'law making' or law creating process;

(b) it promotes certainty and predictability in the law;

(c) it has been regarded as a means of promoting equality of justice;

(d) it has been seen as convenient and efficient to do so;

(e) judges do not like being reversed or overturned on appeal;

(f) as members of a hierarchy with a tradition, the practice of following cases has been seen as a form of judicial co-operation.

It should be borne in mind that, if cases are referred to in this way, civil law courts are careful to stress that either necessity forces them to refer to an instructive case or that the line of case authority is only being utilised as an illustration of some general principle of law, which they can usually find to support their decision. Thus, to answer one of the first questions we posed, it appears to be that civil law countries do regard cases as sources of law in practice, but only in specific circumstances and never actually articulate official recognition of cases as sources of law. David and Brierley (1985) draw the distinction between cases not being sources of legal rules but, nevertheless, being sources of law. This is because, although the cases are referred to in order to ascertain the law, the true source of the law is the legal rule or principle which derives from doctrine, legislation or the Codes.

Case law in the Russian system

Before the collapse of the Soviet Union, in 1991, and the formation of the Russian Federation, the role of judicial decisions in the former USSR was reasonably clear. The purpose of decided cases or judicial decisions was to carry out a strict interpretation of enacted or codified law. It is important to remember the previous Soviet concept and ideological perception of law as an instrument of State policy, and of Marxist/Leninist ideals. Within this philosophical framework, it is easy to appreciate that Soviet judges themselves were subject to enacted law and were not allowed to ignore, or to be ignorant of, government policy. According to the latest Russian edict, proclaimed by Russian President Boris Yeltsin, judges are now to be given independence from State control and, *ex facie*, this means that judges may well begin to play a law making role. In the light of the dramatically changed conditions in the new Russian Federation, this may well become an essential feature of Russian judicial practice. In the past, a number of 'instructions' (administrative edicts) have been passed in response to and incorporating the experience of decided cases. Further, doctrinal works have increasingly referred to decided cases as illustrations of the law, and a summary of judicial decisions has appeared in the official review, *Soviet State and Law*, which has been published since 1938.

However, the disintegration of the USSR, the formation of the Russian Federation and the consequent disappearance of the very foundations of the old Marxist/Leninist ideology from the Russian nation have led to at least the suspension, if not the abolition, of reviews and compilations. It remains to be seen how case law will be interpreted if and when the new Russian Federation achieves stability and a stronger measure of consensus and acceptability.

STYLES OF JUDICIAL DECISIONS

Appellate court decisions

In order to make a meaningful comparison of cases in the different jurisdictions, we shall be concentrating on the styles of appellate judicial decisions, since many of the 'first instance' (trial court/first tier court) civil law decisions either consist of one line pronouncements or are merely laconic statements of principle. Moreover, most of the common law first instance decisions, while generally representative of the style of judgments, are of limited utility in comparative methodological terms, since we would not be comparing judgments at a similar level to those from civil law courts. At the appellate level, there are five distinctive styles of judgments (see Wetter, *The Style of Appellate Judicial Opinions* (1960)).

The five styles of judgments

The five main types of typical judicial styles at the appellate level are:

(a) the English type;

(b) the French type;

(c) the German type;

(d) the Swedish type; and

(e) the American type.

There are, of course, variations within each style, most notably with regard to the English style, where, more than the others, there are several variations on the general approach of English judges. These will be contrasted with the Russian appellate style as it used to exist, pre-1991. Both the style and substance of the Russian judiciary are set to change in view of the sweeping judicial reforms which President Yeltsin wishes to implement. However, the basic civil law/socialist law approach will probably be retained (see, further, Chapter 6).

The English style of judgment

At the appellate level, the style and format of a typical English judgment is, in one sense, no different from that which can be found in first instance or trial court judgments. The appellate court will listen to the oral arguments from counsel from both sides, and then offer its assessment of them, offering, where appropriate, the opportunity for counsel to address counter-arguments. The judges will then, usually, after taking time to consider the evidence and opposing arguments, deliver their judgment. The fact that the case was allowed to reach the appeal stage means that there was doubt as to the law and a choice as to the result. It should be borne in mind that leave (that is, judicial permission) has to be obtained in order for a case to get to the House of Lords (s 1 of the Administration of Justice (Appeals) Act 1934). This is by no means obtained easily.

Ratio and dicta

Each judge will review the salient facts of the case, pose the issues (factual and/or legal) that need to be decided and then review the legal arguments for and against, deciding the issues one way or the other, before coming to a conclusion and decision, usually expressed as a statement of legal principle (the *ratio decidendi*) which will incorporate the most important facts of the case. The *ratio* has been defined as 'the principle that is to be derived from the judge's decision on the basis of the facts that the judge treated as material' (Goodhart (1931)). This will be based on the judge's individual interpretation of the facts. The *ratio* is, strictly, the only part of the judgment that is potentially binding on a future court. Legal points not strictly connected to the *ratio* are considered *dicta* and are said to be *obiter dicta* (uttered in passing), and such statements are not binding on a future court. The difficulty in practice is that it is not always patently obvious or easily discoverable which part of the decision is *ratio* and which is *dicta*.

Sir Rupert Cross, a leading English authority on the doctrine of precedent, even went so far as to say that 'it is impossible to devise formulae for determining the *ratio decidendi* of case' (see Cross (1977) p 76). It is submitted that one method of discovering what the *ratio* of a particular case might be is to examine the issue(s) in the case and then relate this to the judge's statement of principle, which incorporates the key facts of the case. If the judicial statement deals with that issue directly, this is at least one of the *rationes* in the case. The judge will usually give his reasons for his eventual decision and the way he sees them operating so as to lead towards his interpretation of the issues before the court. The analysis could be, and often is, wide ranging and discursive. The judge has the flexibility to choose the facts on which to concentrate and the choice as to which interpretation to adopt regarding, for example, an ambiguous provision or contract clause.

The remarkable fact is that all the English judges presiding in that case, although often varying in their particular emphasis and order of discussion of the facts and issues, will employ the same case law technique or canons of statutory interpretation and operate within this framework in order to reach their particular decision. Moreover, even if, for example, all five House of Lords' judges agree on their reasons for their judgment, their judgment will have been delivered *seriatim*, and no attempt will have been made to co-ordinate the judgments or to present them as a unity. The only visible sign of intra-judicial co-operation will be that one of the judges might deliver a 'leading judgment' with which some of his 'learned brethren' will 'concur'. Two further noteworthy features discoverable from the law report are the names of the presiding judges and a listing of who were in the 'majority' and who dissented. This is very different from the collegial approach of French or German judgments, wherein the judges remain anonymous.

The dissenting judgment

The dissenting judgment is peculiar to the common law tradition. Its style, as one writer has put it, may vary from the 'courteously devastating' to the 'wryly baffled' (see Rudden (1974)). On other occasions, they can be calmly dismissive or patently disapproving. Lord Denning will probably be remembered as one of the most strong minded of dissenting judges, who, at times, was so convinced of the correctness of his position as to disagree with the majority of his learned brethren. Perhaps, the most memorable example of this was in a House of Lords' decision, called *Scruttons v Midland Silicones* [1962] AC 446, where the issue was whether a stevedore could enforce an exclusion clause contained in a separate contract of carriage to which he was not a party. In that case, Lord Denning disagreed with no less than eight of his learned colleagues, as well as with the United States Supreme Court and the Australian High Court.

An example of a dissenting judgment which was calmly dismissive was when Lord Denning called the privity of contract rule (precluding third parties from having an independent right to sue on a contract to which they were not parties) 'at bottom ... only a rule of procedure', in *Beswick v Beswick* [1966] Ch 557. The point to grasp is that, under the English common law tradition, in the event of a disagreement among judges at appellate level, the majority view prevails. Hence, the eventual outcome of a case will depend on how far up the court hierarchy the degree of dissent occurs, not on how many judges *in toto*, supported a particular legal viewpoint. A fairly recent example of this is the 1985 case of *Gillick v West Norfolk and Wisbech Area Health Authority* [1985] 3 All ER 402. No less than five judges agreed with Mrs Gillick's argument that under 16 year old girls should not be allowed to have contraceptive treatment or advice, except with their parent's knowledge and consent, whereas only four disagreed with her. Nevertheless, she eventually lost her case because, in the House of Lords, the highest English domestic appellate court, the Law Lords, voted 3:2 against her. Another useful function of the dissenting judgment is that it provides a useful indicator of those areas of law in which there is some doubt and uncertainty, and which are often developing areas of law. It has been said that English law is often ruled by 'the dead hand of the law' (Maitland), which refers to the English judicial practice of constantly referring to either antiquated procedures or simply old cases and pronouncements by judges who are long dead. The reason for this is the English legal practice of reliance on 'leading cases' in a particular field of law which, although modified to suit changed circumstances and social eras, remain virtually unchanged at their heart. Such a case in the law of tort is *Donoghue v Stevenson* [1932] AC 562, a House of Lords case which has become famous both for its facts (the snail in the bottle) and for the statement by Lord Atkin, uttered 60 years ago, defining the English tort law notion of 'neighbours'. An even more interesting point is that Lord Atkin's statement was, strictly speaking, *dicta* which was later interpreted as a very important *ratio*. Hence, the *ratio* of a case in English law may sometimes be what judges say it is in subsequent cases, rather than what the original court might have stated.

Impact of judgment on future practice

The English appellate judgments are also distinctive for their careful consideration of the impact of their decisions on future practice. This is because they are strongly aware that lower courts will almost always look to their statements for guidance and nearly always follow them and that, if they exhibit sympathy for the unique facts of the case presently before them, they must consider the 'floodgates' argument: will this lead to the floodgates of litigation being opened as a result of this decision? The basic attitude of the English judicial hegemony is not to encourage appeals unless they are absolutely necessary in the interests of justice, or because of a gap in the law or an unresolvable uncertainty in the law (see Annual Practice Statements, issued by the Lord Chancellor's department, stressing that too many lower court appeals are being given leave to appeal to the appeal courts).

Reference to foreign cases in English judgments

As far as reference in English judgments to foreign cases as support for legal propositions or reasoning is concerned, a recent survey of the extent to which such cases are cited is revealing (see Orucu (1994)). Since 1972, when Britain joined the European Community, English courts have only rarely cited continental decisions, except in passing. However, English courts have made frequent reference to Commonwealth and American cases. In the period 1972–93, most reference was made (when made at all) to American cases (40), then to Australia (35), Canada (34) and, finally, New Zealand (27). Scottish cases have also been cited, but even more rarely (23). In 1972, reference was made in 26 out of 602 cases, whereas, in 1993, 30 cases made references to the abovementioned jurisdictions' decisions out of 184 cases. Obviously, such citations would only be made if the need arose to consider a foreign law as in a conflict of laws situation. In such cases, there is a presumption that the law of another jurisdiction is the same as the forum currently considering the case, unless proof to the contrary is presented.

Reference to academic, foreign and comparative literature by English appellate courts

As a general rule, English courts do not refer to the works of academic writers in their judgments, as these are not authoritative, but there are, of course, exceptions. In a number of cases, English judges have actually expressed their gratitude to academics for their comments, particularly in areas where the law is in a state of transition and new law is essentially being made (see *Sidaway v Board of Governors of the Bethlem Royal Hospital and the Maudsley* [1985] AC 871, p 886; *Spiliada Maritime Corp v Causlex Ltd* [1987] AC 460, p 488; and *R v Gomez* [1993] AC 442, pp 489–90). However, it tends to be the case that, once the judge has referred to the academic literature on the area, he proceeds along the lines that have been criticised: see *Re W (a minor)* [1992] 4 All ER 627 where, having referred to 'academic and other writers' and listed a sample of their published criticisms in legal journals and books, the judge then still justified his previous ruling that a child's refusal to consent to medical treatment could be overridden by a person who had parental responsibility for that child and by a court, provided it was in the best interests of that child. He also then reaffirmed his earlier, much criticised approach because it was, in the present case, still seen that it was not in the child's best interests to comply with her wishes.

In the context of reference to foreign literature in English judgments, the case of *White v Jones* [1995] 1 All ER 691 is an example of where the House of Lords used comparative methods by assessing solutions adopted in other legal systems, in this case in German law, to reach its decision in a case of solicitors' negligence, where there was a paucity of suitable precedents. The book by Professor Markesinis (*The German Law of Torts: A Comparative Introduction* (1994)) was expressly referred to by one of the Law Lords.

Distinguishing cases

Previously decided cases can, of course, be 'distinguished' on the basis of their facts, or the law or because they were decided *per incuriam*. Hence, there is leeway for the judges to decide not to follow a precedent on these aforesaid grounds.

The French style of judgment

Cour de Cassation judgments

The French Court of Cassation's judgments tend to be extremely brief and addressed to only one issue. Of course, it is not the approach with every case, but these judgments usually concentrate on an unequivocal statement of the court's finding, but no previous cases are cited. Sometimes, the whole judgment may even be cast in one sentence (sometimes, a very lengthy one!), irrespective of the extensiveness of the facts or the complexity of the legal issue. The subject and the verb occur at the very beginning and very end, respectively, and are divided by a number of 'whereases' (*attendu*) which contain the reasons (*motifs*) which lie behind the judgment. Its length is, thus, more akin to a decree or a series of paragraphs resembling an English court summons.

The lower courts usually employ a number of paragraphs beginning 'considering' (*considerant*), but this is sometimes also employed by the Court of Cassation (see below).

It should be remembered that the Court of Cassation is not a Court of Final Appeal, unlike the House of Lords, and that the court reviews the judgment, not the substantive case, primarily in order to see that lower court judgments are in accordance with the law. The court has the power, if it decides to quash a decision, to remit the case to be reheard or retried by a lower court at the same level as the original court which heard the decision. It is inevitable that the style of French judgments at this level will be quite different from an English appeal court. It is meant to reinforce the French judicial tradition that the judgment is simply a deduction from the principles of enacted law.

Form of French judgment

The typical French law report will usually contain:

(a) the name of the court which heard the case;

(b) a concise statement of the precise issue before the court;

(c) the judgment, collectively stated: '... the court holds ...';

(d) no dissenting (or concurring) judgments apart from the collective judgment.

The judgment will be cast as a deduction from principles of enacted law or doctrine. There will not be any reporting of any arguments for and against the issues before the court and no factual findings on, for instance, the behaviour of the individual defendant or plaintiff. Here is an extract from a Court of Cassation judgment, taken from a note by Puech (Cass Civ 1 December 1969 DS (1970) 422, cited by Rudden (1974)):

> THE COURT ... on the single ground: whereas it appears from the findings of the judgment complained of that Sandrock, being near to a collision between the automobile of Veidt and the moped of Martin, in the course whereof the latter's engine caught fire, attempted to put out the flames with an extinguisher, but was wounded when the petrol tank exploded.
>
> Whereas it is complained that the Court of Appeal ordered Martin to compensate the damage caused to Sandrock, on the ground that a rescue contract had been formed between the parties, but that there can be no agreement without the consent of the parties, and the judgment did not mention that of the victim.
>
> But, whereas, the Court of Appeal did not have to find the express consent of the victim since, when an offer is made in his exclusive interest, the offeree is presumed to have accepted it; that having, within their sovereign power, concluded that a rescue contract had been formed between Sandrock and Martin, the judges of appeal were quite right to hold that the victim was obliged to compensate the damages sustained by one who lent assistance through benevolence; therefore the ground cannot be accepted; for these reasons, reject.

Quite clearly, this highly compressed style of judgment makes it impossible to ascertain the extent to which this case has relied on a previous decision or, indeed, to use it as a precedent for future decisions. It is the commentaries by French doctrinal writers, therefore, to which one has to refer in order to place a French judgment of this nature in context.

An example of a single line judgment is where the Court of Cassation's solitary statement in the judgment was that 'The liability of the defendant to the victim can only be contractual' (see Cass Civ 20 October 1964, DS (1965) 62).

An example of a Court of Cassation judgment, this time containing slightly more factual detail and employing the 'considering' (*considerant*) style, more generally associated with the lower court judgments is:

Cour de Cassation

Prehaut and the Citroen Transport Corporation

v

Peron

Court of Cassation, 1st Civil Chamber, July 15, 1975, President Bellet, Rapporteur Devismes, Advocate-general Granjon, Advocates Le Prado and Lyon-Caen.

Petition for the cassation of the decision of the Court of Appeal of Riom of November 15, 1973.

Decision of the Court

On the ground for cassation:

Having considered Art 1147 of the Civil Code.

Considering that the obligation to transport the passenger safely to his destination, provided for by this Article, is imposed upon the carrier only in the course of the performance of the contract of carriage;

Considering that Jean-Marc Peron travelled in a motor coach of the Citroen Transport Corporation when, at a stop, the driver asked him to take a parcel to a cafe; that in crossing the highway Peron was hit and injured by an automobile;

Considering that in order to hold the driver of the motor coach and the Citroen Transport Corporation liable for the accident, the Court of Appeal relied on the contract of carriage and held that the responsibility for the accident fell on the carrier;

Considering that in so holding, although they found that the accident occurred when the passenger alighted from the vehicle for a reason unconnected with his carriage, the judges of the Court of Appeal have by their erroneous application violated the abovementioned Article of the Civil Code;

For these reasons and without any need to consider the second ground for cassation, this court sets the judgment aside and remits the case to the Court of Appeal of Limoges for further proceedings.

The German style of judgment

Primacy of legislative or codified provisions

German appellate judgments are no different from German first instance judgments in their basic approach to reaching a decision. The starting point is usually a reference to a legislative provision Code provision or legal norm which serves as a basis for a process of reasoning by analogy which, eventually, leads to a decision. A legal rule or norm consists of the legal outcome and the *Tatbestand*, that is, the facts or other circumstances in which the rule is to apply (see Horn, Kotz and Leser, *German Private and Commercial Law* (1982)).

Statute (*Gesetz*) and custom (*Gewohnheitsrecht*) are the only officially recognised sources of law, and all laws normally derive their validity from the constitution which is the ultimate basis of all law. Decisions of the courts are binding only on the parties, since German law does not recognise a practice of precedent, or *stare decisis*, as such. Nevertheless, judges, particularly in the lower courts, devote a great deal of attention to decided cases, especially those of the *Reichsgericht* or of the *Bundesgerichtshof*. As with French law, a whole series of decisions of these two courts which consistently espouse a certain principle, can nearly always be expected to be followed. The persuasive force of German case law is proportionately more strongly weighted, depending on how recent it happens to be. The theory appears to be that an old case might not be followed because it does not accord with current and contemporary social or economic developments, whereas a more recent one might well be followed. Rules developed by decided cases are not strictly regarded as law or even sources of law. However, they are usually seen as contributing to the formation of a rule of customary law.

Exceptions to the rule that stare decisis does not exist

There are four main exceptions to the general rule that precedents have no binding effect:

(a) Federal Constitutional Court decisions are binding on the constitutional organs of the Federal Republic and of the *Länder*, all other courts and public authorities. Indeed, the decisions of this court assume the force of statute if a court decides on the compatibility of an Act or statute with the basic law, or of an Act or statute of one of the *Länder* with a Federal Act or statute.

(b) The Federal Supreme Court (*Bundesgerichtshof*), the highest court in civil and criminal matters, sits in 15 divisions (10 civil divisions and five criminal divisions) referred to as 'Senate'. An individual division or section (*Senat*) for civil matters which does not wish to follow a point of law adopted in an opinion laid down by another Senate for civil matters has to lay the matter before the Great Senate for civil matters of the Federal Supreme Court for decision, and to accept the view adopted by the Great Senate. The same rule applies to the Senate for criminal matters among all similar Senates and in relation to the Great Senate for criminal matters.

(c) A Court of Appeal (*Oberlandesgericht*) which wishes to deviate from an opinion on a point of law adopted in a previous criminal law case by another appeal court or by the Federal Supreme Court is obliged to refer the matter for its decision on the disputed point to the Federal Supreme Court and must then abide by the view adopted by that court.

A similar rule applies to non-contentious matters arising mainly, though not exclusively, in cases such as those relating to the land register, commercial register, probate, guardian and ward. In other words, an appellate court which wishes not to follow a precedent laid down by another Appeal Court or the Federal Supreme Court, in non-contentious cases, must refer the case to the Federal Supreme Court.

(d) Where there was an appeal on a point of law in which the Federal Court had to reverse a judgment of an appeal court or district court and sent the case back for retrial and rehearing, that court is then bound to follow the legal opinion adopted by the Federal Supreme Court.

General style of Federal Supreme Court judgments

As with French judgments, decisions of the Federal Supreme Court are published and presented as unanimous and anonymous judgments of the entire court. This does not mean that the presiding judges never disagree amongst themselves, but that there is no public record of dissenting judgments in the published decision. In the event of dissent, the judges vote in reverse order of seniority, so that the presiding judge votes last and the final decision is reached by simple majority. The final version of the judgment will, in these cases, require careful formulation so as to represent accurately the compromise statement agreed upon by the judges. The length of the judgments is, perhaps, closer to an American report than the longer appellate English law judgment.

Form of American Federal Supreme Court law report

The form of the law report of a Federal Supreme Court judgment will usually contain the following sequence of items:

(a) one or more opening paragraphs stating the propositions of the law supported by the decision. This part of the report forms no part of the decision but, nevertheless, provides a useful summary of the issues in the case;

(b) Articles of the Civil or Criminal Code (or other enactments) which are relevant to the case will be cited next;

(c) the division or section of the court (Senate) which had to decide the case will then be listed;

(d) the date on which the trial was concluded; and

(e) the initials of the parties to the action.

This is the format adopted by the official reports quoted as BGHZ (*Entscheidungen des Bundesgerichtshofs in Zivilisachen*) which are decisions of the civil section of the Federal Supreme Court. There are slight variations on this basic format in other reports, such as the NJW (*Neue Juristische Wochenschrift*);

(f) the facts of the case are then usually cited, abbreviated from the Court of Appeal judgment. Extracts from the appeal court judgment containing the legal reasoning will frequently be included;

(g) the court will then indicate whether it agrees or disagrees with the previous court's reasoning and/or its decision;

(h) it will then consider the appellant's grounds for appeal before giving its own reasons for its conclusions.

The number of facts actually stated in a particular case varies, but they are never as detailed as those in American or English judgments. The facts stated are, of course, much more detailed than French Court of Cassation judgments. If the factual details are considered inadequate, the Federal Supreme Court will state this point but, nevertheless, give its opinion on the law. It will then remit the case back to the lower courts with a direction that they should ascertain the relevant facts in the light of the legal opinion stated by the Supreme Court. In the absence of a doctrine of precedent *per se*, there is obviously no need to search for the case in point or indulge in any detailed dissection of material in order to decide whether a case is 'distinguishable' on its facts. Previous cases may well be referred to and distinguished in judgments at this level, but only in the context of providing illustrative examples of the operation of the legal principle involved, or as an indication of the practice of the court on a given matter to reaffirm a particular argument. Conversely, State Courts of Appeal have been known to choose not to follow a Supreme Court ruling, and it is the degree of appellate court resistance to a particular Supreme Court decision that will determine whether the latter will reconsider its position or assert its position.

Style of legal arguments in judgments

The style of legal arguments that are presented in a Supreme Court judgment is usually 'abstract, highly conceptual and even metaphysical' (Markesinis (1986)). Understanding it presupposes not only a comprehension of the style, but also of uniquely German concepts and their technical application within specialist fields. The other distinctive feature of these judgments is the detailed analysis of the writings of academics, past and present, who have expounded on the subject before the court. German Federal Court judgments sometimes also summarise different academic views on a given subject and even offer a critique of them. The so called 'dominant opinion' on a particular matter is often regarded as strongly persuasive, especially in cases where a straightforward application of a Code or legislative provision is not possible. This 'dominant opinion' (*herrschende Meinung*) is the term applied to the predominant view of a certain rule, as reflected in the majority of academic writings and court decisions. According to Professor Hein Kotz, there were 13 citations referring to 'secondary authority' (academic opinion) per German case, in 1985, compared to 0.77 citations per English case (see Markesinis (1994)). English judges tend not to cite academics' opinions in support or as part of their judicial process of abstraction except in relatively new fields, such as medico-legal cases involving medical ethics, where there might have been very little or no case law on an issue which has arisen. However, with the remarkable growth of reproductive technology in the 1980s and 1990s, there is a discernible rise in the amount of academic legal literature cited by the English courts. However, there is no attitude of deference to such opinions, at best, merely polite approval. This is a noteworthy point of divergence from German judgments.

This deference to academic writing is also found when one refers to commentaries on French cases. It is a practice which is traceable to the rebirth of civil law, in the Renaissance, in the European universities where academics not only commented on legal concepts but, in some cases, actually invented them. One such example is the application of the principle of good faith which is embodied in § 242 BGB, wherein the co-operation between judges and academic writers can be seen in the case law (see RGZ 103, 328, 331, 333 which have expressly followed Oertmann's views).

The Swedish type of judgment

Sweden is generally regarded as a civil law country, hence its style of judgments reflect its primary source of law, namely, Codes which have been historically influenced by the French Code, many of which have now been modernised to adapt to changing social, economic, political and cultural conditions. Sweden's appellate court judgments are, therefore, much closer to the French style rather than the German model; the court is the handmaiden of legislative policy. The tone is impersonal, concise, collegial and brief, yet well crafted. The judges have to stick to the strict facts of the case, and the judge is seen as the interpreter of the law, not the law maker. Unlike the French judgments, however, reasons are given for the decisions, but only those reasons which support the court's opinion. While the submissions of the parties are answered and resolved, there are no references to other courts' decisions which might have referred to those submissions. The Swedish judicial philosophy regarding the provision of reasons in support of a judgment is best described, in Justice Sjogren's opinion, in the following way: 'As a rule, the reasons given in an opinion should, irrespective of the length at which they are presented, be restricted, in a sense, to a minimum because they thereby attain universal applicability' (see Sjogren, Om domskal i tvistemal, TfR 1918, p 44).

In recent times, as a conscious institutional policy, the Swedish Supreme Court has practically abandoned the classical style of judicial exposition in favour of a more modern style. This has meant a somewhat more explicit recognition of the effect that a judgment might have on future cases, although decided cases *per se* are never mentioned. Swedish judgments are also still addressed primarily to the parties in a case, rather than to specialist lawyers, future judges or the academic world. The prime focus of the court is the relevant facts of the case to the virtual exclusion of anything else.

THE RELEVANCE OF OVERRIDING GENERAL PRINCIPLES

In French and German judgments, judges frequently refer to certain general principles of law (*clausulae generales*) as a means of justifying their decision, where the Code provisions or legislative enactments do not cover precisely the particular case before them. This is necessitated by the rule that neither precedent nor doctrine can be cited as the sole ground for decision. On the other hand, even where the Code provisions or statute does cover the situation, judges may prefer room for discretion and flexibility. General principles are, therefore, extremely useful to provide this flexibility and room for manoeuvre. These general principles are usually stated in the introductory Articles of a Code, and may cover areas, such as civil rights or unjustified enrichment. These principles are not immutable and fixed for all time. Their specific content, at any given point in history, will vary with changing ideas of morality, economic and social trends and major political changes. The following are broad headings for the type of general principles usually utilised by the continental courts:

(a) *aequitas*;

(b) *bona fides*/good faith;

(c) good morals and public order;

(d) custom.

Aequitas

On the European Continent, this is referred to as *equité* or *Billigkeit* which does not have a technical equivalent with the English legal meaning (which refers to a distinct branch/division of the law or a body of principles derived from that branch of law). Since the French Revolution, the word '*equité*, has not had favourable connotations in the light of pre-Revolutionary philosophy of 'save us from the equity of Parlements' and has, therefore, not been used very much in legal argument. It only features in certain Code provisions, for instance, Art 1135 of the Code Civil: 'Agreements are binding not only as to what is expressed, but also as to all the consequences which *equité*, usage or law impose upon the obligation according to its nature.' This, clearly, does not refer to any formal rules of 'equity'. On the contrary, French judges will tell you that they decide the case according to law, not equity.

At this point, of course, it is also worth recalling that the notion of law in France is broader than the one generally held in England (see, further, 'Key features of the French legal system', p 69, above). The French conception encompasses the totality of rules devised to establish the structures of society and to regulate people's conduct (Weston (1991)). Hence, the use of several French words (*loi, le droit, la justice*, etc), which all correspond to 'law' in English, but which will mean different things in different contexts! The French notion of law and invoking 'the law', therefore, includes a consideration of social, political and legal rules and is not necessarily linked to litigation.

Of course, French courts apply notions of fairness and justice, although these will simply not be expressed in terms of 'equity'. Situations requiring the court to consider the morality of conditions attached to a gift; or whether *faute* exists; or whether extenuating circumstances exist; or whether an expense incurred by an infant was excessive will be resolved by the French court by using other general clauses, such as *bona fides* or good morals and public order (see below), or even on the basis of certain kinds of recognised custom (see p 261, below). More recently, the French courts have used the 'abuse of rights' doctrine (see below) and propounded the idea that some element of fraud will always taint certain transactions.

Bona fides/*good faith*

Bona fides has probably been the most utilised of the general principles or clauses. This is not to be equated with the English notion of good faith because, although both concepts encompass the notion of fair dealing, they differ on a number of points:

(a) the English notion excludes negligence, but the continental view often regards gross negligence as the equivalent of bad faith;

(b) the continental concept covers a wider field than the English version and includes confidential relationships and minimal standards of conduct expected of parties engaging in commercial transactions.

The Swiss Civil Code provides, in general terms, that 'every person is bound to exercise his rights and to fulfil his obligations in accordance with the principles of good faith', but it (and the Swiss Code of Obligations) lists several prerequisites for the application of the principle in particular contexts.

The German version of this principle is found in the form of *Treu* and *Glauben*. Paragraph 242 of the German Civil Code provides that performance of a contract must always be such as is required by *Treu* and *Glauben*, with due regard to ordinary usages.

Similarly, § 157 of the German Civil Code (and a similar enactment in the German Commercial Code) provides that agreements must be interpreted in accordance with the requirements of *Treu* and *Glauben*, having regard to business practices.

Good morals and public order

Good morals and public order are twin principles which are sometimes invoked by the courts in order to achieve results which are seen to be consonant with public policy. These dual principles may, of course, be utilised in practically any situation, but are applied mainly in relation to contracts. A court will refuse to enforce a transaction on the basis that it is *contra bonos mores*. The key Code provision in French law is Art 6 of the French Civil Code, whereby 'laws involving public order (*ordre public*) and good morals (*bonnes moeurs*) cannot be derogated from private agreements'. These concepts may, thus, be used either as general formulations, supplementing specific statutory provisions, or as a means of invalidating certain specific transactions on one or other of these grounds. The courts may, therefore, nullify a particular transaction by referring to Arts 6 and 1133 of the Civil Code. Article 1133 states that 'A cause is unlawful when it is prohibited by law, or contrary to *bonnes moeurs* or *ordre public*'. It is also possible to invalidate an agreement purely on the basis of these Articles, even if there is no specific violation of any other statute. Under German law, the single concept of good morals has been used, which includes public order and similarly nullifies all transactions which conflict with this overriding precept.

The creative role played by these twin principles has undoubtedly served, on many occasions, to free judges from their constitutional or legislative fetters.

Custom

As a result of France's particular historical development, custom, or usage, assumed unusual significance from about the 14th century, so that court decisions were the *de facto* source of law, and custom that had been judicially approved or recognised became an accepted component of customary law (*droit coutumier*). The French Civil Code still contains several references to custom as a source of decision in relation to the context of consensual transactions. Despite the accepted wisdom that custom is necessarily opposed to the basic framework of written law upon which French law is based, three categories of custom were discernible in classical civil law:

(a) linguistic usages within the statutory framework – *secundum legem* (for example, '*faute*' as the basis of tort liability in Art 1382 of the Civil Code has to be appraised by reference to customary standards of behaviour);

(b) new rules of law which developed independently of a statutory formulation, originating from custom or usages – *praeter legum* (for example, as a source of commercial law (especially consensual transactions), labour law and law of civil procedure); and

(c) customary rules which derogate from a statutory text – *adversus legum*.

A critical issue which has arisen in this last category of custom is whether a statute can be taken to be supervened by a particular custom. French jurisprudence has not been consistent on this question. One example of such a custom is that of 'banking usage' which has been applied to the payment of interest on a current account of reciprocal debts and credits. The courts have applied a particular form of banking usage, despite Art 1154 of the Code Civil which states:

> Interest due upon capital may produce interest either by institution of an action or by special agreement, provided that either in the action or in the agreement the interest in question has been due for at least a whole year.

Another example is the commercial seller's right of repair and replacement which has been judicially approved, although contrary to the Civil Code. From a comparative viewpoint, it can be seen that different types of custom play a much more significant role in civil law countries, such as France, than in common law countries, despite the fact that its express usage (that is, of 'custom') as a term/source of law is studiously avoided by the legislator, and its very notion is opposed to the idea of written law. Indeed, departure from linguistic custom must be justified. This last species of custom, perhaps, most closely resembles the common law maxims or linguistic interpretative devices. English law rarely uses custom as a source of law, except when attempting to ascertain the consistency of a course of dealing between parties engaged in business. Here, certain well established business customs and practices may be offered as evidence in court that certain contractual terms might have been implied as a result of those customary business practices, which must be continuously exercised, certain and reasonable and not in contravention of any legislative enactment (see, for example, *Hutton v Warren* (1836) 1 M & W 466).

Argument by analogy in European courts

In an article published in 1998, Katia Langenbucher (1998) observes that the one of the oldest methods of decision making, argument by analogy, is being utilised by the European courts. This involves the process whereby, whenever the similarity between two situations induces someone to decide once case like another, an analogy is drawn. As she says, it is arguable that every legal tradition employs some version of it to justify their judicial decisions. The interesting point that she makes, however, is that, as European Union countries struggle for recognition of their legal heritage, the way in which arguments by analogy will be used on a European level is likely to combine different approaches. She sees two recurrent patterns in the use of argument by analogy in European law – one typical of civil law, the other of common law. Quite simply, analogical reasoning is used to fill a gap in a Code – rule based argument – whereas common law uses it as a technique for applying the *ratio decidendi* of a precedent to a new case – principle based argument (see Langenbucher (1998) p 481).

CONCLUSIONS

In one form or another, judges from all three major legal families now utilise both statutes and cases in varying degrees and, to that extent, there is a certain amount of convergence between the systems. Nevertheless, the various systems have unique ideological, procedural, linguistic, methodological and conceptual differences which clearly distinguish one from the other. In a world which is beginning to demonstrate a remarkable similarity of economic needs, values and interests, convergence will continue to occur, but true assimilation and wholesale integration of judicial styles appear, at the present time, to be an extremely remote possibility. As far as Europe and the countries of the European Union are concerned, however, if a high degree of European harmonisation of laws becomes a reality, comparatists will relish the fascinating prospect of seeing the development of a unique blend of law, containing international and national judicial styles, emerging from the melting pot of common law and civil law judicial traditions.

SELECTIVE BIBLIOGRAPHY

Allen, *Law in the Making*, 3rd edn (1939) p 151 *et seq*; 7th edn (1964)

Cappelletti, *The Judicial Process in Comparative Perspective* (1989)

Cohn, 'Precedents in continental law' [1935] 5 CLJ 366

Cross, 'The *ratio decidendi* and a plurality of speeches in the House of Lords' (1977) 93 LQR 378

David and Brierley, *Major Legal Systems in the World Today* (1985) pp 133–46

Dawson, *The Oracles of the Law* (1968)

Deak, 'Place of the case in common and civil law' (1933–34) 8 Tulane L Rev 337

Friedmann, 'A Re-Examination of the relations between English, American and continental jurisprudence' (1942) 20 Canadian Bar Rev 175

Goodhart, 'Determining the *ratio decidendi* of a case', in *Essays in Jurisprudence and the Common Law* (1931) p 25

Goodhart, 'Determining the *ratio decidendi* of a case', in Guest (ed), *Oxford Essays in Jurisprudence* (1961) p 148

Goodhart, 'Precedent in English and continental law' (1934) 50 LQR 40

Ireland, 'The use of decisions by US students of civil law' (1933–34) 8 Tulane L Rev 358

Koopmans, 'Comparative law and the courts' (1996) 45 ICLQ 545

Lambert and Wasserman, 'The case method in Canada' (1929) 39 Yale L Rev 1

Langenbucher, 'Argument by analogy in European law' (1998) 57 CLJ 481

Lawson, *A Common Lawyer Looks at the Civil Law* (1953) p 83 *et seq*

Markesinis, 'A matter of style' (1994) 110 LQR 607

Markesinis, 'Conceptualism, pragmatism and courage: a common lawyer looks at some judgments of the German Federal Court' (1986) 34 Am J Comp L 349

Merryman and Clark, *Comparative Law: Western European and Latin American Legal Systems* (1978) Chap 6

Morton, 'Judicial review in France: a comparative analysis' (1988) 36 Am J Comp L 89

Nadelmann, 'The judicial dissent: publication v secrecy' (1959) 8 Am J Comp L 415

Orucu, 'The use of comparative law by the courts', in Bridge *et al* (eds), *United Kingdom Law in the Mid-1990s* (1994) p 440

Pound, 'The theory of judicial decision' (1923) 36 Harvard L Rev 641

Rudden, 'Courts and Codes in England, France and Soviet Russia' (1974) 48 Tulane L Rev 1010

Schlesinger *et al*, *Comparative Law: Cases, Text, Materials*, 5th edn (1988) p 597 *et seq*

Simpson, 'The *ratio decidendi* of a case and the doctrine of binding precedent', in *Essays in Jurisprudence* (1961) p 148

Von Mehren and Gordley, *The Civil Law System* (1977) pp 1127–61

Wetter, *The Style of Appellate Judicial Decisions* (1960)

CHAPTER 9

A COMPARATIVE STUDY OF STATUTORY INTERPRETATION

DEFINING 'STATUTORY INTERPRETATION'

It has been said that 'It would be hard to think of a field of law that needs clarifying more than that of statutory interpretation ... [because] there is a great need to stabilise terms, concepts and premises' (Dickerson (1975)). Key terms, concepts and premises must, therefore, be clarified before undertaking a comparative overview of the current trends in statutory interpretation. In the civil law jurisdictions, the word 'statute' will usually refer to both the law as embodied in a Code (the Napoleonic or German Codes, or derivations thereof), as well as auxiliary legislation. However, the common law understanding of the term primarily covers legislation enacted by Parliament, although this may (as in American jurisdictions) sometimes include codifications and uniform laws. As we have already noted, however, the nature and basis of these 'codifications' is very different from the typical civil law Code.

Defining 'interpretation'

The word 'interpretation', in the context of statutes, may be explained in its broad sense and its narrow sense. In its broad sense, it could indicate the creative activities of a judge in extending, restricting or modifying a rule of law which is expressed or contained in a statutory form. However, in its narrow sense, it could denote the explanation by a judge of the meaning of words or phrases contained in a Code or statute.

GENERAL COMPARATIVE OBSERVATIONS

The different attitudes of the different legal traditions towards the status of legislation have been shaped, largely, by the particular history of that jurisdiction. This has determined a particular legal system's approach to statutory interpretation.

The historical English attitude to the rules of statutory construction has been somewhat negative regarding statutes, in general, as a 'necessary evil'. The 19th century Judge Pollock's view that 'Parliament generally changes the law for the worse' is fairly typical of the time. He goes on to say that the role of the English judge is to keep the 'mischief' of parliamentary interference within the 'narrowest possible bounds'. It must always be borne in mind that case law retained its primacy as the only true source of law in English law, so that statutes should be narrowly construed and that case law should govern any case where a statute did not appear wide enough to cover a given situation.

This antagonistic attitude to statutes has, of course, changed quite considerably, but its historical significance and impact have never fully disappeared.

The English common law method of interpreting statutes is traditionally characterised by the application of three guidelines to construction, called canons of construction, which are deployed to ascertain the 'intention of the legislature'. In more recent times, however, it has become more apparent that an English court does not necessarily simply follow three guides to interpretation in every case and select which to apply to a given situation. If the straightforward application of the three canons of construction exposes ambiguity, absurdity or a repugnant result, the court will then consider other approaches. Thus, where appropriate, an English court will apply several 'aids (or approaches) to construction' and weigh a number of factors relevant to the given situation before reaching a final interpretation.

On the other hand, the typical civil law method of discovering and giving effect to the intention of the legislature is to utilise various theories, such as seeking the 'social and economic purpose of the law'. Thus, both common law and civil law judges appear to seek to give effect to the intention of the legislature and, at one level, will adopt a variety of methods and techniques in pursuit of this aim. At another level, of course, both civil law and common law judges will strive to achieve a result that they consider a just, fair and equitable one, by utilising approaches or theories to produce similar conclusions and principles.

Historically, common law statutory canons were developed originally for 'special statutes', in other words, statutes passed by the legislature to cope with specific urgent problems of the day and these statutory maxims were, therefore, limited to specific problems. On the other hand, civil law rules of interpretation were developed primarily for the construction of Codes, with the eponymous French Civil Code providing the classic model for civil law legislative technique. Of course, civil law jurisdictions also have special statutes which currently outnumber Codes. In fact, cases which are decided under special statutes actually outnumber those decided under Code provisions. However, classical and contemporary civil law jurisprudence derive their focus and ideology from a Code based philosophy. Thus, the primacy of the statutory text as the main and pre-eminent source of law is the cornerstone of the theory and practice of statutory interpretation in civil law jurisdictions. Moreover, it has been the *point d'appui* of the civil law concept of law itself.

METHODS/TECHNIQUES OF STATUTORY INTERPRETATION

The main methods and techniques of statutory interpretation, some of which are common to both civil law and common law traditions, shall now be examined. We commence with civil law techniques, drawing common law parallels whenever appropriate, before turning to common law 'canons of construction'.

Civil law approaches

Grammatical/literal interpretation

In any legal system, the first task of the court is to ascertain the meaning of the particular statutory provision. This usually requires deciphering the meaning of key terms. Civil law and common law judges will usually have a duty to apply a particular legislative enactment strictly, if the meaning of the statute appears to be clearly defined. If only one construction is possible, the next question is whether the court is bound by the words as formulated, or whether there is some basis for changing the literal meaning. As Zweigert and Puttfarken have put it, 'The perimeter of the field of jurisprudence in traditional jurisprudence is marked by the plain meaning rule on the one hand, and reasoning by analogy on the other'.

In civil law jurisprudence, the so called plain meaning rule is often referred to as the *sens clair* principle, which is the equivalent of the old common law doctrine which requires a statute which is 'clear', 'plain' or 'unambiguous' on its face be given the only construction to which it is unequivocally susceptible. Any inquiry into the purposes, background or legislative history of the statute is, in these circumstances, *prima facie* precluded. This will not apply where absurdity or repugnancy would result.

If the words of the statute are ambiguous, then all legal systems need to consider the permissible methods of determining the 'proper construction' of the statute in order to give effect to the legislative intention.

The logical interpretation methodology

Utilising the literal or grammatical meaning approach, the court may conclude that:

(a) the text unequivocally governs the case; or

(b) there are two or more possible solutions/approaches available from which a choice must be made; or

(c) the text, as phrased, is not susceptible to any solution.

According to the logical interpretation approach, it will be permissible to construe the legislative provision not just on its stated terms, but within the context of the entire body of rules comprising the legal system, derived from the same statute, in other laws or from recognised general principles of law.

If the text is unequivocal and can have only one meaning, but applying it would lead to absurdity or repugnance, both common law and civil law courts will disregard a statute's grammatical construction or plain meaning (see Geny, *Methodes d'Interpretation* (1919) Vol II, p 252; and Planiol, *Préparatoires de Droit Civil* (1932) Vol I, 12th edn, No 216 (civil law)). This is also the practice in the common law (see, also, *Beck v Smith* (1836) 2 M & W 191) whose approach and rationalisation is discussed below (see, further, below). Under a French statute, there was a negative added by mistake, and the effect was to purport to punish anyone who got on or off a train while it was not in motion. The Cour de Cassation held that it could not apply the literal meaning rule, and that it could disregard the literal language used in order to avoid reaching an obviously absurd result (Cass Crim 8 March 8 1930, DP 1930/1/101).

If application of the grammatical meaning approach suggests more than one possible interpretation, the text may be construed in accordance with the 'logical interpretation' approach. The possibility of multiple interpretations is especially common under civil law Codes and statutes which are characterised by general clauses, abstract terms and the frequent absence of statutory definitions. One example of a 'logical interpretation' is to consider the context of the legislative provision and its relationship to the other branches of the general body of law. An example from French law involved the case of a theft of a chattel. The question was whether, under Art 2279 of the Civil Code, recovery of a chattel was possible even from a *bona fide* purchaser for value, despite the general principle from that same Article that *bona fide* possession is tantamount to title. The issue was: what was meant by theft (vol) as used in this Article?; was it to be defined under the usage of current speech as meaning any retention without the consent of the owner, or in the narrow penal law sense as set out in Art 379 of the Penal Code? Article 379 states: 'Whoever fraudulently removes a thing which does not belong to him is guilty of theft.' The Cour de Cassation held that 'vol', under Art 2279 of the Civil Code, must be interpreted in the criminal law sense, that is, as defined under the Penal Code, so that acquittal in a criminal prosecution bars recovery of the chattel. This was held even though the Penal Code was not even in force when Art 2279 of the Civil Code was enacted (see Cass Civ 25 March 1891, DP 1892/1/ 301).

Further examples from French cases include two occasions where electricity was held to be a 'thing' within the meaning of Art 379 of the French Penal Code (Cass Crim 3 August 1912, DP 1913/1/439) and to be 'merchandised' within the meaning of a penal statute' (see the Law of 1 August 1905 in Cass Crim 2 November 1945, D 1946/J/8).

If the literal meaning of the legislative provision does not offer any solution to the case at hand, the issue is then whether reasoning by analogy may be permitted. This method seeks to extract an analogy or argument, *a contrario*, based on the logique of the legal system. As explained in the previous chapter, under Art 4 of the Civil Code, a French court must decide a case despite the 'insufficiency' or 'silence' of the law. However, they will not necessarily apply the logical interpretation approach to all laws. This is because of the French legal distinction between codified law (droit commun), sometimes called 'common law', and the law of statutes (lois d'exception), in derogation of the common law of the Codes. The latter are usually construed strictly, particularly when they are first enacted. The expression 'lois d'exception' is used to describe a statute which purports to create an exception to general rules of law without amending Code provisions or transitory legislation enacted in response to emergency situations. Accordingly, courts generally refuse to apply the same broad methods of interpretation to lois d'exception until these new statutes become sufficiently assimilated into the principles of droit commun and may then serve as a basis for logical interpretation. Assimilation may take decades.

The legislative history approach

This mode of interpretation seeks to ascertain the legislative intention by embarking on research into the legislative history of the statute, which is often referred to by the French term 'travaux préparatoires'. It appears that this is an approach which is pursued very much more in civil law countries than in common law jurisdictions. Indeed, common law statutes are not, strictly, supposed to be construed in accordance with their particular legislative history (see p 271, below, for the common law approaches). This method of interpretation appears to raise the issue of the degree of 'weight' to be placed on governmental or administrative views on the meaning of statutes. Such views may be obtained in at least two ways in France. First, in answer to written questions addressed to him by members of Parliament, the minister concerned may indicate how the administration interprets a statute and proposes to enforce it. It should be noted that such answers are not *interpretation authentique* of the statute and are clearly not binding on the courts. They are, on the other hand, indicative of the underlying governmental policy behind a particular enactment. Secondly, directives of instructions to lower administrative divisions by superior authorities may also express administrative policy, the most important of which are sometimes published in special bulletins of the administrative departments, which are available to the public. Once again, however, statements contained in such directives do not have any binding force on the courts.

The teleological approach

A contrasting approach to the legislative historical approach is the teleological approach, also called the 'extensive' or 'progressive' interpretation. It seeks to interpret the legislative text within the context of contemporary conditions. In other words, it presupposes the need to extend the application of a legislative provision beyond the scope of prior legislative intent, and to adapt it to rapidly changing social or economic conditions. One might even question whether this is really interpretation at all, rather than a method of rewriting the statute. However, in France, the teleological approach is widely regarded as a legitimate form of statutory interpretation, largely due to the seminal work of the writer Francois Geny (see Geny, *Méthode d'Interpretation et Sources en Droit Privé Positif* (1919)). In his seminal work, first published in 1900, he urged the frank recognition of the existence of gaps in the statutory framework and argued for 'free scientific research'. His work was greeted with acclaim and inspired other jurists to consider, where appropriate, the social policy behind legislative provisions. Under English common law, there is a similar canon of construction which looks, *inter alia*, at the policy behind the provision and, for example, the 'mischief' it was designed to prevent. The teleological approach has been regarded as particularly appropriate in France which possesses the concept of loi. This is embodied in the Napoleonic Codes as a permanent set of verbal symbols, the meaning of which may change with the times. The theory in the case of loi is that it would not have been possible for the legislature to have considered all the possible future applications of the text, many years after the enactments were passed. Hence, the intention of the legislature would have to be adapted to changed conditions, be they social, economic or technological. The conventional practice of formulating general principles or general terms (*ordre public, bonnes moeurs, equité, faute*) would also necessitate a teleological approach. There are, of course, several caveats to this approach which should be noted.

Scope and limitations of the teleological approach

There are at least three limitations of the teleological approach. First, it cannot be used to reach conclusions directly contrary to those derived from a grammatical or logical interpretation. Thus, the teleological approach can be used only where there is more than one possible interpretation to be placed on a statute, or it is not possible to construe the statutory provision by the application of established general principles of law. Secondly, the teleological approach does not preclude the application of the legislative history approach. Thirdly, French courts tend to demonstrate a preference for the legislative history approach and, as a broad generalisation, it is probably fair to say that the newer the statute or regulation, the less likely it will be for a court to use the teleological method. Conversely, the greater the antiquity of the statute or regulation, the more likely a teleological approach will be used. Thus, it would appear that recent statutes which are ambiguous are invariably interpreted by the legislative history technique, and it is only the Cour de Cassation and Conseil d'État which are more willing to accept the added responsibility of deciding that a particular statute should be decided within a contemporary context, rather than an historical one.

Common law approaches to statutory interpretation

The canons of statutory interpretation

The 'canons of statutory interpretation' refer to certain 'rules' of interpretation or, more correctly, extrinsic aids or approaches to interpretation which are applied by the English courts in a *prima facie* fashion, that is, they will be applied in the first instance, wherever appropriate, to a particular term or phrase in a statute. The three main traditional aids to interpretation are the literal rule, the golden rule and the mischief rule. These have always been subject to a court's perception of 'the intention of Parliament', that is, what Parliament intended to achieve or address in passing that provision. Another very important factor, which is increasingly being taken into account, is the context of a statute (see 'The mischief rule', p 275, below).

The literal rule refers to the principle that the judge must give effect to the ordinary meaning of the words. This is but one method used to ascertain the intention of Parliament. This has sometimes been followed with rather striking results (see *Fisher v Bell* [1961] 1 QB 394; *IRC v Hinchy* [1960] AC 748; *AG v Prince of Hanover* [1957] AC 436). English judges tend to emphasise the predominance of the 'ordinary meaning' of the words and would generally not be prepared to look at the statutory purpose of a statute or any other policies or rationales, unless there is some ambiguity in the words used. This does not mean that an English court has never given effect to a clear literal meaning, only that such an instance must be viewed as exceptional and only within the boundaries of the ambiguity mentioned above, or as a result of the two other main canons of construction. The Interpretation Act 1978 is the only statutory guide, but closer inspection reveals that this is nothing more than a general word saving guide to interpretation, which leaves vast areas of discretion to judges. The 1978 Act states, in s 6, that 'words importing the masculine gender include the feminine' and vice versa; and 'words in the singular shall include the plural and words in the plural shall include the singular'. The 1978 Act therefore simply re-enacts the former 1889 Interpretation Act and consolidates existing enactments being, therefore, more of a lexicographical aid than anything else. It is, thus, not really useful in methodological terms. The other point to note is that the general rule in

English law is that, even when legislative purpose or intent is considered, the statute in point will be interpreted solely in the context of the actual words of that statute or in relation to other parts of the same statute, or the judges might look at previous statutory or case law on the area.

Inadmissible evidence of statutory intent

The strict legal principle has been that two types of 'evidence' are simply inadmissible in an English court's deliberations over a statute's interpretation:

(a) its legislative history; and

(b) sociological and economic studies on the effect of the statute.

Legislative history is the term used to include the parliamentary debates (see *Lyons v Wilkins* [1899] 1 Ch 255, p 264) or preliminary earlier versions of a statutory provision at committee stage, or in a White Paper or Royal Commission Report, which preceded the statute, and these are generally regarded as inadmissible. This is an area where, in terms of strict principle, American courts have tended to differ from English ones in that American courts have been quite prepared to consider both the legislative history and the underlying policy of a particular statute without even considering the plain words of the statute, and their general approach is seen as more substantive orientated, rather than formalistic (see Atiyah and Summers (1987) Chapter 4). However, English law has now relaxed this rule in cases where, for example, the legislation was ambiguous and the literal meaning would lead to an absurdity (see *Pepper v Hart* [1993] 1 All ER 42, below) and in certain specified circumstances.

The other inadmissible material in an English court's process of statutory interpretation has been evidence of results of sociological and economic studies estimating the probable effects of possible interpretations of a statute.

The reality of English judicial practice

As in other areas of English law, theory and practice do not always coincide. Thus, despite the stated rule against admissibility, ancient decisions have intermittently referred to legislative history (for early cases, see *YB* 33 Edw 1 (1305) M Term (Rolls edn) 82; *Ash v Abdy* (1678) 3 Swanst 664) and this has occurred in modern times, for example, *Warner v Metropolitan Police Commissioner* [1969] 2 AC 256; *Beswick v Beswick* [1968] AC 58, p 105; *Sagnata Investments Ltd v Norwich Corporation* [1971] 2 QB 614; *R v Greater London Council ex p Blackburn* [1976] 1 WLR 550, p 556) and, in the early 1980s, the former Lord Chancellor, Lord Hailsham, admitted that he always consulted Hansard (the official parliamentary record of debates), the Blue Books (reports of parliamentary committees) and anything which might have assisted him in clarifying what is meant by a statutory provision (see 1981, HL Reports (5th series) col 1346). On the same occasion, he poured scorn on the idea that the Law Lords did not read these reports. Certainly, if the words are capable of more than one meaning, Lord Reid has stressed that the courts would then be entitled to see why the words were so phrased; practical reasons would not permit debates in either the House of Commons or House of Lords to be cited, but the antecedents of a statutory provision could be examined in the appropriate case (see *Beswick v Beswick* [1968] AC 58, pp 73–74, *per* Lord Reid). The 'practical reasons' mentioned by Lord Reid included the additional time and expense involved in preparing for a case if counsel were expected to read all the debates reported in the parliamentary reports. A more serious substantive objection to allowing admissibility of parliamentary debates is the fundamental principle of separation of powers. The traditional argument put forward has been that the law should be found only by reference to the Act itself, rather than by reference to ministerial statements in Parliament during the passage of a Bill, in order to act as a check on any excessive executive power the government may be wielding, since the government is usually responsible for promoting the particular piece of legislation.

A study of actual judicial practice reveals, nevertheless, that numerous precedents exist for citation of parliamentary material (for yet another example, see *Pierce v Bemis* [1986] QB 384) and reference to Hansard was approved by no less than the House of Lords in *Pickstone v Freemans plc* [1989] AC 66, where an amendment to an Act was made by regulations which, although subject to parliamentary approval, could not be amended by the legislature; and, in late 1992, in *Pepper v Hart* [1993] 1 All ER 42, where the House of Lords held:

(i) having regard to the purposive approach to construction of legislation the courts had adopted in order to give effect to the true intention of the legislature, the rule prohibiting courts from referring to parliamentary material as an aid to construction should, subject to any question of parliamentary privilege, be relaxed so as to permit reference to parliamentary materials where: (a) the legislation was ambiguous or obscure, or the literal meaning led to an absurdity; (b) the material relied or consisted of statements made by a minister or other promoter of the Bill which led to the enactment of the legislation together, if necessary, with such other parliamentary material as was necessary to understand such statements and their effect; and (c) the statements relied on were clear;

(ii) the use of parliamentary material as a guide to the construction of ambiguous legislation would not infringe s 1, Art 9 of the Bill of Rights, since it would not amount to a 'questioning' of the freedom of speech or parliamentary debate, provided counsel and the judge refrained from impugning or criticising the minister's statements or his reasoning, since the purpose of the courts in referring to parliamentary material would be to give effect to, rather than thwart through ignorance, the intentions of

Parliament, and not to question the processes by which such legislation was enacted, or to criticise anything said by anyone in Parliament in the course of enacting it.

Thus, ascertaining the *purpose of the statute* has become a key approach for the English courts which they have used to admit extraneous material where it has been appropriate to do so.

Summary of legislative history position

In general, parliamentary materials have been inadmissible for purposes of statutory interpretation, but the courts as masters of their own procedure retain a residuary right to admit them (see *R v Board of Visitors of Wormwood Scrubs Prison ex p Anderson* [1985] QB 251) in cases where this is the only way in which to give effect to the intention of the legislator; or in those cases specified under *Pepper v Hart* (above). The main reasons for exclusion of these materials which were usually put forward were: their essential and intrinsic unreliability; the cost involved in pursuing them; and the constitutional considerations of 'comity' or the mutual respect and courtesy that should prevail between legislature and judiciary, two organs of the State which should remain separate and independent. Nevertheless, the strict rule of non-admissibility of parliamentary materials has and will be relaxed in those circumstances that the House of Lords and other courts have designated.

The 'golden rule approach' refers to the principle that a judge may depart from the clear meaning of a statute if the result would otherwise be absurd or impractical. Hence, the grammatical sense of the word may be modified to avoid 'injustice, absurdity, anomaly or contradiction' (Lord Simon, in *Maunsell v Olins* [1975] AC 373, p 391). The rationale is that such a result could not reasonably be supposed to have been the legislature's intention. The crucial point here is that the application of this golden rule approach presupposes the existence of a secondary meaning of the words (see *Inland Revenue Commissioners v Hinchy* [1960] AC 748). The *Hinchy* case and others like it (see *DPP v Ottewell* [1970] AC 642; *Wiltshire v Barrett* [1966] 1 QB 312) illustrate that the word 'ambiguity' in the context of statutory interpretation may be applied by the courts to any kind of doubtful meaning of words, phrases or longer statutory provisions. Several English family law cases have given rise to this sort of statutory interpretation, wherein the clear words of a statute have been reinterpreted to give effect to what 'Parliament must have intended', for example, in *Re D (A Minor)* [1987] 1 All ER 20, where the statutory words 'child's development is being avoidably prevented' were read as capable of being construed as 'was being and will be prevented', in order to justify invoking the statute and removing a newborn baby suffering from drug withdrawal symptoms at birth from its drug addicted parents and in *Davis v*

Johnson [1979] AC 264, where protection under a domestic violence statute was, nevertheless, accorded to an unmarried woman who was no longer living with her violent cohabitant at the time of her application, even though the statute gave protection to 'a man and woman who are living together'. In 1994, in the case of *In re M (A Minor)* [1994] 3 WLR 558, the Court of Appeal and House of Lords have once again found themselves in disagreement over the interpretation of a key phrase in a statute, the Children Act 1989, in deciding the meaning of the phrase 'is suffering significant harm'. Under the 1989 Act, a court may make a care order, placing a child within the control of the local authority, if it satisfied itself that a child 'is suffering [or is likely to suffer] significant harm'. The Court of Appeal decided that such an order could not be made if the harm that child had been suffering had, in fact, ceased at the time of the hearing or at the time of disposal of the case. They therefore discharged the care order that had been made with regard to the child in question.

However, the House of Lords disagreed and opined that, in deciding whether to make such an order, the relevant time for application of the 'significant harm' test was the date on which the local authority had initiated the proceedings. Thus, although the child was not suffering any significant harm by the time the hearing had been convened, the House of Lords reinstated the care order with regard to the child.

The mischief rule

The mischief rule or purpose approach, as it is sometimes called, is usually thought to originate from *Heydon's Case*, decided by the Court of Exchequer in 1584 and states that the judge must construe a statute so as to promote its underlying purpose, which is frequently the avoidance of a particular mischief which the general common law did not deal with. Four matters were required by the court to be 'discerned and considered', in order to carry out the 'sure and true interpretation of statutes':

(a) what was the common law before the making of the Act?;

(b) what was the mischief and defect for which the common law did not provide?;

(c) what remedy has Parliament resolved and appointed to cure the disease?;

(d) the true reason of the remedy.

It was further stressed that judges were expected to 'suppress the mischief ... advance the remedy and to suppress subtle inventions and evasions for continuance of the mischief ... according to the true intent of the makers of the Act'.

It is only when the court seeks to ascertain the 'mischief' or defect an Act was passed to remedy that extrinsic materials, such as parliamentary debates or Reports of Royal Commissions, may be looked at if the 'mischief' or defect is not patently obvious on the face of the statute. Such materials are referred to far more frequently in continental and American courts.

In modern times, Lord Denning MR declared that 'we no longer construe Acts of Parliament according to their literal meaning. We construe them according to their object and intent' (see *Engineering Industry Training Board v Samuel Talbot (Engineers) Ltd* [1969] 2 QB 270, p 274). This was following on from the important case of *AG v Prince Ernest Augustus of Hanover* (the *Hanover* case) [1957] AC 436, p 461 where Viscount Simonds listed the meaning of context in the construction of statutes, namely:

(a) other enacting provisions of the same statute;

(b) its preamble;

(c) the existing state of the law;

(d) other statutes in *pari materia*; and

(e) the mischief which the statute was intended to remedy.

Indeed, all the speeches in the *Hanover* case suggest that the object of the statute is something to be taken into consideration in arriving at the ordinary meaning of the statute. The purpose of the statute is relevant at two stages of the judge's deliberations: first, when he is seeking to determine whether the words are *per se* sufficiently precise and unambiguous, and, secondly, if they are not, when he is attempting to resolve any uncertainty arising from the statutory form of words. One example of a case where the purpose approach or golden rule was applied is the case of *Corkery v Carpenter* [1951] 1 KB 102 in relation to the question: 'is a bicycle a carriage?' for the purpose of convicting a drunk and disorderly defendant who had created a disturbance on a highway. The Licensing Act 1872 could only be used to convict the defendant if the bicycle came within the meaning of 'carriage' in the statute. The Divisional Court, on appeal, held that 'carriage' was wide enough to include a bicycle, rejecting the defendant's counsel's reference to the words of the famous 'Daisy Bell' song as an example of how 'bicycle' was not synonymous with 'carriage':

> It won't be a stylish marriage,
>
> I can't afford a carriage
>
> But you'll look sweet upon the seat
>
> Of a bicycle built for two.

The court stressed that 'It does not follow that in every Act of Parliament a bicycle is a carriage' and that it depended on the words of the Act in question and the object of the particular Act. Here, the object was clear: the Act sought to protect the public and preserve public order. For this purpose, 'a carriage can include any sort of vehicle'. A bicycle was therefore a carriage in the context of the present Act 'because it carries'.

Some examples of the sort of questions that have arisen are: 'is a goldfish an "article"?' (*Daly v Cannon* [1954] 1 All ER 315); and 'is orange juice pressed from fresh oranges a "manufactured beverage"?' (*Customs and Excise Commissioners v Savoy Hotel Ltd* [1966] 2 All ER 299).

The overriding point to note is that, if the purpose of a statute is invoked to revoke an ambiguity, it appears to operate only as a rebuttable presumption which can be defeated by some other presumption. It is often seen as another example of contextualising the statute. Every statutory provision has to be read subject to all these canons of construction or approaches.

Filling gaps in a statute

Two approaches to the judicial role in gap filling

There are usually two identifiable approaches to the role of the English judiciary in dealing with situations where there appears to be a lacuna or gap in the statute, in dealing with a case before the court. The first is to consider any law making function an abuse of the legislative function by the judiciary, and the second is to argue that the courts are simply there to ascertain and give effect to the intention of Parliament, and gap filling is only a means of securing this objective. The classical, traditional view is exemplified by Viscount Simonds speaking at the House of Lords stage of *Magor and St Mellons Rural District Council v Newport Corporation* [1952] AC 189, p 191:

> [Filling in the gaps of an enactment] appears to be a naked usurpation of the legislative function under the thin guise of interpretation ... If a gap is disclosed, the remedy lies in an amending Act.

In contrast, Lord Denning had earlier stated in the Court of Appeal stage of the same case that:

> We sit here to find out the intention of ministers and of Parliament and carry it out, and we do this better by filling in the gaps and making sense of the enactment, than by opening it up to destructive analysis ...

Obviously, the courts will be required to resolve the cases before them, even where there are clear gaps in the statute, but it appears that, provided they make it clear that they are merely carrying out an 'interpretative' role rather than a law making or law creating one, it will be acceptable to 'fill' a particular lacuna in the legislation. Seven years later, Lord Denning modified his views in *London Transport Executive v Betts* [1959] AC 213, p 247, even citing the *Magor* case (above) as an authority for the principle that judges cannot fill in gaps which they suppose to exist in an Act of Parliament, but must let Parliament itself do so. Nevertheless, courts may decide whether or not to fill in 'gaps' in the legislation, depending on whether the area of law concerned is seen as essentially regulated by statute law, as in child law, mental health legislation, town and country planning, licensing law or rent restriction Acts. Case law in these areas will certainly be referred to, but only to interpret the legislation. This is the general approach in the United Kingdom, with a notable exception being the Scottish *nobile officium* exercised by the Court of Session in Scotland. Under this power, the court may grant special remedies if these are necessary for the sake of equity and justice. If a statutory scheme is defective, the court may grant an equitable remedy or dispense with a formality, such as a statutory oath as in the case of a petitioner who had become of unsound mind since going bankrupt (see *Henry Roberts* (1901) 3 F 779 (Court of Session)). However, the court is precluded from substituting remedies for those that have already been statutorily provided. In criminal matters, there is a similar power vested in the High Court of Justiciary.

Other linguistic canons of construction/interpretation

There are a number of linguistic canons of construction which the courts also employ to the appropriate statutory provisions. The five most common of these are as follows:

(a) reading text as a whole;

(b) giving technical words their technical meaning;

(c) reading words in their context: *noscitur a sociis;*

(d) the *ejusdem generis* rule and the 'rank' rule;

(e) the *expresso unius* rule.

The first linguistic principle of construing the Act as a whole is exemplified by observations by judges like Lord Halsbury, who stressed that 'you must, if you can, ascertain what the meaning of the instrument taken as a whole in order to give effect ... of the intention of the framer of it' (*Leader v Duffey* (1883) 13 App Cas 294, p 301; see, also, *AG v Prince Earnest of Hanover* [1957] AC 436). This principle gives rise to various other rules, for example:

(a) every part of a legislative enactment must be given some meaning;

(b) the same word should be given the same meaning within the same piece of legislation;

(c) if conflicting statements occur within the same legislation, one should be taken as modifying the other and the provision nearest the end prevails in cases where no other technique of reconciliation is feasible.

The second canon of construction is that technical terms should be given their proper technical meaning as understood by the experts in the field; technical legal terms will be given their normal legal connotation, unless the contrary intention appears. Terms with both technical and ordinary meanings will be construed in accordance with whether the context is seen as technical or non-technical. Nevertheless, a well known example of a court applying a technical (contractual) meaning to a term is the case of *Fisher v Bell* [1961] 1 QB 394, where the court interpreted the shopkeeper's offer for sale of a flick knife in the sense understood by the law of contract, namely, that the mere placing of goods in a shop window did not constitute 'offering [an offensive weapon] for sale' within the meaning of the Restriction of Offensive Weapons Act 1959. Under the law of contract, an 'offer for sale' of goods in a shop window merely constitutes an 'invitation to treat', which means it is merely an invitation for someone to make an offer to buy the goods on display. This case is also an excellent example of how the English court sometimes applies several approaches to a particular enactment, since applying the ordinary meaning was not seen as remedying the mischief the statute sought to rectify and, thus, not further the purpose of the Act and the presence of a 'gap' in the legislation which prevented such knives being sold, hired, lent or given, yet allowed them to be displayed in shop windows meant the courts had to apply a construction which would both give effect to parliamentary intention and avoid an absurd or repugnant result.

The third canon of construction is the term *noscitur a sociis* (it is recognised by its associates) which means that words will be construed in accordance with their surrounding words. Hence, if a statute creates criminal liability for anyone who 'shall unlawfully and maliciously stab, cut or wound any person' and the accused had been indicted for biting off the joint of a policeman's finger, the court proceeded on the basis that it was evidently the intention of the legislature, according to the words of the statute, that the wounding should be inflicted with some instrument and not by the hands or teeth. The accused was therefore acquitted (*R v Ann Harris* (1836) 7 C & P 446; 173 ER 198).

This principle has further given rise to other rules such as the *ejusdem generis* rule and its corollary, the 'rank' principle. The latin term *'ejusdem generis'* (of the same kind or nature) may be applied where it is believed that, where general words come after particular words, the meaning of the general words must be restricted to that of the particular words. The occasion which usually gives rise to this interpretation is where there is a list of class describing words followed by wider, broadly sweeping words, such as 'or any other goods'. There must be a sufficient indication of a category for the doctrine to apply which can be described as a class, even though not specified as such in the legislation. The class must also be narrower than the words it is said to govern. In *AG v Brown* (1920) 1 KB 773, the ambit of s 43 of the Customs Consolidation Act 1876 came under scrutiny when pyrogallic acid was seized aboard a steamship without a licence having been given for the importation of the same. The relevant part of the section reads: 'The importation of arms, ammunition, gunpowder or any other goods may be prohibited.' It was held by Sankey J that the *ejusdem generis* rule should be applied to the phrase 'any other goods', so that the meaning of these words should be restricted to the types of objects specified by the particular words. Hence, 'any other goods' meant goods of the class of arms, ammunition or gunpowder. So, pyrogallic acid was not in the same class as the particular articles set out in the section.

The 'rank principle' which follows from this is that where a list of items of a certain rank or level is followed by general words, those general words could not have been intended to include items or objects of a higher rank than those specified. The example, 'copper, brass, pewter and tin' was held not to include gold and silver (*Casher v Holmes* (1831) 2 B & Ad 592); a list stating 'tradesman, artificer, workman, labourer or other person whatsoever' was held not to include any person above the artisan class (*Gregory v Fearn* [1953] 1 WLR 974).

There are numerous other subsidiary principles but, perhaps, the one that should finally be mentioned is the so called '*expressio unius* principle' which is the short form of the latin maxim *expressio unius est exclusion alterius* (to express one thing is to exclude another). This maxim is occasionally utilised in cases where a statute might well have covered a number of items or matters, but only mentions some of them, in which case the maxim might be invoked to exclude matters or items that have not been specifically mentioned statutorily. The maxim may apply, unless it is possible to argue, in the context of the other rules of construction and taking the statute as a whole, that those matters specifically mentioned were merely examples, or were stated *ex abundanti cautela*. It is important to note that the question of the particular context of the statute is all important and that there is no greater weight given to this maxim above any of the other aids to statutory interpretation. As Lopes LJ put it, this maxim is 'often a valuable servant, but a dangerous master to follow in the construction of statutes or documents'. He discounted its application where the exclusion was the result of inadvertence or accident, or where its application would lead to inconsistency and injustice (see *Colquhon v Brooks* (1888) 21 QBD 52, p 65). These sentiments have been approved in subsequent cases.

Presumptions and precedents

Presumptions are usually only a *prima facie* guide to interpretation and among the most commonly used are:

(a) Parliament is presumed to know the law;

(b) Parliament is presumed to respect common law principles;

(c) Parliament is presumed to legislate prospectively;

(d) Parliament is presumed to act justly and reasonably;

(e) Parliament is presumed to respect international law.

As far as precedents, or decided cases, are concerned, the question has arisen as to whether previously decided judicial interpretations are binding as to interpretation of the same words in a different statute. The general rule is that they are not, since the *ratio decidendi* of each case will be specific to the particular piece of legislation being considered. The most that can be said is that precedents from the same jurisdiction or from other jurisdictions, which have not dealt with the same interpretative issue as the case currently being considered, are of merely 'persuasive' value.

Conflict of statutes with other legal principles

The relationship between statute law and common law is not always an easy one. On the one hand, they appear to co-exist quite happily, almost as two distinct branches of law which occasionally intertwine and feed into one another. On the other hand, there is sometimes the need to resolve which should take precedence if they both regulate a certain area of law. In yet another scenario, common law and statute law appear to form part of the same body of law, which is then applied as an amalgam of both these sources. On one constitutional level, the British Constitution appears to settle the matter of priority as one of its fundamental tenets in that statutes, duly enacted by Parliament, override all and any prior rules and principles whatever. However, the forum in which statutory rules are required to be interpreted and applied will be the common law courts. An opposing academic view was taken by Sir Rupert Cross (1968) who argued that judges received statute fully into the body of the law and Acts could, therefore, be utilised 'by analogy' in the same way as in cases. Professor Atiyah (1985) disagreed, citing several case illustrations, disproving the Cross stance. Nevertheless, he conceded that, before one could assess whether a particular decision or doctrine was 'right' or 'wrong' in an absolute sense, it all depended on what condition the statute book was in at any given point on time. Thus, in planning law, for instance, courts were unwilling to extend 'private law' to it (see *Pioneer Aggregates (UK) Ltd v Secretary of State for the Environment* [1985] AC 132). On the other hand, statutes are not generally taken as intending to interfere with common law rights, unless there are 'plain words' which clearly express this intention (see *Deeble v Robinson* [1954] 1 QB 77, p 81; see, also, *Shiloh Spinners v Harding* [1949] 2 KB 291). Other writers argue that it is all a 'matter of weight which is generally achieved interpretatively' (Bankowski and MacCormick (1991)). It really seems to depend on the particular area of law and, in the same way as judges respond to 'gaps' in the law, the particular interpretation given to a statute will be commensurate with the degree of its comprehensiveness and depend on whether the area of law is mainly statute based. Thus, courts have held that the common law offence of 'motor manslaughter' has not been abrogated by s 1 of the Road Traffic Act 1972 (*Jennings v United States Government* [1982] 3

All ER 104), but have also held that it was undesirable for the prosecution to invoke the common law offence of kidnapping when a child had been kidnapped by its parent in circumstances already covered by the Child Abduction Act 1984 (UK) (see *R v C* (1990) *The Times*, 9 October). In the context of EC law, the position seems to be that British national courts must give effect to clearly expressed community law, even if this means deviating from any domestic law which was in conflict with community law. A British statute may therefore not be as sacrosanct and inviolate as it used to be (*R v Secretary of State for Transport ex p Factortame Ltd (No 1)* [1989] 2 CMLR 353). Ultimately, the issue of whether there is a conflict may be decided on the same criteria of whether 'repugnancy', 'absurdity' and 'inconsistency' will result, and this will very often be determined according to the existing common law interpretative decisions and principles. Thus, there is some truth in both a 'seamless web' theory and a 'separate but interrelated' theory.

Scholarly/doctrinal writing in English statutory interpretation

As explained in Chapter 4, the English common law tradition does not traditionally attach strong persuasive force to the academic writings of its living writers. A well known axiom is that 'the only good academic is a dead one' in the context of the weight to be attached to a particular academic opinion. There are very few references to the works of living authors in English judgments and, when these are referred to, they are not always complimentary. The recent exception is in fields, such as medical law, where the court may be dealing with a new area of legal development, wherein the judges have actually cited an English academic article with approval and even expressed gratitude for the academics' comments (see *Sidaway v Board of Governors of the Bethlem Royal Hospital and the Maudsley Hospital* [1985] AC 871; *Spiliada Maritime Corp v Casulex Ltd* [1987] AC 460; see, also, *R v Gomez* [1993] AC 442). It is important to note that, in strict law, such 'doctrinal writings' (to use the civil law appellation) are not, of course, 'binding' on the court in any way and are only 'persuasive' in the most non-technical sense. However, although foreign and comparative law academic writings were cited with approval in *White v Jones* [1995] 2 WLR 187 by no less than the House of Lords, the more typical approach has been to proceed as they would normally do anyway, despite conceding that there has been strong academic disapproval of their previous decision (see *Re W (A Minor)* [1993] 1 FLR 1, where Lord Donaldson referred to several academic articles which were critical of his approach in a previous case and then proceeded to follow his previous approach, albeit on the grounds that it was again in the best interests of the child).

This is in contrast to the civil law approach (see Chapters 3 and 4), but there is evidence that even English courts are possibly mellowing when it comes to certain fields of law.

Typical structure of English statutes

At the beginning of an Act, the year and chapter number will be found. Thus, the Education Act 1975 is headed '1975 Chapter 2'. An Act may be cited either by its year and chapter number or by its short title. The long title of an Act is usually a description of the aims of the Act, but it should be noted that this description is not meant to be exhaustive, but needs only to be wide enough to cover the contents of the Bill. This is because it may be politically expedient to restrict the number of amendments that may be moved with regard to the particular legislation. The long title of the Education Act 1975 reads:

> An Act to make further provision with respect to awards and grants by local education authorities; to enable the Secretary of State to bestow awards on students in respect of their attendance at adult education colleges; and to increase the proportion of the expenditure incurred in the maintenance of provision of aided and special agreement schools that can be met by contributions or grants from the Secretary of State.

This is usually followed by a date in square brackets which signifies the date when royal assent was obtained, which, in Britain, has not been personally signified by the Sovereign since 1854.

A preamble, which may comprise of more than one paragraph, may then follow, but this is not always the practice. The preamble begins with 'whereas' (as some French judgments do) and continues with an explanation for the passing of the Bill. The enacting paragraph then follows. This, in the British formula, reads: 'BE IT ENACTED by the Queen's Most Excellent Majesty, by and with the advice and consent of the Lords Spiritual and Temporal, and Commons, in this present Parliament, and by authority of the same, as follows.'

The body of the Act consists of sections, a practice dating from 1850, and, where a section consists of several propositions, is usually divided into sub-sections. There is also a marginal note for each section, but not for sub-sections. Each section traditionally deals with one topic and another long established tradition is for sections to contain one sentence, which, in many cases, is very long, purportedly to indicate the unity of thought and policy that underlies it. The practice dates from the era, especially the 19th century, where parliamentary draftsmen were seeking to draft legislation to 'guide the nation' without the aid of detailed preparatory and particularising work, which is today carried out by civil servants and public authorities. If a sentence is very long, the modern practice has been to subdivide it into indented paragraphs and subparagraphs. Major Acts are usually divided into Parts, which designate groups of sections. Matters of detail are usually relegated to Schedules, which are placed at the end of the main body of the Act and might, for example, list repeals of existing enactments. These Schedules are also grouped into titles of paragraphs (similar to sections) and sub-paragraphs, without marginal notes. Modern statutes tend to include definitions, but these have been subject to criticism, since they are not always intended to be all encompassing, exhaustive explanations, but are often meant to distinguish potentially confusing overlaps of terminology, or simply alert the user to the existence of another statutory definition contained in another Act. A definition may commence with the word 'means', which indicates that it is meant to be a comprehensive definition, or with the word 'includes', which suggests that it is merely an 'enlarging definition'. Well known terms are not usually defined on the understanding that their meaning is generally understood, although it might have been thought that terms of art do require definition precisely because there is scope for disagreement over their ambit.

COMPARATIVE OVERVIEW

In the French Civil Code, the organisational structure is similar to Gaius' *Institutions* which divided the compilation of laws into persons, property, wills, intestate succession and obligations. The German Civil Code, on the other hand, greatly influenced by the systematic approach and abstract thinking of its 18th and 19th century scholars, has a different structure, divided into 'Books' or segments, commencing with Book I: General Part, which also contains headings which include persons, legal transactions (including contract and agency), then Book II: Law of Obligations, which expands on contractual and other obligations, followed by Book III: Law of Property, Book IV: Family Law and then Book V: Law of Succession. As has been explained in earlier chapters (see, for example, Chapter 3), distinctive historical factors led to both French and German Codes dividing substantive private law into 'civil law' (non-commercial law) and commercial law, as reflected in the enactment of a Civil Code and a Commercial Code in both French and German systems, and their jurisdictional followers. An area of debate has also arisen in the civil law world over whether there should be a General Part enacted in Codes based on the French model, namely, a separate division which contains those rules which are seen as being generally applicable to all areas of law covered by the particular Code, as a result of their level of abstraction and generality. In some countries, such as The Netherlands, it was decided that a 'General Part' would be included in their Code, but its scope limited to areas of law dealing with rights having a money value. Personal rights are therefore not affected by the rules contained in the General Part. Recent experience in German law itself indicates that it is sometimes difficult to apply all the rules in the General Part to every possible situation, so that the whole premise of an all encompassing corpus of rules is frequently being undermined. Reference to the extremely learned and detailed commentaries on the BGB provisions is now an absolute necessity, as well as the Short Commentary, which consists of around 1,000 pages of cases and is regularly updated (see, also, Chapter 3).

Similarities in approaches between legal systems

There are several similarities which exist between the various systems in their approaches to statutory interpretation. The most significant of these appear to be:

(a) the use of precedents in interpretation;

(b) the use and justification of reasons in judicial interpretation;

(c) the use of certain basic types of argument in interpretation;

(d) the use of 'presumptions'.

The use of precedents

It has become axiomatic to say that common law courts refer to case law, or precedents, to assist in interpreting the statute, whereas civil law courts do not. Yet, various recent studies (see McCormick and Summers (1991)) reveal that, in modern times, nearly all systems, with the notable exception of France, utilise precedents, particularly if these have already interpreted the legislation in question. Even in France, although there is no citation of precedents by the Cour de Cassation, a large number of Articles of the Code Civil have been interpreted by 19th century cases, whose interpretations have remained settled and accepted up to today. The sharp division of executive from judiciary, that is, the separation of powers philosophy, has maintained the *de jure* position of the judge being unable or, indeed, having no need to look further than the statute in order to apply it. In practice, of course, cases continue to be referred to as illustrations, if not sources, of the law as revealed in commentaries on cases by French doctrinal writers. More significantly, Germany, Sweden, Finland, Italy and Poland all utilise precedents to assist them in interpreting the words of a statute where this is deemed to be necessary. The difference is that this has become an almost mandatory practice in Germany and Sweden, but is purely discretionary in other civil law countries, although their utilisation is, in the appropriate case, expected. Of course, in common law jurisdictions, like the United Kingdom and the United States, it has usually been mandatory to use precedents and to observe their binding nature, whereas no such strict *stare decisis* doctrine exists in civil law countries. Flexibility exists in both systems, but for different reasons. Civil law systems retain flexibility because of their freedom not to follow a particular higher court's decision, and the *stare decisis* doctrine in common law countries allows a lower court to deviate from a higher court's ruling by using the techniques of distinguishing and overruling precedents or utilising canons of construction to sidestep a previous decision.

Common judicial arguments on statutory interpretation

Apart from these similarities, no less than 11 basic types of 'judicial argument' have been identified by Summers and Taruffo (1991) as being frequently used by higher courts in all three major types of legal systems:

(1) 'ordinary meaning' arguments;

(2) 'technical meaning' arguments;

(3) contextual arguments;

(4) arguments based on precedents;

(5) statutory interpretation by analogy;

(6) legal concept arguments;

(7) arguments based on general legal principles;

(8) historical/evolutionary arguments;

(9) statutory purpose arguments;

(10) substantive reasoning arguments;

(11) legislative intention arguments.

The first four types of judicial arguments have already been discussed at some length. Argument (5), the argument from statutory analogy, is sometimes applied where a case is not provided for, or only obliquely provided for, in the statute. Here, the approach will be to treat the case in the same fashion as closely analogous cases have been treated in the statute. Alternatively, a statute may be construed as another statute has been construed, by way of analogy. This approach is followed in varying degrees by all legal systems. The countries that tend to invoke this argument are France, Germany, Sweden, Poland, Italy and Finland. It is far less common in the United Kingdom or in the United States.

Argument (6) proceeds on the basis of giving a consistent interpretation or meaning to a recognised general legal concept which appears in a statute. The usual examples are 'contract' and 'corporation'. Argument/approach (7) also seeks to render a consistent interpretation to general principles of law if these are relevant to the case before the court. Uniformity of interpretation, both of substantive and procedural law, is generally the norm. Summers and Taruffo (1991) also identify three senses of 'principles of law':

(a) substantive moral norms previously invoked by judges;

(b) general propositions of substantive law widely applicable within a particular branch of law;

(c) substantive and procedural general propositions of law which are applicable throughout the entire legal system.

Argument (8) has been discussed in the context of reliance on the historical background and historical context of a statute as a guide to interpretation.

However, while this is not wide ranging in common law countries, being concentrated on some narrow areas of law, it is of far greater significance in civil law countries where parts of a Code will have been interpreted within a particular historical context. Argument (9) has already been discussed in the context of giving effect to the purpose of a statute, but 'purpose' may be interpreted either as stated in the express words of a statute, or in accordance with the extrinsic materials or legislative history of a statute, or in accordance with a particular judicial view of legislative purpose. We have already noted the 'mischief rule' and, apparently, some similar form of constructional aid is invoked in all systems. Argument (10) utilises political, social, economic or moral considerations, and this is generally utilised more explicitly in civil law systems or in American higher courts, rather than in common law courts generally. The prerequisites of this approach would usually be a measure of ambiguity, or vagueness, or lacunae, or the need to concretise a general concept, or a conflict between equally plausible arguments. There might even be a combination of these requirements. Argument (11) on the legislature having 'intended' a particular meaning is, of course, used by all systems, as we noted at the outset. Indeed, all systems use some form of 'presumptions' as to legislative intention.

The key difference lies in the amount of weight given to purely linguistic considerations, rather than to extrinsic aids to statutory construction. The United Kingdom stands alone in its formal prohibition of travaux préparatoires. Thus, the so called 'ordinary meaning', or the accepted technical meaning, of the words are the *prima facie* statutory interpretations adopted in the United Kingdom.

Germany also adopts this 'objective' approach, but does not give quite so much weight to linguistic considerations. Remarkably, the presumptions that are employed are also very similar, to the effect that the legislature must be taken to know the ordinary or technical meaning of the words being used; that there is no intention to infringe the constitution; that no absurd or unjust consequences were intended; that statutes are not generally meant to be retroactive; and that treaties should not be violated.

Differences in statutory interpretation between the systems

Apart from differences in judicial attitudes towards the use of precedents as an aid to the interpretation of statutes, there are, of course, other differences in judicial approaches between the three major types of systems. They may be summarised under the following headings:

(a) differences in materials used in argument;

(b) the use of travaux préparatoires;

(c) differences in styles of judicial opinion;

(d) differences in styles of justification;

(e) differences in the level of abstraction;

(f) differences in modes of rationality.

The first category includes 'authoritative' and 'non-authoritative' material, which may also be labelled binding and non-binding materials (see Summers and Taruffo (1991)). Examples of binding material would include the statutory text itself, related statutory texts, relevant constitutional provisions and general principles of law or customary law. Non-binding materials would include dictionaries, technical lexicons, travaux préparatoires and social factors which might have led to the passing of the statute.

The second category is further isolated from the first because it is only the United Kingdom courts that have formally insisted on the inadmissibility of travaux préparatoires, so that counsel may not cite to them records of parliamentary debates and parliamentary committee reports. All other systems, in particular Sweden, ascribe considerable weight to such materials, although specific references to them rarely appear in the actual judicial opinions. Although part of a common law system, the United States Supreme Court has generally been fairly liberal in allowing travaux préparatoires to be admissible. Nevertheless, there appears to be a discernible recent trend in the United States Supreme Court to place more reliance on the ordinary or technical meaning of a statute, and accord less significance or reliance on travaux préparatoires. On the other hand, even in the United Kingdom, official reports of governmental commissions or committees of inquiry have long been permitted by the courts in order to ascertain or clarify legislative intent or purpose, so it is true to say that, while formalistic differences exist, there is indirect acceptance by the United Kingdom courts, of certain types of legislative background material.

The third difference (judicial style) has been dealt with in some detail in this chapter. The fourth difference (styles of justification) focuses on linguistic arguments rooted in the ordinary or technical meaning that is generally attributable to the words/concepts in question, which may or may not be expressed by the citation of the statute itself. Broadly, the difference lies in the recognition or non-recognition of the existence of opposing sets of arguments that exist in relation to the interpretation of a given statute. Sweden, the United Kingdom and, to a lesser extent, Germany appear to recognise explicitly the possibility of opposing arguments, whereas countries like France, Poland and Italy do not. In these latter countries, only the main arguments supporting the chief rationale of the decision are usually mentioned in the published judgments. The fifth difference (level of abstraction) addresses the different levels of abstraction, or levels of sophistication, of judicial reasoning that exist between the various legal systems.

While all systems recognise the need for justificatory reasons to be given in the judgments for a particular interpretation, France appears to be unique in either having extremely brief statements of the law, supported by general principles (for example, 'This decision is taken because it is morally correct'), or an underlying assumption by their judges that the law is clear and does not need further justification. Most of the other systems certainly require more than a bare statement of the law. Thus, at one extreme, a French court may simply state the rule, the facts and the court's interpretation without seeking to justify their decision, while, at the other end of the spectrum, common law jurisdictions, such as the United Kingdom and United States, indulge in long, discursive, sophisticated judgments which marshall arguments for and against alternative interpretations of a given statutory provision, with arguments being further subdivided, and a conclusion reached by deductive reasoning. The eventual decision is presented as the result of judicial choices made in accordance with arguments and conventions of interpretation, rather than on the basis of purely logical argument. The final difference lies in what may be called 'modes of rationality'. This relates to the methods used to rationalise or justify a conclusion or particular decision on the statute's 'meaning'. Again, France stands alone as the only system whose higher courts are seen to focus on the statutory text, utilise a modicum of formal arguments, state the legally significant principle and merely state their rational conclusion derived from that principle. All other jurisdictions, particularly the British and American, have established a tradition of closely argued justifications which, while adhering to the statutory text, are frequently imaginative, innovative and even evolutional. The obvious reasons for this difference in modes of rationality of judgments are cultural, institutional and political. A significant point is French political philosophy which perceives the judiciary as the handmaiden of legislative policy. Thus, where French interpretations tend to be 'positivistic' and formal, American courts are seen as independent bodies which complement the legislature and must be 'instrumentalist', seeking to use the law to further approved and recognised policy and principle. English courts tend to lie somewhere in the middle, rarely as open ended or innovative as American counterparts, but clearly more creative and justificatory (both substantively and logically) than the French. The German Constitutional Court, which has relied increasingly on precedent or case law, is also given to a more discursive and argumentative style, although its justifications for particular statutory interpretations are far more conceptual, abstract and casuistic than the common law courts. It is the only German court that actually issues dissents.

CONCLUSIONS

The latest study suggests that Germany, Italy and Finland appear to be evolving a more distinctive 'rationality model' (see Summers and Taruffo (1991)). This contains elements of both common law and French practice. Thus, while formal reasons and technical language tend to predominate (as in France), the judges are more open about their law making role (as in the United States); again, while complicated long and complex arguments are used (as in the United Kingdom courts), a more 'magisterial' style is employed (as in France). Finally, constitutional and general legal tenets feature prominently in some statutory interpretation cases, as in the United States, but the approach adopted by these courts is not as liberal as that of American courts (in, for example, their sources of law), since they still rely heavily on materials within the system and deploy a classically 'positivist' philosophy, in terms of their mode of argumentation, concepts and authoritative sources. English courts may, in certain circumstances, refer to extrinsic legislative material in construing a statute and, while this took place 'unofficially' until *Pepper v Hart*, that case now makes such a practice more explicitly acceptable within its guidelines. These preliminary findings suggest that, at least in the realm of statutory interpretation, a theory of convergence is developing, but rather more slowly than in other areas. With EC law impinging on the law of its Member States, however, it will surely not be long before a clearly discernible consistency and convergence in statutory interpretation will begin to develop, at least within the European Union countries.

SELECTIVE BIBLIOGRAPHY

Amos, 'Interpretation of statutes' [1933–35] 5 CLJ 163

Atiyah and Summers, *Form and Substance in Anglo-American Law* (1987) especially Chaps 4 and 11

Atiyah, 'Common law and statute law' (1985) 48 MLR 48

Bennion, *On Statutory Law* (1990)

Bennion, *Statutory Interpretation* (1984)

Cross, *Precedent in English Law* (1968)

Cross, *Statutory Interpretation* (1976)

David and Brierley, *Major Legal Systems in the World Today* (1985) pp 108–29

de Vries, *Civil Law and the Anglo-American Lawyer* (1976)

Gutteridge, 'A comparative view of the interpretation of statute law' (1933) 8 Tulane L Rev 1

Kotz, 'Taking civil codes less seriously' (1987) 50 MLR 1

Lawson, 'A common lawyer looks at codification', in *Many Laws* (1977) Vol I, p 48

Marsh, ' The interpretation of statutes' (1967) 9 JSPTL 416

McCormick and Summers, *Interpreting Statutes: A Comparative Study* (1991)

McCormick, *Legal Reasoning and Legal Theory* (1978)

Pizzorusso, 'Italian and American models of the judiciary and of judicial review of legislation: a comparison of recent tendencies' (1990) 38 Am J Comp L 373

Summers and Taruffo, 'Interpretation and comparative analysis', in McCormick and Summers (eds), *Interpreting Statutes: A Comparative Study* (1991) Chap 12

Williams, 'The meaning of literal interpretation' (1981) 131 NLJ 1128, p 1149

Zweigert and Kotz, *An Introduction to Comparative Law* (1977) Vol I, pp 268–74

Zweigert and Puttfarken, 'Statutory interpretation – civilian style' (1970) 44 Tulane L Rev 704

CHAPTER 10

THE LAW OF OBLIGATIONS: A COMPARATIVE STUDY OF CONTRACT AND TORT

INTRODUCTION

In 1953, Prosser declared that, 'when the ghosts of case and *assumpsit* walk hand in hand at midnight, it is sometimes a convenient and comforting thing to have a borderland in which they may lose themselves' (see Prosser, *The Borderland of Tort and Contract* (1953) p 452). In modern English law, the areas of tort and contract are usually placed in separate legal compartments for analytical, pedagogical and conceptual purposes. On the other hand, civil law legal systems group both tort and contract as belonging to one category – the general law of obligations. The common law has adopted the dichotomy since the mid-19th century and, contrastingly, the civil law's treatment of both areas as being part of the same generic law of obligations appears to date from early Roman law.

Yet, in terms of legal theory and legal history, tort and contract are by no means invariably independent or mutually exclusive concepts. In many respects, they are closely related and, as Winfield put it in 1931, 'The segregation of the law of tort from other parts of the law is quite modern' (Winfield (1931) p 8). Winfield himself emphasised the fact that liability in tort arose from the breach of an obligation primarily fixed by law, but in contract it is fixed by the parties themselves. This generalisation was certainly true when liability in contract arose from the mere exchange of promises, but not in more modern times when contractual liability is seen as arising as soon as the plaintiff has conferred a benefit on the defendant, or has incurred loss by relying on the defendant's behaviour (see Dias and Markesinis (1989) p 7).

Indeed, despite their conventional separation, there are situations even within English law, where, for example, a party's conduct may be tortious in character, but may also have contractual overtones. Similarly, the behaviour of a party may be the consequence of a contractual relationship which he has entered into with another, but which may also give rise to tortious liability.

Common examples of overlap between tort and contract arise in English law, for example, in 'economic torts' and certain cases of misrepresentation where a remedy may lie in the tort of deceit (for a fraudulent misrepresentation which induced a party to enter into a contract), or for conduct which induced someone to commit a breach of contract, which may also be regarded as tortious behaviour.

There are several striking differences between common law and civil law systems in their approach to delictual obligations (or the law of tort, in common law parlance) and contractual obligations. These differences are seen in their method of division into separate areas of law, their different remedies and their divergence in bases of liability. While civil law systems group both tortious and contractual obligations under the general area of law which they call the law of obligations, common law systems retain their 19th century division of the law of obligations into the categories of contract, tort and restitution. There are, of course, other types of obligations which, for example, French law is prepared to recognise, but which it will not enforce by legal process. These are called 'natural obligations', using the Roman law terminology from which the concept derives. A typical example is a civil obligation which is unenforceable for technical reasons, such as a statutory limitation period within which to bring the suit. Certain obligations have to be converted into a 'civil act' in order to be actionable and this usually requires a solemn notarial act.

For the purposes of this chapter, we shall compare the historical development of the notion of tortious (or delictual) liability and contractual liability in the two main civil law countries and in English law. We shall also analyse certain common elements such as 'fault' and illustrative situations in tort and contract, as developed in these jurisdictions.

HISTORICAL DEVELOPMENT: A COMPARATIVE ANALYSIS

The early Roman law of obligations

It appears to be well established that Roman law's greatest contribution to modern civil law has been in the law of obligations and, especially, in the law of contract. It is also in the law of contract that common lawyers have most frequently looked to Roman or civil law. But, in Gaius' *Institutes*, followed by Justinian, having dealt with property and succession, he writes about a subject called Obligationes, which he classifies under two headings; those arising from contract (*ex contractu*) or from delict (*ex delicto*). To these categories Justinian added quasi-contract and quasi-delict.

Contracts

Early Roman law

The word *'obligatio'* does not appear to have been used as a legal term until the time of the Empire. Yet, as early as the Twelve Tables, there is mention of a formal act which embodied the bare essentials of an agreement. This was the *stipulatio*, which consisted of an exchange of a question and answer in formal words. In its earliest forms, the prospective creditor/promisee would say: 'Do you solemnly promise [to pay me X ... or to convey to me your house]?' and the prospective debtor/promisor replied: 'I solemnly promise.'

But, the validity of the *stipulatio* derived from its form, not from the agreement which the form embodied. Agreement played no part in early Roman law, being neither necessary nor sufficient. The *stipulatio* thus came to be generally enforceable as a formal promise in which an obligation is imposed on only one party, the promisor or debtor. But, the form of words had to be correct.

Legal historians, such as Nicholas (1962), stress that the idea of contract was one which, as in English law, emerged gradually and probably began with a notion of debt that someone owed someone else a certain sum or thing. The presence or absence of agreement was not a significant consideration. The origins of contract probably lie in the existence of two types of debt – one deriving from a formal act and the other from an informal transfer or payment. The crucial difference between the two is that, whereas the first is a promissory debt, the other is a 'real' debt in that it is limited to the return of something already received from the creditor (Nicholas (1962) p 160).

The implications of the 'promissory debt' for the development of commerce were extremely significant because the needs of a more sophisticated commercial society could be better served by the utilisation of a concept that could be adapted to more complex transactions. Performance of services, or of undertakings incidental to a sale, required a more flexible means of interaction.

Hence, an even more significant development which occurred in certain other transactions (such as sale or hire) was the evolution of the principle of a party being bound by a formless agreement. This meant that a contracting party could be bound when neither had performed their part of the agreement (under an executory contract), a notion which English law recognised only as late as the 17th century. Consensual contracts appear to have been established in Roman law sometime in the first century BC.

The four consensual contracts were:

(a) emptio venditio (sale);

(b) locatio conductio (hire);

(c) societas (partnership); and

(d) mandatum (mandate).

All four of these shared a common denominator: they arose by mere agreement, without the need for any form or any physical act, such as delivery which was a prerequisite for 'real' contracts. The important concept of *bona fides* was also developed through the application of these consensual contracts and, especially, in contracts of sale and hire.

Early English law

Yet, in English law, the notion of an enforceable agreement had appeared at an early stage, but then lost currency until around the late 15th or early 16th centuries. In England, the ecclesiastical courts began to impose spiritual penalties in certain cases of breach of agreement, where no remedy existed at common law. This practice was, however, checked very early by writs of prohibition and does not seem to have made any impact on later law. Much later on, in the 15th and 16th centuries, before the common law courts had created a viable notion of contracts, the English Court of Chancery was apparently establishing a consistent practice of enforcing agreements of several different kinds, without actually deciding the principle upon which it was acting.

Principal feature of contracts in Roman law

The main characteristic of the Roman law relating to contracts is that it consisted of a law of contracts, rather than a doctrinally unified law of contract. There were therefore no generalised rules, but really many different rules governing a recognised list of contracts, and the legal requirements of each contract varied according to its particular species. An informal agreement in Roman law did not constitute a contract, unless it satisfied the legal requirements of this particular contract.

Contracts in Roman private law, thus, became extremely important and various commentators have argued over the nature of contractual obligation. The traditional explanation, however, is that it was the promisor's declaration of his will which made a contract binding, by obliging him to keep his word (*De iure belli*, II II; *De iure naturae*, III 5).

Nicholas (1962) highlights three practical consequences that flowed from the lack of generalised theory:

(a) lawyers were therefore able to determine in detail the 'incidents' of each type of contract in advance, so that these could be adapted to the commercial needs of the particular parties;

(b) since each type of contract had an appropriate form of action, according to the formulary system of the time (see Chapter 3), the plaintiff had to prove that he had entered into the type of contract specified in the formula of his action, or would have his case dismissed at this preliminary stage;

(c) any agreement could be cast in the form of a *stipulatio*, which would then render it legally effective, since the *stipulatio* was a method of contracting, rather than a type of contract. It was the *stipulatio* which gave the Roman system a much needed degree of flexibility as well as generality.

Hence, the classical Roman view, that only certain types of contracts should be enforced, eventually came to be rejected under the influence of canon law, the law merchant (*lex mercatoria*) and natural law. Under these three influences, it came to be accepted that, in principle, any agreement of two parties which had been voluntarily entered into and intended to create legal obligations, should, *prima facie*, be enforced as a contract, irrespective of the presence or absence of what a common lawyer would call 'consideration'. This general principle came to be known as 'freedom of contract'.

Of course, there were many exceptions to the rule, such as the need to comply with certain form requirements, or exceptions based on duress, fraud, illegality or mistake. This was the position on the eve of the age of codification, and the same general principle enunciated above – freedom of contract – was consequently integrated into all the Codes. It is also often stated, and with some justification, that there was no doctrine of consideration in Roman law. However, civil law appears to have developed a doctrine of 'cause' (*causa*) which has been vigorously debated and analysed by legal historians and which has even been incorporated into the French Civil Code.

Cause and consideration in Roman and English contracts

On the question of consideration in contracts, there certainly did not appear to be any rule in Roman law which required that every promise must be supported by 'consideration' as a condition of its validity, in the sense of *quid pro quo*, and equivalent to the English notion of consideration. Under modern English law, consideration has been described as the price of the promise, or 'the price for which the promise is bought' (Pollock). This is, of course, exceedingly vague. It has, however, traditionally been defined as involving either some detriment to the plaintiff or some benefit to the defendant (see *Currie v Misa* (1875) LR 10 Exch 153, p 162; *Thomas v Thomas* (1842) 2 QB 851), but almost invariably involves both and must be of some economic value in order to be legally significant. In fact, the English 'doctrine of consideration' refers to a number of complex rules (see p 301, below). As many legal historians, such as Buckland and McNair (1952), observe, the Romans did not think in terms of consideration in any common law sense, but other writers, such as Lawson (see *Excursus to Buckland and McNair* (1952) p 228 *et seq*), also pointed out that there are apparently four sets of ancient Roman texts which support the similar notion of *causa* or 'cause', in the Roman law, relating to contracts. First, there is a text in the Corpus Juris which suggests that contracts needed *causa* as well as consent in order to be enforceable: see D 2.14.7.4; and D 14.1.49.2 (*cum nulla subest causa praeter conventionem*). Secondly, another set of texts also suggests that an agreement is void or voidable if it is based on an illicit or non-existent *causa*. The central difficulty with the first set of texts is that there were four consensual contracts in Roman law, which existed at the time these statements appear to have been made, which were binding solely on the basis of consent (see above). Cause therefore applies, if at all, to the innominate contracts, and the upshot of it is that 'executed consideration is required where no regimes have been set up for particular contracts' (Lawson, *Excursus to Buckland and McNair* (1952)).

With regard to the second set, Buckland and McNair's analysis (see Buckland and McNair (1952) p 224 *et seq*) suggests that the usage of *causa* varies with the context and certainly does not refer to meanings similar to the English model, but to the failure to perform something which was at the root of the contract, or to an ulterior motive for the transaction which vitiates its legality. Hence, the various Roman contracts which appear to support the notion of *causa* really deal with situations where some fraudulent intention was the real basis of the contract, or recovery of money was ordered because a *causa* (a particular service or undertaking), which was the basis of the whole transaction, was not carried out.

A third Roman origin of cause, unearthed by Lawson, is sometimes called the 'interdependence of promises' which arose from the obligations in a contract of sale. The obligations of the buyer and seller were 'mutually independent', so that neither could refuse to perform his part on the ground that the other had defaulted or was not ready or willing to perform. Nevertheless, classical Roman law mitigated this rule, so that either party could refuse to perform unless the other party was ready and willing to perform his side of the agreement. In cases of failure to pay the price at the agreed time, the insertion of a *lex commissoria* clause into the contract was the solution, since this gave the seller the option of declaring the contract at an end if the buyer did not pay within an agreed time. Once it was inserted, the two promises became interdependent.

A fourth source of the doctrine is the practice that grew up in Roman times of requiring acknowledgment of debts to specify their basis, because of the fear (mainly by the canonists) that vague or abstract promises would pose difficulties of proof and therefore enforceability. The rule therefore emerged that an acknowledgment of debt, *nudum a causa*, could not be enforced. This had nothing to do with consideration.

Nevertheless, the medieval lawyers utilised *causa* as the basis of their system of contract in order to distinguish between promissory transactions which would be legally enforceable and those which would not. The concept has, accordingly, passed into the French Civil Code and into Italian and other European systems, though not into the German system. But, it has been criticised as unmanageable, undecipherable and, in the words of Bonfante, 'the battle ground for metaphysical elucubrations and juridical psychology' (Bonfante, Scr Giur iii, p 125).

The notion of contract in early English law

In the Middle Ages, the word 'contract' was engulfed within the larger idea of property. The medieval usage of the term denoted a transaction involving the transfer of a material thing (*res*), so that the earliest contracts were all 'real' contracts, where the legal duty was based on the delivery of a chattel. Thus, as with early Roman law, the element of agreement or consent did not seem to be relevant, and the majority opinion of legal historians appears to be that agreement was not recognised as a basis of liability (see, for example, Street (1908) pp 1, 5; Holmes (1881) p 264; Pollock and Maitland (1968) p 212; Holdsworth Vol III, p 349; Potter (1958) p 452; Fifoot (1949) pp 225–26). A judicial statement from a 1428 case which is typical of the cases which support the majority view is: 'The ground of the action is a duty' (YB 7 Hen 6, f 5, pl 9).

Professor Simpson (1975) appears to agree with this, to some extent, but points out that the 'duty' was a duty of indebtedness and, although he thinks that medieval law did sometimes enforce parol or verbal agreements, this was not necessarily enforceable in the common law courts. Commentators, such as McGovern and Arnold, also disagree with the majority view, arguing that their research suggests that a wide range and fairly large number of arrangements in the 14th century were analysed in terms of a promise, and the writ of covenant was used for this purpose (see McGovern (1969) and Arnold (1976)). It is submitted that the ambiguous nature of the Year Book accounts and different use of terminology, therein, coupled with the absence of authoritative treatises on the subject, make it impossible to know what the actual legal position was at the time. It is noteworthy, however, that, in the early contracts, any notion of duty seemed to originate from the defendant's receipt of property that was perceived as rightly belonging to the plaintiff. Indeed, as with early Roman law, all the early transactions also seemed to create some 'debt' in the mind of the medieval lawyer.

On the point of terminology, 'covenant' appears to be the medieval equivalent of our legal usage of 'contract', so that, to medieval lawyers, 'covenant' and not contract was the term that signified a legally binding agreement. Thus, although the word 'contract' appears in the Year Books, it does so infrequently and its usage certainly does not seem to correspond to any theory of contract based on agreement. Year Book evidence also suggests that counsel and judges are careful to distinguish 'contract' from a sealed writing. Both Hale and Blackstone treat contract as 'only a means of acquiring ownership or possession'.

The earliest from of a 'real' contract appears to be bailment, wherein the main duty seemed to be the return of the chattel, or its value, to the original owner. English law required the actual delivery of the chattel before it could impose any legal duty. It appears, therefore, that Anglo-Saxon law did not possess any theory of contract and only recognised written agreements under seal, 'real' contracts and the simple contract of suretyship.

The notion of 'contract' was later broadened to include all transactions (consensual or otherwise) which gave rise to the action of debt. Further, another notion associated with the early forms of informal contracts was that of *quid pro quo* (something for something), which was often said to be an essential element of a valid contract. Thus, even in early times, 'contract' was perceived as a bargain involving some element or notion of reciprocal exchange.

It is important to note, however, that, although the notion of *quid pro quo* made its appearance in contracts, like the sale of goods, the doctrine of consideration in the modern or 19th century sense was unknown to lawyers of the 14th and 15th centuries. In any event, all it meant was that, in informal transactions, a duty to pay a debt arose when either performance had been tendered or services had been rendered. Hence, some sort of part performance yielding a benefit to one of the parties must have taken place for some sort of duty to arise. But, this was only relevant to the question of actionability, not the question of when an agreement became binding.

Origins of the modern English law of contract

Actions on the case

The modern law of contract appears to have originated from a form of actions on the case known as *assumpsit* (undertaking). As we have seen in Chapter 4, the early history of the common law saw the establishment of central courts, and the procedure which enabled these courts to summon defendants to answer complaints against them was the form of summons known as the 'writ'. It should be remembered that parol or oral agreements of an informal nature were few and far between in medieval times, since the King's courts were only prepared to recognise agreements which were 'under seal'. Consequently, for a long time, no writ existed for breach of parol agreements.

Thus, there were gaps in the common law of obligations, before the mid-14th century, since there were no writs to deal with informal, unsealed agreements which could be proved by wager of law (production of a certain number of witnesses to prove one's case). Eventually, a new writ of trespass developed, which contained the *vi et armis* (with force and arms) clause, which gave the courts jurisdiction to hear the case. The trespass writ eventually spawned the 'actions on the case', which were actions which local custom classified as wrongs and which were admitted to the courts, even without the *vi et armis* clause, because they were actions based on previous or established cases.

It was against this procedural backdrop that the writ known as '*assumpsit*' was developed from the actions on the case, derived from the original writ of trespass. *Assumpsit* appeared in the mid-14th century, from which the common law developed an action for breach of informal promises. The essence of *assumpsit* was that the defendant had voluntarily assumed an obligation, as illustrated by the case of *Skyrne v Butolf* (1367) YB 3, Ric 2,223, in which the plaintiff, who sought a cure for ringworm from the defendant doctor, alleged that the doctor undertook (*assumpsit*) to cure him for a sum of money which had already been paid. The gist of the plaintiff's claim was that the defendant performed this undertaking or promise so negligently that the defendant suffered injury.

This action was then extended to persons, such as blacksmiths, innkeepers and surgeons in the famous *Humber Ferry Case* (1348) YB 22 Ass, p 141, where the ferryman was held liable for his breach of his undertaking (*assumpsit*) in overloading his ferry such that the plaintiff's mare, which the defendant had promised to carry across the river, perished. The plaintiff sued in trespass, but pleaded a breach of the promise made by the defendant.

These were clearly cases of misfeasance or intentional harm, but the action was later broadened to include cases of non-misfeasance, or unintentional harm, which was established in *Pickering v Thoroughgood* (1533) 93 Selden Society 4. The landmark decision was *Slade's Case* (1602) 4 Co Rep 92, in which it was definitively established that any undertaking or promise could be actionable. In its form, *assumpsit* constituted an action for a detriment suffered by the person to whom the promise had been made, in reliance on that promise. *Assumpsit* therefore shifted the focus of liability, arising from parol transactions, from the delivery of a chattel to whether a promise had been unfulfilled either by defective performance or non-performance.

The doctrine of consideration

As the previous discussion illustrates, the doctrine of consideration began to be developed by the English courts in the mid-16th century as a touchstone of the seriousness of contractual intention. But, this is obviously not the modern day (or 19th century) version of the doctrine. It gradually acquired a technical meaning and became the pivotal prerequisite for the enforceability of promises. By the 19th century, it had become entrenched in the doctrine of English law and, to a certain extent, is the basis of other contractual rules, such as privity of contract. The doctrine itself comprises a number of rules, such as:

(a) past consideration is no consideration – a promise to pay for services already rendered is not usually enforceable;

(b) consideration need not be 'adequate' – it may be a 'tomtit or a canary', but need only be of some value in the eye of the law;

(c) consideration must move from the promisee – a party wishing to enforce a contract must show that he has furnished consideration for the promise of the other party; this is sometimes cited as another of the reasons for the inability of a third party to a contract to sue on such a contract – since he has not provided any consideration for the promise;

(d) performance of an existing duty is not valid consideration – for example, where a duty is already owed under a contract or by law, as with an existing public duty.

In effect, the English courts have the privity rule which denies the third party to a contract a right to sue on a contract to which she or he was not a party, but they have often avoided applying it by utilising a range of devices, for example:

(a) the trust of a promise (*Les Affreteurs Reunis SA v Leopold Walford* [1919] AC 801);

(b) agency – that is, making one of the parties an agent thereby creating an additional contract with the third party (*The Eurymedon* [1975] AC 154);

(c) using s 56 of the Law of Property Act 1925 (LPA 1925), mainly by the late Lord Denning whose efforts to thereby confer rights on the third party were rejected by the House of Lords in *Beswick v Beswick* [1968] AC 58;

(d) recognising a right to claim damages on behalf of another (*Jackson v Horizon Holidays* [1975] 1 WLR 1468).

The English doctrine has come under severe criticism from various commentators and the courts themselves, as well as by the Law Revision Committee (as far back as in 1937), who suggested that an agreement should be enforceable if either the promise was made in writing by the promisor or his agent or if it was supported by valuable consideration, past or present. English legislators and, until recently, the Law Commission have not responded to these suggestions, but, in 1996, after a comprehensive study of contracts, the first *Law Commission Consultation Paper on Privity of Contract and Third Parties* having been published in 1991 (see Law Com CP 121), the Law Commission published their *Report on Privity of Contracts: Contracts for the Benefit of Third Parties* (1996) (Cm 3329) and, at long last, a bill entitled the Contract (Rights of Third parties) Bill is currently proceeding through the British Parliament. We shall look at some of its more salient features.

The Bill has eight clauses and the main change it makes (in cl 1) is a two limbed test: in general, a person who is not a party to a contract – a third party – will be able to enforce a contractual provision which purports to confer a benefit on him or her, if the contract:

(a) contains an express term to that effect; and

(b) on its proper construction, the contracting parties intended to give the third party the right to enforce it.

The third party must be expressly referred to by name, as a member of a class, or as answering a particular description, but need not be in existence when the contract is entered into. The Explanatory Notes clarify that the beneficiary could, therefore, be 'an unborn child, a future spouse or a company which has not yet been incorporated'. The devices of trust, agency and s 56 of the LPA 1925 would, therefore, become redundant as common law exceptions to the general rule of privity.

Since the right given to a third party to enforce a contract made in the abovementioned circumstances would be of limited value if the original contracting parties change their minds, cl 2 regulates the variation and cancellation of a contract. Unless they have specifically made different arrangements in the contract, the parties to the contract will lose the right to vary or cancel the contract to the detriment of the third party if one of three situations apply (see cl 2(1)), namely: (a) if the third party has communicated (by words or conduct) assent to the relevant term to the promisor; (b) if the third party has relied on the term and the promisor is aware of this; and (c) if the third party has relied on the term and the promisor could reasonably be expected to have foreseen that the third party would do so.

If any one of these situations applies, any variation or cancellation can only take place with the consent of the third party. However, in certain cases, the court has the discretion to waive the need for such consent, for example, if his whereabouts are unknown or he has become mentally incapable of giving his consent.

Clause 3 deals with defences, set offs and counterclaims available to the promisor in an action by the third party to enforce the contract. Thus, a void, discharged or unenforceable contract is no more enforceable by the third party than by the promisor. If the promisee has induced the promise by misrepresentation or duress, this may be used by the promisor as a defence to an action brought by the third party. The contracting parties may agree that a set off arising between them from unrelated dealings may be used by the promisor against the third party. It will also be possible for the promisor to rely on defences, set offs or counterclaims against the third party which arise from previous dealings between promisor and third party.

Certain contracts are excluded (see cl 6) from the provisions of the Bill. These are contracts on a bill of exchange or promissory note; terms of a contract of employment as against an employee; contracts for the carriage of goods by sea or, if subject to an international transport convention, by road, rail or air. In addition, the exception for carriage of goods by sea does not apply to reliance by a third party on an exclusion or limitation of liability contained in this type of contract. Hence, there will be no need to rely on agency to give effect to the 'Himalaya' exclusion clause considered in *The Eurymedon* (above). This would apply for the benefit of stevedores.

It remains unclear as to whether the Act (when enacted) would apply to the *Jackson v Horizon Holidays* (above) situation. Ultimately, the case would probably turn on the court's construction of the contract in question as to whether there was a clear intention to benefit the third party. The main parties may clearly decide to specifically benefit a third party under the terms of their contract and know that their intentions will be respected and wishes carried out accordingly. However, they will also retain the right to decide that the provisions of a contract should be framed so that a third party should not have the benefit of the contract and they may change their minds, subject to the rules governing variation and cancellation, discussed above.

It needs to be stressed that the Bill (as it currently stands) is not yet law (at the time of writing in mid-1999), so the current law which has privity as the norm still stands with all its exceptions.

Tortious or delictual liability

Origins and development

Common law

In the early common law, there was no differentiation between crimes and torts. Wrongs were first classified into: (a) felonies; and (b) those that were not felonies. If an offence was punishable by death, dismemberment, escheat or outlawry, it was a felony. The same classification applied if it could be prosecuted by means of the private criminal prosecution, known as an 'appeal of felony', wherein the accused's guilt was decided by battle. If it did not fall within that grouping, it was one of a vast group of offences referred to as 'trespasses' or 'transgressions'. In the famous words of Bracton, 'Every felony is a trespass, though every trespass is not a felony'. Within the group of trespasses, misdemeanours and torts were all mixed in a hotchpot, so that it was impossible to distinguish them.

The word 'trespass' itself was used to mean 'wrong' and applied to many types of actions that involved tortious civil wrongs. Trespass was one of the earliest writs in the royal courts, appearing around 1250, but it possessed criminal overtones and had criminal sanctions. It was directed at serious, direct and forcible breaches of the peace and was the remedy for all such injuries or damage, whether caused to persons, land or chattels. As in France, it was concerned with the punishment of the crime and gave compensation to the injured plaintiff only as supplementary to the sentence.

It developed rapidly during the 13th century and, towards the end of the 13th century, was supplemented by an action of trespass 'on the case' to accommodate wrongful conduct which was neither direct nor forcible, which did not fit within the confines of the original writ of trespass. These sorts of claims were, therefore, granted writs 'on the case', in the light of and on the basis of the particular circumstances.

Thus, there were nominate and specific torts which were directly covered by the original trespass writ and innominate torts which varied according to their individual circumstances.

A scholarly debate developed which focused on the true interpretation of Chapter 24 of the Statute of Westminster II of 1285. For many years, this was thought to have created the authority in the Courts of Chancery to issue writs of trespass on the case (also known simply as 'case'). A subsequent theory was that trespass on the case grew out of the original action of trespass as a natural progression. Professor Milsom has argued, in what has become known as a more modern theory, that trespass was used in obvious cases involving forcible trespass, such as assault and battery and trespass on land, but 'case' was used where the cases were not so obvious. Professor Milsom therefore argues that the term 'case' did not appear until 1370.

After various developments had taken place, wherein the royal courts started to hear the actions on the case by plaintiffs' insertion of the 'with force and arms' formula, it eventually reached the stage where fault was the basic element in actions of trespass on the case, but did not feature in the case of taking someone's personal property or invading someone's land. Here, the nominate torts were used.

Up to the development of industrialisation, during the 19th century, the emergence of fault as a criterion of liability had certainly dominated the English civil liability scenario. However, the notion of fault was found to be inappropriate to the new industrialised 19th century society and new principles were needed to take care of the new phenomenon of 'accidents' which came to include not just fortuitous mishaps, but also harms caused by human errors, predominantly because 'more machines are used and more accidents happen' (see *International Encyclopedia of Comparative Law*, Vol XII, Chapter 1, p 41).

It was probably in England that the industrial revolution had its first impact on the law of tort. Railway trains appear to have been the first source of injuries and actions upon the case for negligence. The process began with an action on the case, supported by an allegation of negligence. This focused the issue on negligence and, after a slow and gradual evolution, the tort of negligence emerged and was unequivocally recognised in the landmark case of *Donoghue v Stevenson* [1932] AC 562, a Scottish appeal which went to the English House of Lords. In a famous passage which has come to be known as the 'neighbour test', Lord Atkin said that a man is required to take 'reasonable care to avoid acts or omissions which he could reasonably foresee would be likely to injure his neighbour' and, in answer to the question 'Who is a neighbour?', he replied, 'persons who are so closely and directly affected by my act that I ought reasonably to have them in contemplation, as being so affected, when I am directing my mind to the acts or omissions which are called into question'.

This was not the first statement (indeed, it was strictly only *obiter dicta*) acknowledging a general theory of duty in negligence, but was the first which gained general acceptance and influenced the whole course of development of the English law relating to negligence. Judges initially only found negligence in cases where an established duty was said to exist (for example, in *Otto v Bolton and Norris* [1936] 2 KB 46, pp 54–55) but, during the period of the 1970s and 1980s, it was accepted as a statement of general principle.

French law

In French law, as in Roman law, only particular torts were actionable and Roman jurists devised a formula (*neminem laedere*: injure no one) which became the basis of Art 1382 of the Civil Code. The French law on torts is essentially a 'praetorian law founded on judicial decisions' (*International Encyclopedia of Comparative Law*, Vol II, Chapter IV, p F-70). The law of early France had three main sources, namely, Germanic customs, Roman law and canon law. Germanic customs were predominant in the field of tort mostly in the North, but also in the South, at any rate, up to the second life or revival of Roman law at the beginning of the 13th century. The Germanic law of the Salic Franks, dating from the 5th century, defined in great detail various offences and the appropriate fines and even prescribed different types of compensation commensurate with the social status of the victim. For example, slaves cost less than an important officer in the army, and a thief had to give compensation not just for the value of the thing stolen, but for the loss of its use. Part of the compensation went to the king and part to the victim or his family.

This was a remarkably sophisticated system for its time. Canon law was later responsible for introducing the intention element in the law, adding to the degree of culpability of the offender. From about the 12th century, Gratian made a clear distinction between damage caused unwittingly and intentionally, which led to a distinction between criminal justice and civil justice. Where criminal law proceeded by a list of specific offences, civil law could develop using more general principles of compensation.

The delict provisions in the French Civil Code are almost completely attributable in their formulation to the French scholar Jean Domat, who, in the 17th century, distinguished between intentional breaches of the law, breaches of contract and mere negligence. Fault was made the criterion of liability. Even when coupled with harm, proof of fault was necessary in order to create liability. As far as the question of what conduct should be considered 'wrongful' was concerned, the French adopted the Roman approach, as expressed by their jurists, and used the criterion of conduct which fell short of the standards of a *bonus paterfamilias* (see *International Encyclopedia of Comparative Law*, Vol XII, Chapter 1, p 36).

Very little progress was made in the period between Domat and the enactment of the French Civil Code. Domat's work inspired Pothier who divided conduct which involved liability in damages into delits and quasi-delits.

German law

Before the enactment of the BGB, the law of tort in Germany was a mixture, with the Gemeines Recht being based partly on traditional types of liability, inherited from Roman law, and other parts of the country being governed by a general clause of liability in tort. The Prussian land law stated in § 1 *et seq* I-6 that 'a person who injures another intentionally, or by gross negligence, must pay full compensation to that other' while 'the person who injures ... another by only moderate carelessness' need only pay for 'the palpable harm cause thereby' (see Zweigert and Kotz (1987) p 293). After seriously considering whether to follow the French Civil Code, the draftsmen of the BGB decided not to adopt a general clause, not least, because they wanted greater precision in the German version, but also because they feared that excessive generality would empower judges to resolve the ambiguities and fill the gaps too frequently, which would be inconsistent with their perception of the judicial function (Zweigert and Kotz (1987) p 293).

Three heads of tortious liability were, therefore, laid down in two paragraphs, supplemented by other specific provisions. Under the first head, § 823I of the BGB, liability for causing injury in an unlawful and culpable manner will arise if the injury affects the victim in one of the legal interests enumerated in the text, namely, life, body, health, freedom, ownership and any other right.

The second head of general tort liability arises under § 823II when 'a statute designed to protect another' is culpably contravened. The kinds of statutes referred to will include all the rules of private and public law, particularly criminal law, 'which are substantially designed to protect an individual or a group of individuals rather than the public as a whole' (Zweigert and Kotz (1987) p 296).

The third head of general tort liability arises under § 826 of the BGB. A person is liable under this provision if he 'intentionally causes harm to another in a manner which offends *contra bonos mores'*.

Law of obligations: contract in civil law

Legal obligations and freedom of contract

French law

In Roman law, in pre-codification times, the contracting parties' consensus was the central and decisive element of the law of contracts. This was also called the principle of 'freedom of contract'. The Civil Code treats obligations in accordance with a classification of their sources, that is, the facts which give rise to the obligation. The draftsmen distinguished between those obligations which arose from the agreement of the parties and those which did not. In the segment dealing with obligations, the first title or chapter deals with contracts, and the second title with other obligations. Non-contractual obligations are subdivided further into those obligations which arise solely from the authority of the law and those which result from a personal act on the part of the debtor. This last group is finally subdivided into obligations which arise from quasi-contracts, from delicts and from quasi-delicts, respectively.

Obligations therefore derive from four sources: contract and quasi-contract, which are broadly similar to the areas covered in English law; and delict and quasi-delict, which are roughly equivalent to the law of tort (excluding areas covered by the law of property). Contract and tort are, therefore, seen as forming one category much more in French law than in English law. The lack of distinction is also facilitated by the view that liability under both heads rests on fault (see 'Fault in the law of contract and tort', p 334, below).

Under the Code, legal obligations arise because the debtor wishes them to arise; in other words, they are created by his will and with his consent. Under Art 1108 of the Civil Code, one element necessary for an agreement is the consent of the party who obligates or 'binds' himself. This indicates that a promise is necessary for an obligation to arise, but not an acceptance. Under the ideology of the Civil Code, an agreement is binding because, and in so far as, the parties have consented to it. Thus, the obligations created by the parties could be modified, altered or rejected by them.

Hence, the norm in the law of obligations was the contractual obligation, and extra-contractual obligations were limited in scope. The Code seeks to ensure that effect is given to the will of the parties.

English law

Of course, the notion of freedom of contract is a dominant principle in English common law as well. The phrase itself has many meanings: (a) freedom to choose to enter into any sort of contracts; (b) freedom to decide whether or not to contract; (c) freedom of each contracting party to fix the terms of his own promise, subject to the agreement of the other party. True or absolute freedom of contract cannot really exist, since parties are rarely completely equal in economic or social terms, and one's freedom to contract is clearly limited by social, commercial and legally acceptable norms, some of which are contained in criminal law and others in the law of contract itself (the contracts that would be void for illegality – contracts to promote illegality or immorality; contracts in restraint of trade).

There has been much academic debate and discussion of this concept which appears to have fallen in and out of fashion from time to time. Professor Atiyah's monumental book, *The Rise and Fall of Freedom of Contract* (1979), surveyed the genesis of the notion and traced political, economic, social and legal influences which have shaped this phenomenon. He concluded that freedom of contract was in decline towards the end of the 1970s but, in the last decade, there has been a strong resurgence of the free market ideology, a revival of interest in the right of the individual to make his own free choices and to be left to make their own mistakes, if that is what they wish to do. Concomitant with this has been the growing distrust of bureaucratic and State controlled decision making. The tremendous rise in the use of administrative and employment tribunals in Britain (see Chapter 4) is not so much an affirmation of belief in the power of quasi-judicial powers, but of the individual's right to an impartial hearing and the right to be heard. Thus, freedom of contract's star has been rising, in the 1980s, and the inevitable tension between legal paternalism and an individual's right to make his or her own contract have come into play yet again.

The use of standard form contracts represents an attempt to introduce generalised terms and conditions of business, primarily for economies of scale. However, these have meant that the average consumer has had to cope with the full might and power of a large commercial enterprise, thus reducing any semblance of equality of bargaining power. The English courts have devised concepts, such as fundamental breach of contract (see Chapter 12), adopted a strict interpretation policy towards widely worded exemption clauses in order to equalise the consumer's bargaining power with that of the large corporation. Parliament has also intervened to pass the Unfair Contract Terms Act 1977 (UCTA) requiring, *inter alia*, that any exemption clause which is sought to be relied upon, must be 'reasonable in all the circumstances'. Schedule 2 of the UCTA lists factors which the court is directed to consider to promote equality of bargaining power in applying the 'reasonableness test'.

However, in 1980, the House of Lords in *Photo Production v Securicor Ltd* [1980] AC 827 appears to have advocated a non-interventionist approach, leaving it to the parties to decide which sort of breaches would entitle the innocent party to repudiate the contract. In other words, the parties' agreement should be the controlling factor. This has been followed in cases, such as the *TLF Prosperity* case [1984] 1 WLR 48, but goes against another earlier House of Lords' case, the *George Mitchell* case [1983] 2 AC 803. Hence, the case law on the English judges' approach to the interpretation of the UCTA indicates:

(a) there are two different approaches to the interpretation of the 'reasonableness' requirement in the UCTA. The *Photo Production* approach suggests a party centred, non-interventionist approach and the *George Mitchell* approach advocates leaving the matter to the discretion of the trial judge;

(b) trial judges seem more likely to operate within the *George Mitchell* approach rather than the *Photo Production* one;

(c) judges seem willing to apply the Sched 2 guidelines which include the strength of the bargaining positions of the parties relative to each other, the presence or absence of an inducement to agree to a term and whether the customer knew or ought reasonably to have known of the existence and extent of the particular contractual term (see the UCTA and Adams and Brownsword, 'The unfair contract terms act: a decade of discretion' (1988) 104 LQR 94).

German law

Freedom of contract, an essential concept to German private law, is protected under the basic law in Germany as part of the general freedom of action (Art 2, para 1 of the Basic Law). As a crucial element of a free economy, contract facilitates private enterprise and promotes the development of economic relationships and commercial enterprise. German law distinguished between the freedom to form contracts and the freedom to decide their content. The freedom to enter a contract or not is limited whenever there is a monopoly of some description. Although there is a general freedom to contract on virtually anything, there are both constitutional and legal limits to this freedom, as with every other legal system.

The limits to contractual freedom are discussed by Horn, Kotz and Leser (1982):

(a) statutory prohibitions under § 134 of the BGB, which include criminal conspiracies and dealings in prohibited drugs;

(b) an assortment of cases where the court decides on their legality, or otherwise, depending on the gravity, the danger or turpitude of the transaction, including medicaments without prescription and transactions to evade tax, which will only be illegal if their principal aim was to evade tax;

(c) prohibition of usurious contracts (§ 2 of the BGB);

(d) a legal transaction will be void if it is 'contrary to good morals' (§ 1 of the BGB).

Apparently, the legislator applies general principles of ethical conduct in order to demarcate the limits within which contractual freedom is permitted. The judges have to give content to this principle and, very much like the English law relating to the tort of defamation, the standard of good moral behaviour has often been described as the 'feeling of propriety entertained by all right thinking people' (see BGHZ 10, 228, 232; BGHZ 69, 295, 297: Supreme Court decisions.

In a codified system, it is particularly noteworthy that it is to case law that one has to turn to discover the types of contracts that have been held contrary to this statutory provision. They include contracts which oppressively restrict personal and economic freedom of movement (BGHZ 22, 347, 355), contracts that pay people for changing their religion (RG Seuff Arch 69, No 48: Imperial Supreme Court decisions), and contracts that benefit one creditor to the detriment of others (BGHZ 55, 34, 35 (1970); BGHZ 30, 149, 153; RGZ 143, 48, 51).

Another restriction on freedom of contract is in the context of immoral transactions, and this is covered by the good faith and fair dealing requirement under the German Civil Code (§ 242), which applies to all obligations and contracts. Paragraph 242 has made it possible to invalidate any part of a legal transaction that is inconsistent with good faith and fair dealing, according to the interpretation of the courts. This resembles the 'blue pencil test' that is sometimes used in English law (see, for example, *Mason v Provident Clothing and Supply Co Ltd* [1913] AC 724) where the offending or illegal part of the contract will be severed from the rest of the contract, provided it is possible to do so without having to redraft the rest of the contract.

Certain rules of the BGB cannot be excluded by contract:

(a) paragraph 276(II) of the BGB, dealing with invalidity of exclusion of liability for intentional fault, and § 248(I), dealing with invalidity of prior agreement to pay compound interest; and

(b) other restrictions dealing with property law, family law, and the law of succession.

Another restriction to contractual freedom relates to formalities, regulated by the requirements of §§ 126–29 and § 313 of the BGB, which are particularly important to sales of land. Failure to comply with these provisions will usually invalidate the transaction (see § 125 of the BGB).

There have also been Acts of Parliament outside the BGB dealing with mandatory rules, which first appeared after the First World War. These protect tenants against eviction by landlords, and employees from dismissal by employers. Although labour law remained separate from the BGB, the mandatory rules for landlords and tenants were integrated into the BGB in the 1960s and 1970s.

The Standard Contract Terms Act (or General Conditions of Business Act) consists of substantive law and provisions which came into force on 1 April 1977. It is designed to protect the weaker party in a transaction, as well as seeking to regulate other aspects of general conditions of business. The three most important provisions are:

(a) the general clause;

(b) the black list; and

(c) the grey list.

If one wishes to ascertain if a clause is void, this may be done by consulting the black list which is a section in the Act which enumerates clauses which are void in every case. Those clauses which are enumerated in the grey list are *prima facie* void, but may not be so interpreted in every case.

If one is unable to find a number in the black or grey list that is similar to the clause being used in any given agreement, the general clause should be consulted, which states that:

(a) provisions in standard contract terms are void if they place the other party at an unreasonable disadvantage to such an extent as to be incompatible with the requirements of good faith;

(b) in case of doubt, an unreasonable disadvantage shall be presumed if a term:

- is incompatible with the fundamental principles of the provision from which it deviates; or

- restricts fundamental rights or duties inherent in the nature of the contract to such a degree as to jeopardise its object (Tonner, 'Characteristics of German contract law' Lecture given at Keele University (March 1990)).

The second part of the Standard Contract Terms Act deals with the right of associations, like consumers' associations, to complain against unlawful individual standard terms (§ 13).

TORT AND CONTRACT: CONTEMPORARY COMPARATIVE ASPECTS

Formation of contracts

French law and common law

The absence of any doctrine of consideration in French law means that agreements of all kinds are legally binding in France, so long as a true consensus has been reached between the parties and provided that, where legally required, there has been compliance with the necessary requirements of form. Hence, French law will recognise the existence of gratuitous contracts, so that any seriously intended agreement is binding and no difficulty arises when a contractual obligation is gratuitously reduced or even discharged.

In addition, there is no conceptual obstacle to the recognition of the binding effect of an offer in the French system. Nevertheless, under the French system, offers may not be freely revoked. In the analysis of offer and acceptance, French law tends to regard a display of priced goods in a shop window or supermarket shelves or in catalogues as an offer, rather than as an invitation to treat. The basis of this is that a display indicates a continuing intention to sell, thus, the buyer's actions, indicating the intention to purchase, mean that the contract is formed from that moment. On the other hand, English law bases its rule on convenience for delaying the moment of completion.

The French law, on the question of acceptance, appears to have been clarified in a 1981 case decided by the Cour de Cassation (Com 7.1.1981, RT (1981) 849). The point to remember is that there are conflicting academic and judicial opinions as to whether the manifestation of acceptance is necessary in French law. Thus, the emission theory argues that the contract is complete as soon as the offeree has emitted a declaration of his acceptance of the offer. A variation of this is the expedition theory which argues that the contract is formed when a letter or telegram has been dispatched accepting the offer. In contrast, the information theory holds that the communication of the acceptance must be received by the offeror before a contract may be said to have been formed. Most decisions have favoured the expedition theory, but the matter had not been definitively settled until this 1981 Cour de Cassation decision.

In the case referred to, an offer to A was to be accepted by C within a set period of 30 days. C actually dispatched his acceptance seven days early, but could not prove that it had been received in time. On the basis of the emission theory, the contract was formed as soon as the offeree 'emitted a declaration of his acceptance of the offer'. Some academic opinion seems to believe that this now resolves the question but, as Nicholas points out, there is less agreement on whether it applies only to the particular situation of lapse or to all cases of revocation of the offer, or whether it is a universally applicable test (see Nicholas (1992) p 74).

On a point of terminology, as Nicholas (1989) points out, the French 'unilateral contract' denotes 'an agreement which creates only rights in one party and duties in the other, as in the case of a gratuitous promise to pay money'. On the other hand, a bilateral contract creates rights and duties in both parties. In English law, a unilateral contract means a promise in return for an act, but this will not be enforceable in French law, unless it can be said that it conforms to the definition of a contract as an agreement, that is, when the offer has been accepted. At that point it will be a bilateral contract (see Nicholas, in Harris and Tallon (eds), *Contract Law Today* (1989) p 19).

German law

Declaration of will

The BGB uses the concept of the declaration of will or intention in regulating the formation of a contract. This comes from the Pandectists and encompasses not only offers and acceptances by persons negotiating a contract, but also unilateral declarations, such as giving notice or effecting a cancellation (see Horn, Kotz and Leser (1982) p 75). Offer and acceptance have to correspond in order to produce a contract, although there is no express provision regulating this in the BGB, which assumes the formation of the contract has already taken place. The offer and acceptance are declarations of intention which occur at different times, the former simply preceding the latter. If, as is common, the contract is the last stage of a series of negotiations, any distinction between offer and acceptance simply fades into insignificance (see Horn, Kotz and Leser (1982) p 76).

Juristic acts

Thus, offer and acceptance are reciprocal juristic acts (acte juridique, Rechtsgeschaft) and the contract to which they give rise is the normal source of obligation. The notion of juristic act embraces all those declarations of intention which are capable of creating, transforming or determining legal relations. Examples are making a will, rescinding a contract, granting power of attorney, transferring property and exercising an option. Unilateral juristic acts are recognised as capable of generating obligations and, apart from the example given above, include the establishment of a foundation, promise of a reward and the acceptance of a negotiable instrument. The Rechtsgeschaft is a concept that gives rise to general rules which govern all juristic acts.

Legal position of offers

There is no specific *'indicia* of seriousness' in German law. But, every offer is irrevocable, unless the offeror has excluded the binding effect of his proposal. As with Swiss law, the only gifts which require a special form are promises to transfer property. All other gratuitous promises, such as a promise to give an interest free loan, or a contract in favour of third parties, or to do or refrain from doing something, are all valid, even if made informally (see Zweigert and Kotz (1977) p 69).

In the case of postal offers, the arrival within the offeree's sphere of influence will be sufficient, even if he is unaware of its existence at the moment of arrival. The offeree need not have read it, but it is sufficient if he had the capacity to do so (see RGZ 50, 191: the lottery ticket case).

The offeror is bound by his offer for a reasonable length of time (§ 145 of the BGB). However, it is common for the offeror to exclude the binding effect of the offer by inserting express words such as 'freibleibend' (subject to change) or 'widerruflich' (revocable). If this is done, then there is only an invitation to make offers or an 'invitation to treat', as English law calls it. This will apply to declarations to the public, as in the case of a catalogue, price list, newspaper advertisement or display in a shop window. Unless an offer and acceptance are given orally or by telephone, they must usually arrive at the recipient's address. There is no equivalent of the 'posting rule', as in English law, where mere posting of a letter of acceptance constitutes an acceptance where negotiations are conducted by post.

Rather than adopting any doctrine resembling consideration or *causa*, German law has opted for 'the construction of the transaction' approach (see Zweigert and Kotz (1977) p 68) in most areas of the law. It is only in the sphere of the law of property that *causa* plays any sort of role, where the *causa* is the right to hold on to something which one has received:

> ... a thing is received with *causa*, and its retention justified by it, if the thing was transferred pursuant to a valid contract, or pursuant to a liability or to a gift ... and if, at the time of the transfer, the transferor knew that he was not obliged to make it. [Zweigert and Kotz (1977) p 69.]

Silence in negotiations

On the issue of silence in negotiations, German law rules that it is not always necessary for the declaration of acceptance to reach the offeror. But, it depends on the individual circumstances of the case. For mail order cases, once a mail order organisation dispatches the goods which have been ordered, this constitutes an acceptance of the offer. In the case of unsolicited goods being sent to a person, unlike English law, he will be treated as having accepted them when he starts to use them.

Apart from these cases, if there is no response to an initial declaration of intention in any written form or by conduct, no legal consequences would normally follow. An exception to this is contained in the German Commercial Code (§ 362) which requires a merchant to make it clear, in certain circumstances, that he is not going to fill an order he has received. If he keeps silent, the legal rule is that the contract will be deemed to have come into force and silence will constitute acceptance of the contract.

German courts have applied this rule to commercial letters of confirmation, which are different from the English approach to counteroffers (or responses to the original offer which includes different terms). In English law, it will depend on whether the response constitutes a counteroffer, which may be accepted or rejected, or whether it is merely a request for information, which does not affect the original offer. It turns on a matter of interpretation of the exact terms. In German law, subsequent to oral negotiations between merchants, if a letter of confirmation is sent on terms which accord with the oral agreement, this will serve as evidence of it, but if it contains different terms from the oral agreement, but is accepted without comment, the agreement will be treated as modified in accordance with the written terms. Here, the letter of confirmation has been held by German courts as having a 'constitutive effect' (see BGHZ 54, 236, 240), which means that the contract will be deemed valid on the terms of the confirmation. The point to note is that, once the letter of confirmation proceeds on the basis that a contract has been formed, a binding contract may now be deemed by the courts to be in existence, despite the fact that no contract was actually crystallised in the original negotiations (Horn, Kotz and Leser (1982) p 76).

If a recipient of a letter of confirmation wishes to reject its contents in any material particular, he should reject it immediately in very clear terms. It does not seem too much to ask of commercial parties to respond in this manner, although it is, of course, quite possible and, no doubt, not uncommon that an oversight might result in a contract being formed, despite silence on the part of the recipient of such a letter.

Culpa in contrahendo

The formation stage of contract may also be affected by the doctrine of *culpa in contrahendo*. This comes from Roman law, in a passage by Modestinus in the *Digest*, as developed by the German jurist, Jhering. As it has come to be known and embodied in the German Civil Code, it recognises that contractual negotiations engender a relationship of trust which obliges the parties to observe a certain standard of care. Thus, whenever a supposed contract fails to materialise, through the negligent misrepresentation and non-disclosures of one of the parties, this would be actionable if the other party suffered damage as a result of being induced to rely upon the representation, even though no contract comes into being.

This is very similar to English law relating to negligent misrepresentation, which also imposes liability in similar circumstances, where the representor had the means to ascertain the true state of facts and where there is a 'special relationship' giving rise to a duty of care between the parties (see *Howard Marine v Ogden* [1978] QB 574). This has been further strengthened in English law by the Misrepresentation Act 1967, which makes it unnecessary to establish a special relationship between the parties, and reverses the burden of proof, so that the representor (rather than the representee, as at common law) must prove, under s 2(1), that he had reasonable grounds for believing and did believe, up to the time the contract was made, that the facts were true. Thus, statutory liability complements and amplifies the liability which also exists 'at common law' (under case law).

The French Civil Code does not refer to this doctrine as such, but it is generally accepted by French jurists and has been cited in various decided cases.

Frustration of contract, impossibility and supervening events

Throughout history, contracting parties have grappled with the problem of non-performance of the contract after its formation (or 'conclusion' in civil law terminology), but before its completion, caused by political, social or economic upheavals beyond their control. Various systems have coped with these situations in different ways, using a variety of approaches. Continental law has utilised notions, such as mistake, abuse of rights, impossibility (which includes financial impossibility within physical impossibility), a want of good faith (in the sense of a want of reasonableness), the collapse of the foundation of the contract and the 'gap filling' doctrine. There is no unity between the different civil law systems, or even within systems, with one system of French courts adopting a different approach from another.

French law

French law proceeds on the basis that a promise to do the impossible is null and void (*impossibilium nulla obligatio*). The principle is widely accepted, although not expressly stated in the Civil Code. It appears to be implicit in a number of Articles such as Arts 1108, 1126–30, 1172, 1302 and 1601 (see Nicholas (1992) p 200). If performance is impossible from the outset, the object is impossible and therefore no contract can exist. If there is supervening impossibility, a contract has already come into existence, but the debtor is no longer under an obligation to perform. Where the non-performance is due to the fault of the debtor or, rather, where he cannot show that the non-performance is due to *force majeure* or *cas fortuit*, a claim for damages will be available. In these circumstances, of course, a claim for performance would not be available.

The scope of *force majeure* in French law is much narrower than the English legal doctrine of frustration. Article 1148 of the Civil Code refers to *cas fortuit*, as well as *force majeure*, but attempts to distinguish these terms have not been successful. According to Cour de Cassation cases, '*force majeure* refers to events which make performance impossible, not to those which make it more onerous' (see, for example, Civ 4.8.1915, S 1916.1.17). This is invoked if a change of circumstances renders the implementation of a contract not just commercially impracticable to perform, but legally or physically impossible to perform.

The impediment to performance must be absolute, unforeseeable and irresistible, as well as unavoidable and insurmountable (see Nicholas (1992) p 203). According to *force majeure*, a contract may be rescinded when the court is satisfied that it has become impossible to perform the contract, as the result of a supervening event which could not have been reasonably foreseen by the parties.

The French civil courts have never accepted any doctrine of imprévision (unforeseeability) which has been applied by the Conseil d'État, as established in a 'leading case' of 1916 (see CE 30.3.1916, S 1916.3.17, D 1916.3.25) and which resembles the English doctrine of frustration. It would seem to be derived from Art 1134 of the Civil Code which stipulates good faith in the performance of contracts and the principle of *rebus sic stantibus*. The doctrine is, therefore, only found in administrative contracts not civil contracts.

German law

In German law, there is a doctrine known as Geschaftsgrundlage or basis of the transaction. This is usually applied under § 242 of the BGB. It recognises that performance of a contract can no longer be insisted upon when, as a result of a complete change in conditions, the performance has become completely different from that originally contemplated by the parties. However, since German courts still insist on compliance with §§ 157 and 242 of the BGB, the doctrine often results in a modification of existing duties under the contract. The doctrine is usually applied strictly and there is no lapse of the foundation of the contract, unless there has been an economic upheaval of a really fundamental character. A total failure of the contractual basis entitles each party to rescind the contract and German law allows this to have a retrospective effect. Consequently, rescission will restore the parties to the status quo, as if the contract had never been concluded.

If there is only a partial failure of the basis of the contract, the courts have the power to vary the terms of the contract, so as to adjust it to the changed circumstances.

As far as other types of impossibility are concerned, the rules have been summarised by Horn, Kotz and Leser as follows:

(a) a debtor will be liable for all irregularities of performance for which he is to blame or is responsible; even if he is not to blame personally, he may be liable if the persons who assisted him in his performance are to blame (a sort of vicarious liability); or

(b) because of the strict guarantee in contracts requiring the procuring and delivery of generic goods; or

(c) because he has assumed the risk by contract; or

(d) because his obligation was 'subjectively' impossible when the contract was formed (see Horn, Kotz and Leser (1982) p 101).

German law distinguishes between objective impossibility, meaning the case where all debtors would be prevented or impeded in the same way, and subjective impossibility, meaning a case where the particular debtor is unable to perform, but someone else is in a position to do so. The final result is not really different from English law, but the different forms of irregularity employed in German law present a more complex scenario than the common law.

English law

In English common law, contractual liability is, in principle, absolute – a party is generally bound to perform what he has promised and is not excused from his performance merely because it turns out to be more difficult, inconvenient and more burdensome than expected. However, the doctrine of frustration was devised to deal with situations involving impossibility of performance. It can be viewed as an exception to the general principle of *pacta sunt servanda* (agreements should be kept) which is basic to both civil law and common law jurisdictions. English law utilised the notion of the implied term to excuse parties from performance (see *Taylor v Caldwell* (1863) 3 B & S 826). It was postulated that certain contracts, by their nature, were subject to an implied condition that the parties should be excused. For example, if it became 'physically impossible' to perform a contract, then parties were discharged from the obligations. This rule was then extended to include legal impossibility caused by a subsequent change in the law. In the course of this development, the broader question of the extent of the court's jurisdiction in litigation concerning contracts was raised. This led to a marked difference of opinion between the Court of Appeal and the House of Lords, in 1951 (see *Br Movietown News v London and District Cinemas Ltd* [1952] AC 166). It was unanimously suggested, by the Court of Appeal, that any uncontemplated change in circumstances was sufficient to justify the court's intervention and the exercise of its discretionary power. The House of Lords, however, equally unanimously disagreed, denying the Court of Appeal's 'inherent jurisdiction' to interfere in such matters and declared that a fundamentally different situation, rather than any unforeseen change, was the prime prerequisite for a contract to be frustrated. Five years later, Lord Radcliffe defined the doctrine in terms which have been approved by subsequent courts (and writers), declaring in *Davis Construction Ltd v Farnham UDC* [1956] AC 696 that:

> ... frustration occurs whenever the law recognises that, without default of either party, a contractual obligation has become incapable of being performed because the circumstances in which performance is called for would render it a thing radically different from that which was undertaken by the contract. *Non haec in foedera veni*. It was not this that I promised to do.

The English courts have indicated that the doctrine which operates to terminate the contract is to be applied within very narrow limits and that mere commercial inconvenience and material loss are not sufficient to invoke it (see, for example, *Tsakiroglou v Noblee and Thorl GmbH* [1962] AC 93).

There is a rather small area covered by the Law Reform (Frustrated Contracts) Act 1943. This Act does not state when a contract is frustrated and its chief feature is that it gives the court the power, subject to certain conditions and excepting instances covered by s 7 of the Sales of Goods Act 1979 or trade practice, to make such adjustment between the parties as the court might consider just.

All other cases of non-performance caused by events beyond the control of the parties, which might occur after conclusion of a contract for the sale of specific or unascertained goods, have to be resolved on the basis of common law rules. Since the adoption of the 'radically different' rule, which Lord Radcliffe called the 'test of the changed significance of the obligation' (see the *Davis* case (above), p 729), an objective interpretation of the common intention of the parties seems to be called for. Hence, the doctrinal differences between the two theories appear to have disappeared and the scope of the judicial discretion has been widened. Today, the court decides in every case whether a 'fundamentally different situation' has been created which qualifies as a legally frustrating event. Hence, each case will have to be decided on its particular set of circumstances and it will be a matter of degree whether the stringent requirements of the doctrine will be met.

Scope of tortious liability

Common law

General

The common law of tort is dominated by the duty of care notion, and English courts, in previous times, had based liability on other torts, such as trespass, conversion and nuisance. Four subsequent House of Lords' cases have added their own glosses to the law of negligence. The first was *Hedley Byrne v Heller* [1964] AC 465, which broadened the scope of liability from physical to economic loss, if caused by a negligent misstatement by someone who would owe a duty of care to the plaintiff, if he voluntarily assumed responsibility to him. The second is *Home Office v Dorset Yacht Co Ltd* [1970] AC 1004, where Lord Reid emphasised that the neighbour principle ought to be applied to all cases of negligence, unless there were good reasons for its exclusion. Further, the House of Lords held that if there is between the defendant and plaintiff 'a sufficient relationship of proximity or neighbourhood such that, in the reasonable contemplation of the former, carelessness on his part may be likely to cause damage to the latter', then a duty of care will be found, so long as there are no policy factors which 'ought to negative, or to reduce or limit the scope of the duty or the class of the person to whom it is owed or the damages to which a breach of it may give rise'.

The third case is *Anns v Merton* [1978] AC 728 which saw another expansion of liability in tort when Lord Wilberforce also strongly supported the notion that a duty of care should be assumed if the parties are proximate, and the duty dislodged or limited only if there are sound reasons of policy for doing so. In the fourth case, *Junior Books v Veitchi* [1983] 1 AC 520, where the Wilberforce approach was used to allow recovery in tort for economic loss (the cost of repair) where the parties, the owner of a building and a subcontractor, were extremely 'proximate' without being in a contractual relationship. Recent indications are that the courts are reverting to more narrow constructions of a 'proximate' relationship.

The elements of an action for negligence are:

(a) a duty of care owed by the defendant to the plaintiff;

(b) a breach of that duty by the defendant;

(c) consequential damage suffered by the plaintiff; which is

(d) caused proximately by the breach.

In fact, these requirements are similar to the civil law requirements that there be negligence, harm and causation.

Liability for nervous shock

In English law, actions for nervous shock were first allowed if they were accompanied by, or flowed from, actual physical injury, so that the courts were less inclined to doubt the seriousness or genuineness of the shock symptoms. Compensation was also allowed where the plaintiff was put in fear of physical injury through the defendant's negligence and suffered nervous shock, but not physical injury as a consequence. A further development which the courts sanctioned was the instance where the defendant had intentionally done an act calculated to cause nervous shock to the plaintiff – in this case through a 'practical joke' which resulted in the plaintiff's nervous shock (*Wilkinson v Downton* [1897] 2 QB 57).

More recently, in *McLoughlin v O'Brian* [1983] AC 410, the House of Lords extended the range of claimants to a close relative or spouse who suffered nervous shock, although he had not actually witnessed the incident wherein the injury had been caused, but had witnessed the extent of the injuries very soon afterwards and had been informed of a fatality in the family in the immediate aftermath of the accident. After this case, although there was difference in opinion as to the exact policy that should be adopted in these cases among the Law Lords, it was clear that the plaintiff must show that he has suffered some form of psychiatric illness through apprehension of injury to himself or shock as a result of injury, or the threat of injury to others, caused by the defendant. The plaintiff must prove that the defendant was negligent, that is, that he owed him, and breached, a duty not to cause him harm by way of nervous shock. Only those who are sufficiently proximate to the victim are owed this duty. There must be proximity to the relationship to the actual victim of the physical harm and to the manner in which they perceive that harm being inflicted. As Lord Wilberforce explained, as regards the means by which the shock was suffered, it must come through sight or hearing of the event or of its immediate aftermath. Further, foreseeability did not, of itself, automatically give rise to a duty of care owed to a person or class of persons.

In the Hillsborough football stadium tragedy of 1989, where 95 people died and about 700 were injured, the question of the scope of liability for nervous shock again went all to the way to the House of Lords (see *Alcock et al v Chief Constable of South Yorkshire Police* [1991] 4 All ER 907). Several psychiatric claims by plaintiffs in close family relationships with the victims of the disaster were brought against the Chief Constable of South Yorkshire, who had accepted responsibility for the overcrowding and, ultimately, the tragedy. In dismissing the appeals and holding that the Chief Constable did not owe a duty of care to to the plaintiffs, the House of Lords made the following important points:

(a) injury by psychiatric illness was more subtle than the ordinary case of direct physical injury suffered in an accident at work or elsewhere, where reasonable foreseeability of the risk was the only test that was needed to determine liability;

(b) liability for injury in the form of psychiatric illness must depend on a relationship of proximity between the claimant and the party said to owe the duty, as well as foreseeability;

(c) the kinds of relationships which would qualify as sufficiently proximate were not confined to husband and wife, or parent and child;

(d) other plaintiffs not present at the football ground all watched scenes from Hillborough on television, but none of these depicted suffering of recognisable individuals. 'The viewing of these scenes could not be equiparated with the viewer being within sight or hearing of the event or of its immediate aftermath', to use the words of Lord Wilberforce (see above), nor could the scenes 'reasonably be regarded as giving rise to shock, in the sense of a sudden assault on the nervous system' (*per* Lord Keith [1991] 4 All ER 907). He stressed that 'the viewing of the television scenes did not create the necessary degree of proximity'.

A subsequent case, heard in 1992 by the English Court of Appeal, confirms this approach. In *Ravenscroft v Rederiaktiebologet* [1991] 2 All ER 470; [1991] 3 All ER 73, the respondent's son had been crushed to death by a runaway forklift truck belonging to the appellants, his employers, who had admitted negligence. But, the appellant had not seen the accident, nor was present at his death in hospital and did not see his body immediately afterwards. In allowing the appeal and denying the mother's claim, the appeal court relied on *Alcock's* case (above), stating that the House of Lords had held that relatives or friends of victims of the Hillsborough stadium disaster, who had suffered nervous shock, were not persons to whom the Chief Constable responsible for policing the stadium owed a duty of care. Sir Christopher Slade LJ conceded that 'the rules of the law of tort which governed recoverability for psychiatric illness resulting from nervous shock might not appear to present a logical and consistent whole', but the *Alcock* case was clear authority for the proposition that 'a claim for damages for psychiatric illness arising from nervous shock was not sustainable in law, unless the shock had arisen from sight or hearing of the relevant event or its immediate aftermath'.

In 1994, in *Page v Smith*, the Court of Appeal heard a case where a plaintiff claimed damages for nervous shock from an accident in which he had not been physically hurt, but in which the psychiatric injury was not reasonably foreseeable. The facts of *Page v Smith* (1994) *The Times*, 4 May were that the plaintiff had suffered no physical injury whatsoever when his car collided with the defendant's car. The plaintiff argued that, for about 20 years, he had been afflicted with ME (myalgic encephalomyelitis) which had manifested itself on sporadic occasions, albeit in a mild form. However, he maintained that the result of the accident was that his condition became chronic and was now permanent. The trial judge had accepted that a well established principle in English law was that the defendant must take the plaintiff as he found him. However, the Court of Appeal disagreed with the trial judge's finding of liability, to the extent that the question whether injury by nervous shock had been reasonably foreseeable was still relevant, even though the plaintiff had been actually involved in the accident. The crucial point in their Lordships' opinions was that, before a defendant could be found to be liable for causing nervous shock to a plaintiff, the plaintiff had to show that his mental/psychiatric injury was reasonably foreseeable. Here, the plaintiff's injury had not been foreseeable in a person of ordinary fortitude as a result of the accident. Farquharson LJ made it clear that, once such liability had been established, the defendant would have been liable for all the consequent mental injury sustained by the victim, even though it was unforeseen and of a kind that would only be suffered by someone who was particularly vulnerable. Hence, it is *prima facie* necessary to establish that liability for nervous shock exists in a case where no physical injury has been suffered, and the plaintiff would have to show that that particular psychiatric injury was itself reasonably foreseeable. In 1996, the House of Lords heard the appeal in *Page v Smith* [1996] AC 155 and drew a distinction between primary and secondary victims. Basically, to be a primary victim one must have been within the zone of physical, as opposed to psychiatric, injury. The plaintiff who was directly involved in a motor car accident fulfilled that requirement and could, in principle, recover compensation for psychiatric loss. All other victims who suffered psychiatric harm were secondary victims and had to satisfy the requirements in *Alcock's* case (see above).

A further development, in December 1998, was the House of Lords holding, in *Frost v Chief Constable of South Yorkshire Police* (1998) *The Times*, 4 December, that police officers who suffered psychiatric injury as a result of being involved in the aftermath of the Hillsborough Football Stadium disaster in Sheffield were not entitled to recover damages against the Chief Constable either as employees or as rescuers. It was stressed by Lord Steyn that 'Nowadays, courts accepted that there was no rigid distinction between body and mind and that a recognisable psychiatric illness resulted from an impact on the central nervous system'.

In addition, the Law Lord stressed:

(a) the pragmatic rules governing the recovery of compensation for pure psychiatric harm did not, at present, include police officers who sustained such injuries while on duty. If such a category were to be created by judicial decision, the new principle would be available to many different situations, for example, doctors and hospital workers who were exposed to the sight of grievous injuries and suffering;

(b) it was common ground that police officers who were traumatised by something they encountered in their work had the benefit of statutory schemes which permitted them to retire on pension. In that sense, they were better off than bereaved relatives who were not allowed to recover in the *Alcock* case;

(c) the law had long recognised the moral imperative of encouraging citizens to rescue persons in peril. Those who altruistically exposed themselves to danger in an emergency to save others were favoured by the law;

(d) in order to recover compensation for pure psychiatric harm as rescuer, it was not necessary to establish that the psychiatric condition was caused by the perception of personal danger. But, in order to contain the concept of rescuer in reasonable bounds for the purpose of the recovery of compensation for pure psychiatric harm, the plaintiff must, at least, satisfy the threshold requirement that he objectively exposed himself to danger or reasonably believed that he was doing so. Without such limitation, one would have the unedifying spectacle that, while bereaved relatives were not allowed to recover, ghoulishly curious spectators who assisted in some peripheral way, in the aftermath of a disaster, might recover. It would be an unwarranted extension of the law to uphold the claims of the police officers.

American law

It is, perhaps, a little surprising that American jurisdictions have not really developed radically in the area of recovery in tort for nervous shock. Having abandoned the original rule, which required contemporaneous personal injury before nervous shock could be compensatable, the majority of jurisdictions, in conformity with s 313 of the Restatement (Second) of Torts, require the plaintiff to be in the danger zone (or zone of foreseeable danger) before he can recover. The controversial case of *Dillon v Legg* (1968) 68 Cal 2d 728, 441 P 2d 912 extended recovery to persons outside the immediate danger zone or zone of foreseeable danger provided:

(a) the 'plaintiff was located near the scene of the accident;

(b) the shock resulted from a direct emotional impact upon plaintiff from the sensory and contemporaneous observance of the accident, as contrasted with learning of the accident from others after its occurrence; [and]

(c) ... plaintiff and the victim were closely related ...' (441 P 2d 912, p 920).

Other Californian courts have not pursued a strict or sometimes easily discernible line in this area, but it seems reasonably clear that different interpretations notwithstanding, 'spatial and temporal proximity' remain 'crucial factors, even though they are likely to be understood differently by different courts' (Markesinis (1990) p 108).

A notable feature of the American development is the apparent extension of recovery to cases of mere 'emotional distress', even where this is not accompanied by physical injury (see, for example, *Molien v Kaiser Foundation Hospitals* (1980) 27 Cal 3d 916, 616 P 2d 813). All the court required in this case was that the emotional distress should be 'serious'. Two Hawaiian cases provide an insight into some judicial attitudes. In the first, *Rodrigues v State* (1970) 52 Haw 156, 472 P 2d 509, 'serious emotional harm' was defined as 'serious mental distress ... found where a reasonable man, normally constituted, would be unable to adequately cope with the mental stress engendered by the circumstances of the case'. In the second, *Campbell v Animal Quarantine Station* (1981) 63 Haw 587, 632 P 2d 1066, five plaintiffs were awarded a total of US$1,000 for the anguish that they suffered when they were told over the telephone that their ageing dog had died from heatstroke the previous day after it had been forgotten in an unventilated van for over an hour and had been left exposed to the Hawaiian sun.

Civil law

French law

Tortious or delictual liability in French law is known as the law of delict or civil wrongs (responsabilité civile) which derives from Roman law, and the further refinement of the early concepts, such as the delict damnum *injuria datum*, which was effected by the continental jurists in the centuries before codification, resulted in the formulation of principles of liability for civil wrongs in the Civil Code. The delict provisions in the Civil Code are expressed in a remarkably concise and compact form, with the entire subject covered in five short Articles, of which Art 1382 is the key provision:

> Any act by which a person causes damage to another makes the person by whose fault the damage occurred liable to make reparation for such damage.

The text does not mean that any damage caused by fault gives rise to liability.

Article 1383 states that:

> A person is responsible for the damage which he has caused whether by positive act, or by his negligence or imprudence.

Article 1384 states that:

> One is responsible for the damage that one causes by one's own act, but also for that which is caused by the act of the persons for whom one ought to answer, or the things that one has under one's control.

Article 1385 states that:

> The owner of an animal, or the person making use of it while it is in his service, is responsible for the damage which the animal has caused, whether it was under his care or had strayed or escaped from it.

Various French doctrinal writers have offered interpretations on these provisions and, in the 19th century, Toullier suggested that Art 1382 applies to actions that cause damage unless the actor is exercising a right. This explanation fell out of favour towards the end of the 19th century and it came to be accepted that the defendant may be liable when it is difficult to identify an injury which infringed the right of the plaintiff, as in cases of unfair competition, seduction or entering into a void contract. After undergoing further scholarly scrutiny, the earlier views have had to give way to induction, so that an examination of the case law in each case needs to be undertaken to ascertain some general rules. The current interpretation is that liability may be excluded if a justification can be found for the activity of the person causing the harm.

The landmark decision of the Cour de Cassation (19.1.14) appeared to establish that liability will exist for the 'custodian' of a 'thing'. The word 'custodian' would cover someone who had use, management, control and disposition of a 'thing'. A 'thing' would include vehicles and vessels, like cars, trains, elevators and ships – any corporeal object. However, such a custodian might avoid liability if he could prove that the damaging occurrence was due to:

(a) *force majeure*, that is, an unforeseen event which either occurred with unforeseeable suddenness or irresistible violence, so that the custodian could not possibly have prevented the harm; or

(b) the fault of the victim; or

(c) the fault of a third party.

The Jand'heur decision (13.2.30 S 1930, I 121) ruled that the 'thing' need not be something that was inherently dangerous, but it must not have played a purely passive role.

In order to recover damages in delict or tort under French law, the plaintiff must show that he suffered damage and that the damage was caused by an act or omission for which the defendant was responsible. The responsibility may exist because the defendant was personally at fault, or because he was vicariously liable for another's fault, or because the damage was caused by a 'thing' in his care. Damage, causality and responsibility have all to be proven.

It is not just physical injury that is recoverable in damages if the delictual requirements are satisfied. Damage to a person's honour is covered, such as damage occasioned by insults, defamation and seduction, deprivations of liberty and invasions of privacy. It also includes mental suffering caused by the death of one's loved ones and the pain and suffering occasioned by physical injuries to oneself. This is called 'moral damage', in French law, and it is not always possible to quantify it in terms of money and in any demonstrably direct way (see Amos and Walton (1967) p 209).

In relation to injuries to the feelings caused by another person's death, there is no textual limitation which restricts the scope of persons who might be potential claimants (Req 10.4.1922, D 1923.1.52; Civ Sect Com 15.12.1923, D 1924.1.69). However, the only limit is the need for proof of real and sufficiently profound sorrow (Amos and Walton (1967) p 210). The courts seem to approach these cases on the basis that it is presumed to exist in the case of certain close relatives, especially the deceased's parents, spouse and children. In other situations, the 'facts and circumstances must point unequivocally to the presence of a continuing and deep injury to the sentiments' (Amos and Walton (1967) p 210). There is therefore no requirement of sight or hearing of the actual event, or being present in its immediate aftermath, as in English law.

An illuminating example of this is how French law treats cases involving landowners exercising their rights in an 'abusive' manner, which French law addresses through the notion of 'abuse of rights' or abus d'un droits which means an abusive exercise of rights (see, also, Chapter 3). English law would approach these sorts of cases falling within 'nuisance' under the law of tort. Three illustrative cases are:

(a) the *Chimney* case (Colmar 2.5.1855, D 1856.2.9);

(b) the *Water Pump* case (Lyons 18.4.1856, D 1856.2.199);

(c) the *Airplane Hangar* case (Affaire Clement-Bayard) (Req 3.8.1915, S 1920.1.300, DP 1917.1.79).

In each case, the defendant purported to act in accordance with his rights over his property: in case (a) to erect a chimney which effectively deprived a neighbour of his access to light in some of his rooms; in case (b) to install a pump, the effect of which was to diminish the water supply of a neighbour's adjoining spring by two-thirds; and in case (c) to erect an immense wooden structure topped with metal spikes which made the launching of zeppelins from the neighbouring hangar difficult, if not impossible.

In each case, the court found no difficulty in finding that the proprietor had abused his right of ownership because the action was carried out with spiteful intent, with the deliberate intention of inflicting harm. The basis of such actions is actually quasi-delictual rather than delictual.

Under English law, all three cases would be treated as instances for which an action might lie in tort (specifically – the tort of nuisance), but in which the results might not have been the same as in the French cases.

Case (b) is very similar to the English case of *Bradford Corporation v Pickles* [1895] AC 587, wherein the defendant stopped an underground stream, which flowed under his land, from flowing to the plaintiff's land in order to compel them to buy his land at an inflated price. The House of Lords found that the defendant was not liable and was merely acting to protect his interests and even said that they would have reached the same conclusion if the defendant had acted maliciously. Motive was said to be irrelevant to liability.

An earlier English case, *Christie v Davey* [1893] 1 Ch 316, had taken a different approach. There, the defendant had blown whistles, banged trays and hammered on the plaintiff's wall solely to annoy the plaintiff in retribution for the annoyance the defendant felt he had been caused by the plaintiff's piano lessons. He was held liable in nuisance for acting so maliciously.

Subsequent English cases, such as the 1936 case of *Hollywood Silver Fox Farm v Emmett* [1936] 2 KB 468, have not followed the *Bradford* case. In the *Hollywood* case, the defendant was found liable in nuisance when he discharged guns on his own land, but close to the boundary of the plaintiff's fox farm, when he knew that the foxes were sensitive to noise and, therefore, acted maliciously. It would appear that *Bradford's* case should be treated as a case involving absolute rights over land and therefore a case of servitudes, where the plaintiff, a corporation, had no legal right to receive water.

German law

The German BGB devotes 30 paragraphs to the law of torts, in contrast to the five Articles of the French Civil Code. However, in essence, the Code proceeds on the basis of three general provisions, §§ 823I, 823II and 826 of the BGB and some specific provisions which deal with a number of particularised tortious situations. In addition, § 824 of the BGB deals with cases of untrue statements which damage one's credit, § 824 requires any person who induces a female person to have sexual intercourse with him to pay compensation, and § 834 deals with the liability of animal supervision.

As Markesinis stresses, 'the Code system of liability is a system of fault based liability' (Markesinis (1990) p 21) and he would analyse it according to three main sets of provisions. First, there are provisions which impose liability for fault (§§ 823I and II, 824–26, 830 and 839); secondly, there are provisions which make liability depend on a rebuttable presumption of fault (§§ 831, 832, 833 (second sentence), 834 and 836–38 of the BGB); thirdly, there is also liability for 'created risks', independent of fault. There are several statutes which deal with these situations, primarily, the Strict Liability Act and the Road Traffic Act. There are also cases where one person is liable strictly, but for some other person's fault (see Markesinis (1990) pp 21–22).

Three further points are stressed by Markesinis (1990) pp 22–23:

(a) the BGB is a typical product of the Pandectist school, 'abstract, conceptual and meticulous in the extreme';

(b) § 823 *et seq* are not an independent and self-sufficient provision of the Code, but must frequently be read in conjunction with other parts of it, especially the general part of the law of obligations and he gives four illustrations:

   (i) contributory negligence of the victim is regulated by § 254I of the BGB 'which makes the obligation to compensate the negligent plaintiff depend on how far the injury has been caused predominantly by the one or the other party (plaintiff/defendant)';

   (ii) the concept of unlawfulness is satisfied 'whenever one of the interests listed in § 823I of the BGB has been infringed in the absence of a legally recognised defence'. But, it is necessary to consult §§ 227–31 of the BGB and their interpretation by case law in order to determine whether the concept has been satisfied;

   (iii) paragraph 847 of the BGB allows monetary compensation for injuries to body or health, or for the deprivation of liberty. This forms an exception to the general rule in § 253 of the BGB which prohibits monetary compensation for harm which is not damage to property, unless otherwise provided by the Code;

   One of the questions which arises in connection with these provisions is whether § 847 can be extended by analogy to cover instances other than the ones for which it expressly provides for in the light of the phrasing of § 253;

   (iv) he also mentions § 278 of the BGB which imposes liability on an employer for the faults of his 'servants' or subcontractors, and has been used to avoid the effect of § 831 of the BGB by shifting the basis of the claim from tort to contract;

(c) the final caveat is directed to common lawyers – not to expect to find in German tort law all the material included in common law tort courses (see Markesinis (1990) pp 22–23).

In order to establish the concept of unlawfulness, according to Zweigert and Kotz (1987), this is satisfied by 'any invasion of one of the legal interests specified in § 823I of the BGB, provided it is not justified by one of the special privileges, for example, self-defence or necessity. They further suggest that culpability or fault is satisfied 'if the harmful conduct is either intentional, that is, accompanied by the intention of invading the protected legal interest, or negligent' (Zweigert and Kotz (1987) p 293). According to § 276 of the BGB, negligence means 'a want of that degree of care which is generally regarded as necessary in society'.

According to Zweigert and Kotz, the courts have applied § 826, the third general head of liability to 'a whole range of cases where one party has caused harm to another by behaviour so offensive and improper as to incur strong disapprobation from the average person in the relevant section of society' (Zweigert and Kotz (1987) p 297).

The experience gained from the case law in this area is that there are considerable areas left uncovered by these three heads of liability, such as gaps in the protection given to rights of personality and for pure economic harm which is negligently caused. The German courts have, therefore, been filling in the gaps and again we see how the courts have, in practice, taken a much more active 'law making' role, though they have proceeded on the basis of merely 'interpreting' the BGB provisions.

As far as injury to feelings is concerned, mere fright, anguish, 'normal' distress or grief which is occasioned by the accident will not be sufficient grounds for recovery of damages. In German law, nervous shock is, 'clearly, injury to health, in the sense of § 823I of the BGB, so long as it entails medically recognisable physical or psychological consequences which would not have been suffered by the ordinary, not over sensitive, citizen' (Markesinis (1990) p 35). As Markesinis points out, the problem of where to draw the line is being treated as a question of legal cause and is being approached increasingly as a matter of policy. The case law indicates that German courts are prepared to allow rights of recovery not just to eye witnessing relatives, but beyond this to persons who suffered trauma from hearing of an accident of a loved one or close relative, that is, cases of 'distant nervous shock'. However, recovery must be limited to cases of recognisable medical illness or nervous shock (see the Federal Supreme Court case reported in BGHZ 56, translated in English and fully discussed by Markesinis (1990) pp 95–103). This approach has been followed in a number of subsequent cases.

In another earlier case, the question was whether the defendants were liable for the plaintiff wife's nervous breakdown which she suffered upon receiving news of her son's death in an accident (see RGZ 133, 270: Markesinis (1990) pp 103–09). The Reichsgericht held, in 1931, that an action could lie, since the plaintiff's wife had suffered injury to her health as a result of the tort. Adequate causality was held to exist. German law has shown that it is prepared to adopt a more liberal view than either English or American law. French law is also fairly liberal in its approach to such cases. Occasionally, of course, an American case demands a suspension of disbelief as in the case of *Campbell v Animal Quarantine Station Station* (1981) 63 Haw 587, 632 P 2d 1066 (see p 324, above, under 'American law'), although animal lovers might well sympathise.

TORT LAW AND TRAFFIC ACCIDENTS

French law

Some brief observations may be made in connection with traffic accidents of one kind or another, as treated in different jurisdictions. In French law, if a collision occurs between a moving vehicle and a properly parked one, the presumption enacted by Art 1384(1) of the Civil Code will not attach to the 'custodian of the car'. However, if the collision occurs at night and the car was not adequately lit or happened to be parked in a place where visibility was poor, the stationary car could well be seen as a 'productive cause of the harm'. If a cyclist is injured by a collision with a van, she cannot sue the custodian of the van if, at the time of the accident, he was travelling at the proper speed on the correct side of the road: see Civ 26 Oct 1949 Gaz Pal 1950.1.79 and Civ 22 Jan 1940, S 1940.1.19. In the latter case (called the *Poyet* case), a car owned by the Société Montbarbon and driven by one Redt, at an excessive speed, suddenly blocked the road at a crossing causing Mr Poyet, who was approaching the crossing on his bicycle, to swerve sharply. There was no contact between Poyet and the car, but he fell from the bicycle and was killed. Having lost her action based on Art 1384 of the Code Civil, on the basis that Art 1384 does not apply unless there had been contact between the object and the victim, Mrs Poyet brought a *pourvoir en cassation* (application for review on legal grounds) to the Cour de Cassation. It was held that, as the absence of contact between the object in question and the damage does not necessarily exclude the causal connection, the decision should be quashed.

In cases where an automobile accident has been caused by something internal which the custodian could not have foreseen, such as a sudden failure of brakes or steering or a tyre exploding, the driver will still be liable for any harm or damage caused because the rules of *force majeure* demand that the event causing the accident must be external to the thing which causes the harm. It must be both unforeseeable and unavoidable in its consequences (see Zweigert and Kotz (1987) p 358).

Drivers falling unconscious at the wheel of the car have also been found liable for the consequences of their actions while still driving (see Civ 18

December 1964, D 1965, 191). This is similar to the English law approach (see 'English law', below). Many cases dealt with custodians of motor vehicles arguing that the unexpected occurrence of a patch of oil on a highway constituted *force majeure*. These claims were rarely accepted and were completely abolished by the Law on Traffic Accidents of 5 July 1985.

As a result of the *Desmares* case (Civ 21 July 1982, D 1982, 449), wherein the Cour de Cassation appeared to say that contributory negligence was irrelevant in reducing the amount of compensation payable, the Law of 85–677 of 5 July 1985 (cited above) was passed. Its main objective was to limit the extent to which the negligence of a traffic accident victim may reduce the amount of compensation payable under his claim for bodily injury or death. This sort of reduction is not permissible if the victim is under 16 or over 70 years old, or if he is at least 80% disabled. Claims may also be reduced if the accident was the inexcusable fault of the victim or the exclusive fault of the victim. But, if the victim is a driver, the law does not protect him. This gap in the law has been addressed by the introduction of a type of insurance marketed by the insurance industry covering drivers and their families.

It has been estimated by Tunc that the result of this legislation and insurance scheme has been that compensation in 85–90% of all accident cases have been awarded independent of the negligence of tortfeasor and victim (see Tunc, *Essays in Memory of Professor Lawson* (1986) p 71). Tort liability for traffic accidents is now largely replaced by a system of insurance protection (see Zweigert and Kotz (1987) p 360).

English law

English law utilises the same general law of tort in dealing with civil or private law claims for compensation for injury, damage or loss caused by traffic accidents. Hence, a duty of care must be held to exist and the usual requirements concomitant with this duty must be proved, on a balance of probabilities. The standard of care required of even a learner driver is that of an average, competently qualified driver (see *Nettleship v Weston* [1971] 2 QB 691). In the case of a driver who lost control of his car through suffering a cerebral haemorrhage which caused him to be unaware of what he was doing and incapable of driving properly, a strict liability approach was adopted and the court held the driver liable in negligence for colliding with another car (see *Roberts v Ramsbottom* [1980] 1 WLR 823). A truck driver has also been held liable for a defect in the brakes which no layman could possibly have discovered (see *Henderson v Jenkins & Sons* [1970] AC 282).

English law allows the defence of contributory negligence to reduce the amount of damages payable to the plaintiff where the plaintiff was also negligent to a certain extent. Under the Law Reform (Contributory

Negligence) Act 1945, damages may be reduced to the extent that the court thinks 'just and equitable having regard to the claimant's share in the responsibility for the damage'. Another possible defence to actions for negligence is the plea of *volenti non fit injuria* which means that a plaintiff is barred from bringing an action that arises from a situation to which he consented.

German law

German law relating to the custodian of a motor vehicle is contained in the Road Traffic Act 1952 and s 7(1) thereof states:

> If, in the course of the operation of a motor vehicle a person is killed ... or injured, or an object is damaged, the keeper of the motor vehicle is obliged to compensate the injured party for the damage resulting therefrom.

Section 7(2) goes on to declare that:

> The duty to compensate is excluded if the accident was caused by an unavoidable event which is not due to a defect in the construction of the vehicle or to the failure of its mechanism.

The provision explains further that an event is deemed to be unavoidable, in particular, if it is:

> ... due to the conduct of the injured party or an animal; and if both the keeper and driver have applied that care which is required in the light of the circumstances.

Hence, unforeseen and unavoidable failure of the parts of a vehicle, such as axle fracture, brake failure, a tyre defect or the seizing up of the steering, will not excuse the custodian or keeper of the vehicle. Liability will only be excluded 'if the accident is due to an "external" event such as the occurrence of black ice or an animal running in front of the vehicle or faulty driving on the part of other motorists' (Zweigert and Kotz (1987) p 349) and the defendant observed all the care necessary in the circumstances.

Liability will also be excluded, or the amount of compensation reduced, if an accident is attributable to:

(a) the behaviour of the victim; or

(b) of a third party not involved in the operation of the vehicle; or

(c) of an animal, and both the custodian and the driver of the vehicle have taken all the care called for in the particular circumstances (see s 9 of the Road Traffic Act 1952 and § 254 of the BGB).

The standard of 'all the care called for in the circumstances' has been described by a German court as 'care going beyond what is usually required ...

extreme and thoughtful concentration and circumspection' seems to be required (BGH VersR 1962, 164). This standard has been affirmed by several subsequent court decisions and, needless to say, is usually very difficult to prove to the satisfaction of the court. If the victim was partially at fault, damages will be reduced accordingly.

It is worth noting that injured passengers in a vehicle can only sue the custodian under the Road Traffic Act 1952 if they were being carried by way of business and for reward, for example, in a taxi or bus. In all other cases, injured passengers would have to use the general provisions of the law of tort or delict (§ 823 *et seq* of the BGB; see Zweigert and Kotz (1987) p 349).

The custodian of a motor vehicle must take out liability insurance in Germany and his victim is given a direct claim against the insurer and will have this right even if he has not insured the vehicle at all, or if the insurer is unidentifiable (in hit and run cases), or insolvent. It has long been demanded that the scope of the custodian's liability be extended (see Zweigert and Kotz (1987) p 377).

FAULT IN THE LAW OF CONTRACT AND TORT

The word 'fault' is derived from the French *faute* which is itself derived from the Latin verb *fallere*. The original meaning of that word was 'to deceive', but it later came to express the notion of failing in some way (see Lawson (1977) Vol II, p 348). Hence, 'fault' here appears to resemble 'default', which is rather vague and general in meaning. As Lawson neatly described it, '[the word] "fault" is not a term of art in the common law' (Lawson (1977) Vol II, p 347).

In the English Law Reform (Contributory Negligence) Act 1945, 'fault' is defined as meaning 'negligence, breach of statutory duty or other act or omission which gives rise to a liability in tort or would, apart from this Act, give rise to the defence of contributory negligence'.

'Fault' occurs rarely in the English common law of contract and features mainly in the sale of goods and in cases where the 'frustration of contract' is said to be self-induced (see 'Frustration of contract, impossibility and supervening events', p 317, above). On the other hand, apart from special cases, the general ground of liability in the civil law system is the fault (*dolus aut culpa*) of the defendant.

The 'duty of care' component, which is an integral part of the common law tort of negligence, is not explicitly stated in the Civil Law Codes. However, the continental courts have also had to face the problem of demarcating the boundaries of liability in delict. In dealing with omissions which cause physical damage to person or property, German law has treated this as governed by § 823 of the BGB. Pecuniary loss is recoverable only where it is a case of malice, and not merely negligence (§ 826 of the BGB).

In French law, *faute* is interpreted not merely as *culpa*, in the sense of negligence, but in the sense of wrongful. This approach approximates the English 'duty of care' characterisation. In French law, therefore, *faute* is a question of law, as duty of care is in English law, so that the judges in both systems have the discretion to delimit the scope of liability for damage resulting from a failure to act with reasonable care. Crucially, any fault which causes damage is actionable irrespective of whether it is a delictual or contractual obligation that has been breached. There is therefore a single concept of fault under French law, and Mazeaud and Tunc define *faute* as an error of conduct and stress that he who conducts himself in an anti-social manner will be at fault. Various writers have seen *faute* in French law as meaning a failure to observe a behavioural norm which the defendant should have respected, or as culpable behaviour on the part of the defendant (see Zweigert and Kotz (1977) p 286).

The justification of the concept of fault in the context of tort has been debated at great length by various commentators. Its advantages appear to be considerably outweighed by its disadvantages. Briefly, the case for retaining some notion of fault is derived from its moral logic, since it is generally accepted that a person should be answerable for the damage he has caused. There is a strong moral content to such a principle and, indeed, fault derives from the canon law notion of sin and the need for atonement for one's sins. Fault also seems necessary to social expectations and socially accepted standards of behaviour. If tort law is seen as a means of ensuring the balance between freedom of the individual and the duties and responsibilities which arise in modern society, then fault is the yardstick which can distinguish the boundaries of liability.

On the other hand, if we accept that the main function of tort is to compensate losses, there is no reason for retention of fault. Fault appears to be a condition of penal liability and should be used to label less serious conduct. In more realistic terms, the tortfeasor's capability to bear the loss, or to pay the compensation for the loss or damage caused, has come to the fore. The idea has grown, particularly in the field of industrial accidents, that the organisation or person best able to afford to pay compensation to the injured party, should be the one who should bear the costs of the loss suffered. Fault fails when confronted with modern technology because it is often the machinery that is really to blame, or because it causes harm which is unforeseeable and which no one could possibly have prevented. The position of the victim has also changed, since the value of the objects which he exposes to being damaged or destroyed is economically much higher. There are also much greater sums which are needed in modern times to compensate the victim for his loss of earnings, in the long and short term.

INTERACTION OF TORT AND CONTRACT

Many criticisms may be levelled at the continuing separation of tort from contract law. While one writer has said that 'contract is productive, tort law is protective' and that 'tortfeasors are typically liable for making things worse, contractors for not making them better', the following are some of the problems which Tunc (1974) has highlighted:

(a) in every country where the distinction has practical consequences, many cases appear not to follow the conventional dichotomy. One writer even called attention to what he labels 'hermaphrodites' (Stevens (1964) 27 MLR 121, p 161) where the cause of action fits either category. Application of the distinction in the common law is compounded by the uncertainty of the criterion;

(b) the complexity of the relationships between tortious and contractual liabilities has led to 'answers which vary from country to country and is itself a complex one in many countries';

(c) among the many criticisms that have been levelled at the distinction, French doctrinal writers have argued that, if you base liability upon fault, and define fault as a violation of a pre-existing legal obligation, there is no justification for distinguishing between tort and contract;

(d) it is often very difficult to say whether damage has been caused within or outside the scope of a contract (see Tunc, in *International Encyclopedia of Comparative Law* (1974) Vol XI, Chapter 1, pp 19–20).

In contrast, Tunc (1974) argues that the scope of the 'obligations' owed by persons in contractual and non-contractual relationships has to be considered carefully. Surely, contractual obligations are owed to persons who have entered into the contract, are involved in its negotiation stages and who might be beneficiaries under it. On the other hand, the 'obligation' of a driver is a general obligation owed to all persons who could be injured by his conduct. It is as different as the rights of ownership are in different situations – rights *in rem* and rights *in personam* – and different durations of limited rights exist, for instance, under bailment as opposed to full legal ownership in English law.

Tunc (1974) therefore advocates not fusion, but unification of the rules of tort and contract, leaving them in separate fields, but making the consequences of liability identical whether liability existed from a breach of a contract or from a tort. The only qualification which he would advocate is that the law should respect any agreement which may have been made between the parties, provided it is not contrary to public policy. He recognises that such agreements would be usual in contractual liability, and exceptional in tortious liability. However, it is possible that the potential perpetrator of a possible private nuisance (or abuse of right) may agree to pay a periodical and reasonable indemnity to the person inconvenienced by his operations and, on the basis of 'assumption of risks', this might be a way of ensuring that all parties reach a satisfactory compromise (see Tunc (1974) p 28).

In fact, some modern systems have already moved toward effecting a desirable fusion in, for example, the English legal system, by allowing plaintiffs a choice of contractual or tortious remedies. The English courts are also beginning to assimilate the rules on remoteness of damage. The Warsaw Convention 1929 and the Brussels International Convention for the Unification of Certain Rules Relating to Carriage of Passengers by Sea (Art 10-1) specifically submit all suits to the same rules. The duality of divisions and regimes has also been rejected by the Czechoslovakian 1950 and 1964 Civil Codes, and the Senegal Code of Civil and Commercial Obligations 1963 has also abandoned the strictness of the old rules, by stating that fault refers to the failure to satisfy a pre-existing obligation, whatever be its nature.

As far as English law is concerned, the differences between 'obligations assumed and [those which are] imposed' (Weir) are being constantly whittled away. Five factors have been identified by Fridman (1977) as responsible for this process:

(a) the rise of the concept of restitution or unjust enrichment, including the idea or practice of 'waiver of tort';

(b) the emergence of a common law remedy for innocent misrepresentation;

(c) the possibility of using *volenti non fit injuria* in a contractual situation to provide a way of avoiding the privity of contract and consideration straitjackets in relation to exemption clauses upon persons not parties to the contract, but who wish to claim its benefit;

(d) the 'advent and extension' of the collateral warranty doctrine which has both contractual and tortious overtones;

(e) the doctrine of promissory estoppel, which, despite contractual roots, has links with principles originating from tort (see Fridman (1977) pp 436–37).

In contrast, Professor Markesinis argues that, particularly in the light of American developments in this area, the common law tort solutions to problems involving an overlap between tort and contract should not be abandoned, but that contract law should be expanded with tort correspondingly restricted (see Markesinis (1987) p 397). No doubt, the debates will continue between various comparatists. In many respects, of course, the struggle to find some sort of compromise between the two branches is symptomatic of a rapidly changing society which is seeking more progressive solutions and modern policies to cope with everyday problems, while attempting to free itself from the philosophical and historical shackles of a bygone age.

COMPARATIVE OVERVIEW

As our comparative survey indicates, there is clearly some basis for saying that, just as civil law places the divisions of contract and tort within a single law of obligations, the common law has also succeeded in blurring the edges of the distinction between tort and contract in a variety of contexts, not least in the area of 'economic torts'.

As far as the formation of contractual obligations is concerned, the analysis of contract in terms of offer and acceptance is basically similar in common law and civil law systems. However, individual problems are not solved in the same way in each jurisdiction. Theoretical differences and the different approaches to commercial and non-contractual contracts in the civil law systems have produced different rules and different results. An offer in France is seen as continuing indefinitely if it is not withdrawn, but in commercial contracts, the offer lapses after a reasonable time. In Germany, every offer is irrevocable unless the offeror has excluded the binding effect of his proposal.

With regard to the so called *indicia* of seriousness in the civil law, French law and other Romanistic systems have flirted with *causa* or cause, as the criterion for distinguishing legally binding transactions from non-legally binding transactions and German law has used the construction of the transaction approach. An important observation is that in the civil law countries, despite the general statements of rules and purported definitions, the application of the law in practice is very much the province of the courts, so that recourse to cases has become ever more significant. English law continues to utilise its much criticised consideration doctrine, but the nature of its detailed rules generally allows some scope for judicial discretion.

In the field of tort, there are many similarities in approach between civil law and common law jurisdictions, particularly in the requirement of a certain standard of care which must be exercised in order to found liability for unintentional harm, and the ubiquitous influence of the industrial revolution. On the question of intentional harm, the common law has proceeded by having specific torts, and continental legal systems categorise particular groups of cases utilising a general clause.

If any appreciable harmonisation of legal systems ever takes place, the legal categories of tort and contract will arguably be one of the most easily adaptable. If the law's clear policy is to provide a remedy in those cases where a breach of a legal rule or norm has occurred, this could be done far more simply by adopting this principle as an explicit policy, and using the contract/tort dichotomy purely as a means of identifying the source of the legal obligation. In this way, particularly in the common law, the ghosts of the past will be exorcised forever and enable claimants to obtain legal redress or compensation more expeditiously and more frequently.

SELECTIVE BIBLIOGRAPHY

A – *Tortious obligations/delictual liability*

Amos and Walton, *Introduction to French Law* (1967)

Catala and Weir, 'Delict and torts: a study in parallel' (1963) 37 Tulane L Rev 573; (1964) 38 Tulane L Rev 701

Dias and Markesinis, *Tort Law* (1989)

Holmes, *The Common Law* (1881) Lecture III

Holyoak, 'Tort and contract after *Junior Books*' (1983) 99 LQR 591

Horn, Kotz and Leser, *German Private and Commercial Law* (1982)

Kahn-Freund, Levy and Rudden, *A SourceBook on French Law* (1991)

Lawson and Markesinis, *Tortious Liability for Unintentional Harm in the Common Law and the Civil Law* (1982) Vols I and II

Lawson, *A Common Lawyer Looks at the Civil Law* (1953)

Lawson, *Many Laws* (1977) Vols I and II

Lawson, *Negligence in the Civil Law* (1950)

Markesinis, 'An expanding tort law – the price of a rigid contract law' (1987) 103 LQR 354

Markesinis, *The German Law of Torts* (1990); 3rd edn (1994)

Tunc, in *International Encyclopedia of Comparative Law* (1974) Vol X1, Chap 1

Weir, in *International Encyclopedia of Comparative Law* (1976) Vol X1, Chap 12

Williams, 'The foundation of tortious liability' (1939–41) 7 CLJ 111

Winfield and Jolowicz, in Rogers (ed), *Law of Tort,* 13th edn (1989)

Winfield, 'The history of negligence in the law of torts' (1926) 42 LQR 184

Zweigert and Kotz, *An Introduction to Comparative Law* (1987) Vol II; 3rd edn (1998)

B – *Contractual obligations*

Amos and Walton, *Introduction to French Law* (1967)

Atiyah, *An Introduction to the Law of Contract* (1979)

Atiyah, *The Rise and Fall of Freedom of Contract* (1979)

Atiyah and Summers, *Form and Substance in Anglo-American Law* (1987)

Buckland and McNair, *Roman Law and Common Law* (1952)

Cheshire and Fifoot, in Furmston (ed), *The Law of Contract* (1990)

Cohn, *Manual of German Law* (1968) Vol I, Chap 3

Cook and Oughton, *The Common Law of Obligations* (1989)

de Cruz, 'A comparative survey of the doctrine of frustration' [1982] Legal Issues of European Integration 51

Dean, 'Unfair contract terms: the European approach' (1993) 56 MLR 581

Fridman, 'The Interaction of tort and contract' (1977) 93 LQR 422

Marsh, *Comparative Contract Law: England, France, Germany* (1994)

Nicholas, *French Law of Contract* (1992)

Nicholas, *Introduction to Roman Law* (1962)

O'Connor, *Good Faith in English Law* (1990)

Owsia, 'The notion and function of offer and acceptance under French and English law' (1992) 66 Tulane L Rev 871

Parry, *The Changing Conception of Contracts in English Law* (1958)

Pound, 'Promise or bargain?' (1959) 33 Tulane L Rev 455

Tallon and Harris, *Contract Law Today* (1989)

Treitel, *Remedies in Contract* (1988)

Trietel, *The Law of Contract* (1987)

Whincup, *Contract Law and Practice: the English System and Continental Comparisons* (1990); 3rd edn (1996)

Zweigert and Kotz, *An Introduction to Comparative Law* (1977) Vol II; 3rd edn (1998)

CHAPTER 11

CORPORATE AND COMMERCIAL LAW

SCOPE OF ANALYSIS

Of the major legal families in the world today, it is the Romano-Germanic jurisdictions and common law jurisdictions that have played dominant roles in the development of a company law ethos. Company law has sometimes been subsumed within the broader category of commercial law, as in the German system. In the former Soviet system, for most of its legal history right up until 1992, the category of commercial law has not featured in the Soviet classification of divisions of law, primarily because of its basic ideology. However, in the light of the dramatic changes which took place between 1990 and 1991, and which have resulted in the disintegration of Communist rule in the former Soviet Union, it is likely that a distinct branch of law known as 'commercial law' may soon develop in the Russian Federation, if their moves toward a capitalist economy eventually prove successful. We shall concentrate on European company law (specifically, France, Germany and EC company law) and contrast this with English company law, for the following reasons. First, it is within Europe that a greater concentration of dominant legal systems can be found. Secondly, the institutions of the European Community (EC) have brought a new dimension to the field of company law. The programme of harmonisation promoted by the EC has the long term goal of creating a new environment for companies at international level as envisaged by Art 54(3) of the Treaty of Rome. Other EC initiatives will also result in more European companies and firms being involved in closer inter-country contact than ever before.

A preliminary point needs to be made regarding our comparative overview of the substantive provisions of these selected jurisdictions. The rules governing company law in France, Germany and England are extremely detailed and overlaid with many subrules and principles. These are primarily there to provide a framework for business enterprise and exigencies, not to be carefully scrutinised in every particular. Thus, we shall focus on certain basic rules and concepts which operate in each of these jurisdictions, with comparative commentary where appropriate. Our coverage will necessarily be selective but is intended to give a flavour of the laws as well as to present an overview.

We also undertake a brief comparative survey of agency or representation in civil and common law countries before examining the shape of EC corporate law. We begin, however, by highlighting some general pitfalls of which we should be wary when undertaking a comparison of company laws.

PROBLEMS IN COMPARISON OF COMPANY LAWS

Several caveats need to be made about the study of different European company laws as with other comparative analyses of substantive topics which have developed in different legal families. These may be summarised as:

(a) terminological;

(b) conceptual;

(c) underlying similarities despite differing terminology; and

(d) systemic.

The terminological caveat refers to the fact that, even if the same term is used to describe a feature or institution of a branch of law, the term can refer to different things, despite the similarity in terminology.

The conceptual caveat refers to the fact that, although legal concepts may exist in every country, these may be understood differently; an example is the concept of share capital.

The third caveat refers to underlying similarities which may exist in spite of *ex facie* differences; for example, although certain countries do not recognise the distinction between authorised and issued share capital, most European countries have the power to issue new shares although this power may be regulated by time limits or by different parties.

The final caveat deals with systemic problems arising from the nature of the legal system of the country where the company is formed or operates. Obviously, where, for example, there is a fused profession, only one legal practitioner may be dealing on behalf of a company. In England, therefore, it may be necessary to be aware of the different functions of a particular legal representative so that a company is aware of the legal ramifications of his actions in relation to the company.

KEY CONCEPTUAL QUESTIONS

Drury and Xuereb (1991) suggest that an analytical framework which goes beyond mere descriptive analysis is required if one is to discover how different systems solve particular problems and why certain solutions are appropriate for one system but not for another. They argue that the underlying concepts, policy considerations and assumptions of each system need to be addressed before the real nature and relative importance of key matters within each system can be properly understood. Among the key conceptual questions that have dominated the study of company law are:

what is a company?; is there a contractual relationship between persons intending to form a company, pre-registration/incorporation?; what are the theories that have underpinned the study of the company?

The significance of these questions will be familiar to company lawyers but it should be noted that, during the last 30 years, we have witnessed a dramatic change in the concept of the company, originating in France. The latest approach is to view the company as the entity that provides a legal structure for the enterprise. Under this new approach, it is no longer critical to determine whether the company is a contract or an institution but rather to ask: what are the social and economic characteristics of that enterprise which has been set up by law? (See Paillusseau in Drury and Xuereb (1991).) Nevertheless, in order to place the new developments in historical and comparative perspective, it is instructive to examine the 'contract theory' and 'institution theory'.

The contract theory is predicated on the basis that 'the company is a contract whereby two or more individuals agree to put something in common, with a view to sharing the possible profits'. This was the definition derived from Roman law, as contained in Art 1832 of the French Civil Code and various other definitions subsequently enshrined in the Italian Civil Code (Art 2247), the Swiss Code of Obligations (Art 530) and the Civil Code of Belgium (Art 1832). This definition endured in France until it was first amended in 1978 and then decisively in 1985 when the Act of 11 July 1985 introduced the one man company in France. The new form of words now reads:

> The société is instituted by two or more persons who agree by way of a contract to combine their assets or their labour in a common enterprise with a view to sharing the profits or benefiting from the savings which result.

A société can be created in the situations provided for by statute, by the voluntary act of a single individual.

This appears to signify a move towards regarding the company as an institution. It is pertinent to note that the word 'société' in French law covers both companies and partnerships. Nevertheless, the words 'contrat de société' have been translated as the 'company contract'. In any event, as soon as the company is registered in France, it becomes a legal entity (see Art 1842 of the Code Civil) and only 'silent partnerships' are not legal entities. It is the judicial conception of the company as a legal entity that has shaped the development of the corporate contract. For example, in 1945 and 1956, the Cour de Cassation acknowledged the legal personality of enterprise committees and of a bankrupt's estate. Hence, the two main consequences of this contract theory are:

(a) the corporate contract creates the company whereby the group of individuals who wish to combine their assets is formed. The group becomes the legal entity when it is registered as a company;

(b) the company is therefore a contract; this organisation is to be effected by the parties themselves and their organisation can only be contractual.

The institution theory stresses the predominance of the legal person over the contract. The company is, as Hauriou puts it:

> ... a concept of work or enterprise which takes shape and has a legal existence in a social environment. To implement this idea, an authority is established which provides the enterprise with organs. In other respects, between the members of the social group concerned with the realisation of the idea, some manifestations of their common will are produced which are directed by the duly empowered organs and regulated by their procedures.

The new conceptual approach has been described by Paillusseau as 'a technique for the organisation of the enterprise'. However, it seems more illuminating to describe it as the legal and institutional framework for the organisation of the commercial enterprise. The notion of the 'enterprise' is apparent not just in French company law but also in its labour law, tax law, accountancy law and competition law. At the pragmatic level, it is clear that the advent of the one man company in French law has rendered the traditional concept of company law obsolete. What exactly is the 'enterprise'?

Paillusseau's enterprise notion

The concept of enterprise, as developed by Paillusseau, has two main features:

(a) the enterprise as a business; and

(b) the enterprise as a focus of interests.

The enterprise as a business would therefore include the production, transformation and distribution of goods, or the supply of services, or some of these features. As with most businesses, it would also include a range of resources, skills, finance, contracts, planning strategies, and decision making procedures.

The enterprise as a focus of interests would assume a particular size, range and complexity depending on the nature of the enterprise, and would inevitably include not just those of the founder or creator of the enterprise. Creditors, partners, shareholders, moneylenders and managers would invariably come into the picture and the unique nature of the enterprise would dictate the role of entrepreneur.

The law provides the statutory framework for the enterprise's structure, functioning, financing, decision making procedures, sale, reorganisation and winding up. Paillusseau suggests five main lines of intervention by the law in determining respective rights and levels of protection to be accorded to parties having an interest in the enterprise. These are:

(a) the protection of different interest groups by means of the dissemination of information;

(b) increasing the rights and protection accorded to certain categories of individuals;

(c) protection of different interest groups through the concept and structure of the company;

(d) using company law to establish an 'institutional equilibrium' between the different interest groups; and

(e) external protection of different interest groups.

In each legal system, the amount of State intervention and State regulation will vary according to the nature, complexity and extent of the interests involved, and it is still accurate to say that the role of contract remains relevant to those situations where parties are capable of a greater degree of self-regulation.

FORMS OF BUSINESS ORGANISATION: A COMPARATIVE OVERVIEW

Corporate terminology in France and Germany

'Company' and 'partnership'

In the continental systems, one term may cover both companies and partnerships in the European continental systems, namely, the French term 'société' or the German term 'Gesellschaft'.

The two main forms of business organisation in Western Europe are:

(a) the partnership where some or all of the members are responsible for the liabilities of the business; and

(b) the limited company, where none of the members has personal liability for the company's debts.

Public and private companies

There are two basic types of limited company in Latin and Germanic countries, namely, the 'share' company (société anonyme (SA): French; Aktiengesellschaft (AG): German) and the limited liability company (société a responsabilité limitée (SARL): French; and Gesellschaft mit beschrankter Haftung (GmBH): German).

The continental 'share' company finds its strict English equivalent in the registered company limited by shares which may be public or private. However, despite the term 'public', the shares are not publicly held or necessarily listed on the Stock Exchange; they need not be held by the public, although they might well be so held.

The difference between share companies and limited liability companies on the continent is distinguishable by utilising a different designation for each type of company. Similarly, in England, under s 25(2) of the Companies Act 1985, the last word of a private company's name must be 'limited' or 'Ltd'. This gives notice to persons dealing with the company that they will not have access to the private funds of the members to satisfy the company's debts. A partnership must not end with the term 'Limited'. Under s 25(1)of the same Act, a public company's name must end with the words 'Public Limited Company' or 'plc'. There is a facility for certain companies in England to dispense with the term 'Limited' for example a private company limited by guarantee (see s 30 of the Companies Act 1985 (UK)).

The English approach to company law

Meaning of 'company' in English company law

A company is an association or organisation with a legal personality distinct from that of the human members who control and administer the organisation. The inclusion of the name 'company' in an association's title does not necessarily mean it is a registered company; the mere adoption of the word carries no legal consequences. When a company is registered, it becomes in law a separate legal entity from its members and this is a fundamental principle of English company law which was established by the English House of Lords in the case of *Salomon v Salomon & Co* [1897] AC 27. The significance of this case is discussed further below. For the moment, it should be noted that the corporate personality is referred to as the 'veil of incorporation' and its members are generally shielded from the legal consequences of the company's actions. However, there are several situations in which the law is prepared to 'lift the veil' of incorporation which are also discussed below (see pp 350–51, below).

Sources of law

English company law is to be found in several companies Acts (Companies Acts of 1948, 1967, 1976, 1980, 1981, 1985, 1989) as well as in the European Communities Act 1972, delegated legislation and stock exchange regulations with regard to listed companies. As is the classic common law style, fundamental governing rules and principles were to be found in case law, which were gleaned from judicial pronouncements, but these have been increasingly supplemented by a mass of legislation and regulation, which have, in turn, been subjected to judicial interpretation which have modified some of the more antiquated principles of law.

Types of business units in the United Kingdom

There are three main types of business units in the United Kingdom, that is:

(a) registered companies;

(b) partnerships; and

(c) sole traders.

Types of companies

There are three types of companies in Britain at the present time:

(a) public corporations;

(b) chartered companies; and

(c) registered companies.

The public corporations are the nationalised industries, such as British Rail and British Gas, which were created and are regulated by their own Act of Parliament so that they do not register under the Companies Act 1985 like registered companies. They are not subject to the control of the shareholders, since there are no shareholders or board of directors.

With the current British Government's privatisation policies, these types are becoming increasingly extinct and there is a question as to whether there will be any such companies left in Britain by the end of the 20th century.

Chartered companies used to be created by Royal Charter, that is, by the power of the Crown, but Royal Charters are no longer used to create trading companies, but are confined to universities and professional organisations, such as chartered accountants and surveyors.

Registered companies, which form the majority of trading associations in the United Kingdom, are created by registration under the Companies Act 1985 and are usually classified by either:

(a) the method by which their liability is limited; or

(b) depending on whether they are public or private.

Methods by which liability may be limited

The two main methods by which liability may be limited are:

(a) by shares;

(b) by guarantee.

Public and private companies

A public company is defined by the Companies Act 1985 as a company limited by shares and guarantee and where:

(a) the Memorandum states that the company is a public limited company;

(b) the company has at least two members;

(c) the name of the company ends in 'plc';

(d) the company has an authorised (nominal) share capital of not less than £50,000.

A private company is not defined in the Companies Act 1985 but, under s 1 of the Act, a private company is any company which is not a public company. Thus, any company which does not fall within the definition of a public company is a private company.

Consequences of incorporation

The most significant effect of incorporation is that the company becomes in law a separate legal entity and becomes a legal personality distinct, and therefore separate, from the members of the company: *Salomon v Salomon* (above). The case also established that the 'one man company' is a legally recognised entity and that incorporation was available to small and large businesses. Thus:

(a) as a result of the separate legal personality theory, the company can make contracts on its own behalf and neither the benefits nor the burdens of such contracts can be claimed by its members. This is the result of the privity of contract doctrine;

(b) the company has contractual capacity and can sue and be sued in its own name;

(c) perpetual succession of the company is possible; the death or incapacity of its members will have no effect on the company or its property. Even if all its shareholders are dead, the company must be put through a 'winding up' procedure if it is sought to dissolve it legally;

(d) the company may own property in its own right, so that the members only have a right to shares in the company but own no direct interest; members are precluded from having any insurable assets in the assets of the company (for example, in the *Macaura* case (1925), the one man owner of the company had no right to claim under an policy when the company owned estate suffered damage by fire, since he had the policy not in the company's name but his own);

(e) under the limited liability principle, the members are not liable for the company's debts if it was a limited company; members would be personally liable for the company's debts if it was an unlimited company.

Companies and contracts

Pre-incorporation contracts

The basic English law rule is that a contract (so called pre-incorporation contracts) made on behalf of a company in the course of its formation but before its formation (or incorporation) does not bind the company. It cannot therefore be ratified by the company after ratification. In *Kelner v Baxter* (1866), a company was about to be formed for the purpose of purchasing a hotel. Before the company was formed, the promoters signed a contract 'on behalf of' the proposed company for the purchase of a quantity of wine. The company was formed, and the hotel was purchased. The wine was also delivered and consumed, but the company then went into liquidation before payment for the wine had been made. The court held that the promoters should be held personally liable for payment of the wine. Any purported ratification by the company, therefore, had no legal effect.

Persons purporting to contract on behalf of the company

Under s 36C of the Companies Act 1985, where a contract purports to be made by a company, or by a person as agent for a company, at a time when the company has not been formed, then, subject to any agreement to the contrary, the contract will take effect as if it had been entered into by the person purporting to act for the company or as agent for it, and he is personally liable on the contract. This section effectively abolishes any distinction that might have existed at common law between signing as an agent of the company and signing to authenticate the signature of the company.

However, a promoter may protect himself from the statutory personal liability imposed by s 36C, by:

(a) agreeing that the promoters' liability shall cease when the company enters into a similar agreement, after incorporation; or

(b) by agreeing that, if the company does not enter into such an agreement within a fixed period, either part may rescind the contract.

Public company trading before issue of certificate

A public company may not commence trading before it has obtained a certificate of compliance with the capital requirements of public companies under s 117 of the Companies Act 1985. This, rather than the certificate of incorporation, is the 'birth certificate' of the English public company. However, if a public company does commence business in contravention of s 117 (above), the transaction will *prima facie* be valid, unless the company fails to comply with its obligations within 21 days of being called upon to do so. Its directors will then be liable to indemnify the other party, if he suffers loss as a result of the company's failure to comply. The company and its officers may also be fined. Clearly, in these circumstances, the law is prepared to 'lift the veil' of incorporation (see, also, below) and go behind the company facade.

Company auditors

The Companies Act 1989 introduces new rules regarding the auditing of a company. They seek to ensure that only persons who are properly supervised and appropriately qualified are appointed company auditors and that audits are carried out in a proper manner and with integrity and independence. The two types of supervisory bodies established under the Act are: (a) Recognised Supervisory Bodies (RSBs) of which all company auditors must be members; and (b) Recognised Qualifying Bodies (RQBs) which will offer the professional qualifications required to become a member of an RSB. The same body can be both a RSB and a RQB. However, the existing professional bodies, such as the Chartered Association of Certified Accountants and the Institute of Chartered Accountants, will probably fulfil both functions.

Under the RSBs' rules, auditing must be carried out properly and with integrity. Two areas have been highlighted by a Department of Trade and Industry consultative document, namely:

(a) the standards of performance of the audit, and compliance with approved auditing guidelines; and

(b) general ethical standards, including rules dealing with independence, objectivity and client confidentiality. Eligible persons who carry out audits must also continue to maintain an appropriate level of competence.

Under English common law, auditors may be liable to the company for loss of dividends if, despite their suspicions, they accept an explanation from an officer of the company (such as a managing director) without undertaking any further investigation (see *Re Thomas Gerrard* [1967] 2 All ER 525, where the auditors were found guilty of negligence and breach of duty under s 333(1) of the Companies Act 1948). If auditors believe that entries in, or omissions from, the books give rise to suspicions, they must make a full investigation into the circumstances (see *Fomento v Selsdon* [1958] 1 All ER 11, where the House of Lords held that auditors were entitled to information relating to certain types of refills of writing instruments, even though they did not appear to be items which were strictly covered by the particular deed of terms).

Lifting the veil of incorporation

Despite the principle that the separate corporate personality of a company prevents outsiders from taking action against the members of a company, so that the members are shielded behind this 'veil of incorporation', there are several examples of cases where the law is prepared to 'lift the veil' or to 'pierce the veil' so as to go behind the corporate personality. This means they will either discover who were the individual members responsible for the particular act or be able to ignore the separate corporate personality of several companies and proceed against the economic entity constituted by the group as a whole. Examples of such instances include:

(a) cases of fraudulent or wrongful trading: s 213(1A) and s 214(1A) of the Companies Act 1985;

(b) cases of individuals using the company to evade their legal obligations (see *Goodwin v Birmingham City FC* (1980));

(c) cases involving holding and subsidiary companies.

In several instances, such as the presentation of financial statements, the companies in a group have been treated as one legal entity. Other examples are where the courts have held that the holding company and its subsidiaries really constitute a single commercial entity: see *DHN Food Distributors v Tower Hamlets LBC* [1976] 3 All ER 462; and where, on the particular facts of the case, the company and its manager have been treated de jure as one person where this was the de facto position: see *Goodwin v Birmingham City FC* (1980). The modern tendency appears to be that courts are more willing to 'lift the veil of incorporation' than hitherto.

Partnership law

Partnership companies

Under s 8A of the Companies Act 1985, it has become easier to set up partnership companies, since such a company is defined therein as 'a company limited by shares whose shares are intended to be held to a substantial extent by, or or behalf of, its employees'.

Differences between partnerships and companies

Under s 1 of the Partnership Act 1890, a partnership is defined as a 'relation which subsists between persons carrying on a business in common with a view to profit'. 'Business' includes any trade, occupation or profession. There are several important differences between partnerships and companies in English law:

(a) A partnership may be created by the express or implied agreement of the partners, and no special formalities are required. Hence, they may be created by conduct, orally or, as is usual, by writing. A company is created by registration under the Companies Act 1985.

(b) A partnership incurs far less expenses than a company from the stage of formation, throughout its life and upon dissolution.

(c) A partnership is not a separate legal person but, as with a company, it may sue and be sued in the firm's name. The partners are personally liable on the firm's contracts but there is no limitation placed on their contractual capacity; such limitations are sometimes written into a company's memorandum and Articles of Association. A company is a separate legal person which may make contracts and, of course, sue and be sued in the company's name.

(d) The liability of a general partner is unlimited, although it is possible for one or more partners to limit their liability. There must, however, be one general partner remaining. A company's liability may be limited by shares or by guarantee. But, limited liability may not be of any practical value for small companies whose directors or majority shareholders will have to give a personal guarantee for loans that are advanced.

(e) Partners have the power to sell goods or personal chattels of the firm, since they own the property of the firm jointly and severally. Companies may, of course, hold property in their own name.

(f) A partnership has confidential accounts, whereas a company is obliged to file accounts at the Company Registry where they are available for public inspection, and accounts for most companies must be submitted to an annual audit.

(g) There is no free transferability of shares for a partnership, and the agreement of all the partners is required before shares may be transferred. A partner may assign the right to his share of the profits but the assignee does not thereby become a partner.

(h) A partnership should generally not have more than 20 persons in a firm, apart from exceptions, such as solicitors, accountants, auctioneers and estate agents. A company must have a minimum of two members but there is no maximum.

(i) All partners are entitled to share in management, unless there is provision to the contrary in the partnership agreement. Members of a partnership who are not managers are still liable as though they were. Only those members of a company who become directors may take part in its management.

(j) A partner is an agent of his co-partners, and may, therefore, bind the firm in contract, provided the contract falls within the scope of the partnership business. A member of a company is not *prima facie* an agent of the company and thus cannot bind the company in contract.

(k) Partners may agree on their own arrangements for drawings of profit and capital, whereas company law requires that dividends may only be declared out of profits, so that there is maintenance of issued capital.

(l) Partnerships have the right to make their own arrangements for the management and organisation of the firm and may carry on any business they wish. A company is fairly tightly regulated in its powers and duties by the Companies Acts; its constitution is clearly laid down in its Memorandum of Association and its internal rules are contained in its Articles of Association.

(m)A partnership may publicise as little or as much as it wishes of its management details, whereas a company has to give far greater publicity to its directorate, charges on its assets and its financial position generally.

(n) A partnership often finds borrowing difficult, since no floating charges are possible, whereas companies generally find borrowing easier.

(o) A partnership ends on the death of a partner, unless there is a specific agreement to the contrary and provision for new members. A company is an artificial and discrete legal entity which is capable of perpetual succession, which may continue irrespective of a change in its members or management.

In English law, therefore, there are many significant differences between partnerships and companies, and each term has its own legal, economic, philosophical and political significance. Of course, the company and the partnership are both means of carrying on a business and the benefits of incorporation (such as a separate legal personality and limited liability) must be weighed against the more intimate relationship of mutual trust and confidence that is more typical of partnerships.

Relevance of partnership to agency

The central feature of a partnership is agency. The English courts have established that the liability of a partner for the acts of his co-partner is similar to the liability of a principal for the acts of his agent. Agency is the relationship which arises whenever one person (the agent) acts (or purports to have the authority to act) on behalf of another person (the principal) and has the power to alter or affect the principal's legal position in relation to the third party. The most important feature of agency is, therefore, the agent's power to alter the legal relationship between the principal and a third party. This can be done by making contracts on the principal's behalf or by disposing of the principal's property.

A crucial distinction is made in English law between the agent's actual authority and his apparent authority.

Actual authority is the authority which the agent actually holds, based on consent between agent and principal, where the principal authorises the agent to act on his behalf, expressly or impliedly; or by operation of law.

Apparent (or 'ostensible') authority is the authority which an agent appears to hold. This may mean either any authority which an agent appears to have (based on the maxim: 'apparent authority is the real authority') or authority which appears to exist but did not, in fact, exist. In this second sense, apparent authority is a form of estoppel, which is pleaded by showing:

(a) a representation was made;

(b) reliance was made on that representation;

(c) alteration of the plaintiff's position took place as a result of that reliance.

Under s 5 of the Partnership Act 1890 (PA), every partner is an agent of the firm and his other partners, for the purposes of the business of the partnership. It indicates that a partner's apparent authority is confined to acts which are connected with the business of the kind carried on by the firm and performed in the usual way. Whether or not a partnership will be bound by a particular act is a question of fact in every case. The test adopted by the courts is an 'objective test'; meaning that the courts would ask whether a reasonable man dealing with the firm would be put on inquiry as to the authority of the active partner who was dealing with the matter in hand (see *Mercantile Credit Co Ltd v Garrod* [1962] 3 All ER 1103).

Company law in France

Types of business organisations

Anyone wishing to carry on a business in France may do so either as a sole trader (enterprise individuelle) or through a corporate body (société) or as a GIE (Groupement d'Intérêt économique), commercial associations which are business entities peculiar to French law. While the sole trader is the simplest form of business organisation, wherein no distinction is made between the capital of the business and that of the trader, the société has a separate legal personality, so there is a distinction between the private capital of its participants and the business capital of the corporate body or company. The liability of the participants for the debts of the société may or may not be limited, depending on its type. Corporate bodies may therefore be divided into two groups depending on the different liability of the participants in each group:

(i) limited liability companies (sociétés de capitaux); and

(ii) partnerships of various kinds where members have unlimited liability for the debts of the société (sociétés de personnes) (see below).

However, although the first type of company corresponds to the English-style limited liability company, and the second is similar to partnerships in English law, there is far less precision in the criteria for the division of these different types of business enterprises. Unlike English law, French law makes a distinction between commercial partnerships and companies (sociétés commerciales) and civil partnerships and companies (sociétés civiles). Different rules will apply depending on whether the société is classified as commerciale or civile. Under Art 1 of the Law of 24 July 1966:

> ... the following forms of société are sociétés commerciales (SA), regardless of their objects: société anonyme, société a responsabilité limitée (SARL), société en nom collectif, société en commandite simple and société en commandite par actions.

Other sociétés will be classified as commercial or civil in accordance with their stated objects.

The following are considered sociétés de capitaux, where the key distinguishing feature is the pooling of capital:

(a) société anonyme (SA), which is the closest in characteristics to an English company;

(b) société en commandite par actions (SCA), which is a partnership limited by shares.

In contrast, those commercial enterprises which are primarily characterised as associations of persons (sociétés de personnes) are:

(a) société en nom collectif (general commercial partnership);

(b) société en commandite simple (limited partnership);

(c) société en participation (undisclosed/sleeping partnership);

(d) société civile (civil partnership).

A French société is based on a contractual agreement, irrespective of whether it is a civil or commercial société.

The SARL (société a responsabilité limitée) is modelled on the German GmbH (see below) and resembles a société à capitaux, although not classified as such. The problem in classification derives from the fact that the capital of an SARL is divided into parts sociales (non-negotiable shares), as it is in a general partnership, and yet the liability of its members is limited to their contributions, which is the same as shareholders in an SA. It is therefore something of a hybrid société.

The société commerciale is now largely subject to mandatory rules and, since 1985, all registration applications for société commerciales have to be made directly to a business formalities centre (centre de formalités des enteprises) which now exists in most départements. The purpose of such a centre is to convey information about the société to the appropriate government authorities, including the greffier of the société's local tribunal de commerce (commercial court). The greffier, which is technically translated as registrar, is an officer of the court who assists judges at court hearings and performs various administrative duties but undertakes no judicial functions. Greffiers are, therefore, not 'registrars' in the English courts' sense, but civil servants. Their functions are closer to 'clerks of the court' in English courts and, among their duties will be to publish the relevant announcement informing the public of the formation of the société commerciale in the *Bulletin Official des Annonces Civiles et Commerciales* (the equivalent of the *Official Gazette*).

No French company may be incorporated for more than 99 years although on the first expiry of this period, its term may be extended by special resolution but for no longer than one other period of 99 years. The French doctrine of *ultra vires* is more restricted in its scope than the English equivalent, although the United Kingdom Companies Act 1989 has greatly reduced the extent of the divergence.

Legislative sources of law

In typical civil law style, the sources of law for the French droits des sociétés are to be found in Codes and legislative enactments. The three main statutes relating to French sociétés are:

(a) Commercial Companies Law (Loi sur les Sociétés Commerciales) 66.537 of 24 July 1966;

(b) Commercial Companies Decree (Decret sur les Sociétés Commerciales) 67.236 of 23 March 1967; and

(c) The General Companies Rules (Dispositions Generales sur les Sociétés) of the Civil Code: Bk III, Title IX, Arts 1832–44.

The first two pieces of legislation apply only to sociétés commerciales and the third applies to sociétés civiles generally and to sociétés commerciales to the extent that they are not in conflict with provisions of the commercial companies law. Other statutory provisions relevant to this area of law include the Commercial Register and Companies Decree (1967) and Economic Co-operation Groups Decree (1967).

Incorporation of a société

It is usually a fairly lengthy process to form a French société, taking an average period of three months, unlike the much speedier processes available in England. The steps required are:

(a) preparation of the Articles of Association (hereafter 'Articles') (les statuts);

(b) signature of the Articles;

(c) payment of registration tax (droits d'enregistrement) and stamping of the document;

(d) opening a société bank account, in return for a certificate from the bank (certificat de dépot) which will acknowledge the share capital deposited;

(e) publication of a notice in a legal gazette, informing the public of the formation of the société;

(f) deposit with the clerk of the commercial court the following: two originals of the Articles (les statuts); two copies of the documents listing the officers of the company (for example, the manager or the directors); two originals of a subscription certificate listing the shareholders; two copies of the report of the special auditor if contributions have been made in kind; and two copies of a declaration (the declaration of conformity or déclaration de conformité) certifying that the proper steps have been taken in conformity with the legal requirements.

Status of a société pending incorporation

Pending the full incorporation of a company, before its registration at the appropriate Register of Commerce (such a company being called une société en formation), a société is still able to enter into contracts en formation, that is, during the period between the signature of the Articles and registration, subject to subsequent ratification of the contract once the company is registered. A clause may be inserted in the Articles, whereby stated obligations to be assumed by the société on its registration will receive automatic ratification by the société on its registration (see modification of this position for SAs and SARLs). Those acting on behalf of a société en formation will generally be personally liable, but this has been modified for SAs and SARLs. A sole trader only requires registration at the appropriate Register of Commerce.

SAs and SARLs

Société anonymes (SAs)

The SA tends to be a large company but closely approximates the English plc in structure and purpose, and, as with the SCA, is the only other form of company which may offer its shares to the public who may become investors. It requires a minimum of seven shareholders, who may be individuals or legal entities, and may be French or foreign, but no maximum number is imposed. Shares cannot be issued before registration of the company in the Commercial Register, or otherwise, the penalty is a fine. Since 1 October 1982, only those corporations listed on a stock exchange may issue or maintain bearer shares and these must be held by authorised institutions, like banks.

An SA may, as with an English plc, obtain finance by different means, such as share issues, debentures, or through public advertisements other than those required by law. Shares must have a nominal value which is fixed by the Articles but, since 1988, there has been no minimum nominal value requirement except in the case of a publicly quoted company whose shares must have a nominal value of at least FF10 expressed in francs, excluding centimes.

Directors run the company and are appointed either by the Articles or by the SA in general meetings, and they may also be removed by the SA in general meetings. Directors generally have to be shareholders in the company. There is usually one managing director and up to 14 other directors. They can be prosecuted and sued for improper management of the SA and, if the company is run fraudulently, heavy fines may be imposed and even imprisonment. If the SA goes into liquidation as a result of a managing director's mismanagement, he may be asked to pay off some of the debts or may be the subject of a personal bankruptcy action, regardless of whether he tried to benefit personally from the fraud. If such an order is made, this means that the managing director will not be permitted to indulge in trading activities for at least five years.

The board of directors of an SA exercises the management powers of the SA as do their English counterparts.

French law requires at least one independent statutory auditor (commissaire aux comptes) to be appointed for a six year period, but, unlike the English company law counterpart, such an auditor has the duty to not just verify that the société's accounts have been drawn up in accordance with the law, but also to report to the public prosecutor if any irregularity or mismanagement of the company of a criminal nature is detected. Further, every time a statutory auditor is appointed, a potential substitute must be named, to allow for the possibility that the appointee retires during the period or is dismissed. Grounds of dismissal include serious misconduct. As we have noted, the United Kingdom Companies Act 1989 has introduced new rules to govern auditors of English companies. In cases where British auditors have been held liable for not carrying out their duties properly, an action may be brought against them by the company through its liquidator under s 212(1A) of the United Kingdom Insolvency Act 1986.

Société à responsabilité limitée (SARL)

The SARL, the most popular form of société, is used extensively in France, and possesses characteristics which are similar to an SA and an English private limited company, in that its members are liable only to the extent of their contributions to the company's capital. However, it also resembles a partnership, in that its participants are treated more like partners than shareholders. Its shares will be made up of non-negotiable shares (parts sociales) which are freely transferable among members, but transfers to third parties (non-members) require the consent of the majority of its members representing at least three-quarters of the corporate capital.

A minimum of only two members is required, with a maximum of 50 members of either individuals or legal entities, which may be French or foreign. Under the Law 85.69 of 7 July 1985, a SARL may be subscribed to, and may continue to exist with, only one shareholder, who may be an individual or a legal entity. He is known as a sole member. This type of SARL is still subject to the same provisions as those governing other SARLs but will be known as an Enterprise Unipersonnelle à Responsabilité Limitée or EURL. If the sole shareholder is a legal entity, it may not also be a EURL, and the sole member who happens to be an individual is not permitted to be the sole member of another EURL.

The management of a SARL may be run by one or more managers (gerants) who may be non-members, but will have full authority and unlimited powers to represent the company and bind the SARL both in respect of third parties and, subject to its Articles (statuts), its members.

The GIE and the GEIE

The GIE

The French GIE (Groupement d'Intérêt économique) is an entity created by Ordonnance No 67-821 of 23 September 1967, to enable any group of businesses to pool their resources to carry on some joint activity whilst maintaining their independence and individuality in other fields of commercial enterprise. It is noteworthy since it is not strictly a corporate body or partnership. The GIE is formed by executing a written agreement between the members and is incorporated by being entered in the commercial register. It may be classified as civil or commercial depending on its stated objects.

Setting up a GIE can enable a group of businesses to co-operate in respect of a number of commercial activities, such as exports or sales, and to co-ordinate their activities in one specialised area, such as distribution, while maintaining their separate identity for other activities.

A GIE may be set up 'for a specified term in order to employ means to facilitate or develop the economic activities of its members, or to increase the profits or benefits of such activities': Art 1 of the Ordinance of 23 September 1967. A GIE must be an extension of the economic activities of its members, and it must have an economic purpose. Two points flow from these requirements. First, each member must retain its economic and managerial independence in non-GIE activities. Secondly, the GIE must actually engage in economic activities. However, an economic activity is not necessarily commercial. For example, if farmers and commercial partnerships form a GIE to provide its members with special services, the GIE will be regarded as civil in character. It will therefore not fall within the jurisdiction of the commercial courts but only within that of the civil courts (that is, the tribunaux d'instance exercising their civil jurisdiction).

A GIE has legal personality and full legal capacity as soon as it is entered in the Commercial Register. It is a separate legal entity from that of its members. It can also be set up without having any share capital. A GIE contracts directly, and its members are jointly and severally liable for its debts provided certain procedures have been carried out, such as service of a formal demand for payment on the GIE by registered letter or service of a written notice delivered by a bailiff (Art 2 of the 1967 Ordinance).

GEIE

The Groupement Européen d'Intérêt économique (GEIE) or European Economic Interest Group is a legal entity which was inspired by the GIE and is designed to facilitate co-operation between businesses in different Member States of the EEC, who wish to combine their resources for certain joint activities, such as research or manufacture. It was created by Regulation 2137/85, on 25 July 1985, by the Council of Ministers, and the Regulation defines its basic characteristics and lists the rules regulating its formation and operation. Individuals, partnerships and companies are all entitled to form a GEIE and, as with the GIE, various joint activities may be undertaken. The basic rules applicable to GEIEs are similar to those of the GIE, but a GEIE is not allowed to issue debentures. GEIEs which are established in France are now governed by the Law 89/377 of 13 June 1989, whereby the GEIEs acquire legal personality, as soon as they have been registered in France on the commercial register.

Partnerships

It will be recalled that, in France, the word 'société' may include both companies and partnerships. Although a partnership is formed by a contract between the parties, there are still de facto partnerships if:

(a) there is a form of contribution by the partners;

(b) a sharing of profits and losses; and

(c) a common intention amongst the partners to achieve a common goal (*affectio societatis*).

French law recognises general partnerships (SNC) (société en nom collectif) and limited partnerships (société en commandite simple). If the latter have a share capital (société en commandite par actions: SCA), they are also recognised by French law, but the SCA has become increasingly obscure. Civil partnerships (sociétés civiles) will be governed by the Civil Code (Art 1841 *et seq*), and are restricted to non-commercial activities. All forms of partnership other than the silent partnership (see below) and the GIE (see p 359, above) must have a corporate capital.

The silent partnership (sociétés en participation) was, for many years, by definition, undisclosed to third parties and is therefore not a legal entity. Accordingly, it need not be registered. Since 1978, a silent partner has the option to decide whether to be disclosed to third parties or to remain secret. Such a partnership may be classified as civil or commercial, depending on the nature of its activities. It cannot have a corporate name and its shares cannot be represented by certificates. Its members remain personally liable for their acts.

Each of the five main types of partnerships (and companies) is referred to as a société commerciale. They are:

(a) the general commercial partnership;

(b) the limited partnership;

(c) the share company;

(d) the limited liability company; and

(e) the partnership limited by shares.

These five types will be regarded as commercial partnerships, irrespective of their objects. Thus, so long as a société has adopted the form of a general commercial partnership or limited partnership, it will still be classified as a société commerciale, even though some of its activities may not be regarded as commercial under French law. On the other hand, if a société has not adopted a commercial form, its classification as a société civile or société commerciale will depend on its objects.

Sociétés civiles or civil companies are unusual in that they are completely governed by the Civil Code (Art 1841 *et seq*). Examples of business activities which such partnerships carry out are in real estate, agriculture and in connection with the exercise of a profession by, for example, doctors, architects, lawyers and accountants. If such partnerships have commercial objects or activities, they will be treated as companies for the purposes of tax. No statutory minimum registered capital is prescribed, and their capital is divided into non-negotiable shares (parts) for which there is no statutory minimum par value. The unanimous prior consent of all partners is required for the transfer of shares, and such transfers must be executed by a written contract of sale and duly registered with the tax authorities.

Any decisions, including a resolution to amend the Articles of a société civile, may be taken at a meeting of the members, usually by a majority vote as laid down in the Articles. However, if the Articles are silent on the type of majority needed to carry an amendment thereof, a unanimous vote will then be required.

The general partnership (SNC) or société en nom collectif is a partnership wherein all partners are deemed to be merchants. This means they will have to abide by the rules applicable to merchants. Liability for the debts of the partnership will be unlimited, joint and several. This form of partnership resembles the English general partnership, but a key difference from the English version is that the French general partnership does possess a separate legal personality.

The limited partnership (SCS) and partnership limited by shares (SCA) are rarely used forms of société, but famous examples of SCAs, which may offer their shares to the public, are Yves Saint Laurent and Michelin. SCAs have:

(a) general partners, who have unlimited personal liability. They manage the partnership in much the same way as their English counterparts;

(b) limited partners, who are shareholders with limited personal liability and do not have the right to manage the partnership, but have the right to supervise its affairs on the lines of the supervisory board of an SA. They are represented by a supervisory board which exercises powers similar to statutory auditors. The rationale behind this fundamental distinction between managers and investors is, apparently, to forestall hostile takeover bids.

Company law in Germany

The political reunification of Germany has given rise to a number of significant developments. Upon the accession of the former GDR to the Federal Republic of Germany, on 3 October 1990, the West German legal system became the law in force in the territory of the former GDR. Special transitional legal provisions will apply to the former GDR area, in some cases, for several years, to enable a proper transition from planned to market economy to take place. The reader is referred to the annexes to the Treaty of Unification for these transitional provisions. For present purposes, we shall proceed on the basis that the law is that which applied to West Germany.

Accordingly, most commercial matters would fall within the jurisdiction of the civil courts, which are traditionally divided into four regional units. The lowest civil court is the Amtsgericht or county court, but claims in excess of DM6,000 have to be brought in the regional or district court, the Landgericht, where each party has to be represented by a German lawyer who has the right to appear at that particular court. A special chamber deals with commercial cases in the Landgericht, which, on request, deals with proceedings between merchants, as well as with other urgent commercial matters.

Commercial parties are also permitted to enter into agreements conferring jurisdiction for disputes concerning property on whichever regional court they choose, so that, particularly between commercial companies, the most convenient forum may be chosen (see Bocker et al (1992) p 3).

Appeals to the Court of Appeal (Oberlandesgericht) are available against decisions of both the Amtsgericht and the Landgericht, but the amount at issue has to be at least DM1,200 in order for leave to appeal to be granted. An appeal to the Federal Supreme Court of Justice (Bundesgerichtshof) on points of law can also be made in cases involving an amount greater than DM60,000, or in disputes concerning matters of fundamental importance. There is no further appeal against the decisions of the small claims court.

The German Civil Code (BGB) also contains the provisions dealing with civil partnerships and the Commercial Code (Handelsgesetzbuch) (HGB) which contains provisions governing commercial partnerships. Special statutes regulate the public company (Aktiengesetz) (AG) and the private company (GmbH-Gesetz) (GmbH), reorganisations and mergers (Umwandlungsgesetz) (UmwG), compositions with creditors (Vergleichsordnung) and bankruptcy (Konkursordnung). There are also special statutes dealing with insurance, banking, mutual funds and the Stock Exchange, but the abovementioned list contains the important Codes and statutes dealing with German company law.

Types of business organisation

Two basic types of legal structures for the formation of a business exist:

(a) the partnership; and

(b) the legal corporation or legal entity, of which the most widespread are the limited company and the public limited company.

Partnerships include the following categories:

- general partnership (OHG);
- limited partnership (KG);
- silent partnership;
- ship-owning partnership (Reederei).

Legal corporations or entities include:

- the limited liability company (GmbH);
- the public limited company (AG);
- the mutual insurance company (VVaG);
- the co-operative company (eG).

There is usually a statutory requirement for most of these companies to be registered in a commercial register (Handelsregister) which is kept at the local county court (Amtsgericht). Companies which are legal entities come into existence upon registration, whereas partnerships and sole trading companies begin their legal existence as soon as they commence their business. In certain cases, fines may be imposed for non-registration of partnerships and sole traders.

Implementation of recent EC Publicity Directives has created another difference between partnerships and legal entities. Legal entities are obliged to publish detailed accounts, whereas partnerships are exempt from this requirement.

Partnerships and sole traders

The question of whether a single businessman and a partnership fall under the rules of the BGB or the HGB depends on their qualification as a 'merchant' (Kaufmann). This is partly dependent on the nature and size of the business. German commercial law is a special law for merchants. The definition of the merchant is, therefore, the basis of commercial law. The first paragraph of the HGB states that, 'For the purpose of the present Code, any person exercising a commercial business activity is a merchant' and § 2 then lists business activities regarded as commercial. These are mainly activities concerning dealing (purchase for resale) and transformation (manufacture) of goods and related activities – brokers, bankers, insurers and transporters. A rule of practice appears to be the value of yearly sales, which, if exceeding a certain amount (say, DM200,000), must be registered if they are regarded as qualifying as merchants who must register their business.

Partnerships and sole trading companies are the most utilised forms of organisation for a business, in the case of small or medium sized family companies. Partnerships trade under the names of their partners and it would seem that incorporation is comparatively rarer in Germany than in other countries, such as Britain. Partnerships between non-merchants are called BGB Gesellschaften – civil partnerships, which is a form that is also available to enterprises who want to form a partnership for a special purpose of short duration. This is often the case with construction businesses or underwriters.

Sole traders

One man businesses can be run as a one man limited company (GmbH) or as a sole trader. Minimum capital investment for a GmbH is DM50,000. Hence, sole trading companies are the norm. Anyone carrying out a business under his or her name can be a sole trader. There is a distinction between 'major' and 'minor' traders (see Bocker *et al* (1992) p 53). The Commercial Code (HGB) only applies to major traders. Minor traders are not allowed to register their company and do not have to comply with the strict requirements of the HGB.

Article 1 of the HGB contains a list of who can be a major trader and among the most important businesses listed are those involved with:

(a) buying and selling goods;

(b) trading with securities (excluding land);

(c) manufacturing of goods;

(d) trade representatives.

If other types of traders wish to be registered as major traders, the registrar must be 'satisfied' that the size of the business justifies registration (proceeding on the basis of, for example, the employment of several employees and a certain amount of bank credit). Estate agents and building businesses do not traditionally form part of the group of major traders.

Although no restrictions exist for the formation of a sole trading company, two notifications must be made:

(a) to the local trade authority; and

(b) to the local tax authority.

Certain businesses, such as auctioneers, brokers, real estate developers, casinos and gambling establishments, have to obtain permission from the local trade authority before commencing trading. Fines may be imposed for non-compliance, but the legal existence of the particular company is unaffected.

A sole trader must use his own name as his trading name. He may add a supplementary phrase describing the nature of his business, such as 'Kurt Wilhelm, Dealer in Quality Watches'. A sole trading company is represented by the proprietor who may confer full commercial powers of attorney to other persons. A sole trading company incurs unlimited personal liability for all debts and obligations which arise in the course of business. Creditors may therefore seize both company assets as well as the sole trader's private assets.

A sale of a trading company may be performed through the transfer of its assets to the purchaser. It is only possible to sell the 'goodwill' and the 'trading name' together with the company. It is therefore possible for the purchaser of the company to continue to use the name of the original proprietor, once he has bought the business.

Partnerships

There are two main types of commercial partnerships in German law: limited partnerships (KG); and general partnerships (OHG), both of which are based on the same basic principles. Their main objective is to pursue a business purpose together, pursuant to which each usually makes a financial contribution or a service. It is also possible, and reasonably common, for a wealthy financial 'backer' to enhance the company's creditworthiness by adding his name to the list of partners.

The liability of the partners will vary according to whether it is a limited or general partnership. All partners will have equal rights, equal standing and full liability in a general partnership but, in a limited partnership, some partners may be fully liable, while others may limit their liability to a fixed sum.

General partnerships (OHG)

According to the HGB or Commercial Code, a partnership of two or more persons, formed for the purpose of running a commercial business under a firm name, is a general commercial partnership (OHG), if the personal liability of none of the partners is limited. There must be a partnership agreement which does not restrict the liability of any partner and designate a firm name, and the OHG must be registered in the commercial register. An OHG is governed by the terms of its partnership agreement, the relevant provisions of the HGB and the provisions of the BGB, if it is a civil partnership, insofar as they are not modified or excluded by the HGB (see Horn *et al* (1982) p 244).

An OHG, under its firm name, can, under Art 124I of the HGB, acquire rights (including rights over real property), incur liabilities, sue and be sued, although it is not a legal entity and does not have a separate legal personality. Hence, it may be a plaintiff or defendant in a court action. Its assets are held by the partners in joint co-ownership and may be seized by the creditors of the OHG pursuant to a judgment against it. Since all partners have equal standing, each of them may represent and conclude contracts on behalf of the company. Contractual provisions for joint representation may be made, but such provisions will have to be registered in the commercial register in order to be legally valid in any third party dealings. Any unregistered restrictions will not affect third parties which act in good faith.

Creditors of the general commercial partnership may take legal action against both the partnership, as such, and against each individual partner. Since, apart from in England, a judgment against the partnership cannot be enforced against a partner and vice versa, it is usually preferable to sue both the company and its most creditworthy partners as joint defendants, in order to secure a claim.

A partner is not usually permitted to sell his or her share in a partnership without the prior permission of all the partners. But, it has now become common practice to insert a clause in the Articles of Associations which allows the sale of partnerships.

Limited partnerships (Kommanditgesellschaft: KG)

The general partnership may be converted into a limited partnership, if some of the partners begin to limit their liability in accordance with Arts 170–75 of the HGB. The firm will then be a commercial business with two types of partner: a general partner; and a limited partner. The latter will be personally liable to the creditors of the KG only up to the amount of his unpaid partnership contribution. If he has paid his contribution and not had it paid back to him, he is not liable to them at all (Arts 171–72 of the HGB). In order to limit the liability of a partner, the partnership contract must name a fixed amount of money which the limited partner is willing to put into the company. This amount has then to be registered and publicised, and the liability of that partner will then be limited to that amount. The partner concerned need only guarantee future payment with no obligation to pay the set sum immediately. If this is done, the creditors may then sue him directly for payment of the fixed sum.

The general partner will remain fully liable and his liability cannot be excluded. Of course, the general partner can also be a limited company (GmbH), in which case the limited partnership is called a GmbH and Co KG, and will enjoy full limitation of liability. As one group of commentators put it, this entity is a 'German peculiarity because it combines the advantages of limitation of liability with the freedom to organise the company structure in a partnership contract' (see Bocker *et al* (1992) p 57). The managing director of the GmbH and Co KG represents this form of partnership, and he will usually hold a share as a limited partner in the KG.

There is also the 'massed partnership' which is gaining in popularity, wherein a large number of limited partners have holdings in the partnership. These are often styled 'investment companies' or 'writing off companies'. This final form of company produce yearly losses for their partners which can be written off for purposes of tax (see Bocker *et al* (1992) p 58).

Limited partners must not consent to the partnership starting business before registration or they will be personally liable, without limit, to any partnership creditors who had no prior notice of their status as limited partners (Art 171 of the HGB). They have a limited role in the management of the company's affairs, unless the Article of Association provides differently, and they cannot represent the KG, unless they have obtained express authority from the general partner to do so, as the general partner is the only official representative of the partnership. They have the right to inspect and check the annual financial statement, to participate in any increase in the internal value of the assets and, subject to the terms of the partnership agreement, may even compete with the partnership.

However, all matters of outstanding importance for the company need to be decided by an assembly of all partners, and any clauses which attempt to abolish voting rights of limited partners are void and unenforceable.

The silent partnership

Unlike the French version of a silent partnership, the German version of a silent partnership has remained true to its name, remaining anonymous and secret. The silent partner is not known to the outside world, so that all third party dealings are handled by the owner of the business. It is a contract between a financier, who acts as silent partner, and the proprietor of a mercantile business (individual, partnership or company) whereby the silent partner receives a share in the profits of another person's business in exchange for his investment in that business. One purpose of such an arrangement might be to provide a member of a family with a source of income without having to involve that person in the management of the business. Creation of a silent partnership can also be useful to avoid inheritance tax in Germany (which is up to 70%), so that children can accrue considerable assets, over many years, and not be subject to inheritance tax, if they are made silent partners at an early age (see Bocker et al (1992) p 61).

The contract setting up a silent partnership should usually be in writing, and the parties may decide the terms on which the arrangement may be made. The silent partner may be made the internal manager of the company by requiring his approval for all external transactions (see Bocker et al (1992) p 60). No registration is required and the company will continue to be run under the name of the proprietor. Third parties will obviously only deal with the proprietor whom they have the right to sue, but the silent investment will be treated as part of the proprietor's assets for these purposes. The silent partner cannot be made personally liable for company debts, since there is no privity of contract between silent partner and third parties (see Bocker et al (1992) p 61).

Of course, the partnership may well provide for the silent partner to have rights in the management of the business or participation in the capital appreciation of the business property.

Limited companies and public limited companies

The limited company (GmbH)

The GmbH is probably the most popular form of company in Germany for small to medium sized businesses. Public limited companies (AG) are more suited to the needs of large businesses. Both corporations have separate legal personality. There are several advantages enjoyed by the GmbH. First, its shareholders and managers will normally avoid personal liability. Secondly, its Articles of Association will usually provide it with greater flexibility than the AG, in relation to the organisation of the company. Thirdly, it can be owned by a single person and the minimum capital needed to effect registration is only DM50,000 up to 50% of which may be inserted by non-cash contributions. Fourthly, it fulfils many functions of an AG, but within a much simpler legal structure.

As a result of these advantages, the GmbH is often called the 'joint stock company of the little man' (see Bocker *et al* (1992) p 61).

As with other corporations and legal entities, the GmbH comes into existence once all the formalities of incorporation have been complied with and upon registration. Before the prescribed procedures have been completed, and full registration has not been effected, something like a quasi-company exists which may commence business, but for which there will be no limitation of liability. All founders and other persons dealing on behalf of the company will be strictly liable for all debts incurred before registration (Bocker *et al* (1992) p 61). Of course, as soon as a GmbH has been registered, its liability is restricted to its assets.

The GmbH operates through the management and the general meeting of the company. Many GmbHs also have an advisory board or some version of a supervisory board. Every GmbH must have one or more business managers who represent it when dealing with third parties. An important point to note is that, even if the company contract or resolution limits the company's management powers, this will only be effective in relation to the company and its members. It will have no legal effect on the company's powers of representation in relation to third parties (see Art 37 of the GmbHG 1892; Law on Limited Liability Companies). As Horn (Horn *et al* (1982) pp 252–53) puts it:

> This is [a] good example of the distinction, so strongly made by the German law of agency, between the external relationship – the power of representation and the internal relationship – the power to manage the business.

Again, although internal restrictions may be imposed, it is not possible to limit the power of attorney of the managing director of a GmbH. Hence, any such restrictions would not be enforceable against a third party.

A GmbH comes to an end on the expiry of the period of time provided in the contract of incorporation, on a resolution carried by the majority of the members, on a court decision, on the commencement of bankruptcy proceedings or on a final determination by the register court that the contract of incorporation is defective (see Art 60 of the GmbHG; Horn *et al* (1982) p 257). Of course, the contract of incorporation may also provide its own grounds for dissolution.

The public limited company (AG)

There are 401 Articles in the Companies Act 1965 (AktG) dealing with the AG, which are also more detailed in coverage, compared to only 84 in the GmbHG. These are more mandatory and offer far less flexibility. This is, perhaps, understandable when it is realised that their purpose is clearly to protect the general public, especially investors.

The AG has a legal personality and is the only company which has a capital that is divided into shares which can be quoted on the market. The AG's closest equivalent is, therefore, the British Public Limited Company. At the end of 1987, there were 2,500 such companies registered in Germany, while only 471 of them had their shares quoted on the stock exchange. It is also possible, though very rare, for a one man AG to be formed. The constitution of an AG is contained in a single company contract.

An extremely complicated formation procedure is required, comprising a number of stages, commencing with a minimum of five founders being required to take up the shares and being obliged to draw up the company contract in notarial form. Articles of Association must contain: shares and capital stock (minimum DM100,000); the face value and number of the shares; the issue price of the shares (minimum face value); and the shares must be held by the founders. A company contract or constitution must contain: the name and location of the company; the object of the company; and the names of the board of directors. Further stages include: the appointment of the supervisory board; auditors, board of directors; a written formation report and submission of a copy of it to the local Chambers of Commerce. The application for registration must include another range of documents, such as the Articles of Association, a report on non-cash investments, documentation on the appointment of all board members, a formation report and a copy of the certificate issued by the local Chambers of Commerce.

The AG will exist as a legal personality, once it is registered, so anyone who acts in the name of the AG before it is properly registered will incur personal liability. As a legal entity, an AG will be liable to all its creditors, as such. Any member of the board of directors or supervisory board could face personal liability if they violate their obligations.

The board of management is responsible for conducting the business of the company and it may act unfettered by any directions from the supervisory board or the shareholders' meeting on how to run the business. Decisions should be taken by members of the board acting jointly or, if the rules permit, by majority decision (see Horn *et al* (1982) p 259). Decisions by a minority or the chairman of the board are not permissible.

The board of management also represents the company in court, wherever necessary, and its members must usually act jointly in order to represent the company. The scope of the managing board's power of representation cannot be limited, since German law does not have any doctrine of *ultra vires*.

It certainly seems plain that any notion of flexibility or freedom to contract on more ad hoc terms has been greatly restricted in pursuance of safeguarding investors and creditors.

The European Economic Industry Grouping (EEIG)

We have already discussed the GEIE in relation to French company law (see p 360, above). Since 1 July 1989, a new European form of company, the EEIG has existed in all EEC member countries. Germany implemented the EEC Directive No 2137–85 by means of an EEIG law which regulates the formation and management of an EEIG, in accordance with the Directive. EEIGs are intended to provide a suitable organisational form for joint ventures between small and medium sized companies from different EEC Member States (see Bocker *et al* (1992) p 69).

In Germany, the EEIG is treated in the same way as a general commercial partnership so that it is not a legal entity, but may be the bearer of rights. It acts though its managing directors, who may represent the company either jointly or severally. Each member is usually taxed according to his national tax law, but German turnover tax may be applicable. No minimum capital is required to form an EEIG. Since it may therefore lack any assets of its own, all members of an EEIG are fully liable to the company's creditors (Bocker *et al* (1992) p 69).

Disclosure provisions

As a result of recent EEC Directives on disclosure, all large AGs and some very large partnerships are obliged to publish their accounts. Disclosure obligations for smaller partnerships and sole traders have also been amplified. In the case of large partnerships: proceeds from turnover; proceeds from holdings; wages, pension, maintenance costs; valuation methods; and the number of employees have to be published. Profit and loss calculations do not have to be published. On the other hand, all AGs, regardless of their size, must publish documents, such as their balance sheet; a list of all shareholders; profit and loss calculation; and annual profits with an account of how they propose to utilise these profits.

The extent of these obligations might well persuade businesses to opt for a GmbH and Co KG, in preference to an AG, when planning which company structure to adopt.

A COMPARATIVE OVERVIEW OF AGENCY

Historical origins

The basic concept of agency exists in civil law and common law jurisprudence and, indeed, has existed in those jurisdictions since earliest times. Civil law systems of the French pattern find in the contract of agency (mandat) the consensual basis for representing another in the process of pre-contractual and contractual negotiations. The contract of mandat dates from the Roman law agreement for management of a patrimony (see Ripert and Boulanger, *Traité Élémentaire de Droit Civil*, Vol II, No 3020 and, further, 'French law', p 375, below). The English common law general principle, recognised from as early as Edward I, is *'Qui facit per alium facit per se'* (any person can act through an agent) and was established for obvious reasons of practical convenience. This basic rule was later modified by case law and statute. The genesis of agency in early English law is traceable to the relationship of master and servant, at least with regard to the history of agency in tort.

In the course of the 13th century, mercantile necessity and canon law cohered to encourage the fairly rapid rise of agents. Thus, the Salman and later the feoffee to uses was an agent for the transference of property. Similarly, the attorney was an agent for purposes of litigation. The records of the medieval courts of the fairs show that a species of commercial agency existed from an early date and that, during the 14th and 15th centuries, the development of trading companies provided further impetus to the need for agents.

Throughout the Middle Ages, canon law also encouraged the development of agency since monks, as corporate bodies, needed agents in order to function, communicate and interact with the outside world. Merchants subsequently borrowed some of the ecclesiastical rules which they then applied to their own agents.

With the rise of negotiable instruments and forms of banking practice, the commercial doctrine of negotiability was one of the earliest instances of deviation from the primitive concept of each party acting for himself. There was also the influence of the law merchant – *lex mercatoria* (see Chapter 12 for an account of the historical development of the law merchant), the body of law that developed from the law and practice of the international fairs.

Other early examples of agency in operation were innkeepers and shipowners/carriers. Such persons, either because of their special status (the innkeeper) or their particular circumstances, such as the remoteness of the ship from the control of others, were charged with a special responsibility for the acts of those under their care, or for the goods in their care. They may well have been more in the nature of insurers, but these individuals were held responsible for the loss of goods, or for damage caused thereto by their servants or agents.

The law in Europe, therefore, recognised from early times that a contract could be made through an agent and that it was the principal and not the agent who would be liable on these contracts, provided they were ratified by the principal.

Further, as mentioned above, since agency derived from the master-servant relationship, agents were seen as a particular class of servant and the sole distinction between 'servant' and 'agent' was to be found in the business in which they were respectively employed. In the last century, however, a disjuncture occurred between the law relating to master and servant and that of principal and agent. This was the result of two developments:

(a) commercial growth led to enormous importance being attributed to the principal-agent relationship as a branch of contract law; and

(b) the law of master and servant became inextricably associated with the law of domestic relations.

The key distinction between master and servant and principal and agent is that, in the latter case, a person becomes the representative of another for the purpose of bringing the principal into a legal contractual relationship with a third party. On the other hand, servants were properly those who were employed to perform services subject to the control and direction of their employer/superior. From the 16th century onwards, certain classes of agents – brokers and factors – were becoming more closely associated with commercial law. Agency had become essential to the necessities of commerce. There clearly came a time when, in the commercial context, the status of servant was eventually transformed into the higher status of an agent. Thus, agency, which began as a status, emerged in modern times as founded on contract and consent.

Modern agency law: common law v civil law

English law

We have already noted the relevance of agency to partnerships, given the special significance of partnerships to English law and we have seen that English law places significance on whether an agent has actual authority or only apparent or ostensible authority. Another important issue is the question of contracts made by the agent on the principal's behalf. In essence, the legal position of the parties will depend on whether the principal was named, disclosed or undisclosed.

If the agent made the contract on behalf of a named principal, the *de jure* contracting parties will be the principal and the third party, the agent being merely a conduit who will drop out of the picture once his work is completed. The principal will be liable provided the agent had express, implied, usual or apparent authority or if he ratifies the agent's acts. The principal may also sue the third party if the agent had actual authority.

Where the agent informs the third party that he is acting on behalf of a principal, but does not disclose the identity of the principal, the legal rights and liabilities of the principal and third party are generally the same as with a named principal, but the agent might nevertheless be liable on a contract if:

(a) he signs the contract in such a way as to assume personal responsibility; this will usually be the case if the agent is sued on a written contract, wherein he appears as a contracting party; or

(b) on the facts of the case, the court decides that this is the correct inference to be drawn.

The agent's personal liability may, ultimately, depend on the particular interpretation or construction that is placed on the contract in question.

German law

In German law (that is, West German law which is applicable to the newly unified Germany since 3 October 1990), the basic concept of agency (Stellvertretung) is very similar to that of English law. However, although several de facto varieties of agency exist in Germany, which include disclosed and undisclosed agency, strictly speaking, German law does not recognise undisclosed agency in the sense that the agent must act in the name of the principal before any legal significance will be attached to the acts of the agent (see § 164(II) of the BGB. This is because under § 164(I) of the BGB, an agent (Stellvertreter) is a person whose conduct in transactions, wherein making and receiving declarations of will occur, has a direct legal effect on the position of the principal (Vertretener).

The disclosed agency

The word 'disclosure' refers to the name or even existence of the principal in dealings between agent and third party. Where the agent reveals he is acting for someone else, this becomes a disclosed or proper agency and the principal has usually to be named. Two contracts are therefore involved in a disclosed agency, one between the agent and the third party, the other between agent and principal, which transfers the rights obtained from the third party to the principal.

If the agent does not reveal that he is acting on behalf of someone else, this is an undisclosed agency, since the principal remains unknown and German law does not recognise any privity of contract between principal and third party.

The commission agent

There are also situations in which an agent does act for an undisclosed principal, such as the agency for commission. This involves a person who is an independent merchant under § 1(II) No 6 of the Commercial Code (HGB) whose business consists of buying and selling goods or securities in his own name on the account of another, called the Kommittent, whereby he earns his commission (§ 383 of the HGB). This type of commission agent is called a Kommissionar and, since he acts in his own name, the agency (and principal) is undisclosed, so that this is not recognised as agency in German law.

There seem to be three contracts involved in the Kommissionar's business:

(a) the contract of commission between Kommittent (the principal) and Kommissionar (commission agent) whereby the Kommittent engages the Kommissionar to buy or sell specific goods for a commission. This comes under § 675 of the BGB, for which the HGB has special rules under §§ 383–405;

(b) the contract of sale entered into between Kommissionar and the third party performed by the transfer of the object of the sale. Since there is no direct contact and no privity of contract between Kommittent and customer, the Kommissionar will usually acquire ownership of all goods purchased on behalf of the Kommittent;

(c) there is the transfer of ownership of the goods from agent to principal or an assignment of his right to claim delivery of the goods from the third party.

In general terms, the commission agent must carry out the business with care and safeguard the interests of his principal, submit accounts or transfer any proceeds of sale to the principal (§ 384 of the HGB). Where the commission agent makes a personal intervention, which is not strictly within the terms of the commission contract, his duty to account and safeguard the principal's interests will be satisfied by showing that he kept to the market or exchange price. If the commission agent goes beyond the Kommittent's instructions, this will be permissible only if he can prove that the final outcome is more favourable to the Kommittent than it would otherwise have been.

French law

The word 'mandat', in French law, refers to the agreement pursuant to which a person is authorised to enter into certain acts of legal significance actes juridiques ('acts in the law') on behalf and in the name of another. Actes juridiques are actions or expressions of will which are intended to alter the legal position of its author. There is no general treatment of agency (also referred to as 'representation') in the Civil Code but, as in Germany, there are commercial agents, independent agents and commission agents. A commercial agent is an individual who carries on 'ordinarily' and 'independently' and 'professionally' (and otherwise than as an employee) the negotiation or conclusion of contracts for the sale, purchase, or letting of lease, or hire of goods or other property or the provision of services, for, and on behalf of, manufacturers, producers or merchants: see Art 1 of the Decree of 23 December 1958. The Decree makes a clear distinction between the commercial agent (commissionaire) and the commission agent to the effect that the former is a representative, whereas the latter acts in his own name on behalf of a principal (commettant).

As a general proposition, the principal is bound only within the limits of the power or authority granted to the agent (see Art 1989 of the Civil Code, which is similar to the English common law position). However, an agent may be liable to third parties in cases where he has not revealed the full extent or scope of his authority (see Art 1997 of the Civil Code).

Commercial agents and commission agents

As far as commercial agents are concerned, the principal will only be liable to third parties for the acts of these agents if these were made within the scope of the commercial agent's authority. However, a commission agent is a party to the contract which he transacts on his principal's behalf, so that he becomes personally liable to third parties with whom he contracts. Since a principal is not a party to the contract made by a commission agent, third parties cannot bring an action against the principal if they wish to have the contract performed. Of course, the corollary to this is that the principal has no direct action against third parties. Nevertheless, an indirect action may be allowed (action oblique), subrogating the plaintiff to the claims of the agent against his principal or against the other party to the contract (see Art 1166 of the Civil Code).

Agents and apparent authority

As in German and English law, an important issue in French law relating to agency is the scope of an agent's apparent or ostensible authority. In the absence of any express Code provision on this matter, court decisions have had to determine this matter. Earlier cases relied upon the Art 1382 concept of fault (faute) as the basis of the principal's liability to an innocent third party. More modern cases suggest that, as in English law, initially, an objective test must be applied, namely: would a reasonable person come to the conclusion, on an objective view of the particular circumstances, that the agent had the requisite authority to act as he proposed to do? If the answer was affirmative, it was then to be ascertained whether the plaintiff's mistaken reliance or belief in the agent's authority was justifiable or 'legitimate'. It would appear that, if these two questions could be answered affirmatively, the burden would then fall on the principal to disprove the justification for assuming the existence of apparent authority, even if there was an absence of fault on his part.

The courts appear to have adopted a policy of protecting a third party who acts in good faith, provided there was nothing in the nature of the transaction to arouse the suspicion of that third party (see *Société Civ Immob Les Genevriers v Bonnin*, Cass Civ 29 April 1969, 1970 DS Jur 23; and *Société Minsallier et cie v Société Lambert et Freèes*, Cass Comm 29 April 1970, JCP 1971 II 16694).

Comparative analysis of agency

The institution of agency or representation has certainly become an indispensable part of modern commercial life. Modern technological developments have changed the context in which agency relationships exist, especially where intricate relationships are involved. With the advent of instantaneous transmission of documents through the use of facsimile machines, agents are receiving far closer scrutiny than before, but there is also the possibility of a speedy response to changes in commercial conditions and, perhaps, less possibility of misunderstanding of contractual intent. The German system of making the agent's power independent of the contractual relationship between principal and agent and of emphasising this independence in the system of the Code has had a considerable influence on all civil law countries. It has, for instance, been adapted into the Swiss Civil Code and the Italian Civil Code.

EUROPEAN COMMUNITY CORPORATE LAW

The notion of European Community (EC) law

EC corporate law is but one component of the many institutions created by the internal market (see Chapter 5 for an overview of EC law). It is 'that part of Community law which enables companies to do business across frontiers in the internal market and which enables third parties to deal with them secure in the knowledge that they may do so within a framework of common standards' (Richards (1991)). Thus, it consists of the creation of a business environment favourable for corporate enterprise and a set of standards of protection for those engaged in corporate dealings. The EEC Treaty provisions embody the spirit of these abovementioned objectives. Article 52 enables nationals of one Member State to establish themselves in another State, without any of the traditional barriers. This includes the right to set up agencies, branches or subsidiaries. The right to set up and manage undertakings is also included in the definition of 'freedom of establishment'.

Article 58 specifies the legal persons that benefit from rights of establishment. The relevant criteria, as set out therein, require companies or firms to be formed in accordance with the law of the Member State and to have either: (a) their registered office; (b) their central administration; or (c) principle place of business to be within the Community.

Article 58 also specifies the types of companies and firms that would qualify under the legislation, namely, those 'constituted under civil or commercial law, including co-operative societies, and other legal persons governed by private or public law' except for those which are non-profit making.

The *Daily Mail* case

The *Daily Mail* case (Case 81/87 *R v HM Treasury and Commissioners of Inland Revenue ex p Daily Mail and General Trust plc* [1988] ECR 5483) which was decided by the European Commission ruled, *inter alia*, that, despite the definition of Art 58, Member States still have the right to impose fiscal and other requirements on the transfer of the company from one Member State to another, without these necessarily constituting a breach of the rights of establishment. Further, clarifying or explanatory legislation may, therefore, be required.

Non-profit making undertakings

In relation to non-profit making undertakings, the EC Commission has never adopted a restrictive view of this aspect. What should be the approach to those undertakings dealing with health, pensions and insurance which often operate as co-operatives or mutualised companies? If their primary purpose is to reduce costs to their members rather than to make profits for distribution, it would appear unduly harsh to classify or regard them as profit making enterprises, simply because they may incidentally make profits. If no clarification is made of the legal position of such enterprises, it will be left to the courts to demarcate the boundaries of acceptable commercial activity. The interim uncertainty is not conducive to true freedom of establishment.

Removal of restrictions on freedom of movement

A general programme to remove restrictions on the freedom of establishment was adopted on 15 January 1992, pursuant to Art 54 which provides for such a programme to be adopted. Article 54 thus supplements Art 58, so that companies which rely only on the 'registered office' requirement for qualifying under Art 58 must also show that they have a tangible link with the economy of a Member State.

Statutory foundations of harmonisation of laws

Various objectives in the pursuit of abolition of barriers to freedom of establishment are defined in Art 54, but the key Article is Art 54(3)(g) which enunciates the task of 'co-ordinating to the necessary extent the safeguards which, for the protection of the interests of members and others, are required by Member States of companies and firms ... with a view to making such safeguards equivalent throughout the Community'. This Article has been used as the legal foundation of the entire harmonisation programme, and the tenor of it suggests that minority shareholders, creditors, employees (that is, company participants and third parties) will continue to be protected by each country's legislation on company law.

Harmonisation of the companies of the financial sector is dealt with by Art 57 which encourages the co-ordination of the provisions laid down by the Member States, with regard to taking up and pursuing activities as self-employed persons.

Nature of EC company law

The Treaty framework provides for two main legal instruments which are available to the legislator, excepting conventions and recommendations. These are the Directive and the Regulation, whereby the Community can create legal entities and means of incorporation. The Community may adopt Directives to implement changes in national or domestic company laws. These Directives have a binding effect as to the result, but leave the national authorities the choice of form and methods (Art 189(3) of the EEC Treaty). A Member State may be brought before the European Court of Justice if a Directive is not incorporated into national law within the stipulated period (Art 169 of the EEC Treaty).

A Regulation is binding in every material particular and is directly applicable in all Member States (Art 189(2) of the EEC Treaty). In the context of company law, the principle of immediate application of Directives is somewhat less significant. Company law proposals require the two reading process before the European Parliament, and the experience, so far, of the EEIG regulation (see p 371) indicates that complementary domestic legislation will usually be a prerequisite to the smooth integration and transition of a particular Regulation into national law. Richards (1991) highlights the variety of provisions that are contained in the Directives:

(a) certain provisions set a minimum (for example, the minimum capital requirement for plcs is 25,000), beyond which the Member States are free to go, but they must respect the overall objectives of each provision;

(b) Member States may sometimes be given alternative means of achieving the same result (for example, the Accounting Directives);

(c) Member States may have an option as to whether to do something or not; they will, of course, then have to observe the rules which regulate the particular option;

(d) company law is also unusual in having a wholly optional Directive;

(e) the Directives sometimes prescribe a minimal margin for manoeuvre.

The question has to be posed as to whether these Directives are too complicated to be readily usable for Member States. It may, however, be argued that a clearly structured framework is better than no framework at all and that Art 54(3)(g) requires the Community to co-ordinate safeguards 'to the necessary extent'.

Directives already in force in the United Kingdom

Directives which have already been implemented in the United Kingdom are now contained in the 1985 and 1989 Companies Acts as follows:

(a) Directives in the Companies Act 1985 are:

    (i) the First Directive (1968) on co-ordination of safeguards required by companies; this includes amendments to the *ultra vires* rule;

    (ii) the Second Directive (1976) dealing with the maintenance and alteration of public company capital; and

    (iii) the Fourth Directive (1978) dealing with company accounts.

(b) Directives in the Companies Act 1989 are:

    (i) the Seventh Directive (1983) dealing with consolidated accounts; and

    (ii) the Eighth Directive (1984) which lays down audit regulations and minimum qualifications for auditors.

Other Directives on prospectuses, mergers and divisions, admission of securities to listing and disclosure of information have also been implemented through the utilisation of delegated legislation, such as the Companies (Mergers and Divisions) Regulations 1987 and the Stock Exchange (Listing) Regulations 1984.

COMPARATIVE CORPORATE LAW: CONCLUSIONS

Comparative analysis reveals that the word 'company' refers to different legal entities in French, German and English law and, thus, between civil law and common law jurisdictions. The difference between a partnership and a company in English law is not merely terminological, but is substantively different. Both civil law and common law jurisdictions have some form of sleeping/silent partner on the premise of a person who provides capital in return for a share of the profits, but who plays either a minimal role or no part in the management of the partnership/company. All systems provide safeguards and penalties against mismanagement of companies and partnerships. Considerable variety exists in the forms of corporate and commercial enterprise.

The sheer flexibility, inventiveness and adaptability of the various forms of the company/partnerships appear to strike a balance between serving the needs of its managers, its members and the demands of commercial fairness. It is the variety of forms which demonstrates the similarity of response on both sides of the English Channel, and the perceived need for such variety to continue to exist, to cope with the rapidly changing commercial world.

However, the EC Directives do not always seem to recognise this fact, and only the Accounting Directives appear to deal directly with this divergence by using a size criterion, rather than a terminological one. Some EC Corporate Law Directives apply indiscriminately to all forms of limited company, while others refer specifically to plcs. Whereas the SA would be the most conventional type of corporate legal entity in France, the vast majority of companies in Germany and the United Kingdom are private limited companies. The EC is also exploring the best way of allowing other associations, such as co-operatives, to participate in the internal market.

There is clearly a hope that Europe is heading towards a 'greater mutual recognition of national laws, on the one hand, combined with more sharply targeted instruments, on the other ... and the European Company Statute falls squarely within this type of approach' (Richards (1991)). However, in the light of the continuing dissension and misgivings over the full implementation of the Maastricht Treaty in EC Member States, there would seem to be some way to go yet, before we can expect to see a high level of harmonisation and widespread co-operation across national frontiers in European corporate and commercial law.

SELECTIVE BIBLIOGRAPHY

Bentley *et al*, *Corporate Law: the European Dimension* (1991)

Bocker *et al*, *Germany: Practical Commercial Law* (1992)

Dickson, *Introduction to French Law* (1994) Chap 10

Drury and Xuereb (eds), *European Company Laws* (1991)

Farrar *et al*, *Farrar's Company Law* (1990)

Foster, *German Legal System and Laws* (1996) pp 318–54

Horn, Kotz and Leser, *German Private and Commercial Law* (1982)

Le Gall, in Pennington (ed), *French Company Law* (1974)

Maitland-Hudson, *France: Practical Commercial Law* (1992)

Murray, 'New concepts in corporate law', in Bentley *et al*, *Corporate Law: The European Dimension* (1991) p 17

Raiser, 'The theory of enterprise law in the Federal Republic of Germany' (1988) 36 Am J Comp L 111

Reith, 'The effect of pre-incorporation contracts in German and English company law' (1988) 37 ICLQ 109

Richards, 'What is EC corporate law?', in Bentley *et al*, *Corporate Law: the European Dimension* (1991) p 1

Teubner, 'Enterprise corporatism: new industrial policy and the essence of the legal person' (1988) 36 Am J Comp L 130

Tunc, 'A French lawyer looks at British company law' (1982) 45 MLR 1

Werlauff, 'The development of Community company law' (1992) 17 EL Rev 207

Wurdinger, in Pennington (ed), *German Company Law* (1975)

CHAPTER 12

SALE OF GOODS

INTRODUCTION

A sale of goods is possibly the most common type of commercial transaction in practically every country in the world. This area of law is predominantly regulated by statutes or Codes, supplemented by case law, in both the civil law and common law world. It derives from the *lex mercatoria* (law merchant) or ancient mercantile law (the body of law that developed from international fairs and mercantile practice: see p 385, below) and is today generally classified as a body of law within 'commercial law'. However, there are significant differences between English law, German law and French law on the basic approach towards the sales of goods. There are, of course, many reasons for this, despite common features of mercantile law having been absorbed into both common law and civil law systems. The current European statutes are all based on creations of the 19th century and there is little doubt that they were products of their time. The French Civil Code of 1804, the English Sale of Goods Act 1893 and the German Civil Code of 1896 all reflect the notion of freedom of contract or the 'autonomy of the parties'. However, in French law, for instance, there is no distinction drawn between the sale of goods and sales of any other type of property, whereas the English common law approach does draw such a distinction. French law treats all sales under the single head of *vente*, which is governed by the general rules stated in Title 6 of Book III of the French Civil Code. However, there are special rules for sales of particular kinds of property, the rules of which are contained in separate legislation. As one might have expected, German law deals with sales of goods in its Civil Code (§§ 433–515), but this should be read together with the entire first part of the Code, the general part of the law of obligations and the general part of the BGB. If the sale is a commercial one, provisions of the German Commercial Code will also apply. The law on general conditions of business (AGBG 1976) and the law on instalment contracts (AbzG 1894) are both also relevant to sales, as well as the all embracing general principle of good faith (§ 242 of the BGB).

German law contains elements of Roman law, Germanic law and the *lex mercatoria*. Most of the principles of German contract law come from the German law of sale, an extrapolation which had already begun by the 19th century and the time of the Pandectists (see Chapter 3). Their agreement of sale concept is also based on the fundamental principle of freedom of contract.

For a variety of historical reasons, the English law of sales of goods is today a combination of statute and case law, predominantly based on the law of contract, but also imbued with distinctive features inherited from its rich and colourful history.

THE HISTORICAL BACKGROUND

Sale of goods in Roman law

In Roman law, the rule was *'periculum rei venditae nindum traditae est emptoris'*, which meant that the risk of a thing sold, but not yet delivered, is on the buyer. Sale – *emptio venditio* – was a contract, but never effected transfer of property. When the *emptio* was *perfecta* (that is, when identity, quality and quantity of the thing had been ascertained and the price had been settled, and when all suspensive conditions (if any) had been fulfilled (Lawson (1949)), the risk fell upon the buyer. Subsequently, if the subject matter of the sale was destroyed, the buyer was, nevertheless, bound to pay the price and, if he paid in advance, he could not recover his payment. The Romans regarded the transfer of property (or ownership) in a sale of goods as an exception to the general principle of *res perit domino* (the risk of destruction falls upon the owner of a thing). Hence, as regards a specific thing of which future delivery has been promised, Roman law took the view that the agreement only produced an obligation that the seller shall convey the thing to the buyer. Indeed, the process of transference of the property (in the sense of ownership) in the goods by sale was seen as consisting of two distinct parts:

(a) the contract or agreement to transfer regulated by the law of obligations; and

(b) the tradition by which the transference is completed, which constituted the right of property.

Germany and The Netherlands follow the Roman law, but France, Italy and English common law see 'property', in the sense of ownership or title, passing by the fact of agreement, that is, when the contract has been formed (or 'concluded', in the civil law parlance). Since there was no 'reception' of Roman law in England in the manner in which it occurred in civil law countries and Scotland, there is no strong Roman law presence in the English law relating to sales of goods, although any features it has in common with French law are attributable, in part, to its *lex mercatoria* inheritance.

The law merchant

The intermingling of concepts and experience in commercial law is not a new phenomenon. The historical development of the 'law merchant' or ancient mercantile law may be divided into two distinct phases:

(a) the law merchant of the Middle Ages; and

(b) the period of National Codifications.

There was also the impact of nationalism and the influence of the leading doctrinal writers of the 19th century.

The Middle Ages

In the Middle Ages, international commercial law evolved in the form of 'a body of international customary rules governing the cosmopolitan community of international merchants, who travelled through the civilised world from port to port and fair to fair' (Schmitthoff (1968)). The prevailing legal situation of the time has been described by one historian as one that developed from the 'law of the fairs born of the peace of commerce' that was 'acting strongly on institutions under the ordinary law, still imbued with its ancient rigours' (Huvelin (1895)).

It is now reasonably well established that this body of law was virtually universally followed and that the jurisdiction of the fairs extended to all parts of the known trading world. The international character of mercantile law was and remains its distinguishing feature. In the Middle Ages, this 'internationalism' was brought about mainly by the unifying effect of the law of the fairs, the universality of the customs of the sea, the special courts dealing with commercial disputes and the activities of the notary public, who handled a great deal of commercial legal work (see Schmitthoff (1968)).

A unique feature of this first phase of development is that international merchants themselves sat in the courts of 'pie powder' (or 'dusty feet') and administered courts at various ports which had 'half tongue juries' (so named because these juries consisted of one half of native and the other half of foreign merchants). The pie powder courts were so known because the term started as a nickname, but came to be known as the official style of the court. Its origins have been variously explained. Coke (*Fourth Institute*, p 272) believed the name originated because justice was administered as speedily as the dust could fall from the feet of litigants, but Cross (*Select Cases of the Law Merchant* (SS) pp i, xiii, xiv) was of the opinion that 'pie powder' referred to the dust on the clothes and boots of the itinerant merchants who used the court. Derivation apart, it seems clear that these courts administered a form of speedy justice, a fact which highlighted the tardiness of the common law courts. Merchants whose livelihood depended on speedy resolution of matters did not relish the stately and contemplative progress of the common law courts and preferred to sort out their affairs as soon as possible.

Thus, the mercantile law of this period was developed by the international business community itself and not by lawyers. By 1622, in England, Chief Justice Herbert could say:

> The custom of merchants is part of the common law of this kingdom of which judges ought to take notice; and if any doubt arises as to them about their custom, they may send for the merchants to know their customs.

Out of this early period came commercial institutions, like the bill of exchange, the bill of lading, the charterparty and even the commercial corporation. As Schlesinger (1900) put it, 'the law merchant, by the end of the medieval period, had become the very foundation of an expanding commerce throughout the Western world'.

National codifications

The second phase of development of the law merchant lasted from the 17th to the 19th century, during which this cosmopolitan and universal law merchant was incorporated into the national laws of various jurisdictions. In England, this transformation and incorporation of the mass of commercial usages into the common law was undertaken by Lord Mansfield (1756–88), when sitting at Guildhall in the City of London with his special jurymen, whom he also met out of court. By clearly stating in his judgments the general principles on which he based his decisions, he gradually managed to give definite form and substance to what became a distinctive and recognisable system of mercantile law. In 1893, the English Sale of Goods Act was passed, which has served as a model or prototype to many countries, European and non-European. In France and Germany, national codifications of commercial law were also undertaken. In France, Colbert, the Minister of Louis XIV carried out his codification on a national scale. His two ordinances, the 'ordinance sur le commerce' (1673) and 'ordinance de la marine' (1681), paved the way for Napoleon's Code de Commerce of 1807. German codification occurred only in the 19th century. In 1834, the Zollverein sponsored a Uniform German Bills of Exchange Act (promulgated in 1848) and, in 1861, the German Confederation adopted a Uniform Commercial Code which was the precursor of the German Commercial Code of 1897.

Despite these early codifications, however, commercial law retained its international flavour and the antecedents of the law merchant and Roman law have survived through the ages. As a result of these developments, commercial institutions which benefited directly were negotiable instruments, insurance and carriage by sea and forms of sales contract were created such as fob and cif, as well as bankers' commercial credits which have become the most frequently used method of payment in the export trade.

Influence of nationalism and contemporary writers

In the 18th century, legal thinkers in Europe had already expressed the need to codify the law to make it more homogeneous and accessible. Adam Smith's book, *The Wealth of Nations* (1776), which included a number of liberalist ideas also included freedom of contract as a concept. Many of his ideas were accepted in France, even before the French Revolution and, undoubtedly, had an impact on the lawyers who drafted the Code Napoleon. Before this, of course, the School of Natural Law had dominated legalistic thinking, in the 17th and 18th centuries, and this particular philosophy also argued that the contract alone should decide the legal effects of agreements and transactions. Furthermore, the Roman law heritage never completely left the scene, as far as French law was concerned, and the 19th century Pandectists also left their mark on German legal philosophy. But, it was not until the 19th century that codification actually took place, in the wake of the emergence of a wave of nationalism and independence and the new Nation States of Europe, such as Italy, Austria, Switzerland and Germany. By the end of the 18th and beginning of the 19th century, largely through the efforts of Lord Mansfield, the modern English law of sale came into its own as a distinct body of law. Many principles of law which were established in the preceding century were embodied in the English Sale of Goods Act of 1893. Even the United States originally adopted a Uniform Sales Act based on the 1893 Act, which was only superseded, in 1951, by their Uniform Commercial Code, which has retained many of the English ideas and juridical components.

KEY ISSUES IN SALES OF GOODS

As far as civil law and common law countries are concerned, the main issues that arise in relation to sales of goods are concerned with:

(a) the legal effects of the contract of sale on the transfer of ownership and risk;

(b) rights and obligations of the seller and buyer under the contract of sale;

(c) warranties as to fitness of the goods; and

(d) remedies of the parties.

It should be remembered that, up to 1992, socialist systems of law have had a totally different view of contracts of sale. Since the adoption of a Marxist/Leninist ideology in several European countries, China and the former USSR, the contract of sale has been seen there as merely a further device, which assists in promoting and implementing the purposes of the State economic plan. However, in view of the collapse of the former USSR and the increasing decline of communism in several Eastern European countries, it is certainly likely that the Westernisation and democratisation of the contract of sale is about to happen. The Russian Commonwealth of Independent States has already begun to implement economic changes which are intended to introduce a more 'capitalist orientated' society which signals the beginning of a new era of private ownership.

COMPARATIVE STUDY OF EUROPEAN CIVIL LAW COUNTRIES

French law

Transfer of ownership

In French law, a commercial contract of sale will be subject to certain special rules found in the Civil Code, Commercial Code and in separate legislation (compare L 13.6.1866). Proof in commercial contracts is governed by Art 109 of the Commercial Code which states the general rule that oral evidence is admissible in any commercial matter in which the court thinks fit to admit it. With regard to the legal effects of a transfer of goods, once the goods have been ascertained and the price agreed upon, the effect of the conclusion (formation) of a contract of sale is that of immediately transferring the property in the goods to the purchaser. This rule will operate unless the parties have expressly or impliedly agreed to postpone the transfer of title (Art 1583 of the Civil Code). If there is a proposed sale of goods which have yet to be ascertained, then the property does not pass until ascertained goods have been appropriated to the contract. In French terminology, there is a need for 'individualisation' of the goods. If there is a contract for the sale of goods 'on approval', then, again, the property or right of ownership in the goods does not pass by reason of the 'conclusion' of the contract until the buyer has signified his approval of the goods.

Responsibility for risk of loss

The question of who bears the 'risk' (of loss, damage or deterioration of the goods) in relation to the goods depends on the particular circumstances involved and the particular arrangement that the parties have entered into. If the contract has been concluded (formed), the buyer would normally bear these risks, even though they have not yet been delivered, since conclusion of the contract itself transfers the property in the goods to the buyer (Art 1138 of the Civil Code). Of course, if the goods have not yet been appropriated to the contract, or where the parties have expressly or impliedly agreed to depart from the principle of the Code, or it is the seller's fault that they have been damaged, the risk of loss or damage remains with the seller. Similarly, the risk is borne by the seller if he delays in making delivery (Art 1138 of the Commercial Code). On the question of future or generic goods, ownership and risk will pass when the goods are ready (*achevée*) for delivery to the buyer in accordance with the contract. Thus, a quantity of rice ordered by the buyer, once put into sacks and labelled with the buyer's name, signifies that ownership and risk of loss have then passed to the buyer. If goods are bought *en bloc*, with reference to the place where they are stored, they are then at the buyer's risk until delivery, provided the seller is not negligent in his care of them. Once goods that have been specifically ordered have been delivered to a carrier, they are then at the buyer's risk, but the buyer retains a right to damages if the goods are then lost or damaged. Goods that require weighing and measuring before delivery will remain at the seller's risk until they have been weighed and measured (Art 1585 of the Civil Code). It is important to bear in mind that all these rules may be overridden by the parties themselves, as already indicated. The parties have a free rein in deciding when the passing of ownership or risk should take place and may agree that the seller shall remain owner until he has been paid. These agreements are regulated by the law of 12 May 1980, which deals with cases of the buyer's bankruptcy. An appeal court has ruled that a seller can rely on a retention of title clause, even though the buyer did not give his written consent to such a clause and that the risk of loss or damage remains with the seller until the price is paid (Cour d'Appel de Metz, 29 October 1980). It should also be noted that French law differs from the Hague Convention on International Sales of Goods 1964, which supports the German approach (see below).

Rights and obligations of buyers and sellers

The seller has a duty to deliver the goods sold as soon as the contract is concluded (Art 1138 of the Civil Code). Of course, the seller's duty to deliver ceases if the buyer fails to pay for the goods on the agreed day (in the case of non-credit transactions) or if he becomes bankrupt: (Arts 1612–13 of the Civil Code). Delivery takes place when the goods are transferred into the control and possession of the buyer (Art 1604 of the Civil Code). The seller also has a duty to guarantee that the buyer is protected against any undisclosed rights of third parties over the goods (Art 1138 of the Civil Code). The buyer is obliged to pay the price and expenses and to take delivery of the goods. Payment should be made at the time and place of delivery, unless the parties have agreed to the contrary. If the contract does not specify where delivery is to be made, it must be at the place where the goods are when the contract is made (Art 1609 of the Civil Code). When goods are not delivered at the agreed time, the buyer has a right to seek cancellation of the contract (Art 1184 of the Civil Code) or apply for delivery to be enforced under Art 1610. The seller may have to pay damages and interest, in any event (Arts 1610–11) but, if there is no agreed stipulation by the parties on this point, the court may decide the time for delivery (Cas Civ 4.4. 1973).

Under Art 1641 of the Civil Code, the seller warrants that the buyer is protected against hidden defects which make the goods unfit for their purpose or reduce their usefulness to such an extent that the buyer would not have bought them or would have paid a lower price had he known of their existence. Thus, four conditions are required to activate this provision:

(a) the defects must have been hidden (*vices caches*) and not apparent on reasonable inspection; second hand goods might not necessarily be covered on the basis that their defects are attributable to their used condition (Civ 10.7.1956, D 1956.719; Civ sect com 11.6.1954, D 1954.697);

(b) the buyer was unaware of them; this will not apply if the defect is so common that the buyer ought to have been aware of it (such as certain types of antique furniture whose antiquity and susceptibility to disintegration have been and are often wrongly assessed, even by experts) in which case the buyer must prove his ignorance of the defect. A usual practice to forestall this occurrence is for the buyer to require the insertion into the contract of the clause 'seller undertakes to supply goods free from defects' for classes of things especially prone to defects;

(c) the defects lessen the fitness or usefulness of the goods; the criterion used is not an aesthetic one, only economic;

(d) the defects antedated the sale; unless, of course, some evidence of such defects was already present at the time of the sale.

All sellers, whether or not they act in the course of a business, are 'caught' by Art 1641. However, French law distinguishes between the professional and non-professional seller in the extent of their liability for defective goods. The professional seller is deemed to have been aware of the faults and will be liable in damages for physical injury and economic loss, whereas the non-professional seller will be obliged only to take back the goods and repay the price (*action redhibitoire*: action for rescission) or repay a part of it if the buyer keeps the goods (*action estimatoire*), unless he was aware of their defects. Either action must be brought promptly, since the Code mentions allowance for a 'brief delay' which may be tolerated, depending on the nature of the defects and the custom of the place where the sale was made. The court has a discretion to simply disallow a claim that has been delayed unreasonably. The buyer may still have a remedy if the merchandise delivered does not correspond with the seller's express or implied description of its quality. If the seller was aware of the defects, the buyer may rescind the contract and claim damages on the ground of fraud (*dol*).

Irrespective of the good or bad faith of the seller and regardless of any undertaking the seller might have given, the buyer may rescind on the ground of an *erreur sur la substance* under Art 1110 of the Civil Code. Claims under this Article must be made within five years of the discovery of the mistake. This type of error exists where the buyer can prove that he was mistaken as to the substantial quality of the merchandise sold; substantial quality would mean that quality which goes to the essence of the thing the buyer wished to acquire in making the purchase. It refers to the identity of the thing which is the basis of the decision to enter into the contract. A relatively recent case in French law involved the seller who wrongly believed that he was selling a painting in the style of Poussin, but not by him. On realising the painting was actually by Poussin, he was allowed to avoid the contract (Cour d'Appel de Versailles, 7 January 1987).

The test applied under Art 1110 is entirely subjective, in contrast to Art 1641 which applies an objective test. A final point is that, irrespective of whether the contract is nullified, a party may be ordered to pay damages if he was to blame for the other's mistake, or acted fraudulently or in bad faith.

On the question of exclusion clauses, the Loi Scrivener Law of 10 January 1978 has been passed to give the government very wide powers to issue decrees to control unfair clauses. Under the decree of 24 March 1978, clauses excluding or limiting consumers' rights against sellers who are in breach of contract may no longer be inserted into contracts. Additionally, clauses entitling sellers unilaterally to change the characteristics of the goods or services contracted for are also forbidden. A second decree has established a model standard form for contracts of guarantee and after sales service relating to domestic electrical equipment (see Decree of 22 December 1987). Another law, the Law of 5 January 1988, enables approved consumer organisations to prohibit the use of particular forms of words in traders' standard form contracts with consumers.

The contractual action known as *'action directe'*, which is unique to French law, may be used where there has been a series of sales of the same thing. At any stage in the chain of sales, a buyer may sue any previous seller, up to and including the manufacturer, for breach of warranty, despite the absence of any contract between them. This has developed from the basic warranty rule embodied in Art 1641 and the basis of *action directe* is that each successive sale implies a transfer of all rights of action relating to the thing sold. Hence, the warranty is attached to, or is part of, the thing sold, so that each successive buyer has the rights of each seller against the previous seller: Cass Civ 12 November 1884. If the person sued is not the first seller in the chain, that person will have an *action recursoire* against any previous seller; and this will continue back to the first seller. Claims for breach of warranty should usually be made within a 'short time': Art 1648. Six to 12 months is the usual acceptable time after discovery of the fault.

Articles 1382–84 enunciate general remedies for any injured party who is unable to establish any contractual or quasi-contractual right. Under Art 1384, every act or omission which damages another person must be paid for by the person at fault. But, French case law has ruled that mere delivery of goods which are not reasonably safe is sufficient to prove fault, unless the supplier can prove that the defect was caused by a stranger or Act of God. Suppliers are vicariously liable for their employees' defective workmanship and also as 'guardians' of things under their control. Physical control is usually the basis of this rule, but there may arguably be liability for defective design or production.

Remedies of buyer and seller

If the seller has not been paid, he may sue for the payment and cancellation of the contract but, in addition, has four special remedies:

(a) a lien on the goods (*droit de rétention*);

(b) a right to take possession (*droit de revendication*);

(c) a prior charge on the goods (*privilege*); and

(d) a right of rescission (*resolution*).

The lien of the unpaid seller entitles the seller to refuse to deliver the goods, so long as he has not been paid the price (Art 1612 of the Civil Code). He is, however, deemed to waive this right where it was provided in the contract that the buyer should be allowed credit. Nevertheless, if the buyer becomes insolvent or bankrupt or if the term of credit expires, the right will automatically revive. The insolvent buyer may still claim delivery of the goods, provided he can find security for payment at the appointed time.

The seller's right to retake the goods exists only if:

(a) no credit has been given, the goods have remained in the buyer's possession, are unchanged in their condition and the claim has been made within eight days of delivery (Arts 2102–24 of the Civil Code); or

(b) where the goods, having been delivered to a carrier, have not yet come into the possession of the buyer or his agent, but the buyer has, in the meantime, become bankrupt or insolvent.

The third special remedy is seldom exercised, since the unpaid seller will usually rescind the sale rather than claim his privilege. Nevertheless, if the eight days have expired or credit facilities have been given and both ownership and possession of the goods sold have passed to the buyer, the seller can compel a judicial sale of the goods and claim payment of the price out of the proceeds in priority to other creditors. This privilege is not available if the goods are no longer in the buyer's possession (excepting the unpaid seller of a motor vehicle, under the terms of D I.30.9.1953 which applies to credit sales), or have perished or where the bankruptcy or 'judicial administration' of the buyer has supervened. Judicial administration (*le règlement judiciare*) refers to a judicially controlled process whereby the court seeks to preserve the bankrupt's business and to restore it to him when the bankruptcy proceedings have been completed. This is to be contrasted with *la faillité* or bankruptcy proceedings of another sort, wherein the object of the court is to wind up the business and terminate the debtor's commercial trading.

The seller's right to rescind is provided for under the Civil Code which states that 'If the buyer does not pay the price, the seller may claim rescission of the sale' (Art 1654 of the Civil Code). Where the goods have already been delivered, the court may give the buyer more time to pay, unless there is a contrary provision in the contract (Art 1183–84 of the Civil Code). The right to rescind is part of the general right to rescind for non-performance in any synallagmatic (two sided) contract (Art 1184 of the Civil Code). It applies regardless of whether the seller has parted with ownership or possession or both. If the buyer fails to collect the goods within the contractually stipulated time, the seller has the automatic right to rescind without first obtaining a court judgment or even without issuing a formal summons to the buyer. In any other situation, the court must pronounce upon the seller's claim to rescind (Art 1184(2) of the Civil Code).

French law distinguishes between a merchant or commercial company and a non-merchant (*société civile*). Broadly, the law leaves the individual creditors to obtain payment as best they can from a non-merchant. However, since there is a public interest in the prompt payment of debts where a commercial company is concerned, there is an elaborate judicial administration involved in settling the debts of the company, designed to preserve equality between the creditors and, if possible, to restore the creditor to commercial viability. Hence, once a merchant debtor has become bankrupt or gone into judicial administration, the right to rescind is lost as soon as the goods have come into his shop or warehouse.

In the case of supervening events which make it difficult or impossible to carry out the performance of the contract, French law also has rules equivalent to the English contractual doctrine of frustration. These are dealt with under the headings of *force majeure* and *imprévision* (unforeseeability) or unforeseen events. French law is far more rigid than the German or English parallels and is applied more strictly. The doctrine of *imprévision* is only found in administrative contracts and there is no similar doctrine in civil contracts. Contracts between private parties cannot, therefore, utilise the doctrine of *imprévision*. Article 1134 of the Civil Code declares that contracts have the force of law, hence the judges cannot change their terms simply in the interests of fairness. *Imprévision* is admitted in contracts to which the French State or another French public body is a party. The Conseil d'État has held that administrative contracts may be revised in 'radically altered circumstances' (*imprévision*). A change in circumstances may render a contract commercially impracticable or more expensive to fulfil, but the contract will, nevertheless, be enforced according to its terms. However, if a change of circumstances renders the contract legally or physically impossible to perform, the doctrine of *force majeure* may be invoked.

If the impossibility is merely temporary, this will not terminate the contract, but simply suspend its execution and only relieve the party from liability for the damage caused by the delay. In the contract of sale, if there is an obligation to deliver a specific thing, the ownership of that item will pass, together with the risk, by virtue of the consent of the parties. If the item perishes before delivery, the obligation to deliver it will disappear, but the obligation of the buyer to pay for the price will remain, unless he can prove fault on the part of the person in whose hands the item perished.

In the famous 1916 case of *Compagnie du Gaz de Bordeau*, the Conseil d'État held that, as a matter of principle, a contract could only be modified with the consent of both parties, but where the whole economic basis of a contract had been altered by executive action, the private individual was entitled to an indemnity from the state agency because of the unforeseen loss it had caused him. A French judge does not have the same discretionary powers afforded to an English judge to terminate a contract completely in these circumstances. A strike or a war will not necessarily be regarded as an event of *force majeure*, but subsequent illegality will usually suffice to terminate a contract by judicial resolution. Article 1148 of the Civil Code permits *force majeure* to be used as a defence to a claim for damages for breach of contract, but only where unforeseeable and irresistible events make it impossible for the contract to be performed. Judicial modification of the terms of the contract may, in exceptional circumstances, be permitted, for example, under Art 1124 of the Civil Code, which allows extension of time for the repayment of debts, or the Law of 9 July 1975 which allows penalty clauses to be nullified.

It should be remembered, however, that, under Art 1147, a debtor may be ordered to pay damages either because of his failure to carry out an obligation or because of his delay in executing it, in every case where he is unable to prove that the delay has proceeded from some external circumstances for which he cannot be made responsible.

German law

General

In German law, there are no rules equivalent to common law concepts of consideration or estoppel. Hence, contracts which have been concluded without consideration are enforceable. However, this is of little practical significance, since sales contracts are invariably entered into so that possession and title may be transferred for a consideration. Moreover, most modern day sales contracts are reduced to writing and standard form contracts are also common in Germany, with German law favouring the 'last shot' rule (that is, the form that was received last will prevail), unless there was a specific contractual stipulation to the contrary or one specifying which form would govern the contract. A creditor's written agreement to accept part payment is binding; full settlement will also be binding on him; and manufacturers' guarantees are directly enforceable, since they are seen as separate from the contract of sale. There is also no general requirement of written form for sales contracts, although contracts for the sale of real property, including mortgages, and concerning the statutes of a company, must be embodied in writing authenticated by a notary or judge (§ 313 of the BGB). Similarly, writing is required in contracts between landlords and tenants and contracts of financial guarantee (§ 766 of the BGB) and hire purchase contracts. Another general principle is that the BGB imposes strict liability in contract upon retailers if their goods and services are not reasonably fit. This rule only applies to the goods or services themselves and does not cover any injury or damage caused to the buyer or his property by usage of the goods. Such claims would require proof of negligence which may be established either though a breach of contract action against the dealer or in a tort action against someone like the manufacturer.

The difference between contractual and tortious liability is clearly highlighted by this approach. Tortious liability is enunciated in §§ 823 and 831 of the BGB, but there is a special rule of strict liability for injuries caused by drugs.

Transfer of ownership

The German code provisions which specifically deal with sale only relate to the contract between the parties and its legal consequences. It is the third book of the Code that deals with the law relating to the ownership of the object which has been sold. The German word 'Kaufvertrag', although translated as 'sale' does not connote the transfer of ownership, but merely that there has been an agreement to sell. The contract of sale creates rights and duties, but it does not, *per se*, transfer property. The property in the goods will pass depending on the rules of § 929 *et seq* of the BGB. German law follows the Roman law principle whereby the transfer of ownership requires transfer of possession. This differs therefore from both French and English law, under which the mere sale will normally transfer ownership of the goods. Thus, a concluded contract will not operate as a conveyance. There is therefore a split between duty and performance which leads to a potential problem if the property is sold twice. In theory, the seller can undertake several conflicting duties to deliver the same piece of merchandise. If the seller then transfers the goods to the second purchaser, the first purchaser is only entitled to sue the seller for damages. It is only in cases where the first purchaser can prove that the second purchaser 'induced a breach of contract' by the seller that the first purchaser may claim the goods from the second purchaser in tort (see BGHZ 12, 308, 318 and RGZ 108, 58).

If the seller goes bankrupt before he can perform the contract and transfer the goods to the purchaser, the purchaser has no right to the merchandise, but is left with a claim in bankruptcy which is generally unsatisfactory.

Responsibility for risk of loss

As far as risk of loss or damage to the goods is concerned, German law states that the risk passes to the buyer only with the delivery of possession (§ 446 of the BGB *'periculum est vendoris'*). This usually, but not always, means that risk passes when ownership is transferred. This differs from Roman law, wherein risk of accidental damage and destruction passed with the completion of the contract of sale (*'periculum est emptoris'*) and from English law, under which *prima facie* risk passes to the buyer with the 'property in the goods', that is, with the transfer of ownership, which usually occurs at the point of conclusion of a contract of sale, irrespective of the transfer of possession (s 20(1) of the Sale of Goods Act 1979) under the *'res perit domino'* rule (the loss falls on the owner). In other words, the goods remain at the seller's risk until ownership passes, which is when the contract is concluded.

In German law, despite the rule that risk passes on delivery, there are exceptions to this rule:

(a) in sales of land, risk passes with either transfer of possession or registration, whichever is the earlier (§ 446(2) of the BGB);

(b) if the place of performance and place of transfer are not identical, then risk passes upon the delivery of the goods to the person or organisation designated to carry out the transfer from the place of performance to the place of delivery (§ 447(1) of the BGB);

(c) the parties may agree that the risk may pass earlier. This is similar to English law where, in the case of cif and fob contracts, the risk passes at the moment the goods are delivered to the ship. German law accords with English law on this point. The German law approach here is that of *'cujus periculum, ejus est commodum'*, so that the burdens and advantages of the thing which has been sold will pass to the purchaser at the same time as the risk passes (§ 446 of the BGB);

(d) there may be a retention of title clause in the contract. Under § 454 of the BGB, such clauses are declared valid. Any problems that arise must be settled by case law. The *Romalpa* clauses (the *Romalpa* case [1976] 2 All ER 552); and see pp 415–17, below), used in common law jurisdictions, are very common, but are rarely contested;

(e) if unascertained goods are destroyed by flood or fire, the seller will only be liable for the buyer's loss in cases of negligence. If the seller has not been negligent, he has no obligation to perform the contract and the buyer has no obligation to pay for the goods;

(f) ownership passes to the buyer only if he obtains actual possession. If the seller has entrusted goods to an independent carrier, risk, but not ownership, will pass, in the absence of a contrary contractual provision.

Duties of buyer and seller

Under German law, the seller is obliged to deliver the goods and transfer ownership in them, while the buyer is obliged to pay the price and take delivery of the goods (§ 433 of the BGB). After delivery, the buyer's main right is to cancel the contract if the goods are defective, but he also has the option to pay a lower price. Unlike Roman and English law, the seller warrants that he has title to the goods he is offering to sell (§ 433(1) of the BGB). This applies not just to things sold, but also to rights. A seller who sells a non-existent right cannot, therefore, argue that the sale is void because of the non-existence of the right. In the case of a defect of title, a purchaser has all the rights that he has in the case of a breach of contract (§ 440 of the BGB). The purchaser will have these rights, even if the seller may not have acted negligently or intentionally. However, the seller will not be responsible for defects of title which are known to the purchaser (§ 439 of the BGB). There are two exceptions to these rules:

(a) in sales of movable property, the purchaser can demand compensation for non-transfer of title after delivery, provided the defect in title has resulted in the merchandise having been delivered to a third party who is entitled to it; or the object has been returned to the seller; or the merchandise has been destroyed (§ 440 of the BGB). This is similar to the Roman principle of eviction, which has also had an impact on English law (see s 12 of the Sale of Goods Act 1979 (United Kingdom));

(b) in sales of immovable property, the seller is obliged to procure the cancellation of all charges on the land, even though they are known to the purchaser (§ 439(2) of the BGB).

The contract of sale gives rise to a number of collateral duties (Nebenpflicten). These are derived partly from the Civil Code, partly from the contract and partly from the general principle of good faith (see p 403, below). One example is the duty of the seller to refrain from competing with the purchaser of his business; another is the duty of the seller to point out to the buyer the existence of any special dangers that are not immediately apparent in the property sold.

Remedies of buyer and seller

Buyer's remedies

Irregularities in the performance of the contract of sale must, first, be categorised before it is possible to know where the various statutory remedies may lie. Various remedies for non-performance by the seller are available to the buyer under the general part of the law of obligations and there are additional rules in the law of sales, particularly for defects in the goods. Two points should be noted:

(a) in the case of a sale of a thing, there is the right of the buyer to demand that the contract be performed, that is, the equivalent of the English action of specific performance except that, in Germany, this 'claim to performance' (Erfullungsansspruch), which entails asking for the transfer of title and delivery of the merchandise, is the standard remedy rather than the exceptional one, unlike the English practice. In Anglo-American law, it is viewed as exceptional and at the court's discretion whether specific performance of the contract should be ordered. Thus, German law frequently adopts the exact opposite of the English common law approach where there is non-performance of the contract by the seller;

(b) if the seller fails to perform and the risk has not yet passed, rules relating to impossibility of performance (which is part of the doctrine of frustration in English law), and delay will apply (see §§ 323–26 of the BGB).

There is some doctrinal dispute as to whether certain cases, wherein the seller was unable to perform his part of the contract, should accurately have been called cases of impossibility or whether they should have been treated within the notion of good faith (*Treu und Glauben*: § 242 of the BGB). However, the key determinant of the seller's liability would appear to be whether he was 'at fault' in some way and therefore responsible for the impossibility of performance. English law regards cases where one party was partly or wholly responsible for the impossibility as 'self-induced frustration' which does not qualify as legally valid frustration. There is no identical conceptual doctrine of frustration in German law, but there is a concept known as a 'fundamental change in circumstances underlying the contract' (Wegfall der Geschaftsgrundlage) which is similar to certain aspects of English law. In German law, where the seller has been responsible in some way for his inability to perform the contract, the buyer has the right to claim damages for non-performance of the sales contract (§ 325 of the BGB). He also has the right to claim damages for lost profits. Should neither party be responsible for the impossibility, obligations for both parties are terminated. Thus, the buyer need not pay anything for goods which were not, in any event, delivered, but neither will he have any right to claim damages.

The rules for delay are similar to those which operate for impossibility (§ 325 of the BGB). Delay has proved to be a more important practical and popular basis for legal actions than impossibility because, as long as non-performance can be proved, the fate of the actual goods is only indirectly relevant to the question of responsibility for the delay. In respect of a unilateral obligation on the part of the seller to deliver on time, this obligation continues in spite of the delay, hence, a right to claim damages will arise for the loss attributable to the delay in supplying the goods. On the other hand, for reciprocal contracts, the buyer has the unique option of fixing an additional time for delay in delivery after it has first occurred, a period of grace (Nachfrist), after which no further obligations will remain under the contract. This is not derived from Roman law, but came into the BGB from the Allgemeines Deutsches Handelsgesetzbuch of 1867. Thus, the buyer may, for example, fix a final date for performance of the contract, so that the seller may either comply by this date or let the date pass, so that the contract may then be resolved by a claim for damages or rescission. The contract is then void and no further claim for performance can be made. If this option of giving a period of grace is not exercised by the buyer, he has the usual right to claim compensation for any loss attributable to the delay. Note that this right to set a subsequent date for delivery exists in addition to any claim for performance, provided, of course, the goods may still be delivered.

Before delay in the legal sense arises, there must, of course, have been an obligation to deliver. Notice is required to put the seller on enquiry, unless the contract has identified the delivery date with sufficient precision, that is, so it is easily identified by reference to the calendar. Words, such as 'as soon as possible' or 'with all speed', will not suffice. A seller may be responsible for a delay in delivery if he deliberately delays performance to satisfy another customer, or does anything or fails to do something which he knows would result in delivery being delayed. This will include failure to employ sufficient workmen to ensure delivery on time, or to get necessary permit permission, or raw materials, or having a shortage of funds, as with any general obligations (§ 279 of the BGB). In other words, the seller must have been negligent in some way before the buyer would be entitled to claim damages. The seller will also be responsible for any fault on the part of those he employs to assist him in performance (§ 278 of the BGB. This last principle resembles the 'vicarious liability' principle utilised in English law. Of course, the seller will not be liable for delays caused by *force majeure*, such as fire, theft, other natural disasters, blockades, wars and similar occurrences over which he has no control, which might have resulted in the unavailability of transport. Such clauses are frequently included in written contracts, particularly in standard form contracts.

The purpose of the award of damages for delay is to compensate for all disadvantages caused by the delay. However, as we have seen, damages constitute only one of the remedies available for breach of contract. Cancellation of the contract or payment of a lower price or a claim for performance (subsequent delivery: § 480 of the BGB) are other possible options for the buyer, depending on the circumstances. The purpose of an award of damages in the context of delay is the same as in English law, as laid down in *Robinson v Harman* (1848) 1 Exch 850, namely, that, 'where a party sustains a loss by reason of a breach of contract, he is, so far as money can do it, to be placed in the same situation ... as if the contract had been performed'. Thus, if the market for the goods has fallen sharply and the buyer has to resell them at a lower price, he would be entitled to the difference between the market price now and its rate when delivery was promised. If the delay results in extra cost being incurred by the buyer, necessitated by giving notice or having to defend a legal action, this will be taken into account in computation of the compensatory figure.

Contributory fault in damages

There is also acceptance of a rule of 'contributory fault' (Mitverschulden) in the law of damages (§ 254 of the BGB) and there is no distinction between direct and indirect (or consequential) losses, although the contract may specify different limitation periods.

Delay also affects the operation of the rules of impossibility. If goods have been accidentally destroyed while the seller was in delay, then he will be liable to compensate the buyer for losses incurred as a result of that destruction, contrary to the general rule regarding impossibility of performance.

Under § 459 of the BGB, the seller of a thing also warrants that, at the time when the risk passed to the buyer, it possesses the following qualities:

(a) it is free from defects diminishing or destroying its value or fitness, for either ordinary use or the use as impliedly or expressly stated in the contract. If there is only a trivial defect in value or fitness, this will not be sufficient (this follows the English *de minimis* principle);

(b) it possesses all the qualities which have been promised.

If this warranty is breached, the two normal remedies provided by § 462 of the Code are the right to cancel the contract (Wandlung) which is the conventional right of rescission, which includes the right to return the goods and the right to demand a reduction in price (Minderung). Rescission is dealt with under § 467 of the BGB and § 472 deals with the Minderung. The reduction of the price is computed by subtracting an amount equal to the deficiency in value from the original agreed price (§ 472 of the BGB). Paragraph 462 also entitles the buyer of defective goods to demand a replacement. Defect is construed in a similar manner to English law. There is no statutory right to have the defect removed and the goods put right, but such a right is frequently incorporated in contracts by the parties or through application of the General Conditions of Business. Instead of bringing a claim for Wandlung (rescission), the buyer may bring a claim for Minderung (abatement of price) or even switch from one remedy to another, unless the seller is relying on the remedy first selected. Apart from the reduction, which is made proportionally, the rest of the sales contract remains intact with all its rights and duties untouched by a claim for a lower price. Actions for breach of warranty must be commenced within six months of purchase. Under the Commercial Code, business buyers must make their complaint immediately after delivery.

The Civil Code also provides a number of other remedies aimed at dealing with a number of special circumstances:

(a) the purchaser has the right to refuse to accept performance and demand damages for non-performance if:

 (i) a quality whose presence has been asserted is lacking (§ 463 of the BGB), but it must be established that the assertion was part of the contract and not merely 'sales talk' preliminary to actual negotiations which was, therefore, not part of the contract;

 (ii) the purchaser has kept silent with malicious intent, despite being aware of a defect and knowing that it would prevent the conclusion of the contract and being aware of his duty to report such a defect under the rule of good faith (§ 242 of the BGB). Mere silence, under these conditions, is sufficient, without the need for any positive act of concealment;

 (iii) the seller has maliciously misrepresented the existence of some qualities or the absence of defects. There is no necessity for any actual promise to have been given. Although not included in the Code, this is a rule derived from customary law, which was introduced by the courts and has commanded universal acceptance by legal writers (see RGZ 132, 78);

(b) in the case of things sold which have been specifically designated in the contract of sale by their particular characteristics (Genuskauf), the purchaser also has the right to demand delivery of an object without defects (§ 480 of the BGB).

These remedies are not available to the buyer in the following cases:

(a) if the purchaser was aware of the defect at the time when the contract was concluded (§ 460 of the BGB);

(b) if the purchaser was ignorant of the defect as a result of his gross negligence and the seller had neither guaranteed that the object was free from that defect nor had maliciously kept silent about it (§ 460). The same rule would apply if the seller had not maliciously asserted that the thing sold was free from defect;

(c) in the case of sales by public auction, where the object has been sold by way of an auction of objects given as a pledge or taken by way of enforcement of a court judgment (§ 461; s 806 of the ZPO (Code of Civil Procedure)).

Seller's remedies

Buyer's failure to pay the price

Paragraph 433(II) of the BGB, requires the buyer to pay the purchase price and take delivery of the goods. The debt, so created, is normally to be paid at the domicile of the seller or by sending the money to him there (§ 270 of the BGB). In modern day practice, mere crediting of the seller's account will suffice to constitute performance of the buyer's promise. The buyer is required to keep himself solvent. The seller may set down a period within which payment should be made; however, once this stipulated period has elapsed, the seller can no longer claim performance of the promise to pay the price of the goods that have been delivered, but only damages will then be available. This claim for damages will usually amount to at least as much as the purchase price. Of course, the seller can still insist on delivering the goods, even if the buyer does not want them. The seller can then claim full damages, including the purchase price.

Impossibility of performance

If the buyer is responsible for impossibility of performance, for example, if he damaged the goods while inspecting them prior to delivery, the seller may still claim for the price and need not perform (§ 324 of the BGB).

Buyer's delay in acceptance of goods

Although there is a general principle, under § 288 of the BGB, which specifies the rate of interest for delay in the payment of money (4% per annum), unless contractually agreed at a higher rate (see § 288I) which applies even if the creditor/seller is not paying any interest himself, the most beneficial right which a seller may claim, nowadays, is the compensation for any interest he has actually paid to his bank during the period of delay (see BGH MDR 1978, 818). If the buyer does not accept the property as agreed, the seller may claim compensation for any harm or loss he has suffered as a result and may even resell the goods if it is a commercial sale (§ 373 of the BGB). This is always subject to the requirement of reasonableness, in § 138. Where acceptance of the property has been made a principal duty under the contract, because the seller has a special reason in disposing of it (for example, perishable goods or if there is a need to clear the particular warehouse), the seller may then stipulate a precise period within which performance by delivery should take place and, if this is not complied with, he may either rescind the contract or claim damages for non-performance.

The principle of good faith in German law

Good faith is a general principle in German commercial law, enshrined in § 242 of the BGB (German Civil Code) which simply states that: 'The debtor is obliged to perform in such a manner as good faith requires, regard being paid to general practice.' As the commentary explains, the aim of the legislator was 'to make people conscious of the true content of the contractual obligation' and the scope of the provision was to be restricted to 'regulating the manner and method of the duty to perform' (I Protokolle zum BGB 303).

Paragraph 242 has been used to elaborate on routine commercial matters, such as what performance entails, and to cover matters, such as the proper packing of goods and the necessary provision of adequate instructions for use with the goods. In this sense, the concept may already be distinguished from the English use of the term 'good faith' which, in the commercial context, applies to buyers of goods who have purchased them from third parties who, unknown to the buyers, were not the owners of the goods. Under s 23 of the Sale of Goods Act 1979 (SGA 1979), purchasers may only defeat the original owner's competing claim to the goods by proving they are *bona fide* purchasers of the goods without notice, that is, they purchased them while unaware of the seller's defect in title. In these circumstances, he may therefore give a good title to a (second) purchaser, provided he is unaware of the defect in title. The specific good faith rules in the SGA 1979 really only deal with 'honesty in fact' and the closely linked concepts of good faith and notice in the SGA 1979 (and the sale of a motor vehicle under the Hire Purchase Act 1964) are really based on commercial convenience and expediency, as exceptions to the general *nemo dat* rule stated in s 21(1) of the SGA 1979. They do not really deal with the broader notions of justice, fairness and reasonableness as specific elements of a principle of good faith. The requirement of good faith in English contract and commercial law is really a requirement of a standard of honesty and fair dealing and, in contracts of insurance, for example, is really an application of well established common law and equitable rules on fraud. In short, English law has had no legislative history of a general statutory requirement that parties should perform their contractual obligations in good faith, nor is there any general principle of common law which implies any sort of duty along these lines. Rather, it deals with the need for goods to be fit for their purpose and of satisfactory quality and all the other prerequisites through concepts, such as 'implied terms' or conditions or warranties, and through certain sections of the Sale of Goods Act 1979, as amended, in 1973, by the Supply of Good (Implied Terms) Act 1973 (the 1973 Act) and, most recently, the Sale and Supply of Goods Act 1994 (the 1994 Act), which implemented changes taking effect after 2 January 1995.

In Germany, § 242 of the BGB has outgrown its original function as it is now being used as a statutory enactment of a general requirement of good faith, a principle of legal ethics (Larenz, *Methodenlehre* (1979)) and, in fact, 'dominates the entire legal system' (Leser (1982)). Its content, today, is seen as primarily 'reliance', whereby it acts as an integrating element in the legal culture and, particularly, through reciprocal reliance which caters to the needs and interests of others (Fikentsher, *I Methoden des Rechts* (1975) pp 109, 179 *et seq*).

In the context of the present chapter, suffice to say that the principle of good faith continues to play an important supplementary role in German sales law, performing an ethical function by giving a legal foundation for ethical values, a contractual function by developing contractual rights and duties and a regulatory function by controlling and demarcating the exercise and scope of rights in conjunction with other business statutes, Codes and principles.

THE ENGLISH COMMON LAW APPROACH

General

The English law of sale of goods originated from the *lex mercatoria* or ancient mercantile law and is predominantly based on principles developed by the law of contract. Until the end of the 19th century, the principles governing sales of goods lay buried in the larger mass of contract law. The 19th century eventually produced the Sale of Goods Act 1893 which remained unchanged on the statute books for 80 years. The sources of the law of sales may now be found in the Factors Act 1889, the Sale of Goods Act 1979 (the '1979 Act'), which consolidates the original Act of 1893 with later amendments, the Unfair Contract Terms Act 1977 and the rules of common law (that is, case law) which have been left intact despite these pieces of legislation. In keeping with the English common law tradition, statutes are not intended, *ipso facto*, to create new rules or procedures, but to consolidate and sometimes clarify the existing law. Indeed, s 62(2) of the 1979 Act declares:

> The rules of the common law, including the law merchant, except in so far as they are inconsistent with the express provisions of this Act and, in particular,

the rules relating to the law of principal and agent and the effect of fraud, misrepresentation, duress or coercion, mistake or other invalidating cause, apply to contracts for the sale of goods.

The 1979 Act therefore makes no attempt to codify systematically existing legislation in any exhaustive way, except that the effect of various provisions has been to codify certain aspects of the law relating to the sale of goods. Hence, as *Bank of England v Vagliano Bros* [1891] AC 107 emphasised, if the Act's provisions were ambiguous in any way, earlier cases may help to resolve the ambiguity; and, if a term had acquired a technical meaning, previous cases may be cited to illustrate this meaning. A necessary corollary of this is that, if a point arose which was not covered by the Act, earlier decisions would have to be referred to and followed. Since it is primarily derived from the law of contract, it is inevitable that a great deal of its key concepts and main remedies have a strong contractual underpinning, supplemented by modified 'commercial law' principles. The 1979 Act defines a contract of sale from other transactions. Section 2(1) states 'A contract of sale of goods is a contract whereby the seller transfers or agrees to transfer the property in goods to the buyer for a money consideration called the "price"'. Further, by s 61(1) of the same Act, the term 'contract of sale' in the Act includes both actual sales and agreements to sell (see, further, p 407, below). The House of Lords, in *Stocznia Gdanska SA v Latvian Shipping Co* [1998] 1 All ER 883, has reaffirmed the proposition that shipbuilding contracts are not to be regarded as contracts of sale.

Key legislative changes that have been made in more recent times are: (a) the Sale of Goods (Amendment) Act 1994 which abolished the rule of market overt in the transfer of title to goods; and (b) the Sale of Goods (Amendment) Act 1995 which allowed buyers to acquire an undivided share/interest in bulk goods under certain circumstances (see p 412, below).

As with the previous civil law analysis, it is proposed to concentrate on the key issues that dominate this area of law under English common law.

Definition of goods under English law

'Goods' are now defined under s 61(1) of the SGA (as amended) as 'all personal chattels other than things in action and money' and, in particular, 'emblements, industrial growing crops and things attached to or forming part of the land which are agreed to be severed before sale or under the contract of sale'. In practical terms, the personal chattels that may be the subject of a sale of goods agreement cover tangible, movable items that English law calls 'things in possession'.

Examples of 'goods', as interpreted under the SGA, continue to be found in recent case law. In *St Albans City and District Council v International Computers Ltd* [1996] 4 All ER 481, the trial judge took the view that computer software was 'probably' goods under s 61(1) of the SGA, since 'programs are, of necessity, contained in some physical medium'. In the Court of Appeal, Sir Iain Glidewell, albeit *obiter*, opined that the disk carrying a program was goods under the SGA, but the program *per se* was not. His view was that the quality of the program stored on the disk was a matter for s 14 of the SGA and, hence, strict liability, in the same way as strict liability would follow in the case of defective instructions in a car maintenance manual. Thus, if a program were directly transferred by the licensor to the user's system without the user receiving any tangible thing, it would fall outside the SGA and the Supply of Goods and Services Act 1982; accordingly, liability would have to exist at common law and the implied term that the parties 'must have intended', in such a case, would be one of strict liability that the program be reasonably fit for its purpose. Bridge (1998) is critical of this view and argues that, while no proper distinction can be drawn between instructions stored on a computer disk and instructions stored in a book, it is not the same for a computer program. Here, it is not the case of a disk being unusable without a program; the disk is merely the 'integument' (outer protective shell/covering) of the program. The hardware is only the means by which the software can be used and enjoyed. In the computer world, 'tangible things are supplied for the purpose of using dominant intangible things' (Bridge). Hence, he argues that this suggests that the supply of software should be classified as the provision of services attracting fault based and not strict liability. If Sir Iain Glidewell's words were to be taken to apply to writers of non-fiction books, then, Bridge suggests, authors should take out liability insurance and preface their work with well drawn exclusion clauses.

Transfer of property and transfer of ownership

Under English law, the basic principle is that whoever is the owner of the goods at any given time must bear the risk of loss, damage or deterioration of the goods. Sections 16–20 of the 1979 Act enunciate the rules relating to transfer of ownership. The statute refers to 'transfer of property as between buyer and seller'. Under the 1979 Act, 'property' refers to the title to the goods, or rights of ownership, as in 'the property in the goods'. Further, the rights expressly dealt with are those which arise between seller and buyer, which are not necessarily identical against the third parties and the world at large. 'Property' or ownership must be distinguished from possession, since the property in goods sold may pass to the buyer, but the seller may, nevertheless, retain possession of the goods. Possession of the goods may also be transferred without transferring the ownership of them, as in hire purchase contracts and contracts whereby the seller has reserved his title (see the *Romalpa* case [1976] 2 All ER 552). Rights of third parties over the goods are covered by ss 21–26 of the 1979 Act. English law does not follow Roman law and so 'property' may pass by agreement.

As far as English law was concerned, the doctrine of the 'passing of property' by consent was combined with the principle of *nemo dat quod non habet* (no one can give a better title than he holds himself) which was subsequently modified by the Factors Act 1889 and the 1893, 1973, 1979 and 1994 Acts (see p 428, below). It also sees problems of risk and ownership as quite separate from those arising from breach of contract. Hence, if the buyer has become owner of the goods, this does not, *ipso facto*, affect his right to repudiate the contract or claim damages for goods which are not in conformity with the contract. If he retains the right to repudiate, ownership will then revert to the seller, although the contract may stipulate that the buyer will be responsible for returning the goods at his own risk. In the United States, Art 2-510 of the Uniform Commercial Code seeks to protect a buyer in these circumstances, so that he will not be at risk, even temporarily. It stipulates that risk of loss remains on the seller until the defect is cured or the goods have been accepted.

Transfer of ownership and risk of loss

Sales and agreements to sell

A clear distinction is drawn between sales and agreements to sell in the 1979 Act:

(a) where, under a contract of sale, the property in goods is passed from the seller to the buyer, the contract is called a sale (s 2(4));

(b) where the transfer of the property in the goods is to take place at a future time or subject to some condition to be subsequently fulfilled, the contract is called an 'agreement to sell' (s 2(5));

(c) an agreement to sell becomes a sale when the time elapses or the conditions are fulfilled subject to which the property in the goods is to be transferred (s 2(6)).

Ownership and responsibility for risk of loss

These distinctions should be noted because the actual moment 'property' or the right to ownership passes is important for the following reasons: first, the risk of loss or damage will pass with the property, that is, with the transfer of ownership (s 20(1) of the 1979 Act), unless otherwise agreed. The risk of accidental damage or loss will, therefore, follow the transfer of ownership under the *res perit domino* principle. It is important to note that the risk of accidental loss or damage will fall on the owner of the goods, irrespective of whether he is in possession of the goods (see *Tarling v Baxter* (1827) 6 B & C 360). Nevertheless, the Act's provisions on, *inter alia*, passing of risk, may be varied by agreement of the parties or by trade custom.

'Risk', within the meaning of s 20, would seem to include only loss or damage caused by accident and without negligence on the part of either buyer or seller.

Secondly, if ownership has passed to the buyer, the seller has the right to sue for the price. Thirdly, if the seller re-sells the goods after ownership has passed to the buyer, the second buyer acquires no title unless he is protected by one of the exceptions to the *nemo dat* rule (see p 428, below). The same sort of principle applies if the buyer re-sells the goods before the property in them, that is, the title to them, has passed to him.

Ownership and unascertained goods

Under s 16 of the 1979 Act, where there is a contract for the sale of unascertained goods (namely, goods identified by description only and not identified until after the contract is made), no property passes to the buyer unless and until they are ascertained. Hence, a particular article or collection of articles must be identified as the unique subject matter of the contract before ownership can pass to the buyer who will then bear the risk of loss, damage or deterioration of the goods.

In *Healy v Howlett* [1917] 1 KB 337, a buyer ordered 20 boxes of fish from the seller. These were separated from a large consignment at a time when the whole consignment had already gone bad. Although the seller had given instructions for the boxes to be appropriated for the buyer, the fish had gone bad before this appropriation had been carried out. It was held that, since property did not pass until appropriation for the buyer had been carried out, when the fish went bad, they still belonged to the seller and so the fish remained at the seller's risk.

Similarly, in *Re London Wine Co* [1986] PCC 121, buyers bought certain quantities of wine which they also identified by specific descriptions, which they then left in the seller's warehouse. The seller went into liquidation and his creditors claimed all the wine in the warehouse. The court held that, even though the quantities and descriptions ordered by the buyers accorded with the wines stored in the warehouse, it was still not necessarily the only wine which could have been used to fulfil the buyer's orders and so property had not passed, and the sellers remained the owners. Hence, the buyers were left with claims for damages from sellers who were insolvent. It is worth noting that, under Art 2-105 of the American Uniform Commercial Code, the buyer of part of an undivided whole becomes owner in common with the owners of the remaining parts.

However, the provisions of the Act can be varied by agreement or trade custom. Thus, if it appears that the parties have agreed that the risk will pass before the property or ownership does, the courts may find such an agreement crucial to their determination of whether the property in the goods has, in fact, passed to the buyer. In *Sterns Ltd v Vickers* [1923] 1 KB 78, the seller agreed to sell 120,000 gallons of spirit, out of a total quantity of 200,000 in a storage tank on the premises of a third party. A delivery order was issued to the buyer, which the third party accepted, but the buyers decided to leave the spirit in the tank for some months for their convenience, during which time the spirit deteriorated. The Court of Appeal held that, although the property in the goods had not passed (because no appropriation had taken place), the parties must have intended the risk to pass when the delivery order was delivered and accepted by the third party. Consequently, the buyer remained liable for the price.

Ownership and ascertained goods

Under s 17 of the 1979 Act, if the contract is for the sale of specific or ascertained goods, the property passes when the parties intend it to pass. In other words, the parties may decide when ownership shall pass if they are dealing with ascertained goods. This may be expressly stated in the terms of the contract. An extremely common practice (see Whincup (1990)) is for a clause to be inserted which says either that ownership shall pass on delivery or when payment is made after delivery. A typical reservation of title clause might read: 'The property in the goods shall remain in the seller until the price and any other payment due to the seller has been discharged in full.' Such clauses are also called retention of title clauses. The seller may, nevertheless, disclaim responsibility for risk and impose liability on the buyer as soon as the latter takes delivery, despite retaining ownership by having a clause in the contract stating the precise legal position and terms of the agreement, to this effect. As with unascertained goods, risk may even pass before delivery by the same device of a clause expressly stating this to be the case, but the buyer will, of course, have to agree to this being so stated. The seller may, therefore, wish to 'reserve title' to the goods until the buyer's outstanding debts are paid and s 19 expressly deals with such clauses and is discussed below (see 'The *Romalpa* case', p 415, below), but, under the 1979 Act, s 17 is also wide enough to enable such reservation of title clauses to be made. If there is no clear statement of the parties' intentions, it may be inferred from the conduct of the parties and the circumstances of the case (s 17(2) of the 1979 Act).

The courts will generally endeavour to give effect to the contracting parties' intentions, as far as they may be discoverable. Nevertheless, a number of business practices have grown up surrounding various types of contracts, despite a lack of written evidence of intention in any given case. For instance, ownership of goods shipped under cif contracts (where the price includes cost, insurance and freight) is usually deemed to pass upon delivery of the documents of title (that is, the bills of lading). In fob contracts (free on board), ownership passes when the goods cross the ship's rail (compare this with the rules on passing of risk which are different for each of these contracts. If a seller retains the documents of title after delivery, the implication appears to be that he still owns the goods (*Cheetham v Thornham* [1964] 2 Lloyd's Rep 17). On the other hand, there are cases, like the *Albazero* [1977] AC 774, which suggest that ownership might be deemed to pass upon shipment of the goods or upon posting the bill of lading. It will clearly turn on the individual circumstances of the case and the court's perception of the parties' intentions. However, if any intentions were expressed after the contract was made, these will be disregarded: *Dennant v Skinner and Collom* [1948] 2 KB 164.

If the parties have not indicated their intention (at the time of contracting) as to when property in ascertained goods should pass to the buyer and it cannot be discovered, even by using all the above means, the matter must be decided by applying the five rules contained in s 18 of the 1979 Act. Section 18 begins by stating:

> Unless a contrary intention appears, the following are rules for ascertaining the intention of the parties as to the time at which the property in the goods is to pass to the buyer.

We now consider the five rules, bearing in mind the words 'unless a contrary intention appears' is an all embracing proviso.

Rule 1 of s 18 provides that, in unconditional contracts for the sale of specific goods in a deliverable state, ownership passes when the contract is made. The term 'unconditional contract' appears to refer to a contract that is not subject to either a condition precedent or condition subsequent, so that it takes effect immediately. 'Specific goods', under s 61 of the 1979 Act, are goods 'identified and agreed upon at the time of sale'. Two contrasting cases are *Kursell v Timber Operators and Contractors Ltd* [1927] 1 KB 298 and *Reid v Schultz* [1949] SR (NSW) 231 (an Australian decision). In *Kursell*, a sale of all the trees in a Latvian forest which conformed to certain measurements, which by a given date had reached a certain size, was held by the Court of Appeal not to be sufficiently specific, as the goods were not sufficiently identified. This was because it was impossible to say then which trees would qualify; not all the trees were to pass, but only those conforming to the stipulated measurements. However, in *Reid*, a sale of all the millable or marketable hardwood timber on a certain site was held to be a sale of specific goods.

'Deliverable state', for the purposes of this rule, refers to the goods being in such a state in which the buyer would, under the contract, be bound to take delivery of them (s 61(5) of the 1979 Act); in other words, if nothing more needs to be done to the goods under the contract. This does not include anything that needs to be done to them to remedy any defects or deficiencies. Hence, if they need to be repaired or dismantled, they are not immediately deliverable and remain the seller's responsibility and he must bear the loss of accidental damage or deterioration. As under all these rules, the parties may agree that the goods concerned are deliverable before anything that needs to be done to them has been completed.

It appears somewhat unsatisfactory to make ownership pass at the time the contract is made, even when the goods remain with the seller, albeit temporarily. Coupled with the rule that the owner then bears the risk of accidental loss or damage, if a buyer orders a specific item in a shop, he therefore becomes the owner of that item. Should it be accidentally damaged before it has been delivered to the buyer, the buyer would still be bound to pay for it. To avoid this, most commercial firms usually insert a clear contrary provision to the effect that risk shall not pass until delivery. Courts have, in any event, shown themselves unwilling to apply r 1 and have been quick to seize any ambiguity or uncertainty in the contract, to find it is unconditional and, therefore, not covered by this rule. As Diplock LJ put it 'In modern times, very little is needed to give rise to the inference that the property in specific goods is to pass only on delivery or payment' *(Ward v Bignall* [1967] 1 QB 534, p 545).

Rules 2 and 3 deal with acts that are required to be fulfilled by the seller. If these necessary acts must be done by the buyer, ownership will pass upon the making of the contract. Rule 2 of s 18 states that, where the contract is for specific goods and the seller is bound to do something to the goods to put them into a deliverable state, ownership does not pass until this has been done and the buyer has been notified accordingly. Hence, if a seller agrees to fix a handle to a piece of furniture which he has sold, ownership will not pass until the buyer has been notified that the work has been carried out (see *Underwood v Burgh Castle Brick and Cement Syndicate* [1922] 1 KB 343).

Rule 3 states that, where the specific goods are in a deliverable state, but the seller is bound to weigh, measure and test the goods to establish their price, ownership does not pass until these things have been done and the buyer is notified accordingly. Clearly, this rule is not applicable to a situation where nothing further needs to be done to the goods to render them deliverable.

Rule 4 deals with goods sent on approval or on sale or return. In this case, ownership of the goods will pass to the buyer only when he informs the seller that he wants them, confirms to the seller that he wants them or in some other way indicates that he wants them. Three examples of the kinds of action that could signify the buyer's intentions were given by Lopes LJ in *Kirkham v Attenborough* [1897] 1 QB 201, p 204:

(a) the buyer may pay the price; or

(b) he may retain the goods beyond a reasonable time for return; or

(c) he may do an act inconsistent with his being other than a purchaser.

In accordance with the third of these possibilities, the buyer may, therefore, sell the goods to someone else and would, it appears, pass a good title, unless the terms of the original contract prohibited him from doing this. If the contract says 'The goods remain the seller's property until paid for or charged', pursuant to the all embracing proviso ('unless a different intention appears'), then ownership will not pass. If the seller holds his buyer as authorised to sell the goods, then the seller may lose them to an innocent third party (s 21 of the 1979 Act).

Unascertained goods

The Sale of Goods (Amendment) Act 1995 introduced s 20A into the Sale of Goods Act 1979, to the effect that, where the goods or some part of them form part of a bulk, the buyer acquires an undivided share in the bulk and becomes an owner in common of the bulk before ascertainment of the particular goods that the seller intends to deliver under the contract. However, there are two conditions to be satisfied. First, the bulk must be identified in the contract or by subsequent agreement by the parties. 'Bulk' is defined as 'a mass or collection of goods of the same kind which ... is contained in a defined space or area ... and is such that any goods in the bulk are interchangeable with any other goods, therein, of the same number or quantity' (s 61(1) of the SGA 1979, as added by the 1995 Act). Secondly, the buyer must have made payment for that share of the goods. In addition, the 1995 Act deals with various matters arising from this change in the law: (i) the size of the buyer's share is a rateable one which will correspond to the ratio between the bulk and the quantity of the goods for which payment has been made to the buyer. Any delivery out of the bulk to a buyer who has made only a part payment will be ascribed to that payment; the buyer's share may increase incrementally as payment is progressively made. Under the unit pricing approach, the size of the buyer's share will correspond directly to the size of the part payment; (ii) diminishing of quantity in the bulk, caused by natural wastage, theft or default of the seller will be borne rateably by the various tenant buyers, according to the size of their respective shares in the bulk (s 20A(4)); (iii) deliveries (including passing of property falling short of a physical delivery: s 61(1)) out of the bulk to individual buyers may override the individual shares of co-owners to whom delivery has not been made. Under s 20B(1)(a) of the 1979 Act, co-owners are deemed to consent to such deliveries out of the bulk to fellow co-owners entitled to receive such delivery. Thus, a buyer receiving delivery in full, in this way, is not required to indemnify fellow co-owners who might subsequently have to suffer a disproportionately large share of diminution that has occurred in the bulk. The consent of co-owners extends to 'any dealing with or removal, delivery or disposal of the goods' by one of their number. This could include a seller's decision to let a buyer have delivery of the goods in the bulk even before the seller receives payment. Section 20(B)(2) appears to offer statutory protection to those who act within the abovementioned consents, so as to be protected from liability in conversion; (iv) the legislation does not seem to affect the contractual rights of those buyers who would benefit from the proprietary rights conferred by s 20A–B.

Michael Bridge (1998) notes four points arising from the 1995 Act amendments: first, the Act appears to create an interim position in the passing of property from seller to buyer: the buyer's undivided share in the bulk will be overridden by the general property in the goods after the buyer's goods have been separated from the identified bulk; secondly, the buyer's undivided share should not be extinguished after ascertainment of the goods just because r 5 of s 18 has not been satisfied; thirdly, the relationship between r 5 of s 18 and s 20A needs to be considered. Bridge argues that it would be a curious property right of the buyer's if it could be unilaterally divested by the seller in separating the buyer's goods from the bulk. Although a buyer will not acquire an undivided interest, under s 20A, until payment is made, once the bulk is exhausted by the other buyer's claims, leaving only the non-paying buyer with a claim to receive goods from that bulk, the property in the goods will pass to that buyer pursuant to s 18, r 5(3) and (4). The unpaid seller will have the protection of a lien over the goods until payment is made: s 39(1)(a) of the SGA. Finally, an undivided interest is now defined as goods under the SGA; yet, a sub-buyer (who may not have been paid) of unascertained goods in a bulk would not automatically become the buyer of an undivided share and the sale of unascertained goods merely because the buyer acquires an undivided share in the bulk upon payment. Thus, the distinction between the sale of an undivided share and the sale of unascertained goods in a specific or identified bulk remains.

Unascertained goods and r 5

As noted above, r 5 must now be potentially undermined by the new s 20A and its requirement of ascertainment, while r 5 maintains a strict approach.

Rule 5(1) of s 18 deals with future or unascertained goods. In other words, it covers goods which are not specific at the time of sale. These were the sort of goods in *Healy* and *London Wine* (above) and are generic or simply unidentified parts of a whole. This rule determines the precise moment after the contract has been made at which the goods become the buyer's property. It states:

> Where there is a contract for the sale of unascertained or future goods by description, the property passes when the goods of that description and in a deliverable state are unconditionally appropriated to the contract by one party with the express or implied assent of the other.

Hence, the goods must be 'unconditionally appropriated' to the contract by the seller or buyer with the express or implied approval of the other.

The case of *Pignataro v Gilroy* [1919] 1 KB 459 is instructive. The seller sold 140 bags of rice to the buyer, 15 bags of which were appropriated by the seller for the contract. The buyer was told where he could collect them. The bags were then stolen, through no fault of the seller, before the buyer was able to collect them. The buyer failed in his action to recover the price paid for the 15 bags. It was held that the buyer had, by his conduct, assented to the seller's appropriation; the seller's appropriation of the bags for the contract, without any objection by the buyer, constituted transfer of title in those bags. The property in the goods (and, therefore, the risk) had passed to the buyer. The bags thus belonged to the buyer when they were stolen.

No appropriation occurs in an fob contract until the goods are shipped (*Carlos Federspiel & Co v Twigg Ltd* [1957] 1 Lloyd's Rep 240). The words of Pearson J, in the *Federspiel* case, are illuminating:

> A mere setting apart or selection by the seller of the goods which he expects to use in performance of the contract is not enough. If that is all, he can change his mind and use those goods in performance of some other contract and use some other goods in performance of this contract. To constitute an appropriation of the goods to the contract, the parties must have had, or be reasonably supposed to have had, an intention to attach the contract irrevocably to those goods, and no others are the subject of the sale and becomes the property of the buyer ... if there is a further act, an important and decisive act, to be done by the seller, then there is *prima facie* evidence that, probably, the property does not pass until the final act is done.

The appropriation must, therefore, be 'irrevocable' and conclusive to be legally effective. It is, perhaps, also worth noting that, if the goods are in the hands of a third party bailee, such as a warehouseman, the goods may still be deemed to have appropriated if, for example, the third party acknowledges that he holds the goods on the buyer's behalf (see *Sterns v Vickers* (1923), discussed above, p 409). The rationale for this decision appears to be that, by giving a delivery order to the buyer, the seller has done all that he can to enable the buyer to collect the goods. In commercial sales, the American Commercial Code (see UCC 2-509) adopts the same approach.

Rule 5(2) of s 18 must be read in conjunction with s 16. Rule 5(2) provides that a seller who delivers goods to the buyer or to a carrier for transmission, without reserving a right of disposal, is deemed to have unconditionally appropriated the goods to the contract. Under s 16, no right of ownership passes until the goods are ascertained.

Reservation/retention of title clauses: s 19

Under s 19, the seller may reserve the right of disposal of the goods until certain conditions are fulfilled, and ownership will not then pass to the buyer until the conditions imposed by the seller have been fulfilled. In brief, this suggests that, if the contract has been appropriately worded, a seller may remain owner of his goods until he has paid for them. The form of words that is frequently used for this retention of title or reservation of title clause has already been suggested and the main purpose of the seller in inserting such a clause is to attempt to give himself the best available security in the event that the buyer becomes insolvent. The opening words of s 18 again come to mind, namely, 'unless a different intention appears', which means that, provided this different intention is suitably worded, a so called *Romalpa* clause (named after the case containing that type of clause: see below) has been utilised as a useful device for hard pressed sellers.

The *Romalpa* case

In the *Romalpa* case [1976] 2 All ER 552), the plaintiffs (AIV), who were a Dutch supplier of aluminium foil, provided in their conditions of sale that 'The ownership of the material to be delivered by AIV will only be transferred to the purchaser when he has met all that is owing to AIV, no matter on what grounds'. After taking delivery of a consignment of aluminium, the purchaser went into liquidation. The plaintiffs, who had not received the purchase price, sought to enforce the above provision so as to secure payment prior to the distribution of the insolvent buyer's assets to the general creditors. The Court of Appeal held:

(a) that the clause enabled the plaintiffs to recover from the insolvent buyer all the unsold foil still on his premises; and

(b) that, since the object of the clause would be defeated unless it impliedly obliged the buyer to hold the proceeds of sale of unmixed foil on trust for the plaintiffs, the plaintiffs had a right to follow such monies into the buyer's bank account and require payment from it.

On the special facts of *Romalpa*, the seller succeeded in recovering the unsold foil and the identifiable proceeds of sold foil from the buyer's liquidator. The remedy of possession appears to be wider than the remedy of lien which is for the price only. Further, the *Romalpa* remedy may be exercised until 'all that is owing' has been paid. In addition, it is wider than the right of stoppage *in transitu*, since the right to stop in transit ends when transit ends. The *Romalpa* remedy is only available after delivery of the goods.

Effect of the *Romalpa* case

The *Romalpa* case was widely regarded as a controversial decision which has resulted in many such '*Romalpa* clauses' being inserted in contracts. The effect of the decision seemed to be to give comfort to sellers who used such clauses, but not to unsecured creditors of companies in the *Romalpa* circumstances. Neither the proceeds of sale nor the buyer's stock in trade would be available to these creditors and even the bank might not be first in priority. Since English law does not require reservation of title clauses to be publicly registered, nor any form of mandatory notice to be given, it appears extremely difficult to discover a company's real creditworthiness. Such a clause, if prudently drafted, however, could still give an unsecured creditor a measure of protection from a buyer's insolvency.

Case law has established that the inference from s 19 is that payment of the buyer's debts must be made in full before property in the goods would pass (see *Mitsui v Flota* [1988] 1 WLR 1145); and that a *Romalpa* clause will not apply once the goods or material in question have been incorporated into other goods or subjected to the manufacturing process. In *Re Peachdart* [1983] 3 All ER 204, leather which was intended to be used in the manufacture of handbags, was sold on reservation of title terms, with the seller being entitled to ownership of both leather and handbags. It was, nevertheless, held that, once goods were incorporated into other goods, they ceased to exist, hence, the supplier's title ceased to exist when the leather had been made into handbags. The seller's claim to the proceeds of the sale of the bags was also dismissed, *inter alia,* on the basis that there was no way of relating the proceeds of the sale of the bags to the value of the leather in them.

In *Clough Mill v Martin* [1984] 3 All ER 982, the material concerned here was yarn which the buyer would spin into fabric. The reservation of title clause stated that the ownership of the yarn remained with the seller until the seller had received payment in full, or the yarn was sold by the buyer in a *bona fide* sale at full market value. When a receiver was appointed, the seller claimed a quantity of the yarn. The receiver refused to return it. The case was heard on the claim for wrongful use (conversion) of the yarn and is not, therefore, a direct authority on the *Romalpa* clause. However, the Court of Appeal upheld the seller's claim and the receiver was held personally liable for wrongful use of goods. Significantly, Oliver LJ suggested that they saw 'no reason in principle why the original legal title in a newly manufactured article, composed of materials belonging to A and B, should not lie where A and B have agreed it shall lie'.

Principle of the *Romalpa* case

The broad principle discernible from the *Romalpa* case appears to be that, if goods have been delivered to the buyer under a contract which contains a stipulation that ownership of the goods is only to pass on payment, the seller may be able to recover the goods, and possibly the identifiable proceeds of sale from the buyer's liquidator, in the event of the buyer's bankruptcy. As a final observation, it would appear that everything turns on the precise wording of the individual clause in each case and the claim to mixed goods and, arguably, their proceeds of sale, will succeed or fail depending on the specificity of the wording of a *Romalpa* clause.

Delivery at seller's own risk

If the seller agrees to deliver specific goods at his own risk, then s 33 of the 1979 Act becomes relevant. Section 33 reads:

> Where the seller of goods agrees to deliver them at his own risk at a place other than that where they are when sold, the buyer must, nevertheless, unless otherwise agreed, take any risk of deterioration in the goods necessarily incident to the course of transit.

The implication of this provision is that the seller would take the risk of unusual or extraordinary deterioration or loss.

Duties of buyer and seller

Conditions and warranties

Under English law, rights and duties granted or imposed under a contract of sale are divided into conditions and warranties. There has also been considerable academic and judicial discussion, prompted by certain leading cases over the proper legal effect of terms of the contract which could not be definitively categorised as either condition or warranty and were sometimes called 'innominate terms'. There are also statutory rules which supplement the common law rules which govern the duties of buyers and sellers. A condition is an essential term, which goes to the root of a contract, the breach of which normally entitles the innocent party to repudiate the contract and claim damages. A warranty is a stipulation of secondary importance, ancillary to the contract, the breach of which only entitles the innocent party to damages, but not to the right of repudiation. Conditions and warranties have been integrated into the Sale of Goods Act 1979 which elaborates and adapts the terminology and concepts to the sale of goods. It is not possible, in a book of this nature, to explore the many terminological and legal difficulties that have been raised by the terms 'condition' and 'warranty', which have been the subject of many decided cases and fairly extensive academic opinion. Suffice it to say that the legal meanings of the words differ from their meaning in common English usage; even more confusingly, they have also been used interchangeably in law. To give an example of each:

(a) the word 'condition' may be used as a condition precedent, or as an essential prerequisite of contractual liability, for example, as in 'If I manage to sell my shares, I will sign the contract'. There will be no liability for breach of the proposed contract if the shares are not sold;

(b) the word 'warranty' (in old English usage) used to mean a promise of any kind, whether of crucial importance or merely subsidiary. Today, it often refers to a manufacturer's guarantee, which may carry no legal consequences whatever, or to an insured party's obligations, the breach of which may nullify the contract, even though the breach was not the cause of the insured 'loss'!

Innominate terms

It may be very difficult, in certain cases, to decide whether a particular term should be regarded as a condition or warranty; thus, the English courts have decided that the final classification of a term may depend on either:

(a) the intention of the parties; or

(b) the nature and consequences of the breach of the contract, rather than on the prior classification of the terms.

In the absence of evidence of intention, the court will consider the consequences of the breach. The leading case, from which (b) is derived, is the Court of Appeal decision, *Hong Kong Fir Shipping v Kawasaki Kisen Kaisha* (the *Hong Kong Fir* case) [1962] 1 All ER 474. This did not involve a sale of goods, but a contract of hire of a ship – a charterparty – in which one of the terms was that the ship should be seaworthy. *Prima facie*, it might have been thought that a ship which was in no fit state to go to sea at all, with no prospect of being repaired sufficiently so as to make it fit to sail again, would surely entitle the charterer to repudiate the contract altogether. Seaworthiness might, therefore, have been regarded as a vital term and thus a condition. However, on the case authorities, seaworthiness was a comprehensive standard and a ship might, therefore, be pronounced unseaworthy for a trifling defect which could be rectified quite easily, but might fail the legal standard. Accordingly, the Court of Appeal held that the shipowner's duty could not be classified beforehand as a condition or warranty, but remained an 'innominate term' until the nature and consequences of its breach could be assessed. Subsequent cases have merely confirmed the existence of such a category which cannot be classified and will be adjudicated upon only when the consequences of its breach are known.

For example, the *Mihalis Angelos* [1971] 1 QB 164 held that some contract terms should still be properly regarded as conditions, so that any breach of them should entitle the innocent party to repudiate the contract; the House of Lords in the *Reardon* case [1976] 1 WLR 989 appeared to say that express contractual conditions in a contract of sale of goods should be subject to the general rules of contract and not the peculiar and specialised rules laid down in the Sale of Goods Act. The position is clearly unsettled and the most that can be said is that judges have a wide discretion in deciding any case of ambiguity.

The uncertainty caused is clearly unsatisfactory from the strictly commercial point of view, since business certainty, at least within a measure of reasonableness, is generally essential to commercial dealings. However, it is still up to contracting parties (or their legal advisers) to devise contracts which will leave no doubt as to the importance that they wish to attach to individual terms of a contract, so that, if the matter comes to court, the judges will have very little room within which to manoeuvre and have no option but to implement the clearly stated wishes of the contracting parties.

Breach of entire and severable contracts

Another possible scenario which the courts have faced is the question of construing when a breach has taken place in the context of entire and severable contracts. The 'entire' contract is a contract in which no payment is due to the seller or supplier of services until he has fulfilled all his commitments precisely in accordance with the terms of the contract. A 'severable' contract is one in which part payment is due as soon as each stage of the contract has been completed. Thus, in the case of an entire contract, the most trivial defect or deficiency in the seller's performance of the contract would, in strict law, amount to a breach of contract which would entitle the buyer to repudiate the contract. However, this might not always be an equitable solution, since the buyer might not be able to return any benefits he might have already received under the contract, thus making an unjustifiable profit. Three points mitigate against interpreting contracts as entire ones. First, judges apply the 'substantial performance' approach which reduces the situation to a breach of warranty, which will not justify repudiation. Secondly, judges are generally reluctant to construe contracts as entire contracts. Thirdly, there is a common law principle that does not allow a whole sum of money to be recovered unless there has been a total failure of consideration. Thus, if a buyer paid some money in advance to the seller in pursuance of a contract, and the seller had already performed part of the contract, the buyer could not usually recover the money unless he received nothing at all in return for it.

Conditions as warranties under the Sale of Goods Act

Under s 11 of the Sale of Goods Act 1979, it is possible for a breach of condition to be treated as a warranty in certain circumstances. Under s 11(2), a buyer may waive a breach of condition by the seller or elect to treat it as a breach of warranty. If a contract is non-severable and the buyer has accepted all or some of the goods, by s 11(4), a buyer must treat a breach of condition as a breach of warranty. However, s 11(4) does not apply to a breach of s 12 which enacts that there is an implied condition that the seller has the right to pass title to the goods. A breach of s 12 will amount to a total failure of consideration, since the transfer of the property on the goods is the essence of a contract of sale. Such a breach cannot, therefore, be treated as a breach of warranty.

Seller's duties

In the 19th century, in the heyday of the *laissez faire* philosophy, the basic rule was that 'the seller was not liable for a bad title unless there was an express warranty or an equivalent to it by declaration or conduct' (*Baron Parke in Morley v Attenborough* (1849) 3 Exch 500, p 512). Thus, the rule was *caveat emptor* (let the buyer beware). However, this was often countermanded by case law and s 12 of the 1979 Act (the Act) now enacts that there is an implied condition that the seller has the right to pass good title to the goods.

Sale by description

Where goods are sold by description, there is also an implied condition under s 13 of the Act that:

(a) the goods will correspond with the description (s 13(1));

(b) if the sale is by sample, as well as by description, the bulk of the goods will also correspond with the sample (s 13(2)).

This has proved to be a source of dispute, in a number of cases, because of the very open endedness of language and its many possible meanings. Among the issues encountered is the question: has this section abolished the distinction between mere representations and contractual terms? Cases, such as *Beale v Taylor* [1967] 1 WLR 1193, appear to suggest that, in practice, this section makes it easier for a buyer to argue that a descriptive statement by the seller is a contractual term and not a mere representation. However, the House of Lords has also suggested that a statement about the goods is only part of the 'description' if it has been used to identify the goods (see *Ashington Piggeries v Christopher Hill* [1972] AC 441). The approach must, therefore, be to analyse the descriptive words to see if they amount to mere representations or form part of the contract. If they are contractual, the normal contractual remedies will be available. If they are misrepresentations, then the usual rules will apply under common law and the Misrepresentation Act 1967. The case of *Grant v Australian Knitting Mills* [1936] AC 35 is also instructive. Here, a buyer of underpants contracted dermatitis because of an excess of sulphite in the garment he purchased. The House of Lords emphasised that a sale may be 'by description', even if the buyer has seen the goods before buying them, provided he relied essentially on the description and any discrepancy between the description and the goods is not apparent. There was therefore a breach of s 13 in that case. There is thus a sale by description, 'even though the buyer is buying something displayed before him on the counter. A thing is sold by description, though it is specific, so long as it is sold not merely as the specific thing, but as a thing corresponding to a description' (Lord Wright in the *Grant* case). His Lordship gave the examples of woollen undergarments, a hot water bottle and a second hand reaping machine. Thus, s 13(3) makes it clear that a sale of goods is not prevented from being a sale by description solely because goods being exposed for sale are selected by the buyer: s 13(3). Hence, many goods may 'describe themselves' by the way they are packed or displayed and the word 'description' in the section does not assume that anything was, in fact, said or written. Hence, whether the goods are new or used, their measurements and packing may all be relevant as to what are essential or merely secondary attributes. As with other aspects of this area of law, a great deal will depend on the consequences of the breach and the cost of the repairs or replacement of the goods. If buyers receive the goods according to their description, but they then turn out to be defective, then their remedy will be under s 14 of the Act, which deals with the rules on satisfactory quality and fitness of the goods for the purpose for which they have been bought (see below). In view of the uncertainty involved in establishing a case, under s 14, buyers may be better advised to attempt to bring their goods within s 13. One method of doing this might be to use extremely precise language, so that the goods are described and identified as clearly and unambiguously as possible, rather than in general terms, such as 'in good condition'.

Implied conditions relating to quality or fitness

Section 14 preserves the basic *caveat emptor* rule (let the buyer beware) under certain circumstances. It declares that there will be an implied condition that the goods will be of satisfactory quality only as provided by its sub-sections or by s 15. The exceptions to the general principle are:

(a) under s 14(2): implied term of satisfactory quality;

(b) under s 14(3): implied term of fitness;

(c) under s 14(4): terms implied by usage; and

(d) under s 15(2)(a) and (c): implied term that, once a sale is by sample, the bulk must correspond with the sample in quality.

Under s 14(2) of the Act, where goods are sold in the course of a business, there is an implied term that those goods are of satisfactory quality unless:

(i) the defects have been pointed out to the buyer before the sale; or

(ii) if the buyer has examined those goods before the sale was made and should have discovered those defects at that time. Section 14(6) makes that implied 'term', under s 14(2), a condition.

The words 'in the course of a business' include a profession and the activities of a government department, local or public authority (s 61(1)) of the Act). It is not necessary to be the manufacturer of the goods and there is no requirement that the business must consist of the buying and selling of the type of goods which are actually sold. Hence, if a milkman sold one of his milk floats, this would still be 'in the course of a business'. Where a person sells the goods as agent for another, for example, a trader selling something on behalf of a non-trader, then the purchaser has the benefit of the statutory protection, unless he knows that the goods are being sold on behalf of a non-trader or the trader took reasonable steps to inform the purchaser of this fact (s 14(5) of the Act). Section 14(2) will cover goods 'supplied' as well as goods 'sold'.

'Satisfactory quality' is now the term used to denote an implied term as to quality. 'Merchantable quality' used to be the term used under the old s 14(6), which was inserted by the Supply of Goods (Implied Terms) Act 1973 and said that goods are merchantable 'if they are fit for the purpose or purposes for which goods of that kind are commonly bought, as it is reasonable to expect, having regard to any description applied to them, the price (if relevant) and all the other relevant circumstances'. This was somewhat unhelpful, since 'merchantability' was defined in terms of reasonable fitness which was the second of the two requirements, but was not itself defined. The key requirement, both under the common law established prior to the s 14(6) definition (that is, pre-1973), is that the goods would not be deemed merchantable if they have defects which make them unfit for their proper use within the terms of the contract description and the particular circumstances of the case. 'Merchantable quality' was a relative concept. So, everything would turn on the actual terms of the contract. Hence, as *Bartlett v Sydney Marcus* [1965] 1 WLR 1013 appears to illustrate, if a car, for example, is being sold as 'second hand with a defective clutch', the car could not be said to be unmerchantable if the defect, once accepted by the buyer, then proved more expensive to rectify than expected. The position would certainly be different if a new car were being offered for sale which proved defective upon examination. *Wilson v Rickett Cockerell* [1954] 1QB 198 suggests that the implied condition as to merchantable quality does not only apply to goods sold, but also to goods supplied under the contract.

The question of the extent of the defects required to entitle a buyer to reject the goods has proved a fruitful source of litigation, where, occasionally, cases have held that even trivial defects rendered the goods unmerchantable (see, for example, *Jackson v Rotax Motor Cycle Co* [1910] 2 KB 937; *Parsons (Livestock) Ltd v Uttley Ingham & Co* [1978] QB 791). However, against this sort of approach is the more common one which is to apply the well known *de minimis* principle, so that defects or deficiencies of a trivial, superficial or cosmetic nature which do not really affect the basic quality of the merchandise will not be afforded relief by the courts and will not, therefore, entitle the right of rejection of the goods to be exercised. It should also be noted that the right to reject the goods can be lost quite quickly when the goods have been used by the buyer for any prolonged period, or been so used substantially or repeatedly.

Clearly, there was discontent with the statutory definition of merchantable quality and this eventually led to the renaming of the term in the Sale and Supply of Goods Act 1994.

The new concept relating to quality of goods is, thus, 'satisfactory quality', which is defined under s 14(2A) and (2B):

(2A) Goods are of satisfactory quality if they meet the standard that a reasonable person would regard as satisfactory, taking account of any description of the goods, the price (if relevant) and all the other relevant circumstances.

(2B) The quality of goods includes their state and condition and the following (among others) are, in appropriate cases, aspects of the quality of goods:

   (a) fitness for all the purposes for which the goods of the kind in question are commonly supplied;

   (b) appearance and finish;

   (c) freedom from minor defects;

   (d) safety; and

   (e) durability.

Section 14(2C)(b) of the Act continues the previous position regarding a buyer who examines the goods before the sale is completed. Such a buyer will not be protected if he actually examined the goods and the defects ought then to have been discovered. If, however, the defect is not discoverable by examination, the seller will then be liable: see *Wren v Holt* [1903] 1 KB 610, where the plaintiff recovered damages for breach of the condition of merchantability where beer had been contaminated by arsenic, a defect which could not have been discoverable on reasonable examination. Under s 14(2C)(a), the seller is not responsible for any matter making the quality of goods unsatisfactory, provided these were drawn to the buyer's attention before the contract was made.

Under s 14(3), where goods are sold in the course of a business and the buyer (expressly or impliedly) makes known to the seller the purpose for which the goods are being bought, there is an implied condition that they will be reasonably fit for that purpose, whether or not that is their usual purpose, unless, in the circumstances, the buyer does not rely, or it is unreasonable for him to rely, on the seller's skill or judgment.

It is usually self-evident what the purpose of most goods is, at least, as far as everyday consumer goods are concerned. Hence, a buyer need only state his requirements in express terms when his needs are more specialised than usual or if they happen to be for unusual purposes. But, the section also requires the buyer to have *prima facie* relied on the seller's skill and judgment in selecting his goods, and reliance is normally presumed. This presumption will be rebutted if, for instance, the buyer has carried out his own expert and detailed examination of the goods; or if the buyer has specified his own design for the goods in which case the quality and workmanship of the goods are still the seller's responsibility, but not the success of the design (*Cammell Laird v Manganese Bronze* [1934] AC 402). As *Wormell v RHM* [1987] 3 All ER 85 suggests, the standard of fitness will depend on the complexity, price and age of the goods, the way they are described and packaged and their instructions as to use. Perfection (however one might define it) is not required of this standard of fitness. Courts frequently allude to the normal expectation and usage of a given product in order to assess the standard of reasonable fitness of merchandise.

It would appear that the buyer has no statutory duty to take defective goods back to the seller to give him the opportunity to remedy the flaw before exercising a right of repudiation, but, if there are potential immediate and serious dangers, the buyer may have no choice but to do so. An example would be cars expressly sold 'subject to service' which means they should be repaired or adjusted after the sale. Unless the buyer returns to the seller to ascertain the extent of the defects, the seller will have had no opportunity to have rectified any problems with the vehicles. For cases which do not have the element of imminent danger, but have frequent breakdowns or many minor defects, the case of *Rogers v Parish* [1987] 2 All ER 232 is instructive. This involved a new Range Rover, costing £16,000 which, six months after purchase, still had an engine that misfired at all speeds and an excessively noisy gearbox and transfer box. Attempts were made to rectify the faults, but, during this time, it was clear that the plaintiff was subjected to driving the vehicle with considerable discomfort and irritation. The appeal court, overturning the lower court, held that the purpose for which this car was required was not merely that of driving from one place to another, but of doing so 'with ... comfort, ease of handling and ... pride in the vehicle's outward and interior appearance'. The defects present in this car were simply well outside the range of expectation, given the price of the car, its newness and the expected value for money. The buyer therefore succeeded in claiming his money back.

There are, therefore, four matters common to ss 14(2) and 14(3) of the Act:

(a) the seller must sell in the course of a business;

(b) this condition applies to all goods 'supplied';

(c) factors taken into account in deciding whether goods are 'of satisfactory quality' and 'reasonably fit' are the age of the goods, the price (if relevant) and all other relevant circumstances (such as the response of the reasonable person to the goods; or their safety or durability);

(d) the condition is one of strict liability; the absence of negligence, on the part of the seller, is no defence. It all depends on the particular situation: if goods have one purpose and they are unfit for that purpose, a buyer would probably succeed under both sub-sections; if the goods are not fit for the buyer's purpose, but suitable for other purposes, the buyer will usually only have a remedy under s 14(3). The goods are statutorily required to be 'reasonably fit', so it is important to bear in mind that the seller is deemed to be guaranteeing the suitability and safety of the goods and will still be liable whether or not he tries or is able to rectify the defect. Hence, the primary liability, under English law, rests on the seller, which means that, if it is claimed to be a manufacturing defect, the seller must then sue the manufacturer under the same section of the Act.

Strict liability is not, however, absolute liability. If the goods are reasonably fit for their purpose, but they nevertheless cause loss or injury, the seller is not liable. Hence, if buyers do not exercise sufficient care in using goods, for example, by incorrect electrical installation, exposure to extreme heat, continued usage while aware of dangers of such usage, the sellers will not be liable for the consequences. There is no set minimum above which the courts will find goods or products unsafe; if a certain type of food has killed someone only on rare occasions, it will still be considered unfit and unsafe, unless it proved dangerous as a result of the buyer's own fault, for instance, by not cooking it properly.

Under s 15(2)(c) of the Act, the implied condition that goods are of satisfactory quality is excluded where there is a sale by sample and the defect could have been discoverable by reasonable examination of the sample, irrespective of whether the goods have, in fact, been examined. Section 15(2) also stipulates that, where there is a sale by sample, there is an implied condition that the bulk will correspond with the sample in quality; and, under s 34, the buyer will have a reasonable opportunity of comparing the bulk with the sample.

Recent developments in 'sale or return agreements'

The case of *Atari Corp (UK) Ltd v Electronic Boutique Stores Ltd* [1998] 1 All ER 1010 dealt with the acquisition of computer games which has been dispersed to a number of buyers' stores. The buyers gave notice that they would be returning large numbers of a particular game at a time when the numbers of returnable stock were unknown. These had not been assembled at a central point and were not immediately available to the sellers. This case raised issues concerning sale or return agreements. The first question concerned whether the buyer's conduct amounted to an acceptance of the goods and was treated as an aspect of construction of the particular arrangement. The sellers had applied for summary judgment under the Rules of the Supreme Court (RSC) Order 14. The Court of Appeal resolved the case by using its powers under

Order 14A, rather than giving the buyers leave to defend. The key issue in the case turned on the point that sale or return buyers are bailees who have an option to decide whether to buy the goods in their possession. Nothing was made of the buyers' duty to pay on 30 November, prior to the expiry of the option period on 31 January. The interpretation of the Court of Appeal was that the notice given by the buyers was valid, since it gave a clear generic description of the goods and the stock to be returned did not have to be immediately ready for collection and could, subsequently, be ascertained. It was therefore unnecessary to decide whether the stock had to be returned. The arrangement between the parties, though treated as a contract, was not construed as an agreement of sale. Phillips LJ opined that the seller could not withdraw his offer to sell, which he thought flowed from the language of s 18, r 4.

If the buyers, despite their non-acceptance of the stock, later sold it or some of it, their earlier notice would remain valid though they would commit the tort of conversion in respect of the sold stock. The sale of return agreement was construed as severable in quantities to be determined by the buyers acting unilaterally when selling on the stock.

Exclusion clauses and defective goods

On the question of exclusion clauses in English law, this is partly dealt with by the Unfair Contract Terms Act 1977 (UCTA), which draws from provisions in the Supply of Goods (Implied Terms) Act 1973 and amends the Misrepresentation Act 1967 and, partly, by case law. But, we focus on the question of defective goods, rather than on any more detailed consideration of this substantial area of law.

Section 6 of UCTA is a very important section which deals with contract clauses or notices excluding the operation of ss 12–15 of the Sale of Goods Act 1979 or equivalent sections of the Supply of Goods (Implied Terms) Act 1973, relating to hire purchase transactions. The section first declares that no seller or owner can escape liability for failing to give a good title to the goods sold or hire purchased. It then draws an important distinction between consumer sales and non-consumer (business) sales or transactions.

As far as consumer sales are concerned, s 12 and ss 13–15 of the 1979 Act cannot be excluded by any clause or notice. Hence, the statutory requirements as to description, sample, satisfactory quality and reasonable fitness cannot be excluded for consumer sales by any such clause. It is also a criminal offence to use such a clause (see Consumer Transactions (Restrictions on Statements) Order 1978). For non-consumer contracts (that is, contracts between businesses), ss 13–15 may be excluded by a clause or notice, but only if the 'test of reasonableness' is satisfied (see below). There is an exception made with regard to exclusion of liability for sales by description, satisfactorability and fitness in the case of 'international sales', under the Uniform Laws on International Sales.

A person 'deals as consumer' when he buys for private use or consumption and not in the course of his own business from a business seller, and sold to a person who does not hold himself out as buying them in the course of a business (s 12 of UCTA). The meaning of sales made 'in the course of a business' has been discussed above (see pp 421–22). The status of the seller should be made plain, since the Business Advertisements (Disclosure) Order 1977 requires the business status to be declared in advertisements. If a private person uses a business agent to sell his goods, the agent will be liable for the quality of the goods, unless the buyer knows that the seller is not acting in the course of a business or reasonable efforts have been made to inform the buyer of this fact (s 14(5) of the 1979 Act). If a business engages in an activity (such as buying a car) which is incidental to their normal business, this will not be 'in the course of the business' unless it is an integral part of it if, for example, it is carried on with a degree of regularity (see *R & B Customers Brokers v United Dominions Trust* [1987] 1 All ER 847). In that case, the purchase of a car, by the company, for the use of their directors was construed as a consumer contract because they were occasional purchases and car buying was not an integral part of the company's business.

The test of reasonableness is stated as a general principle in s 11 of UCTA, which requires contractual and non-contractual clauses to be 'fair and reasonable' clauses at the time the contract was made; and various statutory guidelines as to 'reasonableness' are listed in Sched 2, which is contained in an Appendix to the Act. The crucial time is the time the contract was being made, when the clause should have been known or, at least, in the contemplation of the parties (s 11 of UCTA). The burden of proving that the clause is reasonable is upon the seller or supplier who relies on it. The courts have a wide discretion under UCTA to interpret exclusion or exemption clauses in accordance with their perception of what is 'reasonable' in the circumstances.

Under Sched 2 of UCTA, the court is required to consider, in particular, the parties' relative bargaining power, availability of other sources of supply, any inducements offered to the buyer, whether other suppliers used such clauses, whether the buyer had adequate notice of the clause, whether it was reasonable at the time of the contract to comply with the clause and whether the goods were manufactured, processed or adapted according to the buyer's special needs. There is also a European Directive (EC Directive on Unfair Terms in Consumer Contracts: 93/13/EEC) which deals with unfair contract terms in consumer contracts and which has been brought into effect by statutory instrument which will operate in parallel with UCTA. The Directive does not specifically apply to the sale of goods apart from the fact that its preamble states the need to assist the sale of goods by stimulating competition and provide effective consumer protection by rendering European sales uniform. If a clause amounts to an unfair term within the purview of the

Directive, then it will not be binding on the consumer, so that the contract, apart from the term, will remain in force if it is capable of continuing in existence without the term. In other words, the remaining contract must be able to stand on its own and make sense even without the term.

Transfer of title by non-owner: the nemo dat rule

In some cases, the buyer can acquire a good title to the goods, even though the seller had neither the property nor the right to dispose of the goods either as owner or as pledgee. This is dealt with in the 1979 Act in ss 21–26 under the general heading 'Transfer of Title'. The classic common law position is neatly summarised in the words of Denning LJ (as he then was) in *Bishopsgate Motor Finance Corpn v Transport Brakes Ltd* [1949] 1 All ER 37, p 46, when he said:

> In the development of our law, two principles have striven for mastery. The first is for the protection of property: no one can give a better title than he himself possesses. The second is for the protection of commercial transactions: the person who takes in good faith and for value without notice should get a good title.

This passage deals with the present topic, which may also be described by the maxim *nemo dat quod non habet* (no man gives that which is not his own) and its exceptions. There are several exceptions to the *nemo dat* rule and some of them have been modified by statute. The list of exceptions includes:

(a) sale under order of court;

(b) sale under a common law or statutory power;

(c) estoppel;

(d) agency;

(e) sale under a voidable title;

(f) disposition by seller in possession;

(g) disposition by buyer in possession after agreement to sell;

(h) disposition under Pt III of the Hire Purchase Act 1964.

It is emphasised that the present work is not intended to provide a full discourse and analysis of the many permutations of the sale of goods, but to merely highlight key features and draw comparisons. In that vein, the following may be noted:

On the question of estoppel, s 21 provides that, where goods are sold by a person who is not the owner, the buyer acquires no better title than the seller had unless:

(a) the seller had the authority or consent of the owner; or

(b) the owner is precluded by his conduct from denying the seller's authority to sell.

At common law, a sale by an agent will bind his principal if the agent had actual, apparent or usual authority. Under s 1 of the Factors Act 1889, a mercantile agent is defined as an agent having, in the customary course of his business, authority to sell goods or raise money on the security of goods. This definition includes an auctioneer or broker, but not a clerk or warehouseman. Under s 2 of the same Act, any sale, pledge or other disposition by a mercantile agent in possession of goods or documents of title, with the consent of the owner and in the mercantile agent's ordinary course of business, to a *bona fide* purchaser for value without notice of any defect in his authority is as valid as if expressly authorised by the owner.

Under English common law, sale in market overt used to exist as an exception to the *nemo dat* rule. It is the most ancient of all the exceptions, originating from the 16th century when trading consisted of very simple transactions. However, this exception was repealed by the Sale of Goods (Amendment) Act 1995, so that it is no longer possible for a seller of goods in market overt to transfer a good title to a *bona fide* purchaser.

Under s 23, when a seller of goods has a 'voidable title' (for fraud, but not for mistake), but this title has not been avoided (set aside) at the time of sale, the buyer acquires a good title, provided he buys in good faith without notice of the seller's defect in title. If a seller agrees to sell goods, whereby ownership is transferred, then retains those goods and subsequently disposes of them again to a third party, the delivery or transfer by him of those goods is as valid as if authorised by the owner, provided the second buyer takes in good faith without notice of the previous sale (see s 24 of the 1979 Act and s 8 of the Factors Act 1889). All the first buyer is left with is a personal action against the seller. Note that the seller only needs to retain possession for this exception to operate, although not necessarily as a seller. He may also pass valid title as hirer or trespasser, provided the good faith and lack of notice requirements are satisfied on the part of the second buyer.

The converse to this last situation is where A agrees to sell goods to B and it is agreed that ownership will pass on payment. B then obtains possession or documents of title with A's consent and delivers them to C, who takes in good faith and is unaware of A's ownership. C (subject to the mercantile agency exception) will take good title (s 25(1) of the 1979 Act).

The final exception (s 27 of the Hire Purchase Act 1964) deals with a case where a motor vehicle is held under a hire purchase or conditional sale agreement and the debtor disposes of the vehicle before ownership has passed to him. If the disposition has been made to a private purchaser who: (a) takes in good faith; and (b) without notice of the agreement, the disposition will be valid to pass good title as if the title of the creditor has been vested in the hirer or buyer immediately before the disposition. Notice, in this context, means actual notice (*Barker v Bell* [1971] 1 WLR 983). The word 'disposition' covers any sale, contract of sale, letting under a hire purchase agreement and transfer of property under a provision in such agreement.

Remedies of the buyer and seller

Buyer's remedies

We have already discussed at some length the remedies that are available to a buyer in the context of goods that do not conform to their description, are not of satisfactory quality or are not fit for the purpose for which they have been sold. The right of the buyer to reject the goods or 'repudiate' the contract and the right to claim damages (monetary compensation) in certain circumstances have, by now, become quite familiar in the preceding discussion. Nevertheless, there are six remedies that are available to the buyer, depending on which breaches of contract have occurred:

(a) rejection of the goods;

(b) recovery of the price;

(c) action for damages for breach of warranty;

(d) action for damages for non-delivery of the goods;

(e) specific performance;

(f) tortious action.

Rejection of the goods is available for breach of condition unless the buyer has waived the breach and elected to treat it as a breach of warranty; or the contract is non-severable and the buyer has accepted the goods or part of them (s 11(4) of the 1979 Act). The buyer may recover the price of the goods where he has paid for them if the consideration has failed, for example, if the seller has no title or delivers goods which the buyer validly rejects (s 54 of the 1979 Act). With regard to a breach of warranty, the buyer may set up the loss in diminution of the price or sue for damages under s 53 of the SGA. This section appears to be geared towards general damages which would cover the loss of the value of the goods (see the first limb under the rule in *Hadley v Baxendale* (1854) 9 Ex 341). Section 54 would be available to claim special or consequential damages or special damages under the second limb in *Hadley's* case. If the seller has delayed delivery, damages for delayed delivery are assessed on the basis of the difference between the value of the goods when they should have been delivered and their value at the time of delivery. An anticipatory breach of contract occurs where, before the time of performance, one party informs the other that he does not intend to perform the contract. The innocent party may ignore this proposed repudiation and wait for the date of performance in the hope that it will be performed or accept the repudiation and sue for damages. Specific performance (s 52) is the exceptional remedy in most cases in English law, since it will usually only be ordered if damages are an inadequate remedy. The buyer may also sue the seller and third parties in tort if he is entitled to possession of the goods and possession has been withheld. The buyer may sue the third party under the Torts (Interference with Goods) Act 1977, if third parties wrongfully interfere with the goods, but the buyer must have either possession or an immediate right to possess. A buyer who has resold the goods cannot recover the loss of profit in tort if he cannot recover it in contract, since damages would be computed on the same basis as a contractual claim for non-delivery.

Remedies of the unpaid seller

It will be recalled that, under s 27, the buyer's duty is to accept and pay for the goods. If a seller is unpaid, however, he has the following six remedies under the 1979 Act:

(a) a lien: s 41–43;

(b) a right of stoppage *in transitu*: ss 44–46;

(c) a right of resale: s 48;

(d) a right of retention where ownership has not passed to the buyer: s 47(2);

(e) action for the price: s 49;

(f) action for damages for non-acceptance: s 50.

A lien is the right to retain possession of goods (but not to re-sell them) until the contract price has been paid. Section 41(1) provides that a lien exists in three cases: (a) where the goods have been sold without any stipulation as to credit; (b) where the goods have been sold on credit, but the term of credit has expired; and (c) where the buyer becomes insolvent. Section 41(2) clarifies that the seller may exercise his right of lien, even though he is in possession of the goods as agent or bailee or custodier for the buyer. The rights given under this section are very useful, especially when combined with a power of sale under s 48. Note that the word 'insolvent', in s 41(1)(c), is wider than 'bankrupt' because s 61(4) states that:

> A person is deemed to be insolvent, within the meaning of the Act, who either has ceased to pay his debts in the ordinary course of business or cannot pay his debts as they become due, whether he has committed an act of bankruptcy or not.

After the seller has parted with the possession of the goods to a carrier for transmission to the buyer, he has the right to stop the goods and repossess them if the buyer becomes insolvent (that is, is unable to pay his debts as they become due). The right of stoppage in transit is covered in ss 44–46. Three conditions are required before the right may be exercised:

(a) the seller must be an unpaid seller within the meaning of the 1979 Act;

(b) the buyer must be insolvent; and

(c) the goods must be in course of transit.

This remedy is no longer as important as it used to be, since most export sales are, nowadays, financed by means of banker's commercial credits, which means that a bank in the seller's country pays the seller or accepts bills of exchange drawn by him in return for the shipping documents. Once this occurs, the seller is no longer an 'unpaid seller'. Thus, the right is only important when the sale is on credit. The other method of finance, whereby a bill of exchange is sent together with a bill of lading, while still used, means that, since a bank normally processes the shipping documents, the buyer must honour the bill of exchange before he may obtain the bill of lading and, thereby, the goods. The period of transit commences from the time when the goods are handed to the carrier until the time when the buyer takes delivery of them. There are two methods of exercising the right of stoppage, enunciated by s 46:

(a) by taking actual possession of the goods; and

(b) by giving notice of his claim to the carrier or other bailee or custodier who has possession of the goods.

Transit may also be terminated if the buyer obtains delivery of the goods before the arrival of the goods at the agreed destination; that is, if the carrier hands them to the buyer's agent during transit. If the carrier acknowledges to the buyer that he is holding the goods to the buyer's order or if the carrier wrongfully refuses to deliver the goods to the buyer, transit is also terminated. It should also be noted that the right of stoppage does not, *ipso facto*, rescind the contract.

As a general principle, lien and stoppage in transit do not give the unpaid seller the right to re-sell the goods, but s 48 lists three exceptions:

(a) where the goods are of a perishable nature;

(b) where the unpaid seller gives notice to the buyer of his intention to re-sell, and the buyer does not pay for them within a reasonable time; or

(c) where the seller expressly reserves the right of resale in case the buyer defaults in payment.

The unpaid seller who is still the owner of the goods will have a right of retention coterminous with the right of lien or stoppage. Under s 47, the unpaid seller's right of lien or retention or stoppage in transit is not affected by any sale or other disposition of the goods which the buyer may have made, unless the seller has 'assented' to it. In practical terms, in order for the unpaid seller to have assented, he must have effectively renounced his rights against the goods by, for example, selling goods and agreeing to be paid out of the proceeds of a resale by the buyer (see *Mount Ltd v Jay and Jay Ltd* [1960] 1

QB 159). However, under s 47(2), where a document of title to goods has been lawfully transferred to any person as buyer or owner of goods and that person transfers the document to a person who takes it in good faith and for valuable consideration, then, provided that last transfer was by way of sale, the unpaid seller's right of lien or retention or stoppage in transit is defeated. If the last transfer was a form of pledge or other disposition for value, the unpaid seller's right of lien, retention or stoppage can only be exercised subject to the transferee's rights.

As we have seen, a seller may expressly contract that property in the goods (that is, ownership) will remain his, even after they are delivered, until the contract price or any other debt owing to him by the buyer has been paid (see *Aluminium Industrie BV v Romalpa* (1976) (above)). If this has been done and the seller has not been paid, the seller may re-possess the goods if the buyer, being a company, goes into liquidation or receivership. There is no right to re-possess goods from a buyer who is a private individual, unless he were adjudged bankrupt or if the seller were given some indication that the goods would not be paid for.

There are two personal remedies available to the unpaid seller against the buyer:

(a) an action for the contract price under s 49, where the buyer wrongfully neglects or refuses to pay for the goods contrary to the terms of the contract or where they were due on a specific day irrespective of delivery; and

(b) an action for damages for non-acceptance under s 50, where there is an available market.

In these circumstances, the measure of damages will, *prima facie*, be the difference between the contract price and the market price on the date fixed for acceptance, or in the absence of a fixed date, at the time of refusal to accept. If the buyer has become the owner, the right to sue for the price is available, whereas if the buyer is not yet owner when he rejects the goods, the seller's claim is for damages for breach of contract which will be 'unliquidated damages'. There may also be the right to claim for special damages, under s 54, and for any loss occasioned by the buyer's neglect to take delivery. Under s 37, where the seller is ready and willing to deliver the goods and requests the buyer to take delivery, but the buyer does not take delivery within a reasonable time after such a request, the seller may sue for any loss occasioned by this non-delivery and also claim a reasonable charge for the care and custody of the goods.

The Court of Appeal case of *Peakman v Express Circuits Ltd*, 3 February 1998, suggests that, in actions for damages for breach of warranty under s 53 of the SGA, an award should be made based on the cost of rectifying defects in the goods. In relation to claiming damages under s 53 of the SGA, the case of *Bence Graphics International Ltd v Fasson UK Ltd* [1997] 4 All ER 979 is worth noting. Here, albeit by a majority, the Court of Appeal decided not to follow the well established authority of *Salter v Hoyle and Smith* [1920] 2 KB 11. The general presumption is that damages should be assessed by reference to the value of the subwarranty goods at the time of delivery. In *Bence*, the sellers delivered to the buyers a large quantity of cast vinyl film used by the buyers in manufacturing decals for the container industry. The film failed to survive in a legible state which constituted a breach of express and implied terms in the contract. The lower court treated the film as worthless and awarded the buyers damages amounting to the price paid. The Court of Appeal reversed this decision to the extent that the buyers' damages were limited to the pro-rated contract price for the small quantity of vinyl remaining in their hands. However, there was a difference in approach between the learned judges. Otton LJ took the view that the *Slater* case should be distinguished because, there, it had involved cloth that the buyers bleached and sold on, whereas in the present case the goods sold on by the buyer (decals) were different from those bought by the buyer (vinyl film). However, the other majority judge, Auld LJ, unsurprisingly disagreed with this factual distinction. However, despite adding that the contemplation of losses in subsales displaced the value approach in s 53(3), his conclusion was the same as that of Otton LJ. The dissenting judge, Thorpe LJ, simply decided to rely on the trial judge's finding that the sellers had failed to discharge the burden of showing the parties' intention to displace the presumptive rule in s 53(3). The current judicial view, therefore, appears to be that damages, in a case like this one, should follow the normal remoteness rule and focus on the actual loss caused to the present plaintiff.

The Supply of Goods and Services Act 1982

Certain hire and service contracts are dealt with under the Supply of Goods and Services Act 1982 (the 1982 Act), which came into force in the United Kingdom on 4 January 1983. The 1982 Act has two main parts. Part I amends the law regarding terms implied in certain contracts for the supply of goods and Pt II codifies the common law rules applicable when a person agrees to carry out a service. The Act applies to contracts for services which do not necessarily involve transfer of goods, hence, it applies to contracts 'under which a person agrees to carry out a service'. But, it does not apply to apprenticeships, contracts of employment or services rendered to a company by a director and the services of an advocate before a court or tribunal. Under Pt I, problems that arose with uncertain common law rules and inadequate protection by the Sale of Goods Act either in terms of definition or scope were noted by the Law Commission and their recommendations eventually led to the 1982 Act. Contracts for work and materials, part exchange contracts defined as barter transactions and contracts for the hire of goods which were not originally covered by legislation are now covered. Hence, the 1982 Act applies to 'contracts for the transfer of property in goods' and 'contracts for the hire of goods' and ss 2–5 enact statutory implied terms on the part of the seller which are similar to those in ss 12–15 of the 1979 Act. Sections 1–5 of the 1982 Act deal with goods supplied under contracts for services and ss 6–10 cover those supplied on hire or loan.

The 1982 Act re-enacts the obligations imposed by ss 8–11 of the Supply of Goods (Implied Terms) Act 1973, so that they apply to the contracts covered by the 1982 Act. In the case of contracts for work and materials, such as contracts for installation of central heating, double glazing, burglar alarms, repairs, construction, and so on, the supplier undertakes two obligations:

(a) an obligation pertaining to the goods (as now governed by ss 2–5 of the 1982 Act); and

(b) an obligation pertaining to the work (now governed by ss 13–15 of the 1982 Act).

Hence, in such contracts, there will be, for example, an 'implied term' that, where the supplier is acting in the course of a business, he will perform the service with 'reasonable care and skill' (s 13 of the 1982 Act); if the time for the service to be carried out is not specified by the contract or determined by the parties' course of dealing, there is an implied term that the service will be carried out within a reasonable time (s 14 of the 1982 Act). Finally, if the parties have not specified the consideration for the contract, the party contracting with the supplier will pay a 'reasonable price'. It will be noticed that the 1982 Act implies terms, without using the language of conditions and warranties.

This seems sensible, since the very nature of services will make it impossible to repudiate, in the sense of being returned to their supplier, and so the right of repudiation (contingent upon breaches of condition) is inappropriate. Damages would, therefore, be the proper remedy for breach of these implied terms.

On the question of exclusion clauses, the Unfair Contract Terms Act 1977 (UCTA) has been amended by the 1982 Act in relation to contracts for the supply of goods other than contracts of sale or hire purchase so that:

(a) if the exclusion clause relates to title, it will be void (s 7(3A) of UCTA);

(b) if the exclusion clause relates to description, quality, fitness or sample, it will then depend on whether the buyer deals as a consumer or not. If he does, the clause is void (s 7(2) of UCTA); if he does not, the exclusion clause must satisfy the test of reasonableness as laid down in s 11 and Sched 2 of UCTA;

(c) if the exclusion clause relates to poor quality work, which might amount to a breach of s 13, the clause must also satisfy the reasonableness requirement (as above), unless the negligent work causes personal injury or death, in which case it will be void (s 2 of UCTA).

If there is a complaint concerning defective materials in a consumer contract, the exclusion clause will be void. However, if the materials are of acceptable quality, but the workmanship is negligent, the exclusion clause will, again, have to satisfy the reasonableness requirement (as above). Note that, while a supplier of goods is under an obligation to ensure such goods are reasonably fit for the purpose for which they are supplied, a supplier of services is only able to undertake that he will comply with the normal standards of his trade or profession. Hence, a supplier of services who carries out the contract according to the normal standard expected of him in his trade or profession cannot generally be sued for breach, unless the contract lays down some higher standard or some other special and specific requirement. As a general standard of professional work, English law expects a standard of reasonable care which will be judged in accordance with the view of a responsible body of opinion within that profession (on the question of negligence in English law, see Chapter 10).

THE UNIFORM LAWS ON INTERNATIONAL SALES

In 1964, two international Conventions were adopted at the Hague after nearly 30 years of preparation, involving 30 countries redrafting and negotiation: the Uniform Law on the International Sale of Goods (ULIS) and the Uniform Law on the Formation of Contracts for the International Sale of Goods (ULOF). These are commonly referred to as the Hague Uniform Laws.

This particular version was ratified with reservation by the United Kingdom (that it would only apply if the parties chose it as the law to govern their contract). The Uniform Laws on International Sales Act 1967 came into force in Britain in 1972.

Apart from France, which played a large part in the drafting of the Uniform Laws, all the other five original members of the EEC ratified the Convention. By 1989, there were some 180 reported decisions on the Hague Uniform Laws in the courts of the Member States, except for the English and Scottish courts (see Nicholas (1989) 105 LQR 201, p 202). It appears that these Uniform Laws simply failed to attract sufficient widespread support, despite them obtaining a currency in Western Europe, predominantly because it was seen as representing a narrowly West European origin, despite the 35 countries that were represented at the Hague of which only 19 were from Western Europe.

In any event, further revisions were made and, on 11 April 1980, the UN Convention on Contracts for the International Sale of Goods was adopted at a diplomatic conference of 62 States convened in Vienna by the Secretary General of the United Nations. The Convention became effective on 1 January 1988.

The UN Convention is a radically revised version of the original Hague Uniform Laws. For instance, there are no longer two Conventions, but there is now one Convention which is divided into four parts: Pt I defines the Convention's sphere of application and contains provisions dealing with interpretation, usages and requirements of contractual form. Part II deals with the formation of contract, Pt III contains the main body of rules on sale of goods and Pt IV deals with the public international law framework. Article 92 allows a contracting State to declare that it will not be bound by Pt II or III.

Article 6 provides that, subject to Art 12 (see below), the parties are free to exclude or vary the provisions of the Convention in whole or in part. There is no mention of whether there may be implied exclusion, but this is probably covered. Nevertheless, this has left the situation uncertain, since it is never safe to predict when the courts will be prepared to make such an implication.

The Convention was the result of a successful project under the auspices of the United Nations Committee on International Trade Law (UNCITRAL), set up, in 1966, to promote 'the progressive harmonisation and unification of the law of international trade'.

It is proposed here only to compare and contrast the main points of the approach taken to sale of goods by the ULIS, so that one may compare them with the civil law and common law approaches.

Meaning of 'international sale'

An 'international sale' is defined in Art 1 of the Convention but, like everything else in the Convention (except as provided by Art 12), this is subject to the power to contract out. In other words, parties to whose contract the Convention otherwise applies are bound by it, unless they have excluded its provisions in whole or in part (Art 6).

According to Art 1(1), the Convention applies to contracts of sale of goods between parties whose place of business are in different States:

(a) when the States are contracting States; or

(b) when the rules of private international law lead to the application of the law of a contracting State.

Nicholas (1989) sees the rule in Art 1(1)(a) as being either too wide or too narrow, depending on the circumstances, but it is, at least, straightforward and clear. Article 10 also provides that, if a party has more than one place of business, the relevant place is that which has 'the closest relationship to the contract and its performance'. However, there is clearly some uncertainty of the rule in Art 1(1)(b), since the rules of private international law, which would be the rules of the forum State, would never be realistically predictable.

Sale of goods

The Convention only applies to contracts of sale of goods (Art 1(1)). There is no definition of sale, although the words of Arts 30 and 53 (relating to the obligations of buyer and seller) suggest that a conventional definition will be applied. Sales of goods bought for personal, family or household use (consumer sales) are excluded where there might be a conflict between the Convention and the mandatory rules of domestic law for the protection of consumers (Art 2(a)). Auction sales and sales on execution or otherwise by authority of law are also excluded (Art 2(b) and (c)).

It should be noted that, just as the parties may contract out of the Convention, they may also agree that it shall apply to a transaction in cases where that transaction is, or may otherwise be, inapplicable.

Various other substantive matters connected with the sale of goods are covered and we may usefully highlight the following:

(a) Fundamental breach: this is widely defined in Art 25 and is not without some ambiguity. A fundamental breach is committed by one of the parties 'if it results in such detriment to the other party as substantially to deprive him of what he is entitled to expect under the contract, unless the party in breach did not foresee and a reasonable person of the same kind in the same circumstances would not have foreseen such a result'. This is not quite the same scope as the English version (as propounded by Diplock LJ in *Hong Kong Fir Shipping Co v Kawasaki Kishen Kaisha Ltd* [1962] 2 QB 265, p 266), namely, whether the breach deprived the innocent party of 'substantially the whole benefit which it was the intention of the parties as expressed in the contract that he should obtain'.

(b) Specific performance: the Convention adopts the continental approach which is that it is the norm rather than the exception, being the right of the promisee so that damages are generally merely a substitute for actually carrying out the contract. Nevertheless, the common law position is preserved under Art 28 which allows the court the option not to order specific performance 'unless the court would do so under its own law in respect of similar contracts of sale not governed by this Convention'. Thus, the priority of specific performance remains in jurisdictions to which the provision does apply.

(c) Modification and termination of the contract: this can be done purely by the mere agreement of the parties; consideration is not required. Thus, although the Convention does not expressly deal with the validity of a contract of sale, it impliedly allows the parties to decide on matters connected with its validity.

(d) The seller's obligations: these are in accordance with most national laws, with the seller being bound to deliver goods which are 'of the quantity, quality and description required by the contract and which are contained or packaged in the manner required by the contract'. Articles 35(1) and 35(2) are similar to the 'merchantable quality' definition in the old s 14(6) of the United Kingdom Sale of Goods Act 1979 (SGA) (goods needing to be 'fit for the purpose or purposes for which goods of that kind are commonly bought'), but without the further elaboration of those requirements which follows on in that sub-section (that is, 'having regard to the description ... price (if relevant) and all the other circumstances') of the English statute. Under the current text of s 14(2) of the SGA 1979, there is an implied term that, where the seller sells goods in the course of a business, the goods supplied shall be of satisfactory quality. The new definition has been discussed (above, pp 422–25) under implied conditions relating to quality or fitness.

(e) Article 35(1)(b) is very similar to s 14(3) of the SGA (fitness for purpose known to the seller), subpara (c) is equivalent to s 15(2)(a) of the SGA (sale by sample) and subpara (d) deals with adequacy of packaging.

On the question of when the buyer will lose (wholly or partially) the right to rely on a lack of conformity of the goods, there was no concordance between common law and civil law solutions. Accordingly, another compromise was reached. The buyer must examine the goods as soon as practicable and he will lose his right to rely on the lack of conformity if he does not give notice of it to the seller: (i) within a reasonable time after he discovered it or ought to have done so; (ii) in any case, within two years of the actual handing over of the goods (Art 39). The meaning of 'within a reasonable time' will depend on the buyer's circumstances, but he may also resort to other remedies, such as reduction of the price or damages (except for loss of profit) if he has a reasonable excuse for failing to give notice. But, all this must be within the two year limit.

(f) Remedies of buyer and seller: two remedies for the buyer are stated which will be unfamiliar to the common law: (i) in cases of lack of conformity, the buyer may request the seller to repair the goods, unless this is, in all the circumstances, unreasonable; (ii) if the lack of conformity constitutes a fundamental breach, the buyer may request the seller to deliver substitute goods.

The seller, however, has the right to cure any failure to perform his obligation, including a failure to deliver goods that conform, before the time fixed for performance (as in English law) and, unlike English law, after the time fixed for performance. But, this right is subject to it not causing the buyer unreasonable inconvenience or unreasonable expense and the buyer may still claim damages.

(g) The 'period of grace' procedure: there is a procedure in the Convention which will be familiar to German lawyers, but not to English common lawyers: the Nachfrist (period of grace) remedy. This allows either party to fix an additional period of time to allow the other party to perform

(Arts 47(1), 49(1)(b), 63(1) and 64(1)(b)). During the period specified, the party fixing the period cannot resort to any remedy for breach of contract. The only real benefit of this remedy is to give a party time to consider, or a period of grace, within which he may decide what course of action to adopt in relation to the breach and to encourage the other party to perform. The legal effect of this procedure is confined to three main cases: where the seller has failed to deliver; or the buyer has failed to take delivery; or to pay the price. If the failure is not remedied after the Nachfrist has expired, the other party will be entitled to avoid the contract, regardless of whether the breach is fundamental or not.

(h) Reduction of price remedy: again, this is a civil law remedy whereby the buyer, in the case of non-conformity of goods, is allowed to reduce the price 'in the same proportion as the value that the goods actually delivered had at the time of delivery bears to the value that conforming goods would have had at that time'. This rather convoluted wording basically allows the buyer to set off his losses caused by falls in the value of the goods, but is only really advantageous if the breach is not fundamental.

If the buyer cannot claim damages because the non-conformity is due to an impediment beyond the seller's control, the remedy of reduction of price will protect the buyer. In any event, this remedy will not preclude a claim for damages, which means the buyer will have two remedies in the event of any losses suffered.

(i) Avoidance of the contract: a right to 'avoid' (that is, repudiate, in English law parlance) the contract exists under the Convention, provided it is done within a reasonable time, for: (i) a failure by the other party to perform any of his obligations, which amounts to a fundamental breach; or (ii) if the seller fails to deliver or the buyer fails to pay the price or take delivery of the goods within a Nachfrist fixed by the other party. The effect of avoidance is to release both parties from their obligations under the contract, subject to any damages which may be due.

There is no equivalent of s 11(4) of the SGA where, in the case of a 'non-severable' contract, a buyer cannot reject goods or repudiate a contract if he has accepted them in their entirety or in part. The Convention more closely resembles s 2-601 of the American Uniform Commercial Code .

(j) The rule for damages: Art 74 encompasses the rules in *Hadley v Baxendale* (1854) 9 Exch 341, but is slightly wider in stating that, on the point of foreseeability, all that is required is that a 'possible consequence' of the breach was the loss suffered.

(k) Impossibility of performance: this is covered in the Convention under 'Exemptions', under Art 79, and the first paragraph states: 'A party is not liable for a failure to perform any of his obligations if he proves that the failure was due to an impediment beyond his control and he could not reasonably be expected to have taken the impediment into account at the time of the contract or have avoided or overcome it or its consequences.' Article 79(5) goes on to elaborate on the meaning of 'is not liable': 'Nothing in this Article prevents either party from exercising any right other than to claim damages under this Convention.'

Attention has been drawn (see Nicholas (1989) p 235) to several points: (i) this is different from English contract law dealing with impossibility of performance, in certain ways, the non-performing party has a defence against an action for damages and the impediment does not terminate the contract; (ii) the exemption from liability is in relation to the performance of 'any of his obligations' not just to the performance of the contract as a whole; (iii) the non-performance must be due to an impediment beyond that party's control, which is similar to the French *force majeure* requirements, namely, that the events must be unforeseeable, irresistible, unavoidable and insurmountable (Nicholas, *French Law of Contract* (1992) p 203), but this will be quite familiar to the English lawyer as well. Concepts which are as broad as this, as with notions of fundamental breach, cannot really be pre-empted in their judicial interpretation. Everything will surely depend on the individual circumstances; (iv) this Article's formulation will not include cases amounting to frustration in English law, since there is a focus on 'impediment', but will include English law cases of impossibility.

(l) The passing of risk: subject to Arts 6 and 9, the parties are free to exclude or vary the Convention's terms, apart from Art 12, and will be bound by any trade customs or usages to which they have agreed or any practices they have established among themselves. The Convention deals with two main categories of cases and a residual set of cases. The two categories are: (i) typical international sales cases involving carriage of the goods (Art 67); and (ii) goods sold in transit (Art 68). The residual categories are covered by Art 69.

In (i), for the Convention to apply, this must be a situation where the contract requires or authorises the seller to arrange for the goods to be carried and that the carriage will be by a third party, rather than the seller or the buyer or their servants. Here, if the seller is not bound to hand over the goods at a particular place, the risk passes 'when the goods are handed over to the first carrier for transmission to the buyer in accordance with the contract of sale'. Where the seller is bound to hand over the goods to a carrier at a particular place, the risk does not pass to the buyer until the goods are handed over to the carrier at that place. As Nicholas explains, the policy underlying Art 67 is that risk should pass at the beginning of the agreed transit, since the buyer is usually in a better position than the seller to assess any damage which has occurred in transit and to institute claims in respect of it (Nicholas (1989) p 238).

In (ii), under Art 68, the risk passes to the buyer from the time of the 'conclusion' of the contract – in English law terms, at the time of its formation. The Article goes on to say that, 'if the circumstances so indicate, the risk is assumed by the buyer from the time the goods were handed over to the carrier who issued the documents embodying the contract of carriage'. Following on from this, the Article inserts what English lawyers would call 'constructive notice' because it then says: 'Nevertheless, if, at the time of the conclusion of the contract of sale, the seller knew or ought to have known that the goods had been lost or damaged and did not disclose this to the buyer, the loss or damage is at the risk of the seller.' Thus, it will depend on what the phrase 'if the circumstances so indicate' means.

Article 69 deals with cases not covered by either Art 67 or 68 and states that in such cases:

(1) the risk passes to the buyer when he takes over the goods or, if he does not do so in due time, from the time when the goods are placed at his disposal and he commits a breach of contract by failing to take delivery;

(2) however, if the buyer is bound to take over the goods at a place other than a place of business of the seller, the risk passes when delivery is due and the buyer is aware of the fact that the goods are placed at his disposal at that place;

(3) if the contract relates to goods not then identified, the goods are considered not to be placed at the disposal of the buyer until they are clearly identified to the contract.

Clearly, the general idea is that the seller should bear the risk of loss, so long as he has control of the goods. In para 2 of Art 69, however, if the buyer is to take over the goods from a third party, usually from a warehouse, then the seller is in no better position than the buyer to protect and insure the goods or to pursue any claims which may arise. Hence, the buyer should bear the risk as soon as he is in a position to collect the goods (see Nicholas (1989) p 240). There is, however, a potential problem with para 3 of Art 69 if a case like *Sterns v Vickers* [1921] 1 KB 78 arose. In that case, although the property (or ownership) in the goods had not passed because no appropriation had taken place, it was held that the parties must have intended the risk to pass when the delivery order was delivered, so that the buyer remained liable to pay the price.

Under Art 69(2), the intention seems to be that the risk should pass at once, yet, under para 3 the implication seems to be that risk would not pass until there has been some act of identification or appropriation. Nicholas believes that this conflict was the result of a drafting oversight and suggests that the matter be dealt with as under Art 98(3) of the ULIS which reads: 'Where unascertained goods are of such a kind that the seller cannot set aside a part of them until the buyer takes delivery, it shall be sufficient for the seller to do all acts necessary to enable the buyer to take delivery' (see Nicholas (1989) p 240).

Validity and passing of property excluded

Two important aspects of the contract of sale of goods have been excluded under the Convention: the validity of the contract and the passing of property. Article 4 categorically states that the Convention 'governs only the formation of the contract of sale and the rights and obligations of the seller and buyer' and that it is not concerned with: (a) the validity of the contract or any of its provisions or of any usage; or (b) the effect which the contract may have on the property in the goods sold. Excluded matters will be governed by domestic law.

Passing of property proved to have too many national variations to be reconciled and, in any event, the subject extends outside the law of contract. The Convention does regulate matters, such as the seller's obligation to deliver goods free of third party claims (Arts 41–43) and the passing of risk (Arts 66–70).

Exclusion of validity was also unavoidable because there is a wide spectrum of approaches in national laws on matters, such as mistake and fraud and the practical problem is that national courts might adopt too varied a range of interpretations to maintain any consistency or unity in approach.

Interpretation of the Convention

In the area of interpretation of the Convention and the filling of gaps, Art 7 states: '(1) In the interpretation of this Convention, regard is to be had to its international character and to the need to promote uniformity in its application and the observance of good faith in international trade.' The success or failure of the first part of this provision will clearly depend on the willingness of the national courts to consider the background of the Convention, relevant national case law of domestic tribunals and doctrinal writing. But, it was the interpretation of 'good faith' that proved to be particularly controversial at the Working Committee stage of the Convention process. Basically, the common law States objected to the proposal of the Working Committee to require parties to 'observe the principles of fair dealing' and to 'act in good faith'. They argued that, while the requirements were certainly desirable, the use of the terms was too uncertain and open ended. Another proposal to adopt the German BGB formulation in § 242, thereof, was also considered too risky for commercial certainty. The text finally adopted represents a compromise.

The reference to the 'general principles' for the purpose of filling gaps was included in the hope of discouraging too precipitate a recourse to domestic law (see Nicholas (1989) p 210), but it surely turns on whether a court adopts a restrictive or extensive approach. Article 7(2) requires a court to decide that there is no relevant general principle contained in the Convention before it may refer to domestic law as a source. There is a general requirement for the courts to promote uniformity in the application of the Convention.

As far as trade usages and practices are concerned, Art 9(1) states that the parties are bound by 'any usage to which they have agreed and by any practices which they have established among themselves'. On the other hand, Art 9(2) suggests that a party will be bound by a usage of which he did not know if it is one that is widely known and regularly observed in the particular branch of international trade that is involved and if the court's view is that he ought to have known of it. This resembles the English law notion of an implied term, where a trade custom will be deemed to form part of the contract if the custom is generally accepted by those doing business in the particular trade in the particular place and so generally known that an outsider making reasonable inquiries could not fail to discover it (see *Kum v Wah Tat Bank* [1971] 1 Lloyd's Rep 439, p 444 (Privy Council)).

On the form of a contract that would be acceptable as legally valid, there was inevitable disagreement, but a compromise was reached. Article 11 preserves the right of freedom of form, but Arts 12 and 96 also allow a contracting State, whose legislation requires contracts of sale to be concluded, or evidenced, in writing, to make a declaration that any provision of the Convention that 'allows a contract of sale or its modification or termination by agreement or any offer, acceptance, or other indication of intention' to be made otherwise than in writing shall not apply where any party has his place of business in a State making the declaration. This does not mean that the formal requirements of the declaring State will automatically apply. That will occur only if, under conflicts of laws principles, the declaring State's law is the applicable law.

Article 12 is the only provision that the parties are precluded from excluding under Art 6.

Ratifications

At the time of the UNCITRAL meeting in April 1988, no less than 16 States had ratified or acceded to the Convention and these included Argentina, Australia, Austria, China, Egypt, Finland, France, Hungary, Italy, Lesotho, Mexico, Sweden, Syria, the US, Yugoslavia and Zambia. The Federal Republic of Germany and The Netherlands were then reportedly in the process of ratification and Norway ratified the Convention at the end of 1988. Since 1988, Bulgaria, Byelorussian SSR, Chile, Czechoslovakia, Denmark, Germany,

Finland, Iraq, Spain and the Ukrainian SSR have also ratified the Convention. At the end of its 51 year gestation period, the Convention is, by no means, free from difficulties, but, at the very least, represents a monumental achievement of comparative law, a fusion of different traditions, flawed, but fertile, providing a solid model of a truly international law.

COMPARATIVE OVERVIEW

This comparative study of typically civil law and common law approaches to sales of goods reveals a great many similarities, partly attributable to the common heritage of the law merchant (*lex mercatoria*) or ancient mercantile law, but also attributable to the far reaching changes wrought, first, by the industrial revolution, then, by the impact of nationalism and codificatory tendencies and the dawn of the technological era. It is also increasingly influenced by the unprecedented speed of technological advances which have exposed the archaic and outmoded legal structures in Western Europe and Britain. The wave of consumerism and the legal, social and political movement towards consumer protection, begun in the 1960s and 1970s, have also accelerated the need for change in transactions as fundamental as the sale of goods. Both civil law and common law systems have similar safeguards for consumers, as well as duties imposed on sellers and buyers. One key difference lies in the rules relating to risk of accidental loss or damage. Yet, all three systems allow the parties free rein to decide when the passing of ownership of the goods should take place and may agree that the seller should remain owner until he receives payment. The English Sale of Goods Act, in common with French and German laws, allows contracting parties fairly generous discretion within which to exercise their autonomy and freedom of choice. In cases of supervening events rendering performance of the contract difficult or impossible, all three systems have a legal concept that attempts to deal with it, the French version being the most severe. In the case of remedies, the similarities are certainly striking, although each system inevitably has its own idiosyncrasies and individual nuances. German law is unique in its use of the good faith principle as a general clause applicable and adaptable to a wide range of diverse situations, while English law with no equivalent statutorily regulated doctrine, prefers to deal with each situation on an ad hoc basis, never straying from their underlying requirements of honesty and fair dealing between buyer and seller. All three systems apply variations of similar sorts of rules limiting the scope of damages to losses which are the direct consequences of a breach of contract. All three systems have statutory rules regulating the sales of goods, but, typically, English law statutes are consistently interpreted in the light of existing case law with the aim of giving effect, wherever possible, to the intention of the parties. Civil law codes are more strictly applied, but there is no doubt that there is increasing reliance on case law. In many cases, the differences are rendered nugatory by the basic similarities in approach which often produce the same outcomes. Thus, the marvel of modern European society is that, quite independently, legal systems steeped in different traditions and philosophies are undoubtedly converging at certain levels and in certain spheres of activity.

This is also happening in Eastern Europe, the Russian Federation and, indeed, in other parts of the developed world. A question that must now be addressed is whether the complexity of English law and its many facets of antiquity should, with other European systems, be adapted through legislation, so as to adopt a more unified and 'harmonised' approach, such as that of the UN Convention of Contracts for the International Sales of Goods, so that there will be greater harmonisation of the laws of sales of goods. This law is a mixture of Continental and Anglo-American law, but it represents the concerted effort and combined experience of a vast number of European countries, but a number of non-European countries, such as China, Argentina and Zambia, have also ratified it. The United Kingdom has not yet ratified this Convention, but the United States has already done so. In the light of impending regional European unity, in some form or other, our preceding comparative survey of the sale of goods indicates that there is far more in common than is generally appreciated or realised. In the context of European or global unification or harmonisation of laws, the sale of goods is certainly an area in which there is far more convergence than divergence and in which an impressive measure of consensus has already been reached in regional and international spheres.

SELECTIVE BIBLIOGRAPHY

Atiyah, *Sale of Goods* (1980)

Battersby and Preston (1972) 35 MLR 268

Bewes, *The Romance of the Law Merchant* (1923)

Bocker *et al*, *Germany: Practical Commercial Law* (1992)

Bridge, *The Sale of Goods* (1998)

Cohn, *Manual of German Law* (1968) Vol I, section IX

Daniels, 'The German law of sales' (1957) 6 Am J Comp L 470

Horn, Kotz and Leser, *German Private and Commercial Law* (1982)

Kruse, 'What does "transfer of property" mean with regard to chattels? A study in comparative law' (1958) 7 Am J Comp L 500

Lawson, 'The passing of property and risk in sale of goods – a comparative study' (1949) 65 LQR 352

Maitland-Hudson, *France: Practial Commercial Law* (1991)

Nicholas, 'The Vienna Convention on International Sales Law' (1989) 105 LQR 201

Pennington (1975) 24 ICLQ 277

Schmitthoff, 'The unification of the law of international trade' [1968] JBL 105

Smith, *Property Problems in Sale* (1978)

Wheeler, *Reservation of Title Clauses* (1991)

Whincup, *Contract Law and Practice: The English System and Continental Comparisons* (1990); 3rd edn (1994)

CHAPTER 13

LABOUR LAW

SCOPE OF CHAPTER

This chapter examines labour law and industrial relations as they exist in common law countries, such as Great Britain, and in civil law countries, such as France and Germany. Primary interest will be focused on these three countries. The main comparative objective of our inquiry will be to discover how legal systems with different historical and cultural backgrounds, albeit within the Western hemisphere, have responded to the needs of society at different periods in history and the nature of their employer/employee and employer/trade union relationships. As far as German labour law is concerned, the situation is particularly interesting in view of German unification, in 1990, and its preliminary implications will, therefore, be considered *en passant*.

As with previous substantive chapters, our objective is to examine common legal issues and problems which have arisen in this area, such as the functions of collective agreements, the legislator's role in the development of collective bargaining, the status of collective agreements (is it a contract/statutory instrument?) and, briefly, a comparison of the development of the collective agreement in common law and civil law countries.

As usual, we examine this area from legally significant and, therefore, selective comparative viewpoints with an emphasis on concepts and do not, in any way, purport to undertake a comprehensive substantive survey of the particular legal topic.

HISTORICAL DEVELOPMENT

Great Britain

Early phases of historical development

Great Britain is the country where industrial relations originated and where the first seeds of labour law were sown. It was the 'workshop' of the world and, in the 19th and 20th centuries, the 21 million British citizens who emigrated to America, the British Colonies and overseas dominions brought to these other jurisdictions uniquely English attitudes about industrial relations in the workplace and a typically English common law approach to employer/employee relationships. Britain was the first country to legalise trade unions, in 1824, a legislative step which was in keeping with the *laissez faire* liberal capitalism which dominated Britain between 1820 and 1850. In accordance with the legalisation, the notion of collective bargaining developed and spread to other parts of Europe over the next 70 years or so. Not only did French and German workers visit Britain on fact finding missions to discover how the British style trade unions operated, but British workmen's compensation schemes also served as a model to countries as far flung as Japan.

Yet, in 1852, the law dealing with labour relations was primarily concerned with the individual relationship between employer and employee, reflected in the first book published at that time called *The Law of Master and Servant*. This continued until the commencement of the Second World War. The next phase of development occurred as a result of the dramatic changes in employment practice and industrial relations which were effected during the Second World War. However, collectivism eventually replaced individualism, and the law relating to trade unions and industrial action (strikes, go slows, etc) came into its own and became known as 'industrial law'.

Rights for individual employees

In 1963, Britain became the last country to introduce statutory minimum periods of notice to terminate employment, followed by a series of rights for individual employees, predominantly based on 'unfair dismissal'. In the early 19th century, English employment law had evolved a set of rules concerning termination which were, at bottom, founded on contract. The practical consequence was that individual contract law developed in true common law fashion, that is, when cases came to court. These usually occurred when dismissal had taken place and it became very difficult for the employee to win such cases. It was generally not financially worthwhile to even bring such cases to court. Management was therefore left largely unchallenged and unchecked until about 1972, when a statutory system of job protection was introduced, which was based on a test of 'reasonableness'. Arbitration by an industrial tribunal was offered, as it had been in the past, but the system has never really been able to break free from its contractual antecedents.

After the failure of the Industrial Relations Act 1971, which appears to have miscalculated the desire of employers to use the law and trade unions to co-operate with it, the Labour Government, under Harold Wilson, entered into a 'social contract' with the Trades Union Congress (1974–79) which resulted in a considerable amount of legislation which enhanced the role of the industrial tribunals (which had been established in 1964). There was, however, an ongoing struggle to reconcile collective bargaining with incomes policies and reformist legislation. The victory of the Conservatives, in May

1979, resulted in the abandonment of direct incomes policies, and support for collectivism was replaced by a policy of legal restriction on trade unions, the reintroduction of market regulation and an era of market individualism. In other words, there has been an explicit attempt to restrict collective bargaining.

Content of English labour law

Since the mid-1960s, this area of law has been called labour law, a change generally attributable to the influence of the universities and Professor Otto Kahn-Freund, who apparently first used it. Lord Wedderburn (1986) described the term itself as usually including:

(a) the employment relationship between worker and employee;

(b) the area of collective bargaining between trade unions and employers;

(c) a panoply of rights for individual employees ranging from safety at work to rights relating to job security; equal pay; sex and racial discrimination; and protection of wages;

(d) strikes, lock outs and industrial action generally; interplay of parliamentary statutes and court decisions;

(e) status of trade unions, rights of union members and the role of the trade union movement.

In the course of this chapter, we shall compare the approaches taken by civil law countries, such as France and Germany, to the area of labour law and employment rights.

Current state of labour law: an overview

English labour law's early development was based on contract and this is still very much a feature of the present law. Briefly, it is the individual's contract of employment (and, therefore, its termination and his/her redundancy) that remains the focus, even in the early 1990s, not collective bargaining. The basis of English labour has, thus, been the law of contract, generally case derived, despite legislation in the field which has significantly influenced the development of the law of dismissal and, therefore, the whole of English labour law.

Where government intervention was clearly seen as desirable in the earlier stages of labour law's history, it remains a challenge for the current Labour Government to balance effectively the legal regulation of collective industrial relations, management of the economy and general legal control of labour relations. English labour law may be divided into 'contract based rights, statutory employment protection and collective labour law' (see Rideout (1985)). The historic fourth Tory election victory in May 1992 appeared to seal the fate of policies, such as an unrestricted 'right to strike' and the banning of secondary picketing is set not merely to continue, but to become entrenched. High unemployment and relatively stagnant policies with minimal or negligible rises in social security benefits has led to a widening of the gulf between a group of secure, full time well paid workers and a group of people who remain on the fringe of the core labour market. However, with the Labour Party (now styled 'New Labour') being re-elected in May 1997 after 18 years of Tory government, some expected Britain to eventually return to the pre-Conservative era, at least as far as trade unions were concerned. However, two years on, the advent of 'New Labour' in power suggests to many political observers that the new Labour Government intends to carry on with several of the Tory policies on trade unions and the changes that they have so far brought into force deal with the implementation of the minimum wage. It would appear that the future of trade unionism (not just its political power) remains in doubt and, indeed, the pendulum swing towards privatisation looks set to continue and be part of the industrial scenario into the next millennium.

We shall now turn briefly to the historical development of Germany and France as examples of civil law countries before undertaking a comparative overview of selected aspects of the substantive labour law of Britain, France and Germany.

Germany

Nineteenth century labour law

The history of the labour law of a Germany which was divided into East and West after the Second World War, but was reunited in October 1990 must still consider the period before the founding of the German Reich in 1871. German industrialisation started later than Great Britain so that, in 1848, for example, there was only 5.5% of the population above 14 years of age who were working in factories and in the mining industry, with the remainder working in agriculture or handicrafts. The governing legal principle at that time was freedom of contract. The General German Workers' Association (Allgemeiner Deutscher Arbeiterverein), led by Lasalle, was founded in 1863, with its main objective being to promote the workers' interests by giving everybody the right to vote. However, this and similar associations more closely resembled political parties than trade unions, but are now seen as the first important steps taken towards German free unions or socialist unions. Moreover, the fusion of the second German Workers' Party with the first was the birth of the Social Democratic Party. Even before the German Reich was founded in 1871, therefore, two competing union movements already existed. Kronstein (1952) thus argues that 'collective bargaining has an old tradition in Germany, interrupted only by National Socialism'. In 1873, printers' unions and the association of employers in the printing business agreed that:

(a) union men should be employed by members of the association only on the basis of the conditions stipulated by the two organised groups; and

(b) members of unions should be given preference in employment.

Kronstein (1952) also points out that, from the earliest times, German employers utilised a bargaining platform based on a multi-unit basis (regional or inclusive of all industries), whereas labour bargained through craft unions combining people of similar skill and occupational background.

However, the socialist unions were seen as a danger to the system and the government banned them in 1878. Nevertheless, not only did they survive, but the Social Democratic Party grew ever stronger from election to election and the 1878 law was repealed in 1890.

Eventually, various species of workers' representation groups were formed, with the intention of assisting the workers to be integrated within the enterprise structure and to serve as a foil to the socialist labour movement. These groups were recognised by law and, thus, was formed the dual structure mechanism typical of German collective labour law, namely: (i) a two channel representation by unions; and (ii) works councils. A third group of unions, the Christian union, was formed but, in the early 20th century, the socialist unions were certainly the most important group by a considerable margin of membership and influence.

In the late 1890s, a debate occurred within the socialist unions, wherein collectivism was rejected in favour of increased democratisation and together with increased participation became a cornerstone concept. By 1891, the labour movement had become more reconciled with the works' council. By the early part of the present century, employers' associations had begun to be formed as a response to the labour movement. A critical legitimating factor for the socialist movement was its co-operative attitude towards the government during the First World War which led to its legal recognition as the authentic representative of the workforce.

Impact of the Weimar period

With the split in the Social Democratic party, in 1917, internecine conflict within the working class appeared to take place. But, under the influence of a politically and industrially active labour movement, the Weimar Republic established certain rights for workers. Thus, after the War, when the Weimar Republic was formed, Art 159 of the Weimar Constitution guaranteed freedom of association without limitation for the first time in German history. This basically meant that there was a right to form trade unions and this was complemented by the enactment of the right of equal representation on various 'economic-political' bodies, under Art 165.

During this period, the so called Central Commission of Co-operation (Zentralarbeitsgemeinschaft) was formed by the main organisation of employers' associations and trade unions.

Weiss (1989) highlights three of the most fundamental developments of the time which can be seen as crucial to modern day labour law:

(a) the Act on Works Council of 1920;

(b) the creation of a specific system of labour courts in 1926; and

(c) the establishment of a system of unemployment insurance and placement service in 1927.

A nascent concept of economic democracy also started to develop which intended to give workers a greater say in the decision making process, but which was unable to blossom in the wake of the 1929 global crisis. There followed a rapid decline in the system of industrial relations, and unemployment was extremely high. It was no wonder that collective bargaining fell into disfavour and, with increasing governmental intervention, working standards were continually lowered.

Post-Second World War

Despite the fact that the Nazis dissolved trade unions and employers' associations replacing them with an organisation designed to promote the Nazi State, the effect of the Nazi regime and the Second World War put paid to ideological disunity, which was soon subsumed in the aftermath of the war. The labour movement managed to be reorganised and reconstructed by the allies in a such a way that it began to embrace all manner of ideological and political persuasions within the trade unions. Notions utilised by the Nazis to serve the ends of the Third Reich and which had developed Nazi connotations, such as 'togetherness between the leader of the establishment and his workforce' (Betriebsgemeinschaft) and the 'duty of fidelity' as interpreted by the Nazis, took somewhat longer to practically disappear from the labour force ethos.

The tradition of positive rights, however, is contained in Art 9(3) of the German (formerly FRG) Constitutional Basic Law of 1949, which declares the 'right to form associations to safeguard and improve working and economic conditions'.

Labour law in the former GDR

East German law as an instrument of the State plan

Labour law in the former German Democratic Republic (GDR) – East Germany – was utilised primarily as an instrument to implement the State economic plan. As with other socialist systems, mechanisms were developed in pursuance of the objectives of certain goals of production. There was therefore no free market environment and, thus, no labour market in which individuals could interact in any sort of parity with their employers. Individuals were simply cogs in the wheel of the great State plan, who merely had to conform to the needs of the plan. Labour laws were focused on the collective needs of society, as dictated by the Marxist objectives, and not on any Western style perspective of protection of the worker from exploitation or promotion of equal bargaining power.

Duality of trade union functions

It would appear that the role of the trade union indicated a conflict of interests since, as one commentator explains, 'it was defined as the representative of the workers (as ... in Western countries)' and, yet, 'its main task was to guarantee the performance of the economic plan and thereby execute the Party's and the government's intentions' (see Weiss (1991)). On the other hand, another commentator sees no conflict of interests in such duality of function because the interests of the Party, the government, the trade union and the workers were supposed to be identical (see Mampel, *Arbeitsverfassung und Arbeitsrecht in Mitteldeutschland* (1966) p 75).

No conflict resolution mechanism

It is important to note that any 'agreements' between government and trade unions or between government and industrial entities were not collective agreements in the Western industrial democratic sense. They were yet another means of implementing the plan. Hence, the idea of conflict was never officially recognised or accepted as part of the labour scenario, which meant that no structures or mechanisms for conflict resolution were ever developed.

Minor role of courts

East German courts only played a somewhat minor role, since the only route into court for dismissal cases, for example, was with the support of the trade union and this was by no means easy to obtain. The courts were, in any event, merely another State organ intended to promote the goals of the party. In the absence of any separation of powers, the judiciary, government and Parliament were all seen as having a commonality of function.

Positive rights under East German labour law

Nevertheless, the labour law of the GDR was not without some positive features. It enacted the 'right to get a job' (Art 24 of Die Verfassung der DDR (VERF)) whereby any individual who was willing to work was guaranteed a job. This was not without its difficulties in implementation, since it required a massive administrative undertaking to organise career planning and job distribution and led to a severe surplus of staff which was simply not economically viable in an economy which had such strict market constraints. Another consequence of this statutory right is its effect on female workers. Since women could also avail themselves of this right, this meant that arrangements had to be devised whereby women could work and have a family at the same time. Many Western countries could do worse than follow this example as a positive means of helping the modern working woman.

Transferring the FRG legal system to the GDR

In the early period of transition, in 1990, there was still hope among the GDR population that unification would result in a system of real integration and not simply one which had to adapt to the FRG pattern. Labour law and social security in a unified Germany was, therefore, conceived to become a mixture of the better parts of both systems. Unfortunately, this was not to be and measures soon began to be implemented which made it clear that the FRG legal framework was, indeed, going to be imposed on the former GDR. For instance, since labour courts did not exist in the GDR, the Treaty established the GDR's duty to provide a preliminary and temporary mechanism for resolution of legal disputes during the period in which labour courts were not yet established (see Weiss (1991) p 6).

A new Labour Code was enacted, on 22 June 1990, which introduced a number of provisions which originated from the FRG law. Weiss emphasises that some of the GDR provisions were more favourable to workers than the corresponding provisions in the original FRG, such as longer annual minimum vacations, better protection of pregnant women and better minimum standards for breaks and rest periods during working time (see Weiss (1991) p 6).

According to Art 8 of the Treaty on Political Unification (the Treaty), all law of the original FRG, including individual labour law, was extended to the territory of the former GDR. The five exceptions to this rule are:

(a) where the law involved is one which applies only to specific States of the original FRG;

(b) where the Treaty itself explicitly states exceptions;

(c) where specific provisions of FRG law are either abolished or amended in the context of unification;

(d) where FRG provisions apply only in a modified version until a certain deadline in the former GDR; and

(e) where the Treaty allows GDR provisions to remain valid temporarily until a certain deadline (see Weiss (1991) p 7).

There is, moreover, an attempt to strike a compromise between the GDR and FRG laws. According to Art 30, § 1 of the Treaty, the Parliament of the unified

Germany is supposed to codify, as soon as possible, 'the law relating to the individual employment relationship as well as the protective standards referring to working time, work on Sundays and holidays and the specific protection of women'. Paragraph 2 of this Article further extends this programme to the codification of health and safety standards.

Problems in implementation

Several obstacles to privatisation exist and the conversion from planned economy to market economy is fraught with difficulties. Weiss (1991) highlights four problems:

(a) there is uncertainty as to whether, and to what extent, existing companies can be rescued and privatised, or whether they must be closed down. A 'trust agency' has been established to deal with this problem which carries out evaluation of each industrial unit. Approval of this agency is required before the transformation of the company may take place. Being a bureaucratic organisation, this is a long and slow process which is unfortunately slowing down the restructuring through privatisation;

(b) the infrastructure of the former GDR is in an antiquated and parlous state. As Weiss explains, 'the telecommunication system is simply not functioning; the energy supply system must be totally reorganised; and air pollution and land contamination need to be reduced dramatically' (Weiss (1991) p 9);

(c) there is a serious problem in dealing with the loss of land ownership due to unjustified expropriation during the communist period. The Treaty distinguishes between two periods: expropriations before and expropriations after the foundation of the GDR. Expropriations before the foundation of the GDR are considered to be irreversible, although the original owners may be entitled to compensation. The legislature has broad discretionary power to determine the amount of compensation in each case. Expropriations which occurred after the 1949 founding of the GDR are treated differently under the Treaty: original owners may claim ownership if they can present evidence that they lost property in an unjustified way. Claims have to be filed within a specified period. In the light of these problems concerning the property question, privatisation is greatly delayed and the establishment of regional branches of employers' associations will take time. In the meantime, the functions of employers' associations (as is the case with trade unions) will be performed by the headquarters in the western part of the unified country.

The fourth problem is the lack of a functioning labour court system. As things stand, the arbitration bodies set up under the Treaty only exist on paper in that it is very rare for these bodies to have been created in accordance with the legislation. Labour courts function in a very limited manner. There is the tricky question of which judges should serve on such courts, since any appointments or allocations in this connection could be seen as inappropriate, politically insensitive or simply another example of colonisation, if FRG judges merely replace the former GDR ones.

The treaty provides that specific committees be established by the new States of the former GDR to check the past performance of each judge in the former GDR to decide if he is eligible to continue in the new system. This system has not worked very well and the least of their problems has been that a longer evaluation period has been needed, various GDR judges were simply encouraged to quit for a variety of reasons and there has been a great need to have judges sitting on the various courts. There has therefore been an unavoidable transfer of a significant number of judges from the former FRG.

A number of other problems bedevil the labour market. Since a job was guaranteed in the former GDR to anyone willing to be employed, there is now a severe problem of overstaffing in the 'new' Germany. The rate of unemployment has shot up and only temporary employment is available to these millions of people.

The German Federal government has taken measures to deal with this in the form of vocational training programmes, job creation schemes and placement, as well as 'skilling companies'. These are companies which are run jointly by employers' associations and trade unions and which receive fairly large subsidies from the Federal government. Unfortunately, these skilling companies did not succeed in gaining the co-operation of the employers' associations, although the trade unions have pressed for their creation for some time.

The process of restructuring the economy of a united Germany, in the light of the labour market in the former GDR, will clearly be a long and sometimes painful process. The concept of social partnership has been strengthened and co-operation between social partners and government is apparently occurring on a permanent basis. However, with the removal of the planned economy, many units of public administration have become redundant, from the secret service to departments in the universities. The Treaty on Political Unification terminates employment contracts of employees in such units. These employees will receive 70% of their former net wage until a final decision is made on whether they will be re-employed elsewhere in the public sector (see Weiss (1991) pp 13–14).

Yet another problem facing the restructuring programme is the 'dramatic' (Weiss) wage gap between the original FRG and the former GDR workers. The average wage level of a worker in the former GDR was less than half that of a worker in the western part of the country. The need to equalise wage levels is especially urgent in the public sector. A rather radical rearrangement of the wage structure must be devised before collective agreements will be of any utility, so that job classification according to criteria of skill and performance should replace the pattern in the former GDR.

Key features of contemporary German labour law

Multiplicity of statutes

Contemporary German labour law consists of a variety of statutes. They may be grouped under the following three categories:

(a) individual employment law;

(b) business constitution law;

(c) collective bargaining law.

Individual employment law covers the contractual relationship between an employer and a particular employee. It includes the law of contract and protective laws, such as the law of termination protection.

Business constitution law deals with the internal organisation of large and medium sized firms, including the right of co-determination and internal collective agreements.

Collective bargaining law deals with strikes, the formation of trade unions and collective bargaining agreements.

Operation at different levels of hierarchy

A noteworthy feature of German labour law is that it operates at different levels so that there is a hierarchical relationship between these groups of laws. It could be envisioned as a pyramidal structure with the laws being based on the employment contract, which can be modified by collective agreements, which must comply with the rules of statutory law. They therefore operate according to the following order of priority:

(a) binding rules of statutory laws and regulations;

(b) collective bargaining agreements;

(c) factory agreements;

(d) internal collective agreements;

(e) individual contract (see Bocker et al (1992) p 104).

At the apex of the hierarchical structure is the basic law (Federal Constitution) which provides that 'the right to form associations to safeguard and improve working and economic conditions is guaranteed to everyone and to all trades, occupations and professions' (Art 9, § 3 of the German Basic Law (GG)). This is a mandatory rule which will invalidate agreements, contracts and statutes to the extent that they breach this basic right of association (see Horn et al (1982) p 311).

This order of priority is not adhered to in the case of the 'benefit principle' which permits agreements of a lower ranking to prevail if they are more beneficial for the employee than the collective agreement (Bocker *et al* (1992) p 104).

Further special statutory regulation

Many special statutes have been passed dealing with different aspects of the individual contract of employment, such as notice, protection against unfair dismissal, sick pay, and holiday entitlements. Other statutes deal with the protection of children and minors, expectant and recent mothers and severely disabled persons (see Horn *et al* (1982) p 311).

Many specialist courts

There are, of course, a number of specialist courts which deal with labour law cases: labour courts, labour appeal courts and the Federal Labour Court.

Labour courts deal, *inter alia*, with disputes arising out of the relationship between employer and employee or claims related to strikes and other actions by trade unions. There is a three tiered appeal system in every German district/region and a Federal Labour Court which determines appeals on points of law for the whole country. Parties may be represented by representatives of trade unions before all labour courts except the Federal Court, which requires the parties to be legally represented. Professional and honorary judges sit together to hear labour cases, with trade unions and employers' unions making nominations for honorary judges who are then appointed.

The BGB and contracts of service

The BGB also regulates contracts of service, which are contracts whereby one party 'undertakes to provide the agreed remuneration' (§ 611 of the BGB). These must normally be concluded for an indefinite period of time, since fixed term contracts cannot be concluded unless special circumstances justify them. These circumstances have been specifically listed and confined by the Federal Labour Court to include only the following:

(a) the need for temporary staff;

(b) the need to fulfil a specific task, such as a research project;

(c) seasonal jobs; and

(d) up to 18 months fixed term for a single contract under the employment promotion law (see Bocker *et al* (1992) p 105). Chain contracts are usually treated as contracts for an indefinite period of time.

Paragraph 618 of the BGB stipulates that a person who is entitled to demand a service pursuant to a contract of service must ensure the safety of the premises, installations and equipment with which the other party will come into contact in performing the service. However, since all employees are covered by a statutory scheme of employment which is part of the social insurance system, this provision is simply irrelevant. Employees suffering personal injuries in an accident arising in the course of his employment will obtain compensation under the statutory insurer, but not for pain and suffering. Entitlement does not depend upon proof of anyone's fault and is unaffected by his being at fault himself, unless he caused the accident intentionally. The injured party's survivors are bound by the same rules.

There is no disadvantage to this scheme except in the case of serious injury where the victim would be better off if he could bring a claim against his employer. In that case, he would receive a pension, obtain damages for pain and suffering and an indemnity for all his lost earnings. Separate considerations apply if a third party is responsible for the industrial accident. If he has supplied a defective tool which caused the injury or was a motorist who carelessly injured the workman on his way to or from work (which is an 'industrial accident, in Germany), the workman or his survivors may sue the third party for financial loss not covered by the insurance and for pain and suffering (see Horn *et al* (1982) p 322).

Organisation of unions

The unions in Germany are organised as industrial unions which means that the branch of industry to which a worker belongs, rather than his own trade or skill will determine the trade union to which a worker will belong. It is noteworthy that Art 9, § 3 of the basic law has been used as the source of rights pertaining to union membership and union activities. The German courts have interpreted this Article to mean that 'an individual has not only the right to join a union, but also the right not to join one' (Horn *et al* (1982) p 313).

Operation of collective bargaining

Collective bargaining takes place 'above the plant level' in Germany (Horn *et al* (1982) p 314). Various employers in a number of industries will negotiate with a local section of the appropriate industrial union. In addition, there are consequences on two levels resulting from collective agreements between unions and employers' associations work: first, the 'normative effect' which means that they apply directly to every individual contract of employment between any employer who is a member of the employers' association that is bound by the agreement, and any employee who is a member of the union that is similarly bound; secondly, the 'obligational effects' which generate duties, as with any other contract, for the parties themselves, namely, between the employers' association, on the one hand, and the union, on the other (Horn *et al* (1982) p 315). The most important of these obligational duties is the duty to keep the peace (Friedenspflicht). Basically, for the duration of the agreement, the parties must avoid taking any step which might cause industrial conflict.

If a breach of duty to keep the peace occurs, the affected employer may sue the union for an injunction and damages. As Horn points out, although it is the employers' association that is party to the collective agreement, the courts treat the collective agreement as a contract for the benefit of third parties (§ 328 of the BGB). Accordingly, they allow the individual employer to sue in his own right (see Horn *et al* (1982) p 316).

The union has a right to call a strike if collective negotiations collapse. The employer may retaliate by ordering a lockout, but the legitimacy of this measure has been the subject of intense debate in Germany and the best that can be said is that the Federal Labour Court has held that it is sometimes justifiable to order a lockout in response to a strike.

Legality of strikes

The question of whether the strike is lawful is central in Germany and the matter has been determined by case law. The cardinal point is that strikes can only be lawful if they are called and conducted by a trade union. The rationale is that the function of strikes is to lead to the conclusion of a collective bargain and only unions can be parties to such bargains. Hence, wildcat strikes and strikes called by works councils are unlawful.

However, a strike called by a union is, nevertheless, unlawful if it is called in breach of the union's duty to keep the peace; or if it is called in pursuance of an aim other than those that may be achieved by a collective agreement, namely, 'the improvement of economic and working conditions' of employees (see Art 1 of the Collective Agreements Act; Horn *et al* (1982) p 317). As far as sympathy strikes are concerned, this will only be lawful if the strike in support of which they are called is itself lawful.

Another perspective on legality of strikes has come from the Federal Labour Court which is that a strike will be unlawful if it offends against the 'principle of proportionality'. In other words, if the harm caused to the general public by the strike is out of all proportion to what the union stands to achieve thereby: BAG (Grosser Senat) NJW 1971, 1668 (Federal Labour Court).

The works council

The works council is a distinctive feature of German labour law, which is a body elected by all employees (union members and non-union members) who are 18 years or older and is meant to represent the interests of all workers. It will participate in decisions 'at the plant level on social, personal and economic matters' (Horn *et al* (1982) p 319).

Participation at the company level has existed since the 1950s, wherein workers in the mining industry and (since 1977) in undertakings with more than 2,000 workers, have had the right to choose half the members of the supervisory board.

The Labour Management Relations Act 1972 (the '1972 Act') provides detailed rules for the election of the works councils, their legal position and their powers. The number of workers in each plant will vary with the size of the plant. Works councils have the right to enter into factory agreements with the employer on behalf of the employees. But, its role is to co-operate with the employer so that it is not permissible for it to enter into a confrontational situation with the employer. Indeed, the 1972 Act expressly requires the works council and the employer 'to work together in good faith for the welfare of the workers and the factory' (see Horn *et al* (1982) p 320).

The works council also has several statutory rights and duties. This will vary from a right to be informed or consulted to a right to be involved in some way in decisions taken by the employer. If it is a situation where the works council enjoys a right of co-determination, the employer cannot take steps without its consent, for example, in the employment of new staff, fixing the hours of a working day, including breaks, formulating general rules regarding behaviour in the plant, timing of holidays and provision of sick pay (Art 87 of the 1972 Act). On the other hand, in the case of dismissal procedures, consultation, but not consent, will be required before notice can be given.

'Framework agreements' (Manteltarif) are nowadays entered into which contain important rules on the reciprocal rights of the parties and these often replace statutory law. Short term collective bargaining agreements dealing with wage and salary are also entered into in many industries.

Discriminatory employment practice is prohibited by virtue of Art 3 of the German Constitution. Nobody must therefore be discriminated against as a result of his sex, race, origin, creed or religious and political views. Collective bargaining agreements and statutory law are directly bound by this principle.

The individual employer is also prohibited from discriminating against certain groups of employees. Under the doctrine of equal treatment, arbitrary differences in treatment of employees should be avoided. Article 611(a) of the Constitution gives an action for damages against an employer who discriminates against employees because of their sex. Claims for equal treatment are sometimes initiated on other grounds (Bocker *et al* (1992) p 113).

France

Early history

The notion of *droit du travail* in France is of recent origin. In 1701, Loyseur was still describing a 'master-servant' relationship in his compilation of manorial customs, *Les Oeuvres de Maistre Charles Loyseau*. It was really the customs and conventions of the local community which regulated the rights and obligations arising from services performed for another, rather than any formal, much less written, law. The absolute authority of the patron reigned supreme over workers, servants and apprentices and was derived from the notion of the patriarchal head of the household, which also signified the absolute rights of parents over their children. Rights and duties outside these well established mores were simply non-existent.

It was only when the ideal of a classless society led to the emergence of a working class, ignited by the flames of the French Revolution, that abolition of the privileges of the aristocratic class and of a stratified social structure was even contemplated. The ideals of liberty, equality and the autonomy of the individual were translated into a philosophy that freedom of contract would be the only means of adjusting individual interests in a classless society and that equality of bargaining power should be present in economic and political terms.

The Civil Code thus envisaged workers and employees being linked to patrons within a framework of contractual relationships. Inevitably, the popular ethos of *laissez faire* arose as a reaction against the stifling mass of economic regulation which had swamped the country, leading to the steady rise in the popularity of freedom of contract and the severe restriction of any form of mandatory legislation.

By the early 19th century, French labour law was merely a part of droit civil and assimilated into the general corpus of general rules of law. Present day French labour law can probably trace its legislative development to 1791 when the Assembly of the Revolutionary period enacted two statutes:

(a) one abolishing the guilds which had exercised a monopolistic control over industry; and

(b) the other which forbade the organisation of workers.

Reynard (1952) submits that both these enactments were in keeping with the individualistic spirit of the French Revolution, which placed a strong emphasis on the liberty of the individual and construed it to extend to the 'liberty to work'.

Indeed, the French Penal Code of 1810 even contained an Article prohibiting any concerted action of workers aimed at the improvement of working conditions. This was subsequently repealed.

However, the onset of the Industrial Revolution brought a new awareness of inequality, highlighted by the organisation of large scale industrial enterprises involving substantial numbers of workers under the control of a single, discrete management structure. The sheer speed and extent of the growth of towns and cities accentuated this new consciousness, so that, by 1848, class consciousness and new working environments led to a demand by the working class French industrial worker for special legislation which would protect him from exploitation. Labour law thus started off on the premise of protection for the industrial worker.

The second half of the 19th century saw several statutes passed for the benefit of industrial workers and similar laws were subsequently passed to include farm workers, artisans and employees and agents of business houses. Collective bargaining agreements, international treaties and decisions of arbitration tribunals were all made the subject of the ever widening legislation. In 1864, a statute was enacted limiting the application of the Penal Code provision (see above) and, more importantly, impliedly recognising the right of workers to organise for mutual self-improvement for limited purposes.

In 1884, French labour was basically free to bargain collectively. In that year, penal laws which rendered trade unionism illegal were repealed and unions were recognised as legal personalities with only certain restrictions. This Act gave the courts considerable problems in a number of cases involving the recognition and enforceability of collective agreements. In 1891, the French legislature adopted its first comprehensive enactment in the field of labour law which became the French Labour Code. This substantially codified the rules, which had been evolving in the courts, but also clarified and expanded on them, establishing formal requirements for collective contracts, declaring which persons were to be bound by such agreements, defining the scope of permissible individual agreements, declaring the nature of the obligations that were, thereby, created and designating the parties who had the right to sue for the enforcement of such contracts.

Between 1919 and 1936, the date of the next legislative enactment in this area of law, two important events occurred:

(a) the Confederation Generale du Travail (CGT), which was the most influential and largest of the French labour unions, split into two factions, the CGT and the Confederation Generale du Travail Unitaire (CGTU), as a result of political differences sparked off by the issue of communism. In the light of this sundering of labour forces, collective bargaining experienced a very low ebb, which was not helped by the next event;

(b) the second event was the financial crisis of the early 1930s, which contributed to the depressed condition of collective bargaining. Eventually, a reunion of labour forces took place, to combine again as the CGT, which supported the Popular Front forces in the election, and swept that party into power in 1936. A series of devastating strikes followed, which then led to the Accord of Matignon.

This Accord or agreement resulted from a meeting between the leaders of French labour and industry, presided over by the new Prime Minister, Leon Blum. On behalf of the government, Mr Blum agreed to attempt to codify and implement the terms of this agreement in legislation. Under the Accord, both management and the unions agreed to the immediate conclusion of collective bargaining agreements, to a substantial adjustment in wages and to the establishment of grievance machinery and other procedures for collective bargaining.

These terms were, essentially, embodied in the Act of 1936 which represents the first instance of the French Government actively promoting collective bargaining and which gave a remarkable impetus to the collective bargaining process. There were two significant features in the 1936 Act, namely:

(a) a specialised type of bargaining process by the most 'representative organisations'; and

(b) the principle of governmentally administered extension of contracts so concluded to any outsiders who did not participate in the negotiations.

However, the Act did not secure industrial peace and a wave of strikes followed, particularly when wages and prices failed to keep pace with each other. Employer resistance hardened and, eventually, the government introduced compulsory arbitration in two statutes of 1936 and 1938.

In 1941, during the Second World War, the free trade union movement was completely abolished in France but, although restored in 1946, the relevant Act of 1946 bore the hallmarks of a policy that equated uncontrolled collective bargaining with uncontrolled inflation. A subsequent statute was passed, the Act of February 1950, which is substantially similar to the Act of 1936.

Clearly, the scope of labour law has changed quite radically from the original basic idea of protecting the industrial worker.

Modern labour law

The simplistic notion of patron and worker, as conceived by the Civil Code, is no longer a viable working concept in modern day France. Labour law is now focused on the status of the individuals in the employment arena, so that 'status has, to a large extent, supplanted contract, mandatory rules of law replace contractual arrangements and administrative regulation and adjudication play an important role' (de Vries (1975)). It also includes matters unconnected with the employer/employee nexus, such as social security legislation, administrative regulations, family allowances, tax privileges and old age pensions.

Collective bargaining takes place at different levels. There is a hierarchical structure to the law to the effect that the national agreement constitutes an industrial code, supplemented by regional agreements which themselves supplement local agreements. Article L 132-1 of the Labour Code enumerates a list of different collective agreements arranged in a hierarchy: national agreements; local agreements; and agreements limited to one or several enterprises, or one or several workshops. Article 133-3 lists various items to be regulated in a collective agreement which will be subject to the extension procedure (see below), *inter alia*, the minimum wage for unskilled work, principles for additional pay for skilled work, additional pay for unpleasant, dangerous or unhealthy work, periods of notice for termination, and so on.

The Law of 1971 was passed, modifying certain provisions of the Labour Code aims to strengthen the bargaining procedure, containing the rule that only the most representative unions are allowed to enter into collective agreements. It also seeks to encourage the conclusion of agreements at two extreme levels:

(a) at the plant level; and

(b) at the inter-industry level.

It further aims to make the 'extension procedure' simpler. The extension procedure is a method whereby the Ministry of Labour declares that the agreement is to be binding upon all employers and workers within the area covered by it. Under certain circumstances, it may also be extended to include additional areas. If the extension procedure is implemented, all persons falling within the scope of the agreement are placed in the same position, as if they were members of signatory organisations (see Schmidt and Neal, *International Encyclopedia of Comparative Law* (1982) Vol XV, Chapter 12, p 68).

In more recent times, a new type of collective agreement has appeared – an agreement covering all industries, the 'all embracing collective agreement'.

On the question of the effect of the collective agreement, French law adopts the German approach (see above) so that it governs all those who have signed the agreement as parties, together with those who are, or who become, members of signatory organisations.

Where an employer is bound by a collective agreement, either as a direct signatory or as a member of a signatory organisation, the provisions of that agreement will apply for all contracts of employment entered into by him (Art L 132-10, para 2 of the Labour Code). The purpose of the French legislature has been to bring as many as possible within the scope of the collective agreement.

Ideological pluralism and rights

The Preamble to the French constitution declares that everyone has the right to strike, the right to defend his interests by trade union action and the right 'to belong to the trade union of his choice'. The right of 'choice' between trade unions in France has been called 'ideological pluralism' because, 'from its inception, the modern [French] labour movement was accustomed, in both its industrial and its political wing, to speak the language of political ideology and rights' (Wedderburn (1991) p 42). For most of its history, French trade unions have been divided into groups which have been closely related in structure and in policy to the divided political parties of the left.

The Cour de Cassation, in a 1973 case (21 March), has defined a strike as 'a concerted stoppage of work aimed at pressing ascertained demands on the employer which he refuses to satisfy'. The right to strike must be exercised within the framework of the laws which exist to regulate it.

Classification of the French collective agreement

The French collective agreement has been described as 'nothing more than a declaration of ceasefire' which only lasts for the time being (Schmidt and Neal (1982) p 121). The 'peace obligation' which is imposed depends on the meaning of the statement in the Labour Code Art L 135-1, to the effect that a party is under a duty not to do anything which could prevent the faithful performance of the collective agreement. Any commitment binding a party for a long period of time would be contrary to the policy of the French unions not to submit to restrictions upon the freedom to strike. It should be noted that no peace obligation is imposed upon the individual worker, and the constitutional right is, primarily, a prerogative of the individual. Hence, the peace obligation is of a limited character and may be regarded as nugatory.

The nature of the collective agreement in France has been the subject of considerable debate in France. The basic argument is whether it is primarily a contract, or constitutes a statutory instrument. Modern French writers take the view that it has a mixed character, composed both of contractual elements and of elements of a statutory instrument (Schmidt and Neal (1982) p 104). Schmidt and Neal, however, submit that there are several reasons why it should be classified as a statutory instrument:

(a) only representative unions are permitted to be parties to a collective agreement;

(b) the collective agreement is binding upon all those who are members, or who become members, of an organisation which is a signatory to the agreement. The point is that this rule is not really relevant where the individual employee is concerned. Thus, the effect of Art L 132-10, para 2, is that, when negotiating a collective agreement, the union is acting as the representative of all employees – members and non-members;

(c) government takes an active part in the creation of certain collective agreements, namely, those open to extension (see p 467, above, on 'extension procedure');

(d) Labour Code Arti 133-3 sets out in detail the subjects to be covered by the collective agreement;

(e) the collective agreement, concluded after consideration by a Joint Committee which the Minister of Labour may set up, may be subjected to a special procedure and, by means of a ministerial decree, be extended to cover a certain field of application. Such an agreement will then constitute the law for all enterprises within its field (see Schmidt and Neal (1982) p 105).

It will be seen that the legislature has acted rather like a social reformer in France, subjecting the law on the collective agreement to 'continuous revision in the light of past experience and present needs' (Schmidt and Neal (1982) p 99). The terms of the collective agreement are made a required minimum, with an all embracing character which invalidates private agreements with an employee, but also implies that a collective agreement cannot be used as an instrument imposing duties on an employee.

In France, there is also a distinction between collective and individual disputes. A collective dispute must include 'a procedure to deal with potential collective conflicts and must also contain procedures for revision, modification and termination of the agreement' (Schmiddt and Neal (1982) p 124). Conciliation appears to be the method most utilised to preserve the status quo between the parties in conflict (Schmidt and Neal (1982) p 125).

Labour law has steadily become more systematised and been increasingly subjected to specialised interpretation by doctrinal writers. It has acquired a unique substantive content, approach and methodology, which merits its specialist treatment.

The Superior Court of Arbitration

Separate tribunals and procedures were set up and devised to deal with labour law cases, so much so that, in 1936, the Superior Court of Arbitration (Cour Superieure d'Arbitrage) was created, mainly staffed by judges who were public law jurists. This was entirely independent of the other courts, including the administrative courts, and possessed jurisdiction to issue binding judgments from which there were no rights of appeal. Although it ceased to be operational in 1939, it left a legacy to modern French labour law in its concepts and theories. In declaring itself not bound by the formal French doctrine which disallows courts from establishing precedents, it evolved a 'technique of regulatory decisions' (de Vries (1975)). This meant that courts could, at least, consult and refer to previous decisions where they were hearing similar cases.

Among the other remarkable facets of this Court of Arbitration were:

(a) the possibility of courts reviewing and revising collective bargaining agreements on the basis of changed circumstances;

(b) the shifting of the burden of proof to the employer with regard to termination of employment, limitation of disciplinary powers of management and the reinstatement of employees who were found to be improperly dismissed (see Picard (1931)).

The specialist labour tribunals

The Court of Arbitration's decisions are still cited today as authority in doctrinal writing, but the modern day labour courts are primarily courts of first instance, that is, Conseils de prud'hommes (tribunals consisting of 'men of loyalty and integrity'), numbering over 280, at least one of which exists in each département. These are 'labour conciliation tribunals', or industrial conciliation tribunals, which consist of employers and employees from which there is a right of appeal to the tribunal de grande instance. An appeal may be made to the chambre sociale (social division) of the Cour d'Appel (Court of Appeal) and, thence, to the chambre sociale of the Cour de Cassation.

There are five divisions in these tribunals, each consisting of at least three elected representatives of employees and three of employers. There will always be an equal number of representatives from each group. These divisions may be divided into sections. These courts possess a dual function of adjudication and conciliation. Accordingly, they sit as a conciliation panel and an adjudication panel. All litigants must initially appear before the conciliation panel, which comprises two assessors (one employer and one employee). The adjudication panel consists of four assessors (two employers and two employees). If there is a split decision, a judge from the district court will preside at a rehearing of the case. Urgent interlocutory applications may be heard by two assessors sitting alone and acting for all divisions. If the assessors cannot agree, a district judge will be called upon to resolve the issue.

Current English labour law: Wedderburn's observations

In a paper delivered in 1988 (Wedderburn, 'Freedom of association and philosophies of labour law' (1989) 18 Industrial LJ 1, reproduced in Wedderburn, *Employment Rights in Britain and Europe* (1991) p 198), Lord Wedderburn highlighted five headings which illustrated the labour law programme which the Conservative government appeared to have created:

(a) disestablishing collectivism;

(b) the deregulation of employment law;

(c) union control and ballots for individuals;

(d) enterprise confinement; and

(e) sanctions without martyrs.

These headings are described in considerable detail in his paper and it is proposed here to merely deal with a few salient points. Under (a), he argues that 'the government has removed most of the measures designed to support collective bargaining and to prop up collective organisation', frequently by imposing specified minimum conditions. He also points out that Wages Councils' powers have been reduced and replaced to setting one basic rate – young workers were excluded and wages inspectors have been reduced by administrative means by 35%, since 1979. Further:

> ... privatisation and other pressures for decentralisation or 'flexibility' demand that unions today should move further towards enterprise unionism, while, in some types of 'single union' agreements, the identity of the bargaining union owes more to the preference of the employer granting organising rights to a union, even before any workers have been hired, than to any democratic choice by the workers themselves.

In his view, both law and society have conspired to deregulate the market. There is an absence of a legal duty to bargain with a union democratically 'representative' of the workforce.

Under (b), he focuses on the individual employment relationship which, he says, has also been 'deregulated'. He mentions, *inter alia*, the 'creeping erosion of the floor of rights on employment protection, hand in hand with a gradual reduction of social security rights towards a bare floor on proof of need' (Wedderburn (1991) p 215). This has resulted in a 'diminution of maternity rights, the removal of protection against unfair deductions from wages, the alleviation of the employer's burden of proof, the extension of the employee's qualifying period to two years and similar changes in unfair dismissal law'.

Under (c), he pinpoints 1982 as marking a watershed in the control of the union and the place of ballots. The main objective, it seems clear, was to secure the paramount rights of the non-unionist. Under the 1988 Employment Act, the closed shop ballot is abolished entirely. Although formal freedom of contract is preserved by permitting UMA agreements to be lawful, all the collective pressures to make them effective are outlawed. The rationale put forward by various leading members of the British Government is that individual rights must always prevail against the association or group. The trade union is seen as an obstacle to the competitive market and a threat both to individuals and to private property. Wedderburn sees that this insistence on the so called individual rights, which the State now tries to ensure, will prevail against the trade union as 'the latest marker to characterise the new British labour law'.

Under (d), he observes that the theme running through the legislation, under the Conservatives, is that, if trade unions are to continue, they may need to be confined to the plant or to the enterprise. As he puts it, 'the principle is that the needs of the market demand the confinement of workers' influence within each enterprise – the doctrine of enterprise confinement'. This doctrine is further refined by s 17 of the Employment Act 1988 which introduces a doctrine of 'workplace confinement' so that, under it, each separate place of work must produce its own majority in a separate ballot before industrial action becomes lawful there.

Under the final heading (e) (sanctions without martyrs), Wedderburn turns to the law on trade unions themselves. The immunity of trade unions being limited to trade disputes has been hotly debated and, in 1982, unions were again made liable in tort. In Wedderburn's view, 'this is the key that makes the new system work' for it represents the substitution of union liability for the liability of officials which seeks, thereby, to avoid the 'martyrdom' problem. The sweeping reductions of the immunities, previously enjoyed by trade unions, is predicated upon the perception of unions as an improper restraint of trade in the market and industrial action as an unlawful interference with contracts and property rights. Thus, 'the exposure of union property to civil liability' under common law is the key which makes the machinery work (Wedderburn (1991) p 224).

A few brief comments may be made on Wedderburn's points. In some ways, it must be said, it was events, such as the miners' strike, in the early 1980s, and the 'winter of discontent', which helped the Tories to their second consecutive election victory, in 1983, that led to a backlash of feeling on trade unions and the right to strike 'gone wild'.

In the era of the new Labour Government which won a landslide victory, in May 1997, the trade unions might have been at least hopeful of some reversion to the pre-Tory era of trade union rights. However, at least to date, there is very little evidence of this happening just yet.

COMPARATIVE OVERVIEW

As far as collective bargaining is concerned, there are disparate means of administration. However, Schmidt and Neal ((1982) p 127) see the major distinction between various common law and civil law countries as being:

> ... between countries where entry into a collective agreement relationship represents the statement of a particular status quo between the bargaining parties which is to be maintained within a formalised system of administration, and ... countries in which the collective agreement is viewed as a part of the continuing process of bargaining.

It seems that, although there are several common features in the various jurisdictions, each country is, as ever, a product of its particular history, heritage, political fortunes, culture and distinctive character. 'Rights' abound, but they all exist or function within fairly well defined or (in the English case) deregulated parameters.

Perhaps, the last comparative observations should belong to Lord Wedderburn, the doyen of labour law in both the national and international context. Having surveyed the labour law in a number of European countries, he found that certain values can be found constant in Western and Eastern European countries. First, there is:

... the belief that the task of the law in employment ... is primarily the protection of the worker whose living is obtained, in high technology or in low, by the sale of labour power in the 'workwage bargain'. From that relationship itself springs the need and the right of workers to organise and to take action in free and effective trade unions.

As he stresses, 'The predominance of that need and that right remains in Western and Eastern Europe'.

Secondly, he emphasises that:

... an understanding of collective freedoms which are crucial for workers' self-protection, men and women, young and old, must be rekindled, in the 1990s, after a decade in which the values of fraternity and community have been swept aside in favour of an ideology of commercialised individualism.

As the year 2000 approaches with a new Labour Government, the notion of combining family commitments with work will be implemented as part of a new welfare programme.

Thirdly, he highlights the need for 'free research' because:

... the causes of employment protection and trade union freedom are advanced not by heads buried in the sand, but by liberal inquiry and free expression to which employers and trade unions contribute.

It will be seen that labour law, and the rights that have been gained through its development, is simply another manifestation of the modern day recognition of certain basic rights of the individual in the workplace. In an uncertain economy and time of recession, these rights will increasingly be subjected to intense scrutiny and probable diminution. Even as an economy improves and inches towards relative prosperity and fuller employment, it will take several years before the general workforce derives any monetary or social benefits from the increasing recognition of employment rights. The latest British Labour Government welfare programme is intended to address some of the more pressing needs of the workforce, but other European countries are responding to EC regulation (like the European Works Councils Directive 1994: 94/45/EC) which seeks to emphasise voluntarism, a spirit of closer co-operation with management and special negotiating bodies consisting of employee representatives, to conduct negotiations with central management. Foundations are being laid for notions of 'rights' to be translated into more effective representation of workers and, perhaps, the first five years of the new millennium will see a partial return to trade union bargaining power.

SELECTIVE BIBLIOGRAPHY

Aaron and Wedderburn, *Industrial Conflict* (1972)

Barnard, *EC Employment Law* (1995)

Blanpain, *Labour Law and Industrial Relations of the European Community* (1991)

Blanpain, 'Comparativism in labour law and industrial relations', in Blanpain and Engels (eds), *Comparative Labour Law and Industrial Relations in Industrialised Market Economies* (1993)

Blanpain and Engels, *European Labour Law* (1995)

Bocker *et al, Germany: Practical Commercial Law* (1992)

Clegg, *The System of Industrial Relations in Great Britain* (1970)

Hepple and Friedman, *Labour Law and Industrial Relations in Britain* (1986)

Kahn-Freund, 'Labour law', in Ginsberg (ed), *Law and Opinion in England in the Twentieth Century* (1959) p 215

Kronstein, 'Collective bargaining in Germany: before 1933 and after 1945' (1952) 1 Am J Comp L 199

Maitland-Hudson, *France: Practical Commercial Law* (1991)

Reynard, 'Collective bargaining and industrial peace in France' (1952) 1 Am J Comp L 215

Rideout, 'Labour law in the United Kingdom', in Butler and Kudriavtsev (eds), *Comparative Law and Legal System* (1985)

Rood *et al, Fifty Years of Labour Law and Social Security* (1978)

Schmidt and Neal, 'Collective agreements and collective bargaining', in *International Encyclopedia of Comparative Law* (1982) Vol XV, 'Labour law', Chapter 12

Vranken, *Fundamentals of European Civil Law* (1997)

Wedderburn, *Employment Rights in Britain and Europe* (1991)

Wedderburn, *The Worker and the Law* (1986)

Weiss, 'The transition of labour law and industrial relations: the case of German unification – a preliminary perspective' (1991) 13 Comparative Labour LJ 1

Weiss, *Labour Law and Industrial Relations in the Federal Republic of Germany* (1989)

Whelan, 'On uses and misuses of comparative labour law: a case study' (1982) 48 MLR 285

CHAPTER 14

A NEW WORLD ORDER?

INTRODUCTION

In the 21st century, when comparatists survey the global legal landscape of the early 1990s, and compare it to the global scenario of the 1970s or 1980s, or even further back to the 19th century when so much happened to influence the style, content and legal destiny of those systems, they will note the significant and sometimes dramatic and far reaching changes which two of the world's major countries have experienced – not least, in the early years of the 1990s. Who would have thought that East and West Germany would have become a united nation again, at least in political terms, in 1989–90? Who would have envisaged that the mighty linchpin of the communist bloc, the Soviet Union, would have produced a man who would strive for a new social democracy in the USSR and who, in introducing two terms into popular usage, *perestroika* and *glasnost*, would have caused his own downfall? Even less likely, who would have imagined that the result would have been the disintegration of the USSR into one set of Russian republics forming a Commonwealth of Independent States (now known as the Russian Federation) and another group proclaiming their independence from the new power structure and new President? In the light of the ongoing collapse of communism in Eastern Europe, the 'great socialist tradition' is in danger of disappearing altogether, at any rate, in Europe. Even if rumours of the death of this great tradition have been slightly exaggerated, our approach to the study of major legal traditions, for example, has been radically altered. The Russian republics are presently engaged in returning to their civil law roots or, at any rate, unshackling themselves from the main ideological trappings of communism with the possibility of retention of some of the elements of their Marxist era. The Russian Federation has been in dispute with Chechen, a breakaway republic, so the militaristic aspects of the former USSR continue to haunt the present Russian Government. As more republics rejected communism and declared their independence, they have become novel hybrid systems with civil law and customary law co-existing together with remnants of socialist laws. This would also be an accurate description of the current Russian Federation.

As for the common law world, it could scarcely have been expected in the 1960s that, since the 1980s, the smaller courts and tribunals would account for a 250,000 cases a year, the overwhelming proportion of overall cases that have been heard in England and Wales in the 1990s. Or, that legislation, so reviled in the 19th century by the English jurists as, at best, a necessary evil, would multiply and burgeon to such an extent that, in the 1970s and 1980s, it has become the major law making instrument which accounts for a greater proportion of substantive law than the case law being laid down by the courts. Or, that the one aspect of public law that has grown at a phenomenal rate in England is in the area of 'judicial review' of the administrative actions of public authorities and State-controlled organisations.

In the civil law world, it was, at least, predictable that France and Germany would begin to have recourse to an increasing amount of case law to supplement their 19th century and other Codes to such an extent that their case law has now to be considered a practical necessity and an aid to the interpretation of law. Even if not theoretically admissible, it is a very real, empirical source of law.

As the year 2000 is nearly upon us, and Europe lurches its way towards closer unity via a single Market, having combined to form a Common Market comprised of several sovereign States, it becomes increasingly imperative to consider the implications of a new European law; one which may be interacting at the 'crossroads of legal traditions' (Koopmans (1991)).

The purpose of this chapter is:

(a) to consider the relevance of legal history, noting the agents and catalysts of change;

(b) to examine the new world order (already labelled the 'new world disorder' by some (see Anderson (1992) *New Left Review*, May/June), seeking some explanations for the transformation of the world scenario and consider the contemporary relevance of comparative law to this new order;

(c) to survey the phenomenon of European convergence;

(d) review the so called theories of convergence to consider if legal systems are indeed converging. This will include a brief consideration of the reception of American law in Europe and will reiterate the influence of legal traditions on the development of European Community law, noting, *en passant*, the contribution of the comparative legal method;

(e) to consider whether the world has possibly seen the Last Big Idea (the Fukuyama thesis) – the concept of democracy, which will lead inexorably to complete assimilation of all systems into one politically monolithic entity;

(f) to assess the possibility of convergence occurring between common and civil law systems; and

(g) contemplate the dawn of a new era in world history.

THE SIGNIFICANCE OF LEGAL HISTORY

It seems fair to say that the greatest determinants of legal history have been wars, revolutions, uprisings and great philosophical, ideological, socio-economic and legal movements. Legal history is an integral part of the comparative law enterprise. But, how does one interpret it? Karl Popper (*The Open Society and Its Enemies* (1973) pp 265, 268) observed that:

> There can be no history of the 'past' as it actually did happen; there can only be historical interpretations and none of them final ... the so called 'sources' of history record only such facts as appeared sufficiently interesting to record, so that the sources will often contain only such facts as fit with preconceived theory.

In seeking to place any legal doctrine or principle of legal development within its historical context, it is sensible to heed Popper's thoughts on the question of interpreting history. Although the history of the common law and civil law has been well documented by eminent and fastidious researchers and historians, historical surveys must contain several competing theories. Theories in themselves do no harm, provided they are presented as theories. As the historian Collingwood points out, the historian is well aware that his only possible knowledge of the past is 'inferential' or 'indirect' and never empirical. He suggests that re-enactment of the past in the historian's own mind is what is required in the search for the historical significance of past events (see Collingwood, *The Idea of History* (1973) p 282).

With respect, I would suggest that it is this sort of subjective re-enactment that can often lead to a subjective (and, sometimes, misleading) analysis which one tends to 'fit' into one's preconceived theories. It is therefore suggested that the Popperian method of 'conjectures and refutations' is far more intellectually viable, since this enables an objective critical analysis of historical facts to be carried out (see Popper, *Conjectures and Refutations* (1972)). In essence, the Popperian method involves analysing the strengths and weaknesses of a theory and, after subdividing it to the full extent of its conjectural possibilities, to subject it to rigorous critical analysis. Another technique of this method is to begin with a general concept and proceed to analyse those instances where it does not apply (that is, its exceptions), to see if they undermine it to such an extent as to deny its validity. The method is, therefore, more deductive than inductive.

The historical analysis would then be one of continuous reappraisal and more 'open ended'. Conclusions may therefore be drawn, but these will be deduced without falling prey to the vice of 'interpreting the past in the light of the present' (Fifoot, *History and Sources of the Common Law* (1949) p vii).

A NEW WORLD ORDER?

Global wars and civil strife: historical perspectives

In an editorial published in 1992, Benedict Anderson proffered a very brief glimpse of what he called the 'New World Disorder' and the current global condition (see (1992) *New Left Review*, May/June). It is particularly fitting, in my view, to refer to salient features of his brief survey to place the preceding pages of this book into some sort of historical perspective and to set the scene for future comparative law research.

He begins by referring to one 'deep tectonic movement' which stretched across more than two centuries, the disintegration of the great polytechnic, polyglot and often polyreligious monarchical empires built up so painfully in medieval and early modern times. This emphasises the influence of various Empires that subjugated by force and military might and then left their indelible imprint on the laws, cultures, ideologies and customs of the people they conquered or colonised. The 1770s saw the first nation State born in North America as a reaction to imperial Britain, but which had to undergo 'the bloodiest civil war of the 19th century' before it was able to settle into some kind of stability. Several other great wars also transpired, leading to the emergence of other nation States. Civil wars also ensued in China in the wake of the demise of the Ch'ing Empire, in 1911. Partition in British India, the 30 Years War in Vietnam and the civil strife in Northern Ireland are all seen, by Anderson, as part of the same 'tectonic movement'.

In the midst of all this, another violent revolution produced communism, with Lenin at the heart of the Soviet experiment. However, the Soviet communist bloc, and its latter day Stalinist excesses, was destined to become a superpower enclave which, having seen off Nazism, then proceeded to promote an era of Eastern European communist States with national names. After this came Yugoslavia, North Korea, China, Cuba, Vietnam, Laos and Cambodia.

In the immediate post-Second World War era, the colonial empires of Britain, France, Holland, Belgium and Portugal all went into decline and disintegrated, culminating, in the late 1970s, with a United Nations membership that had quadrupled the original League of Nations which had been formed 50 years before.

The People's Republic of China has emerged as a communist superpower and remains the solitary major bulwark of communism at a time when communism and socialist systems are, to all intents and purposes, turning to some form of Western democracy, with the exception of isolated countries, such as Cuba. Anderson surmises that it is perfectly possible that the People's

Republic of China, in its present form, will also disintegrate and the Tiananmen Square incident certainly supports his view.

Reasons for the transformation of the world order

Mass communications, migrations and ethnicity

Anderson (1992) emphasises that nationalism is by no means dead, but is being constantly refuelled, most recently by a rise in ethnicity, and pinpoints two main reasons for these changes in the world order. First, he attributes these phenomena to mass communications and, secondly, to mass migrations. 'Capitalism and especially industrial capitalism' changed the widespread illiteracy and immobility of peoples who never moved from the country of their birthplace. The mass orientated newspaper and the worldwide dissemination of books, the standardisation of textbooks, curricula and examinations, which also spread to the colonies, meant that 'republicanism, liberalism and popular democracy' would reach nearly all parts of the world.

Mass migration has, in the context of this book, meant that whole communities have travelled and continue to travel to foreign lands, bringing their laws, customs, religions, cultures, languages and traditions with them. People moved not because of disasters or wars, but because of commerce and the promise of economic wealth and social and political aggrandisement.

The current 'ethnicisation' which has occurred throughout the globe, from North America to Australia, and which has existed long before the Arab-Israeli conflict, is indicative of a form of nationalism which is almost always divisive and rarely reconcilable. One reason why the colonising powers almost always left indigenous customs practically untouched was because of the immense local pride that exists in maintaining well established customs.

Ideas whose time has come?

There are, of course, several theories available to explain why the world is in the state it is in, such as the shift in industrial and commercial power from Europe to the United States to the Middle East (because of oil) to Japan, and which is now slowly shifting to the Far East. However, as far as the end of the Cold War and the inexorable shift towards democratic capitalism is concerned, various writers have also speculated on the possible reasons for this. Seyom Brown (1991) offers five possible explanations:

(a) 'imperial overstretch': empires enlarging their sphere of influence and control to the point where their capabilities can no longer sustain their commitments;

(b) hegemonic peace: the presence (or absence) of a dominant great power whose security and well being depend on the perpetuation of a peaceful international order;

(c) 'the Geist whose Zeit has come': the movement towards democratic capitalism is simply a manifestation of the spirit of the times (Zeitgeist) which simply cannot be contained;

(d) the influence of Gorbachev as a 'great man of history': it is arguable that momentous events are brought about partly by great men, such as Gorbachev, who clearly opened Russia to Western influences; and the interaction of Gorbachev's policies of *glasnost* and *perestroika* combined with Zeitgeist is a 'crucial determinant of the drama of history' (Dean Keith Simonton, *Genius, Creativity and Leadership: Historiomatic Inquiries* (1984) p 165. See Brown (1991)).

Brown suggests that it could well be that the explanation for the transformation of world politics is found in all of the above theories. He argues that 'the interpenetrability (let alone simple interdependence) of the various systems that make up the world political system would seem to be a more useful premise on which to understand the kind of systemic change we have been experiencing' (Brown (1991) p 218).

Reasons for the fall of communism in Eastern Europe

In Timothy Ash's *The Magic Lantern* (1990) and William Echikson's *Lighting the Night* (1990), two books on the fall of communism in Eastern Europe, at least five main reasons are suggested for the demise of communism. Echikson's reasons are:

(a) the economic failure of communism; which combined with

(b) the constant struggle of nations who wanted to win freedom.

To these are added three further reasons by Ash:

(a) Gorbachev;

(b) Helsinki; and

(c) de Tocqueville.

Gorbachev, as we have already noted (see above), was a catalyst for change because of his policies of *perestroika* and *glasnost* and a clear message from Moscow that they would not provide any assistance to these countries to protect the status quo. Helsinki is mentioned because it stands for the financial and moral pressure from the West that prevented local communist elites, abandoned by Moscow, from suppressing the wave of change by force. de Tocqueville is also significant because he once described the most important element of a revolutionary situation as 'the ruling elite's loss of belief in its own right to rule'.

It is significant to note that the Communist Party's loss of faith in its legitimate right to rule was a widespread feeling among the middle and upper level bureaucrats, and there was 'a clash of ideology with reality' (Osiatynski (1991) p 829). There was also a loss of popular legitimacy among the local population – the left wing intelligentsia and the workers. The fall of communism was precipitated by 'the emergence of a broad anti-communist coalition in Poland' (Osiatynski (1991) p 832).

THEORIES OF CONVERGENCE

Current convergent trends

From at least the time of Cicero, differences between legal systems have been regarded as inconveniences which have to be overcome. We have seen how the common law and civil law systems are clearly differentiated not just in historical heritage and derivations, but also in a wide range of matters including their sources of law, the structure of their legal professions and legal education, divisions of law, their court structures and fundamental attitudes to law and legal philosophy. Yet, we have also seen that there are clearly similarities in these two systems in the way that they deal with various aspects of sales of goods, contract, tortious liability and in their forms of business organisation. We have also noted that, despite a different attitude towards case law or judicial decisions and legislation, both systems are 'converging' in their use of both these sources of law. In England, there has been a noticeable and fairly dramatic increase in the amount of legislation passed during the last Conservative Government since it first came to power in 1979. In the practitioner's journal, *New Law Journal*, in 1991, the observations of Lord Simon in a House of Lords' debate, which took place on 11 December 1991, were recorded. Lord Simon highlighted current trends which were 'the cause of great constitutional concern': first, the 'aggrandisement of the Executive at the expense of both Parliament and individual rights'; secondly, the dramatic increase in government by regulation in place of statute. He cited as an example the Child Support Act 1991, which has over 100 regulation making powers in its 58 sections, only a dozen of which were subject to the affirmative resolution procedure; and, thirdly, even parliamentary control over the making of regulations was gradually being downgraded, with the use of the negative resolution procedure, in preference to the affirmative procedure, increasingly accepted by both Houses of Parliament. The point was, 'side by side with aggrandisement at the expense of Parliament was an aggrandisement of the executive at the expense of the courts'. Under the Child Support Act 1991, 'individual officials were being given the power to make decisions formerly made by courts of law, with appeals lying to administrative tribunals rather than courts'. There was also an increasing tendency to enact 'Henry VIII clauses' which were clauses containing ministerial power to amend, by regulation, an Act of Parliament without going through the normal parliamentary process.

The English legal system has begun to make more active use of the legislative process, as it did in the 19th century, as a means of implementing more speedy legal reforms rather than to allow the courts to develop the law at their own pace, as they have been doing for several 100 years.

On the other hand, civil law systems are beginning to rely increasingly on case law, particularly in the German constitutional courts and the French administrative courts. Indeed, even in subject areas where Codes and statutes have traditionally been the single authoritative source, the discovery of several 'gaps' in the law has meant that the judges have been given a far greater 'law making role'. Is there, therefore, a convergence of systems? Let us first examine the phenomenon of European convergence, before considering the various theories of convergence.

European convergence

Since 1989, seven countries in Eastern Europe have commenced the transition from one party rule to constitutional democracy. These are Albania, Bulgaria, Czechoslovakia, Hungary, Poland, Romania and Yugoslavia. With the exception of Hungary, whose constitution is a 'patchwork', all the others are currently rewriting their constitutions. The current wave of 'democratisation' is not unprecedented, in some respects, since Japan, Italy and West Germany created democratic constitutions after the Second World War. Nevertheless, as Elster points out, this is a remarkable development because:

(a) all these countries were once under communist rule;

(b) all of them had pre-communist constitutional traditions, although only Czeschoslovakia enjoyed constitutional democracy in the period between the two World Wars;

(c) they are all undertaking simultaneous transitions from central planning to a market economy as well as political modernisation;

(d) the histories of these countries are intertwined;

(e) the developments in 1989 can now be seen as a 'snowballing process in which events in one country inspired and accelerated those in others' (Elster (1991) p 448).

It may be said, therefore, as one writer has, that 'Eastern Europe has ceased to exist' (Osiatynski (1991) p 823). Even more stunning was the pace of events at which the fall of communism took place. There were 'six different phenomena, linked primarily by the chain of events: one revolution unleashed another, in particular, after the collapse of the Berlin Wall' (Osiatynski (1991) p 837).

Writing as a participant in a conference held in Berlin, in 1989, at the European Regional Institute on Comparative Constitutionalism, Gerhard Casper relates that, in all Eastern European countries other than Hungary and the former GDR, new constitutions are being drawn up on the basis of Western European examples, since all these countries aspire to join the Council of Europe and the European Community. All these new constitutions will, in one way or another, implement a form of democratic society and government and, although the State will still regulate many aspects of life, it will also serve as 'the ultimate guarantor of many human aspirations' (Casper (1991) p 445). Thus, the new constitutions will have comprehensive bills of rights, just as their predecessors had, but the private realm will receive constitutional protection. The new constitutions will 'institutionalise judicial review', but will follow the Austrian, German and Italian model of separate constitutional courts having their own procedures (Casper (1991) p 446).

It would certainly appear that a democratisation process is taking place in Europe and, indeed, at least on paper, in most of the former Soviet Russia. As these countries attempt to implement a democratic way of life, this in itself heralds a new legal order. But, it is clearly an order that is dominated by a new pride in one's ethnic origins and represents a return to one's roots and, perhaps, a yearning for past glories. Perhaps it is true to say that the people in these countries no longer want to talk about freedom and democracy as ideals, but simply want to live in a free and democratic society.

What of the rest of Europe? In view of recent legislative developments, Rene de Groot declares that 'it is likely that the legal systems of the European States will form one great legal family with uniform or strongly similar rules in many areas' (de Groot (1992)). Indeed, she asserts that 'To observe that the legal systems of Europe are converging is to state the obvious'. Professor Markesinis, having surveyed the European legal scene, has said that there is 'no doubt that convergence is taking place' (Markesinis (1994)). He mentions:

> ... the convergence of solutions in the area of private law as the problems faced by courts and legislators acquire a common and international flavour; there is convergence in the sources of our law (that is, common law) since, nowadays, case law *de facto*, if not *de jure*, forms a major source of law in both common and civil law countries; there is a slow convergence in procedural matters as the oral and written types of trials borrow from each other and are slowly moving to occupy a middle position; there may be greater convergence in drafting techniques than has commonly been appreciated ... there is a growing rapproachement in judicial views.

Both Markesinis and de Groot argue that the civil law and common law traditions are growing progressively closer in Western Europe and that a new *ius commune* is in the making. The main basis for their assertions is that rules, concepts, substantive and adjectival law and institutional bodies in Europe are converging. In fact, this is readily supportable when one looks at the context of the European Community. Legrand (1996) has argued that these writers are wrong, if one considers the deeper meaning of convergence, because rules are ephemeral and contingent and are basically unreliable guides to how a legal system really operates or how their lawyers really think. He argues that rules are merely surface manifestations of legal cultures and are, therefore, superficial indicators. He submits that rules, thus, do not present the whole picture of what really lies at the heart of a particular legal tradition or culture. Unfortunately, while there is some justification for seeking to ascertain the 'cognitive structure that characterises a legal culture' or mentalité or 'collective mental programme', as he puts it, his argument that it is intrinsically and almost congenitally impossible to understand each other's 'deeper' legal attitude is surely far too sweeping a generalisation to make and undermines the cogency of his approach. In his view, a civilian lawyer can never understand the English legal experience like an English lawyer. Understanding might be achieved, but it has to be a 'different' type of understanding.

Two points may be made to rebut this approach. First, as long as *some* degree of convergence is taking and continues to take place (which he admits is occurring), the case for convergence is already proven. The only scope for debate is: to what extent is it taking place? Secondly, understanding, like convergence, may take place *at different levels*. It may well be that one may never be able to think like another lawyer from a 'foreign' country in every respect so as to almost live that lawyer's professional life, but is there any real need to do so? Does one have to be French to appreciate Monet or German to appreciate Beethoven or, indeed, English to appreciate Shakespeare and the common law? Those who say 'yes' to these questions are falling prey to cultural relativism. Some people will achieve a deeper level of understanding of legal rules and their evolution and socio-legal implications and permutations, while others might only understand them at the basic level *as rules*. Since it is highly unlikely that all the countries of Europe are suddenly going to live together in geographical and culturally identical terms, it is simply unnecessary for the comparatist to get into the mind of the foreign legal system in the sense of getting to know its innermost thoughts and motivations, at least not in the early stages of study and investigation. In short, at the very least, European systems are converging in the context of their commonality of rules, procedures, and institutions. The differences will remain, but the growing similarities are all too apparent.

Philosophies of convergence

There are several philosophies of convergence:

(a) return to the *jus commune*;

(b) legal evolution;

(c) the natural law theories;

(d) the Marxist thesis.

The *jus commune* theory

Basis of the theory

This theory is based on the idea that, in the era before the rise of the nation State, the entire 'civilised world' was governed by one legal system: the Roman-Canonic *jus commune*. The two essential elements of the *jus commune*, fused into a single normative system, were: (i) the Roman law of Justinian's era as rediscovered and developed by the Glossators and Commentators (see Chapter 3) and then received by a large part of continental Europe as the civil law of the Holy Roman Empire (the so called 'Roman common law'); and (ii) canon law, or the law of Roman Catholic Church – the universal Church. The *jus commune* was considered the law of Christendom, ruled by two supreme authorities: the Emperor, the temporal head; and the Pope, the spiritual head (see Cappelletti, Merryman and Perillo, 'The rise of the *jus commune*', in *The Italian Legal System* (1967)). Hence, there was, according to this theory, a 'common law of Europe, a common literature and language of the law and an international community of lawyers' (Merryman and Clark (1978) p 52).

Merryman and Clark (1978) point out the flaws in this particular thesis. To begin with, the medieval *jus commune* only applied throughout Christendom and not to large areas of the world outside it, which would have been entitled to be called 'civilised', even by modern day standards. Further, it was not clear, even within Western Europe, that the *jus commune* was a normal accepted part of the civilised world as it existed then. Hence, although it was sustained by the Church, it seems incongruous to expect nations that were never part of, nor had received nothing of, the *jus commune* to 'return' to it. England, for instance, was never part of the *jus commune*.

A final difficulty with this theory is that it argues on the basis of the disruption caused by the nation State, whereas the nation State actually unified the many diverse laws of the towns, communes, dukedoms and principalities into one major convergence of laws within its jurisdiction. Forcing common law and civil law jurisdictions into accepting one law would offend both group and legal interests.

Reception of American law in Europe

Another development of some considerable consequence has been taking place in Europe since the Second World War – the reception of 'American law' (see Wiegand (1991)). An analogy may be drawn with the 'Latin Middle Ages' wherein the dissemination of the *jus commune* was a European wide phenomenon. The American language has penetrated into everyday French and German (and, incidentally, has also travelled, via television and books, to the Far East as well). With regard to jurisprudence, nearly all fundamental and far reaching changes in European law, during the post-war era, have started from America. Wiegand (1991) explains that American law has now infiltrated to such an extent in Europe that there are:

(a) new business concepts, spawned from the American based practices of leasing, factoring and franchising;

(b) new legal concepts in business and tort law and constitutional law.

In the area of products liability and in 'medical malpractice law' (which has also absorbed the term 'informed consent'), the American approach has been adopted in nearly all European legal systems. American approaches to consumer protection has also influenced European countries (Wiegand (1991) pp 236–46).

As far as concepts are concerned, European systems have started to adopt the 'economic analysis of law' approach which is typically associated with American law as well as an 'interdisciplinary' approach.

Reasons for this 'reception' range from the education of European lawyers (a great many Europeans taking up postgraduate legal training in the United States) to the fact that lawyers occupy key positions in academic institutions, law firms, major banks and private industry, which has already had a fundamental effect on European law and practice. The needs of a post-industrial era and service dominated society have also been readily addressed by American law, so that European law has been quick to draw upon the American solutions to deal with similar needs. Switzerland, in particular, has undergone an American reception in many aspects of its legal scenario. Hence, even if America ceases to dominate European markets in the near future, the seeds have been sown for the 'Americanisation' to continue.

Legal evolution theory

This theory proceeds on the basis that legal change is a natural process which will proceed inexorably and irresistibly because it is controlled by forces beyond human power. Thus, legal systems are at different stages of development and, when they converge, it is because the less developed system is catching up with the more mature one. Since the civil law is much older than the common law, the logical corollary to this thesis is that the common law will gradually become more like the civil law. However, trends toward convergence may be observed in both systems.

While there is more 'codification' in common law countries, particularly in the United States, there is also the phenomenon that civil law judges are becoming more active 'law makers', any jurisprudence constante is being followed more than ever and the rights of the defendant in civil law criminal proceedings are also becoming more like their common law counterparts. In the absence of any universally acceptable criteria, it is extremely difficult to say whether the common law or civil law is more 'developed'. Thus, any discussion of legal evolution, divorced from its socio-cultural or ideological context, is otiose and too abstract to be of any practical value.

Natural law theory

This theory argues that the common nature of human beings will eventually lead to the creation of similar social structures, laws and legal systems. This common nature will therefore be observed and expressed by law (see Merryman and Clark (1978) p 54). Unfortunately, there is no universal consensus about which common characteristics of human beings and human society determine, or ought to determine, the character of the legal system. As Merryman and Clark put it 'The argument that we are all one does not take us very far if there is substantial disagreement about the nature of the one' (Merryman and Clark (1978) p 54).

The Marxist thesis

Marxist theory, which has been discussed in Chapter 6, basically argues that law is mere superstructure. Accordingly, law is merely another instrument for the furtherance of certain economic, social and political ideals. Western bourgeois capitalist nations will all share the same fundamental core values and beliefs and their systems will have converging tendencies, whereas socialist societies will have divergent legal systems which reflect the distinct nature of socialist politics, society and economics. Hence, differences between socialist and Western legal systems are irreconcilable, whereas the legal systems of France, Germany and England are basically reconcilable, since the differences in law tend to be more superficial, similarities being masked by superstructure and terminology.

Of course, the events of the past three years strongly suggest that the socialist system is now in terminal decline and that Eastern Europe is well on the way to adopting a more capitalist and Westernised approach to law and society. As such, although complete privatisation will take many years, perhaps even decades, in the case of certain countries, like Hungary and Poland, convergence in economic, political and social philosophy has already begun to take place between former socialist systems and Western capitalist ones. Of course, the West has already secured international and regional agreements seeking international economic, social and political integration as expressed in the creation of the European Community and the European Union and the conclusion of international treaties, such as the European Human Rights Convention. Convergence of the English derived common law and European continental style civil law has also been set in motion, at least in the field of monetary and economic co-operation and in the field of human rights. The UN Convention on the Rights of the Child, which has received the largest number of signatories of any international treaty in modern times, is indicative of the much closer convergence which exists both within and outside Europe on certain matters.

GLOBAL CONVERGENCE AND THE FUKUYAMA THESIS

In the summer of 1989, an article by a deputy director of the American State Department, Francis Fukuyama, entitled 'The end of history', was published. Its theme was that liberal democracy is the only ideology left in the greater part of the civilised world. This was, by no means, an earth shattering or mould breaking revelation, but Fukuyama's article won notoriety and he went on to write a 360 page book (*The End of History and the Last Man* (1992)) which seeks to clarify to the world his ideas in the article. He explained that his title was merely an example of an idiom that has not been fashionable since the 19th century: Hegelianism. Several writers and philosophers have exposed the flaws in Hegelianism, culminating in a book by Karl Popper, *The Open Society and its Enemies* (1945).

It is not the purpose of this section to discuss the many interesting and sometimes provocative aspects of the book, but it is relevant to the notions of convergence because it argues, *inter alia*, that, in Southern Europe, Latin America, Asia and Eastern Europe, free market economies and parliamentary democracy are, with notable exceptions, fast becoming the norm. He emphasises the victory of the principles of liberal democracy and, more precisely, the liberal idea, rather than liberal practice (see Fukuyama (1992) p 45). Hence, as he puts it, 'for a very large part of the world, there is now no ideology with pretensions to universality that is in a position to challenge liberal democracy and no universal principle of legitimacy other than the sovereignty of the people' (Fukuyama (1992) p 45).

Though there are no longer any serious competitors to it, he raises the question of whether its own internal fissures may not gradually destroy it from within. One of Fukuyama's concerns is that the rights and freedoms of liberal democracy, the safety of the person, equality before the law and the protection of property may not be enough to ensure its survival.

He therefore argues that a society needs to be free in a much wider sense, so as to pursue dreams and aspirations. Tracing this idea to Plato's *thymos* ('courage'; 'public spiritedness'), which Hegel develops as the 'struggle for recognition', he develops his theme that this concept helps to illuminate an understanding of the contemporary world.

Whether one agrees with Fukuyama's ideas, and it should be noted that he does not, in fact, believe that history has 'ended' in any sense, he has highlighted a 'worldwide liberal revolution' while noting the exceptions – China, which will no longer serve as a model for revolutionaries around the world, Cuba, North Korea and Vietnam, Ethiopia, Angola and Mozambique. Authoritarian rulers have been forced to promise free elections in a host of other African countries.

He also places the beginning of this 'revolution' as having occurred in 1974, when the Caetano regime in Portugal was ousted in an army coup and the socialist, Mario Soares, was elected Prime Minister, in 1976. It was also in 1974 that the Karamanlis regime was elected in Greece, which put paid to the era of the colonels who had run the country since 1967. In Asia, the overthrow of the Marcos dictatorship in the Philippines, in 1986, is significant as is the announcement, in February 1980, by FW de Klerk in South Africa that Nelson Mandela would be released and that the African National Congress and the South African communist party would have their ban lifted. In the 1980s, the Chinese communist leadership began permitting peasants, who constituted 80% of the population, to grow and sell their own food. Thus, agriculture was 'de-collectivised' and capitalist market relationships began appearing throughout the countryside and in urban industry as well.

As far as the power of Islamic States is concerned, Fukuyama concedes that Islam has defeated liberal democracy in many parts of the Islamic world, but argues that 'this religion has virtually no appeal outside those areas that were culturally Islamic to begin with' (Fukuyama (1992) p 46). Indeed, he argues that the Islamic world would seem 'more vulnerable to liberal ideas in the long run than the reverse, since such liberalism has attracted numerous and powerful Muslim adherents over the past century and a half'. No doubt Islamic adherents or historians would take issue with him on that point, but the fact remains that there appears to be a worldwide movement towards more liberal ideas and philosophies, which is traditionally associated with Western ideas of liberal democracy. As Fukuyama argues, there were 13 liberal democracies in 1940, 37 in 1960 and 62 in 1992. By his reckoning, there was not a single true democracy in the world until 1776, if one defines democracy as including the 'systematic protection of individual rights'.

By the end of the 1980s, therefore, China, the former Soviet Union and the countries of Eastern Europe had all 'succumbed to the economic logic of advanced industrialisation' (Fukuyama (1992) p 96). Even the Chinese leadership had accepted the need for markets and decentralised economic planning and 'the close integration into the global capitalist division of labour'.

The problem which Fukuyama poses in his final chapters is how far liberal democracy can fulfil the human need for recognition and how far it can become a permanent and stable society – the last stage of history. That, as with many of his other concerns, will surely remain a matter for history itself to answer.

UNIFICATION OF LEGAL SYSTEMS

Strategies of convergence

Three main 'strategies' or modes of convergence have been identified by Merryman and Clark (1978):

(a) active programmes for the unification of law;

(b) transplantation of legal institutions; and

(c) natural convergence.

Unification of law is sought to be achieved through the use of international institutions specifically intended to promote the unification of law – agencies, such as the International Institute for the Unification of Private Law in Rome, the Hague Conference on Private International Law and the UN Commission on International Trade Law. Programmes of international organisations with broader objectives also frequently seek to generalise or standardise legal rules and practices, for example, in the European Community. Other examples of agencies which include unification of law as one of their objectives are the International Labour Organisation, the European Commission on Human Rights and the Organisation of American States.

Unification of law is often attempted through supranational legislation and judicial decision binding on, and applicable within, individual Member States, in the case of regulations of the European Community and the decisions of the European Court of Justice, provisions of treaties and multilateral conventions (for example, the International Copyright Convention). Another recent example of a UN Convention, which has revised an original version of a uniform law, which has had global input is the UN Convention on Contracts for the International Sale of Goods. The objective of unification of law places great store on legislation and focuses on rules of law, along the lines of Savigny and Thibaut's arguments. The practical efficacy of unification will, however, be necessarily circumscribed by the legal structures, institutions and procedures existing within nations which will determine the degree of uniformity in the application and interpretation of rules (see Merryman and Clark (1978) p 58).

Legal transplants

As Alan Watson puts it, 'Borrowing from another system is the most common form of legal change' (Watson, *Legal Origins and Legal Change* (1991) p 73) and legal transplantation has a long history. There was the reception of Roman law in later Europe, the spread of English law through the colonies of the British Empire, even into parts of the United States which had never been under British rule, and the tremendous impact of the French Civil Code on other civil law systems in Europe and abroad, and, latterly, the spread of American law to Europe, especially in places like Switzerland. The so called hybrid or 'mixed jurisdictions' still show the effects of such transplantation in their unique blends of common law, civil law and local customary law (see Chapter 6).

Transplantation may occur voluntarily by, for example, the adoption or imitation of a foreign Code; or involuntarily as when a country is colonised and has a foreign legal system imposed on its indigenous culture. Legal transplants across the common law-civil law boundary inevitably lead to convergence of the two systems. Transplantations may or may not be 'successful', depending on a country's particular conditions for receptivity. While the notions of the condominium and community property system were transplanted quite easily into the United States from the civil law, the Uniform Law on Negotiable Instruments Law, which was widely adopted in the United States, failed in Colombia.

Natural convergence

The basis of this theory is that the legal systems of societies will tend to become more alike as the societies themselves become more like each other. Thus, there are similarities in constitutions in Western democracies and a common international culture brought about by increased international communication and travel, international trade, international organisations, the internationalisation of business and technology and a growing awareness of shared global concerns (pollution, the environment, global warming and so on), student exchange programmes and scholarly exchange schemes.

There are several examples of this type of convergence of civil law and common law: safeguards for defendants in criminal proceedings; adoption of graduated income tax; legal aid schemes; uniformity in definition and protection of individual rights; the rise in judicial review (bearing in mind that this term means different things between America and England, as well as between civil law and common law systems. See Merryman and Clark (1978) p 60).

Of course, as we have seen, there are several notable historically explicable differences between the legal systems of civil law and common law countries, although they have a pronounced concordance of legal principles. The point, perhaps, is that, while there are many practical similarities in their legal solutions, fundamental and deep rooted differences exist in juristic style, philosophy and substance, in court structures and sources of law and, more importantly, in their judicial and administrative ethos, legal divisions and categories and their professional structure and legal education.

Legal transplantation may, of course, affect the speed and direction of change in civil law and common law countries. So may revolutions, even if they are non-violent ones, such as the recent global movement towards the liberal idea and principles of democracy (see 'Global convergence and the Fukuyama thesis', p 488, above).

Convergence and divergence between common law and civil law

Clearly, since the two main Civil Codes were enacted in the early and late 19th century, the drafters could not possibly have anticipated the pace, scale or technology of the modern 20th century. Civil law judges have, therefore, had to create new legal rules to cope with situations which could not have been envisaged by the legislators of the Codes. The French law on torts is, therefore, primarily found in widely published and cited decisions of the courts. Common law judges have always had a high profile and have resorted to judicial law making whenever a 'gap' has appeared in the statute or in cases where the statute has been ambiguous or could produce a manifestly absurd or unjust result (see Chapter 9).

German lawyers and judges continue to rely very heavily on the *Short Commentary on the German Civil Code* for daily practice, which contains thousands of cases. This again resembles common law legal practice, although it should be pointed out that there is no doctrine of binding precedent, as such, on the continent (see Chapter 3).

There has also been a growth in public administration, in Europe, which has accompanied this decline in legislative authority. Members of the public administration itself, sitting in a council of State, decide on the propriety and legality of State administrative actions. In England, there has been a dramatic increase in the use of the application for judicial review of administrative actions and most of the law is laid down by Parliament. Further, most of the non-legislative law is being created by the ever growing network of administrative tribunals. Case law has tended to feature heavily in the German Constitutional Court and French administrative court. However, recent cases tend to indicate that the distinction between public and private law is breaking down both on the European continent and in England. The 1991 English House of Lords' case (*Roy v Kensington and Chelsea and Westminster Family Practitioner Committee* [1992] 1 All ER 705) indicated that the mere assertion of a private law right entitles an individual to proceed by way of an ordinary private law action, rather than be restricted to judicial review, even though he was challenging a public law decision (see Chapter 4).

Apart from these developments, there has been a rise in constitutional power, in the sense that constitutions are increasingly being treated as supreme sources of law, in civil law countries and in the United States. Although the actual technical basis of the constitutional review is by no means identical under civil law and American law, there are common features since, in both types of jurisdiction, there is a move to promote, guarantee and, if necessary, expand individual rights. This is seen by commentators, such as Merryman, as another example of 'decodification', since the Codes are no longer seen as fulfilling a constitutional function (Merryman (1977) p 157). Judges have therefore acquired an enhanced status and expanded role in this context, particularly in the civil law courts.

Finally, there is, of course, the existence and growing influence of European Community law. As a result of *Costa v Enel* (Case 6/64 [1964] ECR 585), Community law prevails over inconsistent national law. As a result of the notion of English parliamentary sovereignty or supremacy, the United Kingdom European Communities Act 1972 has specifically accepted the supremacy of EC law so that Community law has the status of law in the British courts. However, since the 1972 Act is a United Kingdom statute which derives its authority from the British Parliament, it could always be repealed. However, the 1972 Act has created a legislative conduit which will allow EC law to take precedence over and be part of English law, until and unless the 1972 Act is repealed (see Chapter 5).

An analogy could be drawn between Community law and the canon law *jus commune*, since EC law and the European Human Rights Convention could be seen as the foundation of a new *jus commune* 'based on common culture and common interests' (Merryman (1977) p 158).

Convergence between European countries

The dissension surrounding the implementation of closer economic and monetary union through the Maastricht Treaty may not, ultimately, affect the development of the new *jus commune*. The launch of the 'euro', on 2 January 1999, heralds the start of a new era, in which this single currency will link the financial markets around the globe. From New York to Tokyo, London to Hong Kong, in Paris, Madrid and Helsinki and in financial markets across the globe, 100,000 workers devoted their New Year weekend to preparing for the euro launch. But, London remains outside 'Euroland'. Frankfurt will now have tremendous power over 11 countries who are euro players. The euro represents a very real example of European economic co-operation and yet another manifestation of 'convergence' within the European Community itself.

THE DAWN OF A NEW ERA IN WORLD HISTORY

In his Shimizu lecture, published in 1990, Professor Markesinis laments the fact that comparative law is a subject in search of an audience and offers a powerful exposition of 'the value of presenting a foreign system to an unfamiliar audience, primarily through its case law rather than by means of codal provision' (see Markesinis (1990) p 1). Nearly a decade later, it would seem that the time is now ripe for lawyers, judges and students to investigate and utilise the benefits of comparative law. With the impending Single Market, the trend towards convergence of European systems, the growing influence of European Community law on EC Member States, the global village phenomenon and a communality of purpose in the protection and enforcement of human rights, practitioners and international law specialists should seize the opportunity to establish more positive and imaginative programmes for interregional research and practice across national frontiers.

While Eastern European legal systems may be gravitating towards capitalist democracies, basic changes are also taking place in Western Europe. Both the Atlantic Alliance and the European Community are facing fundamental challenges. The North Atlantic Treaty Organisation is facing the current wave of American isolationism and the desires of the Europeans to give defence a 'European identity', whereas the Community itself is grappling with the Danish rejection of the Maastricht Treaty and the dilemma of how far and how fast to expand their economies – assuming there is an upturn in the current economic situation. There is therefore a new European geopolitics which resembles the 19th century style of a fluid, open system of diplomacy. The European Court of Justice has become a source of legal innovation in Europe 'not only because of its position as the Community's judicial institution, but also because of the intellectual strength of its comparative methods'. Thus, the development of European Community law appears to be the 'progressive construction' of a 'many sided edifice' (Koopmans (1991) pp 505–06). It has 'many parents and foster parents' (Koopmans (1991) p 506) so that it becomes increasingly important to know the origins or even existence of different legal doctrines and ideas, so as to cope with a rapidly changing technological world.

CONCLUSIONS

The configuration of the law and legal systems, by the end of the 20th century, will, therefore, depend on a number of variables and imponderables, such as whether new military alliances are formed within Europe, without the United States as a partner, or whether the new united Germany finds itself balancing off France and Russia, as it did in the 19th century. On the other hand, what of the economic power of the Japanese and American economic fortunes? What is going to happen in the 'new Russia' in the next five years or so? What about the new economic power bases in places in the Far East, such as Korea, and the acceleration of the technological revolution?

Although we might appear to have come full circle, there are many elements which will not change and have not changed. The fundamental ideological, doctrinal and religious differences that exist between countries in the Muslim world and the West will be a very long time changing, if at all, although the past five years indicates that nothing is impossible. Newly emergent and poor nations have a greater need than ever to enjoy the benefit of not just Western aid and technology, but also Western experience and advice and, sometimes, Western legal ideas which could galvanise their economies and industries and speed their constitutional and political development, as well as resolve their many domestic problems.

Needless to say, transnational companies are already on the lookout for lawyers who are conversant with more than one system of law and who have an above average understanding of more than one legal system. The ever increasing membership of the European Community, its supranational legal regime and the continuing transplantation of Western ideas to countries all over the world, provide an ideal environment in which the comparative law methodology should not just be used, but will be absolutely essential to an understanding and appreciation of the law. A recent collection of essays, edited by Professor Basil Markesenis, surveys the impact of foreign ideas and foreign influences on English law as we approach the 21st century. Lord Justice Bingham has declared his hope that English lawyers will cease to think of Europe as 'somewhere else' in the 1990s (Bingham (1992)) and Lord Goff has even suggested that comparative law will be the subject of the future (Goff (1988)). English courts frequently refer to American court decisions and those of other Commonwealth countries (see Orucu, 'Use of comparative law by the courts', in Bridge *et al* (eds), *UK Law in the mid-1990s* (1994) UKNCCL) and even the House of Lords has begun to cite foreign and comparative academic writing with approval and appear prepared to adopt a comparative approach where it will assist in its deliberations. Thus, the seeds of cross-fertilisation and integration are well and truly sown (see *White v Jones* [1995] 2 WLR 187).

The contemporary relevance of the comparative law method lies in its potential to facilitate an understanding of the differences between the old world order and the new. However, the enduring value of the comparative law method must lie not merely in its providing a window to the world's legal systems, or in its intellectual merit or in its analysis of substantive doctrines at the international and domestic level. Surely, what comparative law can do is to enable us to look beyond our narrow parochial interests and illuminate our understanding of legal rules and concepts, to remind us that, despite differences in culture, history, law and language, we are all part of the larger community of mankind.

As Koopmans (1996), a former judge of the Court of Justice of the European Communities, has said:

> The 21st century may become the era of comparative methods. As we share so many difficult problems of society, and as we live closer and closer together on the planet, we seem bound to look at one another's approaches and views. By doing so, we may find interesting things, but we may also find ways of coping with the tremendous legal challenges that seem to be in store for us.

In the words of Jerome (*On Getting on in the World* (1889)):

> We are so bound together that no man can labour for himself alone. Each blow he strikes on his own behalf helps to mould the universe.

As a new era in world history beckons, there seems no better time for the comparatist to take up the challenge and to utilise the techniques of comparative law, to think in more global terms so as to acquire a better understanding of the operation of law in a rapidly changing world. There can be few better ways to prepare for the 21st century.

SELECTIVE BIBLIOGRAPHY

Agh, 'The transition to democracy in Central Europe: a comparative view' (1991) 11 Journal of Public Policy 133

Anderson, 'The new world disorder' (1992) New Left Rev 3

Bingham, 'There is a world elsewhere: the changing perspectives of English law' (1992) 41 ICLQ 513

Brady, *Justice and Politics in People's China* (1982)

Brown, 'Explaining the transformation of world politics' (1991) 46 International Journal 207

Casper, 'European convergence' (1991) 58 Chicago UL Rev 441

de Groot, 'European education in the 21st century', in de Witte and Forder (eds), *The Common Law of Europe and the Future of Legal Education* (1992)

Elster, 'Constitutionalism in Eastern Europe: an introduction' (1991) 58 Chicago UL Rev 447

Eorsi, *Comparative Civil (Private) Law* (1979) Pt II, Chap 8

Fukuyama, *The End of History and the Last Man* (1992)

Fukuyama, *Trust* (1996)

Goff, 'Judge, jurist and legislature' (1988) Denning LJ 79

Goodman and Segal (eds), *China in the Nineties* (1991)

Kim, 'The modern Chinese legal system' (1987) 31 Tulane L Rev 1413

Koopmans, 'Comparative law and the courts' (1996) 45 ICLQ 545

Koopmans, 'The birth of European law at the crossroads of legal traditions' (1991) 39 Am J Comp L 493

Legrand, 'European legal systems are not converging' (1996) 45 ICLQ 59

Markesinis, 'Comparative law – a subject in search of an audience' (1990) 53 MLR 1

Markesinis (ed), *The Gradual Convergence* (1994)

McCarney, 'Shaping ends: reflections on Fukuyama' (1993) New Left Rev 37

Merryman, *The Civil Law Tradition* (1985) Chap 20

Merryman and Clark, *Comparative Law: Western European and Latin American Legal Systems* (1978) pp 51–67

Milband, 'Fukuyama and the socialist alternative' (1992) New Left Rev 108

Orucu, 'The use of comparative law by the courts', in Bridge *et al* (eds), *United Kingdom Law in the Mid-1990s* (1994) Pt 2, Vol 15, UK Comparative Law Series, UKNCCL

Osiatynski, 'Revolutions in Eastern Europe' (1991) 58 Chicago UL Rev 823

Piotrowicz, 'The arithmetic of German unification: one into three does go' (1991) 40 ICLQ 635

Rustin, 'No exit from capitalism?' (1992) New Left Rev 96

Vranken, *Fundamentals of European Civil Law* (1997)

Wiegand, 'The reception of American law in Europe' (1991) 39 Am J Comp L 229

INDEX